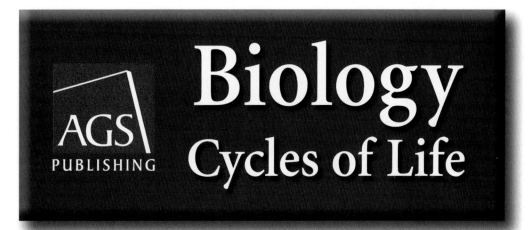

by
Helen M. Parke
and
Patrick Enderle

AGS Publishing
Circle Pines, Minnesota 55014-1796
800-328-2560

About the Authors

Helen M. Parke, Ph.D., is a former secondary and university biology teacher. With 30 years of teaching experience, Dr. Parke has taught science methods courses for undergraduate and graduate level secondary science majors. She has directed centers for science, mathematics, and technology education and is currently Research and Development Manager for Cisco Learning Institute. Dr. Parke designs e-learning professional development for K–12 teachers of mathematics and science.

Patrick Enderle, M.S., received his master's degree in Molecular Biology/Biotechnology from East Carolina University. He has taught biology at the high school, community college, and university levels. He is currently teaching at East Carolina University in Greenville, North Carolina.

Photo credits for this textbook can be found on page 666.

The publisher wishes to thank the following educators for their helpful comments during the review process for *Biology: Cycles of Life*. Their assistance has been invaluable.

Pamela J. Graham, Special Education Teacher/Intervention Specialist, Euclid High School, Euclid, OH; **Debora J. Hartzell**, Lead Teacher for Special Ed, Columbia High School and Lakeside High School, Dekalb County, GA; **Debby Houston**, Research Associate, Florida State University, Tallahassee, FL; **Pamela A. Kazee**, Director, Student Support Services, NE, Clark County School District, Las Vegas, NV; **Denise M. King**, Instructional Coordinator, Leary School of Virginia, Alexandria, VA; **Johnny McCarty**, Special Education Teacher, Science, Flour Bluff High School, Corpus Christi, TX; **Katherine Pasquale**, Euclid High School, Euclid, OH; **Dr. Craig L. Sanders**, Teacher, Richmond Hill High School, East Meadow, NY; **Ann Marie Strozynski**, Director of Secondary Education, Hamtramck, MI; **Susan Sztain**, Teacher, Desert Sands Charter High School, Lanc, CA; **Michelle Villegas**, Biology Teacher, Flour Bluff High School, Corpus Christi, TX

Publisher's Project Staff

Vice President of Curriculum and Publisher: Sari Follansbee, Ed.D.; Director of Curriculum Development: Teri Mathews; Managing Editor: Julie Maas; Editors: Judy Monroe, Jan Jessup; Assistant Editor: Sarah Brandel; Development Assistant: Bev Johnson; Director of Creative Services: Nancy Condon; Senior Designers: Tony Perleberg, Diane McCarty; Production Artist: Mike Vineski; Purchasing Agent: Carol Nelson; Product Manager–Curriculum: Brian Holl

© 2006 AGS Publishing
4201 Woodland Road
Circle Pines, MN 55014-1796
800-328-2560 • www.agsnet.com

Printed in the United States of America
ISBN 0-7854-3972-2
Product Number 94180
A 0 9 8 7 6 5 4 3 2

Contents

How to Use This Book: A Study Guide

Welcome to *Biology: Cycles of Life*. Science touches our lives every day, no matter where we are—at home, at school, or at work. This book covers the biological sciences. It also focuses on science skills that scientists use. These skills include asking questions, making predictions, designing experiments or procedures, collecting and organizing information, calculating data, making decisions, drawing conclusions, and exploring more options. You probably already use these skills every day. You ask questions to find answers. You gather information and organize it. You use that information to make all sorts of decisions. In this book, you will have opportunities to use and practice all of these skills.

As you read this book, notice how each lesson is organized. Information is presented in a straightforward manner. Tables, illustrations, and photos help clarify concepts. Read the information carefully. If you have trouble with a lesson, try reading it again.

It is important that you understand how to use this book before you start to read it. It is also important to know how to be successful in this course. Information in this first section of the book can help you achieve these things.

How to Study

These tips can help you study more effectively.

◆ Plan a regular time to study.

◆ Choose a desk or table in a quiet place where you will not be distracted. Find a spot that has good lighting.

◆ Gather all the books, pencils, paper, and other equipment you will need to complete your assignments.

◆ Decide on a goal. For example: "I will finish reading and taking notes on Chapter 1, Lesson 1, by 8:00."

◆ Take a five- to ten-minute break every hour to stay alert.

◆ If you start to feel sleepy, take a break and get some fresh air.

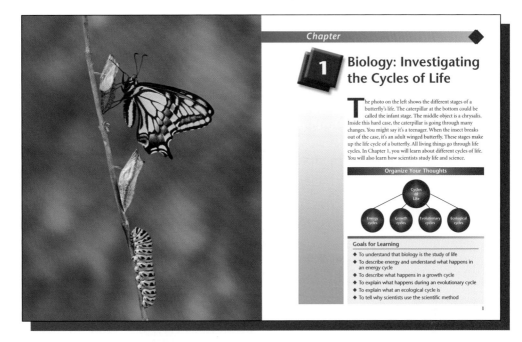

Before Beginning Each Chapter

◆ Read the chapter title and study the photograph. What does the photo tell you about the chapter title?

◆ Read the opening paragraphs.

◆ Study the Goals for Learning. The Chapter Review and tests will ask questions related to these goals.

◆ Look at the Chapter Review. The questions cover the most important information in the chapter.

Note These Features

Notes

Points of interest or additional information that relate to the lesson

Science Myth

Common science misconceptions followed by the correct information

Biology in Your Life

Examples of science in real life with connections to the environment, technology, and consumer choices

■ ● ■ ◆ ■ ◆ ■ ◆ ■ ◆ ■ ◆ ■ ◆ ■ ◆ ■ ◆ ■ ◆ ■ ◆

Biology in Your Life

Achievements in Science

Historical scientific discoveries, events, and achievements

★ ✦ ★ ✦ ★ ✦ ★ ✦ ★ ✦ ★ ✦ ★ ✦ ★ ✦ ★ ✦ ★ ✦ ★ ✦ ★

Achievements in Science

Science at Work

Careers in science

▼◀ ▲ ▼◀ ▲ ▼◀ ▲ ▼◀ ▲ ▼◀ ▲ ▼◀ ▲ ▼◀ ▲ ▼◀

Science at Work

Investigation

Experiments that give practice with chapter concepts

INVESTIGATION 1

Materials
◆ safety goggles
◆ lab apron
◆ flashlight
◆ house plant
◆ insect in a jar

What Is Life?

Biologists study all kinds of life. Life takes on many diverse forms. All life runs through cycles of energy, growth, evolution, and ecology. In this lab you will examine some different forms of life and note their

Discovery Investigation

Experiments with student input to give practice with chapter concepts

DISCOVERY INVESTIGATION 2

Materials
◆ safety goggles
◆ lab apron
◆ 2 clear plastic cups
◆ 20 corn seeds
◆ water

Using the Scientific Method

Scientists answer questions and solve problems in an orderly way. They use a series of steps called the scientific method. How can you use the scientific

Technology and Society

Examples of science in real life with connections to biology, technology, and society

✿ ✿ ✿ ✿ ✿ ✿ ✿ ✿ ✿ ✿ ✿ ✿ ✿ ✿ ✿ ✿ ✿ ✿ ✿ ✿

Technology and Society

Biology in the World

Examples of real-life problems or issues and solutions affecting the United States or the world

BIOLOGY IN THE WORLD

Discovery of Mad Cow Disease

In the mid-1980s, farmers in England noticed that several cows showed strange symptoms before dying. When the animals were examined after death, scientists saw that their brains looked like sponges. Scientists determined the disease that killed these cows was caused by

Math Tip

Short math reminders or tips connected to a lesson

Express Lab

Short experiments that give practice with chapter concepts

Link to

A fact that connects biology to another subject area such as chemistry, environmental science, physics, earth science, social studies, language arts, math, health, home and career, arts, and cultures

Research and Write

Research a topic or question, then write about it

Before Beginning Each Lesson

Read the lesson title and restate it in the form of a question.

For example, write:
What are evolutionary cycles?

Look over the entire lesson, noting the following:
◆ bold words
◆ text organization
◆ notes in the margins
◆ photos and illustrations
◆ lesson review questions

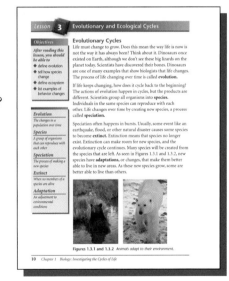

As You Read the Lesson

◆ Read the lesson title.

◆ Read the subheads and paragraphs that follow.

◆ Before moving on to the next lesson, see if you understand the concepts you read. If you do not understand the concepts, reread the lesson. If you are still unsure, ask for help.

◆ Practice what you have learned by completing the Lesson Review.

Using the Bold Words

Bold type

Words seen for the first time will appear in bold type

Glossary

Words listed in this column are also found in the glossary

Knowing the meaning of all the boxed vocabulary words in the left column will help you understand what you read.

These words are in **bold type** the first time they appear in the text. They are often defined in the paragraph.

Biology is the study of life.

All of the words in the left column are also defined in the **glossary.**

Biology (bī ol´ ajē) The study of life (p. 2)

Word Study Tips

◆ Start a vocabulary file with index cards to use for review.

◆ Write one term on the front of each card. Write the chapter number, lesson number, and definition on the back.

◆ You can use these cards as flash cards by yourself or with a study partner to test your knowledge.

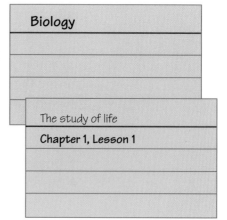

Biology

The study of life

Chapter 1, Lesson 1

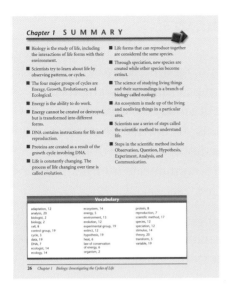

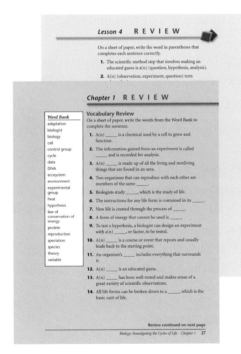

Using the Summaries

◆ Read each Chapter Summary to be sure you understand the chapter's main ideas.

◆ Make up a sample test of items you think may be on the test. You may want to do this with a classmate and share your questions.

◆ Read the vocabulary words in the Vocabulary box.

◆ Review your notes and test yourself on vocabulary words and key ideas.

◆ Practice writing about some of the main ideas from the chapter.

Using the Reviews

◆ Answer the questions in the Lesson Reviews.

◆ In the Chapter Reviews, answer the questions about vocabulary under the Vocabulary Review. Study the words and definitions. Say them aloud to help you remember them.

◆ Answer the questions under the Concept Review and Critical Thinking sections of the Chapter Reviews.

◆ Review the Test-Taking Tips.

Preparing for Tests

◆ Complete the Lesson Reviews and Chapter Reviews.

◆ Complete the Investigations and Discovery Investigations.

◆ Review your answers to Lesson Reviews, Investigations, Discovery Investigations, and Chapter Reviews.

◆ Test yourself on vocabulary words and key ideas.

◆ Use graphic organizers as study tools.

Using Graphic Organizers

Graphic organizers are visual representations of information. Concept maps, flowcharts, circle diagrams, Venn diagrams, column charts, and graphs are some examples of graphic organizers. You can use graphic organizers to organize information, connect related ideas, or understand steps in a process. You can use them to classify or compare things, summarize complex topics, and communicate information. You can also use them to study for tests.

As you read this book, practice making your own graphic organizers. You will find that graphic organizers are helpful tools for learning biology and any other subject.

Concept Maps

A concept map consists of a main concept or idea and related concepts. Each concept—usually one or two words or a short phrase—is written in a circle or box. The organization of concepts in the map shows how they are related.

In the concept map below, Organic Molecules is the main concept. It appears at the top of the map. Carbohydrates, Lipids, Proteins, and Nucleic Acids are all concepts related to Organic Molecules. Each of these related concepts appears in a box below Organic Molecules. Each one is connected to Organic Molecules with a straight line to show they are related. The main concept is the most general. The other concepts are more specific. You will find a concept map at the beginning of each chapter of the book. This simple concept map identifies the main concepts discussed in the chapter and shows how they are connected.

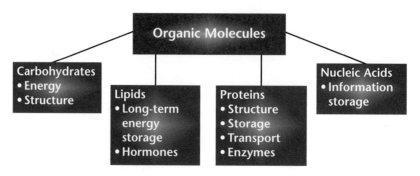

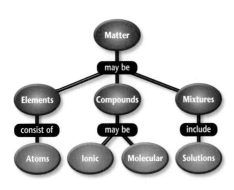

Matter
may be
Elements   Compounds   Mixtures
consist of   may be   include
Atoms   Ionic   Molecular   Solutions

Prophase
The chromosomes in DNA have been copied and paired.

Metaphase
The nucleus disappears. Paired chromosomes line up in the center of the cell.

Anaphase
Paired chromosomes separate and move to opposite sides of the cell.

Telophase
Two nuclei form. The cell divides into two identical daughter cells.

Four Biomes

Tundra	Grassland	Tropical Rain Forest	Desert
cold, dry frozen below the surface	temperate humid	warm wet	very dry
lichens, low shrubs	grasses	palms, tree ferns, vines	cacti
polar bears, caribou, wolves	antelopes, bison, coyotes	bats, birds, monkeys	lizards, snakes, kangaroo rats

The graphic organizer at the left is another example of a concept map. To create this concept map, write the main concept. Draw a circle around it. Next, identify important ideas related to the main concept. Choose a word or a short phrase for each idea. Arrange these under or around the main concept. Draw a circle or box around each idea. Then add lines to link related ideas and concepts. The lines should not cross. You can label the lines to tell why the circles are linked.

Flowcharts

You can use a flowchart to diagram the steps in a process or procedure. The flowchart at the left shows the process of mitosis. Notice it is a vertical chart. Flowcharts can be vertical or horizontal. To make a flowchart, identify the steps to include. Write each step in the correct order, either in a vertical column or in a horizontal row. Draw a box around each step. Connect the boxes with arrows to show direction. You can label the arrows to tell what must happen to get from one step to the next.

Column Charts

You can use a chart or a table to record information and organize it into groups or categories for easy reference. A chart can be a table, a graph, or a diagram. A table is data systematically arranged in rows and columns. To create a column chart, determine the number of items, groups, or categories you want to use. Decide on the number of columns and rows. Draw a chart with that number of columns and rows. Write a heading at the top of each column. Fill in the chart and a title.

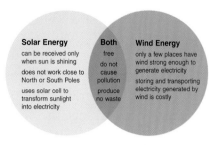

Solar Energy
- can be received only when sun is shining
- does not work close to North or South Poles
- uses solar cell to transform sunlight into electricity

Both
- free
- do not cause pollution
- produce no waste

Wind Energy
- only a few places have wind strong enough to generate electricity
- storing and transporting electricity generated by wind is costly

The Scientific Method

Observation → Question → Hypothesis → Experiment → Analysis → Communication →

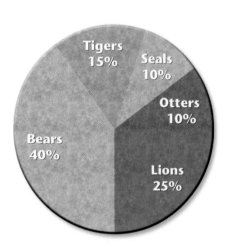

Bears 40%
Tigers 15%
Seals 10%
Otters 10%
Lions 25%

Venn Diagrams

A Venn diagram can help you compare and contrast two objects or processes. To create a Venn diagram, draw two circles of equal size that partially overlap. The circles represent the two things you want to compare. List the characteristics of one in the left circle. List the characteristics of the other in the right circle. List the characteristics both have in common in the area where the two circles intersect.

Circle Diagrams

A circle diagram shows a cycle that repeats. A circle diagram is similar to a flowchart except the last step is connected to the first step. To make a circle diagram, first identify the steps in the process or procedure. Then write the steps in a circle instead of a line. Use arrows to connect the steps. The circle diagram at the left shows the scientific method.

Graphs

You can use a graph to make comparisons and identify patterns among data. Graphs come in many forms such as line graphs, bar graphs, and circle graphs. To create a line or bar graph, draw two perpendicular axes. Label each axis to represent one variable. Add data. Each point or bar indicates a set of values for the two variables. Connect the points or compare the bars to see how the two variables relate. A circle graph shows the size of parts in a whole. To make one, draw a circle. Draw pie-shaped sections of the circle in proportion to the parts. For example, if lions make up one-quarter of a whole population, their section is one-quarter of the circle. Label each section and write its percentage of the whole.

Safety Rules and Symbols

In this book, you will learn about biology through investigations and labs. During these activities, it is important to follow safety rules, procedures, and your teacher's directions. You can avoid accidents by following directions and handling materials carefully. Read and follow the safety rules below, and learn the safety symbols. To alert you to possible dangers, safety symbols will appear with each investigation or lab. Reread the rules below often and review what the symbols mean.

General Safety

◆ Read each Express Lab, Investigation, and Discovery Investigation before doing it. Review the materials list and follow the safety symbols and safety alerts.

◆ Ask questions if you do not understand something.

◆ Never perform an experiment, mix substances, or use equipment without permission.

◆ Keep your work area clean and free of clutter.

◆ Be aware of other students working near you.

◆ Do not play or run during a lab activity. Take your lab work seriously.

◆ Know where fire extinguishers, fire alarms, first aid kits, fire blankets, and the nearest telephone are located. Be familiar with the emergency exits and evacuation route from your room.

◆ Keep your hands away from your face.

◆ Immediately report all accidents to your teacher, including injuries, broken equipment, and spills.

Flame/Heat Safety

◆ Clear your work space of materials that could burn or melt.

◆ Before using a burner, know how to operate the burner and gas outlet.

◆ Be aware of all open flames. Never reach across a flame.

◆ Never leave a flame or operating hot plate unattended.

◆ Do not heat a liquid in a closed container.

◆ When heating a substance in a test tube or flask, point the container away from yourself and others.

◆ Do not touch hot glassware or the surface of an operating hot plate or lightbulb.

◆ In the event of a fire, tell your teacher and leave the room immediately.

◆ If your clothes catch on fire, stop, drop to the floor, and roll.

Electrical Safety

◆ Never use electrical equipment near water, on wet surfaces, or with wet hands or clothing.

◆ Alert your teacher to any frayed or damaged cords or plugs.

◆ Before plugging in equipment, be sure the power control is in the "off" position.

◆ Do not place electrical cords in walkways or let cords hang over table edges.

◆ Electricity flowing in wire causes the wire to become hot. Use caution.

◆ Turn off and unplug electrical equipment when you are finished using it.

Chemical Safety

◆ Check labels on containers to be sure you are using the right substance.

◆ Do not directly smell any substance. If you are instructed to smell a substance, gently fan your hand over the substance, waving its vapors toward you.

◆ When handling substances that give off gases or vapors, work in a fume hood or well-ventilated area.

◆ Do not taste any substance. Never eat, drink, or chew gum in your work area.

◆ Do not return unused chemicals to their original containers.

◆ Avoid skin contact with chemicals. Some chemicals can irritate or harm skin.

◆ If a chemical spills on your clothing or skin, rinse the area immediately with plenty of water. Tell your teacher.

◆ When diluting an acid or base with water, always add the acid or base to the water. Do not add water to the acid or base.

◆ Wash your hands after working with chemicals.

Eye Protection

◆ Wear safety goggles at all times or as directed by your teacher.

◆ If a chemical gets in your eyes or on your face, use an eyewash station or flush your eyes and face with running water immediately. Tell your teacher.

Animal Safety

◆ Do not touch or approach an animal without your teacher's permission.

◆ Handle and care for animals only as your teacher directs.

◆ If you are bitten, stung, or scratched by an animal, tell your teacher.

◆ Do not expose animals to loud noises, overcrowding, or other stresses.

◆ Wash your hands after touching an animal.

Hand Safety

◆ Wear protective gloves when working with chemicals or solutions. Wear gloves for handling preserved specimens and plants.

◆ Do not touch an object that could be hot.

◆ Use tongs or utensils to hold a container over a heat source.

◆ Wash your hands when you are finished with a lab activity.

Plant Safety

◆ Do not place any part of a plant in your mouth. Do not rub plant parts or liquids on your skin.

◆ Wear gloves when handling plants or as directed by your teacher.

◆ Wash your hands after handling any part of a plant.

Glassware Safety

◆ Check glassware for cracks or chips before use. Give broken glassware to your teacher; do not use it.

◆ Keep glassware away from the edge of a work surface.

◆ If glassware breaks, tell your teacher. Dispose of glass according to your teacher's directions.

Clothing Protection

◆ Wear a lab coat or apron at all times or as directed by your teacher.

◆ Tie back long hair, remove dangling jewelry, and secure loose-fitting clothing.

◆ Do not wear open-toed shoes, sandals, or canvas shoes in the lab.

Sharp Object Safety

◆ Take care when using scissors, pins, scalpels, or pointed tools or blades.

◆ Cut objects on a suitable work surface. Cut away from yourself and others.

◆ If you cut yourself, notify your teacher.

Cleanup/Waste Disposal

◆ If a chemical spills, alert your teacher and ask for clean up instructions.

◆ Follow your teacher's directions to dispose and clean up substances.

◆ Turn off burners, water faucets, electrical equipment, and gas outlets.

◆ Clean equipment if needed and return it to its proper location.

◆ Clean your work area and work surface.

◆ Wash your hands when you are finished.

Biology: Investigating the Cycles of Life

The photo on the left shows the different stages of a butterfly's life. The caterpillar at the bottom could be called the infant stage. The middle object is a chrysalis. Inside this hard case, the caterpillar is going through many changes. You might say it's a teenager. When the insect breaks out of the case, it's an adult winged butterfly. These stages make up the life cycle of a butterfly. All living things go through life cycles. In Chapter 1, you will learn about different cycles of life. You will also learn how scientists study life and science.

Organize Your Thoughts

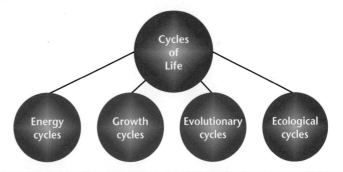

Goals for Learning

◆ To understand that biology is the study of life

◆ To describe energy and understand what happens in an energy cycle

◆ To describe what happens in a growth cycle

◆ To explain what happens during an evolutionary cycle

◆ To explain what an ecological cycle is

◆ To tell why scientists use the scientific method

1

Biology

The study of life

Organism

A living thing; one of many different forms of life

Biologist

A person who studies life

Biology is the name for a whole field of science. Simply put, biology is the study of life. That sounds pretty simple, doesn't it? Yes, but life is complex. Animals and plants are living. An insect flying around your head is part of life. Even the germs that cause you to get sick are living. That gray-green mold on old bread is another form of life. As you can see, many different **organisms** make up life. An organism is a living thing, one of many different forms of life.

Life means more than just a list of these different forms. Life includes how you and other life forms live in our world. Watering a garden is part of life. Birds flying south for the winter are part of life. Eating, drinking, cleaning yourself, even feeding your pets are all parts of life.

Biology is a science that studies all of these things and more. A **biologist** studies life. There are many different types of biologists. Some biologists study plants. Like the biologist in Figure 1.1.1, some biologists study animals. The list of biologists and what they do is long.

Figure 1.1.1 *Biologists study life.*

Cycle

A course or series of events or operations that repeats

Link to ➤➤➤

Earth Science

You might think about life as being present only in places where people live. However, some form of life exists in nearly every place on Earth. Scientists have discovered microscopic life at deep-sea vents on the bottom of the ocean and within thick layers of ice at the poles. They have even found life in the intense heat of rocket boosters!

There are many different ways to study life. How do biologists decide how to study life? They observe the world around them and find something they do not understand. When they find something they do not understand, they ask questions about it. Using different methods, they try to answer those questions. As biologists answer more and more questions, they notice patterns.

One pattern seen in different parts of life is a **cycle.** Saying life runs in cycles means that many of life's activities repeat themselves. It also means that many actions start at one point. These actions go through different steps to return to that same point. Upon returning to that point, they then begin the cycle all over again.

These cycles come in many different forms. Many overlap. This means parts of one cycle may be the starting point for other cycles. It may take a long time for some cycles to get back to the starting point. It may take others less than a second.

To better understand biology, we will look at some cycles that make life work. There are four major groups of cycles. Each cycle is made up of many different individual cycles. The four cycles are Energy, Growth, Evolutionary, and Ecological. As seen in Figure 1.1.2, all of these cycles work together.

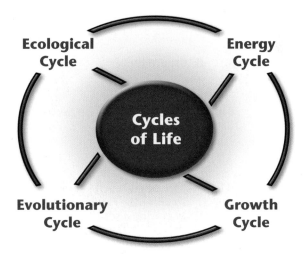

Figure 1.1.2 *Life cycles work together.*

On a sheet of paper, write the word that completes each sentence correctly.

1. Biology is the study of _____.

2. The activities of life run in patterns, or _____.

3. Life is made up of different _____, or forms of life.

On a sheet of paper, write the letter of the answer that completes each sentence correctly.

4. The first step a biologist takes when deciding how to study life is to _____.

A do an experiment   **C** make an observation

B write a paper   **D** make a hypothesis

5. A biologist studies _____.

A soil   **C** weather

B life   **D** rocks

6. Energy, growth, evolutionary, and ecological describe different types of _____.

A cycles   **C** experiments

B organisms   **D** life

Critical Thinking

On a sheet of paper, write the answers to the following questions. Use complete sentences.

7. What is a cycle?

8. List three different examples of life.

9. How might a scientist begin to study the behavior of a spider?

10. What happens when a cycle returns to its starting point?

Objectives

After reading this lesson, you should be able to

◆ define energy and give examples

◆ state the law of conservation of energy

◆ define reproduction

◆ name different parts of life that can reproduce

◆ connect energy and growth cycles

Energy

The ability to do work; found in many different forms

Transform

To change form or makeup

Energy Cycles

Energy is the ability to do work. Think about how you use energy. You use energy to walk, talk, sing, and even eat. You need energy to do anything. Energy is found in many different forms. Energy allows life to do what it is supposed to do. Where does energy come from? The sun serves as the main source of energy for our planet. How does sunlight give you energy to play a game, even when you are inside? The energy from the sun changes into different forms.

Energy can **transform,** or change form, into different types, depending on how it is used. What happens when the energy runs out? Energy never runs out. It just changes completely into other forms.

Express Lab 1

Materials
◆ safety goggles
◆ solar cell with small connecting motor

Procedure
1. On a sunny day, take the solar cell and connecting motor outside. Put on safety goggles.

2. Observe the activity of the motor when the solar cell is exposed to the sun.

3. Cover the solar cell and observe the activity of the motor.

4. Uncover and cover the solar cell 2 or 3 times. Observe the activity of the motor.

Analysis
1. What was the source of energy in this activity?

2. Why did the activity of the motor change when you covered the solar cell?

3. Describe the different ways that energy was transformed during this activity.

A law in science states that energy cannot be created or destroyed. This is called the **law of conservation of energy.** Each time energy changes form, some of it is given off as **heat.** Heat is a form of energy. That means that during any energy transformation, all the energy will not be able to be used in the new form.

So how does energy cycle? Overall, the energy in the universe cycles through different forms. On Earth, energy gets cycled through life in different forms. Figure 1.2.1 shows that different organisms have their own cycles they run through to do work.

We will look at some of the different forms of energy and their cycles in the next sections. Understanding how energy cycles through life lets us see how life operates.

Figure 1.2.1 *Every life form needs energy to do work.*

Growth Cycles

If you use energy to do work, what kind of work are you doing? That answer depends on what part of life you study. A major job of all forms of life is to grow. Growth is found at many different levels.

One of the biggest parts of growth is the making of new life through **reproduction.** Reproduction occurs in many ways from **DNA.** The letters DNA stand for deoxyribonucleic acid, a chemical in an organism that contains the instructions for life. Different cycles are involved in growing. Each cycle ties into the next.

All of these cycles use energy from different energy cycles to run. By growing, the smallest units of life, called **cells,** are able to carry out their job. As cells grow, so do organisms. As organisms grow, they can reproduce and start the cycles all over again in new organisms. One cycle that all life runs is that of life and death.

Reproduction

The process of making new life

DNA

Deoxyribonucleic acid; a chemical in an organism that contains the instructions for life

Cell

The basic unit of life

❀ ❀

Technology and Society

Genetic disorders can cause different kinds of diseases in humans. When a person has a genetic disorder, it means that an important section of his or her DNA does not work properly. Scientists are learning how to insert healthy DNA into human cells to cure a disease. This technique is called gene therapy. The hope is that when cells with healthy DNA are added to a person's body, they will begin to produce new cells that work properly. In time, the new cells would correct the damage and heal the person. Doctors are using gene therapy to help patients with many diseases, including cancer and cystic fibrosis.

Some growth cycles not only help in reproduction, but also in doing work. The instructions found in DNA are turned into action through different cycles. The products of these cycles, such as **proteins,** water, and heat, help a cell to grow and work. These products run their own cycles. As a cell ages, it begins to reproduce itself through different methods.

When DNA and cells reproduce, random events occur that help bring about each organism's uniqueness. You can see in Figure 1.2.2 that each individual has his or her own special group of qualities. This uniqueness in organisms is important for life to continue.

Figure 1.2.2 *Every individual has special qualities.*

On a sheet of paper, write the letter of the answer that completes each sentence correctly.

1. When energy changes form, some energy is _____.

   A lost   **C** given off as heat

   B gained   **D** added as heat

2. A chemical called _____ contains the instructions for life.

   A protein   **C** cell

   B DNA   **D** atom

3. The process of making new life is called _____.

   A reproduction   **C** heat

   B DNA   **D** growth cycle

On a sheet of paper, write the word that completes each sentence correctly.

4. The main source of energy for our planet comes from the _____.

5. The smallest unit of life is the _____.

6. The idea that energy cannot be created or destroyed is the law of _____ of energy.

Critical Thinking

On a sheet of paper, write the answers to the following questions. Use complete sentences.

7. Give two examples of how you used energy today.

8. How are energy cycles and growth cycles related?

9. Explain why the sentence, "Rubbing your hands together creates energy," is an incorrect statement.

10. Why is it important to get enough protein in your diet?

Evolution

The changes in a population over time

Species

A group of organisms that can reproduce with each other

Speciation

The process of making a new species

Extinct

When no members of a species are alive

Adaptation

An adjustment to environmental conditions

Evolutionary Cycles

Life must change to grow. Does this mean the way life is now is not the way it has always been? Think about it. Dinosaurs once existed on Earth, although we don't see these big lizards on the planet today. Scientists have discovered their bones. Dinosaurs are one of many examples that show biologists that life changes. The process of life changing over time is called **evolution.**

If life keeps changing, how does it cycle back to the beginning? The actions of evolution happen in cycles, but the products are different. Scientists group all organisms into **species.** Individuals in the same species can reproduce with each other. Life changes over time by creating new species, a process called **speciation.**

Speciation often happens in bursts. Usually, some event like an earthquake, flood, or other natural disaster causes some species to become **extinct.** Extinction means that species no longer exist. Extinction can make room for new species, and the evolutionary cycle continues. Many species will be created from the species that are left. As seen in Figures 1.3.1 and 1.3.2, new species have **adaptations,** or changes, that make them better able to live in new areas. As these new species grow, some are better able to live than others.

Figures 1.3.1 and 1.3.2 *Animals adapt to their environment.*

Environment

An organism's natural and man-made surroundings

Link to ≻≻≻

Environmental Science

Many advances in technology and the environment come from other organisms. Environmental engineers recently observed microscopic organisms called *bacteria* eating toxic waste on an abandoned industrial site in Michigan. They isolated and released the bacteria onto a test site filled with a poisonous chemical that was harming Lake Huron. The bacteria cleaned the poisons from the site in just a few weeks.

These species become the major species found in an area. Other species will become extinct or keep adapting to survive. At some point, another major event will happen to cause extinction. Speciation starts over again. Evolutionary cycles are some of the slowest to happen. Biologists who study evolution measure time in millions of years. Evolution is present in all areas of biology.

Biologists study life. Life must change, or evolve, to grow. Events that cause evolution are found in DNA, the cell, and the **environment.** The environment is an organism's natural and man-made surroundings. Through evolution, life has changed into many different forms. Scientists group these forms together based on what each form has in common.

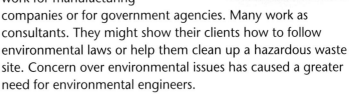

Science at Work

Environmental Engineer

Environmental engineers use their knowledge of biology and chemistry to solve environmental problems. Environmental engineers work on a wide variety of projects. For example, they design water treatment systems and check levels of air pollution. They set up recycling programs, study the effects of acid rain, and protect wildlife.

Some environmental engineers work for manufacturing companies or for government agencies. Many work as consultants. They might show their clients how to follow environmental laws or help them clean up a hazardous waste site. Concern over environmental issues has caused a greater need for environmental engineers.

Environmental engineers have a degree from a four-year college. They also must pass a test to be licensed by the government.

Ecological Cycles

You know that life uses energy to grow and change over time, or evolve. Scientists also look at life in the present. **Ecology** is the branch of biology that studies the relationships of living things with each other and their surroundings. This branch of science looks at how members of the same species and different species live together.

Ecologists look at how organisms act in their environments. The environment has its own cycles that keep everyday life going. **Ecosystems** are made up of all the living and nonliving things in a particular area. As an example, think about a frog in a lily pond. The frog and lilies are living things. The water and rocks are nonliving things. A biologist may want to study why this frog lives in this lily pond.

Ecologists also study the behavior of organisms, or how they respond to stimuli. A **stimulus** is anything to which an organism reacts. The light coming in your bedroom in the morning is a stimulus that causes you, an organism, to wake up.

Organisms' behaviors often occur in cycles. For example, birds fly south for the winter. Then they fly north in the spring. Chipmunks, woodchucks, box turtles, and toads go into hibernation in the winter. As spring approaches, they become active. The way a body receives and sends messages is a cycle. Some cycles happen in less than a second, like body messages. Other cycles take years to run a full course.

Ecology

The study of interactions among living things and the nonliving things in their environment

Ecologist

A person who studies ecology

Ecosystem

All of the living and nonliving things found in any particular area

Stimulus

Anything to which an organism reacts

The Environment

Have you traveled out of the country? If you have, you may have seen government agents searching luggage or vehicles for plants or animals. The movement of plants and animals across international borders is controlled to protect the wildlife that lives in various ecosystems.

Travelers are not allowed to bring plants and animals from one environment into another. Ecosystems build up a balance of life that keeps the population fairly stable. If a plant or animal is released into a new ecosystem, it often can upset this balance.

One example of a disrupted ecosystem is the problem of the African clawed frog in California. African clawed frogs are banned in California, but many people bring them into the state to keep as pets.

Some frogs have escaped into the wild. They have reproduced, creating a new population of wild African clawed frogs. These wild frogs are now causing problems by eating and destroying many of the plants and animals in the state.

African clawed frogs are not from, or native to, California. No animals eat them or compete with them for resources. Without competition or predators, the number of frogs has increased rapidly. State officials are looking for ways to control them.

1. Why are African clawed frogs spreading so rapidly in California?

2. What resources do plants or animals compete for?

3. See if you can identify a plant or animal in your local environment that is not native to the area. Find out if it is disrupting the ecosystem. Write a description that explains how it is disrupting the ecosystem.

Lesson 3   R E V I E W

Word Bank

ecosystem

extinct

speciation

On a sheet of paper, write the word from the Word Bank that completes each sentence correctly.

1. The process of creating new species is _____.

2. A(n) _____ is made of the living and nonliving things in an area.

3. When no members of a species are alive, the species is _____.

On a sheet of paper, write the word that completes each sentence correctly.

4. Changes that make a species better able to live in new areas are _____.

5. The study of living things and their environment is called _____.

6. Two kinds of organisms that cannot reproduce with each other are separate _____.

Critical Thinking

On a sheet of paper, write the answers to the following questions. Use complete sentences.

7. How is a polar bear adapted to living in cold polar areas?

8. How does extinction of a species cause more species to develop?

9. What is an ecosystem? Give an example.

10. You water a wilted plant. The plant becomes healthy. What is the stimulus?

INVESTIGATION 1

What Is Life?

Biologists study all kinds of life. Life takes on many diverse forms. All life runs through cycles of energy, growth, evolution, and ecology. In this lab you will examine some different forms of life and note their different cycles.

Procedure

1. To record your data, make a data table like the one shown here.

Sample	Energy Cycle	Growth Cycle	Evolutionary Cycle	Ecological Cycle	Living/ Nonliving
1					
2					
3					
4					
5					
6					
7					
8					

2. Put on safety goggles and a lab coat or apron. **Safety Alert: Do not open containers or touch samples unless your teacher directs you to do so.**

3. Examine each sample. Use a flashlight if needed. Make a check mark in the Energy Cycle column if you think the sample is involved in an energy cycle.

4. Repeat Step 3 for each cycle. Place a check mark in the column if you think the sample is involved in that cycle.

5. In the final column, decide whether the sample is living or nonliving.

Cleanup/Disposal

Follow your teacher's instructions for disposal of any samples.

Analysis

1. Which samples are living and which are nonliving?

2. Which nonliving samples show some cycles that are common with cycles of living samples? What are the cycles?

Conclusions

1. What forms does energy take while cycling between living things? Describe two examples.

2. Which living samples are a part of the cycles of other living samples?

Explore Further

Think of two or more organisms that are part of a cycle. Create a diagram showing the organisms in the cycle. Label your diagram with the cycle's name.

Specimen

A sample; an individual item or part considered typical of a group or whole

Scientific method

A series of steps used to test possible answers to scientific questions

You may wonder how biologists study all of these different forms of life. There are so many things to look at and understand. Science is a way of learning about the natural world. Scientific knowledge is described by physical, mathematical, and other models.

Scientists use scientific principles and knowledge to investigate living, physical, and designed systems. They ask questions and choose the ones they want to investigate. Different kinds of questions require different methods of scientific investigation. Some investigations involve observing and describing organisms, objects, or events. Others involve collecting **specimens,** or samples, and gathering information. Some require writing test procedures, running experiments, and making and using models.

Biologists have developed different ways to understand life. They use a logical process to explore the world and collect information. This process is called the **scientific method,** and it includes specific steps. Biologists follow these steps or variations of these steps to test possible answers to their questions.

All scientists use the scientific method. They may follow the steps in a different order. They may skip some steps, but they all follow this process. Scientists use the scientific method because scientific knowledge depends on facts that can be tested and retested by other scientists. Scientific explanations must be based on observations and experimental evidence.

Suppose one scientist researches a question and comes up with an answer that proves a fact. Using the scientific method, scientists from anywhere in the world should be able to find the same answer and prove the same fact. Scientists evaluate other scientists' findings. They examine and compare evidence. They communicate their results. If they don't come up with the same facts, they try to figure out why.

Link to >>>

Health

Sickness is often a battle between two life forms for resources. When you are infected with bacteria, you feel bad because a growing number of bacteria are feeding on the resources in your body. The bacteria are also releasing waste products poisonous to you. Your doctor may prescribe an antibiotic, which is a medicine that destroys the bacteria.

The scientific method requires scientists to use many skills. These skills include predicting, observing, organizing, classifying, modeling, measuring, inferring, analyzing, and communicating. The steps of the scientific method are:

1. Observation

2. Question

3. Hypothesis

4. Experiment

5. Analysis

6. Communication

Figure 1.4.1 shows the steps in the scientific method. Let's talk about each step.

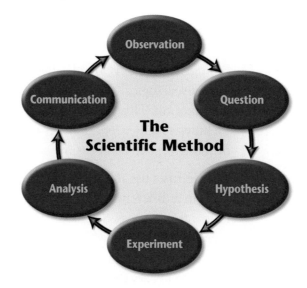

Figure 1.4.1 *The scientific method is a constant cycle scientists use to find answers to many questions.*

Observation. You perform this step without even being aware of it. Look around the classroom. Look at your classmates and all the objects in the room. This first step is simply looking at the world around you, watching life. Scientists also look at the world around them. While they are watching, or observing, they may see something they don't understand. If it interests them, they move to the next step of the scientific method.

Scientists in research teams tend to see things alike. This can lead to bias, or favoring or opposing something without a reason. To guard against this, scientific teams look for bias in the design of their investigations and in their analysis.

Question. You know what a question is. People ask each other questions every day. When scientists see something they do not understand, they ask a question and try to find the answer. The questions biologists try to answer deal with life and all its interactions. They work to find answers to questions like "Why do families look alike?" or "What type of fishes like to live in lakes?" Once biologists have questions, then they can begin looking for answers.

Hypothesis. A **hypothesis** is an educated guess. After asking a question, scientists guess at the answer. Scientists then test their answer to see if it is correct. Scientists usually make their guesses based on what they already know, then use experiments to see if they are right.

Experiment. An experiment is the procedure used to test whether a hypothesis is correct. Biologists perform many different kinds of experiments. The kind they perform depends on the question they are trying to answer. Biologists studying what kinds of fishes live in lakes do not want to perform experiments in a mountain cave. They want to look at lakes, maybe ones on mountains. They do not want to study the plants growing in lakes. They want to look at the kinds of fishes in lakes.

Scientists design experiments to test possible answers to the question. There are two separate groups in a science experiment: the **control group** and the **experimental group.** The control group is the setup in an experiment that has no variable, or factor, changed. The experimental group is the same as the control group, except for one factor to be tested. That factor is called the **variable.** Scientists control the conditions and variables of their experiments to get useful data.

As an example, say you want to see the effect of light on the sprouting of green bean seeds. Seeds grown in no light are the control group. Seeds grown with different amounts of light are the experimental group. The variable is the amount of light the seeds get every 24 hours. Seeds in the variable group will get no light. Seeds in the experimental group will get four hours, eight hours, or twelve hours of light.

Scientists usually perform their experiments many times to be sure they get a similar answer every time. To keep track of all of the **data,** or information, they collect, scientists use different tools such as computers and calculators. Scientists often use special equipment specifically designed for their experiments. Math is also important in experiments. Scientists use math to gather data, analyze data, and to communicate results.

Analysis. After scientists get their results, they analyze them, or make sense of the experiment results. They compare the results to the hypothesis. Scientists need evidence before believing a hypothesis is correct. Scientists see if their results agree with their hypothesis. If the results don't agree, scientists may do more experiments or ask a different question. Sometimes the results answer the question but do not agree with the hypothesis. Remember that a hypothesis is a guess and can be wrong. Sometimes the results and hypothesis match. The answers scientists find often lead to more questions.

Communication. After scientists have checked their results and tested their hypothesis, they truthfully tell others their results. Other scientists may be interested in the same questions, so it is important for scientists to share their information. Scientists publish their methods and results in scientific publications. The Internet, a worldwide network of computers, helps scientists communicate. Scientists use the Internet to share their data and results. They also talk to each other and make the public aware of their findings.

You can use the scientific method to solve problems. The next time you have a question, use facts you know to answer it. If you do not know, research by reading or experimenting.

Scientists check each other's work by repeating the same experiments. If the first results are accurate, then repeated experiments should give the same results. If the same experiments give different scientists the same results, then those results are considered true. This process is called peer review.

Biologists use the scientific method in some way to answer their questions about life. Sometimes they skip some steps or repeat steps. You can use these same steps in your daily life. This doesn't mean that every time you have a question, you have to run an experiment. It means you can solve different problems scientifically.

Scientists judge a new theory by how well scientific data are explained by the new theory.

When new evidence is discovered, scientific ideas and theories may change. A **theory** is a widely accepted idea that explains many different events. Some famous scientists, such as Nicolaus Copernicus and Charles Darwin, were ignored when they first presented their ideas. However, some scientists tested their research and experiments. The experiments always produced the same results. Over time, theories may change as scientists collect and analyze new evidence. For example, scientists once thought the earth was the center of the solar system. Research showed this was not true. We now know that the sun, not the earth, sits at the center of the solar system. In this case, a new theory fit observations better than the old theory.

Finding the answers to questions often leads to asking more questions. When new questions are asked, scientists use the scientific method again. This method is a constant cycle that scientists use to find the answers to many questions. Science is a vast body of changing and increasing knowledge.

★ ✦ ★ ✦ ★ ✦ ★ ✦ ★ ✦ ★ ✦ ★ ✦ ★ ✦ ★ ✦ ★ ✦ ★ ✦ ★ ✦ ★ ✦ ★ ✦ ★ ✦ ★ ✦ ★ ✦ ★ ✦ ★

Achievements in Science

Preventing Infectious Disease

One of the greatest achievements in science has been our understanding of infectious diseases. Before the 1860s, people didn't know much about disease. They didn't know why they got sick, how they got better, or how to keep from getting sick.

Beginning in the 1860s, scientists made many discoveries about disease. The French scientist Louis Pasteur discovered that many diseases were caused by tiny organisms called germs. In Germany, the scientist Robert Koch read about Pasteur's work. Koch began studying germs. Pasteur's and Koch's greatest tools were the microscope and the scientific method. Through many experiments, they concluded that germs cause infectious diseases—diseases that spread from one living thing to another. They also concluded that specific germs cause specific diseases.

Because of the work of Pasteur, Koch, and others, we know how to identify the cause of a disease. We also know how to prevent people and animals from getting some deadly infectious diseases.

On a sheet of paper, write the word in parentheses that completes each sentence correctly.

1. A step in the scientific method that involves making an educated guess is a(n) (question, hypothesis, analysis).

2. A(n) (observation, experiment, question) tests a hypothesis.

3. The answer to a question must be (observed, communicated, hypothesized) to benefit society.

On a sheet of paper, write the word or words that complete each sentence correctly.

4. Computers talk to each other through a worldwide system called the _____.

5. Scientists set up _____ to be tested during an experiment, and then record _____ as they conduct the experiment.

6. Many hypotheses that are supported by testing and accepted can be grouped together in a(n) _____.

Critical Thinking

On a sheet of paper, write the answers to the following questions. Use complete sentences.

7. You set up a tent in the yard for two weeks. When you take down the tent, you notice the grass beneath it has turned yellow. You wonder why. Write a possible hypothesis to explain this observation.

8. Describe an experiment you could do to test your hypothesis for Question 7.

9. The results of an experiment support a scientist's hypothesis. Why is it important to repeat the experiment several times?

10. What happens to a theory or scientific knowledge when new evidence is discovered?

Materials

- safety goggles
- lab coat or apron
- 2 plastic cups
- 20 corn seeds
- water
- vinegar
- paper towels
- eyedropper

Using the Scientific Method

Scientists answer questions and solve problems in an orderly way. They use a series of steps called the scientific method. How can you use the scientific method to answer questions? You will find out in this lab.

Suppose you are watching a news report about acid rain. The report explains that acid rain is rain that has more acid in it than usual. The acid forms from certain kinds of air pollution. The report shows trees that have been damaged by acid rain. You wonder: How might acid rain affect the way a plant starts growing?

Procedure

1. In a small group, discuss the question in the second paragraph above. Then write a hypothesis about how acid rain might affect the way a plant starts growing. The hypothesis should be one that you could test with an experiment.

2. Write a procedure for your experiment. The experiment should take 8 days to complete. Use materials from the Materials list in your procedure. Number the steps. Include any Safety Alerts.

3. Be sure your experiment changes only one variable, or factor, at a time. Include a control group. Remember that a control is a setup for which you do not change any variables.

4. Draw a data table to record your data for 8 days.

5. Have your hypothesis, procedure, and Safety Alerts approved by your teacher. Then carry out your experiment.

Cleanup/Disposal

Before leaving the lab, clean up your materials and wash your hands.

Analysis

1. What variable did you change in this experiment?

2. What changes did you see among the corn seeds after Day 4? What changes did you see after Day 8?

Conclusions

1. Was your hypothesis supported by the results of your investigation?

2. What problems did you have in performing the experiment? What part of the procedure would you change to be more successful?

3. If a hypothesis is not supported by data from an experiment, is that experiment a failure? Explain your answer.

4. How do you think acid rain affects the way plants start growing?

Explore Further

In your group, discuss other variables that might affect how a plant starts growing. Pick one variable your group would like to investigate. Using the scientific method, write a procedure to carry out your investigation.

Discovery of Mad Cow Disease

In the mid-1980s, farmers in England noticed that several cows showed strange symptoms before dying. When the animals were examined after death, scientists saw that their brains looked like sponges. Scientists determined the disease that killed these cows was caused by a *prion.* Prions are proteins that cause disease by changing other proteins.

Prions are a fairly new idea in biology. When DNA was discovered, scientists assumed that DNA created proteins. Proteins are organic compounds that cells use to grow and work. Scientists also assumed that proteins could not be the cause of disease. They thought only bacteria and viruses caused diseases. *Bacteria* are the simplest single cells that carry out all basic life activities. Some bacteria cause disease. *Viruses* are nonliving particles that can cause disease. However, evidence now supports the theory that prions are proteins that cause disease. No DNA or other organism is involved.

The news became more startling in the 1990s when people in England suddenly started becoming sick with Creutzfeldt-Jakob disease. Creutzfeldt-Jakob disease is similar to mad cow disease but affects humans. Scientists examined the prions of infected humans and compared them to prions that cause mad cow disease. They hypothesized that the prions were the same. Testing of beef sold in grocery stores showed the presence of prions.

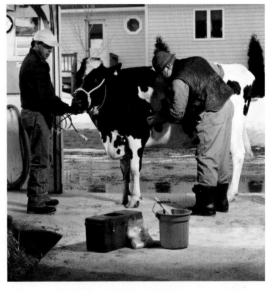

Given this information, many scientists now think that Creutzfeldt-Jakob disease is caused by mad cow prions. The prions are passed on to humans who eat infected beef. Today the United States government closely monitors any outbreak of mad cow disease. The government prevents cows raised near any outbreaks from being sold as beef.

1. What is the difference between mad cow disease and Creutzfeldt-Jakob disease?

2. Describe how these diseases are caused.

3. What evidence supported the hypothesis that Creutzfeldt-Jakob disease is connected to mad cow disease?

- Biology is the study of life, including the interactions of life forms with their environment.

- Scientists try to learn about life by observing patterns, or cycles.

- The four major groups of cycles are energy, growth, evolutionary, and ecological cycles.

- Energy is the ability to do work.

- Energy cannot be created or destroyed, but is transformed into different forms.

- DNA contains instructions for life and reproduction.

- Proteins are created as a result of the growth cycle involving DNA.

- Life is constantly changing. The process of life changing over time is called evolution.

- Life forms that can reproduce together are considered the same species.

- Through speciation, new species are created while other species become extinct.

- The science of studying living things and their surroundings is a branch of biology called ecology.

- An ecosystem is made up of the living and nonliving things in a particular area.

- Scientists use a series of steps called the scientific method to understand life.

- The six steps in the scientific method include Observation, Question, Hypothesis, Experiment, Analysis, and Communication.

Vocabulary

adaptation, 10
analysis, 20
biologist, 2
biology, 2
cell, 7
control group, 19
cycle, 3
data, 20
DNA, 7
ecologist, 12
ecology, 12

ecosystem, 12
energy, 5
environment, 11
evolution, 10
experimental group, 19
extinct, 10
heat, 6
hypothesis, 19
law of conservation
   of energy, 6
organism, 2

protein, 8
reproduction, 7
scientific method, 17
speciation, 10
species, 10
specimen, 17
stimulus, 12
theory, 21
transform, 5
variable, 19

Chapter 1   R E V I E W

Word Bank

adaptation

biologist

biology

cell

control group

cycle

data

DNA

ecosystem

environment

experimental
   group

heat

hypothesis

law of
   conservation of
   energy

protein

reproduction

speciation

species

theory

variable

Vocabulary Review

On a sheet of paper, write the word or words from the Word Bank to best complete the sentence.

1. A(n) _____ is a chemical used by a cell to grow and function.

2. The information gained from an experiment is called _____ and is recorded for analysis.

3. A(n) _____ is made up of all the living and nonliving things that are found in an area.

4. Two organisms that can reproduce with each other are members of the same _____.

5. Biologists study _____, which is the study of life.

6. The instructions for any life form is contained in its _____.

7. New life is created through the process of _____.

8. One form of energy is _____.

9. To test a hypothesis, a biologist can design an experiment with a(n) _____, or factor.

10. A(n) _____ is a course or event that repeats and usually leads back to the starting point.

11. An organism's _____ includes everything that surrounds it.

12. A(n) _____ is an educated guess.

13. A(n) _____ has been well-tested and makes sense of a great variety of scientific observations.

14. A(n) _____ is the basic unit of life.

Review continued on next page

15. A(n) _____ is an adjustment to environmental conditions.

16. The process of life changing over time by creating new species is ____.

17. A ____ studies life and designs experiments with two groups: the ____ and the ____.

18. The idea that energy cannot be created or destroyed is the ____.

Concept Review

On a sheet of paper, write the letter of the answer that completes each answer correctly.

19. The step in the scientific method in which a scientist compares experiment results with a hypothesis is ____.

A analysis

B communication

C observation

D question

20. A heat wave that causes an organism to move to a cooler climate is an example of a(n) ____.

A adaptation

B extinction

C speciation

D stimulus

21. As energy changes form, it is often converted to ____.

A heat

B life

C DNA

D protein

22. The branch of science that studies interactions among living and nonliving things in their environment is _____.

   A botany

   B ecology

   C biology

   D zoology

Critical Thinking

On a sheet of paper, write the answers to the following questions. Use complete sentences.

23. List each step of the scientific method along with a brief description of what happens during the step. Then briefly explain why scientists use the scientific method.

24. What usually causes some species to become extinct? Give two examples of species that are now extinct.

25. Describe the four cycles that are found in biology.

Research and Write

Research a species of plant or animal that is in danger of becoming extinct. Prepare a short report on the species. In the report, include information on the species' native habitat. Tell how many are estimated to exist and why the species is endangered. Describe what is being done to help this species. Present this information to your class.

Test-Taking Tip When you have vocabulary words to learn, make flash cards. Write each word on the front of a card. Write its definition on the back. Use the flash cards in a game to test your vocabulary skills.

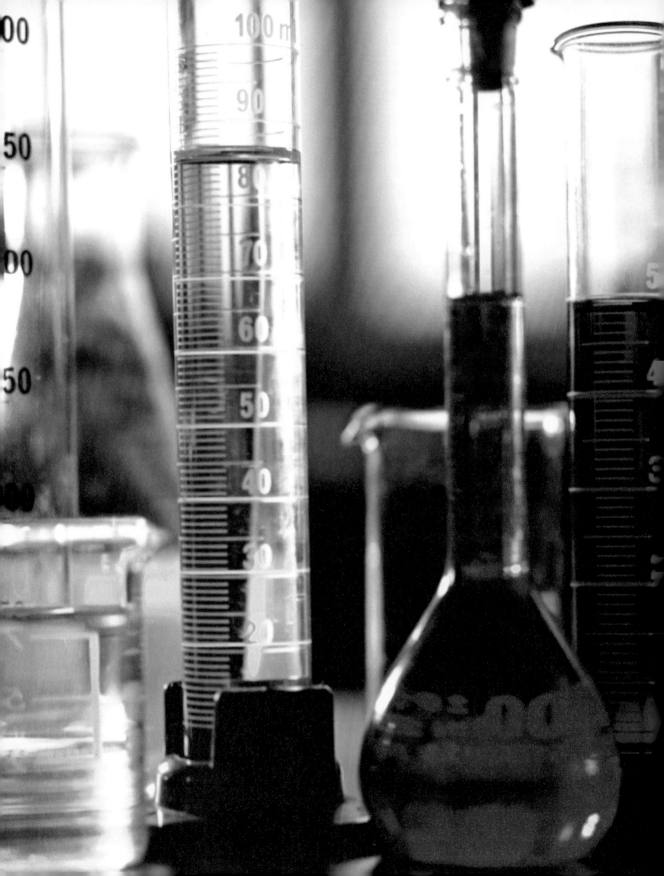

Basic Chemistry

What makes the liquids in the photograph different colors? It's chemistry. You may be wondering what chemistry has to do with biology. Chemistry is the study of matter, and living things are made of matter. To understand the way living things work, you need to know something about chemistry. In Chapter 2, you will learn about the basic structure of matter. You will also learn about matter especially important to living things.

Organize Your Thoughts

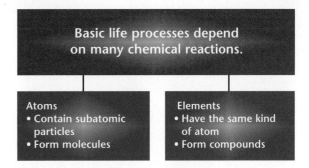

Basic life processes depend on many chemical reactions.

Atoms
• Contain subatomic particles
• Form molecules

Elements
• Have the same kind of atom
• Form compounds

Goals for Learning

◆ To recognize that living things are made of matter
◆ To understand how elements can be recombined
◆ To recognize and understand chemical formulas
◆ To understand that recombining chemical elements results in storage and release of energy
◆ To describe water's unique properties
◆ To recognize that most chemical reactions are acid-base reactions

Objectives

After reading this lesson, you should be able to

◆ explain that all substances are made of matter

◆ recognize that matter has physical and chemical properties

◆ understand that living things are made of matter

◆ explain how energy is released or stored during chemical processes

All living things are made up of **molecules.** A molecule is the smallest particle of a substance that has all the properties of the substance. Each molecule is made up of one or more **atoms.** An atom is the basic unit of **matter.** Matter is anything that has mass and takes up space. **Mass** is the amount of material an object has.

There is great **diversity** among living things, from small mice to large elephants. Whatever the size, living things can be studied at many levels of **organization.**

One level of organization is the **molecular** level. Studying biology at the molecular level requires an understanding of basic **chemistry.** Chemistry is the study of matter and how it changes. **Chemical processes** release and store energy in the bonds of molecules.

Similar activities occur in all cells at the molecular level. This is true for human cells, plant cells, or the cells of **bacteria.** Bacteria are the simplest single cells that carry out all basic life activities.

Molecule

The smallest particle of a substance that has all the properties of the substance

Atom

The basic unit of matter

Matter

Anything that has mass and takes up space

Mass

The amount of material an object has

Figure 2.1.1 *What do these objects have in common?*

Scientists learn about cellular activities in humans by studying the cells of less complex organisms. We will begin our study of living things by learning about matter.

All substances are made of matter. Your desk, a plant, a bicycle, a water drop, and the air are all examples of matter. All matter has properties that are used to describe the matter. How would you describe the difference between your desk and a plant? Think about the differences between water and air.

Matter has **physical properties.** A physical property is a characteristic of a substance that can be observed without changing the substance into a different substance. Physical properties include density, color, boiling point, and freezing point. For example, as matter experiences a change in temperature or pressure, it may experience a phase change, or a physical change.

Express Lab 2

Materials
- safety goggles
- lab coat or apron
- 2 plastic cups
- plastic spoon
- baking soda
- water
- measuring cup
- vinegar

Procedure
1. Put on safety goggles and a lab coat or apron.

2. Put one level spoonful of baking soda into each plastic cup. **Safety Alert: Do not taste or touch any chemicals.**

3. Pour 1/4 cup of water into one cup.

4. Pour 1/4 cup of vinegar into the second cup.

5. Observe what happens in each cup.

Analysis
1. What happened in each cup?

2. In which cup is a chemical change happening?

A temperature change in water may result in solid ice changing to liquid water. Liquid water can then change to water vapor (gas). Salt dissolving in water is another example of a physical change.

Matter has **chemical properties.** A chemical property is a characteristic that describes how a substance changes into a different substance. For example, **elements** combine with each other in **chemical reactions.** An element is a substance that cannot be separated into other kinds of substances. A chemical reaction is a chemical change in which elements are combined or rearranged. The result is a chemically different substance. If you burn a piece of wood, a chemical change occurs. If you pour alcohol on a foam cup, a chemical change occurs. A different substance results.

Living things are made of matter. They need energy to live. You will learn more about energy and matter in this chapter. Energy is stored in the **chemical bonds** of matter. Energy is released or stored during chemical processes that occur in the cells of living things. The force holding atoms together in a compound is a chemical bond. You will learn more about compounds in the next lesson.

Some chemical reactions can take place in less than a second. Other chemical reactions take place over billions of years.

Figure 2.1.2 *What chemical changes occur when a candle burns?*

Word Bank

element
molecular
chemical bonds

On a sheet of paper, write the word or words from the Word Bank that complete each sentence correctly.

1. Energy is stored and released in the _____ of molecules.

2. A(n) _____ is a substance that cannot be changed or separated into other kinds of substances.

3. All living things have similar activities at the _____ level.

Critical Thinking

On a sheet of paper, write the answers to the following questions. Use complete sentences.

4. What are three physical properties of a pencil?

5. What changes take place when you bake a cake? Describe the changes as physical or chemical. Explain how you know.

▼◄▲▼◄▲▼◄▲▼◄▲▼◄▲▼◄▲▼◄▲▼◄▲▼◄▲▼◄▲▼◄▲▼◄▲▼◄▲▼·

Science at Work

Food Chemist

When you eat some of your favorite foods, you probably have a food chemist to thank. Some foods contain natural or artificial flavors designed by a food chemist. Food chemists create new flavors and fine tune the flavors of other foods. The change of even a tiny amount of an ingredient can change the taste of a food.

Food chemists work closely with research and marketing experts to find popular flavors. They must complete a bachelor's or master's degree in chemistry to work in a food laboratory. Many successful food chemists complete a Ph.D.

Materials

- safety goggles
- lab coat or apron
- flask
- water
- hot plate
- rusty nail
- non-rusty nail
- 2 paper clips
- hammer
- magnet
- balance
- crucible
- magnesium strip

Physical and Chemical Properties

Matter has both physical and chemical properties. A change that does not affect the chemical makeup of a substance is a physical change. A chemical change involves a chemical reaction that changes the substance itself.

Procedure

1. Put on safety goggles and a lab coat or apron.

2. Fill a flask two-thirds with water. Place the flask of water on a hot plate. Turn the hot plate on high. Observe what happens to the water as it boils. Turn off the hot plate.

3. Observe a rusty nail. Compare it to a non-rusty nail.

4. With a hammer, straighten a paper clip. Rub this paper clip with the magnet in the same direction about 30 times. Place this paper clip near another paper clip. Observe what happens.

5. Find the mass of the empty crucible and the strip of magnesium.

6. Ask your teacher to ignite the magnesium strip. Let it burn inside the crucible. **Safety Alert: Do not handle or move the crucible while the magnesium burns.**

7. Observe the burnt magnesium. Find the mass of the magnesium ashes and crucible.

Cleanup/Disposal

Follow your teacher's instructions to dispose of the rusty nail and burnt magnesium.

Analysis

1. What happened to the water as it boiled? Was this a physical change or a chemical change?

2. What happened to the nail as it rusted? Was this a physical change or a chemical change?

3. What happened to the paper clip in Step 4? Was this a physical change or a chemical change?

4. Compare the mass of the magnesium strip to the magnesium ashes.

5. Did you watch a physical or chemical change in Step 6? Explain your answer.

Conclusions

1. Write a summary sentence for each of the four changes you observed. Explain what changes took place.

2. Why do you think there was a change in the mass of the magnesium after it burned? What happens to a substance when it burns?

Explore Further

Look for evidence of three physical and three chemical changes in the environment around you. Describe these changes in a list or a paragraph.

Element symbol

One, two, or three letters that represent the name of an element

Compound

A substance that is formed when atoms of two or more elements join together

Elements and Compounds

Most matter is made up of combinations of elements. However, some matter has only one kind of atom. An element is matter that is made up of only one kind of atom. There are 92 elements that occur naturally. The remaining elements have been made in laboratory experiments. Look at the Periodic Table of Elements in Appendix A. Elements are arranged in a periodic table for easy reference. Each element is represented by a **symbol.** The symbol is one, two, or three letters that represent the name of an element. Examples of element symbols are C (carbon), O (oxygen), and Ca (calcium).

There are 25 elements essential to living things. In fact, four elements—oxygen, carbon, hydrogen, and nitrogen—make up 96.3 percent of a person's weight. These same elements make up the matter of most other living things. The other 21 elements are important for many reasons that you will study. The elements that make up the molecules of living things are combined and recombined in different ways.

Elements combine to form **compounds.** A compound is a substance that is formed when atoms of two or more elements join together. Two common examples of compounds are water and table salt. Table salt, NaCl, has equal parts of the elements sodium (Na) and chlorine (Cl). The table salt you use at home may include the trace element iodine as an added ingredient. The thyroid gland requires iodine to function properly.

Water, or H_2O, has two parts of the element hydrogen to one part of the element oxygen. Another example of a compound in living organisms is DNA. DNA carries the instructions to determine the characteristics of an organism. DNA contains the elements carbon, nitrogen, oxygen, hydrogen, and phosphorus.

Subatomic particle

A proton, neutron, electron, or other particle smaller than the atom

Nucleus

An atom's center; made of protons and neutrons

Electron

A tiny particle in an atom that moves around the nucleus; it has a negative electrical charge

Proton

A tiny particle in the nucleus of an atom; it has a positive electrical charge

Neutron

A tiny particle in the nucleus of an atom; it has the same mass as the proton and no electrical charge

Electron cloud

The space effectively occupied by electrons in an atom

Atomic number

The number of protons in the nucleus of an atom

Atoms and Molecules

Elements are made up of atoms. Remember that atoms are the basic units of matter. Atoms are composed of **subatomic particles.** An atom consists of a positively charged **nucleus** surrounded by a negatively charged cloud of **electrons.** Most of the mass of an atom is in the nucleus.

Look at the model of a helium atom in Figure 2.2.1. It shows the **protons** and **neutrons** in the nucleus. Protons are positively charged. Neutrons have no charge. The electrons orbit the nucleus. In real atoms, the **electron cloud** is much larger than the nucleus. Subatomic particles are too small to be seen. The relationship is like comparing the size of a football stadium (electron cloud) to the size of a pea (nucleus).

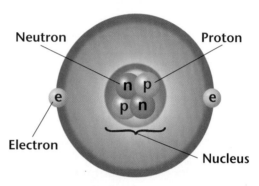

Figure 2.2.1 *The Helium atom has two protons, two neutrons, and two electrons.*

Look at the Periodic Table in Appendix A again. The **atomic number** appears above the symbol for each element. The atomic number of an atom is the number of protons in the atom. The atomic number identifies the element. For example, an atom with six protons is carbon. An atom with one proton is hydrogen. If the atom is neutral (neither negative nor positive), the number of protons equals the number of electrons.

Link to ▷ ▷ ▷

Physics

Physicists constantly search for smaller and smaller subatomic particles. Max Planck pioneered this branch of physics, which is called quantum physics. To honor his work, all subatomic particles are measured in Planck units.

Atomic mass

The average mass of the atom of an element

Isotope

One of a group of atoms of an element with the same number of protons and electrons but different numbers of neutrons

Radioactive

The property of some elements (such as uranium) or isotopes (such as carbon-14) to give off energy as they change to another substance over time

Radioisotope

A radioactive isotope

The **atomic mass** appears below an element's symbol. The atomic mass of an atom is the total mass of the electrons, protons, and neutrons. It is the average mass of the atom of an element. Protons and neutrons are similar in size. Electrons have very little mass and are about $\frac{1}{1836}$ the mass of a proton.

Some elements have **isotopes** that differ only in the number of neutrons. Study Table 2.2.1. Carbon-12 has six protons and six neutrons. Its atomic mass is 12. Carbon-14 has an atomic mass of 14. It has six protons and eight neutrons. Isotopes of the same element have about the same chemical properties because the number of electrons is the same.

Table 2.2.1 Isotopes of Carbon			
	Carbon-12	Carbon-13	Carbon-14
Electrons	6	6	6
Protons	6	6	6
Neutrons	6	7	8

Many elements have multiple isotopes. Some isotopes may be **radioactive.** Radioactive isotopes are called **radioisotopes.** They can be detected because they emit radiation as they decay. For this reason they are also called tracers. Biologists and doctors use radioisotopes to trace the pathway of elements. For example, biologists can date fossils by measuring the ratios of different radioisotopes in the fossil. Doctors can follow chemical processes in the body by tracking the radiation emitted by tracers. However, uncontrolled exposure to radioactive isotopes can harm the molecules in cells. An example is radon gas.

Math Tip

To find the isotope number, add the number of protons and neutrons together. Only the number of neutrons changes between different isotopes.

❊ ❊

Technology and Society

Radon is a radioactive gas. Inhaling high levels of radon gas over time can cause lung cancer. Radon has become a health problem as houses have become more energy efficient. Radon seeps into the house foundation from underground. It cannot escape easily   because of insulation in the roof and tightly sealed window frames. People can buy detection kits to check radon levels in their homes and businesses.

Lesson 2   R E V I E W

On a sheet of paper, write the word that completes each sentence correctly.

1. Isotopes detected by their radiation are _____.

2. A letter that represents the name of an element is called a(n) _____.

3. Protons and neutrons are located in the _____ of an atom.

Critical Thinking

On a sheet of paper, write the answers to the following questions. Use complete sentences.

4. The isotope neon-22 has 10 protons. How many electrons and neutrons does it have?

5. Compare the masses of electrons, neutrons, and protons.

Biology in Your Life

Technology:
The Search for the Perfect Plastic

Think about how many thin plastic containers you used recently. Did you have milk from a plastic jug? Did you carry a bottle of water with you? Before the early 1980s, most products were packaged in glass or heavy plastic. These materials were costly to make. They were rarely recycled and used large amounts of space in landfills.

Today, polyethylene terephthalate, or PET, is the most widely used plastic. PET bottles and packages are much thinner, lighter, and stronger than older plastics. PET bottles are less likely to break than glass bottles.

This new technology benefits communities. Since PET containers are made with less plastic, packaging that is thrown away is more easily compressed. It takes up less landfill space. PET is recyclable.

Recycled PET containers are used mainly as fibers and fleece materials for roofing, shoe insoles, and filters.

1. How are PET containers better for the environment than older plastic containers?

2. What other uses might there be for recycled plastics?

3. Name five PET containers you used recently.

After reading this lesson, you should be able to

◆ explain how to write a chemical formula

◆ interpret a chemical formula

◆ tell how atoms combine to form compounds

◆ give examples of binary compounds

Chemical formula

A set of symbols and subscripts that tell the kinds of atoms and how many of each kind are in a compound

Ion

An atom that has either a positive or a negative charge

Ionic compound

Two or more ions held next to each other by electrical attraction

Empirical formula

The simplest formula for a compound

Scientists use the symbols for elements to write **chemical formulas** for compounds. A chemical formula tells the kind of atoms and how many of each kind are present in the compound. Look at the formula for water: H_2O. Water is a molecule. The formula H_2O shows that each water molecule is made up of two hydrogen atoms bonded to one oxygen atom. The subscript 2 tells you two atoms of hydrogen are in the molecule. Notice there is no subscript after the O. If no subscript appears after the symbol of an element, the compound has only one atom of that element. The formula H_2O shows that one water molecule contains three atoms—two of hydrogen and one of oxygen. Table 2.3.1 shows the chemical formulas for two common chemical compounds.

Table 2.3.1 CH_4 (Methane) and CO_2 (Carbon Dioxide)			
Symbol	**Element**	**Subscript**	**Number of Atoms**
C	carbon	none	1
H_4	hydrogen	4	+4
			5 total atoms
C	carbon	none	1
O_2	oxygen	2	+2
			3 total atoms

Sometimes a compound is not a molecule. **Ions** can form compounds. An ion is an atom or particle that has either a positive or a negative charge. For example, table salt is NaCl. Both Na (sodium) and Cl (chlorine) form ions. NaCl is an **ionic compound.** An ionic compound has two or more ions held next to each other by electrical attraction. The sodium ion has a positive charge. The chloride ion has a negative charge.

Look at Figure 2.3.1. The formula for NaCl has one atom of sodium for every atom of chlorine. This formula is called an **empirical formula.** An empirical formula is the simplest formula for a compound. In comparison, a molecular formula is the same as or is a multiple of the empirical formula.

Radical

A group of two or more atoms that acts like one atom

The molecular formula is based on the actual number of atoms of each type in the compound.

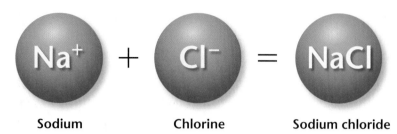

Sodium + Chlorine = Sodium chloride

Figure 2.3.1 *Table salt is an ionic compound.*

Compounds That Contain Radicals

The formulas for some compounds contain groups of two or more atoms that act as if they are one atom. These groups of atoms are called **radicals.** They form compounds by combining with other atoms. The atoms in a radical stay together during a chemical reaction.

The formula for household lye contains the negatively charged radical OH^-. Household lye is a strong chemical used to clean drains. The formula for household lye is NaOH. The OH^- radical contains one atom of oxygen and one atom of hydrogen. The chemical name for lye, NaOH, is sodium hydroxide. More examples of some common radicals are in Table 2.3.2.

Table 2.3.2 Some Common Radicals	
Radical	Name
SO_4	sulfate
ClO_3	chlorate
NO_3	nitrate
CO_3	carbonate
PO_4	phosphate

When a compound contains more than one radical, the radical is written in parentheses. A subscript outside the parentheses tells how many units of the radical are in one molecule of the compound.

Look at Figure 2.3.2. In the formula $Ba(OH)_2$, one barium ion (Ba) combines with two OH^- radicals.

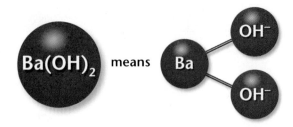

Figure 2.3.2 *One ion of barium bonds to two OH⁻ radicals in Ba(OH)₂.*

When formulas contain radicals with subscripts outside the parentheses, the subscripts multiply the number of atoms inside the parentheses as shown in Table 2.3.3. The compound $Ba(NO_3)_2$ is barium nitrate. The nitrate radical is made up of one nitrogen atom and three oxygen atoms. In barium nitrate, one barium ion combines with two nitrate radicals. Notice in Table 2.3.3 that the compound $Ba(NO_3)_2$ has a total of two nitrogen atoms and six oxygen atoms.

Table 2.3.3 Al(OH)₃ and Ba(NO₃)₂				
Symbol	Element	Subscript	Radical Subscript	Number of Atoms
Al	aluminum	none	not in a radical	1
O	oxygen	none	3	3 (3 x 1)
H	hydrogen	none	3	+3 (3 x 1)
				7 total atoms
Ba	barium	none	not in a radical	1
N	nitrogen	none	2	2 (2 x 1)
O₃	oxygen	3	2	+6 (2 x 3)
				9 total atoms

In more complex molecules, especially in organic substances, the configuration of the formula is important. Parentheses are often required. For example, nitroglycerin, $C_3H_5(NO_3)_3$, consists of three atoms of carbon, five atoms of hydrogen, and three nitrate radicals.

Binary compound

A compound that contains two elements

An important element for healthy teeth is fluoride, which is a form of the trace element fluorine. Tooth decay is less frequent in societies that add fluoride to drinking water and to toothpaste. Fluoride prevents cavities by affecting the metabolism of bacteria that live in the plaque that coats teeth.

Study Table 2.3.4. It shows the chemical formula for $C_3H_5(NO_3)_3$.

Table 2.3.4 $C_3H_5(NO_3)_3$				
Symbol	Element	Subscript	Radical Subscript	Number of Atoms
C_3	carbon	3	not in a radical	3
H_5	hydrogen	5	not in a radical	5
N	nitrogen	none	3	3
O_3	oxygen	3	3	+9 (3 x 3)
				20 total atoms

Naming Compounds

A compound that contains two elements is called a **binary compound.** The name of a binary compound is a combination of the names of the two elements that form the compound. The number of atoms in the compound is not considered when naming a compound. Use the following two rules to name compounds that contain two elements:

◆ The first name of a binary compound is the same as the name of the first element in the compound's formula.

◆ The second name of a binary compound is the name of the second element in the compound's formula with the ending changed to –*ide.* Table 2.3.5 shows how names of some elements are written when they are the second element in a formula.

Table 2.3.5 Naming Binary Compounds	
Element	The Second Element's Name in a Binary Compound
chlorine (Cl)	chlor**ide**
iodine (I)	iod**ide**
fluorine (Fl)	fluor**ide**
bromine (Br)	brom**ide**
oxygen (O)	ox**ide**
sulfur (S)	sulf**ide**

If 250 million hydrogen atoms were placed side by side, the length would be about one inch. Molecules also tend to be small. Many more molecules are in a glass of water than there are glasses of water in the sea.

Look at the formula for a compound to help you determine the compound's name. In Figure 2.3.3, the formula BaO contains the symbols for the elements barium and oxygen. The first name of the compound is the name of the first element, barium. We change oxygen to oxide to form the second name of the compound. BaO is barium oxide.

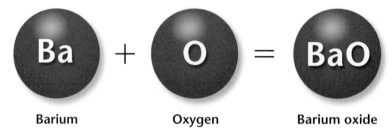

Barium   Oxygen   Barium oxide

Figure 2.3.3 *One ion of barium bonds to one ion of oxygen in BaO.*

Compounds with More Than Two Elements

A compound that contains more than two elements usually has a radical in its formula. The first name of the compound is the name of the first element in the formula. The second name of the compound varies according to the radical in the formula.

Look at the formula $Al(OH)_3$ in Figure 2.3.4. The first name of this compound is the name of the first element—aluminum. The second name identifies the OH radical—hydroxide. The name of the compound is aluminum hydroxide. You can find the names for some common radicals in Table 2.3.2 on page 43. The subscript numbers in a formula with radicals do not affect the name of the compound.

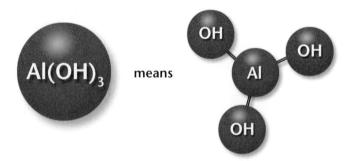

Figure 2.3.4 *One ion of aluminum bonds to three OH radicals in $Al(OH)_3$.*

On a sheet of paper, write the letter of the answer that completes each sentence correctly.

1. The subscript in a chemical formula refers to the _____.

    A atomic mass   **C** number of atoms

    B isotope number   **D** radical state

2. The total number of atoms in a molecule of CH_3OH is _____.

    A one   **C** four

    B three   **D** six

3. A group of atoms, such as OH, is called a(n) _____.

    A isotope   **C** ion

    B radical   **D** binary compound

On a sheet of paper, write the word or words that complete each sentence correctly.

4. The compound $Al(NH_3)_2$ has _____ atoms of nitrogen.

5. When naming a compound with two elements, the ending of the second element is changed to _____.

6. The formula $CaCl_2$ represents the compound _____.

Critical Thinking

On a sheet of paper, write the answers to the following questions. Use complete sentences.

7. In the formula NO_3, what does the subscript 3 mean?

8. How do you name a compound with more than two elements?

9. What is the formula for potassium nitrate?

10. Describe how an ionic compound is formed.

Objectives

After reading this lesson, you should be able to

◆ explain that chemical elements combine and are held together by bonds that contain energy

◆ know that when atoms share electrons, the bond between them is a covalent bond

◆ explain how ions form chemical bonds

◆ explain how electrons fill electron shells

Electron shell

A specific energy level in which electrons orbit the nucleus

Chemical Bonds and Molecules

Combinations of atoms are held together by bonds that contain energy. Electrons are the subatomic particles that mainly determine how an atom behaves when it meets other atoms. Electron behavior determines chemical bonding. To understand this behavior, you need to understand that electrons have energy. All electrons have the same mass. However, electrons vary in the amount of energy they have.

The farther an electron is from the nucleus, the more energy it has. Electrons orbit the nucleus at nearly the speed of light. They orbit in specific energy levels called **electron shells.** Each shell accommodates a certain number of electrons. The number of electrons in an atom determines the number of electron shells in the atom. The shells fill with electrons in a regular pattern from the lowest energy level outward.

An atom has a tendency to fill its outer energy level. An atom becomes more stable when its outermost energy level is filled. An atom shares, lends, or borrows electrons to fill its outer energy level. Electrons in the outermost shell have the highest energy. When an electron absorbs energy, it can move up to a higher energy level.

Look at Figure 2.4.1, which is a model of the sodium atom. Sodium has 11 electrons. Only one electron is in the outer energy level. Sodium tends to lose one electron to another atom to become stable. By losing an electron, the outer level will have eight electrons. It will have the most electrons it can hold.

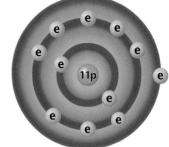

Figure 2.4.1 *The sodium atom has 11 electrons.*

The number of electrons in an atom's outermost shell determines the atom's chemical properties. Atoms whose outermost shells are not filled tend to interact with other atoms in chemical reactions.

Atoms of elements on the right side of the periodic table tend to take electrons. Atoms of elements on the left side of the periodic table tend to give up electrons.

Remember that a chemical reaction is a chemical change in which atoms of elements are combined or rearranged. An atom's chemical properties are determined by the number of electrons it has and by how full or empty its outer electron shell is.

Atoms bond by adding, losing, or sharing electrons. An atom is stable when its outermost energy level is filled. This tendency dictates the kinds of chemical bonds atoms form with each other. When atoms transfer or share electrons, a chemical bond forms. Chemical bonds link atoms together. There are two types of bonds.

Covalent Bonds

One type of bond is a **covalent bond.** Two atoms that share one or more pairs of electrons form a covalent bond. Covalent bonds are shared pairs of electrons. Atoms held together by covalent bonds form molecules.

Look at Figure 2.4.2, which is a model of H_2O, or water. A water molecule is made up of two hydrogen atoms and one oxygen atom. An atom of hydrogen needs a second electron to become stable. This gives hydrogen two electrons in its outermost energy level. An atom of oxygen needs two more electrons to become stable with eight electrons. An atom of oxygen can share two electrons with two hydrogen atoms to become stable. The atoms share their electrons in a covalent bond. The composition of the atoms affects the shape and properties of the molecule.

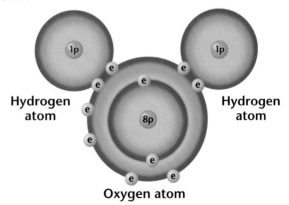

Figure 2.4.2 *Water, or H_2O, is made of covalent bonds between two hydrogen atoms and one oxygen atom.*

An atom has seven energy levels. They are named K, L, M, N, O, P, and Q. Scientists theorize that energy level O can hold 50 electrons, level P can hold 72, and level Q can hold 98.

Different molecules have different shapes depending on the atoms that make up the molecule.

Ionic Bonds

Ions with opposite charges attract and join together in an ionic bond. An **ionic bond** is a type of bonding in which ions are held together by the strong attraction of their opposite charges. An ion forms when an atom or molecule gains or loses one or more electrons. In an ionic bond, a complete transfer of electrons occurs between atoms. One atom gives up an electron to another atom. Look at Figure 2.4.3, which is a model for NaCl, or table salt.

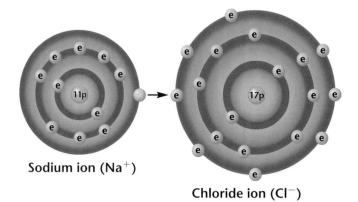

Sodium ion (Na$^+$)

Chloride ion (Cl$^-$)

Figure 2.4.3 *NaCl, or sodium chloride, is an example of an ionic bond.*

The sodium (Na) atom donates one of its 11 electrons to the chlorine (Cl) atom, which has 17 electrons. As a result, the Na atom and Cl atom each have a full outer electron shell. Also, the Na atom becomes positively charged and is written as Na$^+$. The chlorine atom gains an electron and becomes negatively charged. It is written as Cl$^-$. Both charged atoms are called ions. Since opposite charges attract, the two ions are held together by an electrical attraction called an ionic bond.

Look at Figure 2.4.3 again. Keep in mind that when sodium loses an electron, the number of protons in the nucleus remains the same. The Na$^+$ ion now has more positively charged protons than negatively charged electrons. An atom with equal numbers of electrons and protons has no charge. An atom with more protons than electrons is a positively (+) charged ion.

Sodium gives up an electron to chlorine to form the compound sodium chloride. The chlorine atom now has more electrons than protons. When an atom has more electrons than protons, it is a negatively (−) charged ion.

Chemical Reactions

In chemical reactions, atoms change patterns. Inside the cells of living organisms, molecules continually rearrange. The chemical bonds of molecules are breaking and new bonds are forming during chemical reactions. In all chemical reactions there are **reactants** and **products.** A reactant is a substance that is altered in a chemical reaction. A product is a substance that is formed in a chemical reaction. Reactants are rearranged to produce new products.

Remember that as matter is being rearranged, it is neither created nor destroyed. For example, two molecules of hydrogen gas can react with one molecule of oxygen gas to produce two molecules of water. Count the number of atoms on each side of the chemical reaction. You should find the same number of atoms on both sides of the equation.

Reactants		Products
$2H_2 + O_2$	yields	$2H_2O$
hydrogen plus oxygen		water

Atoms share or transfer electrons in all chemical reactions. Because electrons carry and store energy, energy is also shared or transferred. The transfer of energy is important in the chemical processes in living things. For example, plants capture light energy, which is stored in electrons. Energy from electrons is stored in the molecules of an orange. By eating an orange, you access energy stored in the chemical bonds of molecules.

Reactant

A substance that is altered in a chemical reaction

Product

A substance that is formed in a chemical reaction

Link to >>>

Home and Career

Scientists have found that ionized particles in the air impact health. Negatively charged ions may help trap things like pollen that cause allergies. As a result, many home air conditioners and air filters have an ionizer that generates negatively charged ions.

On a sheet of paper, write the word that best completes each sentence.

1. An atom is most stable when its outermost shell is _____ with electrons.

2. An atom that gains or loses an electron becomes a(n) _____.

3. Atoms in covalent bonds _____ their electrons.

Critical Thinking

On a sheet of paper, write the answers to the following questions. Use complete sentences.

4. Why should the number of each kind of atom be equal on both sides of a chemical reaction?

5. Compare and contrast covalent bonds and ionic bonds.

★✦★

Achievements in Science

Early Atomic Ideas

Over 2,500 years ago, the Greek philosopher Thales asked, "What is the nature of matter?" His question started a debate over what was the basic unit of matter. Democritus, another ancient Greek philosopher, said that all matter was made of particles too small to be seen. He called these particles "atoms."

In the early 1800s, British scientist John Dalton published four new ideas about atoms. He said: 1) every element is made of only one kind of atom; 2) every atom of the same element is alike and has the same weight; 3) atoms of different elements have different weights; and 4) atoms of different elements can bond together and form new substances.

Many scientists accepted Dalton's ideas. Later, scientists found that some of Dalton's ideas were not correct. Scientists revised his ideas as new discoveries were made. As scientists continue to make new discoveries, our modern theory of the atom may change.

Organisms are made up of about 70 percent water. The cells in your body have between 70 percent to 95 percent water content. Water has a simple molecular structure.

Study Figure 2.5.1. The oxygen atom has six electrons in its outer shell. It needs two electrons to fill its outer shell. Each hydrogen atom has one electron. Each hydrogen atom needs one electron to fill its outer shell. To form a molecule of water, these atoms share electrons. They make covalent bonds. By sharing, the oxygen atom can have eight electrons in its outer shell. The hydrogen atoms can have two electrons.

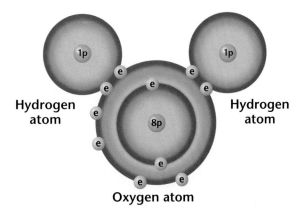

Figure 2.5.1 *Water has a simple molecular structure.*

Look at Figure 2.5.1 again. Notice that the 2 hydrogen atoms bond at an angle with the oxygen atom. This happens because the electrons of each covalent bond are not shared equally between the hydrogen and oxygen atoms. Since oxygen has 8 protons, it pulls electrons more strongly than the 2 hydrogen atoms. The hydrogen nucleus has only one proton. As a result, the oxygen end of the water molecule has a slight negative charge.

Polar molecule

A molecule with an uneven distribution of electron density

Hydrogen bond

A weak electrical attraction between the slight positive charge on a hydrogen atom and a slight negative charge on another atom

Link to ➤➤➤

Health

The cells in the human body require a large amount of water to stay healthy. Drinks containing alcohol or caffeine cause the body to dehydrate. Alcohol and caffeine block the body cells from reabsorbing water.

The end of the water molecule with the two hydrogen atoms has a slight positive charge. A molecule in which opposite ends have opposite electric charges is called a **polar molecule.**

Because of the unequal distribution of charges, water molecules readily form **hydrogen bonds** with each other. A hydrogen bond is a weak electrical attraction. Hydrogen bonds form between a slightly positive hydrogen atom in one molecule and a slightly negative atom in another molecule. Water molecules also form hydrogen bonds with other polar molecules such as sugars and proteins. Because of this, water dissolves these substances. The unique properties of water molecules give water the following characteristics.

Water has a large capacity to hold heat. The faster the molecules in a substance move, the greater the temperature of the substance. Water heats up slowly and holds heat much longer than other matter. As water gets hot, it absorbs and stores a large amount of heat. Some of that heat energy breaks down the hydrogen bond between water molecules. This speeds up the motion of water molecules.

As water cools, the water molecules slow down and form hydrogen bonds. A large amount of heat is released. However, the temperature drops only slightly. In other words, water moderates temperature by releasing heat in cold environments and absorbing heat in warm environments.

This property of water helps control human body temperature. When a person perspires, water evaporates from the surface of the skin. Perspiration draws heat from the skin to maintain a cooler interior temperature compared to the temperature of the external environment.

Water molecules stick together because of hydrogen bonds. These hydrogen bonds make water molecules near the surface of water stick together. These water molecules pull inward and create a strong surface tension. If you drop water onto a sheet of wax paper the water stays as a drop rather than spreading out flat. This property allows water to move from the roots of plants upward to other plant parts in an unbroken column.

Solvent

A substance capable of dissolving one or more other substances

Hydrophilic

Water-loving; polar molecules are hydrophilic

Crystalline

A substance with a regularly repeating arrangement of its atoms

Hydrophobic

Water-hating; nonpolar molecules are hydrophobic

Molecules like sugars contain OH groups that resemble ammonia or water. Water forms hydrogen bonds with these molecules. This bonding results in the solubility of these compounds in water.

Figure 2.5.2 *By standing on water, this insect shows the surface tension of water.*

Water expands as it freezes. As water cools, the molecules move farther apart and eventually form ice. When a substance cools, it usually becomes denser. Ice floats in liquid water. Ice is less dense than its liquid form. Hydrogen bonds hold water molecules farther apart in solid form than in liquid form. Living things can live in liquid water below a frozen surface.

Water is an excellent solvent. A **solvent** is a substance that can dissolve one or more other substances. Water dissolves most biological substances. Because water is polar, it dissolves ionic substances such as table salt and polar molecules such as sugars.

Ions and polar molecules are **hydrophilic.** Hydrophilic means "water loving." For example, sodium chloride is often used in its **crystalline** form. When sodium chloride is added to water, it dissolves. This happens because Na^+ and Cl^- ions are attracted to the polar water molecules and break away from each other. The sodium ions are attracted to the negative end of the water molecule. The chloride ions are attracted to the positive end of the water molecule.

Nonpolar substances such as oils do not mix with water. Oils are **hydrophobic,** or "water hating." Oil and water separate from each other.

Lesson 5   R E V I E W

On a sheet of paper, write the letter of the answer that completes each sentence correctly.

1. A _____ bond forms when two atoms share one or more pairs of electrons.

    A covalent   **C** hydrogen

    B electron   **D** ionic

2. What is the chemical formula for water?

    A HO   **C** HO_2

    B H_2O **D** H_2O_2

3. Water makes up about what percentage of most organisms?

    A 10%   **C** 50%

    B 30%   **D** 70%

On a sheet of paper, write the word that completes each sentence correctly.

4. Water can only dissolve _____ substances.

5. The oxygen atom needs _____ electrons to complete its outer shell.

6. Water beads on waxed cars due to _____ tension caused by hydrogen bonds.

Critical Thinking

On a sheet of paper, write the answers to the following questions. Use complete sentences.

7. Why do you think oil floats on top of water instead of mixing with it?

8. Why does it take the water in a swimming pool some time to heat up during a hot day?

9. How do hydrogen bonds make icebergs possible?

10. Why is water an important part of blood?

DISCOVERY INVESTIGATION 2

Materials

- safety goggles
- lab coat or apron
- clear plastic cups
- sand
- water
- sugar
- salt
- spoon
- thermometers
- heat lamp
- eyedropper
- pipette
- vegetable oil
- plastic water bottle
- freezer
- hot plate
- paper towels

The Properties of Water

Life on Earth owes much to the unique properties of water. These properties include water's ability to resist temperature change, creates surface tension, expand as it freezes, and dissolve certain substances. In this investigation, you will pick one property of water and then develop a procedure to test it.

Procedure

1. Choose one of the following properties of water:

- It holds heat and resists temperature change.

- Its molecules stick together, creating surface tension.

- It expands as it changes from liquid to solid form.

- It is an excellent solvent.

2. Ask a question about the property you have chosen. For example, if you chose that water is an excellent solvent, you could question which substances it will or will not dissolve. Write a hypothesis.

3. Write a procedure that will demonstrate the property you chose. Include Safety Alerts.

4. Choose the materials you need from the materials listed on page 57. Or, create your own materials list. Include your materials list in your lab report.

5. Ask your teacher to approve your hypothesis, procedure, and Safety Alerts. Then obtain the materials you need and perform your procedure.

Cleanup/Disposal

Before you leave the lab, be sure your work area is clean.

Analysis

1. Present your data so that someone who did not see your experiment can evaluate it.

2. If your experiment did not support your hypothesis or was otherwise unsuccessful, evaluate your procedure for problems. Write a new procedure to correct these problems.

Conclusions

1. How did your data answer the question you asked in Step 2 about the property of water?

2. What makes this property important to life? What would be the consequences of losing this property?

3. What causes this property of water?

Explore Further

Choose another property of water from the list. Write a procedure to test it. Include the type of observations and data you would collect.

Acid-Base Chemistry

Many important substances inside cells are **acids** or **bases.** An acid is a substance that can donate a proton (H^+) or accept an electron pair. A base is a substance that can accept a proton (H^+), release OH^-, or donate an electron pair. A base is also called an alkali.

Most of the water in living organisms is in the form of molecules. A small number of water molecules in living organisms dissociate, or break apart, into hydrogen ions (H^+) and hydroxide (OH^-) ions. The hydroxide ion is made up of an oxygen atom and hydrogen atom.

The concentration of H^+ ions indicate the acidity of a solution. It is measured as a **pH** value. The pH is a number that tells whether a substance is an acid or a base. The abbreviation pH stands for potential hydrogen. It is the measure of hydrogen ion concentration in a solution.

If a compound donates hydrogen ions to a solution, it is called an acid. A compound that accepts hydrogen ions is a base. A base decreases the concentration of H^+ in a solution. This increases the hydroxide ion (OH^-) concentration.

Chemical balances and temperature balances in living things are maintained by acid-base reactions. For example, when food is digested in the body, chemical reactions take place. Chemical reactions are involved when nutrients are transported across cell membranes. These are acid-base reactions.

Acid

A substance that can donate a proton (H^+) or accept an electron pair

Base

A substance that can accept a proton (H^+), release OH^-, or donate an electron pair; an alkali

pH

A number that tells whether a substance is an acid or a base

Link to ▷▷▷

Earth Science

Soil pH is an important part of plant health. When the soil becomes too acidic, plant roots cannot absorb nutrients. Farmers and gardeners often add lime, or calcium materials, to the soil. This raises the pH and keeps plants healthy.

Table 2.6.1 provides more information and examples of acids and bases.

Table 2.6.1 Differences Between Acids and Bases		
Solution	**Definition**	**Example**
Acid	A compound that breaks apart into H^+ ions and a negatively charged ion	Vinegar Lemon juice Amino acids Stomach acids
	Accepts an electron pair	Nucleic acids
	Donates a proton	
Base	A compound that breaks apart into OH^- ions and a positively charged ion	NaOH (sodium hydroxide) Baking soda
	Donates an electron pair	
	Accepts a proton	

pH Scale

The strength of an acid or base can be described by a pH scale. Table 2.6.2 on page 61 shows the pH of some common substances. A **neutral solution** has a pH of 7. It is neither an acid nor a base. In neutral solutions, the concentrations of H^+ and OH^- ions are equal. At lower pH values (below 7), a solution is acidic. At higher pH values (above 7), a solution is basic.

The pH scale usually shows a range in value from 0 (very acidic) to 14 (very basic). Each unit on the pH scale represents a tenfold change in the concentration of H^+ ions. For example, lemon juice has a pH of 2. It has 100 times more H^+ ions than an equal amount of tomato juice at pH 4.

In most living cells, the pH is close to 7. A slight change in pH can harm the cell. Changes in the pH of blood are moderated at a safe level through the use of substances called **buffers.** A buffer is a solution that can receive moderate amounts of either acid or base without significantly changing its pH.

A buffer accepts excess H^+ ions when their levels rise. A buffer donates H^+ ions when their levels fall. In other words, a buffer can act like an acid or a base. For example, a change in the pH of a person's blood from 7.4 to 7.0 could cause a coma. Buffers in the person's body keep the pH at a safe level.

Table 2.6.2 The pH Scale of Some Common Substances

On a sheet of paper, write the letter of the answer that completes each sentence correctly.

1. Which of the following is a base?

A baking soda   **C** vinegar

B lemon juice   **D** stomach acid

2. An acid is a(n) _____.

A neutron acceptor

B proton donor

C electron pair donor

D compound that breaks apart OH^- ions

3. Alkali is another word for _____.

A neutral   **C** basic

B acidic   **D** buffer

On a sheet of paper, write the word or words that complete each sentence correctly.

4. A pH of _____ is considered neutral.

5. Vinegar is a(n) _____ because its pH is about 3.5.

6. A solution with a higher concentration of OH^- ions than H^+ ions is _____.

Critical Thinking

On a sheet of paper, write the answers to the following questions. Use complete sentences.

7. What does it mean when we say that water molecules break apart?

8. How does a buffer work to keep pH from changing?

9. How do acids and bases play a role in your diet?

10. Describe the activity of protons when an acid and a base are mixed together.

Blood and pH

Your body works hard to keep itself stable. Your health depends on keeping a steady temperature, fluid balance, and pH.

The pH scale ranges from 0 to 14. Blood pH must stay within a narrow range. A healthy blood pH falls between 7.35 and 7.45. Blood that falls below 7.35 is too acidic and leads to a condition called *acidosis.* A person with acidosis becomes disoriented and could go into a coma.

A pH value above 7.45 means that blood is too basic and causes a condition called *alkalosis.* People with alkalosis may have muscle spasms and convulsions.

Doctors have discovered that sometimes problems with blood pH are linked to too much carbon dioxide or lactic acid in the blood. Carbon dioxide is removed when we breathe out. Problems with blood pH arise when a person has problems breathing or when the body cannot quickly remove waste in the form of lactic acid.

Your blood contains buffers that work as acids or bases to keep your pH in the normal range. Buffers are proteins or ions that can accept or donate protons depending on the pH of the blood.

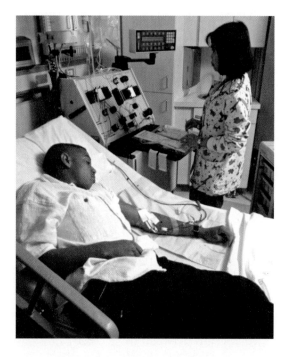

Your body also responds to changes in blood pH by controlling your breathing to keep carbon dioxide at a certain level. People with acidosis or alkalosis are usually treated with oxygen. They also are given artificial buffers to stabilize their blood pH.

1. What is the range of blood pH to maintain good health?

2. How are acidosis and alkalosis alike? How are they different?

3. How do buffers keep a person's blood pH in the normal range?

- All substances are made of matter that takes up space and has mass. Matter has physical and chemical properties.

- Matter can be broken down into elements. Two or more elements can combine to form a compound.

- The basic unit of matter is the atom. Atoms are made of a positively charged nucleus and a negatively charged cloud of electrons. The nucleus is made up of positively charged protons and neutral neutrons.

- Elements called isotopes differ in their number of neutrons.

- Compounds are represented by chemical formulas.

- Ionic compounds are two or more ions held together by an electrical attraction between their charges.

- Radicals are groups of atoms that behave as if they are one ion. Radicals stay together during chemical reactions.

- A compound of two elements is named by stating the name of the first element, then adding the name of the second element with the ending changed to –ide. The names of more complex compounds often use the names of radicals.

- Atoms share electrons in a covalent bond, like in water. Atoms form an ionic bond when one atom gives up an electron to another atom.

- The uneven distribution of electron density between oxygen and hydrogen atoms in a water molecule gives water polarity. Water has the ability to dissolve other polar substances, hold heat, create surface tension, and expand when it freezes.

- A solution can be measured by the concentration of H^+ ions, known as the pH. Solutions with a low pH are acidic. Solutions with a high pH are basic. A pH of 7 is neutral.

Vocabulary

acid, 59	chemistry, 33	hydrophobic, 55	pH, 59
atom, 32	compound, 38	ion, 42	physical property, 33
atomic mass, 40	covalent bond, 49	ionic bond, 50	polar molecule, 54
atomic number, 39	crystalline, 55	ionic compound, 42	product, 51
bacteria, 33	diversity, 33	isotope, 40	proton, 39
base, 59	electron, 39	mass, 32	radical, 43
binary compound, 45	electron cloud, 39	matter, 32	radioactive, 40
buffer, 61	electron shell, 48	molecular, 33	radioisotope, 40
chemical bond, 34	element, 34	molecule, 32	reactant, 51
chemical formula, 42	element symbol, 38	neutral solution, 60	solvent, 55
chemical process, 33	empirical formula, 42	neutron, 39	subatomic particle, 39
chemical property, 34	hydrogen bond, 54	nucleus, 39	
chemical reaction, 34	hydrophilic, 55	organization, 33	

Word Bank

acid

atomic number

base

buffer

chemical bond

chemical reaction

covalent bond

crystalline

hydrophilic

hydrophobic

ionic bond

isotope

matter

neutron

pH

physical property

polar molecule

proton

radical

radioactive

Vocabulary Review

On a sheet of paper, write the word or words from the Word Bank that best complete each sentence.

1. Two atoms are held together by a(n) _____ when an electron transfers from one atom to the other.

2. A(n) _____ molecule can be dissolved in a water solution, but a(n) _____ molecule does not mix with water.

3. The ability of water to change from solid to liquid is a(n) _____ of water.

4. A(n) _____ is a tiny particle in the nucleus of an atom that has a positive electrical charge.

5. Atoms with a(n) _____ share electrons.

6. A(n) _____ of an atom has the same atomic number but a different atomic mass.

7. A solution with a _____ of 7.0 is considered to be neutral.

8. A(n) _____ is a group of atoms that behave like they are one ion.

9. The number of protons in the nucleus of the atom is called the _____.

10. A(n) _____ donates hydrogen ions to a solution, but a(n) _____ accepts hydrogen ions.

11. A(n) _____ has no charge and is found in the nucleus.

12. Anything that has mass and takes up space is _____.

13. A solution that can receive moderate amounts of acid or base without changing its pH is a(n) _____.

Review continued on next page

14. The rearranging of the chemical makeup of matter is called a(n) _____.

15. Water is a(n) _____ because its opposite ends have opposite electric charges.

16. As they change to another substance over time, _____ elements give off energy.

17. Two or more atoms linked by a(n) _____ form a molecule.

18. A(n) _____ substance has a regularly repeating arrangement of atoms.

Concept Review

On a sheet of paper, write the letter of the answer that completes each sentence correctly.

19. The central part of an atom is the ____.

   A nucleus   **C** proton

   B neutron   **D** molecule

20. Water is made up of two ____ atoms and one ____ atom.

   A oxygen, hydrogen   **C** hydrogen, oxygen

   B sodium, hydroxide   **D** carbon, oxygen

21. Which of the following is a radical?

   A H   **C** H_2O

   B O   **D** OH

Critical Thinking

On a sheet of paper, write the answers to the following questions. Use complete sentences.

22. Explain the trend that atoms of certain elements give up or accept electrons based on their position in the Periodic Table.

23. What are the reactants and the product in the following reaction? $C + O_2 \longrightarrow CO_2$

24. Give an example that shows water is an excellent solvent.

25. Explain three ways the special properties of water make it an important biological solvent.

Research and Write

Research the most recent addition to the Periodic Table. Find the name of the element and write a description of it. Include its atomic number, its properties, and a brief description of how the element was created.

Test-Taking Tip To prepare for a test, study in short sessions rather than in one long session. During the week before a test, spend time each day reviewing your notes.

3

Chemistry at the Cellular Level

What do the items in the photograph have in common? All come from living things and all contain organic molecules. When you eat food, your body uses organic molecules for energy and growth. In Chapter 3, you will find out what an organic molecule is. You will learn about the four major kinds of organic molecules that make up living things and what each one does.

Organize Your Thoughts

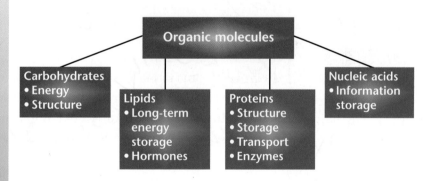

Organic molecules

Carbohydrates
• Energy
• Structure

Lipids
• Long-term energy storage
• Hormones

Proteins
• Structure
• Storage
• Transport
• Enzymes

Nucleic acids
• Information storage

Goals for Learning

◆ To recognize that all living things share common biological molecules

◆ To compare carbohydrates, lipids, and proteins

◆ To identify foods for nutritional balance

◆ To describe the role of DNA and RNA in protein synthesis

Organic Molecules

A cell is made mostly of water. The rest of the cell is mainly molecules that contain carbon. These carbon-based molecules are called **organic compounds.** They are made up of carbon atoms and other atoms bonded together. Look at the structural diagram of an organic molecule in Figure 3.1.1. One line between atoms represents a single bond. Notice that four carbon atoms are bonded in a straight line. Each carbon also bonds to two or three hydrogen atoms.

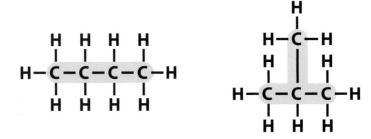

Figures 3.1.1 and 3.1.2 *Here are two examples of carbon-based structural diagrams.*

Organic compound

A compound that contains carbon (except carbon dioxide, carbon monoxide, and carbonates)

Look at Figure 3.1.2. Count the number of carbon atoms and hydrogen atoms in Figures 3.1.1 and 3.1.2. What did you find? Both molecules have the same number of hydrogen and carbon atoms. However, they are different compounds because of their bonding patterns. Figure 3.1.1 is a straight chain carbon compound. Figure 3.1.2 is a branched carbon compound.

Look at Figure 3.1.3. Two lines between atoms represent a double bond. Notice that some carbon atoms form double bonds with other carbon atoms. As a result, each carbon atom can bond with only one hydrogen atom. This structure is called a carbon ring.

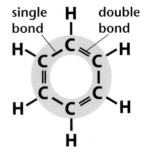

Figure 3.1.3 *This is an example of a molecule with double carbon bonds.*

Functional group

A group of atoms within a molecule that causes the molecule to react in a specific way

A carbon atom can bond with up to four other atoms to fill its outer electron shell. Think about a carbon atom like an intersection of two roads. The carbon atom can form up to four bonds. A carbon atom can bond with another carbon atom. Or, it can bond with other atoms, such as hydrogen or oxygen. This means you can make an endless number of carbon compounds that differ in size and pattern. Unlike carbon, the hydrogen atom can bond with only one atom.

Each organic molecule has a characteristic and complex shape. Molecules recognize each other by shape. The groups of atoms bonded to carbon atoms usually take part in chemical reactions. These groups of atoms are called **functional groups.** A functional group is a group of atoms within a molecule that causes the molecule to react in a specific way. Many organic compounds contain functional groups.

Figure 3.1.4 shows one functional group, the hydroxyl group, or OH. It is found in sugars. The hydroxyl group is hydrophilic. It attracts water molecules. Figures 3.1.5 and 3.1.6 show a functional group called the carbonyl group, or CO. Carbonyl groups are also found in sugars.

Look at Figure 3.1.7. This is another functional group, the amino group, or NH_2. Amino groups are found in proteins. Recall from Chapter 2 that a protein is a compound that cells use to grow and work. Figure 3.1.8 shows a carboxyl group, or COOH. Carboxyl groups are found in proteins.

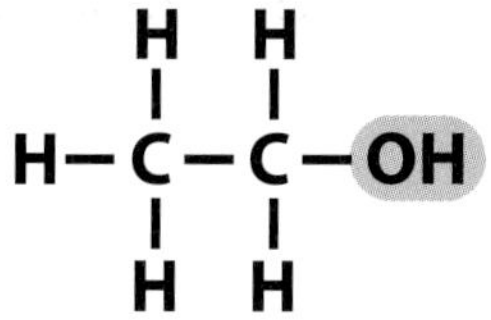

Figure 3.1.4 *Hydroxyl group*

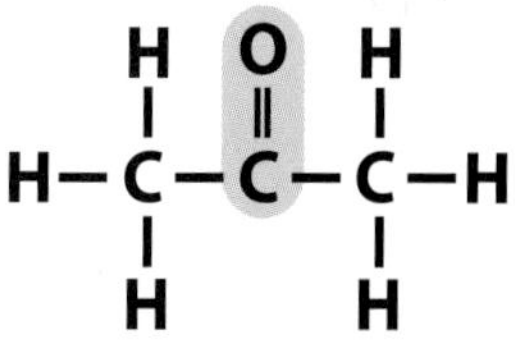

Figure 3.1.5 *Carbonyl group*

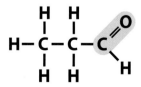

Figure 3.1.6 *Carbonyl group*

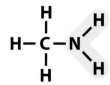

Figure 3.1.7 *Amino group*

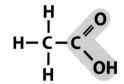

Figure 3.1.8 *Carboxyl group*

Glossary Terms

Hydrocarbon

A molecule that contains carbon and hydrogen

Carbohydrate

A sugar or starch that living things use for energy

Lipid

A macromolecule that is not soluble in water

Nucleic acid

A large macromolecule that stores important information in a cell

Macromolecule

A molecule composed of a very large number of atoms

Monomer

A small molecular structure that can chemically bond to other monomers to form a polymer

Polymer

A very large molecule made from simple units

Amino acid

A molecule that makes up proteins

Monosaccharide

A carbohydrate made of one sugar

If one or more carbon atoms bond to only hydrogen atoms, that molecule is called a **hydrocarbon.** An example of a hydrocarbon is CH_4, or methane. Methane is made up of one carbon bonded to four hydrogens. Methane is abundant in natural gas. It is in the digestive systems of grazing animals like cows. Hydrocarbons contain only carbon and hydrogen. Other organic molecules contain nitrogen, sulfur, or oxygen as well as carbon and hydrogen.

Macromolecules

The four important types of organic molecules are proteins, **carbohydrates, lipids,** and **nucleic acids.** These four large molecules are called **macromolecules.** Macromolecules are made of hundreds or thousands of atoms. Macromolecules are strings of units. The individual units in macromolecules are called **monomers.** Think of a macromolecule like a string of beads. Each bead represents a monomer. The entire string of beads represents a **polymer.** A polymer is a very large molecule made from many small monomers.

Organic molecules are often large. When carbon atoms are joined in long chains or in rings, the molecule is less reactive. The longer the chain, the less reactive the molecule is. Most foods are macromolecules.

Food macromolecules are biological polymers. Biological polymers are chains of repeating units of smaller monomers linked together. The monomers in proteins are **amino acids.** A **monosaccharide** is a carbohydrate made of one sugar. Monosaccharides are the simplest group of carbohydrates. A **polysaccharide** is a long polymer chain made up of monosaccharides. **Nucleotides** are the monomers in nucleic acids.

Unlike nucleotides, lipids are not organized in repeating units of monomers. Lipids are made up of **glycerol, fatty acids,** and other components. Glycerol is a sweet, syrupy alcohol with three hydroxyl groups (OH). Many fatty acids are found in animal and vegetable **fats** and oils. Lipids store large amounts of energy.

Polysaccharide

A carbohydrate that can be broken down by hydrolysis into two or more monosaccharides

Nucleotide

The repeating monomer in nucleic acid; consists of a nitrogen base, a sugar, and a phosphate group

Glycerol

A sweet, syrupy alcohol with three hydroxyl groups (OH)

Fatty acid

A long hydrocarbon with a carboxyl group at the end

Fat

A chemical that stores large amounts of energy

Dehydration synthesis

The process of joining monomers by removing a molecule of water

Hydrolysis

A chemical process in which a molecule is separated into two parts by adding a molecule of water

When cells link monomers into a chain, the process is called **dehydration synthesis.** Dehydration means "removing water." Synthesis means "to put together." When a monomer is added to a polymer chain, a molecule of water forms. The water comes from the release of two hydrogen atoms and one oxygen atom from the monomers. Dehydration synthesis is shown in Figure 3.1.9.

Cells must also break down food macromolecules to access the monomers for assembly into new macromolecules. The opposite process occurs, which is called **hydrolysis.** Hydrolysis means "to break with water." As you can see in Figure 3.1.10, adding water during hydrolysis breaks down bonds between monomers.

Dehydration Synthesis

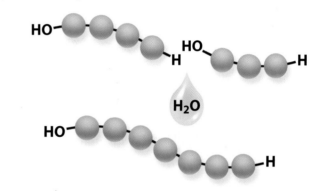

Hydrolysis

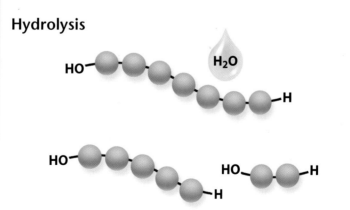

Figures 3.1.9 and 3.1.10 *Figure 3.1.9 shows dehydration synthesis. Figure 3.1.10 shows hydrolysis.*

On a sheet of paper, write the word that completes each sentence correctly.

1. Carbon-based molecules are known as _____ compounds.

2. A(n) _____ is made of many amino acids.

3. Groups of atoms called functional groups are attached to _____ atoms and take part in chemical reactions.

Critical Thinking

On a sheet of paper, write the answers to the following questions. Use complete sentences.

4. How do macromolecules form? Give some examples of macromolecules.

5. Compare and contrast carbohydrates and lipids.

Express Lab 3

Materials
◆ Food labels with Nutrition Facts

Procedure
1. Select one food label.
2. Read the label. Determine the amount of fat, carbohydrates, and protein in one serving of the food.
3. Compare your food label with a different food label chosen by a classmate. Which food is higher in fat, carbohydrates, and protein?

Analysis
1. What kinds of carbohydrates are listed on the label?
2. Calculate the percentage of calories from fat in one serving.

INVESTIGATION 3

Materials
- safety goggles
- lab coat or apron
- wax pencil
- test tubes
- test tube rack
- graduated cylinder
- distilled water
- egg albumin solution
- 5% milk solution
- 5% starch solution
- dropper bottle of biuret solution

Amino Acids and Proteins

Proteins are made of monomers called amino acids. How can you tell if a food contains proteins? In this investigation, you will test for proteins.

Procedure

1. To record your data, make a data table like the one shown here.

Solution	Color	Protein
1. distilled water		
2. egg albumin solution		
3. 5% milk solution		
4. 5% starch solution		

2. Put on safety goggles and a lab coat or apron. **Safety Alert: Do not touch or taste any chemicals.**

3. With a wax pencil, label four test tubes from 1 to 4. Add 3 mL of each solution to the correct tube:

   Test Tube 1 distilled water

   Test Tube 2 egg albumin solution

   Test Tube 3 5% milk solution

   Test Tube 4 5% starch solution

4. Add a dropperful of biuret solution to each tube. Mix gently. Look at the color of each tube. A protein will cause a color change.

5. In your data table, write down your observations.

Cleanup/Disposal

Before leaving the lab, clean up your materials and wash your hands.

Analysis

1. Which tubes contain a protein?

2. What color change do you see if the tube contains a protein?

3. Which tube is a control? Did any of the results surprise you? Explain your answer.

Conclusions

1. What do all proteins have in common?

2. Why do you think Test Tube 1 contained distilled water?

3. Write a new question about testing for proteins that you could explore in another investigation.

Explore Further

Use the same procedure to test for proteins in other foods.

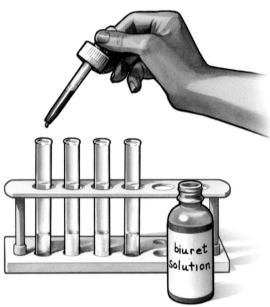

biuret Solution

Objectives

After reading this lesson, you should be able to

◆ explain that saccharides are carbohydrates

◆ understand that carbohydrates store energy used to carry out the many functions of cells

Disaccharide
A sugar formed from two monosaccharide molecules

Saccharide
A simple sugar

Fructose
A form of sugar found in fruit and honey

Glucose
A monosaccharide used as a source of energy in animals and plants

You may call them carbs. Carbs or carbohydrates are sugar molecules in potatoes, pasta, and soft drinks or sodas. These organic compounds contain only carbon, hydrogen, and oxygen. Most carbohydrates are grouped as monosaccharides, **disaccharides,** or polysaccharides. The word **saccharide** means sugar. *Mono* means "one," *di* means "two," and *poly* means "many." This naming refers to the number of sugars in the molecule. A disaccharide has two monosaccharides.

Monosaccharides

Monosaccharides are simple sugars. Monosaccharides are a source of energy for the cell. When monosaccharides are broken down in the cell, energy is released from the bonds and carbon dioxide (CO_2) is given off. Cells also use monosaccharides to make other kinds of organic molecules.

In carbohydrates, the ratio of C, H, and O atoms is 1:2:1. The formula for carbohydrates is $C_nH_{2n}O_n$. The number of carbon atoms equals the number of oxygen atoms. The number of hydrogen atoms equals twice the number of either the carbon atoms or the oxygen atoms.

The two most common monosaccharides are **fructose** and **glucose.** Fructose is found in fruit and honey. Glucose is a source of energy in animals and plants. Look at Figures 3.2.1 and 3.2.2. Notice that fructose and glucose each have six carbons. The chemical formula for both sugars is $C_6H_{12}O_6$. What difference do you see between the fructose and glucose figures?

Figures 3.2.1 and 3.2.2 *Glucose and fructose are isomers.*

Isomer

One of two or more compounds with the same molecular formula but different structures

Starch

A polymer of glucose found in plants

Cellulose

A woody polymer of glucose

Glycogen

The main storage form of glucose found in animal cells

Link to ➤➤➤

Chemistry

Artificial sweeteners provide sweetness but have few or no calories and no nutritional value. Saccharin was the first commercially available artificial sweetener. American chemist Ira Remsen and German chemist Constantin Fahlberg discovered saccharin in 1879. Saccharin is 200 to 700 times sweeter than granulated sugar.

The difference is where the double-bonded oxygen is located in the molecule. Fructose and glucose are **isomers.** Isomers are molecules with the same molecular formula but different structures and shapes.

Remember that the shape of molecules is important. Minor differences in molecules give isomers different chemical properties. For example, fructose tastes sweeter than glucose.

Disaccharides

Disaccharides are two monosaccharides bonded together. Monosaccharides bond when the H from one sugar molecule combines with the OH of another sugar molecule during dehydration synthesis. Two examples of disaccharides are maltose and lactose. Maltose is a disaccharide formed by joining two glucose monomers. Lactose is found in milk. Some people are lactose intolerant, which means they cannot drink milk from cows. They may drink soy milk instead.

Sucrose, or table sugar, is another disaccharide. It is made up of one molecule of glucose and one molecule of fructose. It is obtained from sugarcane and sugar beet roots. In the early 1980s, manufacturers began to change the glucose in corn syrup into fructose. The new product was called high fructose corn syrup (HFCS). Today, HFCS has replaced much of the sucrose in prepared foods such as bread and cold cereals. HFCS has little nutrient value other than being a carbohydrate. Our diets need more complex polysaccharides.

Polysaccharides

Polysaccharides are repeated units of simple sugars. The most common polysaccharides are **starch, cellulose,** and **glycogen.** Starch, cellulose, and glycogen are polymers of glucose. The difference between them is in the way the monomers are linked. In living things, polysaccharides are used to store sugar and to build structural parts of cells. Glycogen is the main storage form of glucose in animal cells. Animals store glycogen in liver and muscle cells. Plants store starch in **plastids.** Cellulose is part of plant cell walls. It provides structure for the plant.

Plastid

A small, special part of a plant cell

Membrane

A wall made of different molecules that separate a cell from its surroundings

Link to ➤➤➤

Health

Fructose is a sugar found in honey and fruits. It is also found in the high fructose corn syrup used in many juices, sodas, and snack foods. Many processed foods contain fructose because it is cheaper to use than sucrose, or table sugar. Fructose can cause digestive problems because it is not easily absorbed by the body. The body can more easily absorb sucrose, which contains glucose.

Carbohydrates and Health

You may have heard the term *carbo-loading,* or eating large amounts of starchy foods the day before a sports event. The body changes starch to glycogen, which is readily available as a source of energy. Starch is the form in which plants store glucose.

Cellulose is important to plant structure because it is a strong, rigid molecule. It is used for plant structures such as stems, leaves, and wood. This strength is why wood is used to build houses. Animals such as cows can change cellulose into a digestible form, but people cannot digest cellulose. For example, we cannot digest wood. If you eat cellulose, it is considered dietary fiber.

Although not a source of nutrients, fiber keeps the digestive system healthy. Vegetables, whole grains, beans, and fruits have fiber. Cellulose is the structural material of plants. Cotton is about 90 percent cellulose. When you use a cotton towel to dry dishes, the towel does not dissolve because it is mostly cellulose.

Figure 3.2.3 shows foods that are good sources of carbohydrates. Carbohydrates are a main source of energy for the body. They are important in cellular functions. For example, they are involved in cells recognizing each other and in the **membrane** structure of cells. A membrane is a wall made of different molecules that separate a cell from its surroundings.

Figure 3.2.3 *Foods high in carbohydrates include whole grains, beans, vegetables, and fruits.*

Carbohydrates also help the body use fats and remove foreign substances. Extra glucose is stored as glycogen or fat in the body.

The average American adult eats about 8 ounces of carbohydrates each day. Some common foods contain mostly carbohydrates. Examples are bread, rice, potatoes, pasta, fruits, vegetables, and baked goods. Many of these foods contain both starch and fiber. The body can digest starch, but it cannot digest fiber.

You may have heard about low carb diets. The nitrogen balance in the body can be harmed if a person does not get enough carbohydrates. The body needs carbohydrates for energy. Without carbohydrates, the body will break down certain tissues to use their proteins. For example, proteins from muscles could be used for energy. This use of protein for energy will harm the body's defense functions.

Healthy Eating

Every day, your body needs many different nutrients to keep healthy. A guide to good nutrition is the Food Guide Pyramid, shown in Figure 3.2.4. The Pyramid can help you choose what and how much to eat from each food group to get the nutrients you need. The U.S. government provides the Food Guide Pyramid and guidelines for a healthy diet and exercise.

Figure 3.2.4 *Food Guide Pyramid. Source: U.S. Department of Agriculture*

Word Bank

glycogen

energy

fructose

On a sheet of paper, write the word from the Word Bank that completes each sentence correctly.

1. Monosaccharides are a source of _____ for the cell.

2. The simple sugar _____ is found in fruits.

3. Animals store sugar in the form of _____ in the liver and muscle cells.

Critical Thinking

On a sheet of paper, write the answers to the following questions. Use complete sentences.

4. How can you recognize the chemical formula of a carbohydrate?

5. Compare and contrast monosaccharides and disaccharides.

▼◄▲▼◄▲▼◄▲▼◄▲▼◄▲▼◄▲▼◄▲▼◄▲▼◄▲▼◄▲▼◄▲▼

Science at Work

Biochemist

Biochemists study the complex chemical reactions in living things. A biochemist combines knowledge of chemistry and biology. They study life processes at a molecular or cellular level. Biochemists work with many kinds of organisms.

Some biochemists work in basic research. Biochemists who work in applied research develop new drugs and medical treatments. Many biochemists work for federal, state, or local governments. Others work for drug companies, universities, or in hospitals or research and teaching laboratories.

Biochemists work independently or as part of research teams. They need strong communication skills to present their research findings and get research funding. A Ph.D. is required to do independent research. Biochemists with a bachelor's or master's degree hold a wide variety of jobs.

Objectives

After reading this lesson, you should be able to

◆ explain that lipids are water-insoluble molecules used for food storage, membranes, and hormones

◆ describe the three main types of lipids

Phospholipid

A lipid with two fatty acid molecules joined by a molecule of glycerol

Steroid

A lipid containing four attached carbon rings

Triglyceride

A lipid made of three fatty acids and one molecule of glycerol

Saturated fatty acid

A fatty acid containing no double carbon bonds and the maximum number of hydrogen atoms

Lipids in the diet are an energy source for cells. Lipids are also important because they carry fat-soluble vitamins and essential fatty acids to cells. Cells need these to make various molecules. A fat-free diet results in a deficiency, or lack, of essential fatty acids in the body. Examples of food containing lipids are butter, lard, and cooking oils.

In living things, lipids are structural parts of cell membranes. They are sources of insulation and a means of energy storage. Lipids are made up of carbon, hydrogen, and oxygen atoms. Examples of lipids are fats, **phospholipids,** and **steroids.**

Fats and Fatty Acids

The three most common forms of lipids in the body are fats, phospholipids, and steroids. Fats are **triglycerides.** Most fats you eat are triglycerides. Your body stores fats as triglycerides. To form a triglyceride, one molecule of glycerol and three fatty acids join by dehydration synthesis. Fatty acids are long hydrocarbons that store large amounts of energy. Fats provide a source of stored energy for your body to use when it needs it. People need to have a stored source of energy or fuel reserve.

Three kinds of fatty acids are **saturated, unsaturated,** and **polyunsaturated.** A saturated fatty acid contains no double carbon bonds and the maximum number of hydrogen atoms. An unsaturated fatty acid contains double or triple bonds and has less than the maximum number of hydrogen atoms. A polyunsaturated fatty acid contains many double or triple bonds. Figure 3.3.1 shows examples of foods that are good sources of saturated and unsaturated fatty acids.

Animal fats such as lard and butter have a high proportion of saturated fatty acids. This arrangement allows them to stack on top of each other. This means they are usually solid at room temperature.

Eating too much animal fat over time may increase the chance of heart disease. Lipid deposits build up in the walls of blood vessels. This reduces blood flow and increases the risk of heart attack.

Some fish oils and vegetable oils, such as corn oil and olive oil, are high in unsaturated fatty acids. Because of the bent shape of their fatty acids, unsaturated oils stay liquid at room temperature. However, tropical plant oils such as cocoa butter are different. Cocoa butter, a tropical plant oil, is an ingredient in chocolate. Because it is a mixture of saturated and unsaturated fatty acids, cocoa butter is solid at room temperature, but melts in your mouth.

Trans fats are unsaturated fatty acids that have been changed to saturated fatty acids. Manufacturers make trans fats by adding hydrogen to vegetable oil. Trans fats increase the stability, or long life, of foods. Trans fats are found in vegetable shortenings, some margarines, crackers, cookies, and snack foods. A small amount of trans fat is found naturally, mainly in dairy products, some meat, and other animal-based foods.

Figure 3.3.1 *Sources of fats include butter, lard, and vegetable oil.*

Lipid bilayer

Two layers of phospholipids

Research and Write

Use the Internet to prepare a group report on the use of anabolic steroids among athletes. Describe the health risks posed by their use.

Phospholipids

Phospholipids are like triglycerides except that a phosphate group replaces a fatty acid chain. The phosphate group interacts with water. Phospholipids contain two fatty acid tails and one negatively charged phosphate head. The tails are hydrophobic (water-hating), which means the fatty acids do not mix with water. The head is hydrophilic (water-loving). The two fatty acid chains position themselves away from water. The phosphate end positions itself toward water. Phospholipids line up with the heads together and the tails together.

Phospholipids can form a double layer called a **lipid bilayer,** or two layers of phospholipids. Cell membranes are made up of a lipid bilayer.

Steroids

Steroids are lipids containing four attached carbon rings. Cholesterol, vitamin D, and hormones are examples of steroids. Cholesterol is an important steroid. It is a common part of animal cell membranes. Various hormones in the body such as estrogen and testosterone are steroids created from cholesterol. However, a high level of cholesterol in the body over time may cause various diseases.

Technology and Society

Food companies use a process called hydrogenation to change liquid corn oil into corn oil margarine. Hydrogenation adds hydrogen to the double-bonded carbon atoms found in unsaturated fats. As a result, the unsaturated double bonds are replaced with single bonds. Hydrogenation increases the shelf life of fats. Foods made with hydrogenated fats can stay fresh a long time. However, hydrogenation also increases the saturation of fats, making hydrogenated foods less healthy.

On a sheet of paper, write the word or words that complete each sentence correctly.

1. In an unsaturated fatty acid, some carbon atoms are joined by _____ bonds.

2. A(n) _____ is a lipid that contains a phosphate group.

3. A(n) _____ fatty acid has no double bonds between carbon atoms.

On a sheet of paper, write the letter of the answer that completes each sentence correctly.

4. A triglyceride is made up of three fatty acids and one molecule of _____.

   A water   **C** phospholipid

   B glycerol   **D** glucose

5. Animal fats such as _____ have a high proportion of saturated fatty acids.

   A butter   **C** olive oil

   B some fish oils   **D** corn oil

6. Unsaturated fatty acids that have been changed to saturated fatty acids are called _____.

   A oils   **C** steroids

   B trans fats   **D** lipids

Critical Thinking

On a sheet of paper, write the answers to the following questions. Use complete sentences.

7. Why are lipids necessary for the body to function?

8. Compare and contrast animal fats and plant and fish oils.

9. Explain the relationship between a diet high in saturated fatty acids and heart disease.

10. What are steroids? Name some examples of steroids.

Materials

- safety goggles
- lab coat or apron
- wax pencil
- test tubes
- test tube rack
- water
- vegetable oil
- unknown liquid
- Sudan III dye solution
- methylene blue dye solution

Testing for Lipids

Lipids contain carbon, hydrogen, and oxygen atoms, but not in the same ratio as carbohydrates. If you were given an unknown substance, how could you tell if it is a lipid? You will find out in this lab.

Procedure

1. To record your data, make a data table like the one shown here.

Solution	Sudan III	Methylene Blue
1. water		
2. vegetable oil		
3. water + oil		

2. Put on safety goggles and a lab coat or apron. **Safety Alerts: Do not touch or taste any chemicals.**

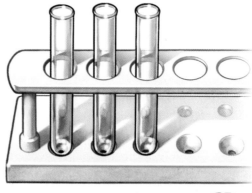

3. With a wax pencil, label three test tubes from 1 to 3. Add the following solutions to the correct tube:

Test Tube 1 2 mL water

Test Tube 2 2 mL vegetable oil

Test Tube 3 1 mL water + 1 mL vegetable oil

4. Add 3 drops of Sudan III to each test tube. Then add 3 drops of methylene blue to Test Tube 3. Shake the test tubes well. Allow them to settle.

5. In your data table, write down your observations.

6. In a small group, discuss how you could determine if an unknown liquid is a lipid. Write a hypothesis that could be tested with an experiment using the unknown liquid.

7. Write a procedure for your experiment. Include Safety Alerts.

8. Have your hypothesis, procedure, and Safety Alerts approved by your teacher. Then carry out your experiment. Record your results.

Cleanup/Disposal
Before leaving the lab, clean up your materials and wash your hands.

Analysis
1. What differences did you notice between Test Tube 1 and Test Tube 2?

2. Explain how Sudan III and methylene blue behave differently as dyes.

Conclusions
1. Was your hypothesis supported by the results of your investigation?

2. How do the structural differences between lipids and carbohydrates explain your results?

Explore Further
In your group, discuss other ways that you could test an unknown substance to determine if it is a lipid.

Proteins are the most complicated molecules in living things. Figure 3.4.1 shows different foods that are good sources of protein. Proteins are made of amino acids. Amino acids contain carbon, hydrogen, oxygen, and nitrogen atoms. Amino acids are often called the building blocks of life. A protein is many amino acids strung together in a certain order. It is then folded into a particular shape.

Twenty different amino acids are found in proteins. The human body contains hundreds of thousands of different types of proteins. Each protein is unique and essential for life. A single cell has about 100 million protein molecules.

Compare this with the 26 letters in the English alphabet. Thousands of words can be made from different arrangements of these letters. Think about how words are made from strings of letters in a particular order. *Bat* and *tab* have the same letters, but the different order of the letters creates different words. The order of amino acids spells out a particular protein.

Figure 3.4.1 *Foods high in protein include meat, poultry, eggs, and dairy products.*

Each of the 20 amino acids has a central carbon atom with four covalent bonds. These bonds link the carbon atom to an amino group (NH_2), a carboxyl group (COOH), a hydrogen atom (H), and an R group.

Contractile

Able to become shorter or longer

Hemoglobin

An iron-containing protein in red blood cells that carries oxygen

Enzyme

A protein that brings about a chemical reaction in an organism

About 25 percent of the protein in your body is collagen. Collagen is a major structural protein. It forms molecular cables, or fibrils, that strengthen the tendons. Collagen also supports the skin and internal organs. Bones and teeth are made by adding minerals to collagen.

The R group can be a carbon side chain, a hydrogen atom, or a functional group. The R group gives a particular amino acid its special chemical properties.

What Proteins Do

Some proteins provide the support needed for hair, feathers, ligaments, and spider webs. Some proteins are used as storage in seeds and eggs. Some proteins are **contractile,** or able to become shorter or longer.

Contractile proteins allow muscles to shorten or lengthen. Some proteins are used for transport. **Hemoglobin** is an iron-containing protein in red blood cells. It carries oxygen. Other proteins are **enzymes.** An enzyme is a protein that brings about a chemical reaction in an organism.

Achievements in Science

Protein Structure

Most proteins are complex molecules containing from 100 to more than 10,000 amino acids. Because they are so large, proteins can be difficult to study. How do scientists discover the molecular structure of a protein?

They start by determining the sequence of amino acids in the protein. To do this, they use acids and enzymes to split the protein at certain amino acids. The English biochemist Frederick Sanger developed this technique. He was the first scientist to show that each protein has a specific amino acid sequence. In 1958, Sanger was awarded the Nobel Prize for Chemistry for his work to determine the amino acid sequence of insulin. Insulin, a small protein made by the body, breaks down carbohydrates and fats.

To find the shape of larger proteins, scientists crystallize the protein. Then they shoot X-rays at the crystal. The X-rays scatter when they strike the crystal and form an image. Patterns within the image reveal the protein's molecular structure and shape.

Peptides

A **peptide** is a compound made up of two or more amino acids. Peptides combine to make proteins. When two amino acids bond, they form a **dipeptide** and a water molecule. The water molecule is removed by dehydration synthesis to form the **peptide bond.** A peptide bond is a covalent bond between two amino acids.

When several amino acids join into a string, the compound is called a **polypeptide.** When the polypeptide chain twists and folds, it forms a protein. In other words, a long chain of amino acids is called a protein. Proteins usually have 100 or more amino acids. The peptide bonds in a protein can be broken by adding water, or hydrolysis.

Making Proteins

To function, proteins must have the necessary amino acids in a specific **sequence** and be folded into a specific shape. A sequence is a continuous or connected series. Proteins loop, coil, and crinkle into complicated shapes. The shapes are like a messy group of wire coat hangers rather than a stack of neatly folded dish towels.

Your **genes** have the instructions to make proteins. A gene is a section of DNA that carries information that a parent passes to its offspring. Each gene is made up of **codons,** which are like the words of the instructions. A codon is a specific sequence of three nucleotides. Each nucleotide contains one of four bases, which are the "letters" of the genetic alphabet. You will find out more about nucleotides in Lesson 5.

Proteins and Health

Proteins are essential molecules used in all types of cellular activity and life. An example of a protein is an enzyme. Most enzymes are proteins. Enzymes are essential for any cell to function. Most proteins in the body are in continuous breakdown and formation. To maintain health, the body must have a supply of amino acids to replace the proteins that are broken down.

Peptide

A compound made up of two or more amino acids; peptides combine to make proteins

Dipeptide

Two amino acids joined by a peptide bond

Peptide bond

A covalent bond between two amino acids

Polypeptide

Several amino acids joined to form a chain

Sequence

A continuous or connected series

Gene

The information about a trait that a parent passes to its offspring; a section of DNA

Codon

A specific sequence of three consecutive nucleotides that is part of a gene

---

Synthesize

To make into a whole substance

Truncate

To shorten

Complete protein

A protein source that provides the body with the essential amino acids

The human body cannot **synthesize,** or make nine amino acids. These nine amino acids are called essential amino acids. The nine essential amino acids are: histidine, isoleucine, lysine, methionine, phenylalanine, threonine, tryptophan, and valine. They must be provided in the diet in adequate amounts because cells cannot make them. A cell will stop making a protein even if one essential amino acid is missing. The result is a **truncated,** or shortened, polypeptide.

A diet that does not include **complete proteins** will negatively affect health. A complete protein is a protein source that provides the body with all nine essential amino acids.

Biology in Your Life

Consumer Choices: Choosing a Vegetarian Diet

Proteins play many roles in the body. The body cannot make nine of the 20 essential amino acids. For cells to make proteins, your diet must include these nine essential amino acids. Complete proteins are those that have all essential amino acids. Eggs, milk, and most meat products are sources of complete proteins.

Most of us get the essential amino acids in our daily diets. For example, the protein in animal products has all the amino acids needed for health. What about a diet that does not include animal products? A vegetarian diet excludes all forms of animal flesh, such as meat, fowl, and fish. Some vegetarians eat eggs and dairy products. Vegetarians who do not eat any animal products are called vegans.

Plant products, such as lettuce, rice, and pasta, do not have all the essential amino acids. Even plant products high in protein, such as beans, are low in one or more of

the essential amino acids. For this reason, a healthy vegetarian diet requires planning. Vegetarians need to eat a wide variety of foods to get all essential amino acids every day. Vegetarians who eat some animal foods regularly, such as eggs or dairy products, probably get enough amino acids.

1. What is a complete protein?

2. Why does a healthy vegetarian diet require careful planning?

3. Describe one example of a healthy vegetarian diet.

Foods such as meat, eggs, and beans are made of giant protein molecules. Enzymes must digest, or break down, the protein molecules before they can be used to build and repair body tissues.

An enzyme in the juice of the stomach starts the digestion, or breakdown, of swallowed protein. The small intestine completes further digestion. Here, several enzymes from pancreatic juice and the lining of the intestine break down protein molecules into amino acids. These small molecules are absorbed from the small intestine into the blood and then are carried to all parts of the body to build cells.

If the temperature or the pH changes in a cell, proteins may come apart and lose their shape. Recall that pH is a number that tells whether a substance is an acid or a base. What happens when you cook an egg? Eggs are a good source of protein. Look at Figures 3.4.3 and 3.4.4. The photos show what happens to an egg as it heats up. The egg white turns from clear to white. The shiny, yellow yolk turns a firm, dark yellow. This happens because the proteins become **insoluble,** or not able to dissolve in water. The proteins form a solid. When this happens, proteins lose their shape and cannot function. A certain protein must have a particular shape to perform a particular job.

Figures 3.4.3 and 3.4.4 *Notice the changes in an egg's protein after heat has been applied.*

Lesson 4   R E V I E W

On a sheet of paper, write the word or words that complete each sentence correctly.

1. When two amino acids join, they form a(n) _____.

2. Genes contain the instructions to make _____.

3. The words for the instructions in genes are called _____.

On a sheet of paper, write the letter of the answer that completes each sentence correctly.

4. Proteins contain _____ atoms, which are not found in carbohydrates.

    A hydrogen   **C** oxygen

    B carbon   **D** nitrogen

5. Contractile proteins are found in _____.

    A seeds   **C** feathers

    B muscles   **D** eggs

6. The shape of a protein resembles _____.

    A beads on a string

    B folded dishtowels

    C a messy group of coat hangers

    D a flat stack of three straight chains

Critical Thinking

On a sheet of paper, write the answers to the following questions. Use complete sentences.

7. Why is the R group in an amino acid important?

8. How are proteins used in the body?

9. What are essential amino acids? Why are they essential?

10. What do you think could happen if a protein in a cell twists into the wrong shape?

RNA

A molecule that works together with DNA to make proteins

Helix

A twisted shape like a spiral staircase

Nucleic acids serve as information storage molecules. They provide the directions to make proteins. Two important nucleic acids are DNA (**d**eoxyribo**n**ucleic **a**cid) and **RNA** (**r**ibo**n**ucleic **a**cid). DNA contains genes, the hereditary blueprints for all life.

Genes are sections of DNA. Genes program the amino acid sequence of proteins. However, RNA must first translate this genetic code in DNA. RNA is essential for protein synthesis. You will learn about this process in Chapter 11.

Both DNA and RNA are polymers. They are both made up of thousands of linked monomers called nucleotides. Nucleotides join to form nucleic acids. Two nucleic acid strands join to form DNA. RNA is one nucleic acid strand.

As seen in Figure 3.5.1, each nucleotide is a complicated molecule with three parts: a sugar, a phosphate, and a base. The sugar and phosphate are the same in all nucleotides. Only the nitrogen base varies. In DNA, the four nitrogen bases are adenine (A), guanine (G), cytosine (C), and thymine (T). These four types of nucleotides can bond in any order. They can form many unique strands of DNA. Figure 3.5.2 on page 95 shows part of a DNA strand and the four types of nitrogen bases.

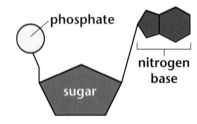

Figure 3.5.1 *A nucleotide is a complicated molecule with three parts.*

DNA is a ladder-like structure. It is made up of two nucleic acid strands twisted together. This structure is called a double **helix.** A helix is a twisted shape like a spiral staircase as you can see in Figure 3.5.3. Covalent bonds between the sugar of one nucleotide and the phosphate of the next nucleotide bond nucleotides together in a strand. This is called a sugar-phosphate backbone. The backbone forms the sides of the DNA ladder.

Ribose

The five-carbon sugar in RNA

Deoxyribose

The five-carbon sugar in DNA

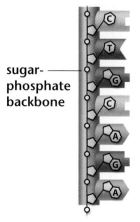

sugar-phosphate backbone

Figure 3.5.2 *Four types of nucleotides make up DNA strands.*

sugar-phosphate backbone

Figure 3.5.3 *The DNA double helix is made up of two nucleic acid strands twisted together.*

The bases in the two strands then bond to form the rungs of the ladder. These bonds are weak hydrogen bonds. When the DNA strands are zipped together into a double helix, it is very stable.

The four steps to make a DNA double helix are:

1. Two nucleic acid strands line up next to each other.

2. The sugar-phosphate backbone of the two strands form the sides of the ladder.

3. The bases of the two strands bond to one another with hydrogen bonds and form the rungs of the ladder.

4. The ladder twists into a spiral to form a double helix.

Only certain bases can bond with other bases. For example, adenine (A) pairs with thymine (T). Guanine (G) pairs with cytosine (C). If the sequence of one strand of the double helix is known, the other strand's sequence of bases can be determined.

RNA differs from DNA in four ways. RNA has an extra OH group, or hydroxyl group. RNA uses a base called uracil (U) instead of the base thymine (T). RNA is a single-stranded molecule and takes various unique shapes. It can even form base pairs with itself so that it can fold into many shapes. RNA uses the sugar **ribose.** DNA uses the sugar **deoxyribose.** Table 3.5.1 shows the differences between DNA and RNA.

Table 3.5.1 Characteristics of DNA and RNA		
Characteristic	**DNA**	**RNA**
Structure	Double-stranded	Single-stranded
Bases	Adenine, cytosine, guanine, thymine	Adenine, cytosine guanine, uracil
Sugar	Deoxyribose	Ribose

On a sheet of paper, write the word or words that complete each sentence correctly.

1. Two important nucleic acids are _____ and _____.

2. DNA forms a ladder-like structure called a double _____.

3. A(n) _____ has three parts: a sugar, a phosphate, and a base.

On a sheet of paper, write the letter of the answer that completes each sentence correctly.

4. In DNA, only the _____ varies from one nucleotide to another.

   A sugar   **C** amino acid

   B phosphate   **D** base

5. Nucleotides are the _____ of nucleic acids.

   A proteins   **C** polymers

   B monomers   **D** amino acids

6. The rungs of the DNA ladder are made from _____.

   A sugars   **C** phosphate

   B carbon and hydrogen **D** bases

Critical Thinking

On a sheet of paper, write the answers to the following questions. Use complete sentences.

7. Compare and contrast the roles and structures of DNA and RNA.

8. What are the three parts of a nucleotide? Which part(s) vary? Which part(s) remain the same?

9. How are the bases in DNA like a four-letter alphabet?

10. Explain why it is important that only certain bases pair with other bases.

Vitamin A and Blindness

Vitamins are organic compounds that the body needs. Each vitamin plays a different role. For example, vitamin A is needed for healthy eyesight. Your body needs vitamin A to make a substance that absorbs light and lets you see. Vitamin A is a fat-soluble vitamin, which means that it is stored by the body.

Your body does not make most vitamins. Instead, they must come from foods you eat. But no one food has all of the vitamins you need. This is why it is important to eat a balanced daily diet that includes a wide variety of foods.

In some parts of the world, many kinds of foods are in short supply. As a result, daily diets may be missing certain vitamins. For example, lack of vitamin A is the most common cause of blindness among children in developing countries. In these areas, many adults and children have poor diets.

Infants are often born with little vitamin A stored in their bodies. After birth, their diets are low in vitamin A. Without enough vitamin A, many children do not develop normal eyesight.

The World Health Organization (WHO) and its partners have found a low-cost solution to vitamin A deficiency. They give young children a high-dose vitamin A capsule every six months. These organizations also train parents to serve the right kinds of foods. A balanced diet means that children will get enough vitamin A as they grow.

1. Why do children need vitamin A?

2. In developing countries, why is vitamin A given to children once every six months instead of daily?

3. For further study, find out what foods contain vitamin A.

- Living things are made of organic compounds. Organic compounds contain carbon.

- There are four main types of organic compounds: carbohydrates, proteins, lipids, and nucleic acids. These four compounds are macromolecules, which are large molecules made of many atoms.

- Some macromolecules are made of repeating units called monomers.

- Carbohydrates are made of simple sugars called monosaccharides. Carbohydrates are made of carbon, hydrogen, and oxygen atoms in a 1:2:1 ratio. Carbohydrates are the body's main source of energy.

- Polysaccharides are made up of repeated units of monosaccharides. Starch, cellulose, and glycogen are examples of polysaccharides.

- Lipids provide long-term energy storage. Oils and fats are examples of lipids.

- A triglyceride is made of one molecule of glycerol and three fatty acids.

- Proteins are made of amino acids. Proteins play many roles in cells, including support, storage, and structure.

- Enzymes are proteins that bring about a chemical reaction in an organism.

- The monomers in nucleic acids are nucleotides.

- Nucleic acids are long strands of nucleotides. DNA is made up of two nucleic acids twisted into a double helix. Genes are sections of DNA. Genes contain the instructions to make proteins. A second nucleic acid called RNA translates the DNA instructions to form proteins.

Vocabulary

amino acid, 72	functional group, 71	monomer, 72	RNA, 94
carbohydrate, 72	gene, 90	monosaccharide, 72	saccharide, 77
cellulose, 78	glucose, 77	nucleic acid, 72	saturated fatty acid, 82
codon, 90	glycerol, 73	nucleotide, 73	sequence, 90
complete protein, 91	glycogen, 78	organic compound, 70	starch, 78
contractile, 89	helix, 94	peptide, 90	steroid, 82
dehydration synthesis, 73	hemoglobin, 89	peptide bond, 90	synthesize, 91
deoxyribose, 95	hydrocarbon, 72	phospholipid, 82	trans fat, 83
dipeptide, 90	hydrolysis, 73	plastid, 79	truncate, 91
disaccharide, 77	insoluble, 92	polymer, 72	triglyceride, 82
enzyme, 89	isomer, 78	polypeptide, 90	unsaturated fatty acid, 83
fat, 73	lipid, 72	polysaccharide, 73	
fatty acid, 73	lipid bilayer, 84	polyunsaturated fatty acid, 83	
fructose, 77	macromolecule, 72	ribose, 95	
	membrane, 79		

Chapter 3   R E V I E W

Word Bank

amino acid

carbohydrate

codon

disaccharide

enzyme

fructose

gene

glucose

hemoglobin

macromolecule

nucleic acid

organic compound

peptide bond

phospholipid

polymer

RNA

starch

triglyceride

Vocabulary Review

On a sheet of paper, write the word or words from the Word Bank that best complete each sentence.

1. A(n) _____ is two simple sugars bonded together.

2. Two amino acids can be joined by a(n) _____.

3. A(n) _____ is a large molecule made of many atoms.

4. Single-stranded _____ molecules translate the code for making proteins.

5. A(n) _____ is a section of DNA that contains hereditary information.

6. A compound that contains carbon is called a(n) _____.

7. A(n) _____ is made up of three fatty acids and a glycerol molecule.

8. A polymer of glucose that stores energy in plants is _____.

9. A(n) _____ is a building block found in proteins.

10. An iron-containing protein in red blood cells that carries oxygen is _____.

11. DNA is made of two _____ strands.

12. A(n) _____ is an organic compound containing carbon, hydrogen, and oxygen in a 1:2:1 ratio.

13. A(n) _____ is a specific sequence of three consecutive nucleotides.

14. A lipid can be a fat, _____, or steroid.

15. A protein that brings about a reaction in an organism is a(n) _____.

Review continued on next page

16. A(n) _____ is a very large molecule made from many simple units.

17. The two most common monosaccharides are _____ and _____.

Concept Review

On a sheet of paper, write the letter of the word or words that complete each sentence correctly.

18. _____ is a sugar found in fruit.

    A Glucose   **B** Lactose   **C** Fructose   **D** Sucrose

19. Animals store glucose in the form of _____ in liver and muscle cells.

    A glycogen   **B** body fat   **C** cellulose   **D** starch

20. During _____, bonds between monomers are broken by adding water.

    A hydrolysis   **C** polymerization

    B dehydration synthesis   **D** carbohydrate loading

21. A complete protein provides the body with the nine essential _____.

    A proteins   **C** carbohydrates

    B amino acids   **D** polymers

22. DNA and RNA are made of units called _____.

    A glycerol   **C** fatty acids

    B amino acids   **D** nucleotides

Critical Thinking

On a sheet of paper, write the answers to the following questions. Use complete sentences.

23. Why are some lipids solid at room temperature?

24. Explain how peptide bonds form.

25. Which kinds of macromolecules store energy? Explain.

Research and Write
Write a report on the role of dietary animal fats in human heart disease. Describe how changes in diet can reduce the risk of heart disease.

Test-Taking Tip When answering multiple-choice questions, read the sentence completely using each choice. Then choose the one that makes the most sense when the entire sentence is read.

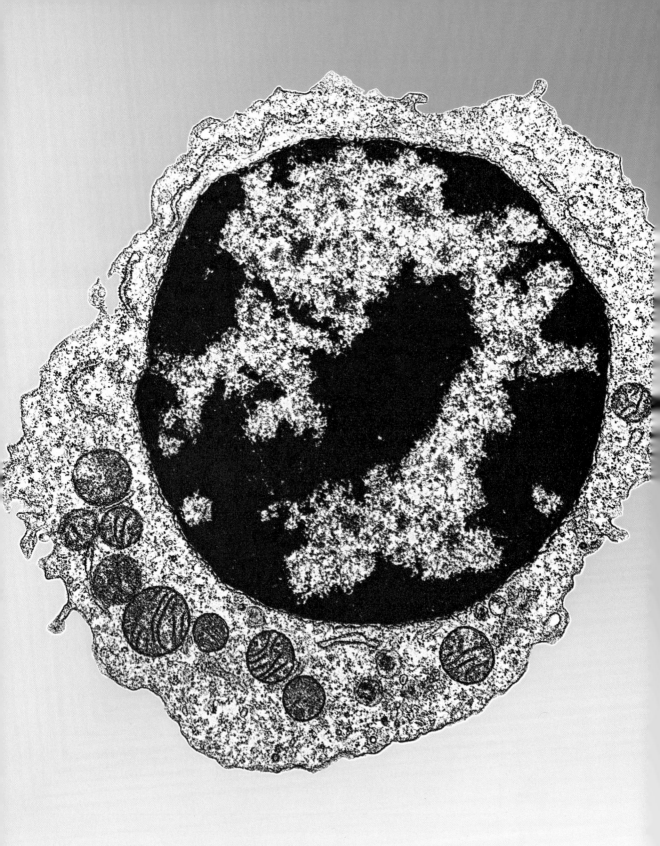

4

Cells: The Basic Units of Life

The object in the photograph is a white blood cell seen through a microscope. Notice that the inside of the cell is organized. This organization is important to large cells like this white blood cell. Some cells do not have the same amount of organization. Yet they do all of the things that make organisms alive. In Chapter 4, you will learn what cells are and what they do. You will also learn about the two basic types of cells that make up living things.

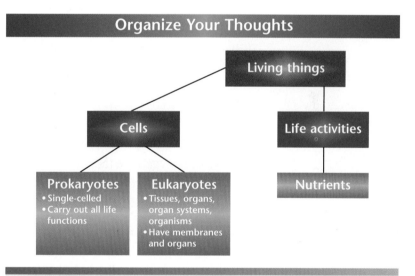

Organize Your Thoughts

Living things

Cells

Life activities

Prokaryotes
• Single-celled
• Carry out all life functions

Eukaryotes
• Tissues, organs, organ systems, organisms
• Have membranes and organs

Nutrients

Goals for Learning

◆ To learn how cells serve as the basic unit of life
◆ To know that cells perform many common activities
◆ To explain how cells use diffusion and osmosis
◆ To understand that cells perform different functions
◆ To explain how cells are grouped by structure

In Chapter 3, you found out that many different types of molecules are in organisms. How do all of these different molecules come together to create a living thing? Organisms get different molecules from the foods they eat. By breaking down food, organisms can harvest all the extra molecules they need to function and live.

Carbohydrate, lipid, protein, and nucleic acid molecules organize themselves into different structures. For example, sometimes proteins and lipids work together to make certain structures. Other times, nucleic acids and proteins work together. The four different types of molecules can work together or separately. They create different structures that help organisms to live.

Organisms are a collection of different combinations of molecules. However, living things are more than a collection of different molecules. All these combinations of molecules come together to form the first level of organization, the cell. A cell is the smallest unit of life.

Major Functions of Cells

The cells in our body perform many important functions. By breaking down food we eat, energy is produced inside cells. Cells use the oxygen we take in. The water in sweat comes from cells. Cells reproduce themselves to make more cells. The instructions for life, found in DNA, are stored in cells.

Nucleic acids, carbohydrates, lipids, and proteins come together in many combinations to make a cell. Each kind of molecule has unique properties, like polarity. These different properties allow each kind of molecule to perform certain actions.

ATP

*Adenosine triphosphate;
a molecule in all living
cells that acts as fuel*

Hormone

*A chemical signal used
to control body function*

Carbohydrates have several functions in a cell. Their main use is for energy. The cell can break the bonds of carbohydrate molecules. When it breaks these bonds, energy is released. This energy is used to make adenosine triphosphate, also called **ATP.** ATP is a cell's main fuel source.

Cells use carbohydrates for other jobs. Many cells communicate with each other using small sugar molecules. Cells use larger complex carbohydrates, such as starch and glycogen, to store energy. Complex carbohydrates also provide support because of their rigid structure.

Like carbohydrates, lipids store energy for cells. Lipids are a form of long term energy storage. Cells use lipids only when carbohydrates are not available. Lipids perform other functions. All cells are surrounded by a membrane. A membrane acts as a barrier for a cell. A membrane separates a cell from the rest of the world.

The main molecules found in membranes are lipids. Lipids are hydrophobic, or water hating. They act as a barrier because they do not mix with water or solutions made with water. Lipids are also the base molecules our body uses to make **hormones.** Hormones are special chemical signals the body uses to direct some of its activities.

Proteins have many different roles in the cell. Many proteins help keep the structure of a cell steady. Other proteins are found inside the membrane. Cells use these proteins to communicate with each other. These proteins also help control what comes in and out of a cell.

Science Myth

Myth: All living things are made of cells, not molecules.

Fact: Living things contain many different kinds of molecules. In living organisms, molecules come together to form the first level of organization, the cell.

Many proteins are used as enzymes. Remember that enzymes bring about a chemical reaction in an organism. Enzymes have specific shapes that determine the kind of job they do. Proteins come in various shapes and sizes. Each protein is unique.

Nucleic acids are the main information molecules in cells. The instructions to make all the proteins we need are in cells found in DNA. The order of bases in a DNA molecule acts as a code to make proteins. RNA helps make the protein coded in DNA. All these different molecules work together to allow a cell to function and live.

Microscopes and Cells

All living things are made of a collection of cells. Cells are so small that we cannot see them with the naked eye. We see cells by using a special piece of equipment called a **microscope.** A microscope is an instrument used to magnify things. Some microscopes use natural light to help magnify an object. These are called light microscopes. Other microscopes use a beam of electrons to create a larger image of an object. These are called electron microscopes.

Microscopes were invented in the late 1500s in Europe. Their invention was important to learning about life. They allowed scientists to see life forms that they normally could not see.

Using the microscope, several scientists made great discoveries about cells. In 1665, Robert Hooke, an English scientist, began to look at thin slices of cork. Cork is a dead wood material. He found that the interior of cork is an ordered collection of little boxes. He looked at other types of plants and found the same pattern. Hooke called these little boxes *cells.* About ten years later, a Dutch scientist named Anton von Leeuwenhoek was the first person to view living cells under a microscope.

The work of Hooke and von Leeuwenhoek was made famous about 150 years later. The new ideas from their research took time to be accepted by other scientists. This is often true in science. In the 1800s, German scientists Matthias Schleiden and Theodor Schwann helped advance a new idea about the cell.

Cell theory

A theory that all living things are made of cells, that cells are the basic units of structure and function in living things, and that cells only come from already present cells

Schleiden showed that all plants are made of cells, and Schwann did the same for animals. Another German scientist in the 1800s, Rudolf Virchow, discovered that cells can only come from other cells.

The Cell Theory

All of these discoveries are grouped together to create the **cell theory.** The cell theory has three parts:

◆ All living things are made of cells. All cells have some structures in common, such as DNA.

◆ Cells are the basic units of structure and function in living things.

◆ Cells only come from already present cells.

Express Lab 4

Materials

◆ safety goggles
◆ lab coat or apron
◆ eyedropper
◆ pond water or hay infusion
◆ microscope slide
◆ coverslip
◆ microscope

Procedure

1. Put on safety goggles and a lab coat or apron.

2. Use the eyedropper to get a drop of pond water or hay infusion.

3. Place the drop on a microscope slide. Hold a coverslip at a 45° angle from the slide and at the edge of the drop of solution. Gently lower the coverslip over the drop. **Safety Alert: Handle glass microscope slides with care. Dispose of broken glass properly.**

4. Use a microscope to examine the slide under low power and then under high power. Describe the different kinds of cells you see.

5. When finished, wash your hands well.

Analysis

1. How many kinds of cells did you find?

2. Were any cells moving? If so, describe them.

Lesson 1 R E V I E W

Word Bank

ATP

microscope

hormone

On a sheet of paper, write the word from the Word Bank that completes each sentence correctly.

1. Another name for adenosine triphosphate is _____.

2. A(n) _____ is a chemical signal our body uses to direct some of its activities.

3. An instrument used to magnify an object is called a(n) _____.

On a sheet of paper, write the letter of the answer that completes each sentence correctly.

4. A cell's main fuel source is _____.

    A DNA   **C** ATP

    B RNA   **D** proteins

5. The cell membrane is mainly made of _____.

    A nucleic acids   **C** proteins

    B lipids   **D** carbohydrates

6. Enzymes have specific _____ that determine the kind of job they do.

    A lipids   **C** starches

    B carbohydrates   **D** shapes

Critical Thinking

On a sheet of paper, write the answers to the following questions. Use complete sentences.

7. What are the characteristics of a cell?

8. How do nucleic acids carry information?

9. Compare and contrast the roles of DNA and RNA.

10. What does the cell theory state?

Materials

- safety goggles
- lab coat or apron
- 100 mL beaker
- sucrose
- warm water (38°C to 43°C)
- glass rod
- 1 envelope active dry yeast
- eyedropper
- microscope slide
- dropper bottle of iodine solution
- coverslip
- microscope

Living Cells

The cell is the basic unit of life. Yeasts are single-celled organisms. In this lab, you will see how yeast cells perform the functions needed for life.

Procedure

1. Put on safety goggles and a lab coat or apron.

2. In a 100 mL beaker, add 4 g of sucrose to 60 mL of warm water. With a glass rod, stir in one envelope of active dry yeast. Let the mixture stand for 10 minutes.

3. Describe the appearance of the mixture in the beaker.

4. Use the eyedropper to place one drop of the mixture onto a clean glass microscope slide. **Safety Alert: Handle glass microscope slides with care. Dispose of broken glass properly.**

5. Add one drop of iodine solution to the mixture on the slide. **Safety Alert: Iodine stains skin and clothing. It is a poison and an eye irritant.**

6. Hold a coverslip at a 45° angle at the edge of the drop of iodine solution. Gently lower the coverslip over the drop. You have prepared a wet mount.

7. Place the wet mount on the microscope stage. Follow instructions from your teacher to focus and adjust the microscope.

8. Observe several yeast cells. Make note of their shape.

Cleanup/Disposal

Before leaving the lab, clean up your materials and wash your hands.

Analysis

1. What is the energy source for yeast cells?

2. What cell structure surrounds each yeast cell?

Conclusions

1. What is the role of the cell membrane?

2. Write a new question about energy and living cells that you could explore in another investigation.

Explore Further

Design a similar procedure to test the effects of temperature on living yeast cells.

Objectives

After reading this lesson, you should be able to

◆ relate a cell's structure to its function

◆ define homeostasis

◆ predict the direction of diffusion

◆ identify the three different kinds of osmotic environments

Homeostasis

The ability of organisms to maintain their internal conditions

A cell's structure determines its function, or the activities a cell can perform. A cell's structure is the collection of molecules that make up that cell. All cells have some structural features in common. All cells have DNA. The difference lies in the code of the DNA. All cellular membranes are made of lipids. But differences in proteins in the membrane create differences in cell function.

How do structure and function relate? The molecules in a cell do different activities. If a cell does not have a certain kind of molecule, it cannot perform a certain function. Some molecules are only present in a cell when it needs to do a certain function. The cell produces many of these molecules when needed, then breaks them down when they are not needed.

There are many different types of activities because there are many different kinds of cells. All cells use some basic functions to stay alive. Many of these activities maintain a biological balance with the cell's surrounding environment. This overall balance is known as **homeostasis.** Homeostasis is the ability of organisms to maintain their internal conditions. In homeostasis, the amounts of molecules inside and outside the cell are kept at certain levels to maintain a balance. Figure 4.2.1 shows the two ways that cells maintain homeostasis.

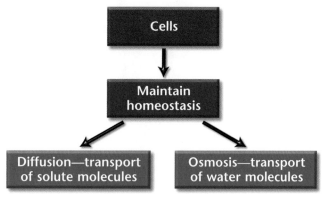

Figure 4.2.1 *Cells maintain homeostasis in two ways.*

Sometimes a cell moves molecules in or out of itself to achieve balance. This activity is called **transport.** Transport means to move molecules from one side of a membrane to the other.

You already know that molecules are constantly in motion. In general, molecules tend to spread out, not group, as they move around. To concentrate molecules means to gather molecules together in one area.

An area having many of the same molecules has a high **concentration** of those molecules. An area of low concentration has only a few molecules. Molecules generally move to an area where they have the most space available. Molecules naturally move from areas of high concentration to areas of low concentration. The movement of molecules from an area of high concentration to an area of low concentration is called **diffusion.**

Figure 4.2.2 shows the process of diffusion. In the first beaker, a sugar cube is dissolving in water. Sugar molecules are moving by diffusion. In the second beaker, sugar molecules have equally distributed themselves in the water. Remember, water is a solvent, a substance that can dissolve one or more other substances.

Figure 4.2.2 *Diffusion is seen when a sugar cube dissolves in a beaker of water.*

Selectively permeable membrane

A membrane that allows some molecules to pass but blocks other molecules from coming through

Concentration gradient

A difference in the concentration of a substance across a distance

Osmosis

The movement of water through a cell membrane

Science Myth

Myth: For best performance, athletes should always have sports drinks during a workout.

Fact: During most exercise, plain water is the best choice to replace lost fluids. Sports drinks may help during long workouts.

Cells use diffusion to control the concentrations of their molecules. A cell's membrane is the main barrier that separates a cell from its environment. Some chemicals can easily cross cell membranes. Large molecules may need help from the cell to pass through its membrane. Polar molecules have difficulty passing through the hydrophobic inside of the cell's membrane.

A cell has a **selectively permeable membrane.** The membrane allows some molecules to pass, but blocks other molecules from coming through. A cell's membrane controls the concentrations of different molecules. A **concentration gradient** forms when different concentrations of a molecule are on either side of the membrane. A concentration gradient is the difference in the concentration of a substance across a distance. Cells use concentration gradients to direct some of their activities. Cells have other ways to control molecule concentrations.

Osmosis: A Special Type of Diffusion

Water is the main solvent for most chemicals in an organism's body. How much water is used to dissolve the chemicals affects the concentration of the chemicals. Cells control the concentration of other molecules by changing the concentration of water molecules. Cells do this by performing **osmosis.** Osmosis is the movement of water through a cell membrane.

Water easily crosses the membrane of a cell. Water also moves from areas of high to low concentration. By moving water molecules around, cells can raise or lower the concentrations of other molecules.

How can scientists tell which molecules move where? Recall that all molecules naturally move from areas of high to low concentration. Moving water molecules around can completely change a cell's inside and outside environment. Three different environments explain the movement of molecules. In these three different environments, the movement of water molecules, or osmosis, is the focus.

Hypotonic

A solution whose solute concentration is lower than the solute concentration of another solution

Solute

A dissolved substance

Hypertonic

A solution whose solute concentration is higher than the solute concentration of another solution

Isotonic

A solution whose solute concentration is equal to the solute concentration of another solution

Equilibrium

A state where concentrations are equal in all parts of an area

Compared to human body fluids, seawater is a hypertonic solution. If a person drinks a lot of seawater, water leaves the body's cells to dilute the salt in the seawater. The body's cells shrink and die. This leads to dehydration and death.

Hypotonic is the first environment shown in Figure 4.2.3. A hypotonic solution has a solute concentration that is lower than the solute concentration of another solution. *Hypo* is a prefix that means "lower." The word *tonic* refers to the **solute** molecules, not water. A solute is a dissolved substance. If the environment outside a cell is hypotonic, it has fewer solute molecules than the environment inside the cell. In other words, water molecules are more concentrated on the outside of the cell than inside the cell. In this type of environment, water molecules will move into the cell. If too much water enters, the cell could burst.

Hypertonic is the second environment. Look at Figure 4.2.4. A hypertonic solution has a solute concentration that is higher than the solute concentration elsewhere. The prefix *hyper* means "higher." If the environment outside a cell is hypertonic, the water concentration is higher inside the cell than outside the cell. In this type of environment, water molecules will move out of the cell. If too much water leaves, the cell could shrink.

If the environment outside a cell is hypotonic, then the environment inside the cell is hypertonic. If the outside is hypertonic, then the environment inside the cell is hypotonic. Hypotonic and hypertonic describe solute concentration. They do not describe water concentration.

Isotonic is the third concentration environment shown in Figure 4.2.5. An isotonic solution has a concentration that is equal to the inside solute concentration of another solution. The concentrations of solute molecules on both sides of the membrane are equal. In this state, the whole environment is in **equilibrium.** Equilibrium is a state of equal concentrations in all parts of an area. Reaching equilibrium with different outside environments is one way cells maintain homeostasis.

Figures 4.2.3, 4.2.4, and 4.2.5 *The same cell is shown in outside environments that are hypotonic, hypertonic, and isotonic. The arrows indicate movement.*

On a sheet of paper, write the word or words that complete each sentence correctly.

1. A cell maintains a biological balance known as _____.

2. When there are different concentrations of a molecule on either side of the cell membrane, a _____ results.

3. A cell reaches _____ when solute concentrations inside and outside the cell are equal.

Critical Thinking

On a sheet of paper, write the answers to the following questions. Use complete sentences.

4. How does a cell maintain homeostasis?

5. Why is a cell membrane selectively permeable?

❋ ❋

Technology and Society

Physiological saline is a sterile solution of sodium chloride. It is isotonic to body fluids. Doctors use it to replace body fluids lost during bleeding, burns, or excessive sweating. Without enough fluid in the body, blood pressure drops. The sudden loss of blood pressure can damage the brain, heart, and kidneys. In medical emergencies, physiological saline saves many lives.

Objectives

After reading this lesson, you should be able to

◆ identify the two major categories of cells

◆ compare the major structural differences between cells

◆ describe the kinds of organisms that cells make

As you have learned, an important cell function is to maintain homeostasis. Cells perform other functions. Cells can be grouped in many different ways, such as by structure. Since structure determines function, these structural groupings can also be the basis of grouping by function.

Prokaryotic Cells

Membranes are the first structures used to group cells together. Some cells have only one membrane. This membrane separates the cell from the outside world. All other cell parts and molecules, including the DNA, float freely inside the cell. This is a prokaryotic cell or **prokaryote.** A prokaryote has only one outside membrane. It has no nucleus or other internal structures.

Prokaryote

A cell with only one outside membrane and no nucleus or other internal structures

Prokaryotic cells are the simplest organisms. Organisms commonly called bacteria are prokaryotes. Remember that bacteria are the simplest single cells that carry out all basic life activities.

Some people think all bacteria are harmful. That is not true. Only some bacteria cause disease. People clean themselves and their surroundings to prevent harmful bacteria from spreading.

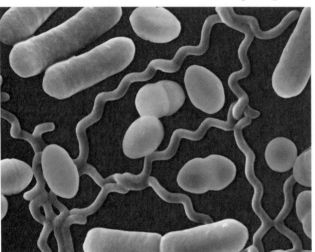

Some bacteria help us live. They help us break down food and use chemicals. Bacteria can also help make different kinds of food, like bread, cheese, and yogurt. Most bacteria are harmless to people. As seen in Figure 4.3.1, most bacteria come in three shapes: rods, spirals, and spheres.

Figure 4.3.1 *Most bacteria are shaped like rods, spirals, or spheres.*

Binary fission

Reproduction in which a bacterial cell divides into two cells that look the same as the original cell

Eukaryote

A cell with several internal structures, including the nucleus, that are surrounded by membranes

Organelle

A tiny membrane-bound structure inside a cell

Link to ➤➤➤

Health

An antibiotic is a drug that kills bacteria. Unlike animal cells, bacteria have a cell wall surrounding the cell membrane. Many antibiotics, such as penicillin, interfere with cell wall production. These antibiotics kill bacteria, but leave eukaryotes unharmed.

Since prokaryotes do not have many specific structures, they do not have many specific functions. Prokaryotes' main goal is to live. To reach this goal, they eat and remove waste from their inside. Both of these functions are controlled by the one membrane that surrounds the cell. To live, prokaryotes must find the right environment. This environment depends on the type of prokaryote. Prokaryotes live in every part of the world. Prokaryotes can be found in any type of environment, even inside other organisms.

Because their structure is so simple, prokaryotes can grow quickly. To reproduce, prokaryotes make copies of their DNA and then divide in two. This process is known as **binary fission,** which we will discuss in Chapter 9. Binary fission is the reproduction of bacteria. In binary fission, a bacterial cell divides into two cells that look the same as the original cell. Prokaryotes reproduce quickly because making cells is simple. One cell can divide enough times to make over a million cells in less than one day!

Eukaryotic Cells

Many prokaryotes live in the world. What about the rest of the organisms on the planet, including humans? These organisms are more complex than prokaryotes. Because of this, they have more complex cells. These complex cells have more structures compared to prokaryotes. If a cell is not prokaryotic, it is a **eukaryote.** A eukaryotic cell has several structures, including a nucleus. In a cell, the nucleus controls growth and reproduction. The nucleus and other cell structures are surrounded by membranes. Eukaryotes include many kinds of organisms, such as mushrooms, molds, plants, and animals.

A eukaryotic cell has more membranes than the one separating it from the outside. The other membranes are found inside the cell and create separate areas called **organelles.** An organelle is a tiny, membrane-bound structure inside a cell. Each organelle has a different function.

All eukaryotic cells have a nucleus. Remember that the nucleus is the information and control center of a cell. It contains most of a cell's DNA.

The nucleus is the main organelle used to identify eukaryotic cells. It is usually the largest organelle inside a cell. All eukaryotic cells have a nucleus surrounded by a membrane. Prokaryotic cells do not have a nucleus surrounded by a membrane.

Eukaryotic cells have other organelles. Each organelle has a specific function. Some organelles produce fuel for the cell. Others help a cell move around. Still other organelles help cells talk to one another. All of these different organelles and their functions are controlled by the activities of the nucleus.

Achievements in Science

Growing Cells in the Lab

Soon after cells were discovered, scientists wanted to learn how living cells function. But they faced a puzzling question: How can you study living cells? In 1907, American scientist Ross Granville Harrison answered this question. He became the first scientist to grow cells outside of an organism. Harrison invented lab techniques to grow frog nerve cells in dishes.

Growing animal or plant cells in an artificial environment is known as tissue culture. Scientists collect one or more cells, and then raise the cells in a special solution called a culture medium. The medium is at a temperature close to that of the organism's normal environment. The cells divide and make new cells. They create a continuous population, or cell line.

From studying tissue culture, scientists have learned that normal cells lose their ability to multiply after 50 to 100 cell divisions. However, cancer cells continue to divide. Many researchers today use the HeLa cell line. These are cancer cells from Henrietta Lacks, who died in 1951 from cancer. Her cells have been a great benefit to modern scientific research.

Since they are complex, eukaryotic cells have many different methods to control their activities. Even reproduction is more complex in eukaryotic cells and happens through a series of steps. We will discuss eukaryotic reproduction in Chapter 9.

Different eukaryotic cells have different amounts and kinds of organelles. The organelles in a eukaryotic cell determine the main function of the cell. A cell's main function affects the kinds of proteins produced by the cell. For example, plant cells have many organelles that store water because they need water constantly. Look at Figure 4.3.2. Muscle cells have many organelles that produce energy. They need energy to work. A cell's structure and its function are closely related to each other. We will discuss different organelles and their functions in Chapter 5.

Figure 4.3.2 *Muscle cells have many organelles that produce energy because these cells need energy to work.*

Lesson 3   R E V I E W

On a sheet of paper, write the word or words that complete each sentence correctly.

1. Structures with different functions inside a eukaryotic cell are called_____.

2. Prokaryotes reproduce by a process called _____.

3. The largest organelle inside a cell is usually the _____.

On a sheet of paper, write the letter of the answer that completes each sentence correctly.

4. The simplest organisms are _____.

   A bacteria   **C** molds

   B plants   **D** animals

5. Prokaryotes contain all of the following except _____.

   A DNA   **C** molecules floating inside

   B a nucleus   **D** a cell membrane

6. Cells found in _____ have many organelles that produce energy.

   A hair   **C** plants

   B skin   **D** muscles

Critical Thinking

On a sheet of paper, write the answers to the following questions. Use complete sentences.

7. How are organelles related to a cell's function?

8. Why is binary fission a fast way for a cell to reproduce?

9. Explain why both prokaryotic cells and eukaryotic cells contain DNA.

10. How could you distinguish a prokaryotic cell from a eukaryotic cell?

DISCOVERY INVESTIGATION 4

Materials
- safety goggles
- lab coat or apron
- microscope slide
- forceps
- *Elodea* leaf
- dropper bottle of distilled water
- coverslip
- microscope
- dropper bottle of 10% NaCl solution

Osmosis in Cells

Water enters and leaves cells by osmosis. In this investigation, you will predict the direction of water movement across a cell membrane. Under what conditions will water enter a cell? Under what conditions will water leave a cell?

Procedure

1. Put on safety goggles and a lab coat or apron.

2. Use forceps to get a small *Elodea* leaf. Use the dropper to put a drop of distilled water onto a clean glass microscope slide. Place the leaf over the drop of water. Carefully place a coverslip on the leaf. **Safety Alert: Handle glass microscope slides with care. Dispose of broken glass properly.**

3. Place the wet mount on the microscope stage. Follow instructions from your teacher to focus and adjust the microscope.

4. Describe what you see. Do you think water is entering the *Elodea* cells or leaving the cells? Explain your answer.

5. In a small group, discuss how you could determine the conditions that cause water to enter and exit the cell. Write a hypothesis that you could test with an experiment.

6. Write a procedure for your experiment. Include Safety Alerts.

7. Have your hypothesis, procedure, and Safety Alerts approved by your teacher. Then carry out your experiment. Record your results.

Cleanup/Disposal

Before leaving the lab, clean up your materials and wash your hands.

Analysis

1. Is distilled water a hypotonic or hypertonic environment compound to *Elodea* cells?

2. In what direction do you think water would move if *Elodea* cells were surrounded by saltwater?

Conclusions

1. Was your hypothesis supported by the results of your investigation?

2. Plant fertilizers contain salts. Why is it important to use the correct amount of fertilizer?

Explore Further

In your group, discuss how you could find out if the events you have just seen are reversible.

Objectives

After reading this lesson, you should be able to

◆ name the four levels of organization in complex organisms

◆ identify examples of each level of organization

Tissue

A group of cells that are similar and work together

Epithelial cell

A skin cell

Nervous tissue

Nerves made from collections of nerve cells

In the last lesson, we looked at the two major classifications of cells: prokaryotes and eukaryotes. Remember that prokaryotes are single-cell organisms that can carry out all the functions necessary for life.

The cells that make up larger organisms have different functions based on their structures. The different kinds of cells are not found everywhere in an organism. All cells do not perform all activities. Different kinds of cells rely on each other to keep an organism alive. Cells in complex organisms are put together in an ordered way.

Cells can be grouped together into **tissues.** A tissue is a group of cells that are similar and work together. For example, skin is made up of **epithelial cells,** or skin cells. Epithelial cells work together as skin tissue to protect parts of your body. Nerve cells work together to form **nervous tissue.** Nervous tissue forms nerves that relay messages to and from the brain. Nerves run throughout your body. Muscle tissue is made of muscle cells that work together to make muscles move.

Figure 4.4.1 *The human body is made up of cells, tissues, organs, and organ systems.*

Tissues can be grouped together into **organs.** The organ is the next level of organization in complex organisms. Organs are a group of different tissues that work together to perform specific functions. The heart is an example of an organ. Muscle tissue in the heart contracts. This movement causes the heart to beat and pump blood. The heart is separated from the rest of the body by a covering of epithelial cells. Nervous tissue relays messages from the brain to the heart.

Organs can be grouped together into **organ systems.** An organ system is a group of organs that work together to perform several connected tasks. The heart, an organ, pumps blood through the arteries. Blood is a tissue made of blood cells. Blood carries oxygen to all the parts of a body. The veins carry blood back to the lungs to get more oxygen for the body. All of these organs and tissues are grouped together in the **circulatory system.** The circulatory system is an organ system that includes the heart, arteries, and veins. It moves blood and gases throughout the body.

Science at Work

Developmental Biologist

During development, a single eukaryotic cell gives rise to dividing cells. These cells become different from one another. This process is called *differentiation.* Developmental biologists find out how cells divide, differentiate, and form tissues and organs. They study how genes control development. Developmental biologists learn about structural changes that take place as an organism develops. They also discover how the environment, drugs, or chemicals affect development.

Developmental biologists often specialize. Many study errors in development that cause diseases or disorders. They seek to understand how development occurs so that diseases or birth defects can be prevented or treated.

Most jobs in developmental biology require a master's degree. A Ph.D. degree is needed to do independent research. Developmental biologists must be patient, curious, and detailed-oriented.

Organ systems are the final level of organization in an organism. Humans, like other animals and plants, have these four levels of organization: cells, tissues, organs, and organ systems. These levels differ for different organisms. We will discuss organ systems found in the human body in Chapters 11 and 12.

Biology in Your Life

Technology:

Artificial Blood

Many accident victims often need blood cells to replace those they have lost. Blood cells carry oxygen throughout the body. Quick replacement of lost blood is needed to survive. A blood transfusion can mean the difference between life and death. However, people must receive blood that matches their blood type.

Supplies of donated blood sometimes run low. Blood must be refrigerated, and it does not stay fresh for long.

Researchers are now developing and testing artificial blood substitutes. These products carry oxygen to body tissues. Artificial blood products do not last a long time in the body. They help a patient survive until the person receives real blood.

Unlike real blood, artificial blood can be given to a person of any blood type. It can be stored at room temperature. Scientists think artificial blood products will soon save lives during medical emergencies.

1. What is the function of blood cells?

2. How does artificial blood differ from real blood?

3. Do you know what blood type you are? If not, how can you find out? Why might it be important to know your blood type?

Lesson 4   R E V I E W

Word Bank

cells

organ system

organ

On a sheet of paper, write the word or words from the Word Bank that complete each sentence correctly.

1. A(n) _____ is made up of different organs that work together to perform a specific connected tasks.

2. A tissue is a group of _____ with similar structures that work together to do a common function.

3. The heart is an example of a(n) _____.

On a sheet of paper, write the letter to complete each sentence correctly.

4. The role of epithelial cells is to _____.

   A protect parts of the body

   B break down food

   C carry oxygen

   D transmit information

5. Blood is an example of a(n) _____.

   A cell   **B** tissue   **C** organ   **D** organ system

6. Messages are carried to and from the brain by _____ cells.

   A muscle   **B** nerve   **C** skin   **D** blood

Critical Thinking

On a sheet of paper, write the answers to each of the following questions. Use complete sentences.

7. Compare the ways in which prokaryotes and eukaryotes perform the tasks necessary for life.

8. Describe the relationship among tissues, organs, and organ systems.

9. Are some tissues found in more than one organ system? Explain your answer.

10. How are organ systems in the body related to one another? Provide an example.

Stem Cells

Many diseases and injuries, such as Parkinson's disease, spinal cord injuries, and damaged heart muscle tissue, involve damage to the body's cells. Currently, many of these diseases and injuries have no cures. New technology in the area of stem cell research may offer solutions.

Stem cells are special cells that can serve as a repair system for the body. They have three properties that allow them to perform this function: 1) They can divide and renew themselves for long periods of time; 2) They do not have a specific task or function; 3) They can become specialized cells, such as muscle cells or nerve cells.

All animals, including humans, start life as one cell. This single cell divides and becomes multiple cells. In three to five days, a small number of stem cells have formed. These cells become hundreds of different kinds of cells that will make up the adult organism. Later in life, stem cells are still present in our bodies. Adult stem cells can replace damaged or worn out cells. Scientists are trying to use adult stem cells as a treatment for diseases that destroy cells.

Doctors treat people with blood diseases such as leukemia by transplanting blood-forming stem cells from bone marrow. Stem cells might be used as replacement cells to treat other conditions.

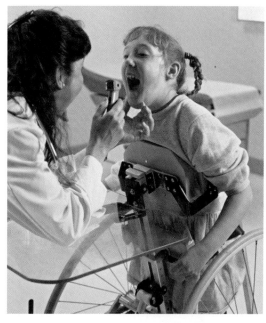

This includes diabetes, spinal cord injury, and Alzheimer's disease. Scientists have been able to cause stem cells to become nerve cells similar to those destroyed by Parkinson's disease. Someday, these nerve cells might replace damaged nerve cells, helping those who have Parkinson's disease.

1. What three properties of stem cells make them special?

2. What kinds of diseases can doctors treat with stem cells? What diseases do they hope to treat in the future?

3. What steps might a doctor take to use stem cells to treat someone who has damaged heart muscle tissue?

- Cells are the smallest units of life. The cell performs many functions necessary for life.

- Carbohydrates, lipids, proteins, and nucleic acids are macromolecules serve different roles in cells.

- Cells can be viewed through a microscope.

- The three-part cell theory sums up the role of cells. First, the cell is an organism's basic unit of structure and function. Second, all living things are made of cells. Third, cells come from other cells that are already present.

- A cell's structure determines its function. Living things maintain a biological balance with their environment. This balance is known as homeostasis.

- A cell maintains homeostasis by transporting molecules in or out through the cell's membrane.

- In the process of diffusion, solute molecules enter or exit a cell as they move from areas of high concentration to areas of low concentration.

- In the process of osmosis, water molecules enter or exit a cell depending on the concentrations of solutes inside and outside of the cell.

- A cell's selectively permeable membrane controls the molecules that enter and exit the cell. Water molecules easily cross the cell membrane.

- There are two kinds of cells, prokaryotes and eukaryotes. Prokaryotes are single-celled organisms that lack a nucleus. Eukaryotes are more complex cells. They contain a nucleus and other membrane-bound organelles.

- Complex organisms are made up of many kinds of cells. Each kind of cell has a different function. Cells with the same function work together to form a tissue.

- A tissue is a group of similar cells with a common function. An organ is a group of different tissues working together to perform specific functions. An organ system is a group of organs working together to perform related tasks.

Vocabulary

ATP, 105	diffusion, 112	hypotonic, 114	osmosis, 113
binary fission, 117	epithelial cell, 123	isotonic, 114	prokaryote, 116
cell theory, 107	equilibrium, 114	microscope, 106	selectively permeable
circulatory system, 124	eukaryote, 117	nervous tissue, 123	membrane, 113
concentration, 112	homeostasis, 111	organ, 124	solute, 114
concentration	hormone, 105	organ system, 124	tissue, 123
gradient, 113	hypertonic, 114	organelle, 117	transport, 112

Chapter 4 R E V I E W

Word Bank

ATP

diffusion

equilibrium

eukaryote

homeostasis

hormone

hypertonic

hypotonic

isotonic

microscope

organ

organ system

organelle

osmosis

prokaryote

tissue

Vocabulary Review

On a sheet of paper, write the word or words from the Word Bank that complete each sentence.

1. In a(n) _____ environment, the solute concentration is equal both inside and outside of the cell.

2. A group of similar cells with similar functions is a(n) _____.

3. The movement of molecules from areas of high concentration to low concentration is called _____.

4. A(n) _____ is a cell with internal structures surrounded by membranes.

5. In a(n) _____ environment, the solute concentration is higher than elsewhere.

6. A biological balance that all organisms work to maintain is known as _____.

7. A scientist would use a(n) _____ to view cells.

8. In a(n) _____ environment, the solute concentration is lower than elsewhere.

9. A(n) _____ is a group of different tissues working together to perform specific functions.

10. The diffusion of water molecules is called _____.

11. A cell with only one outer membrane and no specific internal structures is a(n) _____.

12. A(n) _____ is a special chemical signal the body uses to direct some of its activities.

13. A state where concentrations are equal in all parts of an area is _____ .

14. A group of organs that work together to perform several connected tasks is called a(n) _____.

Review continued on next page

15. The cell's main fuel source is _____.

16. A small, membrane-bound structure in a eukaryotic cell is called a(n) ____.

Concept Review

On a sheet of paper, write the answer that completes each sentence correctly.

17. Cells use diffusion and osmosis to _____.

   A make ATP   **C** move

   B capture prey   **D** maintain a stable environment

18. In cells, the main function of carbohydrates is to _____.

   A act as the major molecule found in membranes

   B provide energy

   C store information

   D help to make chemical reactions possible

19. Prokaryotic cells ____.

   A lack a cell membrane

   B form organs

   C reproduce by binary fission

   D have a nucleus

20. The heart, blood, arteries, and veins work together as a(n) ____.

   A tissue   **C** organ system

   B organ   **D** organism

21. Examples of prokaryotes are ____.

   A bacteria   **C** mushrooms

   B plants   **D** animals

Critical Thinking

On a sheet of paper, write the answers to the following questions. Use complete sentences.

22. A research scientist who is collecting cells places them in an isotonic solution. Explain why the scientist does this.

23. Salt preserves certain foods by removing moisture. Why can salt be used to remove water from foods?

24. How are plant cells, animal cells, and bacteria similar? How are they different?

25. Why are prokaryotes able to reproduce quickly?

Research and Write

With a partner, interview a medical professional and prepare a report on the medical condition known as shock. Describe the causes and treatment of shock.

Test-Taking Tip Take time to organize your thoughts before answering a question that requires a written answer. Jot down notes before answering the question if necessary.

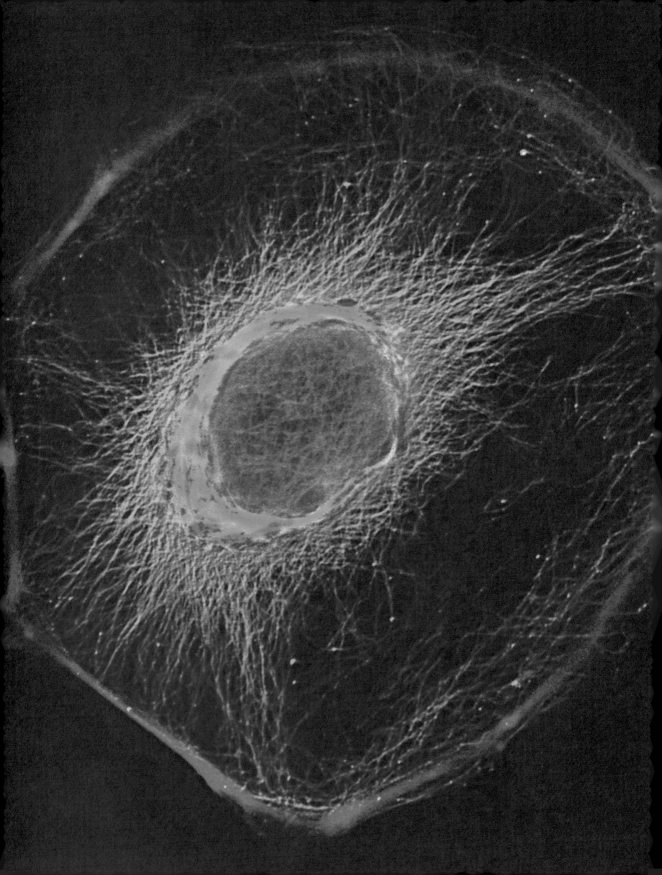

A Journey into the Eukaryotic Cell

5

The object in the photograph may look like something you would see in outer space. However, this is a cell from a mouse. Notice all the structures that make up the cell. Animal cells contain the same types of structures. Plant cells have structures that are different from animal cells. In Chapter 5, you will learn about the many structures in cells. You will also find out how materials move within, through, and around cells.

Organize Your Thoughts

Eurkaryotic cells have membranes.

Plasma membrane outside cell

Membranes create

Controls transport

Provides support and protection

Supports signal pathways

Information organelles

Energy organelles

Factory organelles

Support organelles

Goals for Learning

◆ To identify the structure and activities of cell membranes
◆ To describe information organelles
◆ To describe energy organelles
◆ To understand the endomembrane system
◆ To describe the cytoskeleton
◆ To identify plant cell structures and functions

After reading this lesson, you should be able to

◆ explain the bilayer structure of cellular membranes

◆ identify the function of other molecules found in a cellular membrane

◆ describe a cell's inside environment

Bilayer

Two layers

As you learned in Chapter 4, eukaryotic cells are more complex than prokaryotic cells. For example, eukaryotic cells contain organelles. Organelles are surrounded by membranes that perform special functions. Both cell and organelle membranes are important in determining what a cell does. Membranes control the activities of a cell. Understanding the structure of membranes will help you understand how membranes control cell activities.

Cell Membrane Structure

Cell membranes are made of phospholipids. Remember that a phospholipid is a lipid molecule with a head and a tail. The head is a phosphate group (PO_4) joined to a glycerol molecule. The phosphate group has a negative charge. The head of the molecule is polar and hydrophilic (water-loving). The tail of a phospholipid is made of two fatty acid chains attached to the same glycerol molecule. The fatty acids have no charge. They are nonpolar and hydrophobic (water-hating).

Look at Figure 5.1.1. When phospholipids pack together, the polar heads interact with each other. The nonpolar tails also interact with each other. The phospholipids form a **bilayer,** or two layers. In the bilayer, the hydrophilic heads move to the outside of the layer. The hydrophobic tails move to the inside. This phospholipid bilayer is called a membrane.

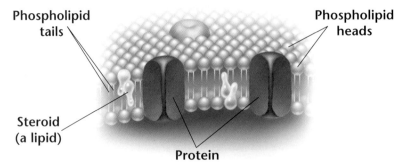

Phospholipid tails

Phospholipid heads

Steroid (a lipid)

Protein

Figure 5.1.1 *Cell membranes are made of two layers of phospholipids.*

Cell Membrane Function

The hydrophilic outside of a membrane allows cells and organelles to interact with their fluid environments. The inside of a membrane is a divider for the cell. The chemical nature of the membrane limits the size and type of molecules that can cross it. Because of this characteristic, the membrane is selectively permeable. Remember that a selectively permeable membrane allows some molecules to pass. It blocks other molecules from coming through. The membrane that surrounds a cell and separates it from the environment is called the **plasma membrane.**

Express Lab 5

Materials
◆ safety goggles
◆ lab coat or apron
◆ medium-sized beaker
◆ warm tap water
◆ vegetable oil

Procedure
1. Put on safety goggles and a lab coat or apron.

2. Fill the beaker about one-quarter full of water. **Safety Alert: Be careful when working with glassware.**

3. Add vegetable oil until the beaker is about half full of liquid.

4. Observe the liquids in the beaker. Gently tilt the beaker back and forth. Observe how the liquids respond to the motion.

Analysis
1. Which liquid is like the head of a phospholipid? Which liquid is like the tail?

2. How did the liquids respond when you tilted the beaker sideways? How is this similar to a plasma membrane?

Although the plasma membrane is selectively permeable, many different molecules can enter and leave the cell. These molecules are often helped by proteins in the plasma membrane. Some membrane proteins are on one side of the membrane. Others stretch across the entire width of the membrane. Some membrane proteins stay in one place. Others float around and through the membrane. The plasma membrane shifts constantly. Phospholipids and proteins move around together. This model of the plasma membrane is called the **fluid mosaic model.** Proteins in the plasma membrane that help molecules to cross are called **transport proteins.** We will discuss the function of transport proteins in Lesson 2.

Extra Cellular Matrix

Animal cells have another layer on the outside of the plasma membrane. This layer is called the **extracellular matrix.** It is a sticky coating made and given off by animal cells. The extracellular matrix keeps cells joined together. It allows them to pass molecules between them. Fibers in this layer connect cells to each other. Those fibers are also connected to the interior of the cell. These connections help similar cells in similar tissues act together.

Inside the Plasma Membrane

Eukaryotic cells contain organelles bound by membranes. These membranes have the same structure as the plasma membrane. They function in the same way because they control the activities of the individual organelles. Organelles process information and energy for the cell. They also provide support and movement.

Inside the cell, organelles float in an area called the **cytoplasm.** Cytoplasm is made of organelles and a fluid called **cytosol.** Cytosol is a water-based mixture of molecules the cell needs. Molecules made by the cell and molecules taken in by the cell move throughout the cytoplasm. Organelles in the cell use or change these molecules.

On a sheet of paper, write the letter of the answer to complete each sentence correctly.

1. The fluid mosaic model describes _____.

　　A the extracellular matrix

　　B the movement of proteins in and out of the cell

　　C the plasma membrane

　　D the organization of organelles in the cytoplasm

2. The characteristics that best describe the tail of a phospholipid molecule are _____.

　　A neutral charge, nonpolar, and hydrophobic

　　B neutral charge, polar, and hydrophobic

　　C negative charge, polar, and hydrophilic

　　D negative charge, nonpolar, and hydrophobic

3. The organelles and fluid in a cell together make up the _____.

　　A cytosol　　**B** plasma　　**C** cytoplasm　　**D** matrix

On a sheet of paper, write the word or words to complete each statement correctly.

4. Unlike prokaryotic cells, eukaryotic cells contain _____.

5. The plasma membrane is _____ permeable.

6. The extracellular matrix is on the outside of the _____.

Critical Thinking

On a sheet of paper, write the answers to the following questions. Use complete sentences.

7. Describe the functions of the plasma membrane.

8. What might happen if a cell's plasma membrane is not partially hydrophobic?

9. Why do cells need a hydrophilic part to the plasma membrane?

10. What is the function of cytosol in a cell?

After reading this lesson, you should be able to

◆ compare active and passive transport

◆ compare exocytosis and endocytosis

◆ list ways animal cells are joined

Passive transport

The movement of molecules across a membrane when the movement requires no energy

Facilitated diffusion

Passive transport that involves membrane proteins

Active transport

The movement of molecules across a membrane when the movement requires energy

The plasma membrane's main function is to control how molecules enter and leave the cell. Some molecules are small enough or have a certain chemical nature so they can cross the plasma membrane. They cross by diffusion. Remember that diffusion is the movement of molecules from an area of high concentration to an area of low concentration.

Diffusion, also called **passive transport,** does not need energy. A cell does not use ATP for diffusion and osmosis (the diffusion of water). Molecules that diffuse across a membrane follow their concentration gradient. They move from a high concentration to a low concentration.

Some molecules have shapes that do not allow them to naturally diffuse. However, they do not require ATP to be transported. These molecules experience **facilitated diffusion.** This type of passive transport uses membrane proteins to help molecules across. The proteins act in one of two ways. One way is when proteins open up a channel in the membrane, like a hole. The channel allows molecules to travel across. The second way is when proteins bind to a specific molecule on one side. Then the membrane opens on the other side to release the specific molecule.

Cells need molecules that cannot passively cross the membrane. To get these molecules, cells perform **active transport.** Active transport is when a cell uses energy to bring a molecule across its membrane. Cells use ATP, the energy molecule, as the fuel for active transport. Transport proteins inside the plasma membrane are involved in active transport.

These proteins use ATP to attach molecules to themselves and then change shape. The proteins push the molecules through the membrane. Transport proteins need energy because the molecules are moving against their concentration gradient. They are going from a low concentration to a high concentration.

Endocytosis

A process in which a cell membrane surrounds and encloses a substance to bring the substance into the cell

Exocytosis

A process in which a substance is released from a cell through a pouch that transports the substance to the cell surface

Sometimes a cell needs to move substances that are too large for transport proteins to handle. The plasma membrane must change its structure to move these substances. The cell uses two processes to do this. One process is to digest needed substances. The other process is to get rid of unwanted substances.

Endocytosis is the process a cell uses to bring large substances inside the cell. Figure 5.2.1 shows this process. The plasma membrane folds inward to surround the substances. The plasma membrane then pinches off the newly formed package. The cell moves the package to where it is needed inside.

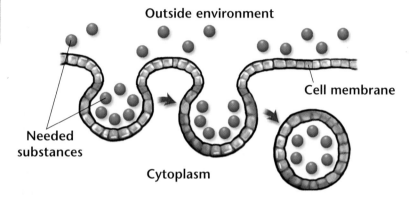

Figure 5.2.1 *Cells use endocytosis to bring in large substances.*

The reverse of this process is **exocytosis.** Figure 5.2.2 shows the process of exocytosis. A cell removes unwanted substances by packing them into a membrane. The cell moves this package to the plasma membrane. The two membranes fuse together. Then the cell pushes the waste outside of the cell.

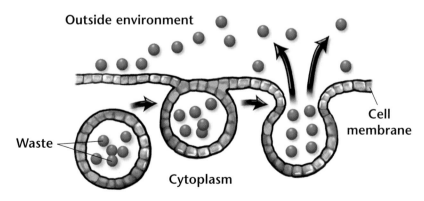

Figure 5.2.2 *Cells use exocytosis to get rid of waste.*

The plasma membrane also helps cells communicate with each other. Carbohydrates on the outside of the plasma membrane act as signals. Cells use these signals to recognize each other. Cells with the same markers stick together and eventually work together as a tissue. When this happens, the plasma membranes form **gap junctions.** Gap junctions are connections between cells made for support and communication. Cells send messages back and forth through gap junctions.

Biology in Your Life

Consumer Choices: Antibacterial Products

You probably have several cleaning products or medicines in your home that are antibacterial or antibiotic. The prefix *anti-* means "against" or "preventing." These products work by destroying cells. Doctors may prescribe antibiotic drugs for bacterial infections. Antibiotics are important weapons against deadly bacterial diseases such as tuberculosis, a lung disease. Antibiotics work in two ways. They cause problems with the cell walls of bacteria, which kills the bacteria. They can also stop bacteria from reproducing.

Most antibacterial soaps and cleaning products contain a chemical called triclosan. Triclosan works by finding active sites on an important enzyme in bacterial and fungal cells. A fungus is an organism that usually has many cells and decomposes material for its food. When triclosan blocks this active site, the cell cannot make some fats it needs to survive.

Many health professionals think antibiotics should be used as little as possible. The more we use them, the less likely they are to work. That is because some bacteria no longer react to the antibiotics.

Instead, they reproduce quickly and create new strains of bacteria that do not react to the antibiotics. Antibiotics do not work on viruses, which cause many common illnesses. Many health professionals also think antibacterial soaps are not necessary. They say washing with regular soap and warm water removes bacteria. Not all bacteria harm humans. Antibiotics and antibacterial products destroy both good and bad bacteria.

1. In what ways do antibiotic drugs work to stop bacteria?

2. How does triclosan in antibacterial cleaning products destroy bacterial cells?

3. What can you do to keep antibiotics working?

Word Bank

active transport

facilitated diffusion

passive transport

On a sheet of paper, write the words from the Word Bank that complete each statement correctly.

1. The type of cellular transport that uses proteins for movement, but not ATP, is called _____.

2. The type of cellular transport that does not use proteins or ATP is called _____.

3. The type of cellular transport that uses ATP and transport proteins is called _____.

On a sheet of paper, write the word or words to complete each statement correctly.

4. The process of removing waste from a cell by fusing the membranes is called _____.

5. Cells communicate with other cells through _____.

6. The process called _____ is used to bring substances into a cell.

Critical Thinking

On a sheet of paper, write the answers to the following questions. Use complete sentences.

7. Describe how facilitated diffusion works.

8. When does a cell need to use energy to transport a molecule across the plasma membrane?

9. Explain how the plasma membrane helps cells communicate with each other.

10. How would the transport abilities of your body's cells be affected if you did not eat properly?

Objectives

After reading this lesson, you should be able to

◆ identify the nucleus of a cell

◆ describe structures found in the nucleus

◆ explain the structure and function of ribosomes

◆ discuss how the nucleus directs cell activities

The rest of this chapter will look at the structure and function of various organelles in eukaryotic cells. One group of organelles controls information in the cell.

The Nucleus

The major organelle that controls information in the cell is the nucleus. It is the largest organelle in a eukaryotic cell. If you look at a cell under a microscope, the nucleus is a large, dark circle. It is surrounded by a membrane called the **nuclear envelope.** This membrane is a bilayer with holes, called **pores,** in it. Pores in the nuclear envelope help the nucleus send and receive messages inside the cell.

Inside the nucleus is a ball of fibers called the **nucleolus.** The nucleolus makes an information organelle called the **ribosome.** Figure 5.3.1 shows a eukaryotic cell and its nucleus.

Nuclear envelope

The membrane surrounding the nucleus of a cell

Pore

A hole in the nuclear envelope used to send and receive messages

Nucleolus

A ball of fibers in the nucleus that makes ribosomes

Ribosome

An information organelle that uses the instructions in DNA to make a protein

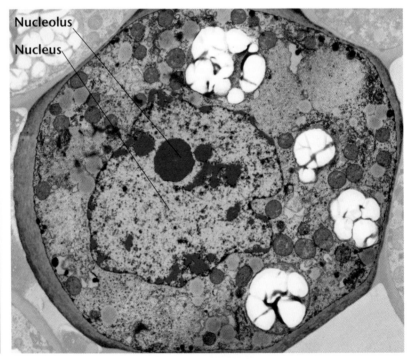

Nucleolus

Nucleus

Figure 5.3.1 *The nucleus is the largest organelle in a eukaryotic cell.*

If the DNA found in one human cell was laid out in one long molecule, it would be about three feet long.

Research and Write

Use the Internet to research DNA mutations. Create a chart listing the activities or materials that cause mutations and the health problems that occur as a result.

The nucleus of a cell acts like the control center. That is because an organism's entire DNA is inside the nucleus. DNA is a double strand of nucleic acid that contains all the directions to make an organism. The entire DNA for an organism is called its **genome.**

How does DNA fit inside a cell's nucleus? First, an organism's DNA in the nucleus is in separate molecules called **chromosomes.** Chromosomes are structures made of DNA and proteins. The proteins bind the DNA molecule and help it fold and coil to become smaller.

This folding is the second reason why DNA fits into a small space. Each chromosome is one molecule of DNA. Many different sets of instructions can be in that DNA molecule. Each chromosome contains different sections called genes. A gene is a specific sequence in DNA that carries instructions to make a specific protein. The proteins made from genes make an organism unique. One way to understand an organism's DNA is to think of it as a set of books. Each chromosome is a book. Each gene is a specific sentence in a book.

Ribosomes

Other information organelles in eukaryotic cells are ribosomes. Ribosomes make proteins from the directions found in DNA. Ribosomes are made from a combination of RNA and other proteins. Remember that RNA is a single strand of nucleic acid made with a different sugar molecule than DNA.

Technology and Society

Scientists use a variety of microscopes to look at cells. Electron microscopes allow scientists to observe cells and their organelles. Electron microscopes work by shooting beams of electrons onto a sample to create an image. Using electrons instead of light allows scientists to see microscopic images in finer detail than ever before. This has allowed scientists to make great progress in their research, especially in the field of medicine.

Ribosomes are found throughout the cell. Ribosomes float freely in the cell or attach to other organelles. They help interpret the instructions found in the genes of a cell. Ribosomes use the sequences of DNA and RNA as a guide. Ribosomes then put together individual amino acids to make a protein. Since a cell is always making many different proteins, large numbers of ribosomes are inside a cell. The small red dots in Figure 5.3.2 are ribosomes.

Because they control the creation of proteins, the nucleus and ribosomes help control cell activities. Most cellular activities require some kind of protein, mainly enzymes. The instructions for these proteins are in genes. The nucleus controls which proteins are made by controlling which genes get used. The cell uses different genes at different times. Ribosomes make proteins. Ribosomes also control which proteins are made first and how quickly they are made.

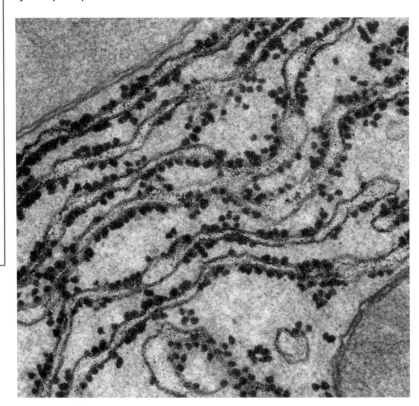

Figure 5.3.2 *The red dots in this cell are ribosomes. Some float freely. Some ribosomes attach to other organelles in the cell.*

Lesson 3   R E V I E W

Word Bank

nucleus

nucleolus

pores

On a sheet of paper, write the word from the Word Bank that completes each statement correctly.

1. Ribosomes are created in the _____.

2. Messages are transported in and out of the nucleus through _____.

3. The largest organelle in a eukaryotic cell is the _____.

On a sheet of paper, write the letter of the answer to complete each sentence correctly.

4. Sections of DNA that code for a particular protein are called _____.

   A chromosomes   **B** genes   **C** genomes   **D** RNA

5. Ribosomes are made up of _____.

   A DNA   **C** DNA and proteins

   B RNA   **D** RNA and proteins

6. A genome includes all the DNA in _____.

   A a gene   **C** an organism

   B a chromosome   **D** the biosphere

Critical Thinking

On a sheet of paper, write the answers to the following questions. Use complete sentences.

7. How can a three-foot long section of DNA fit in the nucleus of one cell?

8. How could a scientist looking at two different cells under a microscope tell which cell makes more proteins?

9. Explain why almost any cell function can be traced back to activity in the nucleus.

10. Why can scientists use a person's DNA to determine if they are likely to develop a disease?

Chloroplast

An energy organelle in plants that harvests energy from the sun

Mitochondrion

An energy organelle that converts energy from bonds in glucose into ATP (plural is mitochondria)

Chlorophyll

A molecule in chloroplasts that traps energy from sunlight

Photosynthesis

A process that chloroplasts use to convert energy from the sun into chemical energy stored in glucose

Cells have many different jobs. All cells take in nutrients, remove waste, reproduce, and most importantly, make proteins. To do these activities, cells use a molecule called ATP as a source for energy. ATP stores energy in its chemical bonds. Energy stored in ATP ultimately comes from the sun. Two organelles, **chloroplasts** and **mitochondria,** harvest and transform the sun's energy for cell use.

Chloroplasts

Chloroplasts are energy organelles found only in plant cells. They harvest energy in sunlight and convert it into other forms. Chloroplasts use a molecule called **chlorophyll** to trap energy. Chlorophyll absorbs energy from sunlight, and then passes that energy to other molecules in the chloroplasts.

These molecules transform the energy through a process called **photosynthesis.** Photosynthesis is a set of many chemical reactions that produce glucose. Energy from the sun is stored in the chemical bonds of glucose. Glucose produced by a plant can be used as a source of energy by other organisms or by the plant itself. We'll discuss the process of photosynthesis in Chapter 8.

Chloroplasts in plant cells have unique structures to harvest light energy. Bean-shaped chloroplasts have two membranes surrounding them. Inside the inner membrane is a space filled with a thick fluid called **stroma.** The sugar-making part of photosynthesis takes place in the stroma.

Link to ➤➤➤

Environmental Science

Plants take in carbon dioxide, use it in photosynthesis, and then release oxygen. People and animals breathe in the oxygen that plants give off. Scientists think that cutting down trees in tropical rainforests contributes to the increase of carbon dioxide in the air. Fewer plants are available to absorb carbon dioxide.

Chlorophyll produces a green color. That is why most leaves are green or have green parts.

In the stroma are membrane sacs, or pouches, called **thylakoids.** Thylakoids contain chlorophyll. Thylakoid sacs are piled together into stacks called **grana.**

Thylakoids are connected to each other inside the chloroplast. Chlorophyll molecules are bound in the membranes of the thylakoids. Chlorophyll traps the sun's energy, transfers the energy into different forms, and stores it in glucose. Figure 5.4.1 shows a chloroplast and its structures.

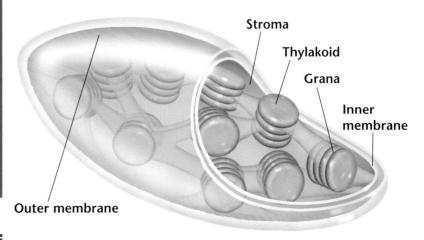

Figure 5.4.1 *Only plant cells have chloroplasts.*

Mitochondria

Mitochondria are energy organelles found in both plant and animal cells. Mitochondria get energy out of glucose so cells can use it. To do this, mitochondria use **cellular respiration.** Cellular respiration uses oxygen to break down glucose molecules. This process involves many chemical reactions similar to photosynthesis. As glucose is broken down, the released energy is stored in the bonds of ATP. We'll discuss cellular respiration in Chapter 7.

Mitochondria are bean-shaped organelles with two membranes. Because mitochondria produce fuel for the cell, they are often called the powerhouse of the cell. **Matrix** is a thick fluid inside the mitochondria.

Cristae

The folded layers of the inner membrane inside mitochondria

Link to ≫≫≫

Chemistry

Photosynthesis is an endothermic reaction, meaning energy is absorbed. Respiration is an exothermic reaction, meaning energy is given off.

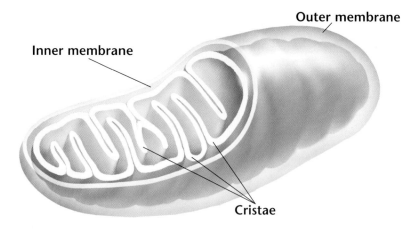

Outer membrane

Inner membrane

Cristae

Figure 5.4.2 *Mitochondria break down glucose to release energy.*

The inner membrane inside the mitochondria folds. This creates many layers. These layers are called **cristae.** The inner membrane contains proteins and other molecules used during cellular respiration. The ATP made from this process diffuses out of mitochondria to the rest of the cell. Figure 5.4.2 shows a mitochondrion and its structures.

Both chloroplasts and mitochondria have a lot of membranes inside of them. The membranes are where the main activities of chloroplasts and mitochondria take place. More membranes means more surface area for a cell. More surface area means more space for photosynthesis and cellular respiration. This helps the cell produce more energy.

Achievements in Science

An understanding of plant disease is important to food growers. Since ancient times, people have lost valuable crops to insects or disease-causing organisms. The first effective use of chemicals for disease control occurred in the late 1800s. Grapes for winemaking were under constant attack from a disease called downy mildew. Alexis Millardet, a French botany professor, noticed that grape plants sprayed with a mixture of limestone and copper sulfate discouraged people from stealing the grapes. The spray also killed the fungus that caused downy mildew.

Millardet's discovery led to the widespread use of a spray called Bordeaux mixture. The spray controls fungi and bacteria that harm plants. Bordeaux mixture is still used today, as are other chemicals, to control plant diseases.

Word Bank

grana

sunlight

cristae

On a sheet of paper, write the word from the Word Bank to complete each statement correctly.

1. The stacks of thylakoids in chloroplasts are called _____.

2. The folded membrane layers in mitochondria are called _____.

3. Photosynthesis captures energy from _____ for use by organisms.

On a sheet of paper, write the letter of the answer to complete each sentence correctly.

4. To break down glucose for cellular respiration, _____ is needed.

   A sunlight   **B** water   **C** ATP   **D** oxygen

5. Mitochondria produce energy in the form of _____.

   A glucose   **B** ATP   **C** matrix   **D** heat

6. Energy is captured for photosynthesis by _____ molecules.

   A ATP   **B** chlorophyll   **C** glucose   **D** cristae

Critical Thinking

On a sheet of paper, write the answers to the following questions. Use complete sentences.

7. Why do mitochondria have folded inner membranes?

8. Why would you expect to find more mitochondria in muscle cells than in fat cells?

9. What part of a plant do you think contains cells with the most chloroplasts? Explain your answer.

10. Humans and animals do not have chloroplasts in their cells and cannot photosynthesize. Why are they still dependent on the sun for energy?

Objectives

After reading this lesson, you should be able to

◆ identify the organelles of the endomembrane system

◆ discuss the function of endomembrane organelles

◆ describe the overall function of the endomembrane system

As you have learned, a main cell activity is to make proteins and other molecules. What does a cell do with these molecules? Eukaryotic cells have a large network of organelles called the **endomembrane system.** The prefix *endo-* means "inside." Endomembrane means "inside the membrane." The organelles in the endomembrane system are mostly made of membranes. Together, these organelles help cells make, adjust, package, ship, and receive many different molecules.

Endoplasmic Reticulum

A member of the endomembrane system is an organelle called the **endoplasmic reticulum,** or ER. The ER is a group of membranes throughout the cell that make different molecules. Two kinds of ER, rough and smooth, work together in the cell.

▼◄▲▼◄▲▼◄▲▼◄▲▼◄▲▼◄▲▼◄▲▼◄▲▼◄▲▼◄▲▼◄▲▼◄▲▼

Science at Work

Endomembrane system

A group of organelles that help a cell make and use different molecules

Endoplasmic reticulum (ER)

An organelle that makes different molecules

Plant Pathologist

Did you know that plants get sick? Plants get diseases caused by bacteria, viruses, and fungi. They also face problems from insects and other organisms.

Plant pathologists examine plants to diagnose their problems and to develop and give treatments. The government uses plant pathologists to keep diseases and pests from spreading. A person with a degree in plant pathology can work for universities, farmers, greenhouses, environmental agencies, or in research.

Plant pathologists need a bachelor's degree from a university. Most government agencies that employ plant pathologists require a master's degree. Working in research or as a professor requires a Ph.D.

Rough ER has ribosomes attached to it. It looks rough under the microscope. Ribosomes make many different proteins that a cell uses or **secretes.** Secrete means "to make and give off." After the ribosomes make proteins, the ER packages and sends them to the next organelle.

Smooth ER acts the same as rough ER, except that it produces other molecules. Smooth ER has enzymes bound inside its membrane, so it looks smooth under a microscope. Those enzymes help the smooth ER make lipids and carbohydrates. Smooth ER also helps cells handle poisonous substances.

Golgi Apparatus

After different molecules are made, the ER sends them to the **Golgi apparatus** for necessary changes. This organelle is a stack of flat membrane sacs. Under a microscope, it looks like a stack of pancakes. Once molecules are ready, the Golgi apparatus packages them. Then it sends the packages elsewhere in the cell or to the outside of the cell.

Vacuoles

Both the ER and Golgi apparatus use organelles called **vacuoles** to send their molecules around. Vacuoles are membrane sacs formed from the membranes of other organelles. They can form from the ER, Gogli apparatus, or plasma membrane. They fuse with other membranes to become part of them. Cells take in materials by forming a vacuole from the plasma membrane.

❁ ❁

Technology and Society

High-Tech Medications

Some new cancer treatments use liposomes, which are hollow bodies made of phospholipids. Liposomes are filled with a cancer drug. The liposomes deliver the drug to cancer cells. The cancer cells absorb the liposomes. The liposomes then break down their phospholipid walls. This releases the drug which poisons the cancer cells.

This ability allows vacuoles to perform several functions. Vacuoles ship molecules within a cell or to the outside of the cell. Vacuoles also store material for later use.

Lyosomes

Another member of the endomembrane system is an organelle called a **lysosome.** Lysosomes are sacs like vacuoles, but they contain special enzymes. The enzymes help the cell digest, or break down, large molecules so it can use them. These enzymes digest many kinds of molecules. They must be contained in lysosomes so they do not destroy the rest of the cell.

A Factory and Delivery Service

The endomembrane system supports the main activities of a cell by making, packaging, sending, receiving, and digesting different molecules. The endomembrane system acts like a cell's factory and delivery service.

Link to ➤➤➤

Health

Chlorophyll is the only natural dye approved by the U.S. Food and Drug Administration (FDA) for use in products. The FDA is a government agency that protects the public's health. The FDA approves the use of chlorophyll in very small amounts. Currently, chlorophyll is used as a coloring in some cosmetics and drugs. Chlorophyll has not been approved as a coloring for food products.

Lesson 5   R E V I E W

On a sheet of paper, match each description with a term in the Word Bank.

1. a packaging and distribution center

2. a storage unit

3. a factory

On a sheet of paper, write the word that completes each sentence correctly.

4. Rough endoplasmic reticulum looks rough under the microscope because it has _____ on its surface.

5. Lysosomes contain _____ that help to digest molecules.

6. Endoplasmic reticulum, the Golgi apparatus, vacuoles, and lysosomes in a eukaryotic cell are made up mostly of ____

Critical Thinking

On a sheet of paper, write the answers to the following questions. Use complete sentences.

7. Describe the two types of endoplasmic reticulum and the materials each makes.

8. Explain what vacuoles do.

9. What does the Golgi apparatus do?

10. How are the organelles of the endomembrane system alike? How are they different?

Objectives

After reading this lesson, you should be able to

◆ describe the primary functions of the cytoskeleton

◆ identify three types of fibers in the cytoskeleton

◆ explain the unique structure of cilia and flagella

Cytoskeleton

A group of fibers running throughout the inside of a cell that supports the cell and helps the cell move

Microfilament

A long cytoskeleton fiber used to move the cell

Actin

A ball-shaped protein used to make microfilaments

Intermediate filament

A rod-like cytoskeleton fiber used to strengthen the cell's shape; organelles anchor themselves to these rods

A group of organelles that helps cells perform many activities is the **cytoskeleton.** *Cyto* means "cell," so *cytoskeleton* means "cell skeleton." That is exactly what it is.

Cytoskeleton Structure and Function

The cytoskeleton is made of many fibers that stretch across the inside of the cell. These fibers give the cell support and help it keep its shape. Some organelles in the cell, like the nucleus, use these fibers to anchor themselves in a certain position in the cytoplasm. Other organelles move around in the cytoplasm, such as lysosomes and vacuoles. They use the cytoskeleton fibers like a train uses tracks. By using these fibers, organelles stay connected to one another. This allows the cell to function as one unit.

The fibers of the cytoskeleton help the cell in movement. If a cell needs to move around, which many do, it needs muscle. That muscle is the cytoskeleton. Cytoskeleton fibers are like the muscles in the human body that stretch and shrink to help the body move. When a cell moves around, the cytoskeleton fibers add more fiber molecule to the moving end. At the same time, the other end of the fibers remove fiber molecules. This causes the end of the fibers to shorten.

Three Types of Cytoskeleton Fibers

The three types of cytoskeleton fibers are made from different types of protein. **Microfilaments** are fibers made of a ball-shaped protein called **actin.** Actin molecules are connected together in long strings. These strings of protein are twisted together to make long fiber molecules. Microfilaments are mainly responsible for moving the whole cell around.

The second type of cytoskeleton fibers are the **intermediate filaments.** These fibers are made from long, string-like proteins. The proteins coil together like rope to form rods that add strength to the shape of the cell. Organelles anchor themselves to these rods.

The third type of cytoskeleton fibers are **microtubules.** Microtubules are made from units of a ball-shaped protein called **tubulin.** Tubulin molecules come together to form a hollow tube that supports the cell's shape. Organelles use microtubules to move around.

Microtubules also work outside the cell. These fibers anchor to and extend out of the plasma membrane. They form two types of structures, **cilia** and **flagella.** Cilia are small, hair-like structures on the outside of some cells. Flagella are long, tail-like structures. Only one flagellum or two flagella are found on certain kinds of cells. Both cilia and flagella help an unattached cell move around. These structures also help move substances across an attached cell. Figure 5.6.1 shows some of the organelles in a eukaryotic cell.

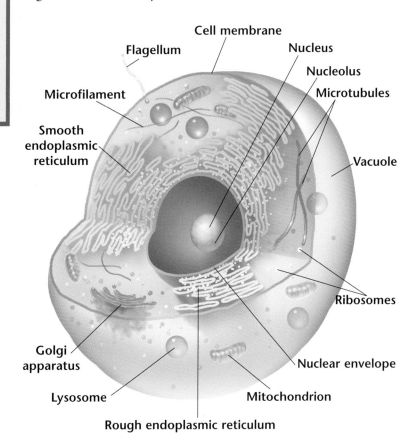

Figure 5.6.1 *Eukaryotic cells contain many organelles with specialized functions.*

Lesson 6 R E V I E W

On a sheet of paper, write the word or words from the Word Bank that match each description.

1. the part of the cytoskeleton mainly responsible for moving the cell around

2. the part of the cytoskeleton that helps organelles move inside the cell

3. the part of the cytoskeleton that adds strength to the shape of the cell

On a sheet of paper, write the word or words that completes each statement correctly.

4. Microfilaments are made up of a protein called _____.

5. Microtubules and microfilaments are made from proteins that are shaped like _____.

6. The word *cytoskeleton* means _____.

Critical Thinking

On a sheet of paper, write the answers to the following questions. Use complete sentences.

7. Describe the two types of microtubule structures that work outside of a cell.

8. Explain how cytoskeleton fiber activity can cause a cell to move.

9. Describe the structure of fibers that make up cilia and flagella.

10. List three ways that the cytoskeleton helps a cell work.

INVESTIGATION 5

Materials

- safety goggles
- lab coat or apron
- tweezers
- onion
- glass slide
- dropper bottle of iodine solution
- coverslip
- microscope
- prepared slide of human cheek cells

Comparing Plant and Animal Cells

All organisms are made up of cells. All cells have some things in common. However, some key differences exist between the cells that make up plants and the cells that make up animals. In this lab, you will examine plant cells and animal cells, noting their similarities and differences. You will learn more about plant cells in Lesson 7.

Procedure

1. Put on safety goggles and a lab coat or apron.

2. Using tweezers, peel a small, thin piece of tissue from an inside section of the onion.

3. Place the piece of onion tissue on a glass slide. Be sure the piece of onion is small enough to fit on the slide. **Safety Alert: Handle glass microscope slides with care. Dispose of broken glass properly.**

4. Add one drop of iodine solution to the onion piece on the slide. **Safety Alert: Iodine stains skin and clothing. It is a poison and an eye irritant.**

5. Hold a coverslip at a 45° angle at the edge of the drop of iodine solution. Gently lower the coverslip.

6. Look at the onion cells under the microscope. Observe the cells at various magnifications until you get a clear, sharp image.

7. Make a drawing of what you see under the microscope. Label your drawing.

8. Next, look at the prepared slide of human cheek cells under the microscope. Make a drawing of what you see. Label your drawing.

Cleanup/Disposal
Before leaving the lab, clean up your materials and wash your hands.

Analysis
1. Which cell parts could you identify in the onion and cheek cells?

2. What differences did you observe between the two types of cells?

Conclusions
1. What organelles were you not able to find as you observed the cells? Why do you think you could not find them?

2. How do the differences in the two types of cells reflect the differences in the organisms the cells belong to?

Explore Further
Observe cells from other sections of the onion. How do they compare with the first cells you observed?

Objectives

After reading this lesson, you should be able to

◆ identify special structures found in plant cells

◆ describe the main functions of special plant structures

Cell wall

The rigid layer of cellulose outside the plasma membrane of plant cells

Plasmodesmata

Openings in the cell wall used for communication and transport of molecules

Central vacuole

Large membrane sac in the center of a plant cell used for water storage

Plant cells are eukaryotic cells. They have organelle structures. We have already discussed one organelle unique to plant cells—a chloroplast. Most plant cells have several chloroplasts, especially if they are in the leaves of the plant. Cells in a plant's roots may not have any chloroplasts because they are not exposed to sunlight. Plant cells have other unique structures.

Plant cells are surrounded by a plasma membrane and a **cell wall.** The cell wall is made of a complex carbohydrate called cellulose. Remember that cellulose is a rigid molecule. It makes the cell wall a firm structure. The cell wall rarely changes shape.

Plasmodesmata are openings in the cell wall. Plant cells use these openings to communicate with each other. Plant cells use their cell walls to connect with other plant cells and to transport molecules. Connected plant cells form plant tissue.

When plants are watered, the water collects each cell in a **central vacuole.** Plant cells have one large central vacuole that takes up a lot of space. Plant cells store water and poisons in the central vacuole, which is usually in the center of the cell. If a plant wilts, it is because of a lack of water in the cells. The cell inside the cell wall will shrivel and die, but the wall will stay firm.

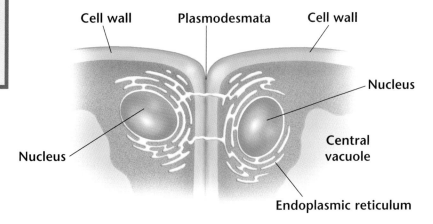

Figure 5.7.1 *Plants cells have some structures that animal cells do not have.*

On a sheet of paper, write the word or words to complete each statement correctly.

1. Plants have _____ cells, meaning they contain membranes and organelles.

2. The cell wall of a plant cell is made from _____.

3. _____ are organelles found in plant cells, but not in animal cells.

On a sheet of paper, write the letter of the answer to complete each sentence correctly.

4. A plant cell contains a(n) _____ that stores water and poisons.

   A cell wall   **C** cell membrane

   B central vacuole   **D** nucleus

5. The purpose of plasmodesmata is to _____.

   A communicate with other cells

   B protect and shape the cell

   C conduct photosynthesis

   D store water

6. Plant cell walls connect with other plant cell walls to create plant _____.

   A organelles **B** megacells **C** vacuoles **D** tissue

Critical Thinking
On a sheet of paper, write the answers to the following questions. Use complete sentences.

7. What would you expect to find in a central vacuole?

8. A plant that is not watered will wilt, but the tissues and cells will stay rigid. Explain what causes plant tissue to keep its shape.

9. Describe a plant part that has lots of chloroplasts and a part that has few chloroplasts.

10. How do plant cell vacuoles and animal cell vacuoles differ?

DISCOVERY INVESTIGATION 5

Materials

- *Elodea* plant
- safety goggles
- lab coat or apron
- tweezers
- eyedropper
- distilled water
- glass slide
- coverslip
- microscope
- prepared slide of onion root tip (longitudinal section)
- prepared slide of corn stem (cross section)

Comparing Plant Cells

The cells in different parts of a plant are different, depending on the jobs of those particular cells. In this lab, you will examine cells from different parts of a plant. You will discover how cells differ according to their functions.

Procedure

1. Put on safety goggles and a lab coat or apron.

2. In a small group, observe an *Elodea* plant. Discuss the structure of its leaves, stems, and roots. Make a table that lists the characteristics of each plant part.

3. Predict what differences you will find in the cells of the three plant parts.

4. Make a wet mount of one *Elodea* leaf using a drop of water.

5. Examine the wet mount under a microscope. Observe the cells at various magnifications until you get a clear, sharp image. Discuss what you see. Record your observations. Make a drawing of the cells you observe. Label the cell parts in your drawing. **Safety Alert: Handle glass microscope slides with care. Dispose of broken glass properly.**

6. Observe the cells in the prepared slide of a corn stem. Discuss and record your observations. Make and label a drawing of the cells.

7. Observe the cells in the prepared slide of an onion root tip. Discuss and record your observations. Make and label a drawing of the cells.

Cleanup/Disposal

Before leaving the lab, clean up your materials and wash your hands.

Analysis

1. What plant organelles did you see?

2. What differences did you notice in the cells and arrangements of cells in the three plant parts?

Conclusions

1. How accurate were your predictions compared with what you observed?

2. As a group, select another type of plant. Predict what you might find in different parts of the plant you have selected.

Explore Further

Research one of the following plant structures: potato, thorn, celery stalk, lettuce, or onion bulb. Is the structure a root, stem, or leaf? What makes this structure different from a typical root, stem, or leaf? What would you expect to find if you examined its cells?

Mitochondrial DNA—A New Tool of Discovery

Forensic investigators use DNA to find criminals. Genealogists use DNA to find ancestors. Genealogists trace or study the history of a person or family. DNA is a great tool, but there are some problems with using it. An individual's DNA is made of a mix of his or her parents' DNA. This means that an almost endless stream of combinations can exist, depending on which chromosomes were passed on. Also, over time DNA can break down when exposed to light or heat.

The discovery that mitochondria have their own DNA is a breakthrough for scientists. Mitochondria make copies of themselves by dividing. This means that the small amount of DNA present in the mitochondria does not change. Also, mitochondrial DNA is only inherited from the mother. The DNA in the mitochondria of your cells is basically the same DNA that existed in your mother's mitochondria and in her mother's mitochondria, all the way back as far as samples can be found. Genealogists use mitochondrial DNA to trace ancestry through many generations of mothers and to make family trees.

Mitochondrial DNA is not as fragile as the DNA that makes up the genome in the nucleus. A genome is the entire DNA of an organism. Some cells have one large mitochondria. Most have thousands. Every cell has mitochondrial DNA.

A small sample of body tissue or blood usually contains enough mitochondrial DNA to test.

Using mitochondrial DNA, investigators have tracked down the parents of political prisoners. Mitochondrial DNA has helped prove the relationship between a parent and his or her children. Recently, scientists used samples from 200,000-year-old bones from Africa to track down what they think is the most direct ancestral mother of modern humans.

1. What property of mitochondrial DNA makes it helpful to criminal investigators?

2. In what kind of situation would mitochondrial DNA not be useful when tracing a family tree?

3. Mitochondrial disorders cause some diseases. What evidence would lead you to think that a disease was inherited through mitochondrial DNA?

- Eukaryotic cells contain organelles with membranes. Cellular membranes are made up of a bilayer of phospholipids.

- The plasma membrane surrounds the cell and controls molecules that pass through.

- Passive transport is when molecules pass through the plasma membrane without needing energy. Facilitated transport is a type of passive transport that uses membrane proteins to help molecules cross the plasma membrane. A molecule requiring energy to cross the plasma membrane undergoes active transport.

- Cells use their membranes to communicate with other cells and their environment.

- The largest organelle in a eukaryotic cell is the nucleus. It contains the nucleolus and the cell's DNA.

- Proteins are produced by the cell using ribosomes and RNA.

- Plant cells contain organelles called chloroplasts that change sunlight into glucose through photosynthesis.

- Both plant and animal cells transform energy from sugars for their use through respiration. This takes place in organelles called mitochondria.

- Eukaryotic cells contain an endomembrane system that packages and transports molecules. This system includes the endoplasmic reticulum, Golgi apparatus, vacuoles, and lysosomes.

- Cells have a network of fibers that make up a cytoskeleton. The cytoskeleton provides support and movement, and anchors organelles.

- Plant cells have a rigid cell wall and one large, central vacuole.

Vocabulary

actin, 154
active transport, 138
bilayer, 134
cell wall, 159
cellular respiration, 147
central vacuole, 159
chloroplast, 146
chlorophyll, 146
chromosome, 143
cilia, 155
cristae, 148
cytoplasm, 136
cytoskeleton, 154

cytosol, 136
endocytosis, 139
endomembrane system, 150
endoplasmic reticulum, 150
exocytosis, 139
extracellular matrix, 136
facilitated diffusion, 138
flagella, 155
fluid mosaic model, 136
gap junction, 140
genome, 143

Golgi apparatus, 151
grana, 147
intermediate filament, 154
lysosome, 152
matrix, 147
microfilament, 154
microtubule, 155
mitochondrion, 146
nuclear envelope, 142
nucleolus, 142
passive transport, 138
photosynthesis, 146

plasma membrane, 135
plasmodesmata, 159
pore, 142
ribosome, 142
secrete, 151
stroma, 147
thylakoid, 147
transport protein, 136
tubulin, 155
vacuole, 151

Chapter 5 R E V I E W

Word Bank

active transport

cellular respiration

chloroplast

cilia

cytoplasm

cytoskeleton

endomembrane
  system

flagella

genome

mitochondrion

nucleolus

passive transport

photosynthesis

plasma membrane

plasmodesmata

ribosome

vacuole

Vocabulary Review

On a sheet of paper, write the word or words from the Word Bank that complete each sentence correctly.

1. A membrane sac that transports and stores molecules is _____.

2. A molecule that moves through a membrane using _____ requires no energy.

3. Made of RNA and proteins, a(n) _____ puts together amino acids to make proteins.

4. The process of _____ transforms energy from sugars to ATP.

5. All the DNA in the cell is contained in the _____.

6. Energy in the form of ATP is required to move molecules through a membrane by _____.

7. Small, hairlike structures made of microtubles are _____.

8. A(n) _____ is an organelle found only in plant cells.

9. Plant cells communicate through _____.

10. An organelle called a(n) _____ transforms energy through respiration.

11. A selectively permeable _____ surrounds the outside of cells and regulates which molecules enter and exit the cell.

12. Ribosomes are made in the _____.

13. Plants use chlorophyll in the process of _____, which traps the sun's energy.

14. The area inside a cell that contains organelles is _____.

15. The endoplasmic reticulum, Golgi apparatus, vacuoles, and lysosomes all make up a cell's _____.

Review continued on next page

16. The _____ is made up of fibers that support and give the cell its shape.

17. Two structures made of microtubules that aid in movement are cilia and _____.

Concept Review

On a sheet of paper, write the letter of the answer that completes each sentence correctly.

18. Both plant and animal cells have _____.

    A mitochondria and chloroplasts

    B chloroplasts and a nucleus

    C a nucleolus and mitochondria

    D a nucleus and a cell wall

19. Molecules move between the nucleus and the rest of the cell through _____.

    A membranes   **C** pores

    B plasmodesmata   **D** vacuoles

20. Facilitated diffusion is a form of _____.

    A active transport

    B passive transport

    C pores

    D neither active nor passive transport

21. Actin makes up cytoskeleton fibers called _____.

    A microfilaments   **C** intermediate filaments

    B pores   **D** microtubules

Critical Thinking

On a sheet of paper, write the answers to the following questions. Use complete sentences.

22. You have discovered an organism that could be a plant or a mushroom. How would you decide what it is?

23. Each organelle of the endomembrane system is surrounded by a membrane. Why is this important?

24. Describe the structures that make up a chloroplast. Also describe which steps of photosynthesis take place at each structure.

25. Why can many physical differences in people be traced to differences in their DNA?

Research and Write

How did some cells develop membrane-bound organelles? Use the Internet and print resources to research the work of American scientist Lynn Margulis. Her work led to what is known as the endosymbiotic theory. This theory is one of the most famous and groundbreaking ideas in biology. Write a short paragraph or make a poster that describes her theory.

Test-Taking Tip If a word on a test is new to you, take the word apart. Compare the parts to other words you know.

6

ATP and Energy Cycles

You can see fireflies easily on a summer night. The photograph shows why. Fireflies give off light. The light is the result of a chemical process that requires energy. That energy comes from an organic molecule called ATP. An ATP molecule transfers energy to an enzyme. The enzyme starts a chemical reaction that gives off light. In Chapter 6, you will learn about the flow of energy in living things. You will also learn how ATP and enzymes are important to the transfer of energy in cells.

Organize Your Thoughts

Chemical reactions in living things

Require energy from ATP

Enzymes speed up reactions.

Enzymes stop reactions.

Goals for Learning

◆ To explain how chemical reactions in cells use or release energy

◆ To describe how ATP transfers energy within cells

◆ To identify the roles of enzymes in cells

◆ To explain how enzymes assist reactions to overcome energy barriers

◆ To describe how enzymes bind with specific molecules

Adenine

A nitrogen-containing compound found in ATP, DNA, and RNA

Metabolism

The collection of the chemical reactions that occur in the cell

Potential energy

Stored energy

Kinetic energy

Energy of motion

The human body does not waste energy, which means it is efficient. Energy is transferred in living things through the breakdown of nutrients. The body takes in food and uses it as a source of energy. If the body cannot use the energy right away, it stores the energy for later use.

Imagine you are watching a race. Where does a person get the energy to run? You may think it comes from simple sugars like glucose. However, the energy comes from the breakdown of glucose in the body. When glucose breaks down, the energy is used to form other molecules. One molecule is adenosine triphosphate, or ATP. ATP provides immediate energy.

ATP is called the energy currency of life. Like currency (money units), the cell can covert, or change, ATP from one form to another. Recall that ATP is a high-energy molecule that stores energy needed by cells. In animals, ATP is assembled in the mitochondria. ATP is made up of ribose, three phosphate groups, and **adenine.** Ribose is a five-carbon sugar. A phosphate group is a group of molecules made up of phosphorus and oxygen. Adenine is a nitrogen-containing compound. Adenine is also found in DNA and RNA.

Potential and Kinetic Energy

Living things need energy to stay alive. Living things use energy for growth, repair, reproduction, and **metabolism.** Metabolism is the collection of chemical reactions that occur in a cell. The following ideas help explain how living things access energy.

Think about lifting a pencil above your head. You provided the energy to lift the pencil. The pencil now has **potential energy,** or stored energy. Potential energy is energy that results from position. If you let go of the pencil, it drops. When the pencil drops, its potential energy transforms into **kinetic energy,** or energy of motion.

Calorie

A unit used to measure the amount of energy food contains

Link to ➢➢➢

Earth Science

Cyanobacteria were the first organisms that were able to photosynthesize and release oxygen. These organisms evolved about 2.5 billion years ago. At that time, they began releasing oxygen into the atmosphere as a product of photosynthesis. This oxygen-rich atmosphere paved the way for modern life.

Remember that energy cannot be created or destroyed. Energy can only be converted from one form to another. Cells take in chemical potential energy and convert it to kinetic energy to use in cellular activities. This cycle is repeated throughout the life of a cell.

Food and Potential Energy

Food has chemical potential energy, especially carbohydrates and fats, which are energy rich. The body processes the potential energy of food to release chemical energy. This process requires oxygen. Inside body cells, food is oxidized. Oxidation releases heat as energy. The energy is used to make ATP.

About 60 percent of the energy from the breakdown of food is converted to body heat. A person needs to keep a temperature of 98.6°F, even in a cold environment. The remaining 40 percent of the energy from food is converted to do work in the cells.

Study the food label in Figure 6.1.1. How many **calories** are in one serving? The calorie is a unit used to measure the amount of energy in food. The calorie count represents the energy content. Calories are energy units.

Nutrition Facts

Serving Size 2 bars (42g)
Servings Per Container 6

Amount Per Serving	2 bars		1 bar	
Calories	180		90	
Calories from Fat	50		25	
		% DV*		% DV*
Total Fat	6g	**9%**	3g	**5%**
Saturated Fat	0.5g	**3%**	0g	**0%**
Cholesterol	0mg	**0%**	0mg	**0%**
Sodium	160mg	**7%**	80mg	**3%**
Total Carbohydrate	29g	**10%**	15g	**5%**
Dietary Fiber	2g	**8%**	1g	**4%**
Sugars	11g		6g	
Protein	4g		2g	
Iron		6%		2%

Not a significant source of vitamin A, vitamin C and calcium.

*Percent Daily Values are based on a 2,000 calorie diet. Your daily values may be higher or lower depending on your calorie needs:

	Calories:	2,000	2,500
Total Fat	Less than	65g	80g
Sat Fat	Less than	20g	25g
Cholesterol	Less than	300mg	300mg
Sodium	Less than	2,400mg	2,400mg
Total Carbohydrate		300g	375g
Dietary Fiber		25g	30g

INGREDIENTS: WHOLE GRAIN ROLLED OATS, SUGAR, CANOLA OIL, CRISP RICE (RICE FLOUR, SUGAR, MALT, SALT), HONEY, SOY PROTEIN, BROWN SUGAR SYRUP, SALT, CINNAMON, SOY LECITHIN, BAKING SODA, ALMOND FLOUR, PEANUT FLOUR. CONTAINS SOY, ALMOND, AND PEANUT INGREDIENTS.

Figure 6.1.1 *Many packaged foods provide consumers with nutrition facts.*

Different types of foods provide different amounts of calories. Each gram of fat contains 9 calories. Each gram of protein or carbohydrate contains 4 calories. This is why one serving of high-fat food contains more energy and calories than one serving of a protein-rich or carbohydrate-rich food.

The potential energy of food does not provide energy directly to cells. Instead, these food molecules are broken down during cellular respiration. Energy is released to make ATP molecules. ATP provides energy for cells to meet their energy needs. In other words, ATP captures, transfers, and stores energy. ATP acts like a type of energy currency.

The process of releasing the chemical energy of food is called cellular respiration. We will discuss this process in detail in Chapter 7. Cellular respiration harvests energy for the cell in the form of ATP. You already know that this process occurs in the mitochondria.

Express Lab 6

Materials

◆ 3 tennis balls

◆ meterstick

Procedure

1. Set one tennis ball on the ground. Set a second tennis ball on a desk or a table. Set a third tennis ball on a shelf or a place that is higher than the desk or table.

2. Push the tennis ball off the desk or table. With a meterstick, measure how high the tennis ball bounces. Record this measurement.

3. Push the tennis ball off the shelf or from the high place. With a meterstick, measure how high the tennis ball bounces. Record this measurement.

Analysis

1. Which tennis ball had the most potential energy?

2. Which tennis ball had the least potential energy?

3. How did you transfer the potential energy of the tennis balls to kinetic energy?

4. What do the bounce height measurements tell you about the kinetic and potential energy of the three tennis balls?

Lesson 1   R E V I E W

On a sheet of paper, write the letter of the answer that completes each sentence correctly.

1. Adenosine triphosphate, or ATP, is used by the body as _____.

  A material to make membranes

  B a reactant to make sugars

  C a means of removing waste

  D a source of energy

2. The energy of motion is called _____.

  A weight   **C** potential energy

  B mass   **D** kinetic energy

3. Calories are units that measure _____.

  A weight   **B** mass   **C** energy   **D** sugars

On a sheet of paper, write the word or words that complete each sentence correctly.

4. Food has chemical _____ energy.

5. Cellular respiration occurs in the _____ of a cell.

6. _____ is made up of ribose, three phosphate groups, and adenine.

Critical Thinking

On a sheet of paper, write the answers to the following questions. Use complete sentences.

7. Describe two ways the body uses energy from food. What proportion is used for each purpose?

8. Where does the energy supplied by ATP come from?

9. How would your eating habits change if you could use only glucose to supply energy to your body? Explain why this would not work well.

10. Explain how ATP operates as a type of energy currency.

Objectives

After reading this lesson, you should be able to

◆ explain how ATP is made from ADP

◆ describe how ATP powers chemical reactions

◆ compare how plants and animals make ATP

ADP

Adenosine diphosphate; a molecule converted to ATP by the addition of a phosphate

Phosphorylation

The addition of a phosphate group to a molecule

Food that you eat is broken down by digestion into macromolecules. Macromolecules travel in the blood to all body cells. Cells take in macromolecules as needed. Inside the cell, energy stored in the bonds of the macromolecules is made available to the cell.

Making ATP and ADP

Recall that mitochondria are sites in cells where energy from food macromolecules is released. This energy is released when bonds in the macromolecules are broken. The energy is used to join a phosphate group to **ADP,** or adenosine diphosphate, to make ATP. Adding a phosphate group to a molecule is called **phosphorylation.**

Because the phosphate groups are negatively charged, they repel each other. It takes a large amount of energy to join them. This means ATP is an energy-rich molecule. The bonds between the phosphate groups in ATP have large amounts of chemical potential energy.

After ATP forms, it moves out of the mitochondria by diffusion to another site in the cell. It is stored until the cell needs energy to cause a chemical reaction to take place. Then ATP is hydrolyzed to provide energy for the reaction. The energy used to make ATP is released when ATP is hydrolyzed, or reacts to water. Hydrolysis removes a phosphate group from ATP. After hydrolysis, an ATP molecule becomes an ADP molecule. ADP is then available to become recharged.

Link to ➤➤➤

Health

ATP provides energy for your body by adding and losing phosphate groups. Phosphate groups are made from phosphorus, a nutrient required for all living things. In addition to being part of your energy cycle, phosphorous is found in your bones and in the walls of your body cells. Foods rich in phosphorus include milk, meat, fish, and eggs.

Figure 6.2.1 sums up this cyclic process. A phosphate group is represented by P_i in the figure.

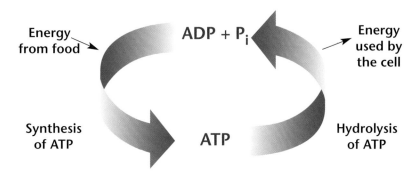

Figure 6.2.1 *In a cyclic process, cells release energy stored in food. This energy is then available for cellular activities.*

Making ATP in Plants and Animals

Plants use the energy in sunlight, carbon dioxide, and water to assemble energy-rich sugars to store as food. Plants use the stored food as a source of energy or to build materials for cells. Plants making food is an example of the transfer of matter and energy between an organism and its environment.

Animals that eat plants use the stored food as a source of energy for cellular processes. Animals that eat plants also use the stored food as a source of raw materials to build and repair cells. This is an example of the transfer of matter and energy between two organisms. Usually organisms can respond quickly to new demands.

Energy from food molecules is used to return ADP to the high-energy state of ATP. In Chapter 7, you will learn more about this process, called the Krebs cycle or the ATP/ADP cycle.

Some macromolecules, such as DNA, are stable and rarely break down. Others break down quickly. For example, the hemoglobin in red blood cells lasts about 100 days. Some enzymes only last a few hours.

Without ATP, life as we understand it could not exist. ATP is the main source of energy for thousands of reactions that occur in all forms of life.

▼◄▲▼◄▲▼◄▲▼◄▲▼◄▲▼◄▲▼◄▲▼◄▲▼◄▲▼◄▲▼◄▲▼◄▲▼◄▲▼

Science at Work

Pharmacy Technician

Pharmacists supply patients with the medicines they need to fight illness. More and more prescriptions today are being written for a growing and aging population.

Pharmacists rely on skilled pharmacy technicians to help them handle the work.

Pharmacy technicians receive prescriptions from doctors and hospitals. They verify insurance information and help the pharmacist with everyday duties. Technicians even help prepare prescriptions under the guidance of a pharmacist.

Pharmacy technicians must have a high school degree. They must also complete a training program or have a two-year degree from a technical school.

Lesson 2   R E V I E W

Word Bank
phosphorylation
energy
ATP

On a sheet of paper, write the word from the Word Bank that completes each sentence correctly.

1. Converting ADP to _____ is a key reaction for all life processes.

2. The addition of a phosphate group to a molecule is _____.

3. Most chemical reactions in cells require _____ to occur.

On a sheet of paper, write the letter of the answer that completes each sentence correctly.

4. The bonds between the phosphate groups in ATP have large amounts of chemical _____ energy.

    A kinetic   **B** potential   **C** rich   **D** low

5. The main source of energy for reactions that occur in all living organisms is _____.

    A diffusion   **C** ADP

    B phosphate   **D** ATP

6. ATP captures _____ when it forms.

    A energy   **B** nitrogen   **C** sugars   **D** fats

Critical Thinking

On a sheet of paper, write the answers to the following questions. Use complete sentences.

7. Describe how converting ADP to ATP is a key reaction in organisms.

8. Explain the process of phosphorylation.

9. Why do you think some macromolecules last longer than others in living organisms?

10. Why is the breakdown and replacement of enzymes in living organisms important?

INVESTIGATION 6

Materials

- safety goggles
- lab coat or apron
- wax pencil
- 6 test tubes
- test tube rack
- maltose solution
- starch solution
- 1% amylase solution
- 250 mL beaker
- warm water
- eyedropper
- iodine solution
- Benedict's reagent

Enzymes in Saliva

Your body uses enzymes to help digest food. When you eat, enzymes in your saliva help break down the sugars in food for your cells to use. In this lab, you will observe how the enzyme amylase found in saliva breaks down starches. You will test reactions with Benedict's reagent and iodine solution. Benedict's reagent changes color from blue to yellow if a sugar, such as maltose, is present. Iodine turns blue or black in the presence of starch.

Procedure

1. To record your data, make a data table like the one shown here.

Test Tube	Contents	Iodine Test	Benedict's Test
1	maltose (sugar)		
2	starch + amylase		
3	starch + maltose (sugar)		

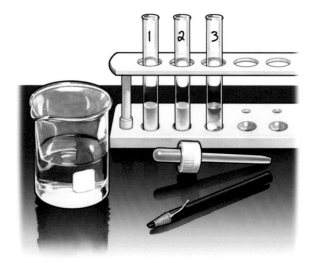

2. Put on safety goggles and a lab coat or apron.

3. With a wax pencil, label three test tubes 1, 2, and 3. Label a second set of three test tubes in the same way and set these aside.

4. Add 2 mL of maltose solution to Test Tube 1.

5. Add 2 mL of starch solution to Test Tubes 2 and 3.

6. Add 4 mL of water to Test Tubes 1 and 3.

7. Add 4 mL of amylase solution to Test Tube 2.

8. To make a warm water bath, fill a 250 mL beaker with 150 mL of warm water.

9. Place all three test tubes in the warm water bath for 15 minutes. Be sure the test tubes stand upright. Do not allow water to enter the test tubes.

10. Remove the test tubes from the water bath. Pour half of the contents of each test tube into the empty test tubes with the same label.

11. For each pair, use the pencil to label one Test Tube I for iodine test and the other B for Benedict's test.

12. Place two drops of iodine solution in Test Tube 1-I. Gently swirl the test tube. Record your observations in the data table. Place two drops of Benedict's reagent in Test Tube 1-B. Gently swirl the tube. Record your observations.

13. Repeat Step 12 for Test Tubes 2-I and 2-B, and 3-I, and 3B.

Cleanup/Disposal

Before leaving the lab, follow your teacher's instructions to clean up and dispose of your materials.

Analysis

1. What happened to the starch when amylase was added to it?

2. Which solutions tested positive for sugar? Which solutions tested positive for starch?

Conclusions

1. Why did you use maltose in one of your test tubes?

2. How does amylase work in your body? Where in your body do these processes take place?

3. Why is it important for you to chew your food well when you eat?

Explore Further

Try the test again using a starchy food such as corn, rice, or potatoes. Be sure you chop up the food before putting it in the test tube. The chopping represents the action of chewing before digestion.

Catalyst

A chemical that helps in a chemical reaction, but is not consumed or changed in the reaction

Enzymes are proteins in living things. They are made of amino acids. Specific enzymes help in the chemical reactions in living organisms. Enzymes help organisms control the chemical environment at the cellular level. Enzymes can speed up chemical reactions. They can also stop chemical reactions from occurring. Enzymes act as **catalysts.** A catalyst is a chemical that helps a chemical reaction, but is not consumed or changed in the reaction.

Living things get energy for cellular processes by breaking down energy-rich food molecules. Getting nutrients and energy from food involves many chemical reactions. These reactions need catalysts. Catalysts lower the energy level required for chemical reactions to occur.

The Role of Enzymes

Most biological catalysts, or enzymes, are specific to certain chemical reactions. Cells create an enzyme with one purpose— to act as a catalyst for one specific biochemical reaction.

Enzymes are part of every chemical reaction in living organisms. They assist digestion, growth, and building of cells. They help break down substances such as vitamins and nutrients. Enzymes also support all reactions involving energy transfer.

Enzymes control the rate and site of chemical reactions. For example, enzymes speed the creation of RNA and DNA. Enzymes also specify the sites for building RNA. Once RNA is formed, enzymes help make proteins that the cell needs.

The breakdown of chemical bonds releases energy. Enzymes control the release of energy in chemical reactions so that the proper amount of energy is released.

The Importance of Enzymes

Enzymes play a very important role in health. An imbalance or lack of certain enzymes can cause many health problems in people. For example, protease is an enzyme that digests proteins. A lack of protease can result in low blood sugar, kidney problems, and bone problems. Another enzyme, amylase, digests carbohydrates. A lack of amylase can result in skin rashes and liver disease.

Lipase is an enzyme that digests fats. If there is not enough lipase in the body, health problems can result. This includes **obesity, diabetes,** and heart and blood vessel disease.

Biology in Your Life

Consumer Choices: Enzyme Products

The human body uses enzymes constantly to do a wide variety of jobs. Some people do not have the enzymes needed to digest certain foods. Taking enzyme products before or while they eat allows them to enjoy these foods.

The most common enzyme-related food problem is lactose intolerance. Lactose is a sugar in dairy products such as milk, cheese, and yogurt. Most people have an enzyme called lactase that allows them to break down and digest lactose.

People who do not have lactase cannot digest lactose. They have stomach problems if they eat dairy foods. Lactose intolerance is common in older people or people of African, Asian, and Mediterranean backgrounds. If you have lactose intolerance, you can use a tablet or liquid product that contains lactase. It will break down the lactose as you eat dairy products.

Other food enzyme products are available to address problems with eating beans and other vegetables. These enzymes help digest the complex sugars in vegetables. The enzymes work the same way lactase does. You add it to your food as you eat, and it helps digest the food in your stomach.

1. Why do some people have trouble eating dairy products?

2. How do enzyme products help people with food intolerances?

3. Do you or someone you know have trouble eating certain foods? If yes, what can the person do to help digestion?

Obesity is a condition of being greatly overweight. Diabetes is an inherited disease in which people have too much sugar in their blood. This results in a high blood glucose level.

People with diabetes may have to take insulin regularly to help in the metabolism of carbohydrates. As seen in Figure 6.3.1, insulin is given by injections, or shots. Insulin is a chemical signal. It causes specific enzymes to work in response to blood glucose levels.

Human **saliva** and the digestive tract have high concentrations of enzymes. Saliva contains an enzyme that converts starches into sugars. Enzymes assist in digestion. The stomach combines the enzyme **pepsin** with acid to speed up the digestion of proteins. Enzymes are carried to the intestines to help the digestion of fats.

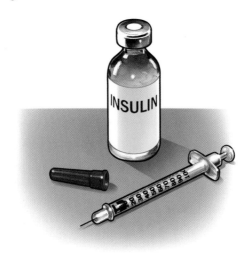

Figure 6.3.1 *People with diabetes may need to take insulin.*

Technology and Society

Engineers use the power of enzymes to clean up polluted soils and streams. They create huge containers of enzymes called bioreactors. These bioreactors are specially mixed to clean up the chemicals in a polluted area. The chemicals are then added to the bioreactor and digested by the enzymes. This process models the way enzymes in your body digest food.

Lesson 3 R E V I E W

Link to ➤➤➤

Home and Career

Researchers are developing coffee plants that produce decaffeinated beans genetically. Normal coffee plants use an enzyme to make the caffeine in their beans. By changing the DNA of the coffee plant, researchers hope to turn off the gene that produces the enzyme. This will produce caffeine-free beans.

On a sheet of paper, write the letter of the answer that completes each sentence correctly.

1. Enzymes allow chemical reactions to occur _____.

  A faster   **C** more often

  B stronger   **D** slower

2. Enzymes work by _____.

  A lowering the energy needed to break bonds

  B adding heat to a reactant molecule

  C making the reactants water-soluble

  D increasing the speed of electrons

3. Enzymes are _____.

  A acids   **B** sugars   **C** fats   **D** proteins

On a sheet of paper, write the word or words that complete each sentence correctly.

4. Enzymes are also called _____ because they support a reaction, but do not change during the reaction.

5. Enzyme action controls the _____ and _____ of a reaction.

6. In humans, _____ and the _____ have high concentrations of enzymes to help the breakdown of food.

Critical Thinking

On a sheet of paper, write the answers to the following questions. Use complete sentences.

7. How do enzymes control chemical reactions?

8. List and describe three health problems caused by an imbalance or lack of certain enzymes.

9. Describe how enzymes assist in the digestion process.

10. Why are enzymes important in living organisms?

Objectives

Objectives

After reading this lesson, you should be able to

◆ describe how pH affects enzyme activity

◆ define activation energy and explain its importance

◆ recognize that an enzyme only works in a specific chemical reaction

◆ recognize that enzymes change shape during chemical reactions, but are not changed chemically

---

Activation energy

The amount of energy needed to start a chemical reaction

Plants transfer the energy from sunlight into food that has chemical energy. Plants use sunlight, carbon dioxide, and water to make energy-rich sugars. Enzymes are involved in the chemical reactions that make these sugars. This process is called photosynthesis, and it is the basis of all life. Only plants perform photosynthesis.

Enzymes are at work wherever there is life. Yeast cells use enzymes when they raise bread dough. Bacteria use enzymes to break down cellulose fiber in the stomachs of cows and termites. Plants, animals, and bacteria use enzymes to control chemical reactions in their cells. Reproduction, growth, metabolism, and synthesis involve enzymes that regulate reactions in all living things.

Some enzymes stop reactions. This keeps the cell from using valuable resources. An example is penicillin, a substance that gets rid of harmful bacteria. Penicillin works by stopping an enzyme that bacteria use to make their cell walls.

Activation Energy

Most chemical reactions in cells need enzymes. A chemical reaction has inputs called reactants and outputs called products. Remember that a reactant is altered in a chemical reaction. To begin the reaction, the chemical bonds of the reactants must be broken. This requires energy, usually heat energy. This energy is called **activation energy.** It is the energy needed to activate the chemical reaction.

Under normal temperatures in organisms, only a few reactants have enough energy to exceed this activation energy. Adding heat would give reactants more energy. This is not an option in living things. Instead, enzymes lower the activation energy of reactions. In other words, enzymes allow reactions to occur at cooler temperatures. Figure 6.4.1 illustrates how enzymes lower the amount of activation energy needed to break the chemical bonds of reactants.

Substrate

A reactant molecule; the molecule on which an enzyme reacts

Active site

The area on an enzyme where the substrate fits in shape and chemistry

Link to ➤➤➤

Health

Most drugs used to treat the HIV virus that causes AIDS stop enzymes from working. These drugs stop the enzymes the virus needs to survive and reproduce. Often the drugs that work against HIV also damage mitochondria. The side effects of HIV drugs are often weakness and failure of body tissues that need lots of energy.

Substrate and Active Site

There are many different kinds of enzymes. Each enzyme works on only a certain chemical reaction. The enzyme recognizes the shape of its reactant molecule. The reactant molecule is called a **substrate.** A substrate is the molecule on which an enzyme reacts.

The enzyme has a special shape called the **active site.** The shape of its active site fits the substrate more snugly. When they come together, the active site changes shape. Think about how your hand changes shape when you shake someone's hand so you have a better fit.

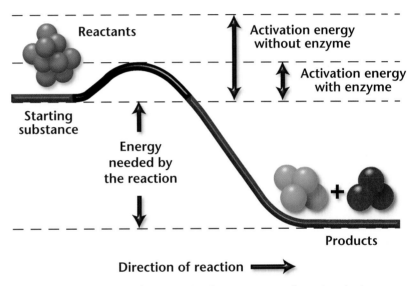

Figure 6.4.1 *Enzymes lower activation energy to allow chemical reactions in the cell to take place.*

Lesson 4   R E V I E W

Word Bank

activation energy

products

reactants

substrate

On a sheet of paper, write the word or words from the Word Bank to complete each sentence correctly.

1. A chemical reaction has inputs called _____ and outputs called _____.

2. The active site of an enzyme fits the _____.

3. The amount of energy needed to start a chemical reaction is called the _____.

Critical Thinking

On a sheet of paper, write the answers to the following questions. Use complete sentences.

4. How does an enzyme work in a chemical reaction?

5. Give an example of an enzyme that stops a reaction.

★ ★

Achievements in Science

Over 18 million people, or 6.3 percent of the population, have diabetes. Diabetes happens when the body cannot produce or properly use insulin. The body secretes insulin. This hormone changes sugar, starches, and other food into energy for daily life. Without enough insulin, the body cannot keep the right amount of sugar in the blood.

People with diabetes must inject insulin and monitor their blood-sugar levels constantly. Man-made insulin first became available in the 1920s. People had to make regular trips to the doctor to have their sugar levels checked and get treatment.

A breakthrough came in the 1940s. Then, Helen Free and her husband, Alfred, invented a test to check blood-sugar levels at home. Anyone could easily use this "dip-and-read" test at anytime. Today, many people with diabetes use in-home tests.

DISCOVERY INVESTIGATION 6

Materials

- safety goggles
- lab coat or apron
- 6 test tubes
- test tube rack
- 2% pepsin solution
- cool tap water
- diluted sodium hydroxide
- diluted hydrochloric acid
- wax pencil
- pieces of boiled egg whites
- eyedropper
- large beaker
- warm water

How Does pH Affect Stomach Enzymes?

Pepsin is an enzyme that digests proteins. The stomach releases pepsin to break down proteins into peptides and amino acids for digestion. The stomach's environment is full of dilute hydrochloric acid, or HCl. HCl is a strong, irritating acid. Pepsin works well in an acidic environment. In this lab, you will create a procedure to test the activity of pepsin over time at different pH levels. You will use pieces of boiled egg as the protein substrate. You will test samples at different times to see how quickly the egg is digested at different pH levels.

Procedure

1. Put on safety goggles and a lab coat or apron.

2. Fill five test tubes half full of the 2% pepsin solution. Be sure each test tube contains the same amount of solution. Create a control by filling a sixth test tube half full of cool tap water. Using the wax pencil, label the control C.

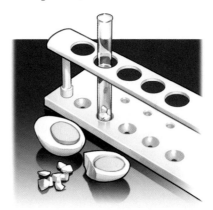

3. Determine the pH levels you want to use in your experiment.

4. You should test a minimum of three pH levels (acidic, neutral, and basic), but you can test up to five. With a wax pencil, number the test tubes. On a sheet of paper, write each pH level and assign it a test tube number. This is your data table. Have your teacher approve your pH levels and data table.

5. Using the eyedropper, add sodium hydroxide to the basic test tube(s) and hydrochloric acid to the acidic test tube(s). Add different amounts according to the variety of pH levels you want. For the neutral pH and control test tubes, do not add either. **Safety Alert: Be careful with diluted hydrochloric acid. Although diluted, it can damage skin, eyes, and clothing. If it spills, rinse the area immediately.**

6. Add a piece of boiled egg white to every test tube. Be sure the pieces are all the same size.

7. Fill the beaker half full with warm water. The water level should be below the top of the test tubes. Place the test tubes in this warm water bath. Be sure the test tubes stand upright with their openings clear of the surface. Water should not enter the test tubes.

8. Observe how the pepsin breaks down the egg whites at each pH level. Record your observations in your data table. At regular time intervals, estimate how much of the egg white is broken down in each test tube. Use your control for comparison.

Cleanup/Disposal
Ask your teacher for guidance in disposing of the solutions. Before leaving the lab, wash your hands.

Analysis
1. How did pH affect the rate at which the egg white was digested?

2. At what pH level did the pepsin work best?

Conclusions
1. What kind of environment does your stomach need to maintain to digest proteins well?
2. Why did you place the test tubes in a warm water bath?

Explore Further
Why do people take antacids? What effect do you think antacids have on your stomach and digestion?

Catalytic Converters

Enzymes and catalysts play important roles in our bodies. These chemicals are also used for other purposes. For example, engineers use catalysts to clean the pollution that comes from vehicles.

The exhaust fumes from cars contain several types of pollution. Among them is carbon monoxide, which is poisonous to animals and humans. Exhaust fumes also include nitrogen oxides, which cause acid rain. Hydrocarbons in exhaust fumes help form smog.

By the 1970s, pollution from cars had become a big problem in the United States. By then, more and more people were driving in cities. The result was a severe drop in the quality of air. Many big cities developed smog problems.

To reduce smog, Congress passed several laws that required cars to have catalytic converters. Today, all cars have catalytic converters that reduce air pollution by as much as 90 percent.

Catalytic converters work by using metals as catalysts to change air pollutants into safer substances. As the exhaust fumes move through the catalytic converter, the metal catalysts cause reactions. The reactions change the pollutants into nitrogen, oxygen, carbon dioxide, and water. Although air pollution is still a

problem in most urban areas, the use of catalytic converters has helped make the air cleaner for everyone.

1. Why were catalytic converters invented?

2. What is an advantage of using catalysts as filters?

3. Besides using catalytic converters, what do you think improves the quality of air?

Chapter 6   S U M M A R Y

- Cells use ATP to provide energy as needed. ATP is made up of a five-carbon sugar, three phosphate groups, and a nitrogen-containing compound.

- Food macromolecules have potential chemical energy in their bonds. Energy from food is released in the mitochondria when these bonds are broken.

- The released energy is used to add a phosphate group to ADP, creating ATP. The bonds that hold the phosphate groups are high in energy.

- When a phosphate group breaks off ATP, it releases energy that the cell uses. The result is an ADP molecule.

- ADP and ATP cycle back and forth, storing and releasing energy as the organism needs it.

- Plants and animals use food as a source of energy for cellular processes.

- Plants and animals use food as a source of raw materials to build and repair cells.

- The energy in plant sugars comes from light energy. Light energy is converted to chemical energy by photosynthesis.

- Matter and energy are transferred between an organism and its environment, and from one organism to another.

- Enzymes are proteins that cause or prevent chemical reactions in living things.

- Enzymes work by lowering the activation energy needed for a reaction to occur.

- Each enzyme works on a specific reactant molecule. The enzyme recognizes the molecule by matching its active site to the molecule.

- Enzymes work to maintain homeostasis, or a stable environment, in living things.

Vocabulary

activation energy, 184
active site, 185
adenine, 170
ADP, 174
calorie, 171
catalyst, 180

diabetes, 181
kinetic energy, 170
metabolism, 170
obesity, 181
pepsin, 182
phosphorylation, 174

potential energy, 174
saliva, 182
substrate, 185

Chapter 6 REVIEW

Word Bank

activation energy

active site

ADP

calorie

catalyst

diabetes

kinetic energy

metabolism

obesity

pepsin

phosphorylation

potential energy

saliva

substrate

Vocabulary Review

On a sheet of paper, write the word or words from the Word Bank that best complete each sentence.

1. The stomach releases the enzyme _____ to aid digestion.

2. A unit used to measure the amount of energy that food contains is a(n) _____.

3. The area on an enzyme where the substrate fits in shape and chemistry is the _____.

4. Together, all the chemical reactions in a cell make up the _____.

5. Food contains _____ that must be released to be used.

6. The process of _____ adds a phosphate group to ADP, creating ATP.

7. A molecule made up of ribose, adenine, and two phosphate groups is known as _____.

8. A chemical that speeds up a reaction, but is not involved in the reaction is a(n) _____.

9. A person who has _____ has trouble regulating the amount of sugar in the bloodstream.

10. As food is chewed, enzymes in the _____ help break down starches for easier digestion.

11. A condition of being greatly overweight is called _____.

12. The energy of motion is also called _____.

13. The amount of energy needed to start a chemical reaction is known as _____.

14. A reactant molecule is a(n) _____.

Review continued on next page

Concept Review

On a sheet of paper, write the letter of the answer to complete each sentence correctly.

15. ATP reacts with _____ to release energy.

   A water   **B** phospholipids   **C** ADP   **D** DNA

16. The bonds in ATP are full of energy because _____.

   A water molecules are being split

   B oxygen is burning food molecules

   C the phosphate groups repel each other

   D the sun's energy is being absorbed

17. When a cell needs energy, ATP is hydrolyzed to produce _____.

   A glucose   **B** oxygen   **C** ADP   **D** ATP

18. ATP is a(n) _____ molecule.

   A energy-poor

   B energy-rich

   C catalyst

   D substrate

19. Enzymes act like _____ in their role of speeding up reactions.

   A water   **B** pH   **C** heat   **D** acid

20. The _____ is the molecule on which an enzyme reacts.

   A catalyst   **C** substrate

   B cell wall   **D** active site

Critical Thinking

On a sheet of paper, write the answers to the following questions. Use complete answers.

21. In what two ways does the calorie content of your food affect your weight?

22. Life would not exist without ATP. Explain why this statement is true.

23. Explain how enzymes allow chemical reactions to occur at cooler temperatures.

24. Give an example of an enzyme that causes a reaction. Give an example of an enzyme that prevents a reaction.

25. Explain the role of enzymes in cells.

Research and Write

You know that enzymes are important to the workings of a healthy cell. Research some health problems and diseases caused by a lack of enzymes or by enzymes that do not work properly. Choose one condition or disease. Make a poster that explains how enzymes are connected to the problem.

Test-Taking Tip When answering a multiple-choice question, first identify the choices you know are not true.

7

Cellular Respiration in Energy Cycles

Like all living organisms, horses get energy from food. How does the energy get to the muscles of the running horses? Cells transfer the energy in food to ATP. The molecules of ATP provide energy when needed. Cells carefully control this process. In Chapter 7, you will learn the process of cellular respiration. You will find out how the right amount of energy is made available to cells to do their work.

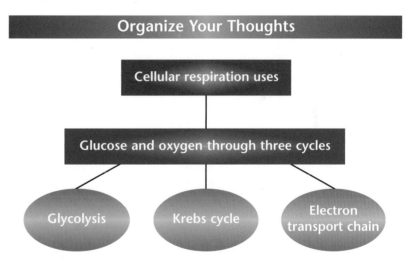

Organize Your Thoughts

Cellular respiration uses

Glucose and oxygen through three cycles

Glycolysis

Krebs cycle

Electron transport chain

Goals for Learning

◆ To understand that cells perform chemical reactions to gain energy
◆ To identify the three stages of cellular respiration
◆ To trace the steps in cellular respiration
◆ To describe various methods to create ATP
◆ To explain how cells control energy reactions

After reading this lesson, you should be able to

◆ define cellular respiration

◆ connect cellular respiration to human breathing

◆ discuss the purpose of redox reactions

Respiration

The process by which living things release energy from food

All cells need energy to do their work. Enzymes use energy in the form of ATP to help reactions happen. Energy is used to move materials in and out of cells. A cell gets this energy from the food an organism eats. How does a cell change the energy from food into the form of ATP? Recall that the reactions a cell uses to create and use ATP are called cellular respiration.

Cellular Respiration

You may have heard the word **respiration.** Respiration is about breathing. When you breathe air in and out, you respire. You breathe in oxygen and breathe out carbon dioxide. Cellular respiration is the process a cell uses to transform chemical potential to energy. The cell uses this energy for metabolism and growth. Study the equation for cellular respiration.

$$C_6H_{12}O_6 + 6O_2 \longrightarrow 6CO_2 + 6H_2O + ATP$$

glucose   oxygen   yields   carbon dioxide   water   ATP

This equation shows that cellular respiration uses O_2 (oxygen) and produces CO_2 (carbon dioxide). This is similar to human respiration. The oxygen in the air you breathe in is used in cellular respiration. The oxygen enters the lungs and is absorbed into the blood. The blood carries the oxygen to all the cells in your body. Cells use this oxygen for cellular respiration.

In addition to oxygen, cellular respiration uses glucose. Recall that glucose has the chemical formula $C_6H_{12}O_6$. Organisms use glucose as their main energy source. You get glucose from the food you eat.

Cellular respiration produces carbon dioxide. This gas is absorbed back into the blood. The blood carries the carbon dioxide back to the lungs. You breathe carbon dioxide out as a gas.

To sum up, you inhale oxygen into your lungs from the air. Your blood carries the oxygen from your lungs to the cells for use in cellular respiration. Your blood carries carbon dioxide produced from cellular respiration back to the lungs, where it is exhaled.

How a Cell Gets Energy from Glucose

How does a cell get energy from glucose? Remember that glucose is a sugar molecule. Glucose has energy stored in its bonds. When these bonds break, they release energy. The energy released is in the form of electrons. The electrons are transferred from glucose to other molecules involved in cellular respiration. The chemical reactions that transfer these electrons are called **redox reactions.**

The word *redox* is formed from two words, **reduction** and **oxidation.** Reduction refers to chemical reactions in which a molecule gains electrons. Oxidation refers to chemical reactions in which a molecule loses electrons. The two words are joined because one molecule gains electrons from another molecule losing them.

Figure 7.1.1 shows that glucose undergoes oxidation and loses electrons during cellular respiration. Through many reactions, the electrons are transferred to the oxygen molecules. As oxygen is reduced, it bonds with hydrogen ions in the cell. The result is water, or H_2O. Water is another product of cellular respiration.

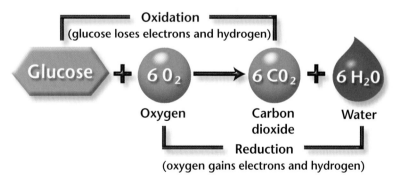

Figure 7.1.1 *Oxidation and reduction are chemical reactions in cells.*

Electron carrier

A molecule that carries electrons from one set of reactions to another

NADH

Nicotinamide adenine dinucleotide; the main electron carrier involved in cellular respiration

Science Myth

Myth: Plants perform photosynthesis instead of cellular respiration.

Fact: All living things carry out respiration. Using energy from sunlight, plants capture carbon dioxide and make sugars during photosynthesis. During respiration, plants release the energy stored in these sugars.

When hydrogen combines with oxygen to make water, the reaction is explosive. Combining hydrogen gas and oxygen gas releases a lot of energy quickly. A cell does not force these two gases together. Instead, it uses many chemical reactions to slowly release this energy in a step-by-step process. As this energy is released, the cell uses it to create ATP.

The slow release of energy happens by transferring electrons through several different molecules. **Electron carriers** are special molecules that help the cell with redox reactions. Specifically, cellular respiration uses an electron carrier called NAD^+.

When electrons are transferred to this molecule, NAD^+ reacts with hydrogen in the cell to form **NADH.** The many reactions involved in cellular respiration produce NADH. The amount of NADH produced helps determine how much overall ATP is produced.

Cellular respiration involves many different chemical reactions. These reactions are grouped into three stages. In Lesson 2, we will discuss the activities and results of each stage.

Express Lab 7

Materials
◆ ingredients list from a food label
◆ dictionary or encyclopedia

Procedure
1. Select a food label.
2. Read the ingredients list on your label. Which items are sugars? Look up unfamiliar ingredients in a dictionary or encyclopedia.
3. Compare your ingredients list with those of your classmates.

Analysis
1. Which food label has the largest number of different sugars?
2. Which food labels list a carbohydrate as the first, second, or third ingredient?

Word Bank

respiration

oxidation

reduction

On a sheet of paper, write the word from the Word Bank that completes each statement correctly.

1. During cellular respiration, glucose undergoes _____ and loses electrons.

2. During cellular respiration, oxygen undergoes _____ and gains electrons.

3. During _____, a cell takes in oxygen and releases carbon dioxide.

On a sheet of paper, write the letter of the answer that completes each sentence correctly.

4. NADH is a special molecule called a(n) _____ carrier.

    A electron   **C** carbon dioxide

    B glucose   **D** oxygen

5. Cellular respiration does not produce _____.

    A CO_2 **B** H_2O **C** glucose   **D** ATP

6. To perform reduction, a cell uses both _____ and oxygen.

    A water   **C** ATP

    B carbon dioxide   **D** glucose

Critical Thinking

On a sheet of paper, write the answers to the following questions. Use complete sentences.

7. Compare and contrast human respiration and cellular respiration.

8. Without oxygen, cellular respiration will stop. Explain why.

9. Describe the two events that occur during a redox reaction.

10. Why do cells need electron carrier molecules during cellular respiration?

After reading this lesson, you should be able to

◆ describe the overall activity of each stage

◆ compare locations of each stage of cellular respiration

◆ discuss the molecules created and used by each stage

Glycolysis

The first stage of cellular respiration in which glucose is first split

Pyruvic acid

A major product of glycolysis

In this lesson, we will discuss the three stages of cellular respiration.

Stage 1: Glycolysis

Glycolysis is the first stage of cellular respiration. It begins the breakdown of glucose. Recall that glucose comes from food an organism eats. Other carbohydrates in food are converted to glucose for glycolysis.

Glycolysis begins by using two ATP molecules. Although cellular respiration makes ATP, some reactions in cellular respiration use ATP. The amount used is small compared to the total amount of ATP made from these reactions.

Figure 7.2.1 shows the process of glycolysis. To begin glycolysis, the cell divides one glucose molecule in half using the two ATP molecules. Each half goes through several reactions. Bonds in the molecules break and release energy in the form of electrons. As a result, NAD^+ is reduced to make two NADH molecules. (The third stage of cellular respiration uses these NADH molecules.) Four ATP molecules are created during glycolysis. These ATP molecules can be used as cellular fuel. In addition, two molecules of **pyruvic acid** are created.

Glycolysis

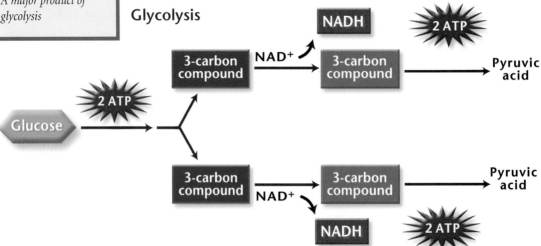

Figure 7.2.1 *Glycolysis is the first stage of cellular respiration. It begins with the splitting of glucose.*

Acetic acid

A sharp-smelling, colorless acid formed from the breakdown of pyruvic acid

Coenzyme A

An organic molecule that helps move the products of glycolysis into mitochondria

Acetyl CoA

A compound made from the bonding of coenzyme A and acetic acid

Krebs cycle

The second stage of cellular respiration

FADH₂

An electron carrier produced by the Krebs cycle

To sum up, glycolysis produces four ATP molecules, two NADH molecules, and two pyruvic acid molecules. These eight products come from one glucose molecule and two ATP molecules. As a result, the overall gain in glycolysis is two ATP molecules.

Recall that mitochondria are the sites of cellular respiration. However, glycolysis does not take place inside of mitochondria. Glycolysis happens in the cytoplasm of the cell. The second and third stages of cellular respiration happen inside of mitochondria.

Before the pyruvic acid molecules can move inside the mitochondria, they need more conversion. The cell breaks off one molecule of carbon dioxide from each pyruvic acid molecule. This creates **acetic acid.** To move into the mitochondria, acetic acid needs help from another molecule called **coenzyme A.** Coenzyme A and acetic acid bond to form one **acetyl CoA** molecule and one NADH molecule. Acetyl CoA crosses the membrane of the mitochondria. It releases acetic acid into the mitochondrial matrix. From one original glucose molecule, two acetic acid molecules enter the second stage of cellular respiration. This stage is called the **Krebs cycle.**

Stage 2: The Krebs Cycle

The Krebs cycle occurs inside of mitochondria in the thick fluid called the matrix. This set of reactions is called a cycle. This is because the beginning and the end of the reactions are the same. Two acetic acid molecules from glycolysis enter the matrix. Each acetic acid molecule bonds to the starting molecule in the cycle. From there, a series of reactions breaks and forms new bonds in the molecules.

As the Krebs cycle continues, two molecules of CO_2 (carbon dioxide) form. They are given off as waste. Most of the CO_2 from cellular respiration is produced here. As the Krebs cycle continues, an ATP molecule is created. The cycle also creates three NADH molecules and one **FADH₂** molecule. FADH₂ is another electron carrier used in the same way as NADH.

ATP, NADH, and FADH$_2$ are the main products of the Krebs cycle, shown in Figure 7.2.2. These products are reactants in the **electron transport chain,** the third stage of cellular respiration. In total, six ATP, eight NADH, and two FADH$_2$ molecules are made from one glucose molecule. This amount includes the two NADH molecules from glycolysis.

Krebs Cycle

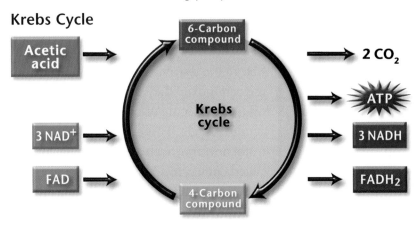

Figure 7.2.2 *The Krebs cycle is the second stage of cellular respiration. Its main products are ATP, NADH, and FADH$_2$.*

Stage 3: The Electron Transport Chain

The third stage of cellular respiration is the electron transport chain. This stage has two parts: an electron transport chain and ATP production. Recall that mitochondria have an inner membrane and an outer membrane with a space between them. The electron transport chain is found in a group of structures inside the mitochondria's inner membrane. In this space are special chains of proteins and electron carriers.

To begin, NADH transfers electrons to the first electron carrier in the chain. From there, the high-energy electrons are passed down the chain of electron carriers. FADH$_2$ also interacts with the electron transport chain. This happens at a point farther down the chain.

Each time the electrons are passed down the chain, a little energy is released. Proteins in the chain use energy to pump hydrogen ions (H$^+$) across the inner membrane of the mitochondria. Hydrogen ions are naturally present throughout the cell. The pumping action of the chain produces a H$^+$ concentration gradient between the two membranes.

ATP synthase

An enzyme at the end of the electron transport chain that helps drive the bonding of a phosphate to ADP to create ATP

As electrons pass down the chain, they lose energy to allow water to form. Electrons from the original glucose molecule lose much of their starting energy. This decrease allows the electrons to react with O_2 and H^+ to form water.

We discussed in Lesson 1 that the formation of water can be an explosive reaction. Why don't cells explode when they form water? The electron transport chain slowly decreases the energy to reduce oxygen. Oxygen also helps pull the electrons down the chain. The cell uses the water formed at the end of the chain in other ways.

With the help of **ATP synthase,** the electron transport chain produces ATP. ATP synthase is an enzyme found in the inner mitochondrial membrane. ATP synthase uses the H^+ concentration gradient to produce ATP.

Remember that the concentration gradient is created by the proteins in the electron transport chain. As H^+ ions collect between the membranes, they move toward areas of lower H^+ ion concentrations. ATP synthase uses energy from this movement to bind a phosphate group to an ADP molecule. The result is a new ATP molecule that the cell can use for energy in metabolic processes. Figure 7.2.3 sums up the electron transport chain.

Electron Transport Chain

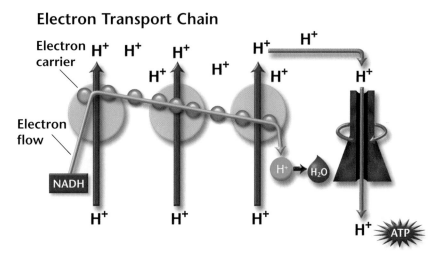

Figure 7.2.3 *The electron transport chain is the third stage of cellular respiration.*

Link to >>>

Earth Science

Over time, some of Earth's carbon is incorporated into minerals such as calcite. Calcite is formed from the shells of marine mollusks and other organisms. These mineral-containing carbon substances are called carbonates. One carbonate mineral, limestone, is used to make cement. Limestone begins to form when marine organisms such as clams and oysters remove minerals from seawater.

The electron transport chain uses all of the NADH and FADH$_2$ made from glycolysis and the Krebs cycle. This means that many H$^+$ ions are pumped into the space between the mitochondrial membranes. In turn, ATP synthase uses the movement of these H$^+$ ions to form ATP.

The electron transport chain alone produces about 34 ATP molecules for one glucose molecule. Cellular respiration produces a maximum of 38 ATP molecules for every glucose molecule. This seems like a lot of energy for the cell, but the cell needs all of it. The high output of ATP from cellular respiration is necessary for cells to live. Some cells use up to 10 million ATP molecules per second.

Figure 7.2.4 shows that cellular respiration is a cyclic process. Cellular respiration includes many individual cycles. One cycle is the Krebs cycle. Another cycle is the movement of H$^+$ ions back and forth across the mitochondrial membrane. This movement drives ATP synthase to produce ATP. The enzymes in these reactions also cycle. Life's most basic processes happen in a cycle.

Cellular Respiration

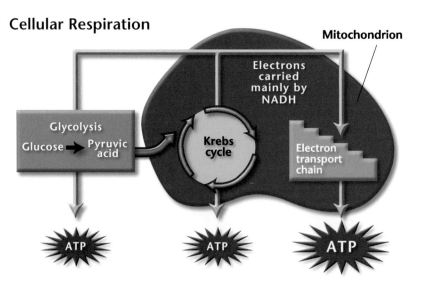

Figure 7.2.4 *Cellular respiration is a cyclic process.*

Lesson 2 REVIEW

On a sheet of paper, write the word or words from the Word Bank that complete each statement correctly.

1. The splitting of _____ begins the process called glycolysis.

2. As electrons are passed down a chain of electron carriers, _____ is released.

3. Three molecules of NADH and one molecule of $FADH_2$ are products of the _____.

Critical Thinking

On a sheet of paper, write the answers to the following questions. Use complete sentences.

4. Which stage of cellular respiration produces the most ATP? Explain your answer.

5. Why is the Krebs cycle considered a cycle?

Achievements in Science

Discovering Biochemical Pathways

Cellular respiration is a set of reactions that occur in sequence. Each reaction is called a biochemical pathway. The product of one pathway becomes the starting material for the next pathway.

Starting in the late 1920s, German scientists Gustav Embden and Otto Meyerhof learned the steps of glycolysis. Glycolysis is the first stage of cellular respiration. These steps are known as the Embden-Meyerhof pathway. In 1937, British biochemist Sir Hans Krebs discovered a series of reactions that became known as the Krebs cycle. The Krebs cycle produces electron carriers, which carry energy to the electron transport chain. Krebs was awarded the 1953 Nobel Prize for Physiology or Medicine.

Then in the late 1930s, biochemist Gerty Cori and her husband Carl F. Cori learned how the body converts glucose to glycogen for short-term energy storage. In 1947, the Coris won the Nobel Prize for Physiology or Medicine. Gerty Cori was the first American woman to receive a Nobel Prize in the sciences.

INVESTIGATION 7

Materials

- safety goggles
- lab coat or apron
- small beaker
- ruler
- bromothymol blue
- plastic wrap
- soda straw

Products of Cellular Respiration

During cellular respiration, cells use glucose and oxygen to make energy in the form of ATP. Cells also release carbon dioxide (CO_2) and water. When carbon dioxide dissolves in water, it forms carbonic acid (H_2CO_3). In this lab, you will see evidence of cellular respiration.

Procedure

1. Put on safety goggles and a lab coat or apron.

2. Using a ruler to measure, pour 1 inch of bromothymol blue into a small beaker. On a sheet of paper, describe the color of the liquid in the beaker. **Safety Alert: Be careful when working with glassware and the solution.**

3. Cover the beaker with plastic wrap. With the soda straw, poke a small hole through the plastic. Fit the soda straw through the hole.

4. Gently blow through the straw into the beaker. **Safety Alert: Be careful not to splash or inhale the solution.**

5. On a sheet of paper, write a description of your results.

Cleanup/Disposal

Before leaving the lab, clean up your materials and wash your hands.

Analysis

1. When you blow through the soda straw, what happens to the color of the liquid?

2. Why does the air you exhale cause this result?

3. What is the source of the carbon atoms in the CO_2 that is released during cellular respiration?

Conclusions

1. What product of cellular respiration causes the result you observed?

2. How do you think exercise affects cellular respiration? Explain your answer.

Explore Further

Use the procedure above to test the effects of exercise on cellular respiration.

Objectives

After reading this lesson, you should be able to

◆ compare aerobic species to anaerobic species

◆ relate fermentation to cellular respiration

◆ describe different products of fermentation

Aerobic

Requiring oxygen

Anaerobic

Not requiring oxygen

Fermentation

An anaerobic process for making ATP

Humans use oxygen to help drive cellular respiration. Because of this, humans are an **aerobic** species. An aerobic species breathes and requires oxygen to live.

Anaerobic Species

Not all species are aerobic. Many bacterial species are **anaerobic.** They cannot use oxygen to drive cellular respiration or other metabolic reactions. In these species, oxygen is a poison. If exposed to oxygen, they are severely damaged or destroyed.

Anaerobic species only exist in places not exposed to the atmosphere or another source of oxygen. Anaerobic species live in closed-in environments with limited resources. They require energy to live. They use **fermentation** to create ATP. Fermentation is an anaerobic process for making ATP.

The reactions for fermentation are the same reactions that occur during glycolysis in cellular respiration. Remember that oxygen is not used in cellular respiration until the electron transport chain. Anaerobic species are prokaryotic and do not have mitochondria.

This is not a problem for anaerobic species. Glycolysis occurs in the cytoplasm, which prokaryotes have. Prokaryotes harvest a small amount of ATP from these reactions. Anaerobic species break down sugars in the same manner. However, the products of these fermentation reactions are different from pyruvic acid.

Technology and Society

Industrial fermentation is the use of fermentation to produce valuable products. Pharmaceutical companies use fermentation carried out by microorganisms to make antibiotics, hormones, and specialized proteins. These proteins include the protein insulin and a variety of antibodies. In many cases, the microorganisms have been genetically changed to produce a specific substance.

Lactic acid

An organic waste produced by anaerobic fermentation

Ethyl alcohol

A colorless liquid waste produced by anaerobic fermentation

Link to ➤➤➤

Social Studies

For centuries, people have used fermentation to bake. By 2600 B.C., the Egyptians were using the fermentation process to make bread. To do this, they maintained an ongoing culture of fermentation microorganisms.

Two Types of Fermentation

The two main types of fermentation are based on the products they form. The first type is **lactic acid** fermentation. This process is shown in Figure 7.3.1. Recall that fermentation is an anaerobic process to make ATP. Lactic acid is an organic waste produced by anaerobic fermentation. Instead of forming pyruvic acid, these reactions use NADH from glycolysis to form lactic acid.

People use anaerobic species to produce certain kinds of food, like cheese and yogurt. Their slightly sour flavor is a result of lactic acid.

People are exposed to lactic acid in another way. Human muscle cells use a lot of ATP and oxygen to function. During major physical activity like exercising, muscle cells need more oxygen. If muscle cells do not get enough oxygen, they use lactic acid fermentation to produce ATP. As muscle cells use these anaerobic reactions, lactic acid builds up in the cells as waste. This buildup causes sore muscles.

Some anaerobic species use another type of fermentation called **ethyl alcohol** fermentation. Ethyl alcohol is a colorless liquid waste product produced by anaerobic fermentation. It is also the main chemical in alcoholic beverages. Ethyl alcohol fermentation breaks down glucose into two products, carbon dioxide and ethyl alcohol.

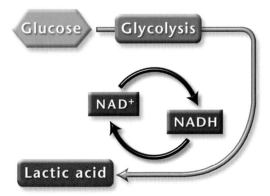

Figure 7.3.1 *During lactic acid fermentation, NADH from glycolysis forms lactic acid.*

People rely on ethyl alcohol fermentation when they use yeast to make bread. Yeasts are aerobic bacteria that perform ethyl alcohol fermentation and glycolysis. When yeasts are put into dough, they separate from oxygen. Yeasts break down the sugars in the dough mixture to get fuel. As they ferment the sugars, they produce carbon dioxide. Bubbles of CO_2 gas are trapped in the dough and cause it to rise. Bakers allow this process to happen so the dough will rise and the taste is right.

Figure 7.3.2 *The spaces in this bread represent carbon dioxide bubbles that escaped during baking.*

Look at Figure 7.3.2. The white, soft part of bread has many tiny air bubbles trapped inside the crust. The spaces are where CO_2 bubbles were trapped during baking.

▼◄▲▼◄▲▼◄▲▼◄▲▼◄▲▼◄▲▼◄▲▼◄▲▼◄▲▼◄▲▼◄▲▼

Science at Work

Certified Athletic Trainer

A certified athletic trainer (ATC) prevents, assesses, and manages injuries resulting from physical activity. An ATC works under the direction of a physician. ATCs cooperate with health care

professionals, administrators, and parents. When a sports injury occurs, an ATC can provide emergency care. ATCs work with patients and other health care team members to develop plans for treatment and rehabilitation.

Certified athletic trainers work in schools, colleges, sports medicine clinics, professional sports programs, hospitals, and the military. Most jobs in athletic training require a bachelor's degree from a college with an accredited athletic training curriculum. After completing a bachelor's degree, people can take a national certification exam to become certified.

On a sheet of paper, write the word or words from the Word Bank that complete each statement correctly.

Word Bank
aerobic
ethyl alcohol
lactic acid

1. Because humans use oxygen, they are a(n) _____ species.

2. Cheese and yogurt are formed by _____ fermentation.

3. The bubbles produced by _____ fermentation cause yeast bread to rise.

On a sheet of paper, write the letter of the answer that completes each sentence correctly.

4. Anaerobic species include certain _____.

    A bacteria   **B** plants   **C** protists   **D** animals

5. Ethyl alcohol fermentation produces all of the following except _____.

    A carbon dioxide   **C** ethyl alcohol

    B ATP   **D** oxygen

6. Lactic acid fermentation occurs in muscle cells when _____ is in low supply.

    A water   **C** oxygen

    B carbon dioxide   **D** ethyl alcohol

Critical Thinking

On a sheet of paper, write the answers to the following questions. Use complete sentences.

7. Describe a situation that could cause lactic acid to build up in human muscle cells.

8. How is fermentation similar to cellular respiration? How is it different?

9. How might an organism benefit by carrying out fermentation instead of cellular respiration?

10. Compare and contrast lactic acid fermentation with ethyl alcohol fermentation.

Materials

- safety goggles
- lab coat or apron
- large beaker
- warm water
  (38° to 43°C)
- large test tube
- solution of yeast and
  sucrose
- one-hole rubber stopper
  with gas delivery tube
- small beaker
- tap water
- limewater

Making ATP Without Oxygen

When oxygen is not present, some species use fermentation to make ATP. What are the products of fermentation? Does temperature affect the rate of fermentation? You will find out the answers to these questions in this lab.

Procedure

1. Put on safety goggles and a lab coat or apron.

2. Fill a large beaker half full with warm water.

3. Fill a large test tube nearly full with the solution of yeast and sucrose. Cap the test tube with the one-hole rubber stopper with the gas delivery tube.

4. **Safety Alert: Be careful when working with glassware.** Place the test tube in the beaker of warm water. Keep the test tube upright. Do not stir or mix the yeast and sucrose solution in the test tube.

5. Fill a small beaker nearly full with tap water. Put the end of the gas delivery tube in the small beaker of tap water. Watch for gas bubbles at the end of the tube. Count the number of gas bubbles released per minute.

6. In a small group, discuss what gas is given off in this setup. Write a hypothesis about how you could identify this gas. The hypothesis should be one that you could test using limewater.

7. Write a procedure and Safety Alerts for your experiment.

8. Have your hypothesis, Safety Alerts, and procedure approved by your teacher. Then carry out your experiment.

Cleanup/Disposal
Before leaving the lab, clean up your materials and wash your hands.

Analysis
1. How do yeast cells make ATP?

2. Is fermentation occurring during your experiment? Describe the evidence that supports your answer.

Conclusions
1. Was your hypothesis supported by the results of your experiment?

2. Does temperature affect the rate of fermentation? Suggest an experiment that you could perform to find out.

Explore Further
In your group, discuss how you could measure the effect of temperature on bread making.

After reading this lesson, you should be able to

◆ relate energy needs to controlling respiration

◆ discuss other molecules that cellular respiration can use

Feedback inhibition

A process used by cells to control metabolic pathways

Cellular respiration and fermentation are the main pathways all life uses to create energy. These regulated and controlled reactions are part of an organism's metabolism. If an organism is resting, its cells do not produce much ATP. Cellular respiration slows down. When an organism is active, respiration reactions work harder to supply energy. Like other metabolic pathways, cellular respiration is strictly controlled. Over time, organisms have developed these controls to save energy.

Many cells use the enzymes involved in these reactions to control the same reactions. The product of a reaction in a pathway can interact with molecules from another reaction in that pathway. For example, the product from one reaction may stop the enzyme of another reaction. When that product becomes concentrated, it causes the enzyme from the other reaction to stop working. The pathway begins to work again when the concentration of the product drops. In this way, a cell can stop a pathway from producing too many molecules. This process of control is called **feedback inhibition.** Feedback inhibition uses energy cycles to control metabolism.

What happens to cellular respiration if glucose is not available? Because cellular respiration is a metabolic process, it interacts with other metabolic reactions. When glucose is not available, cells create glucose from other molecules.

For example, cells use polysaccharides, like starch, by pulling off one glucose monomer at a time. Cells use lipids by breaking them down into parts. By rearranging these parts, cells create molecules needed in different stages of cellular respiration. Feeding these molecules into those stages moves the process along. Because lipids have long fatty acid chains, they store more energy than carbohydrates.

Cells also use proteins for energy. Cells separate proteins into their different amino acids. In this way, cells transform the amino acids into molecules needed in different stages.

The goal of cellular respiration is to obtain energy for the cells of an organism. An organism must eat to provide the molecular fuel for cellular respiration. An organism breaks down food into smaller molecules. The cells of the organism use these molecules for many purposes, including making ATP. When an organism has enough ATP to function, the cells use ATP in other ways.

An organism often stores unused fuel molecules as fat. The fat is stored until the organism uses it. An organism uses fat when its cells cannot find other fuel molecules. For example, people who want to lose weight try to use stored fat molecules. To use this fat, they must limit the number of calories they eat and increase the amount of energy their cells need. By doing both, cells begin to harvest needed energy from stored fat molecules.

Biology in Your Life

Technology:
Carbon Monoxide Detectors

Carbon monoxide poisoning is the main cause of accidental poisoning deaths in the United States. Carbon monoxide is a colorless and odorless gas. When inhaled, carbon monoxide binds to hemoglobin. Hemoglobin is a protein found in red blood cells that carries oxygen throughout the body. Carbon monoxide displaces oxygen. Respiration then slows or stops. Carbon monoxide at low levels causes headaches, nausea, vomiting, and weakness. At higher levels, carbon monoxide can be deadly.

Carbon monoxide is produced when fuel such as wood, gasoline, or oil is burned incompletely. Flame-fueled devices such as gas stoves, water heaters, and grills are sources of carbon monoxide. When these devices are vented properly, carbon monoxide escapes harmlessly to the outside air.

Carbon monoxide detectors in homes save lives. They sound an alarm when there is too much carbon monoxide. When an alarm sounds, people should leave the house quickly and telephone for help.

1. Why is carbon monoxide deadly?

2. How does a carbon monoxide detector work?

3. What flame-fueled devices do you have in your home?

Lesson 4   R E V I E W

Link to ➤➤➤

Home and Career

How are a cell and a thermostat alike? Both use feedback inhibition. A cell uses feedback inhibition to control metabolism. A thermostat also uses this process to control a room's temperature.

A thermostat uses a metal strip that coils and uncoils in response to changes in temperature. The metal strip causes the heat to turn on when the temperature drops below a certain level. It causes the heat to turn off when the temperature reaches a desired level.

On a sheet of paper, write the word that completes each statement correctly.

1. In cells, metabolic pathways are _____ to avoid wasting energy.

2. A metabolic pathway will _____ if it is producing more molecules than necessary.

3. When an organism is _____, cellular respiration slows.

On a sheet of paper, write the letter of the answer that completes each sentence correctly.

4. Organisms will store unused fuel molecules as _____.

   A fat   **B** glucose   **C** water   **D** ATP

5. Cells can break down polysaccharides, like starch, by removing one _____ monomer at a time.

   A lipid   **C** fatty acid chain

   B glucose   **D** amino acid

6. Limiting calories and increasing exercise will cause cells to harvest energy from _____ molecules.

   A polysaccharide   **C** carbohydrate

   B protein   **D** fat

Critical Thinking

On a sheet of paper, write the answers to the following questions. Use complete sentences.

7. How do cells use feedback inhibition to control metabolic pathways?

8. Describe two examples of metabolic pathways used by living organisms.

9. How does cellular respiration harvest energy from food molecules other than glucose?

10. A teaspoon of sugar burns up quickly when lit with a match. Compare the burning of sugar to the breakdown of sugar in the body.

Boosting Cellular Respiration

Think about the last time you exercised hard. Were you out of breath? Were your muscles sore and tired? Providing energy is the job of cellular respiration. This process requires oxygen. When you breathe, oxygen enters your lungs. Oxygen is carried throughout your body by a vast number of red blood cells. Red blood cells travel through your body tissues and deliver oxygen to every cell.

Sometimes red blood cells cannot transport enough oxygen to meet tissue demands. Then the kidneys release a hormone called erythropoietin. Erythropoietin, also called EPO, tells the body to make new red blood cells. Most new red blood cells replace those that are old and worn out.

Blood loss, regular aerobic exercise, or moving to a high elevation also triggers the release of EPO. This causes the body to produce more red blood cells. The extra red blood cells result in more cellular respiration and better delivery of oxygen to body tissues.

Athletes sometimes train at high elevations. This causes their bodies to release EPO and make more red blood cells. Extra red blood cells deliver more oxygen to working muscles. As a result, high elevation training improves speed and endurance.

Sometimes cancer or kidney failure can cause a shortage of red blood cells in people. Doctors may prescribe EPO to increase red blood supply. This helps relieve fatigue. Some athletes take EPO illegally to gain a competitive advantage. However, the dangers of EPO misuse are high. Too many red blood cells cause blood to become thick. This increases the risk of blood clots or stroke.

1. Why do athletes sometimes train at high elevations?

2. Why do you think taking EPO helps people with kidney failure feel less tired?

3. Why is it dangerous for athletes to take EPO?

4. Why does regular aerobic exercise or moving to a higher elevation trigger the release of EPO?

- Living things use cellular respiration to create ATP. Cellular respiration requires glucose and oxygen and produces carbon dioxide, water, and ATP.

- Energy is released from glucose as electrons. Electrons are gained in reduction and lost in oxidation. Glucose is oxidized during cellular respiration.

- Cellular respiration occurs in three stages: glycolysis, the Krebs cycle, and the electron transport chain.

- Glycolysis occurs in a cell's cytoplasm. In glycolysis, glucose splits to produce two molecules of pyruvic acid. Pyruvic acid becomes acetyl CoA, which releases acetic acid for the next stage of cellular respiration.

- In the mitochondria, the Krebs cycle produces the electron carriers NADH and $FADH_2$. These electron carriers are used in the last stage of cellular respiration.

- In the mitochondria, the electron transport chain passes electrons down a series of electron carriers. The released energy is used to make ATP. The electron transport chain makes most of the ATP produced during cellular respiration.

- Fermentation occurs in a cell's cytoplasm. This process does not require oxygen.

- Prokaryotes produce ATP by using lactic acid fermentation, which produces ATP and lactic acid. Lactic acid fermentation can occur in muscle cells. Ethyl alcohol fermentation produces ATP and ethyl alcohol.

- Cells use feedback inhibition to control metabolic pathways. Feedback inhibition stops a pathway when its product is not needed. It starts a pathway when its product is needed.

Vocabulary

acetic acid, 201	electron transport chain, 202	lactic acid, 209
acetyl CoA, 201	ethyl alcohol, 209	NADH, 198
aerobic, 208	$FADH_2$, 201	oxidation, 197
anaerobic, 208	feedback inhibition, 214	pyruvic acid, 200
ATP synthase, 203	fermentation, 208	redox reaction, 197
coenzyme A, 201	glycolysis, 200	reduction, 197
electron carrier, 198	Krebs cycle, 201	respiration, 196

Word Bank

aerobic

anaerobic

ATP synthase

electron carrier

electron transport
  chain

ethyl alcohol

feedback inhibition

fermentation

glycolysis

Krebs cycle

lactic acid

NADH

oxidation

pyruvic acid

redox reaction

reduction

respiration

Vocabulary Review

On a sheet of paper, write the word or words from the Word Bank that complete each sentence correctly.

1. The process of breathing or taking in oxygen is called _____.

2. During the electron transport chain, an enzyme called _____ uses the H^+ concentration gradient to produce ATP.

3. A(n) _____ process is a process that requires oxygen.

4. Glucose is split in half during _____.

5. A(n) _____ is a chemical reaction involving the transfer of electrons.

6. Cells use a process of control known as _____ to regulate metabolic pathways.

7. Any molecule that transports electrons from one set of reactions to another is called a(n) _____.

8. In a(n) _____ reaction, a molecule loses electrons.

9. When oxygen is not present, living things use a series of reactions called _____ to make ATP.

10. The main electron carrier involved in cellular respiration is NAD^+, which becomes _____ after reacting with hydrogen.

11. Glycolysis produces two molecules of _____.

12. Alcoholic beverages and bread are made using an anaerobic process called _____ fermentation.

13. The second stage of cellular respiration is a series of reactions called the _____, which takes place inside mitochondria.

14. During the last stage of cellular respiration, a group of electron carriers called the _____ gradually releases energy from shared electrons.

Review continued on next page

Vocabulary Review

15. A(n) _____ process does not use oxygen.

16. An anaerobic process used to make cheese and yogurt is called _____ fermentation.

17. In a(n) _____ reaction, a molecule gains electrons.

Concept Review

On a sheet of paper, write the letter of the answer that completes each sentence correctly.

18. Cells use _____ to create ATP.

    A DNA   **C** photosynthesis

    B cellular respiration   **D** CO_2

19. After exercise, a buildup of _____ in your muscles can cause soreness.

    A lactic acid   **C** ethyl alcohol

    B carbon dioxide   **D** oxygen

20. Inside the cell, the reactions of the electron transport chain occur in the _____.

    A nucleus   **C** cytoplasm

    B mitochondria   **D** chloroplasts

21. Organisms use _____ as their main carbohydrate energy source.

    A ATP   **B** starch   **C** fats   **D** glucose

Critical Thinking

On a sheet of paper, write the answers to the questions.
Use complete sentences.

22. Compare and contrast fermentation in anaerobic bacteria with cellular respiration in humans.

23. What stage of cellular respiration requires oxygen? Explain the role of oxygen in this stage.

24. Why do cells with a great need for energy, such as heart muscle cells, have more mitochondria than other cells?

25. Anaerobic cells cannot perform cellular respiration. Why?

Research and Write

Write a report on some common anaerobic bacteria. Describe how they can affect the body. Use both print and electronic resources. You might also gather information from a medical professional.

Test-Taking Tip When studying for a test, review any previous tests or quizzes that cover the same information. Be sure you have the correct answers for items you missed.

8

Photosynthesis in Energy Cycles

The giant kelp in the photograph is part of a forest. Like the forests on land, ocean forests play an important role in the cycling of energy. Sunlight shining through the water is taken in and used to make energy-rich molecules. This process is called photosynthesis. The energy-rich molecules made by kelp are food for animals. Now, take a deep breath. The oxygen you just took in may have come from kelp. Kelp uses the same process as land plants to make oxygen. In Chapter 8, you will learn about photosynthesis and how important this process is to life on Earth.

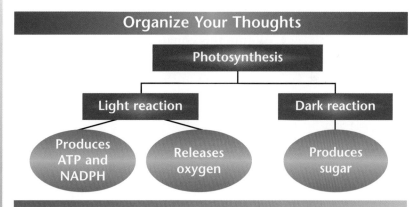

Organize Your Thoughts

Photosynthesis

Light reaction — Dark reaction

Produces ATP and NADPH

Releases oxygen

Produces sugar

Goals for Learning

◆ To understand that photosynthesis is an energy conversion process to produce energy-rich molecules and oxygen

◆ To explain how plants and some microorganisms transform solar energy into chemical energy

◆ To describe the light reaction of photosynthesis

◆ To describe the dark reaction of photosynthesis

Objectives

After reading this lesson, you should be able to

◆ explain how plants change the earth's atmosphere by removing carbon dioxide

◆ identify the relationship between photosynthesis and respiration

◆ explain what chloroplasts do in plant cells

◆ describe how chlorophyll captures light energy

Autotroph

A self-nourishing organism that makes its own food

Sunlight is the source of energy for living things. Living things need energy to grow and to carry out life processes. Recall that living things usually get energy from molecules of glucose. Where does the chemical energy stored in the bonds of glucose come from? The energy comes from photosynthesis. Photosynthesis changes the energy of sunlight into the chemical energy stored in glucose bonds. Photosynthesis is the connection between the sun and the energy needs of living systems.

Photosynthesis

Photosynthesis occurs in plants. Plants are **autotrophs.** An autotroph makes its own food. Plants use energy from sunlight in photosynthesis. They use this energy to combine CO_2 (carbon dioxide) and H_2O (water) to make glucose. Study the chemical equation for photosynthesis.

$$6CO_2 + 12H_2O + \text{light} \longrightarrow C_6H_{12}O_6 + 6O_2 + 6H_2O$$

carbon dioxide   water   energy   yields   glucose   oxygen   water

Within this equation are two important ideas in biology. First, living things need energy to maintain life. The energy usually comes from glucose. During photosynthesis, CO_2 and water molecules are rearranged to become energy-rich sugar molecules.

Second, many living things eat plants, or they eat animals that have eaten plants. Both plants and animals break down glucose in their cells. They use the chemical energy stored in the bonds of glucose. This energy is transferred to the bonds of ATP. The energy in ATP is then readily available as cells need it. Recall that the process of breaking down glucose to form ATP is called cellular respiration.

To sum up, plants use photosynthesis to make glucose. Plants and animals use cellular respiration to harvest the energy in the bonds of glucose.

Green Leaves

Photosynthesis takes place mostly in the leaves of plants or in certain algae and bacteria. If you study a leaf under a microscope, you can see various structures. These structures are important in photosynthesis.

Figure 8.1.1 shows the structures in a leaf. The top layer of the leaf is a transparent waxy layer. It takes in sunlight. This layer also prevents the loss of water from evaporation. A **stoma** is a tiny pore, or hole, that allows gas to move in and out of the leaf. Many stomata are on the underside of a leaf. Stomata take in carbon dioxide and release oxygen.

The veins in a leaf are called **vascular bundles.** They carry water from the roots to the leaf. Vascular bundles also carry food out of the leaf to other parts of the plant.

Mesophyll cells make up the green tissue inside a leaf. They contain organelles called chloroplasts that are the sites of photosynthesis. Chloroplasts contain a green pigment called chlorophyll. A pigment is a chemical that absorbs only certain wavelengths of visible light. You will learn more about wavelengths of light in Lesson 2.

Recall that each chloroplast has an outer and inner membrane. The inner membrane contains stroma, a thick fluid. Suspended in the stroma are thylakoids. Recall from Chapter 5 that thylakoids are sacs arranged in stacks called grana.

Stoma

An opening on the underside of a leaf for gas exchange (plural is stomata)

Vascular bundle

A vein in a leaf that transports water and food

Mesophyll

The green tissue inside a leaf

Science Myth

Myth: Plants obtain the raw materials for photosynthesis just from the soil.

Fact: Plants obtain the materials for photosynthesis from the soil and the air.

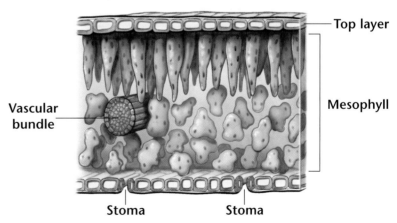

Figure 8.1.1 *The structures in leaves are important in photosynthesis.*

Link to >>>

Earth Science

Plants take in water and minerals from soil. They need minerals in tiny quantities. Each mineral is essential for healthy plant growth. Minerals assist chemical reactions during cellular respiration and photosynthesis.

Chlorophyll molecules and other pigments are in the membranes of the thylakoids. When sunlight strikes the pigments, they absorb the light.

Have you wondered why some green leaves change color in the fall? A leaf is green because of chlorophyll. During the plant's growing season, these green pigments are plentiful. They mask pigments of other colors such as red and yellow. In the fall, the chloroplasts die. Then red and yellow pigments become the main color of the leaves.

Some bacteria carry on photosynthesis although they do not have chloroplasts. Instead, they have photosynthetic membranes within their cells. These membranes allow them to produce sugar.

Express Lab 8

Materials
- lab coat or apron
- 8 paper towels
- tap water
- 10 bean seeds
- 2 containers, such as plastic cups or self-sealing plastic bags

Procedure
1. Put on a lab coat or apron.
2. Moisten the paper towels with tap water.
3. Put 5 bean seeds between the layers of 4 paper towels. Repeat with the other 5 bean seeds and paper towels.
4. Put each set of paper towels and seeds upright in a container.
5. Put one container in a sunny place, such as a windowsill. Put the other container in a dark, lightproof place, such as a closet.
6. After 7 days, examine the seeds. Examine the seeds after 14 days.

Analysis
1. After 7 days, how do the two sets differ? How do they differ after 14 days?
2. Describe the growth form of the seedlings raised in darkness. How is this helpful to the seedlings?

Lesson 1   R E V I E W

Word Bank

chloroplasts

glucose

autotroph

On a sheet of paper, write the word from the Word Bank that completes each sentence correctly.

1. An organism that make its own food is a(n) _____.

2. In photosynthesis, plants change CO_2 and water into _____.

3. Plant cells contain small structures called _____, which are sites of photosynthesis.

Critical Thinking

Write the answer to each of the following questions.

4. Compare cellular respiration and photosynthesis.

5. Photosynthesis does not occur in plant roots. Explain why.

Biology in Your Life

Technology: Fluorescent Lightbulbs for Plant Growth

Have you seen plant growth lamps at a plant nursery or garden center? If you look closely, you will see these lamps use light bulbs with a red or blue tinge. These lightbulbs are designed to produce light that is most beneficial to plants.

Visible light and other forms of electromagnetic radiation are made of different wavelengths of light. Scientists know which wavelengths plants use. Chlorophyll *a* is the most important photosynthetic pigment. It absorbs blue light (short wavelength) and red light (long wavelength).

Ordinary incandescent lightbulbs provide red light, but little blue light. Ordinary fluorescent lightbulbs provide green, yellow, and blue light.

They do not produce much red light. Plant growth lamps contain fluorescent lightbulbs especially made for plant growth. These lightbulbs provide the blue and red light needed for photosynthesis.

1. How do fluorescent bulbs for plant growth differ from ordinary fluorescent bulbs?

2. Fluorescent lightbulbs for plant growth do not contain green light. Explain why.

3. Why would plant growth lamps produce healthier indoor plants than ordinary lightbulbs?

Photosynthesis in Energy Cycles   Chapter 8   **227**

Materials

- safety goggles
- lab coat or apron
- scissors
- 2 *Elodea* sprigs
- heavy-duty thread
- 2 glass rods
- 2 large test tubes
- wax pencil
- 0.25% sodium bicarbonate ($NaHCO_3$) solution
- cooled, boiled distilled water
- test tube rack
- lamp

Oxygen Production During Photosynthesis

During photosynthesis, plants use energy from sunlight to combine carbon dioxide (CO_2) and water to make glucose. Plants release oxygen (O_2) and water. In this investigation, you will see the roles of carbon dioxide and oxygen during photosynthesis.

Procedure

1. Put on safety goggles and a lab coat or apron.

2. Using scissors, remove two healthy sprigs of *Elodea*. Then recut the end of each sprig at a 45° angle. **Safety Alert: Be careful when using scissors.**

3. Use two pieces of thread to tie each sprig to a glass rod.

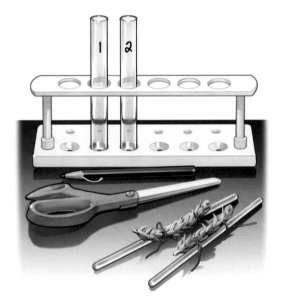

4. With the sprig's cut side up, place each rod into a test tube.

5. With a wax pencil, label the test tubes 1 and 2. Fill Test Tube 1 with 0.25% sodium bicarbonate solution. Be sure the *Elodea* sprig is covered with the solution. Fill Test Tube 2 with boiled and cooled distilled water. Be sure the *Elodea* sprig is covered with the distilled water.

6. Place the test tubes into a test tube rack. Place the rack so that both tubes are 1 meter from the lamp. Turn the lamp on.

7. Wait 5 minutes. Then watch both *Elodea* sprigs for bubbles that form at the cut end. Record your observations. Then turn the lamp off.

Cleanup/Disposal
Before leaving the lab, clean up your materials and wash your hands.

Analysis
1. In which test tube did bubbles appear?

2. What do the bubbles contain?

Conclusions
1. What was the role of the sodium bicarbonate solution?

2. Why did bubbles not appear in one of the test tubes?

Explore Further
Use a similar procedure to test the effect of light on photosynthesis.

The energy produced by the sun travels through space as waves called **electromagnetic radiation.** Electromagnetic radiation is made up of electric and magnetic waves. This radiation reaches the earth in the form of light.

The smallest unit of light is the **photon.** It is too small to be seen. A photon has a fixed amount of energy. Photons of light are **absorbed,** or retained, by pigments in leaves. In this absorption process, photons act like particles of light. However, when photons of light travel from the sun to leaves, they act like waves.

Electromagnetic radiation from the sun is made up of different **wavelengths** of energy. A wavelength is the distance between repeating units of a wave pattern. Light of shorter wavelengths has more energy than light of longer wavelengths. Study the **electromagnetic spectrum** in Figure 8.2.1. This is the spectrum, or range, of wavelengths of electromagnetic radiation. Visible light—the light that humans can see— is in the middle of the spectrum.

Electromagnetic radiation

Radiation that is made up of electric and magnetic waves

Photon

The smallest unit of light

Absorb

To retain

Wavelength

The distance between repeating units of a wave pattern

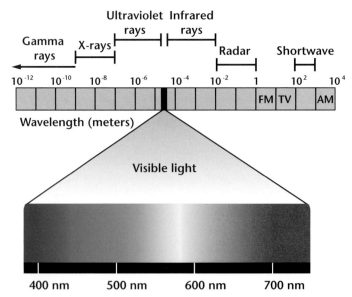

Figure 8.2.1 *Humans can only see a small portion of the electromagnetic spectrum.*

Electromagnetic spectrum

The range of wavelengths of electromagnetic radiation

Link to ➤➤➤

Physics

A prism separates visible light into different wavelengths. The wavelengths are visible as different colors. A man-made prism is a piece of glass or other transparent material cut at precise angles. Objects in nature, such as drops of water, can also serve as prisms. A rainbow forms when tiny water droplets separate light into its many colors.

Humans can see light that is between 400 nm and 700 nm. Nm is the abbreviation for nanometer. A nanometer is one billionth of a meter. Wavelengths of light are measured in nanometers.

Most life depends on the energy of the visible part of the spectrum. Photons of visible light contain just enough energy to excite electrons without hurting the cell. Photons of ultraviolet light contain too much radiation for most biological systems. Photons of infrared light do not contain enough energy to maintain biological systems.

When passed through a prism, we see the different wavelengths of visible light as different colors. Have you seen a rainbow after it rains? The rainbow appears because drops of water act like small prisms.

The Energy of Visible Light and Photosynthesis

Chlorophyll does not absorb all the wavelengths of visible light equally. Chlorophyll *a* is the most important light-absorbing pigment in plants. Chlorophyll *a* does not absorb light in the green part of the spectrum. The absorption of light by chlorophyll *a* is highest at two wavelengths. These wavelengths are 430 nm (blue light) and 662 nm (red light). The rate of photosynthesis at different wavelengths of visible light also shows two peaks. These peaks are close to the absorption peaks of chlorophyll *a*.

❋ ❋

Technology and Society

Commercial greenhouses sometimes use carbon dioxide generators to add carbon dioxide to the air. Carbon dioxide generators are machines that burn natural gas or propane and then release carbon dioxide. This extra carbon dioxide increases the rate of photosynthesis. It helps plant growth. Lower carbon dioxide levels decrease plant growth. This can cause flowers and fruit to drop off the plant.

Besides chlorophyll *a*, plants depend on other pigments. The other pigments, called accessory pigments, absorb light of different wavelengths. One accessory pigment is chlorophyll *b*. It is similar to chlorophyll *a* in structure. Chlorophyll *b* absorbs the orange and blue ranges of the visible spectrum. Plants usually contain about half as much chlorophyll *b* as they do chlorophyll *a*.

Other accessory pigments are **carotenoids.** A carotenoid is a yellow-orange pigment that absorbs blue-green light. Carotenoids pass energy to chlorophyll *a*. Carotenoids also protect the plant by getting rid of extra light energy that could harm chlorophyll. Figure 8.2.2 compares the light absorption of chlorophyll and carotenoids.

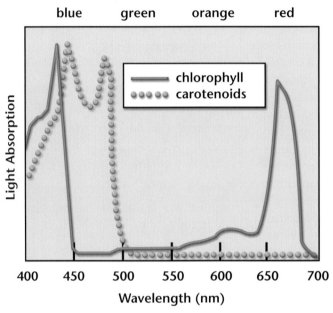

Figure 8.2.2 *Chlorophyll and carotenoids absorb visible light differently.*

The Two Processes of Photosynthesis

Photosynthesis is made up of two processes. Each process is a series of steps. One process is the light reaction. In the light reaction, plant cells convert energy from the sun to chemical energy. This reaction produces ATP and NADPH. NADPH is an electron carrier. The electrons from water are used to form NADPH.

Calvin-Benson cycle

A process in photosynthesis that produces sugar

G3P

A sugar molecule

Reaction center

A special molecule of chlorophyll a in which electron transfer occurs

Link to ➤➤➤

Language Arts

The word *photosynthesis* combines two words. First is the word *photo,* which comes from the Greek word for "light." Second is the word *synthesis,* which comes from the Latin word meaning "to put together." The word *photosynthesis* also describes its two-part nature. During the light reaction, light is captured. During the dark reaction, carbon dioxide is used to make sugar.

The other process is the dark reaction, or the **Calvin-Benson cycle.** During the Calvin-Benson cycle, cells produce sugar from carbon dioxide. ATP produced during the light reaction is the energy source for making **G3P,** a sugar. Some of this G3P is converted to glucose.

Study Figure 8.2.3. Find the relationship between the light reaction and the dark reaction. Notice that both reactions take place inside the chloroplast. To start the light reaction, light strikes the chloroplast. ATP and NADPH are produced. Oxygen is released into the air. In the dark reaction, or Calvin-Benson cycle, the cell produces sugar.

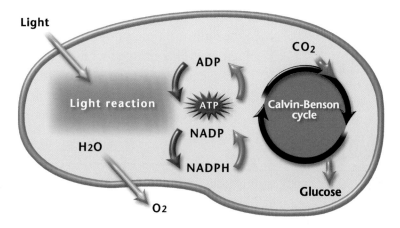

Figure 8.2.3 *In the chloroplast, photosynthesis is made up of a light reaction and a dark reaction. The light reaction produces ATP and NADPH, and the dark reaction produces glucose.*

The Light Reaction

Electrons become excited when photons of light strike pigments. Electrons in the pigments move to a higher energy level. Think of this process as electrons being boosted uphill. The cell transfers the excited electrons to a **reaction center.** A reaction center is a special molecule of chlorophyll *a* in which electron transfer occurs. At the reaction center, the electrons enter an electron transport chain. This chain forms NADPH and ATP. The energy of the excited electrons is captured in these ATP molecules. The ATP and NADPH are used later in the dark reaction to make sugar.

At the same time, the chloroplast splits water molecules into hydrogen and oxygen. It takes a large amount of energy to do this. The energy to split water molecules comes from sunlight. The hydrogen is carried along with the electrons in the electron transport chain.

The Electron Transport Chain

Pigments are arranged on the surface of the chloroplast in groups called **photosystems.** A photosystem is an assembly of proteins and pigments through which electrons are transferred to reaction centers. Photophosphorylation occurs in a photosystem. Recall that phosphorylation is the addition of a phosphate group to a molecule.

In the light reaction, photophosphorylation is a process that generates ATP. In this process, energy-rich electrons from a reaction center lose their energy. The energy loss happens as the electrons move along a chain of molecules called the electron transport chain. The cell uses the energy lost by the electrons to make ATP.

There are two types of reaction centers, Photosystem I and Photosystem II. In Photosystem I, chlorophyll P700 absorbs red light and produces ATP. Then the electrons return to the reaction center. In Photosystem II, chlorophyll P680 also absorbs red light. The electrons in the chlorophyll become excited and move to Photosystem I. Photosystem II replaces these electrons with the electrons gained from splitting water. During this water-splitting process, oxygen is released. The release of oxygen from photosynthesis maintains Earth's supply of oxygen.

To sum up, the light reaction converts solar energy to the chemical energy of ATP and NADPH. Oxygen is released. No sugar is produced. In Lesson 3, you will learn more about the dark reaction.

Lesson 2   R E V I E W

Word Bank

absorb

visible light

more

On a sheet of paper, write the word or words from the Word Bank that complete each sentence correctly.

1. Pigments in green leaves _____ light.

2. Light of shorter wavelengths has _____ energy than light of longer wavelengths.

3. Plants use energy in the _____ part of the spectrum.

On a sheet of paper, write the letter of the answer that completes each sentence correctly.

4. Chlorophyll *a* does not absorb light in the _____ part of the spectrum.

    A blue   **B** green   **C** red   **D** orange

5. A _____ is a yellow-orange pigment that absorbs blue-green light.

    A carotenoid   **C** spectrum

    B chlorophyll   **D** prism

6. Particles of light are called _____.

    A waves   **C** rays

    B photons   **D** electromagnetic radiation

Critical Thinking

On a sheet of paper, write the answers to the following questions. Use complete sentences.

7. What are accessory pigments? Explain what they do.

8. During which process of photosynthesis is light absorbed? During which process is sugar produced?

9. What are reaction centers? Explain what they do.

10. When is oxygen released during photosynthesis?

Materials

- safety goggles
- lab coat or apron
- large flask
- cool tap water
- scissors
- *Elodea* sprig
- heavy-duty thread
- glass rod
- large test tube
- 0.25% sodium bicarbonate ($NaHCO_3$) solution
- meterstick
- lamp
- stopwatch

Light and Photosynthesis

Plants need light to perform photosynthesis. Does the amount of light affect the rate of photosynthesis? You will find out in this lab.

Procedure

1. Put on safety goggles and a lab coat or apron.

2. Fill the flask with cool tap water.

3. Use scissors to cut a healthy sprig of *Elodea*. **Safety Alert: Be careful when using scissors.** Be sure the sprig will fit inside the large test tube. Recut the end of the sprig at a 45° angle. With a piece of thread, tie the sprig securely to the glass rod.

4. With the cut end up, place the glass rod into the test tube. Fill the test tube with 0.25% sodium bicarbonate solution. Be sure the *Elodea* sprig is covered with the solution.

5. Place the test tube into the flask. Place the flask 1 meter from the lamp. Turn on the lamp.

6. Wait 5 minutes. Then watch the *Elodea* sprig for bubbles that form at the cut end. Once bubbles start to appear, count the number of bubbles that form each minute. Do this for 5 minutes, recording your observations in a data table.

7. Write a hypothesis about the relationship between the amount of light and the rate of photosynthesis.

8. Write a procedure for an experiment to test your hypothesis. Include Safety Alerts. Hint: Consider using different distances between the lamp and the *Elodea* sprig.

9. Have your hypothesis, Safety Alerts, and procedure approved by your teacher. Then carry out your experiment.

Cleanup/Disposal

Before leaving the lab, clean up your materials and wash your hands.

Analysis

1. What is the purpose of the water in the flask?

2. At which distance from the light source was the rate of photosynthesis greatest?

Conclusions

1. Was your hypothesis supported by the results of your experiment?

2. Do you think temperature affects the rate of photosynthesis? Suggest an experiment that you could perform to find out.

Explore Further

How could you find out the effects of different colors of light on photosynthesis?

Objectives

After reading this lesson, you should be able to

◆ recognize that the dark reaction uses the ATP and NADPH produced in the light reaction

◆ explain that ATP and NADPH are used to produce energy-rich carbohydrate molecules

◆ describe the Calvin-Benson cycle

◆ describe plants that have adapted to their environment

Think of the Calvin-Benson cycle as a sugar factory. The factory is inside the stroma of the chloroplast. Like a factory, the Calvin-Benson cycle changes its input, mainly carbon dioxide, into a final product. The final product is a small sugar molecule called G3P. The cell uses this sugar molecule to make glucose and other compounds.

One input into the Calvin-Benson cycle is carbon dioxide from the air. A second input is energy from ATP that is made in the light reaction. A third input is high-energy electrons from NADPH, also produced in the light reaction. From these inputs, the Calvin-Benson cycle produces G3P. G3P is an energy-rich sugar molecule.

Figure 8.3.1 shows the four main steps in the Calvin-Benson cycle. In Step 1, CO_2 molecules and the sugar **RuBP** (**ribu**lose **bisp**hosphate) combine to make **PGA** (**p**hospho**g**lycer**a**te). An enzyme assists this chemical reaction. In Step 2, energy from ATP and electrons from NADPH combine to form G3P. In Step 3, G3P produces glucose and other compounds needed for metabolism and growth. In Step 4, energy from ATP is added to the remaining G3P molecules to make RuBP. The Calvin-Benson cycle is now complete and begins again.

RuBP

Ribulose bisphosphate; a five-carbon carbohydrate that combines with CO_2 in the first step of the Calvin-Benson cycle

PGA

Phosphoglycerate; a three-carbon molecule formed in the first step of the Calvin-Benson cycle

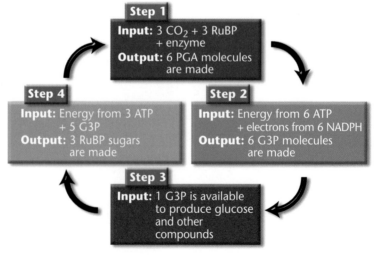

Step 1
Input: 3 CO_2 + 3 RuBP + enzyme
Output: 6 PGA molecules are made

Step 2
Input: Energy from 6 ATP + electrons from 6 NADPH
Output: 6 G3P molecules are made

Step 3
Input: 1 G3P is available to produce glucose and other compounds

Step 4
Input: Energy from 3 ATP + 5 G3P
Output: 3 RuBP sugars are made

Figure 8.3.1 *The Calvin-Benson cycle is like a four-step sugar factory.*

Lesson 1   R E V I E W

On a sheet of paper, write the letter of the answer that completes each sentence correctly.

1. A cell reproduces by dividing to create _____.

    A two daughter cells   **C** two parent cells

    B four daughter cells   **D** four parent cells

2. The size of the cell doubles in the _____.

    A G_1 stage   **B** G_2 stage **C** S stage **D** M phase

3. The process of creating two identical cells is _____.

    A centromere   **C** metaphase

    B interphase   **D** mitosis

On a sheet of paper, write the word or words that complete each statement correctly.

4. A chromosome attached by a centromere to another identical chromosome is known as a(n) _____.

5. During _____, the cell creates a network of spindle fibers.

6. Cells that do not reproduce stay in _____ phase.

Critical Thinking

On a sheet of paper, write the answers to the following questions. Use complete sentences.

7. Why do eukaryotic cells reproduce?

8. Bacterial cells are prokaryotic cells. They divide and split much like human cells do. Why is this not mitosis?

9. What happens during cytokinesis?

10. Give an example of a type of cell that reproduces often and a type of cell that rarely reproduces.

Cancer is a physical condition in which a cell grows without control and divides too much. Human bodies have signal molecules that control cell division. One cause of cancer is when these control systems break. They produce more signal molecules than needed. This causes a cell to divide too much. A cancer cell divides through mitosis. It creates a ball of cells called a **tumor.**

A **benign tumor** grows in only one area of the body. Tumors can spread to other body areas. Cells from the original tumor break away and enter the blood. Tumor cells travel through the body and attach to other areas. Once attached, the cells grow and divide into a new tumor. **Metastasis** is the process of cancerous cells spreading to other body areas. A tumor that has spread is a **malignant tumor.**

Doctors use different methods to rid the body of tumors. If a tumor is found early, doctors can often remove it with surgery. Doctors may treat malignant tumors with radiation therapy. This process uses beams of radiation aimed at the tumor. Radiation kills cells in the tumor by breaking them apart. Doctors may also use chemotherapy to treat cancer. Chemotherapy uses drugs that poison the tumor cells. Because radiation and chemotherapy can hurt normal cells, doctors try to find and remove tumors before they spread.

Cancer

A condition in which a cell grows without control and divides too much

Tumor

A ball of cells made from the extra divisions of a cancer cell

Benign tumor

A tumor that is only in the area where it began

Metastasis

The process of cancer cells spreading from one body area to another

Malignant tumor

A tumor that has spread from its original site to other body areas

Link to ➤➤➤

Health

Every year, more than one million new cases of skin cancer are diagnosed in the United States. Skin cancer causes 9,800 deaths every year. Most skin cancer is caused by too much exposure to the sun. To reduce your risk of skin cancer, use sunscreens, sunglasses, and hats that protect against ultraviolet (UV) rays.

Lesson 2   R E V I E W

On a sheet of paper, write the word that completes each statement correctly.

1. A(n) _____ is a tumor that has spread through metastasis.

2. A condition in which a cell grows without control and divides too much is _____.

3. A ball of cells made from the extra divisions of a cancer cell is a(n) _____.

Critical Thinking

On a sheet of paper, write the answers to the following questions. Use complete sentences.

4. How do the extra cells created by cancer harm the body?

5. How could cancer spread from the lungs to the liver?

❀ ❀

Technology and Society

The DNA microarray, or gene chip, is a cancer-fighting tool. To create microarrays, scientists put hundreds of samples of DNA on a slide. They apply a fluorescent dye to find gene segments that have made proteins recently. Next, they compare gene segments from cancer patients with the gene segments of healthy people. The DNA microarray helps scientists identify the gene segments that are causing the cancer.

The Life Cycles of Cells and Reproduction   Chapter 9   **253**

INVESTIGATION 9

Materials

- safety goggles
- lab coat or apron
- prepared slide of onion root
- microscope

Observing Cell Cycle Phases

Cells grow during interphase. They also make copies of their DNA and organelles during this phase. Cells reproduce to make new cells during mitosis and cytokinesis. As cells enter mitosis, they separate the DNA copies. During cytokinesis, the cells grow larger and divide in two. Making new cells allows an organism to grow larger or replace damaged cells. In this investigation, you will examine the cells of an onion root. You will observe cells in different phases of the cell cycles.

Procedure

1. Put on safety goggles and a lab coat or apron.

2. Examine the prepared slide of an onion root. **Safety Alert: Handle glass microscope slides with care. Dispose of broken glass properly.**

3. Find a cell in interphase. On a sheet of paper, draw what you observe. Label the parts of the cell that you recognize.

4. Find examples of cells in mitosis. Draw examples of a cell in prophase, metaphase, anaphase, telophase, and cytokinesis. Label the cell parts you recognize.

Cleanup/Disposal

When you are finished, return the prepared slide to your teacher.

Analysis

1. What cell parts were you able to identify easily?

2. What cell parts were difficult or impossible to identify?

Conclusions

1. How did you recognize a cell in interphase?

2. What were the main characteristics of the cells in mitosis?

3. How did you identify a cell undergoing cytokinesis?

Explore Further

In which phase were most of the cells you observed? What can you infer about the life of a cell from this observation?

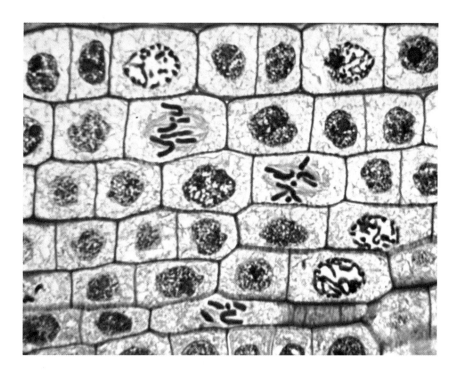

Gamete

A sex cell; sperm or an egg

Egg

The female gamete

Sperm

The male gamete

Somatic cell

A cell that is not a sex cell

Diploid

Having two copies of each kind of chromosome

Homologous chromosome

One of a matching pair of chromosomes that comes from each parent

Gametes, or sex cells, do not perform mitosis. Gametes are cells involved in sexual reproduction. The female gamete is called an **egg.** The male gamete is called **sperm.** Most cells in an organism are **somatic cells,** not sex cells. A human somatic cell has 46 chromosomes in its nucleus. Because there are 23 human chromosomes, each somatic cell is a **diploid** cell. A diploid cell has two copies of each chromosome, called **homologous chromosomes.** One copy of each chromosome comes from the father. The other copy comes from the mother.

Gametes and Meiosis

Gametes are **haploid** cells. They have one set of chromosomes. Both sperm and eggs cells have 23 chromosomes inside their nuclei. Humans create more humans by joining one egg cell with one sperm cell. **Fertilization** is the process of combining an egg cell and a sperm cell. After fertilization, a new diploid cell is formed, called a **zygote.** A zygote goes through many rounds of mitosis, eventually creating a new organism.

Gametes have a special type of reproduction called **meiosis.** Meiosis is similar to mitosis. However, there are some key differences in the formation of haploid cells. In contrast to mitosis, meiosis involves two divisions, meiosis I and meiosis II. In meiosis I, homologous chromosomes are separated from each other. In meiosis II, sister chromosomes are separated. The resulting cells are haploid.

Meiosis I

Figure 9.3.1 shows the four stages of meiosis I. Meiosis I begins with prophase I. In this phase, the sister chromatids for each chromosome shrink. Spindle fibers appear and attach to the centromeres. A special feature of prophase I is synapsis. In synapsis, homologous chromosomes pair together and form a **tetrad.** One copy of each chromosome pairs up with the other copy. Each copy has the same DNA in the same location.

Haploid
Having one copy of each kind of chromosome

Fertilization
The joining of male and female gametes to create a new organism

Zygote
A fertilized cell

Meiosis
A process that results in sex cells

Tetrad
A pair of homologous chromosomes joined together

Crossing over
The process of homologous chromosomes in a tetrad trading pieces of similar DNA

While the chromosomes are paired, they trade DNA pieces with each other. This trade is called **crossing over.** Crossing over makes every organism unique. This process creates different chromosomes that are passed on to offspring.

In metaphase I, the tetrads line up randomly. They line up in the middle of the cell along the metaphase plate. In anaphase I, homologous chromosomes separate. They move toward opposite ends of the cell. Each end now has a haploid daughter nucleus. The nucleus has only one set of chromosomes. Each chromosome is made up of two sister chromatids. In telophase I and cytokinesis, the nuclei and cytoplasm divide in half. Two haploid daughter cells form. Each haploid cell contains two copies of the same set of chromosomes.

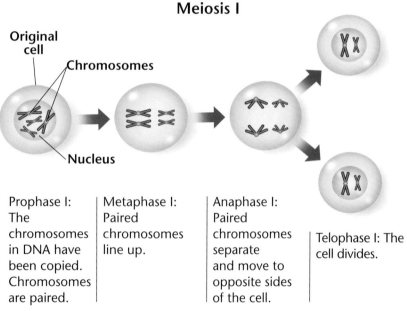

Meiosis I

| Prophase I: The chromosomes in DNA have been copied. Chromosomes are paired. | Metaphase I: Paired chromosomes line up. | Anaphase I: Paired chromosomes separate and move to opposite sides of the cell. | Telophase I: The cell divides. |

Figure 9.3.1 *Meiosis I occurs in four phases.*

Meiosis II

Meiosis II is similar to meiosis I. However, DNA is not copied in meiosis II. Meiosis II starts with prophase II. In this stage, the nuclei and the sister chromatids stay tightly packed. Spindle fibers attach to each pair of sister chromatids. The spindle fibers move the sister chromatids to the center of the cells.

In metaphase II, the sister chromatids reach the metaphase plate. In anaphase II, the sister chromatids separate at their centromeres. The separated chromatids become individual chromosomes. They move to opposite ends of the cells. In telophase II, four nuclei are created. Cytokinesis divides the two cells into four haploid daughter cells. Each gamete cell has 23 chromosomes. When the gametes fertilize, the resulting zygote has a diploid set of 46 chromosomes. Figure 9.3.2 shows the process of meiosis II.

Meiosis II

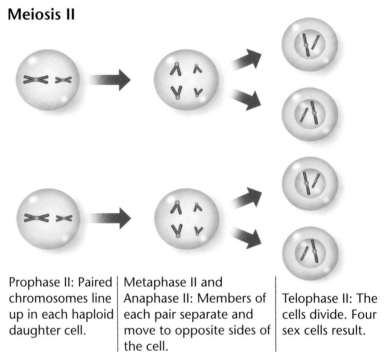

| Prophase II: Paired chromosomes line up in each haploid daughter cell. | Metaphase II and Anaphase II: Members of each pair separate and move to opposite sides of the cell. | Telophase II: The cells divide. Four sex cells result. |

Figure 9.3.2 *Meiosis II creates four new gamete cells.*

Like mitosis, meiosis is a cycle of division and reproduction that supports life. Mitosis and meiosis are alike, but different. In mitosis, one cell undergoes one division, creating two somatic cells. In meiosis, one cell undergoes two divisions to create four gamete cells. Because most cells in an organism are somatic, mitosis occurs more often than meiosis.

Link to ≫≫≫

Social Studies

A group of New York doctors and businessmen formed the American Cancer Society, or the ACS, in 1913. The society's goals were to educate the public about cancer and to raise money for cancer research. Today, the ACS has over 2 million volunteers who work around the world.

On a sheet of paper, write the word or words that complete each statement correctly.

1. Human cells that are not gametes are called _____ cells.

2. Sex cells have a total of _____ chromosomes, and all other cells have a total of _____ chromosomes.

3. Gametes are created during a dividing process called _____.

On a sheet of paper, write the letter of the word or words that complete each sentence correctly.

4. Tetrads form during _____.

   A prophase I   **C** prophase II

   B metaphase I   **D** metaphase II

5. The main difference between meiosis I and meiosis II is that _____ in meiosis II.

   A the nuclei do not divide

   B cytokinesis is not involved

   C no spindle fibers form

   D no new DNA is created

6. After completing meiosis II, human sex cells have a total of _____ chromosomes.

   A 2   **B** 4   **C** 23   **D** 46

Critical Thinking

On a sheet of paper, write the answers to the following questions. Use complete sentences.

7. How do chromosomes during meiosis I change to cause unique offspring?

8. Why are cells that have completed meiosis I not diploid?

9. Describe an egg cell, a sperm cell, and a somatic cell in these terms: diploid, haploid, male, female.

10. What problems would humans have if they reproduced without using meiosis?

Humans reproduce sexually. Their gametes are part of an organ system called the reproductive system. The reproductive system is made of various organs and differs for males and females. The process of creating gametes in males and females also differs.

The Male Reproductive System

Male gametes, or sperm, are made through meiosis. This process, called **spermatogenesis,** takes place in the **testes.** The testes in a sexually active male make more than 200 million sperm cells every day. The testes, also called **gonads,** are the organs that produce gametes in males. The testes also produce the male sex hormone **testosterone.** Testosterone causes male characteristics, such as facial hair and a low voice. Testes are kept in the **scrotum,** a sac outside of the male body. Because the scrotum is outside the body, it is about 2°C cooler than the rest of the body. Sperm cells are sensitive to heat. The lower temperature of the scrotum helps sperm to live. Figure 9.4.1 shows the main reproductive organs of the human male.

Spermatogenesis

The process of making a sperm cell

Testis

The male sex organ that produces sperm cells (plural is testes)

Gonad

An organ that makes gametes

Testosterone

A male sex hormone

Scrotum

A sac that holds the testes

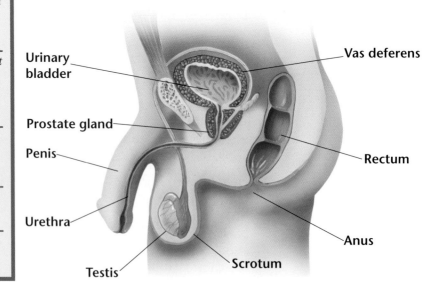

Urinary bladder

Prostate gland

Penis

Urethra

Testis

Scrotum

Vas deferens

Rectum

Anus

Figure 9.4.1 *The male reproductive system is made of many organs.*

Spermatogonia

Early gamete cells that have not grown into sperm

Seminiferous tubule

The tissue in the testes where spermatogenesis happens

Vas deferens

The tubes that connect the testes to the urethra

Urethra

The tube that carries urine and semen out of the body

Semen

A mixture of fluid and sperm cells

Penis

The male organ that delivers sperm to the female body

Ejaculation

The release of semen from the penis

Once a human male is sexually mature, spermatogenesis begins and continues for the male's life. Inside the testes, the original diploid cells that begin meiosis are called **spermatogonia.** They are found in tissue called **seminiferous tubules,** which make up the testes. Once they begin meiosis, they create four haploid sperm cells that are stored until needed.

Sperm cells are released during male sexual activity. When released, sperm cells travel through muscular tubes called the **vas deferens.** These tubes come from each of the testes and carry sperm cells to the **urethra.** The urethra is a tube that carries both **semen** and urine. Semen is a thick, milky fluid that feeds and carries sperm cells outside of the body. When sperm cells reach the urethra, they mix with other chemicals to make semen. Semen is made of mucus, sugars, and enzymes that help the sperm survive outside of the body.

Semen travels down the urethra into the **penis.** The penis is a tube of special tissue that surrounds the urethra. Semen is released through a small opening in the penis tip connected to the urethra. The process of releasing sperm is called **ejaculation.**

▼◄▲▼◄▲▼◄▲▼◄▲▼◄▲▼◄▲▼◄▲▼◄▲▼◄▲▼◄▲▼◄▲▼

Science at Work

Laboratory Technician

Laboratory technicians analyze scientific samples. They may observe cells and run experiments. Laboratory technicians work closely with scientists or doctors. Technicians develop good procedures and follow them carefully. They often read test results and analyze data. A technician uses a variety of  laboratory equipment, including microscopes and culture equipment. Laboratory technicians work with a variety of samples. These samples include plants, animals, chemicals, soils, and blood. Technicians must have a bachelor's degree or a two-year associate's degree in a scientific field.

The Female Reproductive System

Figure 9.4.2 shows the main reproductive organs of the human female. A female's gametes, or eggs, are produced through a process called **oogenesis.** This process happens in the **ovaries.** When a female is born, her two ovaries contain all the cells that will become eggs. These cells, called **oocytes,** are in prophase I of meiosis. When a female becomes sexually mature, the oocytes go through the remaining stages of meiosis. The oocytes grow into egg cells during a monthly cycle.

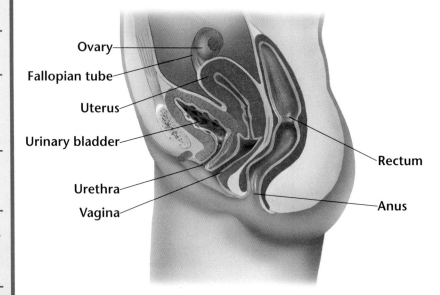

Figure 9.4.2 *The female reproductive system is made of many organs.*

Hormones control this monthly cycle. A main female sex hormone is **estrogen.** At the beginning of the monthly cycle, the ovaries and other organs in the body produce estrogen. As estrogen levels increase during the cycle, one oocyte grows into an egg in one ovary.

This growth begins in a ball of cells called a **follicle.** Each follicle contains the oocyte and other cells that feed and nurture the oocyte. As the follicle grows, the oocyte continues with meiosis. However, meiosis in females produces one egg cell, not four. The other cells from meiosis break down.

Oogenesis

The process of creating an egg cell

Ovary

The female organ that makes egg cells

Oocyte

An early egg cell that has not finished meiosis

Estrogen

A female sex hormone

Follicle

A ball of cells with a growing oocyte found inside

Ovulation

The process of releasing an egg from an ovary

Fallopian tube

A tube through which eggs pass from an ovary to the uterus

Uterus

An organ in most female mammals that holds and protects an embryo

Females are born with about 400,000 oocytes that are produced and stored in the ovaries.

After about 14 days, the follicle releases the egg cell into the **fallopian tube.** This process is called **ovulation.** A fallopian tube is near each ovary. Both tubes connect to the **uterus.**

The inside lining of the uterus grows with blood-rich tissue during the monthly cycle of a female. The lining can hold and nourish a fertilized egg. If an egg is fertilized, it quickly divides and attaches to the lining of the uterus. Here, it develops into an **embryo.**

You can follow the path of an oocyte in Figure 9.4.3. If an egg is not fertilized during a cycle, the egg, blood, and pieces of the lining break off. These materials leave the body through the vagina. This process is called **menstruation.** It signals the end of a female's monthly cycle, about 28 days long. After menstruation, the cycle begins again.

Menstruation continues for many years. Eventually, the ovaries stop releasing eggs. This usually happens between the ages of 45 and 55. This event is called **menopause.** After menopause, a woman stops ovulating.

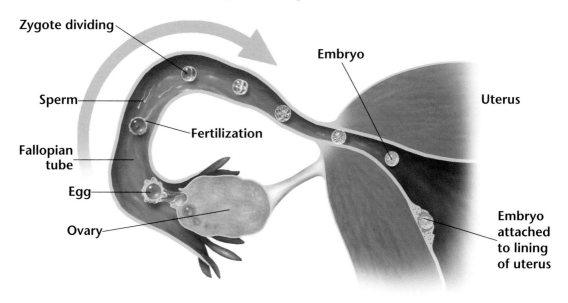

Figure 9.4.3 *A zygote divides in a fallopian tube, becomes an embryo, and attaches to the uterus.*

Lesson 4   R E V I E W

Link to >>>

Physics

Although sperm and egg cells are both haploid gametes, they differ in size and weight. The sperm cell is the smallest cell in the human body. The egg cell is the largest. About 175,000 sperm cells equal the weight of one egg cell.

On a sheet of paper, write the word or words that complete each statement correctly.

1. The male hormone is produced in the _____.

2. A hormone called _____ controls the activities of the female reproductive system.

3. The process of creating a sperm cell is _____, and the process of creating an egg cell is _____.

On a sheet of paper, write the letter of the word or words that complete each sentence correctly.

4. Male facial hair is caused by the production of _____.

   A sperm cells   **C** estrogen

   B semen   **D** testosterone

5. Sperm cells are created in the _____.

   A vas deferens   **C** scrotum

   B seminiferous tubules   **D** testes

6. An unfertilized egg is _____.

   A released from the body through menstruation

   B recycled and returned to the ovaries

   C destroyed and reabsorbed

   D kept in the uterus

Critical Thinking

On a sheet of paper, write the answers to the following questions. Use complete sentences.

7. Contrast the time periods in which eggs and sperm are created.

8. What are three organs of the male reproductive system? What are their functions?

9. Contrast the meiosis of the female oocyte and the meiosis of spermatogonia.

10. What are the pathways a fertilized egg and an unfertilized egg can take?

Objectives

After reading this lesson, you should be able to

◆ describe human fertilization and development

◆ explain childbirth

◆ compare infancy and the teen years

Vagina

The tube-like canal in the female body through which sperm enter the body

Cervix

An opening that connects a female's uterus and vagina

Pregnancy

The development of a fertilized egg into a baby inside a female's body

Gestation time

The period of development of a mammal, from fertilization until birth

Placenta

A tissue that provides the embryo with food and oxygen from its mother's body

For fertilization to happen, sperm must be delivered to the egg. To deliver sperm, an erect penis enters the **vagina.** After ejaculation, sperm enter the vagina and travel through the **cervix.** The cervix is the other opening of the uterus. It connects the uterus and vagina. Sperm travel through the uterus and into the fallopian tubes. One sperm fertilizes one egg.

What Happens During Pregnancy?

The fertilized egg is a diploid cell. It attaches to the blood-rich lining of the uterus. The fertilized egg continues mitosis and becomes a zygote. After a few days, the zygote is called an embryo. It is now a hollow ball of cells. When a fertilized egg attaches to the uterus, the female becomes **pregnant.** Pregnancy is the development of a fertilized egg into a baby inside a female's body. This period of growth in the uterus is called **gestation time.** Human gestation lasts about nine months.

As the embryo grows through mitosis, the lining of the uterus becomes the **placenta.** The placenta is blood-rich tissue that nourishes a growing embryo during pregnancy. The **umbilical cord** connects the placenta to the embryo. The umbilical cord contains blood vessels that provide the embryo with food and oxygen.

A three-week-year-old embryo has three cell layers that will develop into different body parts. Around four weeks, its heart beats and blood vessels have formed. The embryo has a head and buds for arms and legs. The embryo is smaller than a fingernail. In another week, hands and fingers appear. Eyes look like black spots. By week nine, the embryo is called a **fetus.** It has all the major structures found in babies.

By the end of three months, the fetus can suck its thumb. It can turn its head and move its arms and legs. During the next three months of pregnancy, the fetus increases in length and can be active.

Over the last three months, the fetus becomes larger. Muscles and bones become stronger. The fetus has less room to move in the mother's uterus and is usually less active.

Childbirth

When the fetus reaches full size, the fetus and placenta leave the uterus through the vagina. Figure 9.5.1 gives an example of how a baby is positioned in the mother's body. Muscles in the uterus and vagina squeeze together, or contract, and push the fetus and placenta through. The umbilical cord is clamped and cut. Now the baby can survive outside of the mother's body. After this, the cycle of human reproduction can begin again.

Umbilical cord

The cord that connects an embryo to the placenta

Fetus

An embryo after eight weeks of development in the uterus

Adolescence

The teenage years of a human

At birth, the average human baby is 40 to 50 cm long and weighs 2.7 to 4.5 kilogram (7–12 pounds). It is about the size of a small watermelon.

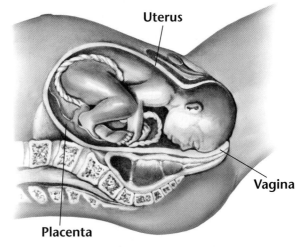

Uterus

Vagina

Placenta

Figure 9.5.1 *A baby leaves the uterus through the vagina.*

Infancy

A human baby, or infant, is born helpless. People must provide constant care for a baby. After a year or so, a baby walks, communicates, and eats solid food. People care for children as they go through the teen years, called **adolescence.**

Rapid growth and physical changes occur during adolescence. The male's voice becomes lower. Hair grows on the face, under the arms, and around the sex organs. For females, hair also grows under the arms and around the sex organs. The breasts enlarge and menstruation begins. Teens learn about becoming an adult. They take on more responsibility. They learn more about themselves and their place in the world.

The Environment:
What Causes Cancer?

Cancer is caused when a cell does not cycle properly and reproduces repeatedly. What causes the cell cycle to go wrong? Scientists know that the cause is often genetic. Some people are more likely than others to get cancer, depending on the genes they inherited.

Some cancers are linked to things encountered in daily life. Things that can cause cancer are called *carcinogens.* Common carcinogens are radiation, tobacco smoke, and asbestos.

Radiation in large doses can damage a person's DNA. If the damage is severe enough, cancer can result. Radiation includes long exposure to the sun. Tobacco smoke contains dozens of carcinogens. Over time, exposure to tobacco smoke can cause lung cancer. This is true even if a person does not smoke.

Asbestos once was a common building material because it does not burn. However, asbestos breaks down into very small fibers that can be inhaled and cause lung cancer. Many countries ban the use of asbestos.

Carcinogens do not cause cancer in all people. Whether someone gets cancer due to a carcinogen depends on three factors: 1) how much of the carcinogen they are exposed to; 2) how long they are exposed to it; 3) and their genetic makeup.

1. Why should you avoid or limit your exposure to carcinogens?

2. How can some people be exposed to carcinogens and stay healthy, while others who are exposed get cancer?

3. What lifestyle changes can you make to lower your chances of getting cancer from a known carcinogen?

Lesson 5   R E V I E W

Word Bank

nine

placenta

fetus

embryo

On a sheet of paper, write the the word or words from the Word Bank that complete each sentence correctly.

1. At week nine, an embryo is called a(n) _____.

2. The human gestation period lasts about _____ months.

3. The umbilical cord connects the _____ to the _____.

Critical Thinking

On a sheet of paper, write the answers to the following questions. Use complete sentences.

4. What kinds of physical changes take place during adolescence?

5. Pregnancies are often referred to as trimesters. A trimester is about three months long. What developments occur in a fetus during the first trimester?

★ ★

Achievements in Science

Cancer in people has been noted throughout recorded history. The word *cancer* was first used by Hippocrates, an ancient Greek doctor. Since then, several doctors have made important discoveries about human cancer. During the 1700s, the Scottish doctor John Hunter began removing malignant tumors from people. Hunter helped develop this surgery. Soon, other doctors began removing tumors for people.

In 1761, John Hill, a British doctor, recognized that tobacco use could cause cancer. An American scientist, Francis Peyton Rous, discovered a virus that caused cancer.

The work of Hill, Rous, and others led to the discovery of other substances that could cause cancer, such as radiation and certain chemicals.

In the late 1800s, Thomas Beatson, a Scottish surgeon, found a link between hormones produced by the ovaries and breast cancer. Beaston's work led the way for hormone treatment of cancer. Scientists discovered radiation in the late 1800s and early 1900s. This discovery led to the use of X-rays to find cancer tumors. Later, scientists discovered how to use radiation therapy to destroy tumors. Today, scientists and doctors worldwide continue to identify sources of cancer and develop new cancer treatments.

Materials

- lab coat or apron
- modeling clay in different colors

Modeling the Movement of Chromosomes

DNA is organized into sections called chromosomes. Each chromosome contains many genes. Human chromosomes come in pairs, with one chromosome coming from each parent. The genes on a chromosome are mixed and distributed during meiosis. In meiosis I, chromosomes trade genetic information by crossing over. In meiosis II, the chromosome pairs are separated and redistributed in gametes.

In this investigation, you will create models of chromosomes with different-colored clay. You will use your models to show how meiosis I and meiosis II cause genes to mix, creating different chromosomes.

Meiosis I: **Meiosis I:**   **Meiosis I:**   **Meiosis II:**

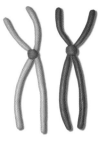   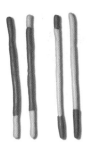

Homologous pair lines up   Crossover   Result   Result

Procedure

1. Form small groups. Select either meiosis I or meiosis II to model.

2. Put on a lab coat or apron.

3. Use the modeling clay to design and create chromosome models. Determine the size and color of your models. Keep your models simple.

4. On paper, diagram the process your group wants to model (meiosis I or meiosis II). Label the activities that occur during each phase of the process.

5. Now use your chromosome models to show each phase of the process. Show how the chromosomes move or change. Use different clay colors to make this clear.

6. Compare the models your group created with the models of other groups. Compare how each group showed that the genes on their chromosomes have moved.

Cleanup/Disposal

When you are finished, return any unused modeling clay to the proper place. Wash your hands in warm, soapy water.

Analysis

1. Compare your models with models of the same process created by another group. How do the two sets differ?

2. Compare your models with models of a different process created by another group. How different are the two sets?

Conclusions

1. In meiosis I, how does the size of the chromosome and the site of crossing over affect the number and type of genes that are transferred? Are some genes more likely to be transferred in crossing over than others?

2. Suppose one of the groups modeling meiosis II used chromosomes that had crossed over in meiosis I as their starting materials. How would this affect offspring?

Explore Further

Compare the models of gamete cells from the end of meiosis II with another group's gamete cells. How much does this affect offspring?

Life Without DNA

All living organisms on Earth have one thing in common—they all use DNA to replicate, or make copies of themselves. A cell's DNA is like a library of all of its parts and activities. DNA controls the production of proteins that make up the cell. It also acts as a blueprint to transmit information from one generation of cells to the next.

Scientists have long wondered how the first DNA molecules were created and whether DNA is necessary for life to exist. They also wonder if other life forms in the universe exist without DNA. Many scientists think RNA may have once done all the work that DNA does now.

Scientists think RNA acts like a messenger for DNA. Scientists have run experiments that show that RNA can behave like DNA as an information carrier. RNA may also act as a protein in carrying out cellular functions.

Recently, scientists have tried to create a type of primitive life-form from RNA. In one experiment, scientists mixed materials that make up RNA with water and a certain type of clay. The materials assembled themselves into a cell-like structure as seen in the photograph. This structure may have been the ancestor to cells as we know them today.

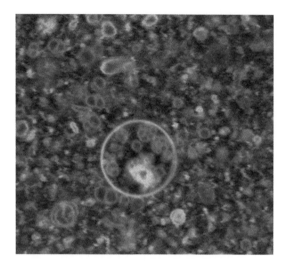

Experiments recreating primitive life without DNA are interesting to both biologists and astronomers looking for life in the universe. Currently, space probes are searching for life based on the life structures we know on Earth. By finding new ways that life can exist, we may be better equipped to search for different types of life elsewhere.

1. What was the importance of the experiment that showed RNA could carry information and do cellular functions?

2. Why do scientists think the first cells may have used RNA instead of DNA?

3. How could information from these RNA experiments be useful in space missions?

- Cells go through cycles. A cell cycle begins when a new cell is created. It ends when the cell divides to make new cells.

- A cell spends most of its life in interphase carrying out its typical cell activities.

- During mitosis, a cell divides to create two daughter cells. Daughter cells from mitosis are identical copies of the parent cell, with the same DNA.

- Cancer is a condition in which cell cycles are uncontrolled.

- Human sex cells, or gametes, undergo meiosis to make new sex cells. Gametes from meiosis are haploid cells and have one set of chromosomes. Cells with two sets of chromosomes are called diploid cells.

- Meiosis I results in two cells with two copies of the same chromosomes. Meiosis II results in four haploid daughter cells, each with one copy of each type of chromosome.

- The male reproductive system produces and delivers sperm to the female uterus to fertilize an egg for reproduction. The female reproductive system produces a haploid egg cell in the ovaries. An unfertilized egg cell is released through menstruation.

- Reproduction takes place when a haploid sperm fertilizes a haploid egg cell. This results in a diploid zygote that grows through mitosis.

- A fertilized egg develops into a zygote, undergoes mitosis, and becomes an embryo. An embryo grows into a fetus, then into a baby.

Vocabulary

adolescence, 266	fertilization, 257	metastasis, 252	spermatogenesis, 260
benign tumor, 252	fetus, 266	mitosis, 249	spermatogonia, 261
cancer, 252	follicle, 262	oocyte, 262	spindle, 249
cell cycle, 248	gamete, 256	oogenesis, 262	testis, 260
centromere, 249	gestation time, 265	ovary, 262	testosterone, 260
cervix, 265	gonad, 260	ovulation, 262	tetrad, 257
cleavage furrow, 250	haploid, 257	penis, 261	tumor, 252
crossing over, 257	homologous	placenta, 265	umbilical cord, 266
cytokinesis, 250	chromosome, 256	pregnancy, 265	urethra, 261
diploid, 256	interphase, 248	scrotum, 260	uterus, 262
egg, 256	malignant tumor, 252	semen, 261	vagina, 265
ejaculation, 261	meiosis, 257	seminiferous tubule, 261	vas deferens, 261
embryo, 263	menopause, 263	sister chromatid, 249	zygote, 257
estrogen, 262	menstruation, 263	somatic cell, 256	
fallopian tube, 262	metaphase plate, 249	sperm, 256	

Chapter 9 R E V I E W

Word Bank

benign tumor

cytokinesis

egg

gonad

haploid

interphase

meiosis

menstruation

mitosis

ovulation

placenta

pregnancy

somatic cell

sperm

zygote

Vocabulary Review

On a sheet of paper, write the word or words from the Word Bank that best complete each sentence.

1. A cell that has undergone _____ results in four cells.

2. A cell that has undergone _____ results in two cells.

3. The process of dividing everything in a cell except the nucleus is called _____.

4. The process of _____ marks the end of the female monthly reproductive cycle.

5. A(n) _____ is a collection of rapidly dividing cells that has not spread from its beginning area.

6. The phase of the cell cycle in which a cell grows and carries out its normal activities is called _____.

7. A(n) _____ cell contains only one copy of each chromosome.

8. The female gamete cell is called a(n) _____.

9. The process of releasing an egg from an ovary is called _____.

10. An organ responsible for making gametes is called a(n) _____.

11. A fertilized cell is called a(n) _____.

12. In the human body, a cell that is not a gamete is called a(n) _____.

13. The _____ nourishes a developing embryo during pregnancy.

14. The haploid gamete produced by males is called _____.

15. The development of a fertilized egg into a baby inside a female's body is called _____.

Review continued on next page

Concept Review

On a sheet of paper, write the letter of the answer that completes each sentence correctly.

16. In mitosis, chromatids line up in the middle of the cell during _____.

   A anaphase **B** metaphase **C** prophase **D** telophase

17. In mitosis, separate nuclear envelopes form around the two sets of chromosomes during _____.

   A anaphase **B** metaphase **C** prophase **D** telophase

18. During meiosis, spindle fibers appear during _____.

   A anaphase **B** metaphase **C** prophase **D** telophase

19. During _____ of meiosis, sister chromatids are separated and pulled to opposite ends of the cell.

   A anaphase I   **C** anaphase II

   B metaphase I   **D** metaphase II

20. Chromosomes are duplicated to create sister chromatids during _____.

   A meiosis I and meiosis II

   B meiosis I and mitosis

   C meiosis II and mitosis

   D mitosis only

Critical Thinking

On a sheet of paper, write the answers to the following questions. Use complete sentences.

21. What is the difference between a cancer cell and a normal cell that is dividing?

22. Some people have cancer tumors removed, and their cancer never returns. Other people with cancer must be treated with drugs and radiation. Explain why.

23. How do cells combine and reproduce to create different combinations of DNA in babies?

24. What is a disadvantage to an organism that reproduces by binary fission? What is an advantage?

25. Describe the production of male and female gametes. Explain how the two work to help humans reproduce. Include the terms *mitosis* and *meiosis* in your description.

Research and Write

Spindle fibers attach to sister chromatids at the centromere. Research to find where the other end of the spindle fibers attach. Compare and contrast how spindle fibers attach in plant and animal cells.

Test-Taking Tip If you cannot think of the right words to answer a question, try recalling pictures. Make a drawing to help you think.

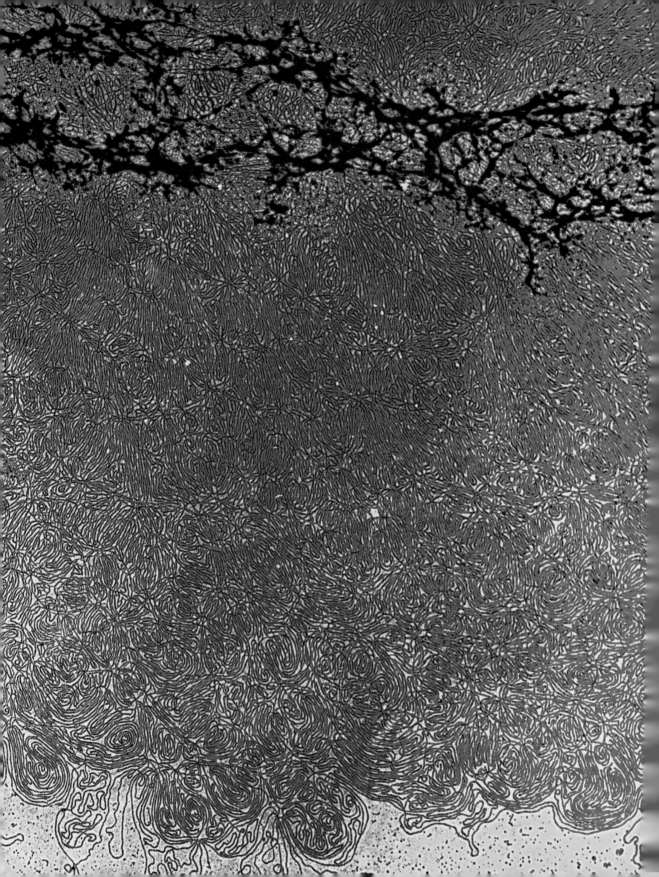

10

Inheritance Patterns in Life Cycles

Look at the photograph of a chromosome. Near the bottom, find the threads that separate from the dark orange mass. These threads are sections of a DNA molecule coiled inside the chromosome. As you know, DNA is genetic material that contains instructions for life. Before DNA could be seen with a microscope, researchers had observed what DNA does. In Chapter 10, you will learn about early research on heredity—the passing of traits from parents to offspring. You will also learn about the structures that store and transmit traits and what can happen if the structures are damaged.

Organize Your Thoughts

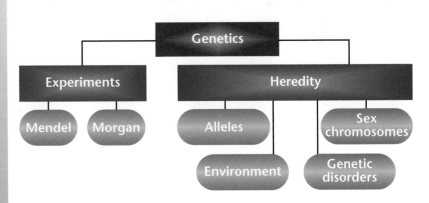

Goals for Learning

◆ To explain how genes pass traits from parents to offspring

◆ To describe the role of chromosomes in heredity

◆ To identify patterns of heredity in humans

Objectives

After reading this lesson, you should be able to

◆ relate heredity to human characteristics

◆ describe Mendel's work with pea plants

◆ identify the law of segregation

◆ identify the law of independent assortment

◆ draw a Punnett square

Trait

A characteristic of an organism

Heredity

The passing of traits from parents to offspring

Cross-fertilization

A process in which pollen from one plant fertilizes the eggs in a flower of a different plant

Pollen

Tiny grains containing sperm; the male plant gamete

Many families have characteristics common among all the members. Some offspring have the same eye or hair color as a parent. Others have the same nose shape as a grandparent. All organisms, including humans, pass **traits** to their offspring during reproduction. A trait is a characteristic of an organism. A trait can be a physical characteristic like eye color, height, or face shape. Traits are inherited through gametes. **Heredity** is the study of how traits are passed from parents to offspring.

Mendel's Studies

The science of heredity began in the mid-1800s. An Austrian scientist named Gregor Mendel noticed common traits in pea plants. Each trait had two forms. For example, pea plants were tall or short. Flowers were purple or white. Mendel decided to study seven traits. He studied plant height, flower position, flower color, seed color, seed shape, pod color, and pod shape. Mendel studied almost 20,000 pea plants.

To begin, Mendel grew many generations of plants until he had true-breeding for each trait. True-breeding plants have offspring that always show the same form of the trait. For example, true-breeding tall plants always produce tall plants.

Mendel now began to cross-fertilize. **Cross-fertilization** is a process in which **pollen** from one plant fertilizes the eggs in a flower of a different plant. Pollen is the male plant gamete. Mendel used pollen from a tall plant to fertilize an egg of a short plant. He made similar crosses between plants with opposite forms of traits.

The F_1 Generation

Mendel called the first round of plants the parental generation, or the **P generation**. The P generation is the first two individuals that mate in a genetic cross. Mendel called the offspring the **F_1 generation**.

The F_1 generation plants were **hybrids.** Hybrids are the offspring of two different true-breeding plants. The parent plants differed only in one trait. Another name for this type of cross is a **monohybrid cross.** Mendel carried out monohybrid crosses to study each of the seven traits. The offspring from monohybrid crosses always gave similar results. For every trait, he saw only one form of that trait in the F_1 generation. The other form seemed to disappear. Mendel wondered if the form truly had disappeared, or if something else was happening.

The F_2 Generation

Mendel then used F_1 plants to fertilize each other, creating an F_2 **generation.** Mendel found two results. First, some offspring in the F_2 generation showed the same trait forms as the F_1 generation. Second, the trait forms that had disappeared in the first cross now appeared. These traits had only been hidden in the F_1 generation.

For example, Mendel's pea plants had a gene for tall plants and a gene for short plants. When he crossed a true-breeding tall plant and a true-breeding short plant, all F_1 generation plants were tall. When he crossed F_1 generation plants, some F_2 generation plants were tall. Some were short. The short gene had been hidden by the tall gene in the F_1 generation. This means a gene can take two or more forms. **Alleles** are different forms of the same gene.

Recall from Chapter 9 that an organism receives an allele from each parent. When the parent gametes fertilize, two alleles are inside the new cells. These alleles can be the same or different. If the alleles are the same, both genes show the same form of a trait. If they are different, one is a **dominant gene** and shows its form of the trait. The other allele is a **recessive gene.** It is hidden by the dominant gene and does not show its form of the trait.

Link to ➤➤➤

Language Arts

The term *F₁ generation* means "first filial generation." Filial means "of or relating to a son or daughter."

Law of Segregation

From his results, Mendel came up with the **law of segregation.** This law states that pairs of homologous chromosomes pull apart in meiosis. Each gamete receives one gene of a pair. Genes that come together with the same alleles are **homozygous.** Genes that come together with different alleles are **heterozygous.** The dominant allele is displayed in a heterozygous pair.

Law of Independent Assortment

Mendel wondered if certain trait forms and their alleles were inherited together. For example, would round seeds always be yellow? Would wrinkled seeds always be green? To find out, Mendel made **dihybrid crosses.** He used a P generation that differed in only two traits. Each parent displayed two dominant trait forms or two recessive trait forms. He crossed these plants with each other. His F_1 generation always displayed both dominant trait forms. Next, he let the F_1 plants fertilize each other. If certain alleles always inherit together, he would see only those allele pairings in the F_2 generation.

Sidebar

Law of segregation

A law that states that pairs of homologous chromosomes separate in meiosis and each gamete receives one gene of a pair

Homozygous

Having chromosomes that contain an identical pair of genes for a particular trait

Heterozygous

Having chromosomes that contain a pair of genes that do not code for the same trait form

Dihybrid cross

A cross between two plants that differ in two traits

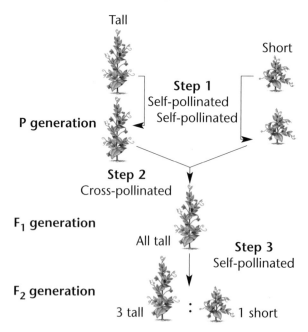

Figure 10.1.1 *Mendel's studies involved three generations. The results were always the same.*

For any two traits, Mendel's results always showed the ratio of 9:3:3:1. For example, for seed color and shape, the F_2 generation had nine yellow round seeds and three green round seeds. It also had three yellow wrinkled seeds and one green wrinkled seed. He saw the same ratio for all pairings of his seven traits.

From these results, Mendel came up with the **law of independent assortment.** This law states that each pair of chromosomes separates on its own in meiosis. Four pairings of alleles are possible. Figure 10.1.1 sums up the results of Mendel's experiments.

Punnett Squares

A model called a **Punnett square** can help explain the results of Mendel's crosses. The Punnett square in Figure 10.1.2 shows Mendel's cross of true-breeding tall plants with true-breeding short plants.

TT stands for a pure tall parent plant, and *tt* stands for a pure short parent plant. The capital *T* stands for the dominant gene for plant height (tallness). The lowercase *t* stands for the recessive gene for plant height (shortness). As Figure 10.1.2 shows, all F_1 pea plants were tall. But they also carried the recessive gene for shortness.

Law of independent assortment

A law that states that each pair of chromosomes separates independently of other pairs of chromosomes in meiosis

Punnett square

A model used to represent crosses between organisms

Science Myth

Myth: More dominant alleles exist than recessive alleles.

Fact: The frequency of a specific allele is not due to its dominance. Frequency is the number of times an allele appears. The frequency of an allele is due to whether the allele helps an organism survive.

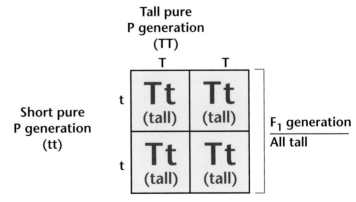

Figure 10.1.2 *This Punnett square shows Mendel's F_1 generation.*

Math Tip

In Mendel's F_2 generation, he always got three tall plants and one short plant.

Mendel grew another generation of pea plants, the F_2 generation, by crossing the F_1 generation. Mendel saw that some short pea plants showed up in the F_2 generation. The Punnett square in Figure 10.1.3 shows Mendel's results. Three dominant allele plants showed up for every one recessive allele plant. In other words, for every three tall plants, there was one short plant. Mendel wrote this ratio as 3:1. Figure 10.1.3 sums up the results of Mendel's experiments.

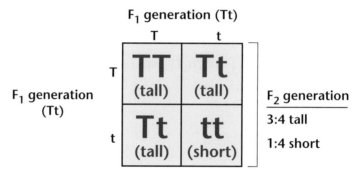

Figure 10.1.3 *This Punnett square shows Mendel's F_2 generation.*

In Mendel's dihybrid crosses, the F_2 generation results were always the same. He always got the ratio 9:3:3:1. For example, he made dihybrid crosses for seed color and shape. He always got nine yellow round seeds, three yellow wrinkled seeds, three green round seeds, and one green-wrinkled seed.

Link to ➤➤➤

Chemistry

Many genetic disorders are caused by a mistake in a chemical pathway. For example, a missing enzyme causes a rare genetic disorder called phenylketonuria (PKU). The enzyme breaks down phenylalanine, an amino acid. Without the enzyme, brain damage occurs. Babies with PKU can be identified at birth and placed on a low-phenylalanine diet. Foods high in phenylalanine include milk and eggs.

Word Bank

monohybrid
crosses

F$_2$

homozygous

F$_1$

On a sheet of paper, write the word or words from the Word Bank that complete each sentence correctly.

1. Recessive genes can be hidden in the _____ generation, but can reappear in the _____ generation.

2. If genes come together with the same alleles, they are _____.

3. To study a single trait, Mendel carried out _____.

Critical Thinking

On a sheet of paper, write the answers to the following questions. Use complete sentences.

4. What are true-breeding plants?

5. In each generation, Mendel counted the number of pea plants having each trait form. Why was this important?

Math Tip

To find the probability in Step 4 of Express Lab 10, multiply 0.5 by 0.5.

Express Lab 10

Materials
◆ safety goggles
◆ 2 coins

Procedure
1. Put on safety goggles.

2. Probability is the likelihood that a specific event will occur. Toss a coin into the air. What is the probability that the coin will land head up? Tail up?

3. Toss the second coin. Does the way that the first coin landed affect how the second coin landed?

4. What is the probability that both coins will land head up? To find out, multiply the separate probabilities of each event.

Analysis
1. How is each coin toss similar to an allele?

2. How can you use a Punnett square to show your results?

Objectives

After reading this lesson, you should be able to

◆ compare dominant and recessive alleles

◆ describe how alleles work together

◆ relate the influence of the environment on traits

◆ explain linked genes

Genetics
The study of heredity

Simple dominance
One allele is dominant to a recessive allele

Genotype
An organism's combination of genes for a trait

Phenotype
An organism's appearance as a result of its combination of genes

Pairs of alleles come together during fertilization of a female gamete by a male gamete. As the zygote develops, the pairs of alleles are copied many times. Pairs of alleles exist in all cells except haploid gametes. Pairs of alleles work together in different ways. Some pairs behave differently from other pairs.

Simple Dominance

Let's look at how different alleles are created. Over time, DNA changes. Recall that genes make up chromosomes, which are sections of DNA. When the gene for a certain trait changes, it may produce a change in the form of that trait. The new form may help the organism survive better. If the organism reproduces, it will pass the new gene and allele to its offspring. Even if the allele does not help survival, it will still pass on the new trait form to its offspring.

Genetics is the study of DNA changes and how genes are passed through generations. Genetics is the study of heredity.

The most common relationship among alleles is **simple dominance.** In simple dominance, one allele is dominant to a recessive allele. When two dominant alleles come together in a homozygous pair, the dominant trait shows. When two recessive alleles come together in a homozygous pair, the recessive form of the trait shows. What happens when a dominant allele and a recessive allele come together in a heterozygous pair? The dominant form of the trait shows. Many human genes have simple dominance.

Genotypes and Phenotypes

An organism's combination of genes for a trait is called its **genotype.** The genotype of Mendel's F_1 pea plants was *Tt*. These plants were tall. What an organism looks like as a result of its genes is its **phenotype.** An organism has both a genotype and a phenotype for all traits.

Determining Unknown Genotypes

How can scientists tell if an organism with a dominant form of a trait has homozygous or heterozygous allele pairs? They perform a **testcross.** In a testcross, an individual of unknown genotype, but dominant phenotype, is bred with a homozygous recessive individual. The appearance of the offspring from the testcross will indicate the genotype of the unknown parent. A testcross relies on simple dominance.

Other Allele Relationships

Less common relationships also exist among alleles. Some genes have **multiple alleles.** A multiple allele is a genetic trait with more than two alleles. An example of a multiple allele is human blood type. As seen in Figure 10.2.1, people have A, B, AB, or O blood type.

These blood types are created by three different alleles: A, B, and O. The A and B alleles are dominant. The O allele is recessive. A person with blood type A has two A alleles or an A allele and an O allele. A person with blood type B has two B alleles or a B allele and an O allele. A person with blood type O has two O alleles.

Testcross

A test that determines an unknown genotype of an organism by crossing it with a homozygous recessive organism

Multiple allele

One of more than two forms of a gene

Link to ≫≫≫

Environmental Science

Changes in global temperature can change the way a trait appears. For example, in some rabbits a black coat is controlled by an enzyme. This enzyme is active only at low temperatures. In temperate climates, most rabbits are mostly white. Only the cooler regions of the body—the tips of the feet, tail, ears, and nose—are black.

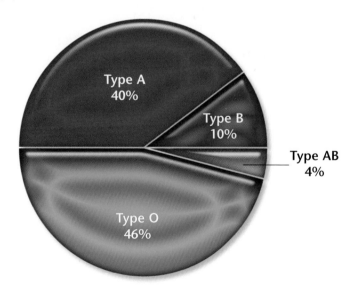

Type A
40%

Type B
10%

Type AB
4%

Type O
46%

Figure 10.2.1 *There are four blood types in the United States.*

People with blood type AB have both an A and B allele. Both alleles display their trait form. The two alleles have **codominance.** Codominance is when two different alleles come together and both show their trait form.

Another relationship between alleles is **incomplete dominance.** In heterozygous pairs, the dominant allele usually hides the recessive allele. In incomplete dominance, the dominant and recessive alleles work together. These create a trait form that is between the dominant and recessive trait forms. For example, red is a dominant color in snapdragon flowers. White is a recessive color. The heterozygous pair produces pink flowers. Pink is between the dominant red and recessive white.

In **pleiotropy,** one gene affects many traits. An example of pleiotropy is a genetic disease called **sickle-cell disease.** A different allele for a protein in red blood cells causes sickle-cell disease. Look at Figure 10.2.2. The gene that affects the protein also affects cell shape. This causes red blood cells to become sickle shaped. Sickle-shaped red blood cells have difficulty passing through small blood vessels. Less blood reaches the body. Tissue that does not receive normal blood flow becomes damaged.

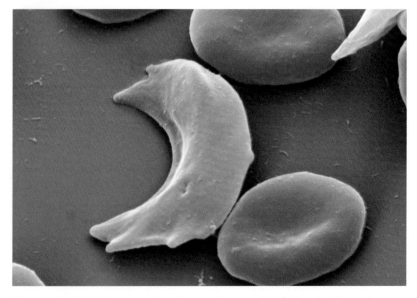

Figure 10.2.2 *Compare the shape of normal red blood cells and sickle-shaped red blood cells.*

Polygenic trait

A trait controlled by two or more genes

Linked gene

A gene close to another gene on a chromosome, causing their alleles to be inherited together

Linkage map

A map that shows distances between linked genes on a chromosome

A trait controlled by two or more genes is called a **polygenic trait.** Examples of human polygenic traits are eye color, skin color, and height. Many genes are involved in polygenic traits.

Linked Genes

When genes are on separate chromosomes, they sort independently during meiosis. **Linked genes** located on the same chromosomes tend to be inherited together. They tend to stay together during meiosis. Sometimes, the alleles of linked genes are separated. Scientists count the number of separations in a group of organisms. Then they create a **linkage map** of the separations. A linkage map tells the distance between different genes on the same chromosome.

The Role of Genetics and Environment

When scientists study traits of organisms, they look at genes and the environment. All organisms live in a unique environment. Environmental factors often play an important role in developing genes or alleles. For example, several genes affect the color of human skin. However, skin color can change based on how much sunlight it absorbs. Traits of all organisms are affected by the organisms' environment. Traits are also affected by organisms' inherited genes.

Science Myth

Myth: Probability indicates the actual outcome of a genetic cross.

Fact: Probability is the likelihood that a specific event will happen. Probabilities are used only to predict the possible outcome of a genetic cross.

❀ ❀

Technology and Society

The blood of people with hemophilia lacks a substance that allows it to clot. In the most common form of hemophilia, the missing clotting factor is called factor VIII, or antihemophilic globulin (AHG). To treat hemophilia, physicians give people clotting factors. The clotting factors come from donated human blood. To prevent blood-borne diseases, clotting factors are heated.

Biology in Your Life

Technology:
Genetic Testing

Genetic testing is the process of examining a person's DNA to search for a disease or a disorder. Some genetic tests looks for large evidence. This includes a missing or extra chromosome or piece of a chromosome. Other tests look for smaller evidence. This includes an extra or missing base in a gene.

Many genetic tests look for inherited disorders that appear in families. Testing can reveal if a person is a carrier for genetic diseases such as cystic fibrosis or Tay-Sachs. A carrier is an organism that carries an allele, but does not show the effects of the allele. Cystic fibrosis is an inherited disease that affects sodium in the body. It causes respiratory and digestive problems. Tay-Sachs disease is fatal. Harmful amounts of a fatty substance collect in the brain's nerve cells.

Both parents must be carriers to have a child with cystic fibrosis or Tay-Sachs. People with a family history of these and other genetic disorders can be tested before deciding to have children.

Scientists have developed genetic tests for several types of cancer that show up in families. Most forms of breast and colon cancer are not inherited. However, a small number of people carry an allele that greatly increases their risk. For these persons, a genetic test shows if they need regular screenings for cancer.

1. What is genetic testing?

2. When might people want to know if they are carriers for cystic fibrosis or Tay-Sachs?

3. Why is it helpful for people to know if they have an allele for an inherited type of cancer?

On a sheet of paper, write the word from the Word Bank that completes each statement correctly.

1. In simple dominance, one allele is _____ to its _____ allele.

2. What an organism looks like as a result of its genes is its _____.

3. Two alleles have _____ when both produce their trait.

On a sheet of paper, write the letter of the answer that completes each sentence correctly.

4. In AB blood, the A and the B alleles have _____.

   A simple dominance   **C** codominance

   B pleiotrophy   **D** incomplete dominance

5. To perform a testcross, scientists cross an organism with an unknown genotype with a _____ organism.

   A homozygous recessive   **B** heterozygous

   C homozygous dominant   **D** true-breeding

6. A ratio of 3 tall plants to 1 short plant suggests that _____.

   A height is controlled by pleiotropic alleles

   B tall is dominant and short is recessive

   C short is dominant and tall is recessive

   D the alleles for height are codominant

Research and Write

Use the Internet and print resources to write a report on Manx cats. Manx cats do not have a tail. Explain how not having a tail in these cats is controlled by a deadly allele.

Critical Thinking

On a sheet of paper, write the answers to the following questions. Use complete sentences.

7. Why are linked genes often inherited together?

8. How is a linkage map created?

9. Explain the inheritance of blood type in humans.

10. Describe an example of a polygenic trait in humans.

Materials
◆ paper
◆ pencil

Using Punnett Squares

A Punnett square is a tool used to predict the possible offspring of a cross. In a Punnett square, a capital letter stands for a dominant allele. A lowercase letter stands for a recessive allele. Each parent carries two alleles. If the parent is true breeding, the alleles are the same. In this investigation, you will use Punnett squares to predict the offspring of genetic crosses.

Procedure

1. In pea plants, a flower color of purple is dominant over the color white. Use capital P to stand for the allele for purple. Use a lowercase p to stand for the allele for white. In his experiments, Mendel crossed a true-breeding purple-flowering plant with a true-breeding white-flowering plant. On a sheet of paper, write the symbols for these two parental (P-generation) plants.

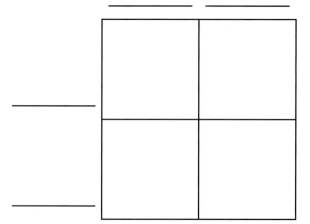

2. Draw a Punnett square like the one shown on page 290. Separate and write each of the alleles from one parent in the indicated spaces along the top. Separate and write each allele from the other parent along the side. Fill in the four boxes in the Punnett square. Each box shows the F_1 combination of the allele from one parent (along the top) with the allele from the other parent (along the side).

3. Draw a new Punnett square. Cross two F_1 plants with each other. The new Punnett square will show the resulting F_2 individuals.

Analysis

1. What allele combinations and flower colors are possible among the F_1 plants?

2. What allele combinations are possible among the F_2 plants? What flower colors are possible? Write the ratios of combinations and flower colors in this generation.

Conclusions

1. Why did Mendel use true-breeding plants for each parental cross?

2. Write a new question about genetic crosses that you could explore in another investigation.

Explore Further

Use the procedure above to show the offspring of a dihybrid cross.

Objectives

After reading this lesson, you should be able to

◆ describe how an organism's sex is determined

◆ compare different types of sex chromosomes

◆ explain how sex-linked traits are inherited

Sex chromosome

A chromosome that determines the sex of an organism

Autosome

A chromosome other than a sex chromosome

An important trait in an organism is its sex, whether it is male or female. Chromosomes other than **sex chromosomes** are called **autosomes.** Sex chromosomes determine the sex of an organism. Recall that all organisms have two sex chromosomes in each cell, except for gamete cells. Only one sex chromosome is present in gamete cells. The types of sex chromosomes that pair up determine the sex of an organism.

Determining the Sex of an Organism

Humans have two types of sex chromosomes, X and Y. A human zygote with two X chromosomes (XX) is female. A human zygote with an X and a Y chromosome (XY) is male. During meiosis, the sex chromosomes separate. The sex chromosomes that pair in fertilization depend on the sex chromosomes in the gametes.

The sex of an organism depends on the Y chromosome. If a Y chromosome is present, the zygote becomes male. It produces certain chemicals found in males. If a Y chromosome is not present, the zygote becomes female. It produces certain chemicals found in females. The Punnett square in Figure 10.3.1 shows a 50 percent chance of producing either a female or male offspring.

Female parent

	X	X
X	XX (female)	XX (female)
Y	XY (male)	XY (male)

Male parent

Figure 10.3.1 *Human sex chromosomes determine the sex of an offspring. The chance of producing either a female (XX) or male (XY) is 50 percent.*

Some human females and males have an extra X chromosome. Some human males have an extra Y chromosome. The extra chromosome comes from an error during meiosis in one of their parent cells.

Sex chromosomes of many organisms follow this XY pattern. Other patterns also determine sex. In many insect species, only the X sex chromosome exists. Males have one X chromosome. Females have two X chromosomes. Other species have the ZW sex chromosome system. In this system, male organisms have two Z sex chromosomes (ZZ). Females have Z and W chromosomes (ZW).

Genetic Disorders

Sex chromosomes carry many genes in their DNA. Not all of these genes are involved in deciding sex. An organism's sex chromosomes determine **sex-linked traits.** This is true in people, especially for the X chromosome. The X chromosome contains genes important for other functions. Genes on the X chromosome may control genetic diseases such as **hemophilia.** People with hemophilia have blood that does not clot. Because the gene involved in hemophilia is sex-linked, it is inherited differently in males and females.

Every person gets an X chromosome from her or his mother. The mother only has an X sex chromosome in her gametes. The father's gametes can have an X or a Y chromosome. The sex of an offspring depends on which chromosome is present in the sperm that fertilizes the egg. The inheritance of sex-linked traits is also controlled by the pairing of sex chromosomes.

Let's look at hemophilia. Its allele is on the X chromosome. The allele for hemophilia is recessive. A mother with hemophilia carries two alleles for hemophilia. Any X chromosome she passes on will have the hemophiliac allele. This means a son will receive the hemophiliac allele and have hemophilia. Any daughters may or may not have hemophilia. This depends on if the father's X chromosome has the hemophilia allele.

Carrier

An organism that carries an allele but does not show the effects of the allele

Daughters with normal blood can have two normal alleles or one normal and one hemophiliac allele. A **carrier** is an organism that carries an allele but does not show the effects of the allele. For any disorder, a human carrier has one dominant normal allele and one recessive allele. Carriers pass these alleles to offspring. For hemophilia, if a father has a normal allele, the daughter will be a carrier. If a father has the hemophiliac allele, the daughter will have hemophilia.

Sex-Linked Inheritance

In the early 1900s, an American scientist named Thomas Morgan studied chromosomes and genes. He used fruit flies because their cells have four pairs of chromosomes. The chromosomes are large and easy to see under a microscope. He also used fruit flies because they reproduce quickly. It is easy to tell the male fruit fly from the female.

▼◀▲▼◀▲▼◀▲▼◀▲▼◀▲▼◀▲▼◀▲▼◀▲▼◀▲▼◀▲▼◀▲▼

Science at Work

Genetic Counselor

Genetic counselors help people understand the chances of inheriting a genetic disease. Many people who see genetic counselors have a family history of an inherited disease or disorder. A genetic counselor can help them understand medical information about inherited diseases.

Genetic counselors are members of a team of health professionals. They work with physicians, nurses, dieticians, social workers, and lab technicians. Most genetic counselors work in university medical centers or private hospitals.

Genetic counselors enjoy helping people and working as part of a team. They need experience in biology, nursing, genetics, public health, or psychology. Any jobs require graduate degrees in medical genetics and counseling.

Sex-linked inheritance

The passing on of traits with genes located on the X chromosome

Fruit flies usually have red eyes. Morgan noticed that one male fruit fly had white eyes. To produce an F_1 generation, he mated the white-eyed male with a red-eyed female. All offspring had red eyes. Morgan concluded that the allele for red eyes was dominant in fruit flies.

Morgan mated the flies from the F_1 generation to produce an F_2 generation. Some offspring had red eyes and some had white eyes. All white-eyed flies were males. None of the females had white eyes. Morgan concluded that eye color in fruit flies is a sex-linked trait.

Morgan showed that the father plays an important role in determining the sex-linked traits of offspring. The father shares the one copy of his X chromosome. A disorder allele on his X chromosome is passed to all of his daughters. The father is the only source of Y chromosomes for his sons. **Sex-linked inheritance** has special patterns. The genes on one chromosome may or may not be found on the other chromosome. Sex-linked inheritance is the passing on of traits with genes located on the X chromosome.

The Punnett squares in Figure 10.3.2 show Morgan's results. Notice that only the X chromosome carries a gene for eye color. The genotypes $X_R X_R$ and $X_R X_r$ represent a red-eyed female fly. The genotype $X_R Y$ represents a red-eyed male. White-eyed males have the genotype $X_r Y$.

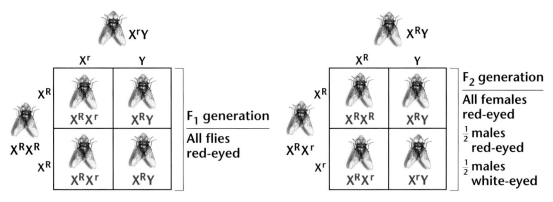

Figure 10.3.2 *These Punnett squares show the results of Morgan's experiment with fruit flies.*

Lesson 3 REVIEW

Word Bank

autosome

sperm

Y

On a sheet of paper, write the word or letter from the Word Bank that completes each sentence correctly.

1. A(n) _____ is a chromosome other than a sex chromosome.

2. A sex-linked gene is found on the _____ chromosome.

3. The sex of an offspring depends on the _____.

Critical Thinking

On a sheet of paper, write the answers to the following questions. Use complete sentences.

4. A man cannot be a carrier for hemophilia. Why.

5. Why do sex-linked disorders usually occur in men?

★ ★

Achievements in Science

Discovering Genes for Genetic Diseases

Hard work and new ideas help researchers find disease-causing genes. For example, in 1979, Dr. Nancy Wexler studied families in Venezuela where Huntington's disease was common. This genetic disease destroys the nervous system. She collected family information and blood samples from thousands of people. She then traced the inheritance of Huntington's disease.

Based on Wexler's data, scientists found the Huntington's gene in 1993. An error in the gene causes it to make a defective protein. This protein builds up in the brain, resulting in death.

Finding a gene is often the first step toward finding a cure. Genomics is the development of new treatments based on an organism's genes.

In 1996, Dr. Kári Stefánsson began a genomics project. He collected modern disease information and genetic data. He also studied historical records from over a thousand years ago. Stefánsson identified parts of genes shared by related people and some disease-causing genes. Based on his data, scientists can now find treatments and cures for some diseases.

DISCOVERY INVESTIGATION 10

Interpreting Pedigrees

A pedigree is a chart that traces a family's genetic history for a certain trait. In this lab, you will learn how to interpret a pedigree.

Procedure

1. On a sheet of paper, copy the pedigree shown below. Circles represent females. Squares represent males. A horizontal line between a male and a female represents marriage. A vertical line that comes down from a married couple leads to their children. A Roman numeral indicates each generation.

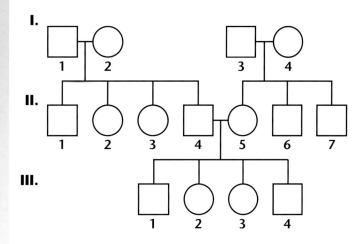

2. Read the following information. It applies to the pedigree on page 297.

- Attached earlobes are attached to the side of the head. Free earlobes are not attached to the side of the head. Persons I-3 and I-4 have free earlobes. So does their son, II-7. Their daughter, II-5, and son, II-6, have attached earlobes. Their daughter's husband, II-4, also has attached earlobes.

- Person I-1 has type A blood. His wife, I-2, has type B blood. They have four children: son II-1 (type O), daughter II-2 (type AB), daughter II-3 (type A), and son II-4 (type B).

3. Write a procedure describing how you could determine the possible phenotypes and genotypes of the Generation III individuals.

4. Have your procedure approved by your teacher. Write the possible phenotypes and genotypes for Generation III.

Analysis

1. Write the phenotypes and genotypes of the persons described in Step 2.

2. Which two persons are adopted?

Conclusions

1. Is either the earlobe trait or blood type trait a sex-linked trait? Explain your answer.

2. What are the possible phenotypes and genotypes for Generation III?

Explore Further

How can a pedigree reveal a child's risk of inheriting a genetic disease?

Karyotyping

A karyotype is a picture of the chromosomes from an individual cell. In the 1920s, scientists prepared a karyotype to show the four chromosomes of the fruit fly. In the mid-1950s, scientists determined that humans have 46 chromosomes.

To prepare a karyotype, a tissue sample (usually blood) is obtained from the organism. Then researchers add a substance to the blood sample to start cell division. This is done because chromosomes are only visible when a cell is undergoing mitosis or meiosis.

Researchers then add a chemical to stop the dividing cells at metaphase. Then they treat the cells with a solution that causes them to swell. The cells are placed on microscope slides.

Next, researchers stain the cells with dyes to create banding patterns in each chromosome. Because the banding patterns are unique, researchers can recognize each chromosome.

Finally, researchers photograph the chromosomes. They cut out the photos and arrange them in pairs according to size.

Researchers can identify genetic disorders with karyotypes. Humans usually have 22 pairs of autosomes and one pair of sex chromosomes. A karyotype can show an abnormal chromosome number. Researchers also spot missing or extra material within a chromosome.

1. What are the steps to prepare a karyotype?

2. Why are dividing cells used for karyotyping?

3. Why do researchers use karyotypes?

Chapter 10 SUMMARY

- Scientist Gregor Mendel studied the inheritance of genetic traits by working with garden peas. Mendel summed up his work in two laws.

- The law of segregation states that an organism has two genes for each trait, one from each parent. The two genes separate during meiosis and come back together in fertilization.

- The law of independent assortment states that alleles separate independently of each other in meiosis.

- A genotype is an organism's combination of genes for a given trait. A phenotype is the appearance that results from the genotype.

- Multiple alleles occur when more than two alleles govern a genetic trait.

- In simple dominance, one allele is dominant to a recessive allele.

- In codominance, both alleles display their form of the trait. In incomplete dominance, both alleles work together to create a new form of the trait.

- Two or more pairs of genes at the same time determine a polygenic trait.

- Sex chromosomes determine the sex of an organism. All other chromosomes are autosomes.

- A human male has an X and a Y sex chromosome. A human female has two X chromosomes.

- A carrier is an organism that carries an allele but does not show the effects of the allele.

- Genes found on the X chromosome are called sex-linked genes.

- Human females can carry a sex-linked trait. Males who inherit a sex-linked allele will show it. Females must have two copies of a sex-linked allele to show it.

Vocabulary

allele, 279
autosome, 292
carrier, 294
codominance, 286
cross-fertilization, 278
dihybrid cross, 280
dominant gene, 279
F_1 generation, 279
F_2 generation, 279
genetics, 284

genotype, 284
hemophilia, 293
heredity, 278
heterozygous, 280
homozygous, 280
hybrid, 279
incomplete dominance, 286
law of independent assortment, 281

law of segregation, 280
linkage map, 287
linked gene, 287
monohybrid cross, 279
multiple allele, 285
P generation, 279
phenotype, 284
pleiotropy, 286
pollen, 278
polygenic trait, 287

Punnett square, 281
recessive gene, 279
sex chromosome, 292
sex-linked inheritance, 295
sex-linked trait, 293
sickle-cell disease, 286
simple dominance, 284
testcross, 285
trait, 278

Chapter 10 R E V I E W

Vocabulary Review

On a sheet of paper, write the word or words from the Word Bank that complete each sentence correctly.

Word Bank

allele
carrier
codominance
dihybrid cross
F_1 generation
F_2 generation
genotype
heredity
heterozygous
homozygous
hybrid
incomplete dominance
law of independent assortment
law of segregation
monohybrid cross
multiple allele
P generation
phenotype
Punnett square
recessive gene
sex chromosome
sex-linked trait

1. The study of how traits are passed through generations is called _____.

2. A(n) _____ involves parents that differ in only one trait. A(n) _____ follows the inheritance of two traits.

3. The original pair of individuals involved in a cross is called the _____.

4. Each different form of the same gene is called a(n) _____.

5. The _____ are the offspring of the original organisms involved in a cross. When this second generation of individuals produces offspring, the new generation is the _____.

6. A(n) _____ will be hidden unless the individual is homozygous.

7. The _____ states that an organism has two alleles for each trait, one from each parent, which come together during fertilization.

8. A(n) _____ is the product of gametes from two different sources.

9. A(n) _____ is the physical form of a trait produced in an organism. A(n) _____ is an organism's combination of genes for a certain trait.

10. According to the _____, alleles separate independently of each other during meiosis.

Review continued on next page

11. If both alleles of a gene are the same, the gene is _____. If both alleles of a gene are different, the organism is _____.

12. A trait controlled by a(n) _____ has more than two alleles for that gene.

13. When two different alleles come together and both produce their form of the trait, that pair of alleles is in _____.

14. A(n) _____ is a tool used to predict the possible results of a genetic cross.

15. When a trait is controlled by _____, the resulting form is between the dominant and recessive form.

16. A trait determined by the X or Y chromosome is a(n) _____.

17. A(n) _____ determines whether an individual is male or female.

18. For a recessive genetic disorder, a(n) _____ has one dominant normal allele and one recessive allele.

Concept Review

On a sheet of paper, write the letter of the answer that completes each sentence correctly.

19. Recessive traits often reappear in _____.

   A the parental generation   **C** the F_2 generation

   B the F_1 generation   **D** heterozygous individuals

20. A(n) _____ shows the distances between genes located on the same chromosome.

   A pedigree   **C** dihybrid cross

   B linkage map   **D** Punnett square

21. A carrier can transmit a genetic disorder when they pass on _____.

    A one dominant normal allele

    B one recessive abnormal allele

    C one dominant abnormal allele

    D one recessive normal allele

Critical Thinking

On a sheet of paper, write the answers to the following questions. Use complete sentences.

22. In Mendel's studies, why did one form of a trait seem to disappear?

23. How can a testcross determine the unknown genotype of an organism?

24. How can you tell if the inheritance of a trait is sex-linked?

25. A scientist crossed a red-eyed female fruit fly with a white-eyed male fruit fly. All F_1 offspring had red eyes. Then the scientist bred the F_1 flies to create an F_2 generation. All F_2 females were red-eyed. One-half of the F_2 males were red-eyed. One-half were white-eyed. Why were none of the F_2 females white-eyed?

Research and Write

With a partner, prepare a report on Tay-Sachs disease. In addition to using the Internet and the library, interview a doctor or other healthcare professional. Describe the cause of the disease. Explain why it is more common in certain populations.

Test-Taking Tip Answer all questions you are sure of first. Then go back and answer the others.

11 Genetic Information Cycles

Genes that produce traits are part of DNA. Scientists can determine much of the information that DNA stores. Lab images of DNA show patterns of dark and light bands like the ones in the photograph. By interpreting these patterns, scientists have made maps of the genes in chromosomes for many living things. In Chapter 11, you will learn about DNA and how it transmits genetic information. You will find out how scientists use knowledge of DNA to understand and treat certain diseases.

Organize Your Thoughts

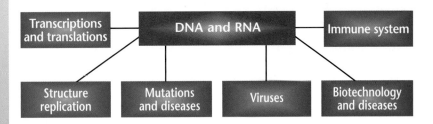

Goals for Learning

◆ To describe the structure and function of DNA

◆ To identify that viruses are special pieces of DNA

◆ To explain some changes in DNA that can lead to health problems

◆ To explain that organisms have systems to fight diseases

Sugar-phosphate backbone

The negatively charged backbone of a nucleic acid strand

Nitrogenous base

A nitrogen-containing molecule attached to a nucleotide

Guanine (G)

A double-ringed nitrogenous base found in DNA and RNA

As you know, traits are inherited from parents through the activities of chromosomes in cells. A trait is a characteristic of an organism. DNA stores information about an organism's traits. Recall that chromosomes are sections of DNA. Chromosomes contain genes for traits. An allele is one of several forms that a particular gene can take. Alleles differ slightly in their molecular structure. These slight differences determine the traits that an organism inherits. DNA stores the genetic information of an organism.

The Parts of DNA

To understand how DNA instructs life, let's look at the parts of DNA. Remember that DNA is a nucleic acid. It is made up of many smaller molecules called nucleotides. Nucleotides have three parts. One part is a sugar molecule. DNA has the sugar deoxyribose. RNA, the other nucleic acid, has the sugar ribose. Both sugar molecules have five carbon atoms along with oxygen and hydrogen atoms.

Nucleotides also have a phosphate group. This group is important for creating nucleic acid strands. The phosphate group of one nucleotide forms a covalent bond with the sugar of another nucleotide. The repeating pattern of bonded nucleotides forms a long strand called a **sugar-phosphate backbone.** The phosphate groups are negatively charged. This causes the nucleic acid strand to have a negative charge.

Nucleotides also have a **nitrogenous base.** The nitrogenous base is a molecule made of carbon, nitrogen, hydrogen, and oxygen. It is attached to the sugar of the nucleotide. Study the base structures in Figure 11.1.1. The double-ringed bases are adenine (A) and **guanine (G).** The single-ringed bases are **thymine (T), cytosine (C),** and **uracil (U).** DNA nucleotides have a phosphate group, deoxyribose, and A, G, C, or T. RNA nucleotides have a phosphate group, ribose, and A, G, C, or U.

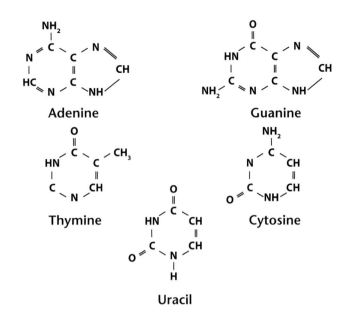

Thymine (T)

A single-ringed nitrogenous base found in DNA

Cytosine (C)

A single-ringed nitrogenous base found in DNA and RNA

Uracil (U)

A single-ringed nitrogenous base found only in RNA

Figure 11.1.1 *There are five nitrogenous bases found in DNA and RNA.*

James Watson and Francis Crick used tin and wire to make DNA models. Their research earned them the Nobel Prize.

Research and Write

Prepare a report on the research of Rosalind Franklin. Describe how her X-ray studies of DNA helped Watson and Crick discover its structure.

The Discovery of DNA's Structure

For many years, scientists wanted to know the structure of DNA. In 1949, Austrian scientist Erwin Chargraff researched the DNA of many organisms. He found the amount of adenine always equaled the amount of thymine. He also found that the amount of guanine always equaled the amount of cytosine.

In the early 1950s, British scientists Rosalind Franklin and Maurice Wilkins took X-ray photographs of DNA. Their photographs did not show details of the structure. However, they did show that the shape of DNA was a helix.

Meanwhile, British scientists James Watson and Francis Crick were also trying to determine the structure of DNA. They built many models. None worked. Then they saw one of Franklin's X-ray photographs. Using this photograph, Watson and Crick created a new model of DNA. Their model was two strands of nucleotides that wound around each other. The strands formed a double helix. A double helix is a twisted shape like a spiral staircase. Watson and Crick put the sugar-phosphate backbone on the outside of the double helix. They put the nitrogenous bases on the inside.

Watson and Crick thought the nitrogenous bases on one strand formed hydrogen bonds with nitrogenous bases on the other strand. The hydrogen bonds kept the two strands of nucleotides the same distance apart. Watson and Crick wondered how the bases were paired between the two strands. They knew the pairings were due to the size of the bases and the forming of hydrogen bonds.

Watson and Crick turned to Chargraff's discovery. They found that the nitrogenous bases follow a pattern called **complementary base pairing.** Each base always pairs with its complement base. Adenine in one strand always pairs with thymine in the other strand. Guanine always pairs with cytosine. The pairing of a single-ringed base with a double-ringed base maintains the same distance between strands. The sequence of nucleotides along the length of each DNA strand can vary. Watson and Crick published their model in 1953. It was a milestone in biology.

Express Lab 11

Materials
- ◆ paper
- ◆ pen

Procedure
Erwin Chargraff analyzed the amounts of nitrogenous bases in the DNA of various organisms. Some of his results are shown in the table below.

Analysis
1. Which nitrogenous bases are single-ringed bases? Which are double-ringed bases?

2. How do Chargraff's results vary? What do his results suggest about DNA?

Organism	Adenine	Guanine	Cytosine	Thymine
Human	30.4%	19.6%	19.9%	30.1%
Ox	29.0%	21.2%	21.2%	28.7%
Sea urchin	32.8%	17.7%	17.3%	32.1%

On a sheet of paper, write the word or words in parentheses that complete each statement correctly.

1. DNA contains the sugar _____ (deoxyribose, ribose, guanine), and RNA contains the sugar _____ (guanine, deoxyribose, ribose).

2. Complementary pairing of _____ (phosphate groups, nitrogenous bases, sugars) ensures that the strands of DNA maintain an even distance.

3. In DNA, adenine pairs with _____ (thymine, ribose, cytosine) guanine pairs with _____ (thymine, guanine, cytosine).

On a sheet of paper, write the letter of the answer that completes each sentence correctly.

4. In RNA, the base _____ replaces thymine.

   A uracil   **B** guanine   **C** adenine   **D** cytosine

5. A molecule of DNA contains two _____.

   A phosphate groups   **C** sugar molecules

   B nitrogenous bases   **D** nucleotide chains

6. A nucleotide contains each of the following except a(n) _____.

   A nitrogenous base   **C** amino acid

   B sugar molecule   **D** phosphate group

Critical Thinking

On a sheet of paper, write the answers to the following questions. Use complete sentences.

7. What is the role of nucleotides in DNA structure?

8. Explain how DNA resembles a twisted ladder.

9. What is complementary base pairing?

10. How did the work of other scientists help Watson and Crick determine the structure of DNA?

Replication
The process DNA uses to copy itself

Bacteriophage
A virus that infects bacteria

Virus
A type of germ that is not living

Marker
A material, such as an atom, used to mark an item

Semi-conservative replication
A model of DNA replication in which an old strand of DNA is used to make a new strand of DNA

The process of copying DNA in a cell is called **replication.** Scientists discovered this process in the 1950s.

The Experiments of Hershey and Chase

How did scientists learn that DNA transferred information from parents to offspring? Until the 1950s, some scientists thought proteins were the genetic material. Other scientists thought that DNA was the genetic material.

To find out, American scientists Alfred Hershey and Martha Chase ran experiments in 1952. They used **bacteriophages** containing both DNA and protein. Bacteriophages are **viruses** that infect bacteria. You will learn more about viruses in Lesson 4.

Hershey and Chase put special atoms called **markers** into the DNA and protein of the viruses. The markers identified the DNA and the protein. Viruses with the marked atoms infected bacteria. The bacteria reproduced. The offspring bacteria had DNA and proteins. However, only the DNA contained markers. The experiments of Hershey and Chase showed that DNA passed from parent to offspring.

DNA as a Template

Scientists wondered how instructions in DNA were passed from parents to offspring. Watson and Crick thought that complementary base pairing was important. Recall that complementary base pairing in DNA is the matching of single-ringed bases with double-ringed bases.

American scientists Matthew Meselson and Franklin Stahl proved this theory during 1957 and 1958. They also showed that DNA is copied through **semi-conservative replication.** In this process, the original molecule serves as a **template** for making new DNA molecules. A template is a pattern used for copying.

Template

A pattern used for copying

Origin of replication

A site where DNA replication begins

Replication bubble

An area in which DNA replication is occurring with both strands unwound and being used as templates

Replication fork

The end of a replication bubble in which DNA polymerase is actively adding nucleotide bases to a new strand

DNA polymerase

An enzyme that adds new nucleotide bases to a new strand during DNA replication

While reproducing, the double helix unwinds. The strands separate. Each old strand becomes a template for a new strand. Remember that in DNA, adenine pairs with thymine, and guanine pairs with cytosine. As new nucleotides form and bond, they make a new strand to complement the old strand.

DNA replication creates two DNA molecules from the unwound original molecule. Each new DNA molecule contains one old strand and one new strand. This makes the two DNA molecules semi-conservative. Using this method, the instructions in DNA can be copied many times.

How DNA Replicates

DNA replication begins in areas of DNA molecules called **origins of replication.** These areas have nucleotide bases arranged in certain orders called sequences. Sequences of bases are the signals for all processes involving DNA. Each molecule of DNA has several origins of replication.

Recall from Chapter 9 that chromosomes reproduce in S phase. Each chromosome is made of one piece of DNA and proteins. In S phase, the DNA molecule unwinds at each sequence. As the strands unwind, they create **replication bubbles.** Several bubbles are on every DNA molecule during replication. The bubbles grow on each side as new strands are made inside. The growing bubbles combine into larger bubbles. All the bubbles grow together and create two new molecules of DNA.

In the replication bubbles, enzymes help in DNA replication. To begin, enzymes unwind DNA at the origin of replication. This creates a small replication bubble. There is a **replication fork** on each side of the bubble. At the replication fork, new nucleotide bases attach, creating the new strand. **DNA polymerase,** an enzyme, helps bond the new nucleotides. These nucleotides are complementary to the nucleotides on the template strand.

Leading strand

The side of the replication fork where the newly made DNA is in one piece

Lagging strand

The side of the replication fork where the newly made DNA is in several small pieces

DNA ligase

An enzyme that bonds all pieces of newly made DNA to make one strand

DNA polymerase uses both old strands as templates. It bonds the phosphate group of a new nucleotide to the sugar of the last nucleotide in a growing strand. DNA polymerase adds bases in only one direction. At each replication fork, one new strand is made as one piece. This side of the fork is called the **leading strand.** The other side of the fork, called the **lagging strand,** is made from many small pieces of DNA.

As DNA polymerase adds bases, the new strand at each fork becomes longer. The replication bubbles grow and combine. **DNA ligase,** an enzyme, connects the pieces of the new DNA strand. DNA ligase makes sugar-phosphate bonds between nucleotides. When all the small pieces of DNA have been bonded together, two new DNA double helixes are created. These two new strands have the same sequence of nucleotides. Figure 11.2.1 shows DNA replication.

DNA replication occurs constantly in organisms. DNA is replicated every time a cell divides. Replication produces exact copies that are passed to new cells through mitosis or meiosis. The cycle of division, growth, and reproduction keeps life going. It allows genetic information to be passed on.

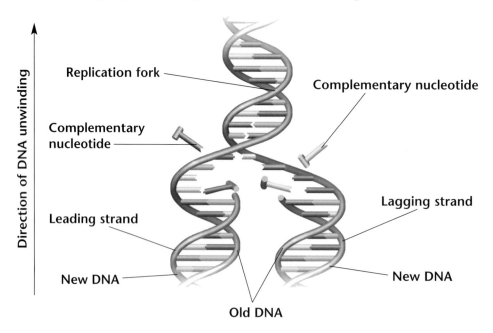

Figure 11.2.1 *DNA replication occurs constantly in organisms.*

Word Bank

DNA

DNA polymerase

viruses

On a sheet of a paper, write the word or words from the Word Bank that complete each sentence correctly.

1. During replication, an enzyme called _____ adds new nucleotide bases to the new DNA strand.

2. Experiments performed by Hershey and Chase showed that _____ is passed from parent to offspring.

3. Bacteriophages are _____ that infect bacteria.

On a sheet of paper, write the letter of the answer that completes each sentence correctly.

4. During replication, DNA _____.

   A is used to make RNA   **C** directs protein synthesis

   B remains intact   **D** is copied

5. When DNA is replicated, the original molecule serves as a(n) _____.

   A template   **B** replication fork   **C** enzyme   **D** marker

6. Before DNA replication can begin, the DNA must _____.

   A undergo translation   **C** join with a ribosome

   B unwind   **D** leave the nucleus

Critical Thinking

On a sheet of paper, write the answers to the following questions. Use complete sentences.

7. What is semi-conservative replication?

8. When does DNA replication occur?

9. What happens at a replication fork?

10. Compare and contrast the roles of DNA polymerase and DNA ligase.

Materials

- safety goggles
- lab coat or apron
- paper models for sugar, phosphate group, cytosine (C), thymine (T), adenine (A), guanine (G)
- large sheet of paper
- tape
- wooden craft sticks
- ruler

Modeling DNA

DNA is made of two strands of nucleotides arranged in the form of a double helix. Each nucleotide is made of a sugar called deoxyribose, a phosphate group, and one of four nitrogenous bases.

Procedure

1. Put on safety goggles and a lab coat or apron.

2. Place a large sheet of paper on your desk. The paper represents the width of a DNA molecule.

3. Select a model of deoxyribose and a model of a phosphate group. Position them along one side of the paper. Show how they form the sugar-phosphate backbone of one strand of the double helix. Tape them to the paper.

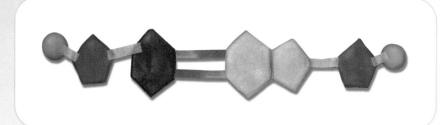

4. Select two nitrogenous bases for your first base pair. Follow the rules of complementary base pairing. Tape one base to the sugar of one strand. Tape the second base to the other sugar.

5. Position wooden craft sticks to represent hydrogen bonds between the bases. **Safety Alert: Broken craft sticks may have sharp edges. Do not use them.**

6. Select another sugar model and phosphate group model. Position them along the other side of the paper. They represent the second side of the sugar-phosphate backbone of the second strand. Be sure the sugars are directly across from each other. Then tape down the models to the paper.

7. Repeat Steps 2 through 6, adding two more nitrogenous bases to your DNA molecule.

8. Use a ruler to measure the widths of the two sets of base pairs in your model. Record your data.

Cleanup/Disposal
When you are finished, put away the tape and ruler.

Analysis
1. Are the two sets of base pairs in your model equal in width? Explain your answer.

2. Which nitrogenous bases can be correctly paired?

Conclusions
1. A DNA double helix is the same width throughout. What does this suggest about base pairing?

2. Write a new question about DNA structure that you could explore in another investigation.

Explore Further
Combine your finished model with other students' models to create a longer double helix.

Transcription

The creation of an RNA molecule using the bases in a DNA molecule as a template

Translation

The creation of a protein using the bases in an RNA molecule as a template

RNA polymerase

An enzyme that adds RNA nucleotides to a new RNA molecule

Messenger RNA (mRNA)

An RNA molecule that carries instructions for the order of amino acids in a protein

Instructions in DNA are found in the order of its nitrogenous bases. Genes are certain sequences of DNA found on the chromosomes. Bases in these sequences are a code. A cell reads the code and gives directions to make proteins. These proteins become enzymes or other structures that allow life to continue.

To read the code in DNA, a cell uses RNA, enzymes, and other molecules. Two processes happen when a cell reads the instructions in DNA: **transcription** and **translation.** Through these processes, genetic information flows from DNA to RNA to protein.

Transcription and RNA Splicing

The first step in making a protein is the reading of DNA. This step is called transcription. It happens inside the nucleus of a cell. Transcription produces complementary RNA to DNA sequences. When a cell needs to make a protein, it uses **RNA polymerase,** an enzyme. RNA polymerase helps make a molecule of **messenger RNA,** also called mRNA.

Messenger RNA helps interpret, or read, the DNA code. To make messenger RNA, RNA polymerase attaches to specific sequences called **promoters.** Promoters are located at the beginning of genes. RNA polymerase attaches to the promoter sequence on one DNA strand. The promoter sequence determines which strand goes through transcription.

After RNA polymerase attaches to the promoter sequence, it unwinds the DNA. Then it begins creating an RNA strand. RNA polymerase moves down the DNA. It brings in RNA nucleotides complementary to the DNA nucleotides. Finally, RNA polymerase comes to a **terminator** in DNA. Terminator sequences stop RNA polymerase and transcription. The new strand of mRNA is released. The new mRNA is an RNA copy of the DNA gene.

During transcription, RNA polymerase adds RNA nucleotides. Ribose is the sugar of RNA nucleotides. If a cytosine base is in the DNA nucleotide, RNA polymerase adds a nucleotide containing guanine to the new RNA. RNA polymerase adds a uracil nucleotide for every adenine nucleotide in DNA.

Cap and tail structures are then added to the ends of the new mRNA strand. It also undergoes **RNA splicing.** During this process, enzymes cut out certain parts of the mRNA strand. These parts, called **introns,** do not produce proteins. The strand parts that produce proteins are called **exons.** After these changes, mRNA leaves the nucleus.

Ribosomal RNA (rRNA) and **transfer RNA (tRNA)** are made in the nucleus by transcription of certain genes. These two RNAs are important in translation. Translation is the next step in making a protein.

Translation

Translation happens in a cell's cytoplasm. Translation produces proteins based on the sequence of nucleotide bases in mRNA. An organism's **genetic code** is found in codons. Codons are sets of three bases in mRNA. Codons can be any combination of the four RNA bases. Each combination codes for a specific amino acid. Recall that amino acids are the building blocks of proteins. The AUG codon is the start signal for translation. UAA, UAG, and UGA are the three stop codons. They signal the end of translation.

Translation uses ribosomes in the cytoplasm. Ribosomes are made of rRNA and protein. At the start of translation, the rRNA in ribosomes line up with the mRNA. The ribosome moves down the mRNA until it reaches the start codon. Then tRNAs enter the ribosome with amino acids attached.

Anticodon

A complementary three-base sequence to the codon found in tRNA

Link to >>>

Environmental Science

The sun's ultraviolet (UV) radiation can cause the joining of thymine bases in DNA. If the joined thymine bases are not fixed by repair enzymes, they interfere with DNA replication. They may cause skin cancer. The earth is protected from UV radiation by a layer of ozone molecules. The use of chemicals called CFCs has caused ozone levels to decrease.

Each tRNA has a base sequence called an **anticodon.** Anticodons are complementary to the codons in mRNA. For example, if an mRNA codon is GAU, the tRNA anticodon is CUA.

For each mRNA codon, the tRNA with the complementary anticodon binds to it. This tRNA brings an amino acid, which becomes attached to a growing protein chain. The ribosome moves down the mRNA. The ribosome trades used tRNAs for new tRNAs. The chain of amino acids grows. Finally, the ribosome reaches a stop codon. Translation stops. The amino acid chain releases and folds into a protein. The mRNA leaves the ribosome.

▼◄▲▼◄▲▼◄▲▼◄▲▼◄▲▼◄▲▼◄▲▼◄▲▼◄▲▼◄▲▼◄▲▼

Science at Work

Pharmaceutical Researcher

Pharmaceutical researchers work in teams to discover and develop new drugs. A pharmaceutical researcher may be trained as a chemist, a biologist, a virologist, or a physician. A virologist studies viruses. Scientists working to discover new drugs can identify and test molecules that could be used as a drug. After a new drug is developed, it must be tested to ensure that it is safe and effective. Pharmaceutical researchers study how the drug is absorbed and used by the body.

The growing field of genomics has increased the pace of new drug development. Genomics is uncovering new information about genes and the proteins they make. In turn, scientists are learning more about the roles of these proteins. Many pharmaceutical researchers are studying the interaction of a person's genetic makeup and his or her response to a drug.

Pharmaceutical researchers must be willing to learn new things. They must also work as team members.

Transcription and translation happen constantly inside of cells. Cells must make proteins they need, such as enzymes. An mRNA created in transcription is translated many times before it is lost. Then the genetic information cycle starts over again by creating another mRNA.

Mutations

How do genes change to make alleles? Alleles are created by **mutations.** Mutations are changes in a DNA sequence. Mutations happen for several reasons. Sometimes, DNA mutates randomly and naturally.

Mutations are also caused when mistakes happen during DNA replication and transcription. DNA polymerase usually corrects these mistakes. Another cause of mutations is **mutagens.** Mutagens are physical or chemical materials that cause changes in DNA. Mutagens include ultraviolet radiation from the sun, tar and nicotine in cigarette smoke, and X-rays.

Some mutations are harmless. Others can be harmful. Mutations can change the structure of an amino acid that becomes part of a protein. This change can cause the protein to not function.

One type of mutation is a **substitution.** Substitution occurs when one nucleotide base is replaced with another. This can change a codon structure in mRNA. As a result, a different amino acid might be built into a protein.

Deletions happen when nucleotides are removed from DNA. **Insertions** happen when extra nucleotides are added to a DNA sequence. These types of mutations can greatly change the amino acid structure of a protein.

Any of these mutations create new alleles—new forms of a gene. New alleles can cause a new phenotype to be displayed in organisms.

Lesson 3 REVIEW

Word Bank

cytoplasm

mutagen

mutations

nucleus

transcription

translation

On a sheet of paper, write the word from the Word Bank that completes each sentence correctly.

1. RNA molecules are made during _____. Proteins are made during _____.

2. Changes in the sequence of DNA are called _____. Such a change might be caused by a _____.

3. Transcription takes place in the _____. Translation occurs in the _____.

On a sheet of paper, write the letter of the answer that completes each statement correctly.

4. Molecules of mRNA and tRNA line up with the cell's _____ to begin translation.

   A DNA   **B** ribosomes   **C** nucleus   **D** cell membrane

5. Introns are removed from mRNA because they _____.

   A lack protein-making instructions

   B slow down transcription

   C are missing uracil

   D contain mutations

6. When _____ occurs, a nucleotide is removed from DNA.

   A a substitution   **C** a deletion

   B an insertion   **D** transcription

Critical Thinking

On a sheet of paper, write the answers to the following questions. Use complete sentences.

7. Compare and contrast introns and exons.

8. Why are promoters and terminators needed?

9. Describe the roles of tRNA.

10. Describe the role of rRNA.

Link to >>>

Chemistry

Chemical mutagens cause mutations. Some chemical mutagens are like normal nitrogenous bases. However, they pair incorrectly during replication. An example is 2-amino purine. This compound is similar to adenine. Other mutagens cause chemical changes in bases. This changes their pairing abilities. Nitrous acid changes cytosine to uracil, which then forms hydrogen bonds with adenine instead of guanine.

Objectives

After reading this lesson, you should be able to

◆ describe the structures of viruses

◆ compare the life cycles of viruses

◆ discuss how vaccines work

Parasite

An organism that absorbs food from a living organism and harms it

Capsid

The protein shell of a virus

Evolve

To change biologically

The path of genetic information from DNA to RNA to protein supports life. Living things use genetic information to grow, function, and reproduce. Viruses use this path only to survive. Viruses are not living and do not produce their own energy. They do not have organelles. They cannot reproduce by themselves.

Viruses are pieces of DNA or RNA wrapped in a protein shell. Viruses are cellular **parasites.** Parasites need other living things to grow and reproduce. Viruses use cells to make molecules and reproduce.

The Structure of Viruses

Viruses have two main structures. One structure is the **capsid.** It is the outside protein shell of the virus. It is made of protein and has different shapes. Some viruses have molecules on the outside of this shell to help them attach to cells.

The second structure in a virus is its genetic material. This can be DNA or RNA. The genetic material of a virus contains genes to make more viruses. Viral genetic material is smaller than cellular genetic material. Just one mutation in viral DNA can have a great effect on that virus. Viruses can quickly change, or evolve. Figure 11.4.1 shows an influenza, or flu, virus.

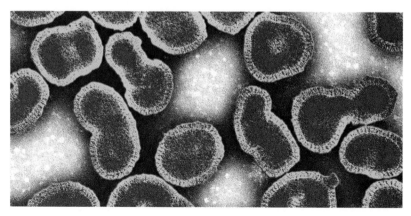

Figure 11.4.1 *This is an influenza, or flu, virus. It can be passed from person to person.*

Many viruses cause colds in people. These different viruses are almost the same except for small mutations. Doctors cannot cure colds because there are so many variations.

How Viruses Infect

Scientists group viruses by what organism they **infect,** or use for their needs. Some viruses only infect plants that have RNA. Many animal viruses infect only certain species. They do not harm other animal species. However, viruses can mutate to infect new species.

When a virus infects an organism, it attaches to the membrane of a cell, called the **host cell.** The virus opens a hole in the membrane. It pushes its genetic material inside. Once inside, two pathways are possible for the genetic material.

The first pathway is the **lytic cycle.** In this cycle, the virus uses the host to make more viruses. The host cell makes copies of the DNA or RNA and new capsid proteins. This process continues until the cell is full of viruses. Then the cell bursts open and dies. New viruses are released.

Science Myth

Myth: Antibiotics treat a cold.

Fact: Viruses cause colds. Antibiotics are effective only against bacteria. Doctors sometimes prescribe antibiotics for people with colds to treat other bacterial infections, such as strep throat. These infections sometimes occur because a cold weakens the immune system.

The second pathway is the **lysogenic cycle.** In this cycle, viral DNA hides itself in the host's DNA. Viral DNA can hide for years. If the cell undergoes stress, the viral DNA comes out and switches to the lytic cycle. Because viruses can hide, it is hard to cure a viral infection.

Vaccines

As seen in Figure 11.4.2, there are many **vaccines** available to fight viral diseases in people. By getting a vaccine, an individual introduces a virus to his or her **immune system.** The immune system is a natural defense system against disease. The immune system remembers what a virus looks like. The immune system identifies and destroys cells infected by that virus. You will learn more about the immune system in Lesson 6.

The measles vaccine and other vaccines are made from very weakened viruses. Vaccines for influenza, also called flu, and other vaccines are made from dead, whole viruses. Other vaccines are made with parts or products of a virus.

Figure 11.4.2 *This young girl is receiving a vaccine.*

Word Bank

genetic material

host cell

parasites

On a sheet of paper, write the word or words from the Word Bank that complete each sentence correctly.

1. Viruses are cellular _____, using other cells to make molecules and reproduce.

2. Viruses can be grouped according to the kind of _____ they infect.

3. When a virus invades a host cell, it pushes its _____ inside the cell.

On a sheet of paper, write the letter of the answer that completes each sentence correctly.

4. A virus contains a(n) _____.

   A type of nucleic acid   **C** nucleus

   B organelle   **D** ribosome

5. Viruses have two main structures, a(n) _____ and genetic material.

   A organelle   **C** host cell

   B vaccine   **D** capsid

6. Some vaccines are made from _____.

   A capsids   **C** RNA

   B severely weakened viruses   **D** antibiotics

Critical Thinking

On a sheet of paper, write the answers to the following questions. Use complete sentences.

7. Why are viruses nonliving?

8. Why does a vaccine work only against a specific virus?

9. Compare and contrast the lytic cycle and the lysogenic cycle.

10. Why can viruses evolve quickly?

Link to ➤➤➤

Language Arts

The word *vaccine* comes from the Latin word *vacca,* which means "cow." In 1796, British physician Edward Jenner gave the world's first vaccination. He used the harmless cowpox virus to protect people against smallpox. Cowpox virus is related to the smallpox virus. Smallpox is a deadly disease.

Objectives

After reading this lesson, you should be able to

◆ define biotechnology and how it works

◆ describe new products made through biotechnology

◆ identify medical conditions caused by changes in genetic information

◆ relate the activities of chromosomes to disease

◆ identify the genetic parts of cancer

Scientists use genetic information to help make life better. **Biotechnology** uses living organisms and their genetics to make medicines and better food crops. Biotechnology changes an organism's genetic makeup to make new molecules, such as proteins. These molecules are used to help that organism, or other organisms.

How Biotechnology Changes Genetic Makeup

How does biotechnology change genetic makeup? Scientists have figured out the DNA sequence of various simple organisms. Scientists compare these genes and their proteins to human genes and proteins. They have found many similarities, even with bacterial genes and proteins. Bacteria are valuable organisms in biotechnology.

Bacteria are simple organisms with only one chromosome. They have small rings of DNA called **plasmids.** Plasmids have few genes on them. Plasmids can be passed from one bacterium to another. **Biotechnologists** use plasmids to make new gene products.

Because bacterial DNA is simple, it can take on new genetic information easily. Biotechnologists take interesting genes and put them into bacterial DNA. First, they use enzymes called **restriction endonucleases** to cut out the gene. These enzymes recognize certain nucleotide base sequences. They break DNA molecules at that sequence.

Biotechnology

The use of organisms and their genetics in industry to make products

Plasmid

A small, circular piece of DNA, usually found in bacteria

Biotechnologist

A scientist who studies biotechnology

Biotechnologists then insert the gene into another piece of DNA, usually a plasmid. To do this, they cut the plasmid with restriction endonucleases. They mix in the desired gene. Then they use DNA ligase to bond the genetic material together. The new gene becomes part of a plasmid. Then biotechnologists put the new plasmids into bacteria. The process of adding foreign DNA to a bacterial cell is called **transformation.**

The bacteria treat the new plasmids like their own genes and make proteins from them. Biotechnologists also use the DNA of cows, pigs, and other organisms to take on new genes and make new proteins.

Improvements Through Biotechnology

Biotechnologists improve many medicines and foods. For example, biotechnologists have developed a new way to make insulin. People with diabetes do not produce enough of the protein insulin. They need insulin shots regularly. Biotechnologists have removed and copied the human insulin gene and put it into bacteria. The transformed bacteria make insulin. Most insulin used to treat diabetes is made this way.

Biotechnology has improved other medicines, such as antibiotics. Antibiotics are medicines that help people fight infection caused by bacteria.

Biotechnology has improved farming and growing crops such as cotton. Plants can take on new genetic information easily. Farmers often spray chemicals on plants to stop insects from destroying them. Some plants make these chemicals naturally. Biotechnologists put the genes of plants that make these chemicals into plants without them. Biotechnology helps more crops survive. Figure 11.5.1 shows a cotton plant that has been improved through biotechnology.

Figure 11.5.1 *Biotechnology has improved many crops, including cotton.*

Genetically modified food

A food product with genes that have been changed

Down syndrome

A medical condition caused by cells having an extra chromosome 21

Nondisjunction

Chromosomes that do not separate during anaphase, resulting in extra chromosomes in some cells

Growth factor

A protein that helps control the growth and division of cells

Scientists also have improved the flavor and freshness of fruits and vegetables through biotechnology. Food changed through biotechnology must be labeled **genetically modified food.**

Understanding the Genetics of Diseases

Knowledge of genetic information has helped scientists understand the genetics of diseases and other medical conditions. Some conditions are caused by the number of chromosomes in cells. One such condition is **Down syndrome.** People with Down syndrome have cells with three copies of chromosome 21.

Nondisjunction causes Down syndrome. Nondisjunction occurs when chromosomes do not separate during meiosis. This causes some gametes to have extra chromosomes that are passed on to offspring. Extra chromosomes give humans cells too much information. This causes conditions like Down syndrome.

Small mutations in DNA sequences for particular proteins cause many diseases. Some mutations change the amino acid order by changing or removing an amino acid. Proteins with these mutations do not function normally.

Sickle-cell disease arises from an amino acid change in the protein hemoglobin. People with sickle-cell disease have jagged and curved red blood cells. Normal red blood cells are smooth and round. Hemoglobin in red blood cells carries oxygen to other cells.

Link to ➤➤➤

Social Studies

DNA plays an important role in forensic science. Forensic science is used in the justice system, often to solve crimes. DNA analysis can help identify potential suspects whose DNA may match evidence left at a crime scene.

People with sickle-cell disease have hemoglobin that makes crystals. The crystals cause the sickle shape. One mutated nucleotide base in a gene causes the different hemoglobin.

Problems with DNA can cause cancer. Cancer starts when cells do not stop growing and dividing. This extra growth leads to tumors. Mutations in certain genes cause tumors. These genes produce **growth factor** proteins. Growth factors control when and how fast cells grow and divide. Changes in the genes for these proteins can cause them to not work or to work too much.

Much research focuses on the changes in cells that lead to cancer. Research has helped doctors determine if someone is at risk to develop cancer. People can take genetic tests to find out if they have mutations associated with most cancer.

Doctors can test people to see if they have genetic diseases. These tests look for odd DNA sequences or proteins that are not functioning. Science, including biotechnology, makes treating and curing some diseases possible.

Technology and Society

Many scientists think that a person's entire genome can soon be placed on a digital chip. A genome is all the genetic material in all of the chromosomes of an organism. Doctors could then use this DNA information to diagnose and treat diseases. Over time, scientists will develop more diagnostic tests that can be run on genome chips.

Lesson 5   R E V I E W

Word Bank
plasmids
restriction endonuclease
transformation

On a sheet of paper, write the word or words from the Word Bank that complete each sentence correctly.

1. Small rings of bacterial DNA are _____.

2. Enzymes called _____ cut DNA molecules at specific sequences.

3. The addition of foreign DNA to a cell is known as _____.

On a sheet of paper, write the letter of the answer that completes each sentence correctly.

4. _____ are useful organisms in biotechnology.

    A Bacteria   **C** Growth factors

    B Proteins   **D** Antibiotics

5. Down syndrome results from _____.

    A a deletion   **C** a substitution

    B nondisjunction   **D** antibiotics

6. A disease called _____ is the result of uncontrolled cell growth.

    A sickle-cell disease   **C** diabetes

    B Down syndrome   **D** cancer

Critical Thinking

On a sheet of paper, write the answers to the following questions. Use complete sentences.

7. What is biotechnology?

8. Describe one way that biotechnology might benefit you or a member of your family.

9. How do biotechnologists produce insulin?

10. What advantages do bacteria offer biotechnologists?

◆ paper
◆ pencil

A Faulty Protein

The nucleic acid DNA contains the directions for making proteins. A mutation is a change in the sequence of DNA nucleotides. In this investigation, you will learn how a mutation can affect a blood protein called hemoglobin, causing sickle-cell disease.

Procedure

1. Write the following DNA nucleotide sequence on a sheet of paper:

    T G A G G A C T C C T C.

2. Write the complementary mRNA sequence.

3. Table 11.1 on page 331 shows the possible codons in mRNA. Each codon, or set of three nucleotide bases, codes for one amino acid. Use this table to translate the mRNA sequence in Step 2. Write the amino acid sequence that the mRNA sequence will produce.

4. Write the following DNA nucleotide sequence:
    T G A G G A C A C C T C.
Does this DNA sequence match the one in Step 3?

Analysis

1. In Step 2, what is the complementary mRNA sequence? How many codons does it contain?

2. In Step 3, what is the amino acid that the mRNA sequence will produce?

3. In Step 4, what is the complementary mRNA sequence for the DNA sequence? What is the amino acid sequence that this mRNA sequence produces?

Conclusions

1. What process is occurring in Step 2?

2. What process is occurring in Step 3?

3. Identify the DNA mutation shown in Step 4. What type of mutation is this?

Explore Further

When might a genetic mutation fail to affect a protein? Change the DNA sequence in Step 1 to show how a gene can undergo a mutation and still produce a normal protein.

First Base	Second Base				Third Base
	Table 11.1 Codons in mRNA				
	U	C	A	G	
U	UUU } Phenylalanine UUC UUA } Leucine UUG	UCU UCC UCA } Serine UCG	UAU } Tyrosine UAC UAA } Stop UAG	UGU } Cysteine UGC UGA } Stop UGG } Tryptophan	U C A G
C	CUU CUC } Leucine CUA CUG	CCU CCC } Proline CCA CCG	CAU } Histidine CAC CAA } Glutamine CAG	CGU CGC } Arginine CGA CGG	U C A G
A	AUU AUC } Isolecine AUA AUG } Start	ACU ACC } Threonine ACA ACG	AAU } Asparagine AAC AAA } Lysine AAG	AGU } Serine AGC AGA } Arginine AGG	U C A G
G	GUU GUC } Valine GUA GUG	GCU GCC } Alanine GCA GCG	GAU } Aspartic acid GAC GAA } Glutamic acid GAG	GGU GGC } Cysteine GGA GGG	U C A G

Objectives

After reading this lesson, you should be able to

◆ identify the three methods of nonspecific defense

◆ describe the inflammatory response

◆ discuss how the body has specific defenses against disease

◆ compare the functions of B cells and T cells

Infectious disease

An illness that can pass from person to person

Pathogen

A germ

Lymph system

A human organ system that transports hormones and human immune cells throughout the body

White blood cell

A cell of the immune system

The human immune system is made up of a system of organs and cells that fight disease. It also protects against some cancer cells. If enough germs get into the body, they can start causing an infection. An **infectious disease** occurs when viral or bacterial germs invade body cells, causing sickness. The invading organisms are called **pathogens.**

The Lymph System

The immune, nervous, endocrine, and **lymph systems** work together to regulate internal body functions and behavior. The lymph system is a network of small vessels and organs. The organs include the spleen, thymus, and lymph nodes. Lymph nodes contain billions of **white blood cells.** White blood cells multiply rapidly to fight germs. During illness, lymph nodes fill with millions of extra white blood cells and dead germs. When you are healthy, lymph nodes are about the size of a pea or grape. When you are ill, lymph nodes can swell to the size of a golf ball.

The lymph system carries hormones and other chemicals throughout the body. White blood cells use the lymph system to travel. The immune and lymph systems defend against disease in two ways, **nonspecific defense** and **specific defense.**

Nonspecific Defense

The first part of nonspecific defense is the skin. Skin keeps out most invaders. It covers most of the body. Body areas without skin that are exposed to the outside environment have a mucus cover. Mucus is a thick fluid given off by cells. Mucus protects the surface of body areas. Mucus traps pathogens. Chemicals in mucus make it hard for pathogens to survive.

If the skin and mucus barriers are broken, pathogens can infect a person. Then the second part of nonspecific defense begins to work. **Complement proteins** fight pathogens. They open holes in the membranes of invading pathogens. They also signal the **phagocytes.**

Phagocytes are a type of white blood cell. Phagocytes eat infected and foreign cells. They move around the body in the blood. Phagocytes find pathogens or infected cells and surround them. Then they bring the invaders inside their membrane. Enzymes in phagocytes break down the infected cells or pathogens.

The third method of nonspecific defense is the **inflammatory response.** Cells near an infection site send out chemical signals. The signals increase blood flow to the area. Complement proteins arrive. They signal phagocytes. When phagocytes arrive, they eat infected cells and pathogens. After the invaders are gone, the damaged tissue heals.

The body sometimes uses fever in the inflammatory response. Fever results from an increase in body temperature. This stops bacteria from growing and helps phagocytes work faster.

Specific Defense

Specific defenses use the **lymphocytes.** Lymphocytes are a type of white blood cell. There are two types, **B lymphocytes** and **T lymphocytes.** Each lymphocyte has thousands of receptor proteins in its membranes. Receptor proteins recognize **antigens.** Antigens are molecules or pieces of molecules not usually found in the body. Antigens are often molecules in bacterial membranes or viral capsids.

B lymphocytes mainly defend against bacteria and viruses found in body fluids outside of cells. B lymphocytes produce antibodies in response to antigens found in body fluids. An antigen receptor on a B lymphocyte binds to the matching antigen receptor on a pathogen. The B lymphocyte then grows and produces an identical B lymphocyte through mitosis. These soon form millions of identical B lymphocytes.

Each B lymphocyte produces and secretes antibodies specific to the antigen on the pathogen. The binding of antibodies stops the pathogen from reproducing. It also causes pathogens to stick together. Phagocytes then destroy the clumps of pathogens.

Antigen

A foreign molecule that activates the immune system

Cytotoxic T cell

A lymphocyte that scans for antigens and then destroys infected cells

T lymphocytes work differently than B lymphocytes. They directly attack host cells that contain bacteria or viruses. Host cells are infected body cells. Every T lymphocyte has receptors for a specific antigen. A pathogen that has infected a body cell displays its antigens on the surface of the body cell. The antigens bind to the receptors on the matching T lymphocyte.

The T lymphocyte then grows and produces an identical T lymphocyte through mitosis. These soon form millions of identical T lymphocytes. The identical T lymphocytes develop into **cytotoxic T cells.**

The cytotoxic T cell binds to an infected cell's membrane. They secrete a protein which pokes holes in the membrane. The infected cell spills fluid, breaks open, and dies. Phagocytes then restore the dead host cell.

★★★

Achievements in Science

Finding HIV

In 1981, doctors in California and New York were puzzled. They were seeing several young men with an unusual kind of pneumonia. Pneumonia is a lung disease. Other men had a rare form of cancer.

Within months, scientists learned that a new disease was in the United States. This disease weakened the immune system, resulting in death. The disease was named acquired immune deficiency syndrome, or AIDS. Researchers worldwide looked for the cause of AIDS.

In 1983, Dr. Luc Montagnier in Paris reported that he had found a new virus, LAV, associated with AIDS. Several months later, Dr. Robert Gallo announced that a virus caused AIDS. He named the virus HTLV-III. In 1986, the AIDS virus was renamed human immunodeficiency virus, or HIV.

The identification of AIDS and its cause was an important first step in the fight against AIDS. Scientists have developed drugs that slow the progress of the disease. However, there is no cure. From 1981 through 2003, 20 million people worldwide have died from AIDS.

Helper T cell

A lymphocyte that scans for antigens

Macrophage

A large white blood cell that eats pathogens and cellular waste

Memory cell

A lymphocyte that is activated if an antigen causes another infection

Immunity

The ability of the body to fight off a specific pathogen

Both B lymphocytes and cytotoxic T cells get help from a type of lymphocyte called a **helper T cell.** Like all lymphocytes, every helper T cell has receptors that recognize a specific antigen on macrophages. **Macrophages** are white blood cells that eat pathogens. Helper T cells secrete chemicals that attract both cytotoxic T cells and B lymphocytes.

Immunity

Most of the cells involved in overcoming an infection die. However, some B lymphocytes and T lymphocytes live in the body. The become **memory cells.** A memory cell is a lymphocyte that is activated if an antigen causes another infection.

Thanks to memory cells, the immune system remembers some antigens. These antigens will activate lymphocytes that have receptor proteins specific to the antigens. If a pathogen tries to invade a second time, memory cells recognize it right away. They divide quickly and make active lymphocytes to fight the pathogen. They then get rid of the pathogen before it can cause a disease.

People develop **immunity** from diseases. Immunity happens when antigens cannot cause sickness because lymphocytes remember the antigen and destroy it. For example, people are sick with chickenpox only once. After the first infection, the immune system identifies and destroys newly infected cells.

Word Bank

antigens

lymph

nonspecific

On a sheet of paper, write the word from the Word Bank that completes each sentence correctly.

1. When the body is attacked by a foreign substance, the _____ defenses are the first to react.

2. Foreign molecules called _____ activate the immune system.

3. A network of small vessels and organs known as the _____ system carries chemicals throughout the body.

Critical Thinking

On a sheet of paper, write the answers to the following questions. Use complete sentences.

4. How does the inflammatory response fight infection?

5. How do people develop immunity from a certain pathogen?

Biology in Your Life

Technology: Vaccine Delivery

In the past, most vaccines were given as a shot. There are needle-free options for some vaccines. A nasal vaccine that protects against influenza, or flu, contains inactive flu viruses. The vaccine is sprayed up the nostrils and enters the blood.

People can get a vaccine by a needle-free injector. The injector uses a jet of helium gas to deliver the vaccine to the blood. Other devices use a spring to shoot drugs into the muscle or just below the skin. People can swallow some vaccines. A fatty acid surrounds tiny, vaccine-filled particles. The fatty acid protects the vaccine from being broken down and digested in the stomach. When the drug reaches the lower intestine, it is absorbed and enters the blood.

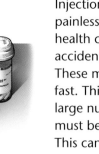

Injection-free methods are painless. They protect health care workers from accidental needle pricks. These methods are also fast. This is important when large numbers of people must be vaccinated quickly. This can happen during flu season, for example.

1. Why can a viral vaccine be delivered in a nasal spray?

2. Most vaccines cannot be swallowed. Explain why.

3. What are advantages of needle-free vaccination for you?

The Human Genome Project

Launched in 1990, the Human Genome Project was a 13-year research effort to analyze human DNA. The U.S. Department of Energy and the National Institutes of Health funded the project. One goal of the Human Genome Project was to identify all genes in human DNA. Another goal was to determine the base pair sequences that make up each gene.

Researchers also studied the genes of several other organisms. These included certain species of bacteria and yeast, the fruit fly, and laboratory mice. Researchers can use genes from these simpler organisms to study similar genes found in humans.

Scientists completed the sequencing of the human genome in April 2003. The information gained from the Human Genome Project helped create a new field of study called genomics. Genomics is the study of genes and their functions.

During the Human Genome Project, scientists identified about 1.4 million locations in human DNA in which single-nucleotide DNA differences, or SNPs, occur. These differences make each person unique. SNPs will make it possible to find the DNA sequences for heart disease, diabetes, arthritis, Alzheimer's disease, and certain forms of cancer.

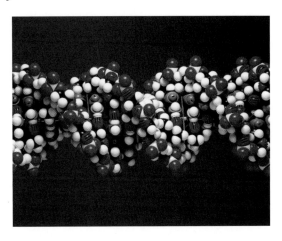

Scientists are using genomic information from the Human Genome Project to find new ways to diagnose and treat genetic disorders and diseases. Detailed genetic maps will make it possible to develop treatments that target the cause of the disease instead of the symptoms. Scientists will be able to design new drugs to match a person's genetic makeup. These custom drugs will be based on a person's genetic profile.

1. Why did scientists want to discover the DNA sequences of other organisms?

2. What is genomics?

3. How can the Human Genome Project lead to the development of new drugs?

- The double helix structure of DNA allows it to carry coded instructions to make proteins.

- Each nucleotide in DNA contains the sugar deoxyribose, a phosphate group, and one of four nitrogenous bases. Each base follows a pattern called complementary base pairing: adenine pairs with thymine, and guanine pairs with cytosine. RNA is a single strand of nucleotides. RNA nucleotides contain uracil instead of thymine and ribose instead of deoxyribose.

- Two new copies of DNA form during DNA replication. During replication, the double helix unwinds. Each strand serves as a template for a new strand.

- Transcription is the creation of an RNA molecule. During translation, a protein is created based on the sequence of bases in mRNA.

- A virus is a nonliving particle. A virus invades a host cell to reproduce.

- Biotechnology is the use of organisms and their genetics to make medicines and improve food crops.

- The immune system defends the body against infections. Nonspecific defenses, such as the inflammatory response, are the body's first line of defense. Specific defenses, such as antibodies, attack infected cells based on the presence of certain antigens.

- Immunity results when the immune system recognizes previous antigens.

Vocabulary

anticodon, 318
antigen, 334
B lymphocyte, 333
bacteriophage, 310
biotechnologist, 325
biotechnology, 325
capsid, 321
complement protein, 333
complementary base pairing, 308
cytosine, 307
cytotoxic T cell, 334
deletion, 319
DNA ligase, 312
DNA polymerase, 311
Down syndrome, 327
evolve, 321
exon, 317
genetic code, 317

genetically modified food, 327
growth factor, 327
guanine, 306
helper T cell, 335
host cell, 322
immune system, 323
immunity, 335
infect, 322
infectious disease, 332
inflammatory response, 333
insertion, 319
intron, 317
lagging strand, 312
leading strand, 312
lymph system, 332
lysogenic cycle, 323
lymphocyte, 333
lytic cycle, 322
macrophage, 335

marker, 310
memory cell, 335
messenger RNA, 316
mutagen, 319
mutation, 319
nitrogenous base, 306
nondisjunction, 327
nonspecific defense, 333
origin of replication, 311
parasite, 321
pathogen, 332
phagocyte, 333
plasmid, 325
promoter, 317
replication, 310
replication bubble, 311
replication fork, 311
restriction endonuclease, 326
ribosomal RNA, 317
RNA polymerase, 316

RNA splicing, 317
semi-conservative replication, 310
specific defense, 333
substitution, 319
sugar-phosphate backbone, 306
T lymphocyte, 333
template, 311
terminator, 317
thymine, 307
transcription, 316
transfer RNA, 317
transformation, 326
translation, 316
uracil, 307
vaccine, 323
virus, 310
white blood cell, 332

Chapter 11 R E V I E W

Word Bank

anticodon

antigen

biotechnology

DNA polymerase

host cell

immunity

lymphocyte

messenger RNA

mutation

nitrogenous base

nonspecific
defense

phagocyte

plasmid

replication fork

restriction
endonuclease

ribosomal RNA

semi-conservative
replication

specific defense

transcription

transfer RNA

transformation

translation

vaccine

virus

Vocabulary Review

On a sheet of paper, write the word or words from the Word Bank that best complete each sentence.

1. The building block that makes up a nucleic acid is a(n) _____.

2. During _____, a protein is created from the coded sequences of bases in the RNA molecule.

3. Nucleotide bases are attached to a new strand of DNA at the _____.

4. An enzyme called _____ bonds new nucleotides to the nucleotides on the template strand.

5. When _____ occurs, an RNA molecule is created based on the sequence of bases in a DNA molecule.

6. A molecule called _____ interprets the DNA codes and carries the coded instructions for the order of amino acids in a protein. Another molecule called _____ delivers the correct amino acids. During translation, _____ helps position the amino acids.

7. Three complementary base units known as a(n) _____ ensure that the correct amino acid is delivered.

8. A(n) _____ is made up of nonliving pieces of DNA or RNA wrapped in a protein shell.

9. A white blood cell that has receptor proteins that recognize antigens is a(n) _____.

10. DNA is copied during _____.

Review continued on next page

11. The ability of the immune system to recognize and remember an antigen is known as _____. A(n) _____ contains a weakened virus that prepare the body to fight and destroy cells infected by that particular virus.

12. In DNA, a(n) _____ can be cytosine, thymine, adenine, or guanine.

13. The use of organisms and their genetics to make medicines and improve food crops is called _____. A(n) _____ is a small circular piece of DNA.

14. A(n) _____ is a change in the sequence of DNA.

15. A foreign molecule that activates the immune system is called a(n) _____.

16. A virus infects an organism by entering a(n) _____.

17. Scientists use an enzyme called _____ to cut a DNA molecule and remove a specific sequence. During a process known as _____, foreign DNA is added to a bacterial cell.

18. When any foreign substance appears, the immune system will first use its _____ to attack. Later, the immune system will use its _____ to attack infected cells based on the presence of antigen molecules.

Concept Review

On a sheet of paper, write the letter of the answer that completes each sentence correctly.

19. A vaccine helps the body _____.

    A make new DNA   **C** fight viruses

    B repair mutations   **D** make proteins

20. A molecule called _____ carries the genetic code from the nucleus into the cell cytoplasm.

  A mRNA   **C** rRNA

  B tRNA   **D** DNA polymerase

21. A specific defense is a(n) _____.

  A inflammation   **C** skin barrier

  B fever   **D** lymphocyte

Critical Thinking

On a sheet of paper, write the answers to the following questions. Use complete sentences.

22. Compare and contrast transcription and translation.

23. What would happen to the human body if helper T cells disappeared?

24. Why is DNA replication called semi-conservative?

25. Compare and contrast antigens and antibodies.

Research and Write

Write a report on the development of the vaccine for polio.

Test-Taking Tip To answer a multiple-choice question, read every choice before you answer the question. Cross out the choices that you know are wrong. Choose the best answer from the remaining choices.

Human Body Systems

Think about what the swimmer in the photograph must do to create motion through water. Every body system is involved in producing and controlling motion. Muscles, bones, skin, lungs, heart, ears, eyes, brain, and stomach are all in action at the same time. Imagine building a machine that could move like a swimmer! In Chapter 12, you will learn about the systems of the human body. You will find out how the systems interact and how their activities are coordinated.

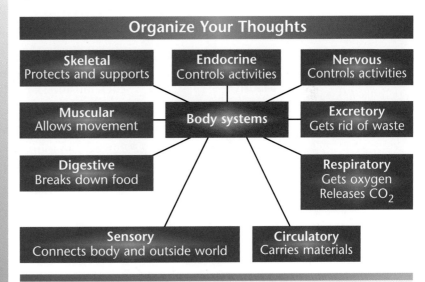

Organize Your Thoughts

Skeletal
Protects and supports

Endocrine
Controls activities

Nervous
Controls activities

Muscular
Allows movement

Body systems

Excretory
Gets rid of waste

Digestive
Breaks down food

Respiratory
Gets oxygen
Releases CO_2

Sensory
Connects body and outside world

Circulatory
Carries materials

Goals for Learning

◆ To describe the digestive, respiratory, and circulatory systems
◆ To explain the excretory and nervous systems
◆ To describe the sensory and endocrine systems
◆ To explain the skeletal and muscular systems

343

People need nutrients, minerals, and vitamins from food to live. The human body uses these materials as a source of energy and to build and maintain new cells. The body breaks down food in the digestive system. The main part of the digestive system is the digestive tract. The digestive tract is a long tube that is open at each end of the body. The digestive tract begins at the mouth, where food and liquids enter the body. The tract ends at the anus, where wastes leave the body. The journey of food through the digestive system takes about 24 to 33 hours. As you read about digestion, refer to Figure 12.1.1, which shows the digestive tract.

The Four Stages of Digestion

The first stage of digestion is **ingestion.** Food is taken into the mouth. The teeth chew food into a soft pulp. While food is in the mouth, a **reflex** triggers the release of saliva. A reflex is an automatic response. As you know, saliva is a liquid produced by glands in the mouth. Saliva helps in chewing and starts digestion. Food mixes with saliva and becomes moist and slippery. Saliva also kills bacteria in food. An enzyme in saliva called salivary amylase begins to break down starch and glycogen.

Ingestion

The intake of food; the first stage of digestion

Reflex

An automatic response

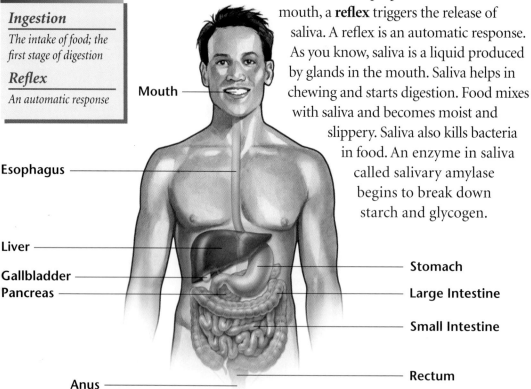

Mouth

Esophagus

Liver

Gallbladder

Pancreas

Stomach

Large Intestine

Small Intestine

Rectum

Anus

Figure 12.1.1 *The human digestive tract can measure up to 30 feet.*

Pharynx

The passageway between the mouth and the esophagus for air and food

Peristalsis

The movement of digestive organs that pushes food through the digestive tract

Gallbladder

The digestive organ that stores bile

Chyme

The liquid food in the digestive tract that is partially digested

Villi

The tiny, fingerlike structures in the small intestine through which food molecules enter the blood

Bile

A substance made in the liver that breaks down fats

Bacteria can cause an ulcer, or a break, in the stomach lining. Ulcers can be treated with antibiotics.

With the help of the tongue, the food passes to the **pharynx.** The food enters the esophagus. The esophagus connects the mouth and the stomach. The food moves through the esophagus by **peristalsis,** or waves of muscle contraction.

Once food enters the stomach, the second stage of digestion begins. The swallowed food mixes with digestive juices from the liver, **gallbladder,** pancreas, and glands in the intestinal wall. The digestive juices contain enzymes that further digest food. Thick muscles in the walls of the stomach contract. They mash food into a soup called **chyme.**

Stomach acid is very strong. It can dissolve an iron nail. However, the stomach is protected by a lining of mucus. Stomach lining is replaced every three days.

The third stage of digestion is absorption. Chyme enters the small intestine. The small intestine is the longest part of the digestive tract. If unrolled, it would be nearly 20 feet long. The small intestine has fingerlike projections on its surface called **villi.** Villi increase the rate of absorption of food and minerals into the blood.

In the small intestine, enzymes continue to chemically break down food. During this process, the gallbladder releases **bile.** The liver makes bile, a substance that breaks down fats. As chyme arrives in the small intestine, bile flows from the liver to the gallbladder and into the intestine.

Nutrients from food are now small molecules. They can pass through the lining of the small intestine and into the blood. Nutrients are carried to the liver and other body parts to be processed, stored, and distributed. The liver works like a food-processing factory. The liver stores some nutrients. It also changes nutrients to different forms, then releases them into the blood. The nutrients travel to each body cell. Cells absorb the small molecules, such as amino acids and simple sugars. The cells then reassemble these molecules for growth and repair or for ATP production.

The fourth stage of digestion is elimination. Undigested food moves to the large intestine and water is recovered. Useful substances are absorbed through the walls of the large intestine and released into the blood. Undigested material passes out of the digestive tract as **feces** through the **rectum** and anus.

Humans absorb 80 to 90 percent of the organic matter in food. Humans cannot digest the cellulose from plant cell walls. Vegetables and fruits are not absorbed as completely as meat, fats, and simple carbohydrates.

Glucose and Glycogen

During digestion, liver cells and muscle cells store glucose as glycogen. Liver cells take up glucose from blood. They store excess glucose as glycogen and change it back to glucose when needed. Glycogen is made of many glucose units. Glucose is the main fuel molecule for the body's cells.

Hormones regulate metabolism. For example, the glycogen storage areas may be full. If people eat more calories than needed, the extra calories are stored as fat in adipose, or fat, cells. If people eat fewer calories than needed, the stored fuel is removed from the storage areas. It is then used as fuel for the body's cells.

Link to ➤➤➤

Environmental Science

Escherichia coli, or *E. coli*, is a bacterium commonly found in the digestive tract of humans. Although humans interact with *E. coli* often, nearly all strains are harmless. Sometimes, a bacteria strain harmful to humans can develop. It might be passed along in food. That is why it is important to follow clean practices in food packaging and food preparation.

Express Lab 12

Materials

◆ Food products with nutrition labels

Procedure

1. Study the food labels of two different types of food.
2. Look at the ingredients list on each label. Note the amount of fiber in each type of food.

Analysis

1. What is the connection between cellulose and fiber?
2. How much fiber is recommended each day as part of a healthy diet?
3. Why is fiber important to a healthy diet?

Word Bank

anus

chyme

mouth

villi

On a sheet of a paper, write the word from the Word Bank that completes each sentence correctly.

1. The surface of the small intestine has fingerlike projections called _____ that increase the rate of absorption.

2. Food that has been mashed into a soup in the stomach is _____.

3. The digestive tract begins at the _____ and ends at the _____.

On a sheet of paper, write the letter of the answer that completes each sentence correctly.

4. Your body's metabolism is regulated by _____.

    A hormones **B** glucose **C** enzymes **D** adipose cells

5. The body stores extra glucose as _____.

    A sucrose   **B** ATP   **C** bile   **D** glycogen

6. Bile aids digestion by _____.

    A neutralizing stomach acid

    B breaking down fats

    C converting glucose to glycogen

    D storing vitamins and minerals

Critical Thinking

On a sheet of paper, write the answers to the following questions. Use complete sentences.

7. Why is it helpful for the small intestine to have villi?

8. How do nutrients reach all the cells in the body?

9. List the three roles that saliva plays in digestion.

10. Why does the strong acid in the stomach not dissolve the organs in the digestive system, including the stomach?

After reading this lesson, you should be able to

◆ identify the function and parts of the respiratory system

◆ describe the process of gas exchange in the lungs

◆ describe the process of breathing

◆ list some respiratory diseases

Epithelium

A thin layer of cells forming a tissue that covers body surfaces and lines some organs

Capillary

A blood vessel through which oxygen and food molecules pass to body cells

Glottis

The opening to the windpipe

Larynx

The voice box

Body cells use oxygen to release energy from food. This process is cellular respiration. During this process, carbon dioxide is produced as waste. The body takes in oxygen and releases carbon dioxide into the environment. The exchange of oxygen and carbon dioxide occurs in the lungs. That is why the lungs are the most important organs in the respiratory system.

Oxygen from inhaled air diffuses across the **epithelium** in the lungs into the blood. The epithelium is a thin layer of cells forming a tissue that covers body surfaces and lines some organs. The blood circulates to the body's tissues through **capillaries.** Capillaries are blood vessels that have a wall that is one cell thick. Oxygen and food molecules pass through the capillaries to body cells. Carbon dioxide, a waste product of the body, diffuses from the blood into the lungs to be exhaled.

Respiration

Respiration begins when air is inhaled. Air enters the nose through the nostrils. Small nasal hairs filter the air. The nostrils warm and humidify the air. Then the air flows to the pharynx. The digestive tract and respiratory tract cross at the pharynx.

When the **glottis** is open, air passes through. The glottis is the opening to the windpipe. When food is swallowed, the **larynx** moves up and tips the epiglottis over the glottis. The epiglottis is a thin, soft material. It prevents swallowing and inhaling at the same time.

From the larynx, air passes to the **trachea.** The trachea divides into two branches called bronchi. Each **bronchus** leads to one lung. The lungs have a spongy texture and are lined with cilia and mucus. Cilia are hair-like structures. Mucus traps dust, pollen, and other particles. The cilia move the mucus up where it is swallowed. This process cleans the respiratory system.

| **Trachea** |
| The tube that carries air to the bronchi |
| **Bronchus** |
| A tube that connects the trachea to a lung (plural is bronchi) |
| **Bronchiole** |
| A tube that branches off the bronchus |
| **Alveolus** |
| A tiny air sac at the end of each bronchiole that holds air (plural is alveoli) |

In the United States, nearly 87 percent of lung cancer cases are connected to smoking.

From the bronchi, the lungs branch into **bronchioles.** At the tip of each bronchiole is a cluster of air sacs called alveoli. An **alveolus** is a tiny air sac. There are millions of alveoli. Gas exchange happens at the alveoli. Oxygen enters the alveoli and dissolves in the moist mucus. It diffuses across the epithelium into a network of capillaries. Capillaries are wrapped around the alveoli. Capillary walls are very thin and close to each other. Oxygen easily seeps through them and into the blood. At the same time, carbon dioxide in the blood seeps into the alveoli. Carbon dioxide is removed from the body when exhaled.

Breathing

Figure 12.2.1 shows the respiratory system. Breathing alternates between inhaling and exhaling. During inhalation, the muscles around the lungs and the diaphragm contract. The diaphragm is a strong, thin muscle below the lungs. The rib cage expands and lung volume increases. Air rushes into the lungs. During exhalation, the diaphragm and other muscles around the lungs relax. Lung volume decreases. Air is pushed up the breathing tubes and out the mouth and nostrils.

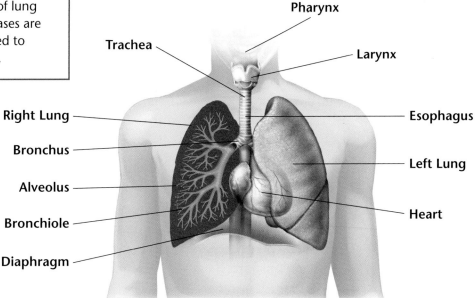

Figure 12.2.1 *The respiratory system takes in oxygen and gets rid of carbon dioxide.*

Sleep apnea

A condition in which short periods of not breathing occur during sleep

Asthma

A condition that narrows or blocks the airways and makes breathing difficult

Bronchitis

An inflammation of the bronchial tubes

At rest, you usually breathe about 12 times a minute.

The contracting and relaxing of muscles control the rate of expansion (increase) and constriction (decrease) of the lungs. That means you can control your breathing by holding your breath. You can breathe deeper or faster. Breathing is usually automatic. You breathe without thinking about it.

Sometimes this automatic system does not work correctly. People with **sleep apnea** stop breathing up to 300 times a night. When breathing stops, oxygen levels decrease. Then carbon dioxide levels increase in the blood. The decreased oxygen and increased carbon dioxide usually signal the brain to breathe. The person wakes up so breathing can restart.

Changes in altitude can change breathing. As altitude increases, atmospheric pressure decreases. Decreased pressure reduces the amount of oxygen that enters the blood. To get more oxygen, mountain climbers breathe more quickly as they climb. They also lose carbon dioxide faster.

Respiratory System Diseases

Some people have respiratory system diseases. **Asthma** is a condition that narrows or blocks the airways. This causes shortness of breath and makes breathing difficult. The airways narrow when they overreact to certain substances, such as dust, smoke, or cold air.

Bronchitis is another respiratory system disease that reduces airflow. Over time, exposure to lung irritants causes bronchitis. Irritants include cigarette smoke and air pollutants. Cystic fibrosis is a genetic disease. It causes mucus to build up in the lungs and clog the airways.

The circulatory system, which you will learn about in Lesson 3, works together with the respiratory system. The respiratory system supplies oxygen to the body and gets rid of carbon dioxide. This process supports the work of cells. The circulatory system transports these gases from the lungs to the cells and back to the lungs. This process is a continual cycle.

Word Bank

carbon dioxide

cystic fibrosis

oxygen

sleep apnea

On a sheet of a paper, write the word or words from the Word Bank that complete each sentence correctly.

1. An inherited respiratory disease is _____.

2. A condition that causes a person to stop breathing at night is _____.

3. Gas exchange involves taking in _____ and getting rid of _____.

On a sheet of paper, write the letter of the answer that completes each sentence correctly.

4. The _____ traps dust and other particles in the lungs.

   A alveoli   **B** cilia   **C** glottis   **D** mucus

5. Respiration begins when _____.

   A the lungs stretch   **C** air is inhaled

   B the diaphragm contracts   **D** the mouth opens

6. An increase in altitude changes breathing by _____.

   A slowing carbon dioxide loss from blood

   B reducing the amount of oxygen entering the blood

   C increasing dehydration in blood

   D decreasing muscle activity in the diaphragm

Critical Thinking

On a sheet of paper, write the answers to the following questions. Use complete sentences.

7. Why can't a person breathe when swallowing food?

8. How does oxygen taken in by the lungs reach the body's cells?

9. Why are the lungs the most important organs in the respiratory system?

10. Describe three respiratory diseases.

Objectives

After reading this lesson, you should be able to

◆ identify the major parts of the circulatory system and their functions

◆ compare and contrast arteries and veins

◆ trace the flow of blood through the heart

◆ describe the parts of blood and explain their functions

Cardiac

Relating to the heart

The circulatory system transports gases, nutrients, hormones, and antibodies within the body. Blood delivers oxygen and nutrients to the body's cells. Blood also carries away waste materials.

The Heart

Figure 12.3.1 shows the heart. The heart is the main organ of the circulatory system. It pumps blood through the body. The heart is about the size of a fist. It is located between the lungs in the chest cavity. The heart is made mostly of thick muscular tissue called **cardiac** muscle. The heart contracts and relaxes in a regular manner know as the heartbeat. The heart works automatically. A person does not have to think about it to make the heart beat.

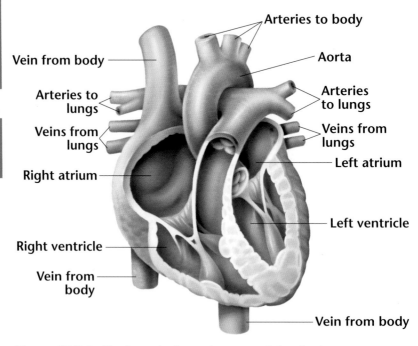

Vein from body

Arteries to lungs

Veins from lungs

Right atrium

Right ventricle

Vein from body

Arteries to body

Aorta

Arteries to lungs

Veins from lungs

Left atrium

Left ventricle

Vein from body

Figure 12.3.1 *The heart is the main organ of the circulatory system.*

The heart has two sides, left and right. Each side has an upper chamber called the **atrium** and a lower chamber called the **ventricle.** The atrium is the smaller chamber and has thin walls. It receives blood from the body. From the atrium, blood flows into the larger ventricle. The ventricle has thick, strong walls that contract to pump blood.

How Blood Circulates

Blood travels in one direction to form a circle pattern. Arteries are blood vessels that carry blood away from the heart. An **artery** carries blood full of oxygen. The **aorta** is the largest artery. Arteries become smaller as they move away from the heart.

From the aorta, blood flows through arteries to the heart muscle. Other branches lead to capillaries in the head, arms, stomach, and legs. From capillaries, the blood travels to body cells. **Interstitial fluid** fills the space around body cells. It exchanges nutrients and wastes with the blood. Blood gives up oxygen and picks up carbon dioxide produced by cellular respiration.

Blood that contains waste products flows back to the heart through **veins.** A vein carries blood to the heart. Oxygen-poor blood from the head, arms, and neck goes to a large vein called the **superior vena cava.** Another large vein called the **inferior vena cava** carries blood from the trunk and legs. These large veins take blood into the right atrium of the heart. The oxygen-poor blood flows into the right ventricle.

Only one artery carries blood high in carbon dioxide. This artery carries oxygen-poor blood from the right ventricle to the lungs. As blood flows through capillaries into the lungs, it loads oxygen and unloads carbon dioxide. Oxygen-rich blood returns from the lungs to the left heart atrium and to the left ventricle. The left ventricle pumps the oxygen-rich blood into the aorta, and the cycle repeats.

Atrium

A heart chamber that receives blood returning to the heart (plural is atria)

Ventricle

A heart chamber that pumps blood out of the heart

Artery

A blood vessel that carries blood away from the heart (plural is arteries)

Aorta

A large vessel through which the left ventricle sends blood to the body

Interstitial fluid

A fluid that fills the space around cells and exchanges nutrients and wastes with blood

Vein

A blood vessel that carries blood back to the heart

Superior vena cava

A large vein that carries blood from the head, neck, and arms to the heart

Inferior vena cava

A large vein that carries blood from the trunk and legs to the heart

Connective tissue

The supporting framework of the body and its organs

Plasma

The liquid part of blood

Platelet

A tiny piece of cell that helps form clots

Link to ➤➤➤

Chemistry

Red blood cells are one of the few human cells that do not contain DNA. As they mature, red blood cells lose their cell nucleus. DNA is stored in the nucleus. Mature red blood cells also contain no mitochondria.

Heart valves prevent blood from flowing backwards. A defect in a valve is called a heart murmur. It sounds like hissing as blood squirts backward through a valve. The elastic walls of arteries expand when they receive blood from the ventricles. When you take your pulse, you can detect this movement. A pulse represents the rhythmic stretching of the arteries. Blood pressure is the contractions of the ventricles, which cause stretching.

The heart beats about 70 times a minute in adults who are sitting or standing quietly. That is over 100,000 beats per day pumping more than 7,000 liters of blood. Some body hormones increase heart rate. An increase in body temperature also increases heart rate. A fever causes body temperature and pulse rate to increase. Exercise increases heart rate, which delivers more oxygen to the muscles to do the extra work.

Capillaries in the brain, heart, kidneys, and liver are always filled with blood. The amount of blood varies in other body sites. After eating, blood is moved to the digestive tract. You may feel cold after eating because of this. During exercise, blood is moved away from the digestive tract and sent to the skin and muscles.

Blood Cells

Blood is **connective tissue.** Connective tissue is the supporting framework of the body and its organs. Blood contains cells held in **plasma.** Plasma is the liquid part of blood. The three types of blood cells are red blood cells, white blood cells, and **platelets.**

Red blood cells, also called erythrocytes, transport oxygen. Hemoglobin is a protein in red blood cells that contains iron. Hemoglobin transports oxygen.

White blood cells are larger than red blood cells. There is about one white blood cell for every 700 red blood cells. White blood cells fight infection in the body. White blood cells usually stay outside the circulatory system in the interstitial fluid.

Fibrinogen

A protein in the platelets that forms into threads, creating a clot

Thrombus

A clot of blood formed within a blood vessel

Cardiovascular disease

A disease of the heart and blood vessels

Atherosclerosis

A disease that harms the arteries by narrowing them

Hypertension

High blood pressure

Science Myth

Myth: The blood in arteries is red. The blood in veins is blue.

Fact: All blood is red. Blood vessels near the skin look blue because you look at blood through skin. Illustrations often have red for arteries and blue for veins. This is to show that arteries carry more oxygen than veins.

Platelets are pieces of cells used in blood clots. A protein in the platelets, called **fibrinogen,** forms into threads, creating a clot. An inherited defect in clotting is hemophilia. A person who has hemophilia can have trouble stopping the flow of blood, even from a minor cut. The blood does not clot well.

In some people, platelets form a clot, or a **thrombus,** when there is no injury. A thrombus blocks the flow of blood. A thrombus can form in people who have heart disease.

Heart Diseases

Diseases of the heart and blood vessels are called **cardiovascular diseases.** Cardiovascular diseases cause more than half of all deaths each year in the United States. Heart attacks and strokes result from a thrombus that clogs an artery. A blocked artery causes cardiac muscle tissue to die. Blocked arteries in the brain can cause a stroke.

Many people who have had a heart attack have **atherosclerosis.** This disease causes a buildup of fatty substances. Over time, this buildup causes blood vessels to harden and narrow. The risk of a heart attack or stroke increases. Another condition called **hypertension,** or high blood pressure, increases the chance of stroke or heart attack. Hypertension happens when the force of blood against the artery walls is too strong.

Keeping Fit

Being overweight increases a person's chances of cardiovascular diseases. Most people become overweight because they eat too many calories and do not exercise enough. Exercise has many more benefits than helping maintain a healthy body weight. Regular exercise makes the heart stronger and more efficient. It helps strengthen muscles, bones, and joints. It also helps reduce the risk of diabetes, colon cancer, and cardiovascular and other diseases.

Everyone needs exercise to stay healthy. Most people should be physically active daily for at least 30 minutes. Keeping fit can include playing sports, walking, biking, or swimming.

Lesson 3   R E V I E W

Word Bank

arteries

atrium

plasma

On a sheet of a paper, write the word from the Word Bank that completes each sentence correctly.

1. The _____ is the smaller chamber of the heart.

2. The liquid part of blood is _____.

3. Atherosclerosis is caused by fatty substances that are deposited on the inner walls of _____.

Critical Thinking

On a sheet of paper, write the answers to the following questions. Use complete sentences.

4. How does cardiovascular disease cause a heart attack?

5. What part of red blood cells helps to transport oxygen?

Biology in Your Life

Consumer Choices: What Does Blood Pressure Mean?

The American Heart Association estimates that about 25 percent of adults have high blood pressure. High blood pressure is also called hypertension. Many people do not know when they have hypertension. It often does not cause obvious problems.

Blood pressure tells how hard the heart works to pump blood throughout the body. Sometimes arteries get clogged or become narrow. Blood moves slower through the body and the heart must work harder. This builds pressure. The person may be at risk for heart attack or stroke.

Smoking, too much alcohol, and high stress can cause hypertension. To control hypertension, doctors tell people to exercise regularly and lose weight, and eat more fruits, vegetables, and whole grains.

People may have to take medications to reduce hypertension.

1. Why can someone who feels healthy have high blood pressure?

2. What are dangers of high blood pressure?

3. Do you know someone who has high blood pressure? What do they do to treat it?

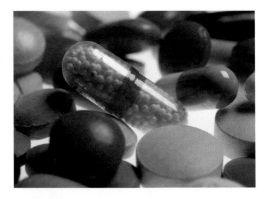

Materials
- graph paper
- clock with a second hand

How Exercise Affects Heart Rate

Heart rate is usually measured by taking a person's pulse. Each time your heart beats, it sends blood rushing through your arteries. The arteries stretch a little as blood rushes through them. You can feel this stretching as a small bump or beat at a pressure point. The easiest pressure points to use are on your neck or on the inside of your wrist. By counting the beats, you will find your heart rate, or pulse rate. In this lab, you will find out how your heart rate changes with exercise.

Procedure

1. To record your observations, draw a table like the one shown below on a sheet of graph paper.

2. To find your resting heart rate, take your pulse. To do this, sit quietly in a chair for two minutes. Then place your first two fingers on your inner wrist near the base of your thumb. Press lightly to feel your pulse. If you do not feel a pulse, move your fingers around a little until you do.

Activity	Heart Rate
Sitting quietly	
After running for 1 minute	
After resting for 2 minutes	
After resting for 4 minutes	
After resting for 6 minutes	
After resting for 8 minutes	
After resting for 10 minutes	

3. Watching the second hand on a clock, count the beats you feel for exactly one minute. Record this number in your table.

4. Run in place for one minute. **Safety Alert: Tell your teacher if you should not do this physical activity.**

5. Immediately measure your heart rate for one minute. Record this information.

6. Sit quietly for one minute. Then measure your heart rate for one minute. Repeat until you have recorded five measurements after your run.

7. On graph paper, make a graph from your data to show how your heart rate changed before, during, and after exercise.

Analysis

1. How did exercise affect your heart rate?

2. What happened to your heart rate when you stopped exercising and rested?

Conclusions

1. What needs do you think your heart responded to when your heart rate changed?

2. What do you think heart rate tells you about the level of exercise you are performing?

Explore Further

Measure your heart rate for one minute while you run in place. At the same time, have a partner measure your respiration rate (the number of breaths you take in a minute). How are respiration rate and heart rate related?

Lesson 4 — The Excretory System

Objectives

After reading this lesson, you should be able to

◆ explain how the excretory system regulates water balance in the body

◆ explain how the excretory system removes waste from the body

◆ describe how hormones control water absorption in the body

Ureter

A tube that carries urine from the kidney to the urinary bladder

Urine

Liquid waste formed in the kidneys

The excretory system regulates water balance in the body and removes waste. Wastes from interstitial fluid are carried by blood capillaries. The capillaries deposit the waste at a collection point for removal from the body. The excretory system also regulates the chemical makeup of body fluids. It keeps the proper amounts of water, salts, and nutrients in the body fluids. The excretory system includes the kidneys, **ureters,** bladder, urethra, liver, lungs, and skin.

Your cells make nitrogen wastes, which are poisonous. The excretory system gets rid of these wastes. The body has two bean-shaped kidneys. The kidneys are the main organs of the excretory system. Each kidney is about 10 centimeters long. Blood flows to and from the kidneys through the renal artery and renal vein. The kidneys take the nitrogen wastes from the blood and form **urine.** Urine leaves each kidney through the ureter. The ureter is a duct, or body tube. A ureter from each kidney drains into the bladder. From the bladder, urine leaves the body through the urethra. Follow the path of urine through the excretory system in Figure 12.4.1.

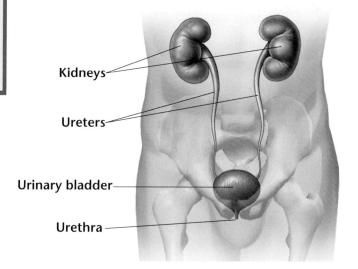

Kidneys

Ureters

Urinary bladder

Urethra

Figure 12.4.1 *The body produces about 1.5 liters (6 cups) of urine in one 24-hour period.*

Nephron

A small tube that is the excretory unit of the kidney

Glomerulus

A group of capillaries that make up a tiny tube in nephrons

Antidiuretic hormone (ADH)

A hormone that controls the absorption of water back into the body

Epidermis

The thin outer layer of skin

Dermis

The thick layer of cells below the epidermis

Fatty layer

The layer of skin that protects organs and keeps in heat

Perspiration

A liquid waste made of heat, water, and salt released through skin

Nephrons filter about 125 milliliters of body fluid per minute. They filter all body fluid about 16 times every day.

Inside the kidney are millions of **nephrons.** A nephron is a tiny tube made up of the **glomerulus,** a group of capillaries. Blood flows into the kidney from the renal artery. The renal artery branches into capillaries in the glomerulus. Pressure from the arteries causes water and solutes from blood to filter into the nephrons. Fluid flows through the nephrons into a collecting duct. Capillaries surrounding the nephrons receive fluids and solutes. Nephrons filter water and solutes from blood. They replace water and molecules in the blood. They secrete waste products from surrounding capillaries into the ureters.

Antidiuretic hormone, or **ADH,** controls the absorption of water back into the body. A low fluid level in the blood causes the release of more ADH into the blood. ADH causes the kidneys to increase water absorption and produce less urine. This puts more water into the blood. When there is too much fluid, ADH in the blood is reduced. The kidneys absorb less water and produce more urine. Infection, poisons such as mercury, and genetic diseases can harm kidney function.

Many wastes leave the body through the skin. Figure 12.4.2 shows the three layers of skin. The **epidermis** is the top layer. It protects the deep layers of the skin. Under the epidermis is the **dermis.** This thick layer of skin contains blood vessels, nerves, and glands. The next layer is the **fatty layer.** It protects the body's organs and keeps in heat.

The body carries water and salt to sweat glands. These wastes form **perspiration.** Thousands of sweat glands in the skin release perspiration through pores on the skin's surface. Perspiration cools the body when water evaporates from the skin.

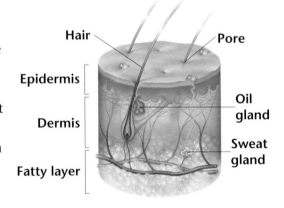

Figure 12.4.2 *Skin is made up of the epidermis, dermis, and fatty layer.*

Lesson 4   R E V I E W

Word Bank

ADH
dermis
mercury

On a sheet of a paper, write the word from the Word Bank that completes each sentence correctly.

1. Kidneys can be damaged by poisons such as _____.

2. Absorption of water back into the body is controlled by _____.

3. The three layers of skin are the epidermis, the _____, and the fatty layers.

On a sheet of paper, write the letter of the answer that completes each sentence correctly.

4. The _____ is not a part of the excretory system.

   A kidney   **B** liver   **C** stomach   **D** skin

5. A nephron is made up of a group of _____ that together make up the glomerulus.

   A arteries   **B** capillaries   **C** veins   **D** ureters

6. Urine leaves each kidney through a _____.

   A ureter   **C** renal vein

   B renal artery   **D** bladder

Critical Thinking

On a sheet of paper, write the answers to the following questions. Use complete sentences.

7. What kinds of wastes are released through the skin?

8. Describe the path that wastes take as they are processed by the kidneys.

9. How does ADH control activity in the excretory system?

10. What three functions does a nephron perform?

For all your body systems to work, they need to be coordinated. Body parts have to know what to do and when to do it. Your nervous system coordinates all your body parts. It is the body's communication network. It is also the most complex body system.

The nervous system is made up of two systems. The central nervous system is made up of the brain and spinal cord. The central nervous system controls the activities of the body, including the sense organs. The peripheral nervous system is made up of nerves outside the central nervous system. The peripheral nervous system carries messages between the central nervous system and other body parts.

The Brain

The brain is at the center of the nervous system. It is divided into five areas: the **brain stem, cerebellum, limbic system, diencephalon,** and **cerebral cortex.** The brain stem connects the brain and the spinal cord. It controls automatic activities including heart rate, digestion, respiration, and circulation. It coordinates muscles that move without you thinking about them, such as stomach muscles.

Above the brain stem is the cerebellum. This area of the brain controls balance. It also helps muscles work together so that you walk and write smoothly. The limbic system registers your feelings, especially fear, anger, and pleasure.

The front of the brain is called the diencephalon. It includes the **thalamus** and **hypothalamus.** The thalamus directs incoming sensory messages so that you see, hear, and smell. The hypothalamus regulates hormones, the pituitary gland, body temperature, and other activities. The **pituitary gland** produces secretions that regulate basic body functions. You will learn more about the thalamus, hypothalamus, and pituitary gland in Lesson 7.

Brain stem

The part of the brain that controls automatic activities and connects the brain and the spinal cord

Cerebellum

The part of the brain that controls balance

Limbic system

The part of the brain that registers feelings

Diencephalon

The front of the brain

The cerebral cortex makes up most of the brain. Most high-level functions take place in the cerebral cortex. The cerebral cortex is made up of two halves. Each half is divided into four lobes: frontal, parietal, temporal, and occipital. Each lobe is responsible for different body functions. Some lobes are involved in vision, hearing, touch, movement, and smell. Others are involved in thinking, reasoning, and memory.

Areas in the frontal lobes are used for short-term memory. Short-term memory stores a small amount of information for a short time, about 35 to 40 seconds. If the information is needed for a longer period of time, long-term memory is activated. Long-term memory stores information in the brain for a long time. If the information is needed, it is brought into working memory. Figure 12.5.1 shows the human brain.

The Spinal Cord

The spinal cord is a thick bunch of nerves that start at the brain stem and go down the back. The spinal cord runs through the backbone. The backbone protects the spinal cord. The brain sends and receives information through the spinal cord. Thirty-one pairs of spinal nerves branch off from the spinal cord.

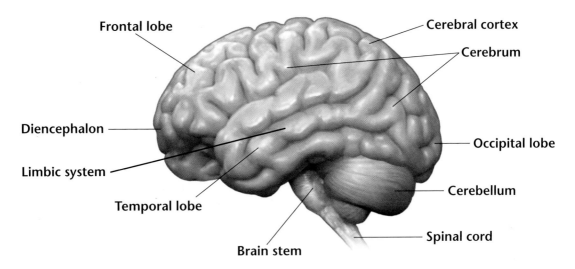

Figure 12.5.1 *The human brain is at the center of the nervous system.*

Neurons

Information moves through your body by traveling along many nerve cells. Nerve cells are called **neurons.** Neurons send signals in the form of electrical signals throughout the body. These messages are called impulses. An impulse quickly carries information from one neuron to the next. Neurons do not touch each other. Impulses must cross a small gap, or **synapse,** between neurons.

An impulse travels from one end of a neuron to the other end. When the impulse reaches the end of a neuron, a chemical called a **neurotransmitter** is released. The neurotransmitter moves into the synapse and touches the next neuron. This starts another impulse.

Each neuron has a cell body. Thin, spider-like **dendrites** branch out from the cell body. Dendrites receive information from other cells. Each neuron also has an **axon,** a long, wire-like nerve fiber that extends from the cell body. The axon carries information to other cells. The axon's ends are branched and have button-shaped axon bulbs.

With the help of neurotransmitters, nerve impulses travel along the axon. Then they jump across synapses to other nerve cells. Find the parts of the two neurons in Figure 12.5.2.

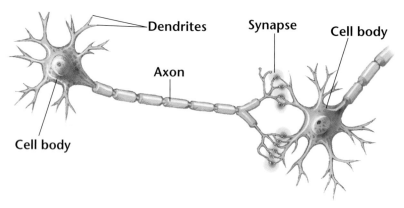

Figure 12.5.2 *Neurons transmit information throughout the body.*

Amyotrophic lateral sclerosis (ALS) is a rare disease that destroys nerve cells in the spinal cord. A person with ALS slowly loses motor abilities and becomes paralyzed. People with ALS lose the ability to move, but still think clearly. Lou Gehrig, a Yankee baseball player, had ALS. ALS is also known as Lou Gehrig's disease.

The nervous system has three types of neurons. Sensory neurons carry impulses from sense organs to the spinal cord or brain. Motor neurons carry these impulses to muscles and glands. Inside the spinal cord, association neurons receive impulses from sensory neurons and send them to motor neurons. All of this happens in an instant. Impulse speeds between neurons can be more than 200 miles per hour.

Reflex Actions

Sneezing, coughing, and blinking are reflex actions. They happen automatically. Many reflex actions protect the body from injury.

Achievements in Science

People once thought that the food they ate changed into blood. Blood was then burned up as energy. In 1628, William Harvey, a British doctor, published a description of the circulatory system. Other doctors criticized Harvey's work. Over time, however, they accepted the idea that blood circulates constantly in the body.

In 1818, James Blundell, another British doctor, performed the world's first successful blood transfusion. A blood transfusion is the transferring of blood from a donor to another person. A donor is someone who donates, or gives, blood. Since then, doctors have saved millions of lives by blood transfusions. In 1901, Austrian scientist Karl Landsteiner discovered that proteins in blood cells create different blood types. Doctors soon realized they needed to match blood types in transfusions. Today, all blood is typed and matched between donors and the people who receive donated blood.

In 1967, Christiaan Barnard, a South African doctor, transplanted the world's first human heart. He took the heart of a woman who had just died and placed it into the body of a 55-year old man. The man lived 18 days. This historic event led to successful transplants of hearts and other organs.

Lesson 5   R E V I E W

Word Bank

central nervous
  system

electrical impulses

synapses

On a sheet of a paper, write the word or words from the Word
Bank that complete each sentence correctly.

1. Gaps between neurons are _____.

2. Nerves cells transmit information as _____.

3. The _____ is made up of the brain and the spinal cord.

On a sheet of paper, write the letter of the answer that
completes each sentence correctly.

4. The control center of the body is the _____.

    A heart   **C** brain

    B spinal cord   **D** hypothalamus

5. The part of the brain that is responsible for balance is the
_____.

    A cerebellum   **C** brain stem

    B limbic system   **D** cerebral cortex

6. The limbic system of the brain is responsible for _____.

    A movement   **C** memory

    B body temperature   **D** feelings

Critical Thinking

On a sheet of paper, write the answers to the following
questions. Use complete sentences.

7. Describe the parts that make up a nerve cell.

8. How does the brain handle information for short-term
and long-term memory?

9. What are the functions of the brain stem?

10. Describe how a nerve impulse travels through a nerve cell
to another nerve cell.

Objectives

After reading this
lesson, you should
be able to

◆ describe how
   sensations that
   begin as forms of
   energy are
   detected by
   sensory receptor
   cells

◆ explain how
   the brain
   distinguishes any
   type of stimulus

◆ name the five
   sensory receptors

◆ trace the
   interactions
   among the
   senses, nerves,
   and brain that
   allow humans to
   cope with their
   environment

The sense organs connect the body with the outside world. The five main sense organs are the eyes, ears, skin, nose, and tongue. Receptor cells in these organs receive information about the outside world. Receptor cells send impulses to your brain through sensory neurons. Your brain processes these impulses. Then you see, hear, feel, smell, and taste.

How the Sensory System Works

The nervous system transmits and understands sensory information. Once sensory information gets to the brain, it is sent to an integration center. When the information is received, signals from the integration center communicate to **effector cells.** Effector cells are muscle or gland cells that carry out the body's responses to stimuli. Recall that nerves carry information along nerve pathways by transmitting electrical impulses.

Sensations begin as different forms of energy, such as mechanical energy, light, heat, and chemical energy. The five types of **sensory receptors** are mechanoreceptors, pain receptors, photoreceptors, thermoreceptors, and chemoreceptors. Each receptor is a specialized neuron that can detect a tiny stimulus. A photoreceptor can detect a single photon of light. A chemoreceptor can detect a single molecule that creates an odor or a taste.

Mechanoreceptors respond to stimuli such as pressure, touch, stretch, motion, and sound. These are forms of mechanical energy. Receptors that detect touch are close to the surface of the skin. Receptors responding to pressure and vibration are in deep skin layers. Other receptors, such as hair cells in the ear, detect motion through movement.

Pain receptors are in the epidermis. Recall that the epidermis is the outer layer of the skin. Pain receptors respond to high temperature, heavy pressure, or specific chemicals. These stimuli result in a reaction. For example, if you touch a hot stove (stimulus), you will remove your hand quickly (reaction).

Effector cell

A muscle or gland cell that carries out the body's responses to stimuli

Sensory receptor

A specialized neuron that detects sensory stimuli, then converts them to nerve impulses that go to the brain

Photoreceptors detect energy as different wavelengths of radiation, such as visible light. Thermoreceptors respond to heat or cold. They help regulate body temperature. Chemoreceptors respond to specific molecules. Taste buds on the tongue detect sour and sweet, for example.

When a sensory receptor cell detects stimuli, it sends a signal to the brain. Information about sounds or visual objects is sent to the temporal lobes of the brain. Information about motion and location is sent to the parietal lobes of the brain. Once the brain is aware of sensations, it interprets them. Then we see, hear, feel, smell, and taste.

The Sense of Sight

The human eye is an organ that detects colors and forms images of objects. Figure 12.6.1 shows the parts of the eye. Light rays enter the eye through the **cornea.** The cornea is a clear layer of tissue that light passes through. The cornea bends rays of light toward the **pupil.** The pupil is the dark, round opening in the center of the **iris.** The pupil opens and closes to control the amount of light that enters.

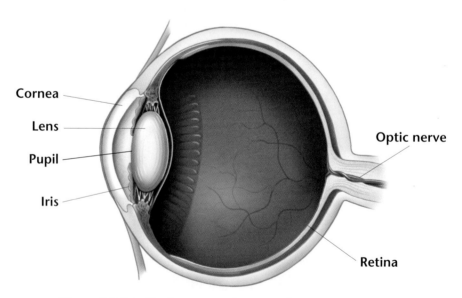

Figure 12.6.1 *The human eye is a complex organ.*

Behind the pupil is the lens. The lens focuses light rays onto the **retina.** The retina lies at the back of the eye. The retina has a membrane that contains photoreceptors. Photoreceptors change light rays into electrical impulses. The impulses are sent through the **optic nerve** to the brain. The brain translates the impulses into the images you see.

The Sense of Hearing

Your ears transform sound waves into electrical impulses. Review Figure 12.6.2 as you read how the ears work. When something makes a sound, it sends sound waves, or vibrations, into the air. The outer ear collects sound waves. The waves enter the ear opening and go down the ear canal. The vibrations strike the tympanic membrane, or **eardrum.** The eardrum is a thin tissue that vibrates, or shakes, when sound waves strike it.

The vibrations pass through three small bones in the middle ear. The bones are called the malleus, incus, and stapes. The sound waves enter the inner ear. They cause fluid in the **cochlea** to vibrate. The cochlea is a hollow, coiled tube that contains fluid and thousands of mechanoreceptors. Mechanoreceptors vibrate when sound waves strike them. These cells send impulses to the **auditory nerve,** which goes to the brain. The brain interprets the impulses as sounds you hear.

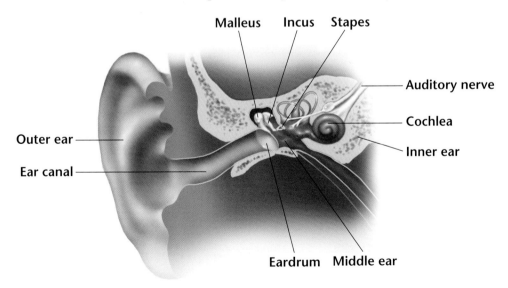

Figure 12.6.2 *The ears are sensory organs.*

The Sense of Touch

The skin receives messages about heat, cold, pressure, and pain. Sensory receptors in the skin send nerve impulses to the brain. The brain interprets the impulses to tell if something is cold, hot, smooth, or rough. The fingertips and lips have the most receptors and are very sensitive to touch.

The Senses of Taste and Smell

Taste buds are receptor cells on the tongue that can sense taste. The four kinds of tastes are sweet, sour, bitter, and salty. When food touches the tongue, taste buds send impulses to the brain. The brain interprets these impulses as tastes.

Much of the sense of taste depends on the sense of smell. Receptors in the nose sense smells. The brain needs these impulses from the nose and impulses from the tongue to interpret taste.

Technology and Society

Some people who wear corrective lenses—eyeglasses or contact lenses—decide to have laser surgery. Laser surgery, also called LASIK, uses computers to map the cornea of the eye. The cornea is cut and reshaped using a laser, knife, or heat device. The corrected cornea transmits a sharper image to the brain. LASIK surgery corrects vision problems.

Lesson 6   R E V I E W

Word Bank

cochlea

cold

heat

sensory receptor

On a sheet of paper, write the word or words from the Word Bank that complete each sentence correctly.

1. Thermoreceptors respond to _____ or _____.

2. The _____ is an organ in the ear that transforms vibrations into nerve impulses for the brain to interpret.

3. A specialized neuron that detects sensory stimuli is a(n) _____.

On a sheet of paper, write the letter of the word or words that complete each sentence correctly.

4. _____ receptors are located in the epidermis of the skin.

    A Pain   **B** Touch   **C** Vibration   **D** Motion

5. _____ cannot be detected by a mechanoreceptor.

    A Pressure   **B** Touch   **C** Sound   **D** Light

6. The _____ controls the amount of light that enters the eye.

    A pupil   **B** iris   **C** retina   **D** cornea

Critical Thinking

On a sheet of paper, write the answers to the following questions. Use complete sentences.

7. What are different types of sensory receptors? What do they do?

8. How do effector cells work in the body?

9. Explain how the parts of the eye transmit stimuli to the brain.

10. People sometimes ask, "If a tree falls in the forest and no one is around, does it make a sound?" What is the scientific answer to this question?

The endocrine system can take minutes, hours, or days to act. It takes time for hormones to be produced and carried in the blood to target organs.

The endocrine system produces hormones, which regulate body functions. Table 12.7.1 lists glands in the body that produce hormones. Figure 12.7.1 shows that glands are found throughout the body. There are more than 30 different hormones. Hormones affect everything from kidney functions to growth and development. They work by attaching to certain cells, then changing the function of the cells.

Table 12.7.1 Eight Glands and What They Do	
Gland Name	**What It Does**
Adrenal glands	Increase metabolic activity and raise the level of glucose in the blood
Gonads	Produce sperm in males and estrogen in females
Hypothalamus	Regulates the pituitary gland
Pancreas	Regulates the level of glucose in the blood
Pineal gland	Secretes melatonin to regulate sleep
Pituitary gland	Maintains water and salt balance
Thymus gland	Helps certain white cells develop and plays a part in the body's defenses
Thyroid gland	Regulates calcium in the blood

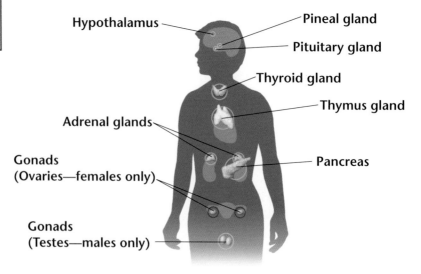

Figure 12.7.1 *The glands secrete more than 30 different hormones in the body.*

Each gland must secrete the correct amount of hormones for the body to work properly. After hormones reach the cells, the cells send a chemical signal back to the gland. This signal tells the gland to continue or to stop secreting the hormones. This process is called a feedback loop.

The body reacts when it is stressed. People under stress sweat more, their heart beats faster, and they breathe faster. This is the stress response. When a person feels scared or excited, the adrenal glands secrete a hormone called adrenaline. Adrenaline causes stress changes in the body.

The stress response can be negative if it goes on for a long time. A person can become depressed. The stress response can also be positive. If you are running a race, your heart rate increases and more oxygen is sent to your muscles. Adrenaline increases the amount of glucose in your muscles. After the race, your body returns to normal.

▾◂▴▾◂▴▾◂▴▾◂▴▾◂▴▾◂▴▾◂▴▾◂▴▾◂▴▾◂▴▾◂▴▾◂▴▾◂▴▾◂▴▾◂▴▾◂▴▾

Science at Work

Forensic Technician

Forensic technicians investigate crimes. They collect and analyze physical evidence. They perform tests on weapons or substances such as fiber, hair, tissue, or body fluid. Forensic technicians use technology, including DNA analysis, to investigate crimes.

Forensic technicians prepare reports on their findings. They provide information to investigators.

When criminal cases go to trial, forensic technicians often provide testimony (information). Their testimony can include laboratory findings about the substances and materials found at a crime scene.

Forensic technicians must have a high school degree and an associate's degree or two years of specialized training. Many obtain a four-year college degree and become forensic investigators.

Word Bank

glucose

gonads

hormones

On a sheet of a paper, write the word from the Word Bank that completes each sentence correctly.

1. The endocrine system produces _____ that regulate body functions.

2. Sperm and estrogen are produced in the _____.

3. The pancreas regulates the level of _____ in the blood.

Match the following descriptions with the correct gland. Write the letter of your answer on a sheet of paper.

4. increases metabolic activity and raises the level of glucose in the blood

5. maintains water and salt balance

6. regulates calcium in the blood

    A thyroid gland   **C** adrenal gland

    B pituitary gland   **D** thymus gland

Critical Thinking

On a sheet of paper, write the answers to the following questions. Use complete sentences.

7. Explain how the feedback loop works between cells and glands to regulate the release of hormones.

8. What are five glands and their functions?

9. How do the adrenal glands respond to stress?

10. What is the stress response?

Objectives

Objectives

After reading this lesson, you should be able to

◆ identify the functions of bone

◆ explain how bones and muscles work together to produce movement

◆ describe the different kinds of muscle

Skeletal system

The network of bones in the body

Red marrow

The spongy material in bones that makes blood cells

Osteoporosis

A disease in which bones become lighter and break easily

The Skeletal System

The 206 bones of the human body make up the **skeletal system.** The skeleton has five major jobs. First, it protects vital organs such as the brain, heart, and lungs. For example, the rib cage protects the lungs and heart. Vertebrae protect the spinal cord. The pelvis protects reproductive organs. The skull protects the brain. Second, bones give the body shape. Bones form a framework that supports the softer tissues of the body.

Third, the skeletal system allows movement. Because muscles are attached to bones, when muscles move, bones move. The body has big bones, small bones, flat bones, wide bones, and bones with unusual shapes. The variety of bones helps a person move in different ways. Fourth, blood cells are formed in bones. Bones contain spongy material called **red marrow.** Red marrow has special cells that make blood cells. Fifth, bones store minerals such as calcium, phosphorous, and magnesium.

Bones

Bones are alive and change constantly. They have nerves and blood vessels. Bones are built up and broken down throughout life. This is a normal process. For example, enzymes break down bone tissue when the body needs calcium. Calcium is released into the blood. If calcium is not replaced in bone tissue, a person can develop **osteoporosis.** Osteoporosis is a disease in which bones become lighter and break easily. Exercising on a regular basis and taking in more calcium can help prevent osteoporosis.

A typical bone has an outer layer of hard bone. This layer is strong, dense, and tough. Beneath the hard bone is a layer of spongy bone. It looks like a honeycomb. It is light and slightly flexible. In the middle of some bones is red marrow. The red marrow makes blood cells.

Most bones start out as cartilage. Cartilage is a thick, smooth, tough tissue. It is softer than bone. Parts of your body are cartilage. Feel the end of your nose and outer ear. These body parts are made of cartilage. Before birth, the entire skeleton is cartilage. It is gradually replaced by bone. Infants have about 350 bones. As people grow, some bones fuse together.

Cartilage covers the end of each bone. Where two bones meet, cartilage at the bone ends is covered by a thin film of slippery fluid. This keeps bones from scratching and bumping against each other when they move. Strips of strong tissue called **ligaments** connect bones to each other. Ligaments stretch to allow the bones to move.

Joints

Bones meet at joints. Three types of joints allow for flexibility in movement. One type of skeletal joint is the ball-and-socket joint. This joint allows the arms and legs to rotate. Figure 12.8.1 shows another type of joint, the hinge joint. The knee is a hinge joint. Hinge joints allow movement only in one direction. A third type of joint is the pivot joint. This joint allows limited rotation. The forearm at the elbow is a pivot joint.

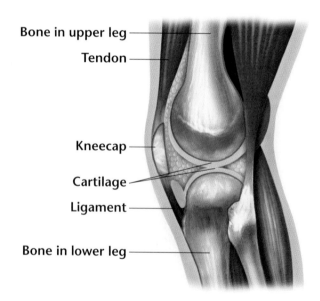

Bone in upper leg
Tendon
Kneecap
Cartilage
Ligament
Bone in lower leg

Figure 12.8.1 *The knee is a hinge joint.*

The Muscular System

The muscular system consists of more than 640 muscles in the human body. Almost half the body's weight is muscle. The skeletal and muscular systems work together to produce movement. Tough strips of tissue called **tendons** attach muscles to bones.

Muscle tissue is made up of long cells. Muscles can contract, or shorten, when they receive a signal from the brain. Muscles pull on tendons when they contract. Tendons pull on the bones and cause limbs to move. Muscles are attached in antagonistic pairs. This means the muscles in a pair work against each other. One muscle pulls the body part one way. The other muscle pulls it back. As one muscle pulls, the other muscle relaxes and stretches.

There are three types of muscle tissue: skeletal, smooth, and cardiac. Most muscle is skeletal muscle. Skeletal muscles are attached to bones. Skeletal muscles cause voluntary movement. This means you can choose when to use them. **Voluntary muscles** are in your face, arms, and legs.

Smooth muscle is found in the lining of the digestive tract, arteries, and other organs. Smooth muscles are **involuntary muscles.** This means that you cannot choose when to use them. These muscles use peristalsis, or wavelike motions, to do their job. For example, food moves through the digestive tract by peristalsis. The heart is made of cardiac muscle. Cardiac muscle is involuntary.

Tendon

A tough tissue that attaches muscles to bones

Voluntary muscle

A muscle that a person can control

Involuntary muscle

A muscle that a person cannot control

Link to ➤➤➤

Home and Career

Some people choose to donate their organs when they die. They are often given a special symbol on their driver's license to tell others of their wish. Currently, not enough organs are donated to fill the need for saving lives. If you want to become an organ donor, tell your family and friends so that they are aware of your wish.

Lesson 8   R E V I E W

Word Bank
involuntary
red marrow
tendons

On a sheet of a paper, write the word or words from the Word Bank that complete each sentence correctly.

1. Muscle actions that activate the heart and lungs are _____.

2. New blood cells are created in the _____.

3. The skeletal system is connected to muscle tissue by _____.

On a sheet of paper, write the letter of the answer that completes each sentence correctly.

4. Muscles move the body by _____.

    A twisting   **B** lengthening   **C** pushing   **D** pulling

5. The area of the skeletal system that protects the heart is the _____.

    A skull   **C** rib cage

    B backbone   **D** limb and pelvis

6. The skeletal system does not _____.

    A stimulate growth of the body

    B protect the vital organs

    C give shape to the body

    D allow movement

Critical Thinking

On a sheet of paper, write the answers to the following questions. Use complete sentences.

7. Why do some people develop osteoporosis?

8. What are the three types of muscle tissue? Where is each type found?

9. Is breathing a voluntary muscle action or an involuntary muscle action? Explain your answer.

10. Describe the three types of skeletal joints that allow movement.

DISCOVERY INVESTIGATION 12

Materials

- safety goggles
- lab coat or apron
- assorted materials to model joints such as screws, washers, hinges, ball-like lollipops, bottle caps, craft sticks, pipe cleaners, modeling clay, push pins, glue

Constructing Models of Human Joints

The human skeletal system uses three types of joints that allow movement. The ball-and-socket joint allows rotation. The hinge joint moves back and forth in one direction. The pivot joint allows limited rotation. By working together, these joints allow the human skeleton to move in many different ways.

In this investigation, you will be given a variety of materials to make your own models of these joints.

Procedure

1. In a small group, write a procedure with Safety Alerts to make one type of joint. You may use any of the materials listed. Write the procedure as if you were giving directions to another person.

2. Put on safety goggles and a lab coat or apron.

3. Follow your procedure to construct the model. **Safety Alert: Be careful when working with materials that have sharp edges.**

Cleanup/Disposal

When you are finished, clean up your area and put extra materials away.

Analysis

1. What factors did you consider when making your joint?

2. Where is the actual joint located in the human body?

3. What are the limitations of your joint model?

Conclusions

1. Describe how your joint model is different from the body joint it represents.

2. What limitations did you have with the materials?

3. What are the advantages of body joints compared to mechanical joints?

Explore Further

Add a motor or pulley system to make your model move. Try to mimic the movements of the body joint. Be creative in your materials and methods.

Blood Donations

You probably have seen blood drives. You or family members may have donated blood. People often need blood when a natural disaster or medical emergency happens in a community. The need for blood during emergencies is constant and urgent. A supply of blood for emergencies must always be available.

The donor's blood type must match the blood type of the person receiving the blood. Blood type is determined by the types of proteins on the surface of red blood cells. Donated blood that does not match can clot, causing death for the person who receives it. A person with type AB blood can only donate blood to other AB blood types. However, people with type AB blood can receive blood from all other blood types.

For this reason, people with AB blood are called universal receivers. People with type O blood can donate to all blood types, but they can receive only type O blood. People with type O blood are called universal donors.

Health professionals must test donated blood for disease agents, such as the viruses that cause AIDS and hepatitis. Hepatitis is a liver disease. New screening procedures include testing for the nucleic acids that make up harmful viruses.

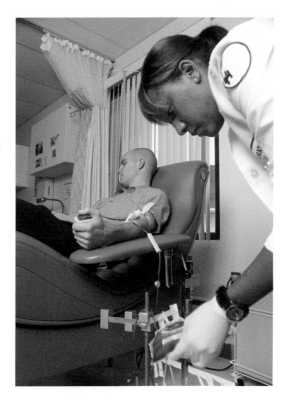

These new tests are more accurate than older tests. Older tests looked for antibodies. These new tests are also faster than the old tests. This allows donated blood to be used more quickly.

1. What steps are taken to be sure a community's blood supply is safe?

2. Every medical facility keeps a supply of type O blood. Why?

3. What must health professionals do to blood that has been donated?

Chapter 12 S U M M A R Y

- During digestion, food changes into a form that can enter cells. The large intestine eliminates undigested food.

- The respiratory system brings oxygen into the lungs and releases carbon dioxide from the lungs.

- The circulatory system moves materials to and from cells. The heart is the main organ in this system. Blood contains different cell types that bind with oxygen, prevent bleeding, and fight infection.

- The excretory system removes waste and regulates water balance in the body. The kidneys filter the blood to get rid of toxic wastes. The wastes leave the body as urine.

- The nervous system controls and coordinates body activities. Impulses carry information from nerve cell to nerve cell. The brain is the control center.

- The five main sense organs are the eyes, ears, skin, nose, and tongue. Sensory receptors in sense organs gather information and send nerve impulses to the brain.

- The endocrine system produces hormones that regulate many body functions.

- The skeletal and muscular systems work together to produce movement. Blood cells are made inside some bones. Bones store minerals, protect organs, and give the body shape.

Vocabulary

alveolus, 349
antidiuretic hormone (ADH), 360
aorta, 353
artery, 353
asthma, 350
atherosclerosis, 355
atrium, 353
auditory nerve, 369
axon, 364
bile, 345
brain stem, 362
bronchiole, 349
bronchitis, 350
bronchus, 349
capillary, 348
cardiac, 352
cardiovascular disease, 355
cerebellum, 362

cerebral cortex, 363
chyme, 345
cochlea, 369
connective tissue, 354
cornea, 368
dendrite, 364
dermis, 360
diencephalon, 362
eardrum, 369
effector cell, 367
epidermis, 360
epithelium, 348
fatty layer, 360
feces, 346
fibrinogen, 355
gallbladder, 345
glomerulus, 360
glottis, 348
hypertension, 355
hypothalamus, 363

inferior vena cava, 353
ingestion, 344
interstitial fluid, 353
involuntary muscle, 377
iris, 368
larynx, 348
ligament, 376
limbic system, 362
nephron, 360
neuron, 364
neurotransmitter, 364
optic nerve, 369
osteoporosis, 375
peristalsis, 345
perspiration, 360
pharynx, 345
pituitary gland, 363
plasma, 354
platelet, 354
pupil, 368

rectum, 346
red marrow, 375
reflex, 344
retina, 369
sensory receptor, 367
skeletal system, 375
sleep apnea, 350
superior vena cava, 353
synapse, 364
tendon, 377
thalamus, 363
thrombus, 355
trachea, 349
ureter, 359
urine, 359
vein, 353
ventricle, 353
villi, 345
voluntary muscle, 377

Chapter 12 R E V I E W

Word Bank

artery

capillary

chyme

effector cell

epithelium

fibrinogen

glottis

ligament

nephron

neuron

peristalsis

plasma

red marrow

sensory receptor

synapse

tendon

trachea

Vocabulary Review

On a sheet of paper, write the word or words from the Word Bank that best complete each sentence.

1. A(n) _____ is a cell that specializes in conducting electrical impulses throughout the body.

2. A(n) _____ detects stimuli and converts them to nerve impulses that are sent to the brain.

3. Food is pushed along the digestive tract through the action of _____.

4. The _____ must be closed when swallowing food in order to protect the windpipe.

5. Information from an integration center goes to a(n) _____, which carries out the body's response.

6. Blood cells are made in _____.

7. A(n) _____ connects bones to each other.

8. Oxygen that is breathed in diffuses across the _____ into the blood.

9. A bone is connected to a muscle with a(n) _____.

10. Nerve impulses pass between two nerve cells through a(n) _____.

11. Food that is being digested takes the form of _____ when it enters the small intestine.

12. A small tube that is the excretory unit of the kidney is a(n) _____.

13. The liquid part of blood is _____.

14. Blood reaches an individual cell through a(n) _____.

Review continued on next page

15. Air travels through the _____ to reach the bronchi.

16. The protein in blood that forms clots is _____.

17. Blood traveling in a(n) _____ is moving away from the heart.

Concept Review

On a sheet of paper, write the letter of the answer that completes each sentence correctly.

18. Blood in an artery is usually _____.

    A rich in oxygen and moves toward the heart

    B poor in oxygen and moves toward the heart

    C rich in oxygen and moves away from the heart

    D poor in oxygen and moves away from the heart

19. High-level functions such as learning, thinking, and memory functions are carried out by the _____.

    A cerebral cortex   **C** limbic system

    B cerebellum   **D** spinal cord

20. The liver works to help the body by _____.

    A producing stomach acid

    B processing food to get nutrients

    C releasing bile into the stomach

    D extracting water from waste

21. Platelets can form a clot, or a _____.

    A red blood cell   **C** plasma

    B white blood cell   **D** thrombus

Critical Thinking

On a sheet of paper, write the answers to the following questions. Use complete sentences.

22. Why must muscles work in pairs to allow a complete range of movement?

23. Describe the two main systems that make up the nervous system.

24. Describe the process of respiration.

25. How can the stress response be negative or positive?

Research and Write

Investigate government regulations for the handling and preparation of food products. What new technologies are being introduced in the meat industry to prevent food from becoming infected by pathogens? Describe some arguments that support these methods. Describe some of the criticism of the methods.

Test-Taking Tip Read test questions carefully. Identify questions that require more than one answer.

13 Evolution and Natural Selection

C an you see the leopard in the tree in the photograph? The leopard's spots help it blend with the spotted pattern in the tree bark. This keeps the leopard hidden. The spots make the leopard a better hunter. Traits like the leopard's spots are called adaptations. Adaptation improves the chance that an organism survives and reproduces in an environment. In Chapter 13, you will learn about biological evolution. You will find out how species adapt through natural selection.

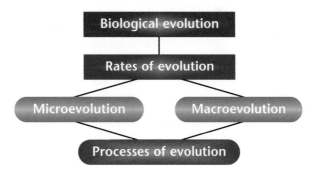

Organize Your Thoughts

Biological evolution

Rates of evolution

Microevolution — Macroevolution

Processes of evolution

Goals for Learning

◆ To describe the theory of evolution and the evidence that supports evolution

◆ To describe the rates of evolutionary change

◆ To explain how changes occur in the gene pool

◆ To define natural selection, microevolution, and macroevolution

Objectives

After reading this lesson, you should be able to

◆ define evolution

◆ state the two theories that came from Darwin's work

◆ explain why Mendel's work supported evolution

◆ describe the theory of modern synthesis

Fossil

The remains or impressions of an organism that lived in the past

Population

A group of organisms of the same species that live in the same area

Biological evolution

The change in the gene pool of a population over time

Gene pool

The genes found within a population

Millions of different types of organisms live on the earth today. They differ in structures, behaviors, and genes. Living things are also alike in many ways. They reproduce, use energy, and exchange substances with the environment. Living things share the same pattern of genetic code. How do scientists explain the differences and similarities in living things?

To answer this question, scientists look at the history of living things. They do this by looking at **fossils** in rocks. Fossils are the remains or impressions of organisms that lived in the past. Fossils show that ancient organisms are like modern organisms, but are also different. Scientists look at other types of evidence that support a theory called evolution. Evolution is the changes in a **population** over time. You will study these types of evidence in Lesson 2. Scientists use the theory of evolution to explain the similarity and differences in living things.

Biological evolution is the change in the gene pool of populations of organisms over time. **Gene pool** is the genes found within a population. Biological evolution explains how living things that appear to be different are related. This theory also explains how differences develop among living things.

Lamarck's Ideas About Evolution

In the early 1800s, French scientist Jean Baptiste de Lamarck published ideas about evolution. He thought a relationship between fossils and modern living things was due to the idea that life evolves. He thought organisms change as they adjust to changes in the environment. The changes are passed to offspring.

For example, Lamarck thought ancient giraffes ate the lower leaves on trees. To eat the higher leaves, they stretched their necks. Lamarck thought stretching caused offspring to be born with longer necks. He thought a giraffe's long neck was an **acquired trait.** An acquired trait would come from an organism's behavior and is passed to offspring. Scientists rejected Lamarck's ideas. However, scientists accepted the idea that adaptation resulted from interactions between living things and their environments.

Darwin's Theories of Decent with Modification and Natural Selection

From 1831 to 1836, British scientist Charles Darwin sailed around the world. On his travels, Darwin studied living things. He observed that organisms were alike in many ways, but were also different.

Darwin suggested organisms living today descended, or evolved, from organisms that lived millions of years ago. These early descendants spread to different areas. Then they changed to fit different ways of life. Darwin called this idea **descent with modification.** This theory states that more recent species of organisms are changed descendants of earlier species.

On his travels, Darwin observed that species created large numbers of offspring. However, not all survived. He also observed great variation among members in a population. He suggested individuals with survival traits best suited to their environment are more likely than others to reproduce. Darwin called this idea **natural selection.**

In 1859, Darwin published his ideas in a book, *On the Origin of Species.* Natural selection is the process by which organisms best suited to the environment survive, reproduce, and pass their genes to the next generation.

Darwin explained evolution with two ideas. His first idea was **common descent.** He stated that present organisms are related to past organisms. Darwin thought all species had come from one or a few original life-forms. For example, he thought all birds and mammals came from an animal that lived in the distant past. Darwin's theory explains why organisms have offspring that are similar. Common descent basically says that evolution occurs in nature.

Darwin's second idea was natural selection. Darwin thought that natural selection explained how evolution occurs. In this theory, new variations within populations happen constantly. Some variations give individuals an advantage in survival. These individuals produce more offspring than individuals without the variations.

Adapt

To change genetically over generations to become more suited to the environment

Modern synthesis

A theory that states evolution involves changes in a population's gene pool over time

Link to ➤➤➤

Social Studies

By examining the DNA of many people, scientists have found that we are all very closely related. The genetic diversity between any two humans is very small. Scientists have evidence that all humans descended from a very small population in northern Africa. These people lived between 70,000 and 140,000 years ago.

Individuals in a population with traits best suited to the environment increase in numbers. They are more likely to survive. They are also more likely to pass their genes to their offspring. The entire population **adapts** to its environment as more offspring with the favored traits are created. Over many generations, the entire population and the whole species evolve with the adaptations.

Sometimes, natural selection can cause a new species to arise from an old species. The new species cannot reproduce with the old species. The two species often become separated by natural barriers, such as rivers and mountains. This reproductive separation causes the two species to evolve differently.

The Transfer of Genetic Material

Remember from Chapter 10 Gregor Mendel's experiments with pea plants. In 1866, Mendel determined how traits combined to produce patterns of inheritance. Based on Mendel's data, scientists later determined how genetic material was passed to offspring. In all organisms, genes carry the information about traits from parents to offspring.

Modern Synthesis

Darwin and Mendel laid the groundwork for the modern study of life. Darwin explained that all living things are connected. He proposed the theory of natural selection to explain how organisms changed. Mendel developed the theory of genetics. Recall from Chapter 10 that genetics is the basis for biological inheritance.

Today, scientists support a theory of evolution called **modern synthesis.** The theory of modern synthesis explains that populations evolve. Individuals do not evolve. Modern synthesis combines the ideas of Darwin, Mendel, and other scientists. Modern synthesis states that evolution involves changes in a population's gene pool over time. Genes determine the traits of all living things.

Lesson 1 REVIEW

Word Bank

acquired trait

common descent

gene pool

On a sheet of paper, write the word or words from the Word Bank that complete each sentence correctly.

1. Darwin's idea of _____ states that today's organisms are related to past organisms.

2. The theory of modern synthesis states that evolution involves changes in a population's _____.

3. Lamarck's ideas about evolution stated that a giraffe's long neck was a(n) _____.

On a sheet of paper, write the letter of the answer that completes each sentence correctly.

4. Mendel developed the theory of _____.

    A natural selection   **C** evolution

    B modern synthesis   **D** genetics

5. Darwin thought _____ was needed for a species to change.

    A extinction   **C** genetic mutation

    B natural selection   **D** an acquired trait

6. A current theory of evolution is _____.

    A species isolation   **C** behavior change

    B barrier   **D** modern synthesis

Critical Thinking

On a sheet of paper, write the answers to the following questions. Use complete sentences.

7. Describe the process Darwin thought caused a species to evolve into another species.

8. Describe the modern synthesis theory of evolution.

9. What are fossils? What do they show scientists?

10. What were Lamarck's ideas about evolution?

Sedimentary rock

The rock formed from pieces of other rock and organic matter that have been pressed and cemented together

Fossil record

The history of life on the earth, based on fossils that have been discovered

Scientists use different types of evidence to support the theory of modern synthesis. Scientists have found fossils of organisms similar to modern organisms. They have found patterns in the way living things are distributed on the earth. Organisms that look different may have similar body structures. Scientists have also found that the DNA of each species is different, but alike. Let's look at each type of evidence of evolution.

Fossil Record

Fossils are evidence that species lived long ago. The earth today is very different than it was billions of years ago. The continents were once in different locations. The climate was different. Scientists have found that **sedimentary rock** contains a **fossil record,** or diary, of the earth's history. Sedimentary rock is rock formed from pieces of other rock and organic matter that have been pressed and cemented together. Sedimentary rock often has layers.

By examining the fossils in each rock layer, scientists can estimate when certain organisms lived. Fossils in the lower layers represented species that lived before species in the upper layers. The fossil record also shows how organisms have changed over time. By comparing fossils to modern organisms, scientists have found many similarities.

Biogeography

Scientists have found patterns in the way living things are distributed, or spread out, on the earth. The study of the geographical distribution of fossils and living organisms is called **biogeography.** For example, kangaroos are only found in Australia. Scientists think kangaroos evolved in isolation from regions where other animals diversified.

Biogeography

The study of the geographical distribution of fossils and living organisms

Charles Darwin observed that the animals on the Galapagos Islands were similar to animals in South America. The Galapagos Islands are a group of islands 600 miles west of Ecuador in South America.

Darwin thought that Galapagos species evolved from animals that came from South America. He thought the differences between parents and offspring happened through natural selection. By using biogeography, scientists today have evidence that supports Darwin's observations.

Express Lab 13

Materials
- marker
- 3 flat sponges

Procedure

1. Form small groups.

2. Using a marker, make a shape like an ✕, ☐, or ○ on the long side of each sponge. Make each mark different. The marks represent fossils. The sponges represent layers of rock.

3. Put the sponges on top of each other so that the fossils face you. Observe the order of fossils from top to bottom.

4. Hold the layers of sponges tightly on both ends. Moving your hands toward each other, push inward against the sponges. Observe what happens to the order of fossils from top to bottom.

Analysis

1. Which fossil is the oldest in Step 3?

2. How did the order of fossils change in Step 4?

3. What does a scientist need to know about a rock to tell if one fossil is older than another fossil?

Comparative Anatomy

To look for clues suggesting evolution, scientists compare the **anatomy** of species. Anatomy is the structure of an organism. **Comparative anatomy** is the study of anatomy of animals of different species. Sometimes species look different, but their structures are similar.

Look at the front limbs of the four animals in Figure 13.2.1. Notice how similar the bones are. The limbs are **homologous structures.** Body parts that are similar in different animals are homologous structures. However, the function of the limbs differs for each animal. Some scientists think homologous structures appeared in an ancestor common to all organisms.

Anatomy

The structure of an organism

Comparative anatomy

The study of anatomy of different species

Homologous structure

The body parts that are similar in related animals

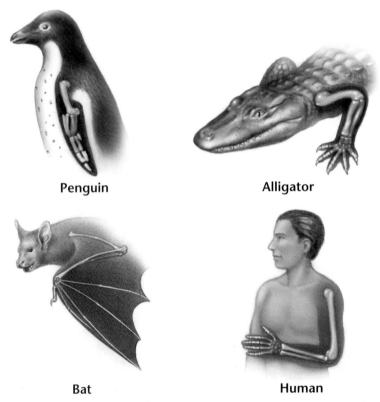

Penguin   Alligator

Bat   Human

Figure 13.2.1 *The front limbs of these different animals are similar.*

Molecular Biology

Scientists use **molecular biology** to examine the basis of life. Molecular biology is the study of the biochemical and molecular processes within cells. Scientists use molecular studies as evidence of evolution. For example, scientists use DNA analysis to show that life has evolved. They have found that similar forms of organisms have more recent common ancestors than less similar forms. They have also found that the early stages of embryos of different animals are very similar.

The evidence for these patterns is in the DNA sequences of organisms. Remember that a cell makes a new copy of its DNA before dividing to produce two daughter cells. Cells may make mistakes when copying its DNA nucleotides. A few nucleotides may change each time a cell divides.

Over time, two organisms with a common ancestor will have differences in their DNA sequences. The more cell divisions that occur, the more differences in DNA sequences will result. By comparing these differences, scientists can understand how species are related.

Scientists have methods to find the sequence of DNA nucleotides in chromosomes. In 2003, the Human Genome Project identified the entire sequence of human DNA. Recall from Chapter 5 that a genome is the entire DNA found in a cell. Scientists also have found the sequences of other species' genomes. By comparing these sequences and other evidence, scientists are putting together the history of life on the earth.

Link to ➤➤➤

Chemistry

Scientists once thought prokaryotes did not have organelles. Recently, they discovered a primitive organelle that exists in some bacteria. These tiny organelles are like pouches. These pouches contain enzymes. The pouches are also found in some eukaryotes. Scientists think this may be an important evolutionary link between bacteria and eukaryotic cells.

Lesson 2 REVIEW

Word Bank

molecular biology

nucleotides

sedimentary rock

On a sheet of paper, write the word or words from the Word Bank that complete each sentence correctly.

1. Pieces of rock and organic material pressed together form _____.

2. DNA sequences between two related organisms will often have a few different _____ due to copying errors.

3. The study of biochemical and molecular processes within cells is _____.

On a sheet of paper, write the letter of the answer that completes each sentence correctly.

4. The layers of sedimentary rock form a _____.

    A biogeography   **C** continent

    B fossil record   **D** climate

5. The body structures of some species support Darwin's theories because they _____.

    A have similar functions   **C** are the same

    B have similar limbs   **D** are very different

6. The study of biogeography includes information about the location of _____.

    A rocks   **C** fossils and living organisms

    B homologous structures   **D** the fossil record

Critical Thinking

On a sheet of paper, write the answers to the following questions. Use complete sentences.

7. How could a scientist use DNA sequences of two organisms to find which is more closely related to a common ancestor?

8. What can scientists find by examining the fossil record?

9. Why did Darwin think animals on the Galapagos Islands evolved from animals in South America?

10. How has the Human Genome Project contributed to knowledge about evolution?

Objectives

After reading this lesson, you should be able to

◆ define geologic time

◆ explain how a rock's age determines a fossil's age

◆ describe how the geologic time scale relates to evolutionary change

◆ explain how continental drift and plate tectonics relate to evolutionary change

Geologic time

All the time that has passed since the earth formed

Paleontologist

A scientist who studies fossils

Many modern organisms are very different in structure and behavior from organisms that lived in the past. For example, modern horses are much larger than early horses. Early horses had four toes on each foot. As the horse evolved, its four toes became a single hoof.

The diversity of organisms today and in the past is the result of evolution. Evolution has occurred on the earth over many millions of years. Scientists look for evidence of evolutionary change in the earth's history.

Geological Time

Most events in the earth are compared to **geologic time.** Geologic time is all the time that has passed since the earth formed. Scientists estimate that the earth is about 4.6 billion years old. They base this estimate on meteorites and moon rocks. Meteorites are pieces of rock that hit the surface of a planet or moon after traveling through space. Both meteorites and moon rocks formed about the same time as the earth.

Fossils are an important record of the earth's history. Recall from Lesson 1 that fossils are the remains or impressions of organisms preserved in rocks. Fossils are evidence that certain kinds of life existed.

Paleontologists are scientists who look for and study fossils. Their findings have formed a fossil record. The fossil record tells about the organisms that once lived on the earth. The fossil record also shows how organisms have changed over time.

A fossil can be a preserved organism or an impression of an organism. Fossils of an organism's activities are called trace fossils, such as foot prints.

The oldest known rocks on the earth are in Greenland. They are about 3.8 billion years old.

Paleontologists can determine the relative ages of fossils by comparing their locations in rock. Relative age shows whether a fossil is older or younger than another fossil. Fossils in lower layers of rock are older than fossils in upper layers of rock. The lower rock layers were formed first. More recent rock layers contain fossils that look more like existing species.

Paleontologists can also estimate the actual ages of fossils. Actual age tells the number of years ago a fossil formed. Scientists use **radioactive elements** to date fossils. A radioactive element decays to form another element. This decay happens at a constant rate. To determine the age of fossils found in a rock, paleontologists compare the amounts of different elements in the rock.

Geologic Time Scale

Using fossils, paleontologists have put together the **geologic time scale.** This table is shown in Appendix D. The geologic time scale is a table that divides the earth's history into different time periods. The table shows the kinds of organisms that first appeared during each time period.

Scientists have found small fossils that show evidence of bacteria living 3.5 to 3.8 billion years ago. They have found evidence that animals of two or more cells lived 670 million years ago. However, the organisms that lived between these two dates did not have hard body parts. They seldom became fossils.

In the Cambrian period about 570 million years ago, there was a dramatic change on the earth. At the beginning of this period, animals with hard shells and other body coverings appeared. Fossils from the Cambrian period show that a variety of **invertebrates** lived in the seas. An invertebrate is an animal that does not have a backbone.

The earliest **vertebrate** fossils are from about 500 million years ago. A vertebrate is an animal with a backbone. Early **amphibians** and **reptiles** appeared next. An amphibian is a vertebrate that lives at first in water and then on land. A reptile is an egg-laying vertebrate that breathes with lungs.

Dinosaurs appeared about 225 million years ago. They disappeared suddenly about 160 million years later. Birds and mammals appeared in the fossil record about 200 million years ago.

Geologic Time

One of the greatest scientific theories is that geologic time represents billions of years. Using radioactive dating methods, scientists measure the age of radioactive elements and fossils. Scientists used this new knowledge along with an understanding of **plate tectonics.** Plate tectonics is a theory that states the earth's crust is made of large sections of crust that move. Scientists knew evolutionary change that resulted in new species occurred very slowly. The rate of evolutionary change happens over millions of years.

The study of plate tectonics discusses the theory of **continental drift.** This theory states that the major landmasses of the earth move. In 1912, German scientist Alfred Wegener published the theory of continental drift. He thought the earth's continents were once a single, large landmass. Wegner thought this landmass began to break up about 200 million years ago. The continents slowly moved to their present positions. Figure 13.3.1 shows their movement. For a detailed map of the continents today, see Appendix E.

Plate tectonics

A theory that the earth's surface is made of large sections of crust that move

Continental drift

A theory that the major landmasses of the earth move

225 million years ago   180 million years ago   Present day

Figure 13.3.1 *The theory of continental drift states that the major landmasses move over time.*

As evidence, Wegener found fossils on one continent that were similar to those on other continents. He thought mountain ranges and rock layers continued from one continent to another. In the 1950s, scientists used new instruments to determine if Wegener's theory was supported. They did this by mapping the ocean floor.

Scientists found long mountain ranges called mid-ocean ridges along the ocean floor. Mid-ocean ridges wind along the entire earth. Scientists found that **magma** once pushed apart the **plates** on which continents were located. Magma is hot, liquid rock inside the earth. Magma pushes up when volcanos erupt. A plate is a large section of the earth's **crust,** or outer layer, that moves. By the late 1960s, scientists accepted the theory of continental drift.

The theory of continental drift led to another important theory in science—plate tectonics. This theory states that the earth's crust is made of large sections, or plates. Most plates include ocean crust and continental crust. Over a long time, plates move. The positions of the continents change. Thus, as the continents moved apart, each became a separate evolutionary area. The living things of the different biogeographic regions diversified. The living things of different biogeographic regions adapted and evolved.

Link to ➤➤➤

Earth Science

In 2003, paleontologists uncovered the complete skeleton of an ancestor to the modern guinea pig. Guinea pigs are rodents which are small gnawing mammals. The skeleton belonged to the largest rodent ever discovered. Unlike modern rodents, this ancestor was the size of a horse. It measured over 9 feet long and weighed more than 1,500 pounds.

Lesson 3 **REVIEW**

Word Bank
continental drift
geologic time scale
paleontologist

On a sheet of paper, write the word or words from the Word Bank that complete each sentence correctly.

1. A scientist who studies fossils is a _____.

2. The _____ is a measurement of the earth's history, divided into time periods.

3. Today's continents may have existed as one large landmass that separated due to _____.

On a sheet of paper, write the letter of the answer that completes each sentence correctly.

4. Fossils before the Cambrian period are rare because _____.

  A little life existed then

  B little sediment existed to form fossils

  C organisms lacked hard parts

  D organisms lived mainly in the ocean

5. Plate tectonics states that the earth's crust is made of _____.

  A plates   **C** meteorites

  B magma   **D** moon rocks

6. A fossil found under a layer of rock is usually _____.

  A younger than the rock

  B older than the rock

  C evolved from the rock

  D made from a different type of rock

Critical Thinking

On a sheet of paper, write the answers to the following questions. Use complete sentences.

7. Why do scientists think the earth is 4.6 billion years old?

8. What is the theory of continental drift?

9. What is the theory of plate tectonics?

10. How do scientists find the actual age of a fossil?

- about 50 blue plastic chips
- about 50 white plastic chips
- blue pencil
- red pencil

Natural Selection in Action

Mutations are random changes in DNA. Mutations create differences in organisms. When the environment changes, some organisms can survive and reproduce due to characteristics from mutations. Natural selection may remove organisms without these characteristics. Then their genes are less likely to be passed on. In this investigation, you will demonstrate how a mutation affects the survival rate and reproduction of organisms in a certain environment.

Procedure

1. Make a data table like the one shown on page 403.

2. Scatter 12 white plastic chips and 12 blue plastic chips on your desktop. The white chips represent organisms that can survive in temperatures above

0°C. This is the normal temperature range for the species. The blue chips represent organisms of the same species with a mutation. The mutation allows them to survive in temperatures below 0°C and in the normal temperature range. These organisms are cold-tolerant. The desktop represents the environment for all the organisms. Record the number of blue chips, white chips, and total chips.

3. In the first event of this investigation, the temperature is above 0°C. To have the organisms reproduce, add a white chip or a blue chip for each pair of chips of the same color. For example, in the first round of reproduction, you start with 12 white chips (6 pairs). Add 6 more white chips to the environment. You also have 12 blue chips (6 pairs). Add 6 more blue chips to the environment. Record the number of white chips, blue chips, and the total chips after this event.

4. Follow the directions and events described by your teacher. After each event, allow your organisms to reproduce as in Step 2.

5. Make a graph to compare the population growth of the white and blue organisms. Label the *y*-axis "Number of Organisms." Label the *x*-axis "Time" and mark off increments of 10,000 years. Use a blue pencil to track the population of the blue chips. Use a red pencil to track the population of the white chips.

Cleanup/Disposal

When you are finished, return the materials to your teacher.

Analysis

1. How was the number of normal-range organisms (white chips) affected by cold weather?

2. How was reproduction by both normal-range and cold-tolerant organisms affected by a colder climate?

Conclusions

1. If the climate stays cold, what predictions can you make about the blue and white populations?

2. What would happen if the climate became warmer?

3. What information is missing from this investigation?

Explore Further

Try the simulation again introducing the missing element referred to in Question 3.

	Start	1st Event	2nd Event	3rd Event	4th Event	5th Event
Blue						
White						
Total						

Objectives

After reading this lesson, you should be able to

◆ describe processes that add new alleles to the gene pool

◆ describe processes that remove alleles from the gene pool

The diversity of organisms today and in the past is the result of evolution. There are processes that allow evolution to continue. There are also processes that slow evolution. Remember that individual organisms do not evolve. Although they change as they grow and develop, these changes are not evolution. Evolution is the change that occurs in the gene pool of a population over time. A population is made up of individuals of the same species that live in the same place. Members of the same species mate and reproduce. How do changes in the gene pool of a population occur? They can occur through mutation, recombination, gene flow, genetic drift, and natural selection.

Mutation

Recall that random change in the nucleotide sequence of DNA is a mutation. Mutations are the source of new genetic variations. Radiation or chemicals in the environment can change genes. Germ-cell mutations can occur in an organism's gametes, or germ cells. Genes can change if they are copied incorrectly during DNA replication. For example, one nucleotide in a DNA strand could replace another nucleotide. This could change the protein made by RNA. If the protein function changes, this could harm the organism.

A mutation could help an organism. A mutation sometimes results in a trait that improves an organism's chances for survival. An organism that survives is more likely to reproduce. The favorable mutation is passed to offspring. As the mutation is passed on to future generations, it becomes more common within the population.

Technology and Society

One of the most common causes of skin cancer is exposure to the sun's ultraviolet (UV) rays. These rays damage the DNA in skin cells. This can create a mutation that causes skin cancer. Recently, scientists developed a skin lotion with DNA-repair enzymes that enter the cells. Scientists hope enzyme lotions can also be developed to treat other skin diseases.

Science Myth

Myth: A gene and an allele are the same thing.

Fact: A gene is a segment of DNA that codes for a particular product, such as a protein. Mutations of the same gene create different alleles, or forms of the trait. For example, one allele for eye color may code for green eyes. Another allele may code for brown eyes.

Mutations are important because every individual has thousands of genes. Many populations have thousands or millions of individuals. Over time, mutations become the source for variation in genes.

The variation is then subject to natural selection. For example, some insects are resistant to chemicals used to destroy them. Insects that are resistant to the chemicals survive and reproduce. The gene for resistance is passed to the offspring. This means the offspring are also resistant to these chemicals.

Recombination

Every chromosome in sperm or egg cells is a mixture of genes from the parents. This is due to a process called **recombination.** Recombination is the creation of new combinations of alleles in offspring. Remember that an allele is a different form of the same gene.

Think of recombination as reshuffling. Recombination is a process of evolution. It adds new alleles and combinations to the gene pool.

Here is how recombination happens. Genes are at specific locations along the chromosomes. Most sexually reproducing organisms have two of each chromosome type in every cell. One chromosome is inherited from the mother. The other chromosome is inherited from the father. Recall that when an organism produces gametes (sex cells), the gametes have only one of each chromosome.

During meiosis, each chromosome of a pair breaks in several places. The chromosome pieces are rejoined to form two new chromosomes. Later, these chromosomes are split into two cells that divide and become gametes. Both chromosomes are a mix of alleles from the mother and the father because of recombination.

Recombination creates new combinations of alleles. Alleles that arise at different times and different places can be brought together. Recombination can occur between genes and within genes.

Gene Flow

A population may gain or lose alleles when it combines with another population. New individuals can enter a population by moving from another population. If they mate, they can bring new alleles to the local gene pool. This is called **gene flow.**

Suppose that pollen from a population of white flowers is blown to a population of red flowers. Recall that pollen is the tiny grains of a seed plant that contain sperm cells. If the pollen fertilizes the red flowers, new alleles are introduced. Over time, genetic differences between the two populations will be reduced.

Genetic Drift

One generation in a population represents the gene pool of the previous generation. The size of the population could greatly decrease if disaster strikes. Natural disasters include floods, droughts, fires, and earthquakes. Natural disasters often happen by chance.

A population that survives a disaster may not represent the parent population's gene pool. Some alleles may be removed. These changes result in loss of gene variety. The population cannot adapt well to a quickly changing environment. This leads to **genetic drift.** Genetic drift is the random changes in the gene pool of a small population.

All populations have genetic drift. Genetic drift can greatly change small populations. The loss of gene variation could reduce the ability of a population to adapt to environmental change. It can lead to an **endangered** species or the **extinction** of a species. An endangered species, such as the cheetah in Figure 13.4.1, has almost no organisms left. Extinction is the death of all members of a species.

Figure 13.4.1
Cheetahs are an endangered species.

Today, there are only three small populations of cheetahs in the wild. The loss of gene variation and loss of their **habitat** raise concerns about the future of cheetahs. Habitat is the place where an organism lives.

Hardy-Weinberg Equilibrium

Hardy-Weinberg equilibrium

A principle that states the frequencies of alleles in a population do not change unless evolutionary factors act on the population

Scientists must study and analyze population's gene pools to understand how they change. To do this, scientists must first assume that a population is in **Hardy-Weinberg equilibrium.** What is this principle? Hardy-Weinberg equilibrium means that frequencies of alleles in a population do not change unless evolutionary factors act on the population. In other words, a population stays in Hardy-Weinberg equilibrium unless outside factors change its gene pool. Gene flow and genetic drift are factors that can take a population out of Hardy-Weinberg equilibrium, for example.

Godfrey Harold Hardy and Wilhelm Weinberg are the two scientists who came up with this principle. For their idea to work, they had to make assumptions about a population. The main assumption is that a population does not change. This means its gene pool does not change. For this to happen, the population size must be large. The population also cannot experience natural selection, mutation, or other changes. However, in the natural world, populations usually change. The Hardy-Weinberg equilibrium is useful because it provides a starting point to understand when a gene pool is changing.

Scientists use the Hardy-Weinberg principle to predict genotype frequencies. The Hardy-Weinberg principle is written as an equation: $p^2 + 2pq + q^2 = 1$. This equation describes each of the possible allele combinations in a population. The p and q represent the frequency of the dominant (p) and the recessive (q) alleles in a population. Since all the alleles for a certain point will be dominant or recessive, then $p + q = 1$ (or 100%).

This means that all homozygous dominant individuals would have two dominant alleles ($p \times p = p^2$). Recall that homozygous means having an identical pair of genes. Homozygous recessive individuals would have two recessive alleles ($q \times q = q^2$). Heterozygous individuals would have one of each allele. Those pairs can be made in two different ways. This depends on which parent donates an allele ($2 \times p \times q = 2pq$).

Natural Selection

Natural selection can increase or decrease the number of times an allele appears in a population. Natural selection that weeds out harmful alleles is called negative selection. Natural selection that increases the number of helpful alleles is called positive selection. You will learn more about natural selection in Lesson 5.

Summing Up

As you know, evolution is a change in the gene pool of a population over time. Evolution can occur due to various processes. Processes that add new alleles to the gene pool are mutation, recombination, gene flow, and natural selection.

Processes that remove alleles are genetic drift and natural selection. Genetic drift removes alleles randomly from the gene pool. Natural selection removes the frequency of harmful alleles from the gene pool. The genetic variation in a population results from the balance between these processes.

▼◀▲▼◀▲▼◀▲▼◀▲▼◀▲▼◀▲▼◀▲▼◀▲▼◀▲▼◀▲▼◀▲▼

Science at Work

Paleontology Technician

A paleontologist studies fossils to learn about ancient life. Paleontology technicians assist paleontologists by collecting and preparing fossil specimens. They may work with a paleontologist to collect and record data and to catalog samples. In addition, paleontology technicians may create fossil displays for teaching.

To become a paleontology technician, a high school degree and some technical training is required. Most technicians have a degree in college or go to a technical school. Some may be able to work with a paleontologist in an entry-level job. As they take on more responsibilities, they can earn the title of paleontology technician.

On a sheet of paper, write the word that completes each sentence correctly.

1. Recombination shuffles genes by recombining _____.

2. Genetic drift can lead to the formation of a(n) _____ species.

3. Individuals do not evolve, but _____ evolve.

Critical Thinking

On a sheet of paper, write the answers to the following questions. Use complete sentences.

4. Explain how gene flow and genetic drift affect a population.

5. Can individuals experience evolution? Explain.

Achievements in Science

Scientists continue to learn about the genes that make living things function. One research area is the human Y chromosome in males. The Y chromosome is more likely than other chromosomes to contain mistakes and lose pieces. These mistakes are passed on to male children. There is no second Y chromosome in males to correct mistakes.

The Y chromosome is inherited only by males. By analyzing the Y chromosome, scientists can track male ancestors. In 2003, scientists mapped the Y chromosome.

They found that most genes on the Y chromosome are involved in producing sperm. They also found that genes on the Y chromosome affect body size. This finding supports a theory that the changing of the Y chromosome over time helps males. These changes make males bigger and stronger.

Currently, scientists are collecting blood samples from males worldwide. They will use the Y chromosome sequencing to track where the first people lived. They will also try to determine how people have moved throughout the world.

Artificial selection
_____

A process of changing a species by people who select the breeding of certain traits

British scientist Charles Darwin published *On the Origins of Species by Means of Natural Selection* in 1859. The book presented his ideas about evolution and natural selection. Darwin became famous for his ideas. You will learn more about natural selection in this lesson.

Artificial Selection

Darwin knew that people who bred animals and plants used variations among the offspring of the parents. For example, breeders mated pigeons. The offspring had different colors, beaks, necks, feet, and tails. The breeders then selected specific traits in the offspring. They bred those offspring.

Darwin called this process **artificial selection.** Through artificial selection, pigeon breeders created many different-looking pigeons. Figure 13.5.1 shows an example of a pigeon created by artificial selection. All pigeons belong to the same species. However, they have differences in their genetic makeup.

Figure 13.5.1 *Pigeon breeders can create many different-looking pigeons through artificial selection. Here is an example of a pigeon created by artificial selection.*

The sickle-cell allele occurs most often in areas of Africa where malaria is common.

Darwin knew that animals living in the wild struggled for survival. Some birds, for example, were good at finding scarce food in a severe winter. They also avoided being eaten by larger animals. These birds had a better chance of surviving and reproducing offspring.

Darwin called this process natural selection. He chose this term to show that artificial selection was different than natural selection. In natural selection, events in the natural environment determine which animals survive. The animals that survive can then mate to produce offspring.

Natural Selection

Natural selection keeps life going over time. Environments always change. New generations must adapt to survive and reproduce. If they did not adapt, individuals would die as their environment changed.

Natural selection does not always stop a new allele from increasing. If a new allele helps the organism survive, natural selection will favor it.

An example of natural selection is the allele of sickle cell. Variation in a single gene determines whether red blood cells are shaped normally or sickled. The sickle shape prevents cells from carrying normal levels of oxygen.

About one in every 500 African Americans has sickle-cell disease. This disease results from being homozygous (having an identical pair of genes) for the recessive sickle-cell allele. One in every 11 African Americans is heterozygous and a carrier. This means they do not get the disease. But they may pass the recessive gene to their children.

Heterozygous individuals are more resistant to **malaria** than individuals who are homozygous. Malaria is a disease in the tropics caused by a parasite. This parasite is a major cause of death in certain areas of Africa. Heterozygous individuals pass on both sickle-cell alleles and normal alleles to offspring. Thus, both alleles remain in the gene pool.

Technology: Safe X-rays?

Have you had X-rays taken at a doctor's or dentist's office? You were probably given protective clothing to wear. Doctors and dentists commonly use X-rays to learn about people's health and dental problems.

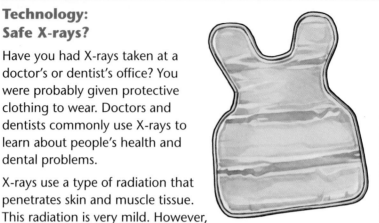

X-rays use a type of radiation that penetrates skin and muscle tissue. This radiation is very mild. However, any radiation that penetrates a cell could damage the cell's DNA. Severe damage can cause a mutation that could lead to cancer or other health problems.

Cells with damaged DNA due to X-rays work quickly to repair the damage. Cells with mild damage from X-rays often will self-destruct. Then they do not pass on DNA damage.

To reduce possible DNA damage, health professionals use precautions when giving X-rays. They use X-rays only when necessary. They use the lowest dosage of radiation needed. Health professionals cover areas not being viewed by X-rays with protective lead aprons. People who operate X-ray machines use lead shields as protection.

1. What possible damage to cells can result from X-rays?

2. How do cells respond to DNA damage?

3. If you get an X-ray, what safety precautions should be used?

Word Bank

artificial selection

environment

reproduce

On a sheet of paper, write the word or words from the Word Bank that complete each sentence correctly.

1. Natural selection gives an advantage to some organisms that make them more likely to survive and _____.

2. Without being able to adapt, species would die as their _____ changed.

3. Changes in a species caused by people who breed the species for certain traits is _____.

On a sheet of paper, write the letter of the word or words that complete each sentence correctly.

4. _____ alleles for sickle-cell disease remain in the gene pool.

   A Two   **B** One   **C** Four   **D** Zero

5. Sickle-shaped red blood cells help prevent _____.

   A oxygen   **B** malaria   **C** alleles   **D** mosquitoes

6. _____ individuals pass on both sickle-cell and normal alleles to offspring.

   A Old   **C** Heterozygous

   B Homozygous   **D** Recessive

Critical Thinking

On a sheet of paper, write the answers to the following questions. Use complete sentences.

7. Compare and contrast natural selection and artificial selection.

8. A person breeds dogs for a specific color. How does this affect the genetic makeup of the population of the dogs?

9. Why is the sickle-cell allele in the human population?

10. How does natural selection help ensure that a population survives over time?

Materials
◆ Blood Type Allele Chart
◆ coin

Tracking Blood Type Alleles

A person's blood type is determined by the inheritance of one of three alleles—A, B, or O—from each parent. The alleles together determine the blood type of that person. The allele combinations that create blood types are shown in the following table:

Blood Type	Allele Pairings	
A	AO	AA
B	BO	BB
O		OO
AB		AB

In this investigation, you will track alleles and blood types in a family. You will also examine how alleles are passed from parents to offspring.

Procedure

1. On a sheet of paper, copy the Blood Type Allele Chart on page 415. The chart represents three generations of a family. For each person, the top two squares show the person's blood type alleles. The bottom square shows the blood type that resulted from the combination of the two alleles.

2. Fill in the allele blanks for Child W and Child K. Determine each child's blood type.

3. Determine the blood types of Spouse W and Spouse K.

4. Choose which alleles will be passed from the second generation to the third generation. You may want to flip a coin to determine the allele a grandchild will receive.

5. Determine the blood types for all grandchildren.

Analysis

1. What blood types are possible for the grandchildren from Child W and Spouse W? Explain your answer.

2. What blood types are possible for the grandchildren from Child K and Spouse K? Explain your answer.

3. What allele was removed from the Child K–Spouse K branch to result in Grandchildren L and M?

Conclusions

1. What effect does the O allele have on determining blood type?

2. In this investigation, is it appropriate to use a coin flip to determine the alleles that are inherited? Explain your answer.

3. How could the offspring of Grandchild L or Grandchild M reclaim the lost allele?

Explore Further

A blood type also has a Rh factor. Parents pass on a positive Rh allele or a negative Rh allele. Go through the chart again and assign Rh alleles to all blood types.

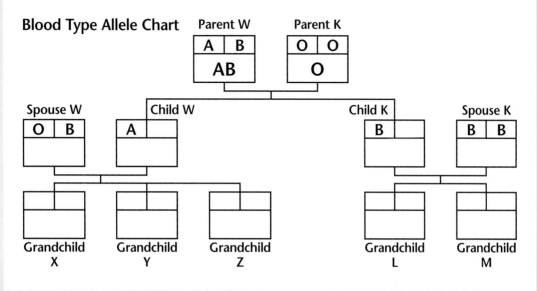

Blood Type Allele Chart

Scientists refer to evolution as **microevolution** and **macroevolution.** Microevolution are the minor changes in a population's allele-frequencies from generation to generation. These changes may be due to these processes: mutation, gene flow, genetic drift, and natural selection.

Macroevolution refers to large-scale changes over long periods of time. Macroevolution produces evolutionary trends. Macroevolution also includes mass extinctions that have occurred during the history of life. These extinctions involved losses of large numbers of species. Macroevolution may result in the evolution of new species.

Scientists sometimes have difficulty telling the difference between microevolution and macroevolution. Over time, tiny mutations like those in microevolution can build up in populations. Eventually, a new species can result. This is macroevolution.

Scientists have shown the process of microevolution in the laboratory. To explain the process of macroevolution, scientists use the fossil record.

An Example of Microevolution

Scientists have studied many examples of microevolution. One example happened in England in the 1800s. During this time, scientists kept track of moths named *Biston betularia.* The moths were either light or dark in color.

Before 1848, dark moths made up less than two percent of the population. However, the **frequency**, or numbers, of the dark moth began to increase. By 1898, 95 percent of the moths in English cities were dark. Scientists noted that there were fewer dark moths in rural areas.

Microevolution

The minor changes in a population's allele-frequencies from generation to generation

Macroevolution

The large-scale changes in a population over long periods of time

Frequency

The rate of occurrence

Over 50 years, the moth population had changed from mostly light-colored moths to mostly dark-colored moths. Figure 13.6.1 shows the two moths. Scientists wondered why this change happened. The color of the *Biston betularia* moth is mainly determined by one gene. The change in the number of the dark moths meant a change in the gene pool. Dark moths meant a change in the allele-frequencies of the moth gene pool. A change in the gene pool of this population is evolution.

The increase in the numbers of the dark moth was due to natural selection. The Industrial Revolution took place in the late 1800s. During the Industrial Revolution, people used power-driven machines in factories to make goods. People built factories in the cities.

As the machines ran, they gave off a black powder called soot. The soot covered the nearby birch trees. The trees became dark. Moths landed on these trees. When birds looked for moths to eat, they saw only the light-colored moths.

The dark moths stayed alive because the birds could not see them. The dark moths reproduced. The greater number of offspring from the dark moths caused their increase. These members in the population of moths were naturally selected to live and reproduce.

Figure 13.6.1 *Scientists in the 1800s kept track of the light-colored and dark-colored moths named* Biston betularia.

Overproduction

When organisms produce more offspring than can survive

Differential reproduction

When individuals leave more offspring than other individuals

Link to ➤➤➤

Health

Many professional sports teams use drug tests. They use the tests to be sure that athletes do not cheat by using performance-enhancing drugs. Performance-enhancing drugs are often swallowed or injected by needles. Today, some athletes may be putting performance-enhancing genes directly into their muscles. Scientists are working on tests to detect the genetic changes caused by this action.

Darwin's Four Main Ideas of Natural Selection

Darwin's ideas can be applied to both microevolution and macroevolution. The following four ideas sum up his theory of natural selection:

• Organisms tend to produce more offspring than can survive. This is called **overproduction**. For example, frogs lay thousands of eggs. Only a few live to be adult frogs.

• Individuals in a population vary in many traits. Frogs in a population may differ slightly in color, length, or speed. Alleles for specific traits are inherited.

• Individuals with alleles best suited to the environment are more likely to survive.

• Individuals with alleles best suited to the environment usually leave more offspring. The offspring survive and reproduce. This leads to **differential reproduction** within a species. Differential reproduction is when individuals leave more offspring than other individuals. Over time, the gene pool in the population changes.

Phenotypes and Evolution

An organism's phenotype is determined by its genes and its environment. Remember that a phenotype is an organism's appearance. For example, people are larger now than in the recent past. This is a result of better diet and new medicines. It is not a result of gene changes.

Phenotypic changes are not necessarily due to evolution. There is no change in the genes. In other words, a phenotypic change is not passed on to an organism's offspring. Most changes due to environment are slight, such as size differences. However, large-scale phenotypic changes are due to genetic changes. Thus, they are considered evolution.

Scientific Study of Evolution

Scientists seek to understand nature—how natural facts and events relate to other natural facts and events. Scientists look for causes and effects. They have developed explanations for the diversity of living things due to natural selection. Scientists continue to develop better explanations for the causes of natural facts and events.

Scientists use theories to group together scientific information. Scientists can never be sure an explanation or theory is complete and final. For that reason, scientists continue to investigate theories. Scientists change theories if new scientific information is accepted after repeated experiments or observations.

The theory of evolution talks about experiments and observations that show life has changed over time. This theory explains why there are different kinds of life on the earth. Changes in living things, as shown in the fossil record and in the DNA of organisms, support the theory of evolution. Based on many tests and careful analysis, scientists are confident about the theory of evolution.

In this chapter, you have learned that **evolutionary biology** provides new insights into the world. Evolutionary biology is the study of genetic changes within and among populations of organisms. This includes genetic changes that are occurring or have occurred.

Evolutionary biology links basic scientific research to knowledge needed to meet important needs of society. This includes preservation, or the saving of the earth's environment. You will learn more about preservation in Chapter 19.

Lesson 6   R E V I E W

Word Bank

evolutionary
  biology
macroevolution
microevolution

On a sheet of paper, write the word or words from the Word Bank that complete each sentence correctly.

1. Large changes in gene frequency over a long period of time is _____.

2. Evolution that involves small gene changes over a few generations is _____.

3. The study of genetic changes within and among populations of organisms is _____.

On a sheet of paper, write the letter of the answer that completes each sentence correctly.

4. An organism's phenotype is determined by its _____.

  A mutation   **C** microevolution

  B macroevolution   **D** genes and environment

5. The formation of a new species can result from _____.

  A macroevolution   **C** phenotypes

  B microevolution   **D** macroevolution or microevolution

6. The increase in the numbers of black moths in England in the 1800s was due to _____.

  A genetic drift   **C** natural selection

  B gene flow   **D** recombination

Critical Thinking

On a sheet of paper, write the answers to the following questions. Use complete sentences.

7. Why do scientists support the theory of microevolution?

8. Describe how microevolution caused a change in the populations of light- and dark-colored moths in England during the 1800s.

9. What evidence exists for macroevolution?

10. What are Darwin's four main ideas that sum up his theory of natural selection?

Problems with Animal Breeding

All dogs carry defective, or not perfect, genes. Defective genes are usually recessive. A recessive gene is hidden by a dominant gene.

Since genes come in pairs, normal genes hide most defective genes. Dogs usually have four to seven defective genes in their DNA. In contrast, humans usually have 10 to 12 defective genes.

Most people who breed animals have a purpose. For example, people breed race horses for their speed. Breeding closely related animals allows breeders to get traits they want.

When dogs are bred, there is some inbreeding. Inbreeding is the breeding of closely related individuals to get desired characteristics and to remove unwanted characteristics. With inbreeding, two closely related animals share genes for certain traits. When these two animals are bred, the desired form of a trait, such as a specific fur color, appears.

While good traits are achieved through inbreeding, some bad traits are also found in the offspring. If inbreeding continues, the bad traits build up. This leads to genetic problems.

Some human populations have been inbred. Sometimes this happens because of isolation. Isolation can occur because of barriers like mountains. Mutations are concentrated in inbred populations. For example, hemophilia often appears in some royal families when relatives marry and have children.

1. Why are most defective genes not a problem for an organism?

2. Why do people inbreed some domestic animals?

3. Some states have laws that do not allow marriage between closely related people such as first cousins. Why are these laws in place?

- Life on the earth is diverse. Organisms change constantly. New species form. Some species become extinct.

- Charles Darwin stated organisms evolve into different species over time. He also stated the theory of natural selection, in which organisms with some traits survive better than others. They breed more offspring, and the traits become more common.

- Gregor Mendel's experiments showed that traits in organisms are passed on through genetic material. Mendel's discoveries and Darwin's theories explained how a population's gene pool changes over time.

- New species arise from parent species when similar organisms become reproductively isolated from each other.

- Fossils give clues about older life-forms, including body structures and how long ago they lived. Scientists find evidence for evolution in fossils, distribution of organisms, anatomy, and molecular biology. Scientists can date fossils relatively by their position in the earth. They can date fossils more exactly with radioactive dating.

- The position of the continents has changed due to continental drift.

- Mutations occur randomly. This causes diversity within populations. Diversity can help organisms survive and reproduce.

- Mechanisms of microevolution are genetic drift, gene flow, mutations and natural selection.

Vocabulary

acquired trait, 389
adapt, 390
adaption, 389
amphibian, 398
anatomy, 394
artificial selection, 410
biogeography, 393
biological evolution, 388
common descent, 389
comparative anatomy, 394
continental drift, 399
crust, 400

descent with modification, 389
differential reproduction, 418
endangered, 406
evolutionary biology, 419
extinction, 406
fossil, 388
fossil record, 392
frequency, 416
gene flow, 406
gene pool, 388

genetic drift, 406
geologic time, 397
geologic time scale, 398
habitat, 406
Hardy-Weinberg equilibrium, 407
homologous structure, 393
invertebrate, 398
macroevolution, 416
magma, 400
malaria, 411
microevolution, 416

modern synthesis, 390
molecular biology, 395
natural selection, 389
overproduction, 418
paleontologist, 397
plate, 400
plate tectonics, 399
population, 388
radioactive element, 398
recombination, 405
reptile, 398
sedimentary rock, 392
vertebrate, 398

Chapter 13 R E V I E W

Vocabulary Review

Word Bank

acquired trait

anatomy

artificial selection

biogeography

biological evolution

extinction

fossil

gene flow

gene pool

genetic drift

macroevolution

microevolution

molecular biology

overproduction

plate tectonics

radioactive element

recombination

On a sheet of paper, write the word or words from the Word Bank that complete each sentence

1. A(n) _____ provides direct evidence of a species that once lived.

2. The _____ are all the genes present in a species or population.

3. A species that has difficulty surviving may face _____ and disappear.

4. Small-scale changes in gene frequencies in a population that occur over a few generations is _____.

5. Large evolutionary changes in a population over a long period of time is _____.

6. A(n) _____ decays, or breaks apart, to form another element.

7. A theory from the 1800s said that a(n) _____ comes from an organism's behavior.

8. New combinations of alleles in offspring are created through _____.

9. The theory of _____ says that the earth's surface is made of large sections of crust that move over time.

10. The random changes in the gene pool of a small population is _____.

11. A process that adds alleles to or removes alleles from a population is _____.

12. The study of the geographical distribution of fossils and living organisms is _____.

13. A change in the gene pool of a population over time is _____.

Review continued on next page

14. Organisms tend to practice _____ by producing more offspring than can survive.

15. People change a species through _____, which is the breeding of organisms for specific traits.

16. The structure of an organism is _____.

17. The study of DNA and its expression in cells is an area of _____.

Concept Review

On a sheet of paper, write the letter of the answer that completes each sentence correctly.

18. Darwin's theory of common descent stated that all organisms _____.

   A evolve at a constant rate

   B evolve due to acquired traits

   C evolve until they are selected

   D evolved from past organisms

19. The deeper a fossil is found in sedimentary rock, the _____.

   A older the fossil is

   B more likely the fossil has evolved

   C less complete the fossil is

   D more worn the fossil is

20. The earliest organisms to appear on the earth were _____.

   A algae   **B** fishes   **C** plants   **D** bacteria

21. When two populations combine, the result is often _____.

   A recombination   **C** gene flow

   B genetic drift   **D** mutation

Critical Thinking

On a sheet of paper, write the answers to the following questions. Use complete sentences.

22. What is the theory of modern synthesis?

23. How do mutations create genetic diversity? Why do some mutations not cause any change?

24. How does the allele that causes sickle-cell disease both help and harm people?

25. Do mutations that survive through natural selection always improve a species? Explain your answer.

Research and Write

Work with a partner to research two hoaxes about evolution and fossils. People have found fake fossils and presented them as real. Some fake fossils have fooled scientists. Write a description of the hoaxes. Include how scientists proved that the fossils were not real.

Test-Taking Tip Before writing out an answer on a test, read the question twice to be sure you understand what it is asking.

14 Speciation and Punctuated Equilibrium

The bird in the photograph is a medium ground finch. Charles Darwin observed this species in the Galapagos Islands. Just as Darwin thought, the key to this bird's success is the size of its beak. The kinds and sizes of seeds that these finches eat change every year, depending on the rainfall in their area. Variation in the trait of beak size helps the species adapt to changes. In Chapter 14, you will learn about the formation of species, or speciation. You will also learn about the rates at which speciation occurs.

Organize Your Thoughts

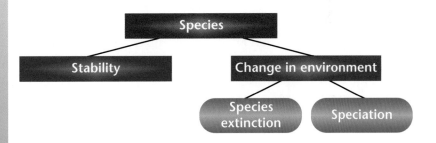

Goals for Learning

◆ To define speciation and explain how it occurs
◆ To identify the classification systems of living things
◆ To identify conditions for speciation to occur
◆ To describe conditions that affect the survival of species

Objectives

After reading this lesson, you should be able to

◆ describe methods scientists use to classify living things

◆ describe Charles Darwin's speciation ideas

◆ list causes of speciation

◆ explain the biological species concept

◆ explain the ecological species concept

◆ describe three types of speciation

Classify
To group

Mammary gland
A milk-producing structure on a mammal

Morphology
The study of differences in body forms of organisms

In Chapter 13, you learned that living things are similar, but different. To study living things, scientists classify organisms into groups based on their similarities and differences. **Classify** means "to group." For example, scientists classify humans into the group *Homo sapiens.* Humans belong to a larger group called mammals. Mammals are animals that have **mammary glands.** Mammary glands are milk-producing structures on a mammal. Humans also belong to a larger group called animals.

You have also learned that scientists make decisions about how to compare and contrast living things. They may use **morphology** to classify living things. Morphology is the study of the differences in the body form of organisms. For example, the body form of a bird differs from the body form of a cat. Scientists classify birds and cats into different morphology groups. Scientists also classify living things based on differences in **biochemistry,** body function, or behavior.

Species: Most Specific Level of Classification

Scientists group members of a population into a classification level called species. As you know, a species is a group of living things that can breed with each other. They produce offspring that are like themselves and are **fertile.** Scientists classify animals and plants by a classification system. Species is the most specific level of the classification system. You will learn more about this classification system in Lesson 2.

Darwin's Theories on Speciation

Scientists want to find what causes differences in living things to happen. To find the answers, scientists investigate how a species changes over time. Scientists also study how one species evolves into two or more different species.

Charles Darwin, a British scientist, traveled around the world from 1831 to 1836. He wanted to learn how and why living things change over time. To find out, Darwin studied many organisms, including the finches on the Galapagos Islands.

The Galapagos Islands are on the equator in the Pacific Ocean. They are 600 miles (960 kilometers) west of Ecuador, South America.

Darwin observed that the Galapagos finches looked alike. However, some groups of finches did not reproduce with each other. He noticed that the different species had specific differences. Some had beaks for eating seeds. Others ate insects. Some finches had beaks like a woodpecker. They used their beaks to drill holes in tree bark. Then they held a cactus spine in their beaks to dig out insects. Some finches lived on the ground. Others lived in trees.

Darwin found 13 species of finches on the Galapagos Islands. He wondered if these species had a common ancestor. The ancestor would be the original species. Finding the ancestor of the finches would help Darwin figure out how speciation happened. Today, scientists think the original species of finches came from Central or South America. The 13 species of Galapagos finches developed from the original species. This speciation took several million years.

Causes of Speciation

As you know, speciation is the creation of new species. There are different explanations as to how speciation occurs. Geographical barriers can separate the members of a population. Recall that a population is a group of organisms of the same species that live in the same area.

Over time, if separated populations come into contact and members interbreed, speciation does not occur. However, if members from the separated populations do not reproduce with each other, speciation occurs. Populations that do not reproduce with each other are **reproductively isolated.**

Any factor that prevents two species from reproducing living, fertile offspring contributes to reproductive isolation. Over time, the gene pools in each of the separated populations change. The populations can no longer **interbreed** even if they come in contact with each other. That is because they are reproductively isolated. Recall from Chapter 13 that a gene pool is the genes found within a population.

Biological species concept

A principle that defines
a species as populations
that can interbreed and
produce offspring

Insects are the
most diverse
organisms on the
earth.

Defining Species: Biological Species Concept

Scientists classify sexually reproducing species using the **biological species concept.** This principle defines species as groups of interbreeding populations reproductively isolated from other groups. Species cannot interbreed with members of another species. Reproductive barriers between species isolate their gene pools.

Genetic exchange is possible among members of a species. However, genetic exchange is not possible among members of different species. Look at the horse and donkey in Figure 14.1.1. Horses and donkeys are closely related. If these two species interbreed, the offspring are mules. A mule is not fertile. For this reason, scientists classify horses and donkeys as two species.

Fireflies may look similar, but different species of fireflies do not mate. Many factors prevent mating. For example, the two species may live in different habitats of an area. They do not come in contact with each other. This reproductive isolation occurred with Darwin's finches. Some finches lived in trees. Some lived on the ground.

Different species of fireflies may breed at different times of day or in different seasons. Male fireflies use specific signals to attract females. A firefly from one species would not use or recognize the signals of another species.

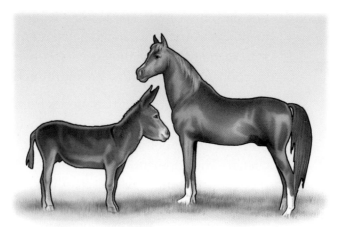

Figure 14.1.1 *How are a donkey and a horse alike? How are they different?*

Defining Species: Ecological Species Concept

Scientists cannot use the biological species concept for species that reproduce asexually. **Asexual reproduction** involves one organism and no egg or sperm. Scientists define asexually reproducing species by the **ecological species concept.** This principle states that species are defined based on their **niche.** A niche describes the way of life of a species, or how a species adapts to a role in its environment.

A niche refers to more than an organism's physical surroundings. It includes the organism's living and nonliving interactions with its environment. Sometimes scientists define species by both the biological species concept and the ecological species concept.

Two Classification Questions

To classify living things, scientists usually ask two questions. First, does a species differ from other species? Second, will a species remain different in the future? Scientists answer the first question by looking at structure, reproduction, and niches.

To answer the second question, scientists decide if a **subspecies** will become isolated. A subspecies is a division of a species. If a subspecies becomes isolated, natural selection or genetic drift will produce different gene pools. Remember from Chapter 13 that genetic drift is the random change in the gene pool of a small population.

Mechanisms of Speciation

Before a new species arises, the gene pool of a population is cut off from other populations of the parent species. The population with the isolated gene pool now evolves on its own. This reproductive isolation can follow two different development paths in forming a new species. One path is **allopatric speciation.** The other path is **sympatric speciation.**

Allopatric speciation means that similar organisms do not interbreed due to a physical barrier. A physical barrier could be mountains, forests, deserts, rivers, or oceans. A physical barrier isolates populations. This occurred with the finches on the Galapagos Islands.

Asexual reproduction

Reproduction that involves one parent and no egg or sperm

Ecological species concept

A principle that defines species as populations that can interbreed and produce offspring based on their niche

Niche

The way of life of a species

Subspecies

A division of a species

Allopatric speciation

When similar organisms do not interbreed due to physical barriers

Sympatric speciation

When similar organisms live nearby, but do not interbreed due to differences in behavior

---

Sympatric speciation occurs when a **subpopulation** becomes reproductively isolated while living among the parent population. The lack of interbreeding occurs because of differences in behavior. Sympatric speciation is not a common method among animal species. However, sympatric speciation accounts for about 25 percent of plant species. This mechanism accounts for many plant species grown for food.

Biology in Your Life

The Evolution of Dogs: The Environment

Dogs have evolved for the last 10,000 to 14,000 years for one main purpose—to coexist with humans. Dogs originally evolved from wolves. They have changed greatly and are now very different animals. Scientists have studied dogs to learn how having them as pets could cause so many changes. The answer probably depends on how dogs first became tame and began to coexist with humans. Scientists have several theories about how this happened, but do not know for sure. Perhaps less aggressive wolves found that they could get food from humans by begging. Perhaps tamer wolves were not frightened by humans and began to live near their garbage.

The evolution of wolves into dogs marked several distinct changes. Many of these changes cannot be explained. For example, many breeds of dogs and other pets developed short legs. Their tails became curled. Their ears became floppy. Other traits are more logical. For example, dogs have much smaller teeth than wolves. This makes sense because pets do not need their teeth for hunting and tearing meat from bones like wolves do.

Scientists also are studying how foxes change when they are selected over several generations to become pets. Many of the same traits, such as short legs and floppy ears, begin to show up as well. These traits are not essential in pet animals. They may develop because they are located close to desirable traits in the genome.

1. What theories try to explain how wolves started to become pets?

2. What kinds of traits developed in dogs as a result of becoming pets?

3. Why do scientists think other traits also developed?

Word Bank
fertile
morphology
speciation

On a sheet of paper, write the word from the Word Bank that completes each question correctly.

1. To group organisms, scientists use _____, or the differences in body form.

2. Organisms that are the same species can breed and produce living, _____ offspring.

3. The creation of a new species is _____.

Critical Thinking

On a sheet of paper, write the answers to the following questions. Use complete sentences.

4. How does Darwin's study of the Galapagos finches relate to the concept of niche?

5. What can cause speciation to occur?

Express Lab 14

Materials
◆ buttons or other objects

Procedure

1. Examine the buttons or other objects. Each object represents a different organism.

2. Working with a partner, develop a way to group these organisms into different "species."

3. When you are finished, be prepared to explain your method to your classmates.

Analysis

1. What are the unique characteristics of each species?

2. Which species are most closely related? How can you tell?

3. List more characteristics to classify these organisms if they were actual living things.

Genus

A group of similar species

Kingdom

A group of similar phyla or divisions

Phylum

A subdivision of the animal kingdom (plural is phyla)

Division

A subdivision of the plant kingdom

Scientists use a system to group and classify extinct and living species of organisms.

Linnaeus Classification System

In 1753, Carolus Linnaeus, a Swedish scientist, developed a new system to classify plants and animals. Scientists use his system today to classify new organisms. Linnaeus grouped species by physical characteristics.

Under the Linneaus system, each species has a two-word name. The first word is the **genus.** For example, maple trees belong to the genus Acer. The scientific names of all maple trees begin with the word *Acer.* The second word is the species. The scientific name of the sugar maple tree is *Acer saccharum.* The scientific name of the red maple is *Acer rubrum.*

In the Linneaus system, each organism belongs to seven levels. Look at Figure 14.2.1. From the most general to the most specific, the seven layers are: **kingdom, phylum or division,** class, order, family, genus, and species.

Scientists have used the Linneaus system for over two centuries. You will learn more about this classification system in Chapter 15.

Levels of Classification

KINGDOM

PHYLUM OR DIVISION

CLASS

ORDER

FAMILY

GENUS

SPECIES

Figure 14.2.1 *Each organism belongs to seven levels in the Linneaus system.*

Link to >>>

Language

Most species have Latin or Greek names. The scientific name for humans, *Homo sapiens,* comes from two Latin words. *Homo* means "man" and *sapiens* means "wise." Some species are named after the people who discovered or named them. For example, Johann Wilhelm Weinmann discovered and named *Weinmannia silvicola,* a tree native to New Zealand.

Study Figures 14.2.2 and 14.2.3. The figures show two species, the fruit fly and the sweetbay magnolia. How are these species alike? How do they differ?

Grouping Species by Ancestors

In the 1960s, scientists also began to group species by ancestors. Scientists continue to use characteristics that are alike in species to group them. Some characteristics include DNA, biochemistry, and morphology.

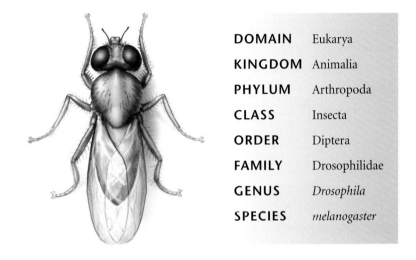

DOMAIN	Eukarya
KINGDOM	Animalia
PHYLUM	Arthropoda
CLASS	Insecta
ORDER	Diptera
FAMILY	Drosophilidae
GENUS	*Drosophila*
SPECIES	*melanogaster*

Figure 14.2.2 *Fruit fly,* Drosophila melanogaster

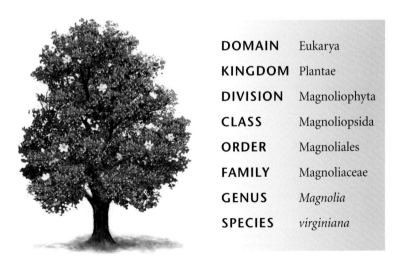

DOMAIN	Eukarya
KINGDOM	Plantae
DIVISION	Magnoliophyta
CLASS	Magnoliopsida
ORDER	Magnoliales
FAMILY	Magnoliaceae
GENUS	*Magnolia*
SPECIES	*virginiana*

Figure 14.2.3 *Sweetbay magnolia,* Magnolia virginiana

Three-Domain System

Recently, scientists began using a **three-domain system.** In this system, scientists classify living things into three broad groups: Bacteria, **Archaea,** or **Eukarya.** The fruit fly, sweetbay magnolia, and human belong to the Eukarya domain. You will learn more about the three-domain system in Chapter 15.

Differences Used to Classify Species

Scientists look for differences in living things to classify an organism as a member of a population. The difference must be clear and constant. Scientists often ignore small differences when classifying species.

Sometimes scientists cannot isolate one main difference when assigning an organism to a species. For example, they look at several factors to assign a tree to the correct species. They may compare the color of flowers, buds, and bark. They also compare the number of flowers, and the shape of the leaves and fruit.

Three-domain system

A system that classifies all living things into three broad groups

Archaea

The domain of prokaryotic organisms that are not bacteria

Eukarya

The domain of eukaryotic organisms

★ ★

Achievements in Science

Discovering Human Ancestors

Humans are the only living species that belong to the genus *Homo.* Modern humans and our ancestors are hominids. Hominids walk upright on two legs and have thumbs for gripping. Early hominid fossils generally belong to the genus *Australopithecus.* This genus is an ancestor to the *Homo* species.

Raymond Dart, an Australian scientist, found the first hominid fossil in 1924. He found a skull that was larger than an ape's skull. The skull was about 2 million years old and resembled both humans and apes. Dart named this organism *Australopithecus africanus.*

In 1974, American paleontologists working in Ethiopia found a nearly complete skeleton of *Australopithecus afarensis.* They named the 3-million-year-old skeleton Lucy. In 1994, another group of American paleontologists found a 4.4-million-year-old skeleton. Scientists classified this skeleton as a new genus, *Ardipithecus ramidus.*

Between 1997 and 1999, Yohannes Haile-Selassie found fossil fragments of a subspecies of *Ardipithecus ramidus* in his native Ethiopia. He called the new fossils *Ardipithecus ramidus kadabba.* These fragments are about 5.2 million years old. Scientists continue to search for evidence of the earliest hominids and fill in the gaps of human ancestry.

Word Bank

genus

morphology

species

three-domain
system

On a sheet of paper, write the word or words from the Word Bank that complete each question correctly.

1. Scientists use the _____ to classify living things into three broad groups.

2. The first word of a scientific name is the _____ of the organism. The second word is the _____.

3. Scientists use DNA, biochemistry, and _____ to name and classify living things.

Critical Thinking

On a sheet of paper, write the answers to the following questions. Use complete sentences.

4. List the seven levels of Linneaus classification from most general to most specific.

5. Why do scientists consider many factors when assigning an organism to a species?

Technology and Society

Recently, scientists have begun looking for new organisms in the world's oceans. To do this, they sample seawater and analyze DNA. Currant data shows that there is more life and diversity in the sea than scientists had thought. The first sample of seawater contained 1.2 million unrecorded genes and 1,800 new microorganisms.

INVESTIGATION 14

Materials

- safety goggles
- lab coat or apron
- gloves
- wax pencil
- 2 nutrient agar petri dishes
- Bunsen burner
- inoculation loop
- bacteria culture
- forceps
- antibiotic disk

Natural Selection in Bacteria

People use antibiotics to destroy bacteria that can cause disease. Medicines, soaps, and other cleaners may contain antibiotics. Antibiotics kill bacteria or change their ability to reproduce or function. Through natural selection, some bacteria adapt and become resistant to antibiotics. This makes it more difficult to kill harmful bacteria with antibiotics. In this investigation, you will observe the effects of natural selection in bacteria.

Procedure

1. Put on safety goggles, a lab coat or apron, and gloves.

2. Using a wax pencil, label the bottom of one petri dish A. Label the bottom of the other petri dish B. Write your name and the date on the bottom of each petri dish.

3. Follow your teacher's instructions to light the Bunsen burner.

4. To sterilize the inoculation loop, pass it through the flame. **Safety Alert: Be careful when working with an open flame.**

5. Collect a small amount of bacteria culture by putting the inoculation loop on the surface of the bacteria culture. With the inoculation loop, make a zigzag streak from top to bottom on the nutrient agar in petri dish A and petri dish B. Do not break the surface of the nutrient agar.

6. Using the forceps, pick up an antibiotic disk. Put the disk on petri dish A.

7. Cover both petri dishes. Put both petri dishes in a light- and temperature-controlled area as directed by your teacher.

8. Over the next three days, check your petri dishes every 24 hours. Record your observations.

Cleanup/Disposal

When you are finished, clean your lab area. Dispose of used petri dishes according to your teacher's directions. Wash your hands well with soap and warm water.

Analysis

1. Compare the growth of the bacteria on petri dish A and petri dish B.

2. Describe the differences in the bacterial growth between your petri dish B and the petri dish B of other classmates. What factors cause these differences in growth?

Conclusions

1. What effect did the antibiotic disk have on the bacteria population on petri dish A?

2. What is occurring on petri dish A? What changes are occurring in the bacterial population as a result?

3. What problems can result by using antibiotics too often?

Explore Further

Take a sample of bacteria growing close to the antibiotic disk from petri dish A. Streak this sample onto a clean petri dish. Add an antibiotic disk. Cover the petri dish. Put this dish in a light- and temperature- controlled area as directed by your teacher. Check your dish every 24 hours over the next three days. Record your observations. Compare the growth of the bacteria on this dish with the growth on your petri dish A from the investigation. What could cause the differences in bacteria growth?

Speciation occurs when a single species becomes two or more species. Speciation usually takes much longer than a person's lifetime to happen. To study speciation, scientists look at changes in the geography of the area where populations live. Scientists then look at how the characteristics of living things differ between geographic areas. For example, related species could live in nearby areas, but are separated by a barrier.

How Speciation Occurs

Scientists think speciation begins when members of a species become separated by geography. The species becomes two populations that live in different environments. Members of each species do not move between the populations. The two populations do not interbreed. They do not exchange genes. Over time, they evolve with differences in the gene pool.

The two populations become very different. If they come together, they cannot interbreed. The two populations are reproductively isolated. Scientists classify members of the two populations as separate species.

The Rate of Speciation

Scientists think speciation happens by different methods. Recall from Chapter 13 that speciation may be the result of many smaller changes occurring. These changes occur over a vast period of time.

In the 1800s, Charles Darwin explained that the origin of species is through adaptation by natural selection. Isolated populations evolve differences gradually as they adapt to the environment. Paleontologists find evidence of gradual changes in the fossil record.

Stasis

Showing little change over time

Punctuated equilibrium

A theory that states species stay the same for a long time, then new species evolve suddenly due to global changes and mass extinctions

In the 1930s, two American scientists, Theodosius Dobzhansky and Ernst Mayr, published a new theory about speciation. They thought members of a species separated by geography, such as a barrier, become separate species. Dobzhansky and Mayr thought that geographic isolation happens before speciation. Their theory is called allopatric speciation, which was discussed in Lesson 1.

Both theories link environmental change with evolution. Darwin's theory of natural selection is linked with environmental change. The Dobzhansky-Mayr theory states that speciation happens in populations isolated by geography. The change in geography results from environmental change. This means changes in the environment are related to speciation.

Punctuated Equilibrium

Some scientists support the sudden appearance of new species. These scientists think speciation occurs in thousands of years rather than in millions of years. They think that species are in **stasis** most of the time. Stasis means showing very little change over time.

Some species can survive without change for millions of years. Then, a huge change happens in the environment. For example, a meteor crashes into the earth. Or the sea level rises because polar ice caps melt. This pattern of speciation is called **punctuated equilibrium.**

The punctuated equilibrium theory states that species stay the same for long periods of time. Then, the species changes quickly because of changes in the environment. Changes in the environment change the living conditions of species.

Scientists have found examples of punctuated equilibrium over the past 1.65 million years. For example, the earth has had four main periods of global warming. During periods of global warming, glacial ice moved into North America, Europe, and Asia. As a result, ecosystems moved south. Recall from Chapter 1 that an ecosystem is the living and nonliving things found in an area.

Plant and animal species survived if they could live in the changed areas. These species stayed the same. Other species became extinct. They could not live in the changed areas. Or they did not move away from the original area to a new area where they could survive.

Coordinated Stasis

Paleontologists study life in the past by studying fossils. As you know, fossils are the remains or impressions of organisms that lived in the past. The findings of paleontologists have formed a fossil record that shows how organisms have changed over time.

Paleontologists think evolution happens in a common process. The ancestors of species that live in an area evolved in the same way. Many species show similar patterns of evolution. After extinction, new species often appear at about the same time. Scientists call this pattern **coordinated stasis.**

Science at Work

Scientific Illustrator

A scientific illustrator creates art for scientific purposes. A scientific illustrator may create drawings, paintings, or models. The art must be accurate.

Scientific illustrators work in all areas of science. They often work with scientists. For example, a scientific illustrator might work with a paleontologist. The scientific illustrator would make a painting of a newly discovered dinosaur. A scientific illustrator's artwork may appear in museums, brochures, magazines, textbooks, and other books.

Most scientific illustrators have a high school degree and some science education from a university or technical school. Many have completed a degree from an art school. Many scientific illustrators have computer training to create images, models, and animation.

An example of coordinated stasis is a global cooling that began about 2.8 million years ago. Cooler and drier conditions in Africa resulted. The African ecosystems changed suddenly.

As seen in Figure 14.3.1, dry grasslands replaced wet forests. Some species survived. Other species moved. Some species became extinct because they could not adapt to the new environment. At the same time, animal species moved to the African grasslands. Speciation also occurred during this time.

To sum up, classifying the many living things on the earth is a continuing process. Scientists debate about how organisms evolve. They look for evidence as to whether living things gradually change over time, as Darwin thought. Or they look for evidence as to whether punctuated equilibrium leads to the diversity in species.

Figure 14.3.1 *The African grasslands replaced wet forests due to global warming about 2.8 million years ago.*

Word Bank

coordinated stasis

punctuated
  equilibrium

stasis

On a sheet of paper, write the word or words from the Word Bank that complete each question correctly.

1. A species that shows little change over time is in _____.

2. A pattern where most new species appear at about the same time is _____.

3. A theory says species stay the same for a long time, then change quickly because of environmental changes. This theory is _____.

On a sheet of paper, write the letter of the answer that completes each sentence correctly.

4. Today, most species are in _____.

  A change   **C** stasis

  B coordinated statis   **D** isolation

5. When glacial ice moved into North America, some organisms survived without changing by _____.

  A breeding with new species

  B reproducing in larger numbers

  C using fewer resources

  D moving to new areas

6. A pattern where most species appear at about the same time is _____.

  A speciation   **C** coordinated stasis

  B punctuated equilibrium   **D** stasis

Critical Thinking

On a sheet of paper, write the answers to the following questions. Use complete sentences.

7. Describe the Dobzhansky-Mayr theory.

8. Explain why closely related species are often located near each other.

9. How do scientists study speciation?

10. What often happens when a species becomes geographically divided into two populations?

DISCOVERY INVESTIGATION 14

Materials

- safety goggles
- lab coat or apron
- moss plant
- fern plant
- coniferous tree branch
- flowering tree branch

Plant Evolution

The DNA of life forms changes over generations. Many changes are slight and make little difference in the lives of the organisms. Environmental changes can cause organisms to change. Environmental changes allow some organisms with slight differences to grow and reproduce better than other organisms. Over time, these differences may cause new species to develop. In this investigation, you will examine several types of plants. You will determine how changes caused new species of plant life to develop.

Procedure

1. Put on safety goggles and a lab coat or apron.

2. Examine the plants your teacher provided. Read the notes and descriptions that go with each plant.

3. In small groups, observe and discuss each plant. Record your observations. Your teacher will help guide your discussion and answer questions.

4. Use the notes provided by your teacher and your own observations to answer the Analysis questions.

Cleanup/Disposal

When you are finished, clean your lab area.

Analysis

1. What differences did you see between the moss and the other plants? Would each difference be an advantage or disadvantage? Explain your answer.

2. How are the moss and the fern different from the other two plants?

3. The coniferous plant and the flowering plant are adapted to what kind of niche?

4. What advantage does the flowering plant have compared to the other three plants? Why do you think this is an advantage?

Conclusions

Using your observations and the information provided, determine the order in which the four plants evolved. List the four plants, in order, from the earliest to the most recent.

Explore Further

Research the physical and biological characteristics of blue-green algae. Do you think blue-green algae evolved sooner, the same time, or later compared to the four plants in this investigation? Explain your answer.

Objectives

After reading this lesson, you should be able to

◆ explain the effect of mass extinction on surviving species

◆ describe the process of speciation in new areas

◆ define instantaneous speciation

◆ explain the genetic health of a species

◆ describe the current loss of species in the world

Mass extinction

The dying out of large numbers of species in a short period of time

Community

A group of different populations that live in the same area

Many factors affect the survival of species. You will learn about some of these factors in this lesson.

Mass Extinction

Scientists have found periods of **mass extinction** from the fossil record. Mass extinction is the dying out of large numbers of species in a short period of time. A species becomes extinct when its habitat is destroyed. Recall from Chapter 13 that a habitat is the place where an organism lives.

A species can become extinct if its environment changes. For example, if the ocean changed a few degrees in temperature, many organisms would die. Some species may become extinct. Other species would not become extinct. Over time, they would adapt to their new environment.

One mass extinction happened 250 million years ago. Another mass extinction happened 65 million years ago. Some scientists think a large comet or asteroid hit the earth both times. As a result, the earth's crust moved and volcanoes erupted. Hot, liquid rock inside the earth pushed up through volcanoes. Sunlight may have been blocked for many years. Plants and animals died from lack of food.

Other scientists think a gradual process of volcanic eruptions and continental drift caused the two mass extinctions. As you have learned, continental drift describes how the major landmasses of the earth move. Species that survive mass extinction fill new roles in the changed environment.

Diversity in New Areas

Species in a new area go through a cycle in populating and creating diversity. For example, after an island forms, many species move to the island. The species interact with one another. They form a **community.** A community is a group of different populations that live in the same area.

Co-adaptation

One species becoming
dependent on another
species

**Instantaneous
speciation**

A new species formed
in one to several
generations

Many scientists
think a meteor hit
the earth and
caused the
extinction of
dinosaurs.
Scientists have
found a large
meteor crater
measuring about
112 miles (180
kilometers) in
diameter on the
ocean floor. This
giant crater is on
the Yucatan
Peninsula of
Mexico and in the
Gulf of Mexico.
The crater is the
same age as the
extinction of the
dinosaurs.

Rapid evolution then occurs. The new populations adapt to the island's environment. Speciation occurs if members of the population are geographically isolated and do not come together to interbreed.

Scientists have found examples of speciation on the islands of Hawaii. They have found a small number of original species on the islands. These species evolved into many species over hundreds or thousands of years. That is a short time compared to evolution in other areas of the world.

Some of these new island species interacted regularly. As they continued to evolve, they underwent **co-adaptation.** Co-adaptation happens when species interact so much that they change in response to each other. Over time, these species become dependent on each other for survival.

The land along the equator has more species than areas north or south of the equator. There are more species in a large landmass than a small island. For example, South America has more species than small islands in the Pacific Ocean. The more stable an area, the more species there are in the area. This happens because the species have more time to adapt. This process results in more diversity.

A new species can be formed in a few generations. For example, plants in one generation can create offspring that cannot breed with the parent plants in only one generation. This is an example of **instantaneous speciation.**

Sympatric speciation sometimes produces new species in a short time. For example, some fruit flies breed on one kind of a plant. Others breed on a different kind of plant. Still others breed at different seasons. These differences happen because existing genes mutate or recombine in a short time. It is possible for a new species to form within a few years. Most species do not form that quickly.

Genetic Health of Species

Scientists have observed that the size of a population influences the genetic health of a species. When a population falls below 100 individuals, harmful genes in the population occur in greater frequencies. This can result in death. In large populations, harmful genes occur less frequently.

Biologists think a population with 50 members is too small for genetic health. They are concerned when the population size becomes too small to remain healthy. Populations of 500 or more members usually stay healthy. In Chapter 13, for example, you learned that scientists are concerned about the small cheetah population.

Today's Loss of Species

Today, scientists around the world are concerned that some species are disappearing quickly. Species are disappearing at almost a thousand times faster than they are forming. This extinction is mainly because people are changing the environment.

In one person's lifetime, it is possible to lose half the species of the world. That would mean a huge change in a short period of time. It took thousands or millions of years for most species to develop. Scientists want to protect living things from extinction.

Link to ➤ ➤ ➤

Earth Science

Scientists have found a layer of metal called iridium in ancient rock layers. Iridium formed about the time dinosaurs disappeared. Iridium is rare on the earth, but it is very common in meteors.

Word Bank

community

instantaneous
  speciation

mass extinction

On a sheet of paper, write the word or words from the Word Bank that complete each question correctly.

1. A group of different populations that live in the same area is a(n) _____.

2. A new species that forms in only one generation is an example of _____.

3. The fossil record shows that periods of _____ are followed by diversity in organisms.

On a sheet of paper, write the letter of the answer that completes each sentence correctly.

4. The more stable an area, the more _____ are in the area.

A instantaneous speciations   **C** mass extinctions

B endangered species   **D** species

5. When organisms populate a new area and are isolated geographically from other populations of the same species, _____.

A the population decreases   **C** speciation occurs

B mass extinctions occur   **D** evolution slows down

6. A species becoming dependent on another species is _____.

A co-adaptation   **C** population

B instantaneous speciation   **D** community

Critical Thinking

On a sheet of paper, write the answers to the following questions. Use complete sentences.

7. Describe two theories for the mass extinctions that occurred 250 million and 65 million years ago.

8. What is instantaneous speciation?

9. Why is a large population generally healthier than a small population?

10. What current trends are scientists observing about speciation and extinction?

Discoveries of New Species

Scientists have identified over 2.5 million species alive on the earth today. Many more species remain to be discovered. Scientists are constantly searching for new species of plants and animals. Many places, such as rainforests, are dense with organisms and have not been fully explored by scientists.

Scientists estimate that they have identified only a small percentage of the bacteria on the earth. Bacteria and other microorganisms are too small to be observed in the environment. They must be observed under a microscope to be identified.

Not all newly discovered species are tiny. In 2001, scientists discovered a new species of evergreen tree in Vietnam. The tree, found clinging to the side of a rock, was named the Golden Vietnamese Cypress.

In 2003, British scientists discovered a new plant species. They named the species *Senecio eboracensis.* The plant resulted from the mating of two different weed plants. It evolved into a separate species. This happened because of a change in the plant's flowering time. It flowered at a different time than the parent plants and could no longer reproduce with them.

The discovery of new plant species provides information about the environment and ecosystem they belong to. Plants are also a common source of medicine. Finding new plants may lead to the creation of important new medical treatments.

1. Why are many species undiscovered?

2. What caused the plant discovered in Britain to be considered a separate species?

3. What benefits can result from the discovery of new plant species?

Chapter 14 SUMMARY

- Scientists classify all organisms into groups. Scientists use morphology, biochemistry, body functions, and behavior to classify organisms.

- A species is the first level of classification. Members of the same species are very similar to each other. They can breed with one another to produce fertile offspring.

- Scientists classify sexually reproducing species by the biological species concept. They classify asexually reproducing species by the ecological species concept.

- Living things change over time. New species sometimes emerge as a result of these changes. Mechanisms of speciation include allopatric speciation and sympatric speciation.

- Scientists give every species a two-part scientific name. The scientific name is made up of the genus and the species.

- Scientists use the Linneaus system to classify animals and plants. Each organism belongs to seven levels. These levels, from general to specific, are: kingdom, phylum, class, order, family, genus, and species.

- Speciation, or the creation of new species, happens when a single species becomes two or more species. Speciation usually occurs because two populations of the same species separate. They evolve and cannot breed with each other.

- Speciation often follows periods of mass extinction. Populations that survive take over new resources.

- Currently, scientists believe that species are disappearing much faster than new species are emerging.

Vocabulary

allopatric speciation, 431
Archaea, 436
asexual reproduction, 431
biochemistry, 429
biological species concept, 430
classify, 428
co-adaptation, 448
community, 447

coordinated stasis, 442
division, 434
ecological species concept, 431
Eukarya, 436
fertile, 429
genus, 434
instantaneous speciation, 429
interbreed, 430

kingdom, 434
mammary gland, 428
mass extinction, 447
morphology, 428
niche, 431
phylum, 434
punctuated equilibrium, 441
reproductively isolated, 429

stasis, 441
subpopulation, 432
subspecies, 431
sympatric speciation, 431
three-domain system, 436

Chapter 14 REVIEW

Word Bank

allopatric speciation

Archaea

asexual reproduction

co-adaptation

coordinated stasis

Eukarya

genus

kingdom

mass extinction

morphology

niche

punctuated equilibrium

reproductively isolated

stasis

subspecies

sympatric speciation

three-domain system

Vocabulary Review

On a sheet of paper, write the word or words from the Word Bank that best complete each sentence.

1. Reproduction that involves one parent and no egg or sperm is _____.

2. A system that classifies all living things into three broad groups is the _____.

3. A theory that states species stay the same for a long time, then new species suddenly evolve due to global changes and mass extinctions is _____.

4. The study of differences in body forms of organisms is _____.

5. A population in _____ is not changing.

6. Two populations that were separated by a barrier become different species through _____.

7. A subpopulation becomes a different species by being reproductively isolated even when living with the parent population through _____.

8. A(n) _____ describes the way of life a species, or how a species adapts to its role in its environment.

9. The domain of prokaryotic organisms that are not bacteria is _____.

10. The domain of eukaryotic organisms is _____.

11. A group of similar phyla is a(n) _____.

12. A group of similar species is a(n) _____.

13. A(n) _____ occurs when large numbers of species disappear suddenly.

Review continued on next page

14. A division of a species is called a(n) _____.

15. A pattern where most species appear at about the same pattern is _____.

16. Two populations of birds that no longer reproduce with each other are _____.

17. Species that are dependent on each other have developed _____.

Concept Review

On a sheet of paper, write the letter of the answer that best completes each sentence.

18. In the species name *Homo sapiens,* the word *Homo* is the name of the _____.

   A kingdom   **B** family   **C** genus   **D** species

19. If parents belong to the same _____, they can produce fertile offspring.

   A kingdom   **B** speciation   **C** niche   **D** species

20. Sympatric speciation means that subpopulations _____.

   A are reproductively isolated while living among the parent population

   B are geographically separated form the parent population

   C can breed with each other to produce fertile offspring

   D are created due to a period of mass extinctions

21. A species that survives mass extinction _____.

   A eventually becomes extinct

   B becomes weak

   C diversifies to fill niches

   D undergoes a period of stasis

22. Scientists classify sexually reproducing species by the
_____.

   A ecological species concept

   B biological species concept

   C punctuated equilibrium theory

   D coordinated stasis pattern

Critical Thinking

On a sheet of paper, write the answers to the following
questions. Use complete sentences.

23. Place these seven classification levels of Linnaeus in order
from the most specific to the most general: class, family,
genus, kingdom, order, phylum, species.

24. A biologist is studying a new tree whose leaves are the
same shape as another familiar tree. Should the biologist
classify the new tree as the same species as the familiar
tree? Explain your answer.

25. How do mass extinctions cause diversity in other species?

Research and Write

Use the Internet and print resources to select a country in which
species are becoming extinct. Identify and investigate some
endangered species. What are people doing to preserve plant and
animal diversity in that country? Share your research with the class.

Test-Taking Tip   When studying for a test, learn the most important points. Practice
writing this material or explaining it to someone else.

15

Phylogenies and Classifying Diversity

A patch of mushrooms grows on the tree trunk in this photograph. The mushrooms began with the growth of a single spore. Then they appeared when conditions were right for reproduction. Scientists think life on the earth began with one living cell. Life then spread throughout the earth's surface. The millions of different species we see today gradually replaced earlier, simpler life-forms. In Chapter 15, you will learn about the evolutionary history, or phylogeny, of the major groups of living things. You will also learn how biologists classify living things.

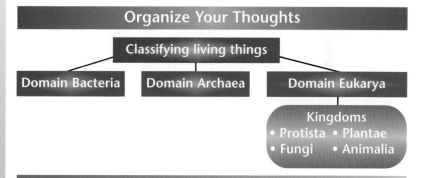

Organize Your Thoughts

Classifying living things

Domain Bacteria   Domain Archaea   Domain Eukarya

Kingdoms
• Protista • Plantae
• Fungi   • Animalia

Goals for Learning

◆ To describe the three domains for living organisms

◆ To name and describe the four kingdoms of the domain Eukarya

◆ To name and describe characteristics of protists, fungi, and the three main groups of plants

◆ To list the eight common features of animals and to describe the characteristics of invertebrates and vertebrates

Taxonomy

The science of classifying organisms based on the features they share

Taxonomist

A scientist who classifies and assigns scientific names to organisms

Humans have about 100,000 million bacteria living in every square centimeter of their skin.

In Chapter 13, you learned that scientists use different systems to group and classify organisms. **Taxonomy** is the science of classifying organisms based on features they share.

Taxonomists classify and assign scientific names to organisms. They assign a two-part Latin name to each species. They classify species according to several classification systems. You will study the three-domain system in this chapter.

The Three-Domain Classification System

Taxonomists use three domains to represent the highest level of classification. Figure 15.1.1 shows the three domains: bacteria, archaea, and eukarya. As you learned in Chapter 14, taxonomists classify living things into other levels. After grouping organisms into a domain, they classify organisms into kingdom, then phylum (for animals) or division (for plants and fungi). The next levels are class, order, family, genus, and species. In this chapter, you will learn about the features of each domain and kingdom. You will also learn about the evolutionary history and features of some animal phyla and plant divisions.

The Domain Bacteria

Recall from Chapter 1 that bacteria are the simplest single cells that carry out all basic life activities. There are thousands of species of bacteria. Bacterial cells live as individuals or in clusters. Some bacteria move. Others never move.

Figure 15.1.1 *Scientists classify living things into three domains.*

Bacteria are prokaryotes. Bacterial cells do not have a nucleus or other organelles. Bacteria have cell walls like plants. However, their cell walls lack a protein found in plant cell walls. Bacteria live on or in nearly every material and environment on the earth. They live in soil, water, and air.

Some bacteria perform photosynthesis. They make food from sunlight and get rid of oxygen. Other bacteria absorb food from the material they live on or in. Some bacteria can cause disease in animals.

Other bacteria are helpful. For example, millions of *E. coli* bacteria live in the stomach. They help the body digest food. They also produce some vitamins the body needs.

The Domain Archaea

The Dead Sea is located at the lowest point on the earth's surface, 390 meters (about 1,300 feet) below sea level.

Archaea are prokaryotes that look like bacteria. Although archaea have genes like eukaryotes, their genes are only found in the domain Archaea. Many archaea live in extreme conditions. For example, some live in polar ice or very salty conditions such as the Dead Sea in Jordan. Archaea have molecules and enzymes that protect them from extreme temperatures and harsh conditions. Many archaea also live in ordinary temperatures and conditions. Archaea have a pigment in their cells that reacts with light to make ATP.

The Domain Eukarya

All eukaryotes belong to the domain Eukarya. Some eukaryotes are single-celled organisms. Others have many cells that do different tasks. Taxonomists classify eukaryotes as animals, plants, fungi, or protists. Recall that protists are one-celled organisms and have plantlike or animal-like properties.

Eukaryotic cells are usually larger than prokaryotic cells. Every eukaryotic cell has organelles that include a nucleus, DNA, chromosomes, and ribosomes. Most eukaryotes also have Golgi apparatus and mitochondria. Plants and algae have chloroplasts that carry out photosynthesis.

Link to ➤➤➤

Health

Viruses are not living, but they have their own genetic material. Viruses contain DNA or RNA. A subset of RNA viruses are retroviruses. The HIV virus that causes AIDS is a retrovirus.

Many eukaryotes have flagella for movement or cilia to sense the environment. Reproduction occurs by mitosis. In most eukaryotic animals and plants, sexual reproduction occurs by meiosis. You will learn more about the domain Eukarya later in this chapter.

Nonliving Viruses

Recall that viruses are not living things. Taxonomists do not classify them in a domain. As you know, a virus is made up of genetic material inside a capsid, a protein coat. Viruses are everywhere. They infect all types of living things. However, viruses are specific to certain living things. For example, plant viruses infect certain plants cells and not animal cells. Scientists classify viruses by the kind of organism they infect, their shape, and the molecules they use.

Express Lab 15

Materials
◆ pictures of pets

Procedure
1. Bring to class a photograph, drawing, or magazine picture of a pet.
2. Using all of the pictures brought by your classmates, create your own classification system for the pets. Organize them in a way that makes sense. Create three or more different levels of organization.

3. Create an organizational chart for your classification system.

Analysis
1. On what features did you base your classification system?
2. How is your classification system similar to the three-domain system? How is it different?

On a sheet of paper, write the word from the Word Bank that completes each sentence correctly.

Word Bank
archaea
domain
living
taxonomist

1. Viruses are not _____ things and are not classified in a _____.

2. A _____ classifies and assigns scientific names to organisms.

3. Many _____ live in extreme conditions.

On a sheet of paper, write the letter of the answer that completes each sentence correctly.

4. _____ are members of the domain Eukarya.

   A Fungi   **B** Bacteria   **C** Virus   **D** Archaea

5. In most eukaryotic cells, sexual reproduction is by _____.

   A ribosomes   **B** mitosis   **C** meiosis   **D** pigments

6. The science of classifying organisms based on shared features is _____.

   A ecology   **C** biogeography

   B paleontology   **D** taxonomy

Critical Thinking
On a sheet of paper, answer the following questions. Use complete sentences.

7. Compare the organisms that make up the domain Bacteria and the domain Archaea.

8. How can bacteria be helpful? How can they be harmful?

9. You are given a sample of single-celled organisms. You must classify the sample as bacteria or eukarya. By using a microscope, what clues could you look for?

10. People cannot be infected by a virus carried by a plant. Explain why.

INVESTIGATION 15

Materials

◆ pictures of different organisms

Classifying Organisms

Scientists classify all organisms by domain, kingdom, phylum or division, class, order, family, genus, and species. In this investigation, you will see that the more related organisms are, the higher the classification level they share.

Procedure

1. Note the differences and similarities between the organisms in the pictures.

2. On a sheet of paper, make a classification chart. To start, list the three domains. Choose one organism from the pictures to represent each domain. List each organism next to its domain on your chart. Write a brief description of each organism and why it is classified in its domain.

3. Choose one organism from the pictures to represent each kingdom. List these on your classification chart. Write a brief description of each organism and why it is classified in its kingdom.

4. List the remaining organisms from the pictures on your chart.

462   *Chapter 15   Phylogenies and Classifying Diversity*

Cleanup/Disposal
When you are finished, be sure your lab area is clean.

Analysis
1. What differences did you see in the sizes of the organisms in the three domains?

2. Where are the organisms in each domain usually found?

Conclusions
1. What features do scientists use to classify organisms into domains?

2. What differences did you notice between organisms in different kingdoms?

Explore Further
Say that you have discovered a new species. Make some notes about this new organism. Include its size, where it lives, and how and what it eats. Trade your information with a classmate. Decide how you would classify each other's organisms.

Objectives

After reading this lesson, you should be able to

◆ name the four kingdoms in the domain Eukarya

◆ describe the kingdom Protista

◆ describe features of three types of protists

◆ name three classification levels in the kingdom Protista

◆ describe features of algae

◆ describe features of slime molds

Protozoan

A protist that ingests food and usually lives in water (plural is protozoa)

Algae

A protist that makes its own food and usually lives in water

Euglena

A protist that make its own food

The domain Eukarya has four kingdoms: Protista, Fungi, Plantae, and Animalia. This lesson will discuss the kingdom Protista. The kingdom Protista is made up of many eukaryotic organisms such as protozoa, **algae, euglenas,** and **slime molds.** Most protists are one-celled organisms. A few have many cells. Some protists make their own food. Others absorb food from outside sources. All protists carry out basic life activities.

Protozoa

A **protozoan** is an animal-like protist that moves. Protozoa have stomach-like parts for digesting food. Some protozoa have properties of animals and plants. They behave like animals by getting food and moving. They eat bacteria, other protozoa, and fungi. In turn, they give off nitrogen, an element needed by plants. Some protozoa make their own food in sunlight. There are about 65,000 species of protozoa. They live in many different environments.

Most protozoa are harmless. A few can cause disease. For example, a type of **amoeba** can live in the human intestines. It feeds on red blood cells and causes **dysentery,** a disease of the intestines.

There are three groups of protozoa. The largest group is the ciliates. These one-celled organisms have cilia, or hairlike structures that help them move around. An example of a ciliate is the paramecium. Look at Figure 15.2.1 on page 465. The paramecium is covered by cilia. The cilia move the paramecium through water and sweep food into its mouthlike opening.

The second group of protozoa is the amoebas. Find the amoeba in Figure 15.2.1. Amoebas move by **pseudopods.** A pseudopod sticks out like a foot and pulls an amoeba along. Amoebas also use their pseudopod to surround food and bring it inside.

The third group is the flagellates. They are the smallest protozoa. They have one or more flagella. Recall that flagella are long, whiplike tails that help move protozoa and other organisms through water.

The euglena in Figure 15.2.1 is a flagellate. One flagellum is shown. Euglenas behave like both plants and animals. Like plants, they make their own food in sunlight. Like animals, they absorb food from the environment. They absorb food when sunlight is not present.

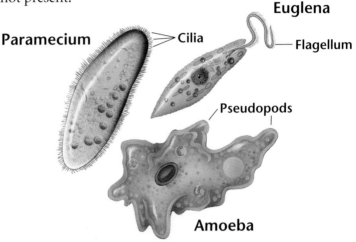

Figure 15.2.1 *Protozoa probably evolved about 1.5 billion years ago.*

Algae range in size from microscopic organisms to large seaweed. Some seaweed can grow as long as a football field.

Other Protists

Brown algae belong to the division Phaeophyta. They are the largest and most complex algae. They are often called seaweed. There are also red algae and green algae species. Algae are plant-like protists. They grow in moist areas, on trees, and on rocks. Most algae live in fresh water and saltwater. You may have seen algae that grow as a green scum on a pond or lake. The green scum is thousands of tiny algae.

Some algae get their nutrients from living things. For example, *Pfiesteria* produces harmful substances that stun passing fish and cause bleeding sores. *Pfiesteria* feed on the fish blood and fluids. Most algae make their own food. They use energy from sunlight and release oxygen. Algae produce a large amount of the oxygen that other organisms use. However, algae are not plants because they do not have roots, stems, or leaves.

Slime mold

A protist that lives as an individual cell, then joins other slime mold cells to form a community that produces spores

Spore

A reproductive cell of some organisms

Diatoms are another example of useful protists. A diatom has a hard shell made out of silica. Silica is used to make glass. Shell remains of diatoms are used to make paint for roads and grit for toothpaste.

The Phylum Amoebozoa

The phylum Amoebozoa is made up of **slime molds.** This phylum is in the kingdom Protista. Slime molds are like fungi and animals. They have amoebalike cells that digest fungi and bacteria. They usually grow on damp soil, rotting logs, or other decomposing matter in moist areas. Many slime molds are yellow or red. Some are white.

If food or water is scarce, slime molds gather together and form one structure. The new community becomes a slimy covering and moves toward food or water. Once they move to their new location, they begin to reproduce. Some slime mold cells become **spores.** A spore is a reproductive cell. When food and water are present, a spore becomes a new slime mold cell.

★ ✦ ★ ☆

Achievements in Science

The History of Classification Systems

An ancient Greek, Aristotle, developed the first classification system. His system had four categories: plants, animals with blood, animals without blood, and other things. Scientists used Aristotle's classification system for centuries.

In 1753, Carolus Linnaeus developed the classification system that scientists use today. Linnaeus took Aristotle's system and expanded it. He made it more complex. Linnaeus introduced hierarchy, in which organisms in larger categories are divided into smaller and more precise groups.

Linnaeus grouped organisms into the animal kingdom or the plant kingdom.

Then he used differences in how the organisms looked or functioned to further classify them. His hierarchy levels are kingdom, phylum, class, order, family, genus, and species.

Through the years, scientists have expanded Linnaeus's classification system. They have analyzed the chemical structures of organisms and their DNA. As a result, they adjusted how some organisms are classified. They expanded the kingdom level to include more organisms. They also added the domain level above the kingdom level. The domain level represents genetic differences between organisms.

Lesson 2   R E V I E W

Word Bank

cilia

pseudopod

sunlight

On a sheet of paper, write the word from the Word Bank that completes each sentence correctly.

1. Protozoa use _____ to move and capture food.

2. Amoebas use a _____, or false foot, to move and to surround food.

3. Most algae get their energy from _____.

On a sheet of paper, match each term with one of the descriptions listed below.

A algae   **B** protozoa   **C** slime molds

4. protista that act like animals

5. protista that behave like plants

6. protista that act like fungi

Critical Thinking

On a sheet of paper, answer the following questions. Use complete sentences.

7. In what ways do humans use diatoms?

8. In what ways are protozoa dangerous to humans?

9. Describe the positive and negative impact that algae have on humans.

10. Describe the life cycle of a slime mold.

After reading this lesson, you should be able to

◆ describe the kingdom Fungi

◆ describe features of fungi

◆ describe lichens

Mold

A fungus that grows quickly on a surface

Hyphae

Threadlike fibers containing membranes and cytoplasm

Mycelium

The underground feeding network of a fungus

The fungus *Armillaria ostoyae* is the size of 1,600 football fields. It weighs hundreds of tons and may be the world's largest organism. *Armillaria ostoyae* is between 2,400 and 8,500 years old.

Have you seen mushrooms in the grocery store or **mold** on bread? Both are members of the fungi kingdom. You will learn about the kingdom Fungi in this lesson.

Some fungi are single-celled, such as yeast. Most fungi are bunches of many cells, such as mushrooms or mold. Fungi are eukaryotic organisms. Their DNA is in the cell nucleus. Some fungi look like plants. However, fungi cannot carry on photosynthesis. Fungi are more closely related to animals than to plants. Scientists have identified about 100,000 fungi species.

Fungi decompose, or break down, dead organisms for food. They absorb sugars through their cell walls. To take in more complex food, fungi give off enzymes. The enzymes break down complex food into simpler forms. The fungi then absorb the food. After fungi digest the food, they give off carbon and nitrogen. Other organisms use these chemicals.

Fungi usually grow in slightly acidic environments. They do not need much moisture. Fungi live in soil, in houses, on plants and animals, and in fresh water and seawater. Some fungi spread by forming reproductive spores, or sex cells. A fungus can produce trillions of spores. Wind, water, birds, and animals carry away the spores. If conditions in the new areas are right, the spores will grow into new fungi.

Most fungi are made of **hyphae.** Hyphae are threadlike fibers that contain membranes and cytoplasm. Hyphae form a mat called a **mycelium.** This is the underground feeding network of fungi. Although fungi cannot move, hyphae grow and spread quickly. Some hyphae can grow up to a kilometer (0.62 miles) in one day. The mushroom you see growing on the ground is the reproductive structure of the fungus. Most of the fungal body lies underground as mycelium.

Lichen

An organism that is made up of a fungus, a green alga, and a cynobacterium

Cyanobacterium

A blue-green algae

Link to ➤ ➤ ➤

Social Studies

The potato famine caused by the fungus *Phytophthora infestans* resulted in a large wave of immigration from Ireland to the United States. These immigrants included the great-grandparents of President John F. Kennedy.

Helpful and Harmful Fungi

Some fungi are useful, such as the fungus in penicillin. Penicillin is an antibiotic used to destroy bacteria that cause disease. People add fungi to milk to make cheese. People use yeast, a fungus, to make bread rise.

Some fungi cause diseases in plants, animals, and people. The fungus *Phytophthora infestans* caused the Great Potato Famine in Ireland in the mid-1800s. Millions of people died when this fungus ruined their potato crops. Fungi ruin about a quarter to half of harvested fruits and vegetables each year. Fungi can harm wood in houses, clothing, and some plastics, such as shower curtains.

Lichens

A **lichen** is made up of a fungus, a green algae, and **cyanobacterium.** Taxonomists classify lichens as a species. The algae provide food. The bacteria provide nitrogen. The fungi provide a physical environment for growth. Lichens are usually found on rocks and trees. Some lichens are thousands of years old. There are two lichens in Figure 15.3.1.

Figure 15.3.1 *Lichens are usually found on rocks and trees.*

Biology in Your Life

The Environment: Nature's Recycling System

What would happen if everything that died did not decompose, or break down? The surface of the earth would soon be covered in dead plants, animals, and microorganisms. Decomposition is part of the cycle of life. Fungi and bacteria constantly decompose organic matter. The leftovers are used by living organisms for growth, repair, and reproduction.

People use microorganisms to break down organic material in a process called composting. People compost because this process gets rid of waste. Composting provides fertilizer, or nutrients, for crops and gardens. Composting also reduces the amount of material in landfills.

Many things can be composted, such as leaves, wood, and grass clippings. Newspapers, coffee grounds, and food waste also can be composted. Composting is easy. To begin composting, pick a place and pile material there. Add a little water regularly. To speed up composting, turn the compost pile regularly. This allows air to enter the pile and allows gases to escape.

Microorganisms present on the composted materials begin to decompose. This raises the temperature in the pile. As the temperature increases, material decomposes more quickly. After a few weeks, you have compost—a fine-textured, fertile material. You can spread compost on top of soil, or dig it into soil.

1. What is composting?

2. What kinds of organisms are used for composting?

3. How can you begin composting? What happens during the process of composting?

On a sheet of paper, write the word from the Word Bank that completes each sentence correctly.

Word Bank

acidic

hyphae

mycelium

1. The bodies of fungi are made of single strands of _____.

2. Fungi grow best in slightly _____ environments.

3. The body of a fungus that looks solid is a mat of fibers, or the _____.

On a sheet of paper, write the letter of the answer that completes each sentence correctly.

4. Molds and mushrooms are both _____.

   A lichens   **B** fungi   **C** bacteria   **D** algae

5. Lichens are a combination of fungi, algae, and _____.

   A bacteria   **B** cyanobacteria **C** moss   **D** spores

6. Scientists have identified about _____ species of fungi.

   A 1,000   **B** 10,000   **C** 100,000   **D** 1,000,000

Critical Thinking

On a sheet of paper, write the answers to the following questions. Use complete sentences.

7. How do fungi digest food?

8. Where can fungi live?

9. What are lichens? How do the three parts of lichens interact?

10. How can fungi help people? How can they harm people?

Seed

A plant part that contains a beginning plant and stored food

Fern

A seedless vascular plant

Moss

A nonvascular plant that has simple parts

Gymnosperm

A nonflowering seed plant

Angiosperm

A flowering seed plant

Vascular plant

A plant that has tubelike cells

Plants are eukaryotes that perform photosynthesis. Most plants live on land. Scientists have named more than 260,000 kinds of plants. Possibly tens of thousands of plants have not been found and named.

The kingdom Plantae is in the domain Eukarya. Scientists classify plants by body parts, such as **seeds,** roots, tubes, stems, and leaves. The three main groups of plants are **ferns, mosses,** and seed plants. Seed plants are divided into **gymnosperms** and **angiosperms.** You will learn more about each group in this lesson.

Vascular and Nonvascular Plants

Seed plants and ferns are **vascular plants.** Vascular plants have tubelike cells. These cells form tissue called **vascular tissue.** The tissue forms tubes that transport food and water throughout the plant. Vascular plants have leaves, stems, and roots.

Vascular plants are made of two types of tissue. One type is **xylem,** which is made of dead cells. Xylem transports water and minerals from the roots to the leaves. As you know, photosynthesis occurs in leaves. The second type of vascular tissue is **phloem.** Phloem is made up of living cells. Phloem takes sugars in the leaves to the roots. Photosynthesis does not occur in the roots.

Roots anchor plants in soil and rock. Roots absorb water and minerals, which are carried upward to the stems and then to the leaves. Some fungi live close to the roots of plants. The fungus absorbs minerals from the soil and shares them with the plant. In turn, the plant provides the fungus with some of the food it makes. The plant and fungus both benefit. This is called **mycorrhiza.**

Vascular tissue is important to plants. It allows food and water to be transported throughout the plant. A plant can grow tall because its leaves and stems do not need to be near the soil. A plant also grows tall because vascular tissue is thick. It provides support for the plant.

Vascular tissue

A group of plant cells that form tubes through which food and water move

Xylem

The vascular tissue in plants that carries water and minerals from roots to stems and leaves

Phloem

The vascular tissue in plants that carries food from leaves to other parts of the plant

Mycorrhiza

A close relationship in which a fungus and the roots of a plant live together and help each other

Nonvascular plant

A plant that does not have tubelike cells

Rhizoid

A rootlike thread of a moss plant

Alternation of generations

A life cycle of mosses, algae, and some protists that alternates between a haploid phase and a diploid phase

Nonvascular plants are short and small because they do not have tubelike cells. They do not have tubes to transport water or provide support. They also do not have leaves, stems, or roots. Nonvascular plants usually grow in damp, shady areas on the ground and on the sides of trees and rocks.

The Phylum Bryophyta

Mosses belong to the phylum Bryophyta, a level in the kingdom Plantae. Scientists think mosses were the first plants to appear on the earth. A moss is a nonvascular plant that has simple leaflike and stemlike parts. Mosses grow in beds or clumps. They are low-growing plants.

Mosses need constant contact with moisture. They live in moist, shady areas. They get water through rootlike threads called **rhizoids.** Mosses have a waxy outer coat that prevents them from drying out.

Plants like mosses, algae, and some protists have a life cycle called **alternation of generations.** This means the life cycle takes turns, or alternates, between a haploid phase and a diploid phase. Recall that a haploid cell has one copy of each kind of chromosome. A diploid cell has two copies of each kind of chromosome.

The diploid phase in plants produces spores. A plant in this phase is called a **sporophyte.** Spores are produced by meiosis. This means a spore is a haploid reproductive cell. A spore can develop into an adult without fusing with another cell.

 Science Myth

Myth: A plant makes tissue from the water and minerals it gets from soil.

Fact: Plant tissue is made from carbon. A plant gets carbon by taking in carbon dioxide from the air.

A spore then gives rise to a **gametophyte.** A gametophye produces gametes, or sex cells, by mitosis. The gametes fuse and give rise to the diploid phase. The sporophyte and gametophyte generations alternate in a plant's life cycle.

In mosses, millions of tiny spores form inside spore capsules on the end of a sporophyte stalk. Ripe spore cases break open. They shoot many spores into the air. Wind, rain, and animals carry the spores to new areas. There the spores grow by mitosis. They form gametophytes, or mature sex cells. The male gametophytes release sperm that swim through water to eggs in a female gametophyte. The diploid zygote develops as a sporophyte. The life cycle of the moss goes on.

▼◄▲▼◄▲▼◄▲▼◄▲▼◄▲▼◄▲▼◄▲▼◄▲▼◄▲▼◄▲▼◄▲▼◄▲▼◄▲▼

Science at Work

Museum Guide

Museum guides teach students and visitors about the exhibits in a museum. The work of a museum guide varies, depending on the type of museum. For example, a guide in a natural history museum may describe fossils in exhibits. A guide in a science exploratory museum may perform experiments and demonstrations.

Guides must enjoy teaching and working with people. They must be able to answer questions for students and visitors.

To be a guide, a person must have a high school degree and complete training in the museum. Guides must stay current on changes in museum displays and in the research relating to the museum. Many guides get a higher degree. Then they may move to museum positions such as education director, display developer, or museum curator.

Link to ➤➤➤

Environmental Science

Some plants can tolerate air pollution better than other plants. Plants such as the Gingko tree are regularly planted in big cities.Gingko trees are not harmed by smog that damages many other plants.

The Phylum Polypodiophyta

Ferns belong to the phylum Polypodiophyta, a level in the kingdom Plantae. Ferns developed after mosses appeared. Scientists have found over 12,000 species of ferns. Many ferns live in tropical forests and temperate forests. Ferns are vascular plants. Fern leaves, or **fronds,** are usually large and flat.

On the underside of fronds are **sori.** Sori are small, round clusters that contain spores. Each cluster releases many haploid spores. These spores grow into tiny gametophytes on or just below the soil surface. On the underside of the gametophyte are sperm and egg-producing structures. Like mosses, fern sperm have flagella. The sperm swim through water to fertilize eggs. The zygote grows into the new sporophyte.

Over thousands of years, pressure and heat have changed the buried remains of ancient ferns and other plants and animals into coal. Coal, oil, and natural gas are **fossil fuels.** Fossil fuels provide energy for people. The amount of fossil fuels on the earth is limited. Scientists are looking into alternative sources of energy. You can learn more about different kinds of energy in Appendix F.

The Phylum Coniferophyta

After ferns appeared, gymnosperms such as **conifers** developed next. Conifers belong to the phylum Coniferophyta, a classification level in the kingdom Plantae. Gymnosperms are the first seed plants. Seed plants use seeds to reproduce. A seed is a plant part that contains a beginning plant and stored food.

The beginning plant is called an embryo. A seed has a coat that protects the embryo and holds in moisture. When conditions are right, the embryo grows into a full-sized plant.

Gymnosperms are nonflowering plants. The largest group of gymnosperms is conifers, or cone-bearing plants. Common conifers are pine trees, junipers, firs, cedars, redwoods, and spruces. Scientists have found about 700 species of conifers. Conifers can grow very large and tall, such as the giant redwoods in California. Gymnosperms are the main source of lumber and paper.

Most conifers have green leaves all year. They are called evergreens. The leaves are shaped like needles. They do not lose water as easily as the bigger leaves of other trees. Because of their needles, conifers can survive well during dry periods.

Gymnosperm seeds are uncovered. They are under the scales of the cones. The reproductive organs of gymnosperms are in cones. Some cones are female. Some cones are male. Male cones are smaller than female cones. During reproduction, male cones release millions of pollen grains into the air. Some pollen grains reach female cones. The pollen grain grows a tube that reaches eggs in the ovary. When the pollen and egg meet, fertilization takes place.

The Phylum Anthophyta

After conifers appeared, angiosperms, or flowering plants, developed. Flowering plants belong to the phylum Anthophyta, a classification level in the kingdom Plantae. Most plants are angiosperms. Scientists have found about 250,000 species. Seed plants have the most advanced vascular tissue of all plants.

Study Figure 15.4.2. The flower is the part of an angiosperm that contains eggs and sperm. In a flower, the **stamens** are the male reproductive organs. The stamen includes the anther and filament. They produce pollen. Pollen contains sperm.

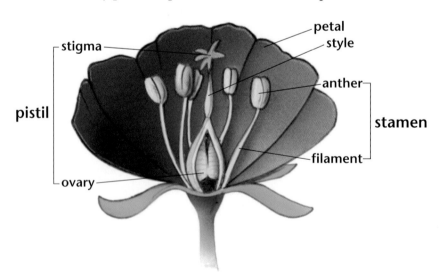

Figure 15.4.2 *A flower contains male and female reproductive organs.*

Pistil

The female organ of reproduction in a flower

Stigma

The upper part of the pistil on the tip of the style

Nectar

A sweet liquid that many flowers produce

Pollination

The process by which pollen is transferred from the stamen to the pistil

Germinate

To start to grow into a new plant

The **pistil** in a flower is the female reproductive organ. The upper part of the pistil is the **stigma,** which is sticky to catch pollen. The stigma is on the tip of the style. The lower part of the pistil is the ovary, which contains eggs.

Flowers attract insects and birds. They land on flowers to drink **nectar,** which is a sweet liquid many flowers produce. While insects and birds drink, pollen sticks to their bodies. They carry the pollen to the pistil of the same flower or other flowers. Wind, rain, and animals also spread pollen. **Pollination** occurs when pollen is transferred from the stamen to the pistil.

After pollination, the pollen grain grows a tube. The pollen tube grows down through the pistil to the eggs in the ovary. When the pollen inside the tube meets an egg, fertilization takes place. The ovary grows to become a fruit. Inside the fruit are seeds. The fruit protects the seeds. When the fruit is mature, it drops from the plant or is carried by another organism to a different area. For example, birds may eat the fruit. They will carry and drop the seeds in new areas. The seeds will **germinate** if conditions are right. The seeds then grow into new plants.

Angiosperms are valuable plants. They are a source of food for many living things. People use angiosperms for medicine and for fibers to make clothing. Some flowering plants are used to make perfume. Figure 15.4.3 sums up the three main groups of plants: mosses, seedless plants, and seed plants. Appendix G provides more information about the plant kingdom.

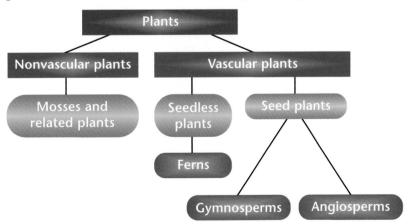

Figure 15.4.3 *Plants are classified according to their structures.*

Lesson 4   R E V I E W

Word Bank

conifers

rhizoids

sporophyte

On a sheet of paper, write the word from the Word Bank that completes each sentence correctly.

1. Mosses get water through rootlike threads called _____.

2. Most _____ have green leaves all year.

3. The seed of an angiosperm germinates to produce a _____.

On a sheet of paper, write the letter of the answer that completes each sentence correctly.

4. A plant is a _____.

    A one-celled eukaryote

    B one-celled prokaryote

    C multicellular eukaryote

    D multicellular prokaryote

5. Pollen is a _____.

    A female gametophyte   **C** male gametophyte

    B female sporophyte   **D** male sporophyte

6. Small, round clusters that contain spores on fronds are _____.

    A cones   **B** flowers   **C** seeds   **D** sori

Critical Thinking

On a sheet of paper, answer the following questions. Use complete sentences.

7. Describe the male and female parts that make up a flower.

8. How do plants and fungi work together to get nutrients?

9. Describe the two types of vascular tissue in plants.

10. How are ancient ferns and other plants connected to the way humans get energy today?

Objectives

After reading this lesson, you should be able to

◆ describe eight common features of organisms in the kingdom Animalia

◆ define vertebrates and invertebrates

Heterotroph

An organism that cannot make its own food

Multicellular

Made up of many cells

Blastula

A hollow ball of cells formed by cell divisions of a zygote

Animals are eukaryotes. The kingdom Animalia is in the domain Eukarya. Scientists have classified more than 1.5 million animals. Over half of these species are insects. New species are discovered every year. Scientists think there may be millions more species to find and classify.

Eight Common Features of Animals

Most animals share eight common features. One feature is that animals are **heterotrophs.** They cannot make their own food. They must eat food to supply energy and material for cell growth and repair. Animals eat live or dead organisms. Digestion occurs inside the animal's body.

Most animals have coordinated movement. They can also move quickly. Animals move by means of muscle cells. A nervous system controls their muscular and skeletal systems.

Another feature is that all animals are **multicellular.** They have many cells. This is true for tiny animals that can be seen only under a microscope and for huge animals such as whales and elephants.

Most animals are diploid. This means that most animals have two copies of each chromosome. One copy is inherited from the father. The other copy is inherited from the mother. Only their sex cells (sperm and egg) are haploid. They have one copy of each kind of sex chromosome.

Most animals reproduce sexually. They produce gametes, or eggs and sperm. Egg cells are much larger than sperm. Animal sperm cells have a flagella, which move the sperm cells.

When an egg is fertilized, it becomes a zygote, or a fertilized egg cell. The zygote divides again and again to form a hollow ball of cells called a **blastula.** All zygotes of animals develop a blastula. The formation of a blastula is another feature of animals. Cells within the blastula form three layers. These layers will become different parts of the body.

Only animal cells do not have rigid cell walls. This gives animal cells the ability to move. Remember from Chapter 11 that macrophages are white blood cells that move to different body parts. There, they surround and digest pathogens. If macrophages had rigid cell walls, they could not do this.

The cells of most animals are organized into tissues. Remember that a tissue is a group of cells that work together to perform a task. For example, muscle cells contract for movement. Here is a list of the eight features of animals:

- Heterotroph
- Coordinated movement and can move quickly
- Multicellular
- Diploid
- Reproduce sexually
- Develop a blastula
- No rigid cell walls
- Have tissues

Invertebrates and Vertebrates

Animals are either invertebrates or vertebrates. As you know, an invertebrate is an animal without a backbone. A vertebrate is an animal with a backbone. You will study invertebrates in Lesson 6, and vertebrates in Lessons 7 and 8.

Word Bank

heterotrophs

invertebrate

nervous system

vertebrate

On a sheet of paper, write the word or words from the Word Bank that complete each sentence correctly.

1. Animals are _____ because they cannot make their own food.

2. Most animals have coordinated movement because their muscular and skeletal systems are controlled by a(n) _____.

3. A(n) _____ is an animal without a backbone, and a(n) _____ is an animal with a backbone.

On a sheet of paper, write the letter of the answer that completes each sentence correctly.

4. An animal zygote divides to form _____.

   A sperm   **B** an egg   **C** flagella   **D** a blastula

5. The cells of most animals are organized into _____.

   A tissues   **B** blastulas   **C** diploids   **D** haploids

6. All animals are _____, meaning they have many cells.

   A made up of rigid cell walls

   B haploid

   C multicellular

   D invertebrates

Critical Thinking

On a sheet of paper, answer the following questions. Use complete sentences.

7. In animals, what happens when an egg is fertilized?

8. How does having a nervous system help animals?

9. How are all animals alike as heterotrophs?

10. What are the eight features that most animals share?

Invertebrates make up about 97 percent of all animal species. Recall from Chapter 13 that an invertebrate is an animal without a backbone. Invertebrates belong to more than 30 phyla. You will learn about eight phyla in this lesson.

Phylogeny is the origin and evolution of a species. Scientists use comparative anatomy and molecular biology to investigate animal phylogeny. In this lesson, you will learn about eight of the many phyla that belong to the kingdom Animalia and their evolutionary history.

The Phylum Porifera

The phylum Porifera is sponges. Sponges are the simplest animals. Their bodies are made up of two layers of cells. They do not have tissues or organs, and they do not move. They live in water and strain food from the water. Each cell of a sponge can sense and react to the environment. Scientists have found about 9,000 species of sponges.

The Phylum Cnidarian

Cnidarians appeared after sponges. Cnidarians include jellyfish, corals, and hydras. There are about 10,000 species of cnidarians. All live in water. All have **radial symmetry.** Radial symmetry is an arrangement of body parts that resembles the arrangement of spokes on a wheel. Cnidarians also have armlike **tentacles** with stinging cells. The tentacles capture food and push it into a baglike body cavity for digestion.

The Phylum Platyhelminthes

Flatworms developed after cnidarians. Flatworms are flat and thin. Their bodies have a left half and a right half. The halves are the same. This body type is called **bilateral symmetry.** Flatworms include planarians, flukes, and tapeworms. There are about 20,000 species of flatworms and most are parasites.

Phylogeny
The origin and evolution of a species

Cnidarian
A group of invertebrates including jellyfish, corals, and hydras

Radial symmetry
An arrangement of body parts that resembles the spokes on a wheel

Tentacle
An armlike body part of cnidarians that is used to capture food

The Phylum Nematoda

Roundworms, such as pinworms and hookworms, belong to the phylum Nematoda. They developed after cnidarians. There are about 90,000 species of nematodes, and there are probably more. Like flatworms, roundworms have bilateral symmetry. Roundworms live in wet soil or water. They eat dead leaves and other material. Some eat insects that destroy plant roots. Other roundworms destroy the roots of plants. Some roundworms live in humans and can cause them to become sick.

Roundworms have a complete digestive tract. This is a digestive tube with two openings. Animals with a complete digestive tract process food as it moves through different organs.

The Phylum Annelid

The annelids, or **segmented worms,** developed after roundworms. The round body of segmented worms is divided into many sections, or segments. Segmented worms live in moist soil, saltwater, and freshwater. There are more than 15,000 species of annelids.

Earthworms and leeches are two species of annelids. Earthworms tunnel through the soil to eat small food particles. Their tunnels loosen the soil and allow air to enter. This helps plants grow. Some leeches eat small invertebrates. Others attach to the skin of a vertebrate and feed on its blood. While feeding, the leech secretes a chemical so that the blood does not clot. Scientists are investigating this chemical as a medicine.

The Phylum Mollusca

Snails, slugs, oysters, clams, and octopuses belong to the phylum Mollusca. There are about 150,000 species of **mollusks.** Most live in saltwater and freshwater. They can swim quickly to find food. Some mollusks live on land. Mollusks have bilateral symmetry.

Every mollusk has a head, body, and muscular foot. The foot moves the animal around. Mollusks have soft bodies that contain organs. A hard outside shell protects most mollusks. The animal can fit inside this shell for protection.

Radula

A tonguelike organ covered with teeth that is used for feeding

Arthropod

A member of the largest group of invertebrates; this group includes insects

Crustacean

A class of arthropods that includes crabs, lobsters, crayfish, and pill bugs

Arachnid

A class of arthropods that includes spiders, scorpions, mites, and ticks

Exoskeleton

An external skeleton

Molting

The process by which an arthropod sheds its exoskeleton

Snails have a coiled shell. Slugs have a small internal shell. Snails and slugs make up the largest group of mollusks. Oysters, mussels, and scallops are protected by two shells hinged together. The hinged shells open and close. These animals live in mud or sand and use their foot for digging. Squid have a small internal shell, and octopuses have no shell. The brain of an octopus is large. Octopuses have good sense organs.

Mollusks feed by using a **radula.** A radula is a tonguelike organ covered with teeth that is used for feeding. A garden snail uses its radula to cut out pieces of leaves to eat. A squid's radula can rip apart food.

The Phylum Arthropoda

Arthropods belong to the phylum Arthropoda. There are about a million species of arthropods. They are the largest group of invertebrates. They make up more than three-fourths of all animal species. The five main groups of arthopods are **crustaceans,** millipedes, centipedes, **arachnids,** and insects.

Arthropods have segmented bodies with jointed legs. Most arthropods have antennae that allow them to feel, taste, and smell. Their body is covered with an **exoskeleton,** or an external skeleton. The exoskeleton can be thick or it can be very thin in places such as joints. As they grow, arthropods shed their exoskeleton and secrete a larger one. This process is called **molting.**

❀ ❀

Technology and Society

DNA technology helps scientists classify organisms accurately. For example, nautilus mollusks were once classified into five species. Using DNA analysis, scientists found only two species of nautilus mollusks. Scientists are examining fossils for DNA evidence of ancient viruses that may have caused extinctions.

Crabs, lobsters, crayfish, and shrimp are crustaceans. There are about 40,000 species of crustaceans. Most live in freshwater and saltwater. One group, called pill bugs, lives under moist leaves. Many crustaceans have five pairs of legs. Some legs have claws to help the animal handle food. The two legs closest to the head usually have powerful claws for protection.

Millipedes and centipedes have many body segments. They live on land and eat decaying plant matter. There are about 10,000 species of millipedes and 2,500 species of centipedes. Millipedes have two pairs of short legs on each body segment. Centipedes have poison claws that they use in defense and to paralyze insects and other animals. They have a pair of long legs on each body segment and can run quickly.

Arachnids are spiders, scorpions, mites, and ticks. There are about 70,000 species of arachnids. Most live on land. They have four pairs of legs and a pair of feeding limbs. Spiders produce threads of silk to spin webs and build nests. Spiders eat insects caught in their webs and nests. Some spiders catch small fish or frogs. Spiders inject their prey with poison to capture it. Scorpions use a stinger to inject poison into their prey. Mites and ticks live on mammals, including humans. Mites feed on hair and dead skin. Ticks feed by piercing the skin and eating blood.

There are about one million species of insects. They live almost everywhere, except in the deep ocean. Mosquitoes, flies, ants, and beetles are insects. Insects have three body parts: a head, thorax, and abdomen. The head has antennae and a pair of eyes. Mouth parts are varied for biting, chewing, and piercing skin.

Insects have three pairs of legs and one or two pairs of wings. Because insects can fly, they can escape predators. They can find food and move to new habitats. Insects are the only invertebrates that can fly.

Many insects go through **metamorphosis.** Metamorphosis is a major change in form that occurs as some animals develop into adults. **Complete metamorphosis** is the changes in the animal's form during development in which earlier stages do not look like the adult.

Look at Figure 15.6.1. The complete metamorphosis of a butterfly has four stages. The first three stages do not look like the adult butterfly. Some young insects, like grasshoppers, resemble adults. This is called **incomplete metamorphosis.** Crickets and cockroaches also develop by incomplete metamorphosis.

Many insects are pests. Fleas, ticks, and mosquitoes carry microorganisms that cause diseases. Grasshoppers and caterpillars destroy crops. They also serve as food for other organisms. Other insects are helpful. They make useful products such as honey, wax, and silk. Many insects pollinate flowers, which produce fruits.

The Phylum Echinodermata

Echinoderms belong to the phylum Echinodermata. Sea urchins, sand dollars, sea cucumbers, and sea stars belong to this group. All 7,000 species live in marine environments. Most do not move. Some move slowly. Echinoderms do not have body segments. They have radial symmetry. For example, starfish have parts that come out from the center like spokes.

Echinoderms have an **endoskeleton,** or an interior skeleton. They have a network of canals filled with water. These canals circulate water. The canals branch into **tube feet.** The tube feet attach firmly to surfaces and also move echinoderms.

Complete Metamorphosis

Stage 1
A butterfly egg hatches into a caterpillar.

Stage 4
After a few weeks, the pupa molts into an adult butterfly.

Stage 2
A caterpillar feeds on leaves, molting several times as it grows.

Stage 3
When a caterpillar reaches its full size, it molts into a form called a pupa.

Figure 15.6.1 *A butterfly metamorphosis has four stages.*

Table 15.6.1 sums up the eight phyla covered in this lesson.

Table 15.6.1 Eight Invertebrate Phyla		
Phylum	**Description**	**Examples**
Porifera	Body wall of two cell layers; pores and canals; no tissues or organs; live in water; strain food from water	sponge
Cnidarian	Baglike body of two cell layers; one opening leading into a hollow body; tissues; radial symmetry; live in water	jellyfish, coral, hydra
Platyhelminthes	Flat, thin body; three cell layers; organs; digestive system with one opening; nervous system; bilateral symmetry; most are parasites	tapeworm, planarian, fluke
Nematoda	Round, slender body; digestive system with two openings; nervous system; bilateral symmetry	hookworm, pinworm
Annelid	Round, segmented body; digestive system, nervous system, circulatory system; bilateral symmetry; most are not parasites	earthworm, leech
Mollusca	Soft body covered by a fleshy mantle; move with muscular foot; some have shells; all have organ systems; bilateral symmetry; feed by using a radula	snail, slug, clam, oyster, scallop, squid, octopus
Arthropoda	Segmented body; jointed legs; most have antennae; all have organ systems; external skeleton	
	• Crustacean—two body parts; usually five pairs of legs two pairs of antennae; breathe with gills	crayfish, lobster, crab, shrimp, sow bug
	• Many body segments; from 15 to over 100; one or two pairs of legs in each segment	millipede centipede
	• Arachnid—two body segments; four pairs of legs; no antennae	spider, scorpion, tick mite
	• Insect—three body segments; three pairs of legs; one pair of antennae; most have two pairs of wings	fly, beetle, grasshopper, earwig, silverfish, water strider, butterfly, bee, ant
Echinodermata	Covered with spines; body has five parts; radial symmetry; live in ocean	sea star, sea urchin, sand dollar

Lesson 6 R E V I E W

Word Bank

radial symmetry

radula

sponges

On a sheet of paper, write the word or words from the Word Bank that complete each sentence correctly.

1. Mollusks feed by using a _____.

2. The simplest animals are _____.

3. Sea urchins, sand dollars, and sea cucumbers have _____.

On a sheet of paper, write the letter of the answer that completes each sentence correctly.

4. Three-fourths of all animal species are _____.

    A crustaceans   **C** annelids

    B arthropods   **D** poriferas

5. Flatworms have a body type called _____.

    A radial symmetry   **C** radula

    B bilateral symmetry   **D** exoskeleton

6. Insects have _____ pairs of legs.

    A five   **C** three

    B four   **D** two

Critical Thinking

On a sheet of paper, answer the following questions. Use complete sentences.

7. Compare and contrast an endoskeleton and an exoskeleton.

8. Compare and contrast arachnids and insects.

9. Name and describe the three body parts of a mollusk.

10. Gardeners say that a garden filled with earthworms is good. Explain why.

Scientists have classified about 50,000 species of vertebrates in the kingdom Animalia. The phylum Chordata is part of the kingdom Animalia. **Chordates** are vertebrates, or animals with backbones.

Features of Vertebrates

Vertebrates have three unique features. First, they have a skeleton inside their body. The skeleton is made of bone and **cartilage.** Cartilage is a soft material. Some invertebrates have an internal skeleton, but it is not made of bone. Second, vertebrates have a backbone. A **vertebra** is a bone or a block of cartilage that makes up a backbone. A backbone is made of many small vertebrae. Third, vertebrates have a skull. The skull surrounds and protects the brain.

Vertebrates live in most land habitats. Fish, which are vertebrates, live in freshwater and seawater.

The Phylum Chordata

Chordates share four common features when they are an embryo. First, they develop a **dorsal** nerve cord. The hollow nerve cord includes the brain and spinal cord. Second, a stiff **notochord,** or rod, develops along the dorsal side of the embryo.

Third, chordate embryos develop **pharyngeal slits,** or openings in the wall of the pharynx. The pharynx is the tube that connects the mouth to the digestive tract and windpipe. Fourth, chordate embryos have a tail that goes beyond the anus.

All chordates, including humans, have these features in their embryonic stage of development. These four features may be present for only a short time in some embryos.

Chordate
An animal that, in its embryo stage, has a dorsal nerve cord, a notochord, pharyngeal slits, and a tail that goes past the anus

Cartilage
A soft material found in vertebrate skeletons

Vertebra
One of the bones or blocks of cartilage that make up a backbone; (plural is vertebrae)

Dorsal
The back part of an animal

Phylogeny

Vertebrates developed about 550 million years ago. The oldest vertebrate fossils are those of fish with no jaws. About 440 million years ago, ancestors of the first fish with jaws and a soft skeleton appeared. Bony fish evolved next.

About 370 million years ago, most amphibians resembled modern species. They became the first vertebrates to live on land. Reptiles arose from amphibians about 300 million years ago. Scientists think birds and mammals evolved from reptiles. Birds appeared about 220 millions years ago. Mammals are older, appearing 300 million years ago.

Eight Classes of Vertebrates

Scientists divide vertebrates into eight classes. Four classes are made up of different types of fish. These include fish without jaws, fish with jaws and soft skeletons, and bony fish. The other four classes are amphibians, reptiles, birds, and mammals.

Class Myxini and Class Cephalaspidomorphi

There are four classes of fish. One is the class **Myxini,** or hagfish. Another is the class **Cephalaspidomorphi,** which are lampreys. The fish have a skeleton made of soft cartilage. Both classes of fish have no jaws or scales.

Class Chondrichthyes and Class Osteichthyes

Class **Chondrichthyes** includes sharks, rays, and skates. Chondrichthyes have a flexible skeleton made of cartilage and paired fins. For example, sharks have a row of sensory organs along each side of the body. They sense changes in water pressure. This means they can detect vibrations caused by nearby fish. Chondrichthyes are fast swimmers. They have good sight and powerful jaws with rows of sharp teeth. Chondrichthyes swim to force water over their **gills** so they can breathe in oxygen.

The class **Osteichthyes** consist of bony fish. This includes tuna, trout, bass, salmon, goldfish, and many others. These fish have a jaw, scales, and a skeleton made of bone and paired fins. There are about 30,000 species of osteichthyes. They live in saltwater or freshwater. They have a keen sense of smell and eyesight.

Glossary sidebar

Operculus

A protective flap over gills that allows a fish to breathe without swimming

Swim bladder

A gas-filled organ that allows a bony fish to move up and down in water

Larva

The immature form of an animal that looks different from the adult form

Amniotic egg

The egg of a vertebrate that lives on land

Cold-blooded

Having a body temperature that changes with the temperature of the surroundings

Ectotherm

An animal whose main source of body heat is its environment

Link to ➢➢➢

Language Arts

The word *amphibian* comes from two Greek words meaning "double life."

Bony fish have an **operculus.** This is a protective flap over their gills so they can breathe without swimming. Bony fish are covered with scales that protect the fish. Many bony fish also have a **swim bladder.** By changing the amount of gas in this organ, a bony fish can move up and down in water.

Class Amphibia

Amphibians belong to the class Amphibia. There are about 4,000 species of amphibians. Amphibians have four legs and a skeleton of bone. They produce jellylike eggs that develop in water. A frog is an amphibian. Frogs lay eggs in water, but live on land. A frog egg develops into a tadpole that lives in water. The tadpole is the **larva** stage. The tadpole has gills and a long tail. During metamorphosis, a tadpole grows legs and lungs and loses its gills and tail. It develops into an adult frog.

The skin of amphibians is thin. To keep from drying out, most amphibians live near water or in damp environments like swamps and rain forests. Their eggs do not have shells and would dry out if not in water. Amphibians breathe with lungs or through their skin as adults

Class Reptilia

Reptiles belong to the class Reptilia. There are about 6,500 species of reptiles, including snakes, lizards, turtles, alligators, and crocodiles. All reptiles have scales that waterproof their skin. Reptiles breathe in oxygen through their lungs. They have a skeleton of bone and claws. They also produce **amniotic eggs.** An amniotic egg has four membranes and is covered by a shell. The shell protects the egg on land. Some reptiles live on land. Some live in water.

Fish, amphibians, and reptiles are **cold-blooded** animals. They are **ectotherms.** Their body temperature changes with the temperature of their surroundings.

Dinosaurs were reptiles that appeared about 235 million years ago. They ranged in size from a four-story house to a modern cat. They became extinct about 65 million years ago.

The blue whale is the largest animal that has ever existed. Today, it is an endangered species.

Class Aves

Birds belong to the class Aves. There are about 8,600 species of birds. Like reptiles, birds produce amniotic eggs. They have scales on their legs. Unlike reptiles, birds have a bone structure for flying. Most birds fly. The bones of birds are hollow, strong, and light. Some birds, like eagles, have wings adapted to soar on air currents. Other birds like hummingbirds flap their wings constantly to stay in the air. Some birds, such as ostriches, do not fly.

Birds have feathers. Their feathers are made of protein. Feathers on their bodies help to regulate their body heat. Birds have no teeth. They use a gizzard to grind food. Female birds have only one ovary and lay eggs covered by a hard shell. All birds breathe with lungs and have a horny beak. Birds and mammals are **warm-blooded** because their body temperature stays the same. Warm-blooded animals are **endotherms.** They create body heat through metabolism.

Class Mammalia

Mammals belong to the class Mammalia. There are about 4,500 species of mammals. Most mammals live on land. There are about 1,000 species of mammals that have wings and fly, like bats. Other mammals live in water. These include blue whales, dolphins, and porpoises.

One feature of mammals is hair that covers most of their body. Hair helps keep a constant body temperature. A second feature mammals have is mammary glands on the chest or abdomen. Mammary glands produce milk for young offspring. A third feature mammals have is lungs.

Two mammals are egg-laying, the duck-billed platypus and the spiny anteater. After their eggs hatch, the young lick milk secreted onto the mother's fur.

Marsupial

A mammal with a pouch

About 300 species of mammals, such as kangaroos and koalas, are **marsupials.** Marsupials are animals with pouches. Marsupials give birth to tiny embryos that mature inside a pouch on the mother's abdomen. Milk is secreted inside the pouch for the embryos. More than 4,000 species of mammals have young that develop inside the mother. These include mice, tigers, elephants, dogs, cats, and humans.

Table 15.7.1 sums up the phylum Chordata.

Table 15.7.1 Vertebrates		
Group	Description	Examples
Chordata Phylum	Internal skeleton of bone or cartilage; skull; sexual reproduction; bilateral symmetry Embryo—dorsal nerve cord, notochord, pharyngeal slits, tail	
Class Myxini Class Cephala-spidomorphi	Skeleton of cartilage; no scales or jaw; breathe with gills; live in water; cold-blooded	hagfish lamprey
Class Chondrichthyes	Skeleton of cartilage; toothlike scales; jaw; paired fins; breathe with gills; live in water; cold-blooded	shark, ray, skate
Class Osteichthyes	Skeleton of bone; bony scales; jaw; paired fins; breathe with gills; live in water; most have swim bladder; cold-blooded	trout, salmon, swordfish, goldfish
Class Amphibia	Skeleton of bone; moist, smooth skin; breathe with lungs or through skin as adults; young live in water, adults live on land; four legs; eggs lack shells; cold-blooded	newt, frog, toad
Class Reptilia	Skeleton of bone; dry, scaly skin; claws; breathe with lungs all stages; four legs except snakes; eggs have shell; cold-blooded	turtle, snake, alligator, lizard
Class Aves	Skeleton of bone; feathers; wings; beaks; claws; breathe with lungs all stages; eggs have shell; warm-blooded	hawk, goose, quail, robin, penguin
Class Mammalia	Skeleton of bone; hair; mammary glands; breathe with lungs all stages; young develop within mother; warm-blooded	bat, kangaroo, mouse, dog, whale, seal, human

Lesson 7   R E V I E W

Word Bank

amniotic eggs

ectotherms

endotherms

shells

On a sheet of paper, write the word or words from the Word Bank that complete each sentence correctly.

1. Warm-blood animals are _____, and cold-blooded animals are _____.

2. Amphibians usually stay in the water because their eggs do not have _____ and would dry out on land.

3. Like reptiles, birds produce _____.

On a sheet of paper, write the letter of the answer that completes each sentence correctly.

4. The bones of _____ are light and hollow.

    A amphibians   **C** mammals

    B birds   **D** reptiles

5. Reptiles get oxygen through their _____.

    A lungs   **C** skin

    B gills   **D** swim bladder

6. By changing the amount of gas in its _____, a bony fish can move up and down in water.

    A notochord   **C** operculus

    B swim bladder   **D** lungs

Critical Thinking

On a sheet of paper, answer the following questions. Use complete sentences.

7. Describe the four classes of fish.

8. What are three features of mammals?

9. Describe some key differences between a shark and a tuna.

10. Describe some key differences between amphibians, reptiles, birds, and mammals.

Materials

- dichotomous key
- specimens or photos of several insects

Using a Dichotomous Key

To identify the species of an organism, scientists often use a dichotomous key. A dichotomous key allows the user to trace a path about the features of an organism. The user makes choices along the path based on observations about the organism. The dichotomous key splits into branches according to these choices until the user reaches the name of the organism. In this investigation, you will use a dichotomous key to identify the genus and species of several insects.

Procedure

1. Get a dichtomous key from your teacher.

2. Choose a specimen. Observe the specimen. **Safety Alert: Do not touch or harm the specimen.**

3. Look at the first branch of the dichtomous key. Determine which path to follow based on the features of your specimen.

4. Continue making observations and following the dichotomous key until you reach the name of the insect.

5. Use the dichotomous key to identify other specimens.

Cleanup/Disposal

When you are finished, be sure your lab area is clean.

Analysis

1. What kinds of observations did you need to make to identify your specimens?

2. What type of information is used in a dichotomous key?

3. What type of information is not used in a dichotomous key?

Conclusions

1. To be effective, should a dichotomous key include descriptions of all organisms that could be identified? Explain your answer.

2. In Investigation 15, you used descriptions and names to classify organisms. How is using a dichotomous key more helpful than relying on descriptions and names?

Explore Further

Using objects in everyday life, create your own dichotomous key. For example, create a dichotomous key that identifies different cars. Test your dichotomous key by having someone identify one object.

Objectives

After reading this lesson, you should be able to

◆ define homo sapiens

◆ list features of humans

Culture

The languages, religions, customs, arts, and dress of a people

Bipedal locomotion

The ability to walk upright on two feet

Life span

The number of years an individual lives

Link to ➢➢➢

Language Arts

Homo sapiens comes from Latin and means "wise man."

Humans are classified as kingdom Animalia, phylum Chordata, subphylum Vertebrate, and class Mammalia. The species of humans is called *homo sapiens.* Humans are unique compared to other species. Humans develop language, have intelligence, and have **culture.** Culture is the languages, religions, customs, arts, and dress of a people. Humans use technology. They are naturally curious. They ask questions and find answers.

Humans have **bipedal locomotion.** They walk upright on two feet. Their hands have four fingers and one thumb. Human hands have opposable thumbs. Genetics, environmental conditions, and cultural factors like diet influence the body size of humans. Humans have the highest brain-to-body mass ratio of all large animals. Dolphins are second. Sharks have the highest brain-to-body mass ratio among fish. Octopuses have the highest ratio among invertebrates.

Homo sapiens are widespread on the earth. They are one of the most numerous mammals. Humans have a growing population. There are about 6.5 billion people on the earth today. Asia is the continent with the greatest population of humans. The rest live mainly in the Americas, Africa, and Europe.

Humans have much experience in changing their habitats. Humans change the environment by farming, building cities, developing transportation, and manufacturing products. This allows them to live in many areas of the world.

In wealthy nations, the human **life span** is about 80 years. Life span is the number of years an individual lives. The longest recorded life span for a human is 120 years. As new technology and new medicines are discovered, scientists think the average human life span will increase.

bipedal locomotion

brain

species

On a sheet of paper, write the word or words from the Word Bank that complete each sentence correctly.

1. There is only one _____ of humans.

2. Humans use _____, meaning they walk upright on two feet.

3. Humans have the highest ratio of _____ to body mass of any animal.

On a sheet of paper, write the letter of the answer that completes each sentence correctly.

4. The scientific name for humans is _____.

   A *Homo erectus*

   B *Homo habilis*

   C *Homo neanderthalensis*

   D *Homo sapiens*

5. Most humans live in _____.

   A the Americas   **C** Africa

   B Asia   **D** Europe

6. Unlike other mammals, human hands have _____.

   A five fingers   **C** fingernails

   B skin   **D** opposable thumbs

Critical Thinking

On a sheet of paper, write the answers to the following questions. Use complete sentences.

7. What factors influence the body size of a human?

8. Why do scientists think the human life span will increase?

9. How do humans change their environments?

10. What are some features specific to humans?

The Link Between Dinosaurs and Birds

Until the 1980s, most scientists thought that dinosaurs were heavy, slow creatures that looked like large lizards. Scientists get information about dinosaurs and other extinct animals mostly from fossils.

Recently, scientists have found many more dinosaur fossils. These fossils suggest that dinosaurs may be closely related to birds.

Recent fossils found in China show that dinosaurs had birdlike features. A dinosaur fossil of an early tyrannosaur shows clear imprints of feathers. Another smaller dinosaur was fossilized in a sleeping position. This position looks similar to the way modern birds curl up when they rest. These and other fossils show that many dinosaurs were small and quick. Some dinosaurs, for example, were the size of a chicken and could move fast.

The discovery of a dinosaur with feathers provided clues about the purpose of early feathers. Large dinosaurs like the tyrannosaur did not fly. Scientists think that feathers kept dinosaurs warm. After millions of years of evolution, birds began to use feathers on their wings for flight.

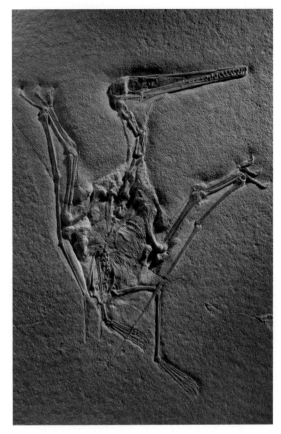

1. How do scientists learn about dinosaurs?

2. What evidence links dinosaurs to birds?

3. What purpose did feathers probably serve for dinosaurs?

Chapter 15 S U M M A R Y

■ Scientists classify living organisms by their features and evolutionary history. The highest level of classification is the domain. Organisms are classified into the domains Archaea, Bacteria, or Eukarya.

■ The kingdom Protista includes protozoa, algae, euglena, and slime molds. Members of the kingdom Fungi are eukaryotes with bodies made of strands of hyphae.

■ Plants are classified into phyla by their evolutionary advancements. Phylum Bryophyta is mosses, and the phylum Polypodiophyta is ferns.

■ The phylum Coniferophyta is conifers, and the phylum Anthophyta is flowering plants.

■ Kingdom Animalia includes organisms that are multicellular eukaryotes. Animals are classified as invertebrates or vertebrates. Invertebrates include sponges, cnidarians, flatworms, mollusks, annelids, arthropods, and echinoderms. Vertebrates include fishes, amphibians, reptiles, birds, and mammals.

■ There is only one species of humans, called *homo sapiens*.

Vocabulary

algae, 464
alternation of generations, 473
amniotic egg, 491
amoeba, 465
angiosperm, 472
arachnid, 484
arthropod, 484
bilateral symmetry, 483
bipedal locomotion, 497
blastula, 479
cartilage, 489
cephalaspidomorphi, 490
chondrichthyes, 490
chordate, 489
cnidarian, 482
cold-blooded, 491
complete metamorphosis, 485
conifer, 475
crustacean, 484
culture, 497

cyanobacterium, 469
dorsal, 489
dysentery, 465
ectotherm, 491
endoskeleton, 486
endotherm, 492
euglena, 464
exoskeleton, 484
fern, 472
flatworm, 483
fossil fuel, 475
frond, 475
gametophyte, 474
germinate, 477
gill, 490
gymnosperm, 472
heterotroph, 479
hyphae, 468
incomplete metamorphosis, 486
larva, 491
lichen, 469
life span, 497

marsupial, 493
metamorphosis, 485
mold, 468
mollusk, 483
molting, 484
moss, 472
multicellular, 479
mycelium, 468
mycorrhiza, 473
myxini, 490
nectar, 477
notochord, 490
nonvascular plant, 473
operculus, 491
osteichthyes, 490
pharyngeal slit, 490
phloem, 473
phylogeny, 482
pistil, 477
pollination, 477
protozoan, 464
pseudopod, 465

radial symmetry, 482
radula, 484
rhizoid, 473
roundworm, 483
seed, 472
segmented worm, 483
slime mold, 466
sori, 475
spore, 466
sporophyte, 474
stamen, 476
stigma, 477
swim bladder, 491
taxonomist, 458
taxonomy, 458
tentacle, 482
tube feet, 486
vascular plant, 472
vascular tissue, 473
vertebra, 489
warm-blooded, 492
xylem, 473

Chapter 15 R E V I E W

Word Bank

algae

alternation of
generations

angiosperm

bilateral symmetry

gametophyte

gymnosperm

heterotroph

hyphae

larva

metamorphosis

mold

molting

phylogeny

pseudopod

slime mold

sporophyte

xylem

Vocabulary Review

On a sheet of paper, write the word or words from the Word Bank that complete each sentence correctly.

1. A(n) _____ consumes organic material for nutrition.

2. The _____ of a species includes information about its origin and evolution.

3. A body made of left and right halves that are the same is known as _____.

4. A protist that is yellow, red, or white and is like fungi and animals is a(n) _____.

5. An amoeba uses a(n) _____ to surround food and to move.

6. Mosses, algae, and some protists have a life cycle known as _____.

7. A protist that makes its own food and usually lives in water is _____.

8. During _____, arthropods shed their exoskeleton and secrete a larger one.

9. A fungus that grows quickly on a surface is a(n) _____.

10. A plant that is diploid is the _____.

11. A plant that is haploid is the _____.

12. Some organisms undergo _____, which involves several stages, as they develop into an adult.

13. A nonflowering seed plant is a(n) _____.

14. The bodies of fungi are made of strands of _____.

15. One stage of metamorphosis between embryo and adult for some organisms is the _____ stage.

16. A flowering plant is a(n) _____.

Review continued on next page

17. The _____ is the vascular tissue in plants that carries water and minerals from the roots to the stems and leaves.

Concept Review

On a sheet of paper, write the letter of the answer that completes each sentence correctly.

18. The order of classification from highest to lowest level is _____.

    A domain, kingdom, phylum, class, order, family, genus, species

    B domain, species, kingdom, phylum, class, order, family, genus

    C species, domain, kingdom, phylum, class, order, family, genus

    D species, kingdom, phylum, class, order, family, genus, species, domain

19. The domain Eukarya has four kingdoms: Protista, Fungi, Plantae, and _____.

    A Protozoa   **C** Cnidarian

    B Animalia   **D** Phaeophyta

20. Bony fish have a(n) _____, or a protective flap over their gills.

    A radula   **C** swim bladder

    B notochord   **D** operculus

21. The phylum of plants that have vascular tissue but no seeds is _____.

    A Anthophyta   **C** Bryophyta

    B Coniferophyta   **D** Polypodiophyta

Critical Thinking

On a sheet of paper, write the answers to the following questions. Use complete sentences.

22. In what ways are birds, amphibians, and reptiles alike? In what ways are they different?

23. How are the four classes of fish alike? How are they different?

24. List the kingdom, phylum, and class of the species *Homo sapiens*.

25. Name the three groups of protozoans. Describe the structures each group uses for movement and catching food.

Research and Write

Do research to find information on key fossils of primitive humans. Explain the importance of each fossil find. Use this information and photos or art to create a poster. Include a map that shows where each fossil was found.

Test-Taking Tip To choose the answer that correctly completes a sentence, read the sentence using each answer choice. Then choose the answer that makes the most sense when the entire sentence is read.

Chapter

16 Behavioral Biology

Behavior is a response, or reaction, as a result of a stimulus. The bear's genes and changes in sunlight tell the bear that winter is coming. It's time for the bear to put on fat. The salmon know it's time to reproduce. Their genes tell them to return to their birthplace. They will lay eggs there. Some behaviors are innate, such as the salmon returning to their birthplace. Other behaviors are learned, such as the bear catching salmon. In Chapter 16, you will learn about animal behavior and its role in animal survival. You will also learn some processes that control animal behavior.

Organize Your Thoughts

Behavior

Innate behavior

Learned behavior

Communication as behavior

Help animals survive

Goals for Learning

◆ To recognize that behaviors are responses to stimuli
◆ To identify behaviors as innate or learned
◆ To identify ways that animals communicate
◆ To recognize that behaviors help organisms survive

505

Objectives

After reading this lesson, you should be able to

◆ define and give examples of internal and external stimuli

◆ define and give examples of innate and learned behavior

You have probably watched animals over a period of time. You may have observed how a goldfish swims toward food. You may have watched how two dogs play. You may have observed how birds fly in flocks. These are examples of animal **behavior.** Behavior is the way an organism acts.

Behavioral biology is the study of the behavior of living things. A scientist who studies the behavior of animals is an **etholologist.** Ethologists observe animal behavior and then try to find out why the animals behaved in certain ways. Ethologists usually study animal behavior in their natural environments, such as flocks of birds flying. They also study behavior through experiments.

Behavior is usually observable. Scientists observe animals to see how they get food, reproduce, and avoid danger. Animals that are flexible in their behavior can adjust when their environment changes. These animals will change their behavior to fit the new environment.

Ethologists identify factors that shape behavior. They want to understand what stimuli cause animals to show a certain behavior. They also want to understand how behavior works and how animals learn a behavior.

Internal and External Stimuli

When organisms act, they are reacting to a stimulus. Recall from Chapter 1 that a stimulus is anything to which an organism reacts. For example, you eat because you feel hungry. Hunger is an **internal stimulus.** The behavior of eating is your reaction to this internal stimulus. A bird's song is an **external stimulus.** Birds use songs to attract mates. An external stimulus is one that occurs in an animal's environment.

Behavior

The way an organism acts

Behavioral biology

The study of the behavior of living things

Ethologist

A scientist who studies the behavior of animals

Internal stimulus

A stimulus that occurs inside of an organism

External stimulus

A stimulus that occurs outside of an organism

Sometimes animals may show the same behavior in all environments. Animals may also show certain behaviors only in certain environments. An animal's responses to external stimuli can result from interactions with members of its own species or other species. An animal also responds to nonliving elements in its environment.

Innate Behavior

Some responses are **innate behavior.** This behavior is inherited and does not have to be learned. Innate behavior is present at birth. For example, a spider's ability to spin a web does not require learning. When young spiders hatch, the mother dies. The young spiders make webs without seeing their mother make one.

Inheritance shapes behavior. Most animal behavior stays the same over time. This type of innate behavior is called **fixed action pattern behavior.** The behavior always occurs the same way. One species of spiders always spins webs by following the same steps in the same order. The behavior of web spinning is the same. Another species of spiders spins different webs. This species may use different steps in a different order.

Learned Behavior

Animals behave by observing and learning. This is called **learned behavior.** Animals invent and learn new behaviors. For example, scientists observed Japanese snow monkeys. These monkeys live near the ocean that surrounds Japan. The scientists threw pieces of potatoes near the monkeys. The monkeys wanted to eat the potatoes, but the pieces were covered with sand. The monkeys tried to brush off the sand, but the sand would not come off.

Then a female monkey dipped a piece of potato in the ocean. The water washed the sand away. She ate the potato. Some of the monkeys watched and learned this behavior. Other monkeys saw the behavior, but did not imitate it.

Innate behavior

A behavior that is present at birth

Fixed action pattern behavior

A behavior that always occurs the same way

Learned Behavior

A behavior that results from experience

Link to >>>

Chemistry

Plants respond to stimuli. Tropisms are growth responses. They cause plants to grow toward or away from a stimulus. Tropisms are usually regulated by plant hormones, or chemicals, such as auxins. Phototropism is the growth of a plant toward or away from a light. Gravitropism is a plant's growth due to gravity.

The scientists tried another experiment. They threw grains of wheat near the monkeys. The monkeys could not get the sand off the small grains. A monkey put a handful of grain into the water. The sand sank. The grains of wheat floated on top of the water. The monkey skimmed off the wheat grains and ate them. Other monkeys watched and learned this new behavior. The new behavior was shared by imitation.

These experiments show that both genes and the environment affect behavior. Eating is an innate behavior. The snow monkeys modified their behavior by using a new method to clean their food. Figure 16.1.1 shows a group of Japanese snow monkeys.

Behavior Evolves Through Natural Selection

Scientists study behavior as evolutionary principles. They determine if a behavior is innate or learned. They also track changes in behavior over long periods of time. Patterns of behavior have evolved to ensure the reproductive success of a species. These changes in behavior evolved through natural selection.

Figure 16.1.1 *Some animals, such as Japanese snow monkeys, are flexible and can adapt to environmental changes.*

Scientists also investigate why certain behaviors are more favored by natural selection. They might ask, for example, why the mating behavior of many bird species occurs in the spring. This behavior may be due to available food in the spring for offspring.

Express Lab 16

Materials
- 3 copies of a maze puzzle
- stopwatch or clock with a second hand

Procedure
1. Work with a partner. Get a copy of a maze puzzle from your teacher.

2. Decide who will keep time and who will solve the maze puzzle. Time the person solving the puzzle. Stop timing the person when the puzzle is solved. Record this time.

3. Get another copy of the same maze puzzle. Have the same person solve the puzzle and the same person keep time. Record the time.

4. Get a third copy of the maze puzzle. Switch jobs with your partner.

Analysis
1. How did the time differ between the first attempt and the second attempt to solve the maze puzzle? What caused this difference?

2. How did the time in Step 4 compare to the first two times? What factors were different for the partner who solved the maze puzzle in Step 4?

3. Is the ability to solve the maze puzzle innate or learned?

On a sheet of paper, write the word or words from the Word Bank that complete each sentence correctly.

Word Bank

ethologist

innate behavior

learned behavior

1. A(n) _____ is a scientist who studies the behavior of animals.

2. A behavior that results from experience is _____.

3. A(n) _____ is a behavior that an animal is born with.

On a sheet of paper, write the letter of the answer that completes each sentence correctly.

4. A stimulus that occurs inside of an organism is a(n) _____.

    A internal stimulus   **C** innate behavior

    B external stimulus   **D** learned behavior

5. A stimulus that occurs outside of an organism is a(n) _____.

    A internal stimulus   **C** innate behavior

    B external stimulus   **D** learned behavior

6. The study of the behavior of living things is _____.

    A fixed action pattern behavior

    B stimuli

    C behavioral biology

    D learned behavior

Critical Thinking

On a sheet of paper, write the answers to the following questions. Use complete sentences.

7. How are behaviors linked with evolution and natural selection?

8. Compare an external stimulus and an internal stimulus.

9. Where does a spider's ability to spin a web come from?

10. Describe how snow monkeys learned new behaviors.

INVESTIGATION 16

Materials

- safety goggles
- lab coat or apron
- shoebox and lid
- scissors
- 6 paper towels
- tap water
- 10 sow bugs
- small lamp

Investigating Animal Behavior

Animals often react when their environment changes. They adapt to the change or move to a more suitable environment. Sow bugs often live under rocks in gardens and yards. They eat decayed organic material. In this investigation, you will observe what type of environment sow bugs prefer.

Procedure

1. Put on goggles and a lab coat or apron.

2. Make half of your shoebox dark. Make the other half open to light. To do this, use scissors to remove half of the shoebox lid. **Safety Alert: Be careful when using scissors to cut the shoebox lid.**

3. Dampen the paper towels with tap water. Put a layer of damp paper towels in the entire bottom of the box.

4. Put the sow bugs in the middle of the box. **Safety Alert: Handle the sow bugs gently. Do not harm them.** Put the lid on the box. Half of the box should be dark and half should be exposed to the light. To make the exposed half lighter, shine a small lamp onto it. Be sure the lamp only lights up half of the box. Keep the other half dark.

5. Wait five minutes. Count how many sow bugs are in the light half and how many are in the dark half of your box. Record the numbers.

Cleanup/Disposal

After handling the sow bugs, wash your hands. Follow your teacher's instructions for collecting the sow bugs and disposal of material. When you are finished, be sure your lab area is clean.

Analysis

1. In Step 5, how many sow bugs were in the light half of the box? How many were in the dark half?

2. What was the stimulus in this investigation? Describe the behavior the sow bugs displayed in response to this stimulus.

Conclusions

1. What type of environment do sow bugs prefer?

2. Do you think the behavior of the sow bugs in this investigation is innate or learned?

3. Why might sow bugs display this type of behavior?

Explore Further

Sow bugs are usually found in dark, damp environments. Design another investigation to determine whether sow bugs prefer a damp environment or a dry environment. Write a hypothesis. Have your procedure and Safety Alerts approved by your teacher. Conduct your investigation. Do your results support or refute your hypothesis?

Objectives

After reading this lesson, you should be able to

◆ describe parental care, courtship, defensive, and territorial behaviors

◆ give examples of spatial learning, imprinting, and observational learning

◆ give examples of inheritance and learned behavior together

◆ explain how behaviors help animals survive

Simulate

To make the same conditions as the natural or original conditions

Parental care behavior

The caring for offspring by a parent

Courtship behavior

A behavior that helps attract a mate

Scientists investigate stimuli that trigger behaviors. To do this, scientists usually set up lab conditions to observe a behavior. For example, if a bird mates at a certain season, scientists might create lab conditions to **simulate** the season. Then, when placed in these conditions, the bird might show mating behavior, such as singing.

Scientists ask many questions to better understand animal behavior and why it happens. They may ask: How does a behavior affect an animal's chances of survival and reproduction? What are the stimuli that bring on a response? Has the response been changed by recent learning? Does a behavior change as an animal ages? What early experiences are necessary for a certain learned behavior? How does a behavior in one species compare with similar behavior in related species?

Categories of Innate Animal Behavior

Ethologists study many types of animal behavior. They want to find out how much of a behavior is due to inheritance or to learning. Ethologists group innate behaviors into various broad categories.

One category is **parental care behavior.** This type of behavior ensures that offspring survive. For example, newly hatched birds open their mouths to get food from their parents. The young birds do this although their eyes are not yet open. This is an example of innate behavior. To live, the young birds must eat as soon as they are born. They have no time to learn how to eat.

Another category of innate animal behavior is **courtship behavior.** This behavior is used to attract a mate. Courtship behavior also helps animals recognize their own species. Courtship behavior differs for different animals. A male peacock displays his colorful tail to attract a female peacock. Other birds attract a mate with a certain song. Crickets have special mating sounds.

Defensive behavior

A behavior to avoid or protect against predators

Predator

An organism that eats another organism

Prey

An organism that is eaten by another organism

Warning coloration

The bright colors or patterns on animals that scare off predators

Instinct

A pattern of innate behavior

Mimicry

A method of defense in which a species looks like another poisonous or dangerous species

Aggressive behavior

A behavior that warns predators not to approach

The light flashes that fireflies make in the summer are a form of courtship communication. The male makes a pattern of flashes. The female flashes back her response.

Defensive behavior is another category of innate animal behavior. In defensive behavior, animals avoid or protect themselves against **predators.** A predator eats another organism called its **prey.** Avoiding predators is very important to stay alive. Some animals improve their skills at avoiding predators. This is an example of animals adapting an innate behavior.

Some animals show certain defensive behaviors so that predators do not eat them. One example is **warning coloration.** Some species of wasps that can sting their predators are brightly colored. This warning coloration is a stimulus. It modifies, or changes, the behavior of predators. Based on experience or **instinct,** predators will not attack wasps with warning colorations. An instinct is an innate behavior.

Animals also use **mimicry** in defensive behavior. For example, hoverflies are colored like wasps but do not sting. Because some predators do not eat wasps, they also do not eat hoverflies. These predators think hoverflies are stinging wasps.

Some behavioral changes are defensive. For example, wolves may show **aggressive behavior** by growling and showing their teeth. They also flatten their ears. Aggressive behavior warns predators not to approach. These behaviors tell the predator that the hunted animal will fight. Rattlesnakes shake the rattle on their tail to warn predators that their bite is poisonous. Aggressive behavior is innate.

Animals sometimes combine aggressive behavior and warning coloration. For example, an amphibian may have a brightly colored belly. Recall from Chapter 15 that an amphibian is a vertebrate that lives in water and then on land. The rest of the amphibian's body is colored to blend with its surroundings. If threatened, the amphibian shows its belly. The colored belly tells a predator that the amphibian is poisonous.

Glossary Terms

Territorial behavior
A behavior that claims and defends an area

Releaser
A stimulus that brings out a certain behavior in another animal

Spatial learning
Learning by recognizing features

Imprinting
Learning in which an animal bonds with the first object it sees

Observational learning
Learning by watching or listening to another animal

Landmark
An object used to mark a location or position

Territorial behavior is another category of animal behavior. A territory is an area defined by an animal. The animal usually defends its territory from other animals of the same species. Territorial behavior helps animals survive. Animals can court, mate, produce offspring, and raise their young in their territories. Territorial behavior is an innate behavior.

Austrian ethologist Konrad Lorenz and Dutch ethologist Niko Tinbergen studied stimuli that cause territorial behavior. These stimuli are called **releasers.** Lorenz and Tinbergen studied territorial behavior in adult male robins.

During mating season, adult male robins often claim their territories with song. If this does not stop other male birds, the territorial birds display aggressive behavior. They attack other male robins that come into their territory. However, adult male robins do not show aggressive behavior toward young males. That is because the young males do not have red feathers yet. The red breast feathers on other adult males are the releasers for territorial behavior.

Innate and Learned Behavior Combine

Many patterns of behavior are a combination of innate and learned behavior. An animal's behavior may depend on both genetic inheritance and the environment. Three examples of animal behavior that have both genetic and learned parts are **spatial learning, imprinting,** and **observational learning.**

Spatial learning. To investigate spatial learning, Tinbergen looked at the behavior of a species of wasp. He wondered how an animal learns to recognize features in its area. He wanted to find out if a wasp can learn to find its nest by using **landmarks.** A landmark is an object used to mark a location or position.

Tinbergen observed that a female wasp digs an underground nest for each larva. The female wasp returns to her nest to care for each larva. Tinbergen wondered how each wasp found her nest. Did she use landmarks?

Link to ➤ ➤ ➤

Social Studies

Scientists think the first signs of aggressive behavior between groups of people, appeared over 3,000 years ago in a village in Mexico. There is evidence that a protective wall was built around the village. Scientists think that war did not occur until groups of people began to live together and gathered large amounts of resources.

To test this hypothesis, Tinbergen placed pinecones in a circle around the nest of a female wasp. The wasp continued to go to her nest. Then Tinbergen moved the pinecones away from the nest and put them in a circle. As you can see in the top half of Figure 16.2.1, the female wasp went to the center of the pinecone circle.

Next, Tinbergen put the pinecones into a triangle around the nest. Then he arranged rocks in a circle near the nest. Look at the bottom half of Figure 16.2.1. The female wasp flew to the rocks in a circle. Based on his experiments, Tinbergen showed that a landmark signals a wasp to its nest. The wasp used spatial learning.

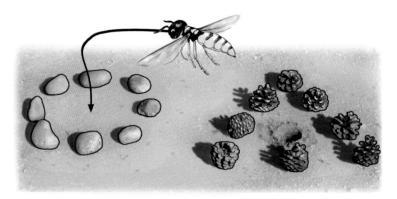

Figure 16.2.1 *A digger wasp finds her nest by noting how landmarks are arranged.*

For their work in behavioral biology, Konrad Lorenz and Niko Tinbergen received a Nobel Prize in 1973.

Imprinting. Konrad Lorenz found that young birds bond with the first object they see. This behavior is called imprinting. Lorenz observed that young geese and chickens follow their mothers soon after they are hatched. He discovered this response could be transferred to another stimulus.

In one experiment, Lorenz removed goose eggs from their nest. He hatched the eggs in a lab. The baby geese saw Lorenz first. They imprinted on him. They thought Lorenz was their mother and followed him everywhere. The young geese did not recognize their real mother or other adults.

Lorenz repeated the experiment. This time he used boots and baby ducks. The young ducks imprinted on the boots.

Lorenz found that once imprinting is set, it cannot be changed. Imprinting helps animals survive. A result of imprinting is a strong bond that forms between a newborn and a parent. Young animals stay close to their mother. The mother feeds and protects her young. Lorenz also found that learning determines the result of this inherited behavior.

Observational learning. Birdsongs are both innate and learned. A bird raised alone will sing. Singing is innate behavior for birds. However, young birds must hear an adult male sing the species song. The song gets imprinted on the young birds. This type of behavior is called observational learning. Animals learn by watching or listening to another animal. As the young birds mature, they practice the species song. Their song eventually matches their memory of the imprinted song.

Science Myth

Myth: Some birds, such as parrots, can use human language.

Fact: Some birds can be taught to mimic human sounds. These birds say certain words or phrases. However, they are only reproducing what they hear. They do not understand the words. They are not communicating.

Young birds raised in isolation that do not hear the species song cannot sing it. This means there is a period of time for young birds to learn the species song. As the birds mature, they perfect the song. This is another important period of time for learning the species song. If a bird becomes deaf after singing the song as a mature adult, it will continue to sing the song correctly.

Achievements in Science

Animal Behavior Research

Many scientists have contributed to the field of animal behavior. In the early 1900s, Russian scientist Ivan Pavlov investigated how dogs could be conditioned to show behavior. Conditioning is learning in which an animal connects one stimulus with another stimulus. Pavlov observed that dogs make saliva when they smell food. He rang a bell whenever he served food to the dogs. Soon the dogs associated the sound of the bell with food. The dogs made saliva whenever they heard the bell, whether food was present or not. The dogs' response was conditioned.

Austrian scientist Karl von Frisch studied the behavior of honeybees. He discovered that bees sense and react to different wavelengths of ultraviolet light. His most famous discovery was that honeybees communicate with each other through dance patterns.

These and many other scientists used patience, observation, and scientific methods to study animal behavior. Their work has provided insight into the animals with whom we share the earth.

Word Bank

defensive behavior

imprinting

observational
learning

On a sheet of paper, write the word or words from the Word Bank that complete each sentence correctly.

1. Animals avoid or protect themselves against predators in _____.

2. Young birds form an attachment, called _____, to the first thing they see after they hatch.

3. Learning by watching or listening to another animal is _____.

On a sheet of paper, write the letter of the answer that completes each sentence correctly.

4. Rattlesnakes shake the rattle on their tail to _____.

A attract a mate   **C** warn predators

B help find food   **D** direct other rattlesnakes

5. Learning by recognizing features is _____.

A aggressive behavior   **C** spatial learning

B parental care behavior   **D** imprinting

6. Some amphibians display a brightly colored stomach to show that they are _____.

A male   **B** female   **C** young   **D** poisonous

Critical Thinking

On a sheet of paper, write the answers to the following questions. Use complete sentences.

7. Why is parental care behavior important? Give an example.

8. Describe Niko Tinbergen's experiments to determine how a female wasp finds its nest.

9. How do most birds learn to sing the species song?

10. How do animals use warning coloration and mimicry to protect themselves?

Objectives

After reading this lesson, you should be able to

◆ define communication

◆ identify and give examples of social behaviors

◆ give examples of animal communications

◆ describe how communications can work together

◆ explain how communication helps animals survive

◆ give an example of an advanced communication system

Communication

Sending information

Sociobiologist

A scientist who studies how animals communicate and interact with each other

Social behavior

The interaction between two or more animals

When a bird sings, it is communicating. When a frog croaks, it is communicating. When a baby bear calls for its mother, it is communicating. In this lesson, you will learn different ways animals communicate.

What Is Communication?

Communication is sending information. People use language, speech, writing, art, and music to communicate. But there are other ways to communicate. Animals use actions, such as showing their teeth or wagging their tails. They also use smells and sounds. Communication has a purpose. Birds sing to find a mate or protect their territory. Dogs bark to warn that a stranger is approaching.

Social Behavior

Sociobiologists study how animals communicate and interact with each other. **Social behavior** is the interaction between two or more animals, usually of the same species. Some types of social behavior are aggressive behavior, courtship behavior, and **cooperation.** Social behavior influences the survival and reproduction of animals. Social behaviors are important adaptations in many species.

There are many types of aggressive behavior. In **agonistic interaction,** individuals have contests. Many species display aggressive behavior when they compete for food, find mates, and protect their territory. Birds, for example, sing songs during these contests. These songs warn other birds away.

Recall from Lesson 2 that animals establish a territory to protect their food supply and offspring. Some animals show aggressive behavior if their territory is threatened. They may also tell other members of their species about approaching predators. These are examples of aggressive behaviors.

Cooperation

A type of social behavior in which two or more individuals work or act together

Agonistic interaction

A type of social behavior in which individuals have contests and show aggressive behavior

Matched submission

A type of social behavior in which a threatened animal yields to a dominant animal

Dominant

Having the most influence or control

Signal

A behavior that causes a change in the behavior of another animal

Scent

Having a smell or odor

Competitor

An animal that tries to get the same resources as another animal

Another aggressive behavior is **matched submission.** A threatened animal shows submission to a **dominant** animal. For example, a small dog has a bone. A large dog wants the bone. The large dog snarls at the small dog. The large dog is showing aggressive behavior toward the small dog.

The small dog rolls over and shows its belly to the large dog. This behavior shows that the large dog is dominant. The large dog stops its aggressive behavior and takes the bone. Some species show behavior to indicate that the submissive animal is accepted.

You learned about courtship behavior in Lesson 2. Courtship behavior is a social behavior. Selection of a mate is important to ensure survival of the species. A **signal** is a behavior that causes a change in the behavior of another animal. Animals make signals to attract or keep the attention of a possible mate. Courtship signals are often a display of body parts, a call, or the release of a **scent.**

These signals are unique to a species. They make sure individuals mate with a member of their own species. Animals that form a lasting bond with one mate often show the same signals to each other. An example is a victory display shown between two penguins at their nest site.

Cooperation is when individual animals work together for the common good. For example, ants work together in an anthill to feed and raise offspring.

Communication Signals

Social behavior depends on methods of communication. Communication has three parts: sending a signal, receiving a signal, and responding to a signal. There are many kinds of signals and messages. A signal may be calls or sounds, facial expressions or body positions, scents, or specific movements. For example, when a bird sings, its message may tell **competitors** to stay away. Or the song may be a call for a mate. Other birds hear this stimulus and respond to it.

Some animal signals are related to food. Food calls tell a mate, offspring, or members of a group about a food source. Honeybees perform a dance that tells other honeybees where to find food. The dance patterns show other bees the direction and distance of flowers from the hive. Honeybees communicate by the pattern of their flight and how they move their bodies. This group of behaviors is called cooperation.

Some animals give alarm calls to signal that a predator is nearby. Alarm calls tell members of their species to run for cover. Sometimes members of other species will also hide. Instead of hiding, some animals may stop moving or gather into a group to reduce the risk of attack.

Metacommunications are signals that change the meaning of the next set of signals. For example, a dog shows a play face to another dog. This tells the other dog that the next aggressive signal is a play fight. It is not aggressive behavior.

Some predators deceive, or fool, prey by communication. For example, the angler fish has a small growth that hangs in front of its jaws. The growth looks like a lure, or food. When a small fish bites the fake lure, it is close to the mouth of the angler fish. The angler fish quickly captures the small fish.

❋❋❋❋❋❋❋❋❋❋❋❋❋❋❋❋❋❋❋❋❋❋❋❋❋❋❋❋❋❋❋❋❋❋❋❋❋

Technology and Society

Scientists are developing new technology that allows people with disabilities to communicate effectively. People who are paralyzed may not be able to speak. They may not be able to use their hands to write or gesture. Scientists are developing a computer chip to be put into the brain. The computer chip would allow a person to control a computer cursor and keyboard using only their thoughts.

Link to ➤➤➤

Cultures

Humans, chimpanzees, and orangutans display cultural behavior. Cultural behavior is a behavior that is invented within a group and passed to the next generation. Cultural behavior in chimpanzees and orangutans includes activities such as using a tool to find food. These behaviors are found in some cultures, but not in others.

Signals Working Together

Animal communication often involves displaying a part of the body or a specific movement. Often these two communications occur together. The animal's movement shows off the body part.

Look at the bill of the adult herring gull in Figure 16.3.1. A parent herring gull shows its bill to its chicks in the nest. The bill of a herring gull is yellow with a red spot near the tip of the beak. When the parent returns to the nest with food, the parent stands over the chicks. The parent taps its bill on the ground in front of the chicks. This stimulus causes the hungry chicks to make begging responses. In turn, this action stimulates the parent to put the food in front of the chicks. The chicks eat the food. Once the chicks are fed, the parent leaves to find more food.

This communication cycle involves a body part, which is the red-spotted bill of the parent. It also includes a movement, which is the tapping on the ground. This helps the chicks see the red spot on the parent's bill. The red color causes a begging response from the herring gull chicks.

Animals have body parts to aid in communication. One example is the tail of the peacock. Sociobiologists think its tail is used in courtship behavior. Courtship behavior can lead to the growth of a feature that helps in selecting a mate.

Figure 16.3.1 *The red spot on the bill of the adult herring gull causes the chicks to beg.*

Scent Signals

Some animals communicate by odor. These chemical scent signals are called **pheromones.** Scent glands in the body make pheromones. Chemical signals are common among mammals and insects. Cats and dogs mark their territory with urine. Some hamsters have scent glands on their sides. To mark their territory, they leave their scent by rubbing their cheeks against objects.

Bees carry a pouch that contains material from their hive. When the bees return to their hive, they release the material. The odor of the material tells other bees that they are members of the hive. They can then enter the hive.

Advanced Signals

Alarm calls and courtship signals are innate responses to stimuli. Do animals understand the meaning of the signals they give and receive? This is a key question in the study of animal **cognition,** or knowledge.

Some signaling systems show an advanced understanding of communication. An example is the alarm calls by vervet monkeys. Vervet monkeys make different alarm calls in response to different predators.

Science at Work

Social Worker

Social workers help people function within their environment, maintain relationships, and solve personal problems. Social workers work one-on-one with a person or a group of people. A social worker may help two or more people communicate with each other so they can work together.

Both private organizations and government agencies employ social workers. Health care organizations and social service industries employ social workers. Most social workers specialize in providing a specific type of help.

To become a social worker, a bachelor's degree in social work, psychology, sociology, or a related field is required. Some positions in the health industry require a master's degree. Social workers must be licensed or certified by their state.

Their alarm calls are different for a leopard, snake, or eagle. The alarm calls allow other vervet monkeys to respond to the predator. Vervet monkeys develop the ability to make alarm calls over time.

Summing Up

Behavioral biology is the study of how animals react to stimuli and respond to predators and competitors. Behavioral biologists study mating behavior in animals. They study how animals interact with their own species to increase their chances of survival.

Biology in Your Life

**Technology:
Instant Wireless Communication**

Over the years, people have created new ways to communicate with each other. The invention of the telegraph and the telephone in the 1800s allowed people to communicate over long distances. Today, cell phones and the Internet allow people to communicate quickly from nearly anywhere.

A new form of communication technology is radio frequency identification (RFID) chips. These tiny computer chips hold a lot of information. A radio receiver reads the information instantly.

Some companies use RFID chips in their products. The chips are very inexpensive. They are tiny and can be put on or into every product. When a product is shipped or sold, a radio reader identifies it and tracks it instantly. A computer then shows how many items have been sold or shipped at any time.

In the future, a tiny RFID chip with medical information could be put under a person's skin. Using the RFID chip, a doctor could

identify the person and get medical history instantly. RFID chips could be used to buy items in stores. You would take the items you want to buy and go to the front of the store. As you walked through the doorway, computers would read the identification of the items you bought. Computers would also read your credit card information from an RFID chip that you carry. This could mean no more lines at the cash register!

1. What does RFID stand for?

2. How are RFID chips used today?

3. In the future, how could RFID chips help you communicate instantly?

Lesson 3   R E V I E W

Word Bank

metacommunication

agonistic interaction

signal

On a sheet of paper, write the word or words from the Word Bank that complete each sentence

1. Individuals have contests and show aggressive behavior in _____.

2. A signal that changes the meaning of the next set of signals is _____.

3. A _____ is a behavior that causes a change in the behavior of another animal.

On a sheet of paper, write the letter of the answers that complete each sentence correctly.

4. A _____ is a chemical that has an odor.

   A metacommunication   **C** scent

   B pheromone   **D** cognition

5. Honeybees signal the location of food to other honeybees by _____.

   A releasing a scent   **C** dancing in patterns

   B changing color   **D** making sounds

6. Pheromones are _____.

   A chemical signals   **C** patterns of behavior

   B changes in appearance **D** mating behaviors

Critical Thinking

On a sheet of paper, write the answers to the following questions. Use complete sentences.

7. What are the three main parts of communication?

8. Give an example of how animals use alarm signals to communicate.

9. Give an example of how animals use pheromones to communicate.

10. Why do scientists think peacocks display colorful tails?

Materials

◆ index cards

Exploring Human Communication

People rely on spoken or written language to pass on information. They also use nonverbal methods to communicate. Some people may not realize that they use nonverbal communication. In this investigation, you will explore some ways humans communicate without using written or spoken language.

Procedure

1. In your group, discuss nonverbal ways animals and humans communicate. Examples are gestures, sounds, and body position. Record each example on an index card. Label the backs of the index cards Method.

2. Divide your group into two subgroups. One subgroup is the performers. The other subgroup is the audience.

3. In each subgroup, think of scenarios involving animal behavior. Examples are aggression and cooperation. Record each example on a card. Label the backs of the cards Scenario.

4. Have the performers select one of their scenario cards. Do not show the card to the audience.

5. Have the audience select an index card from the method pile. Put this card face up on the table so everyone can see it.

6. Have the performers act out the scenario using the communication method on the card. Have the audience interpret the scenario and discuss what clues made the communication successful.

7. Alternate between the performers and audiences to interpret scenarios. Continue until all the scenario cards are used. Replace the method card after each scenario so it can be reused.

Cleanup/Disposal

When you are finished, be sure your lab area is clean.

Analysis

1. What clues led your subgroup to interpret the scenarios?

2. How do emotions play a part in communication?

Conclusions

1. What communication characteristics are associated with aggressive behavior, defensive behavior, and cooperative behavior?

2. Although people use spoken language to communicate ideas, words are only part of the communication. How do sounds and gestures communicate ideas? Give examples.

Explore Further

Gestures, tones, and expressions may send a different message from the words humans use. Design another investigation in which some students make truthful statements and others make untruthful statements. Try to decide who is untruthful.

Behavior Studies of Twins

Animal behavior is determined by a mix of genetics and the environment. By studying twins, scientists can discover which behavior may be caused by the environment and which may be caused by genes.

Twins can be either fraternal or identical. Fraternal twins come from the union of two different eggs and two different sperm cells. Identical twins come from the same egg and sperm. The fertilized single egg splits. This creates two babies with the same DNA.

Since identical twins have the same DNA, most differences should be caused by their environment. Identical twins often share many behaviors. Some identical twins have been separated at birth and raised separately. Years later, as adults, they are still very similar.

Studying fraternal twins also provides information about how the environment shapes behavior and other traits. Scientists compare differences between fraternal and identical twins. For example, scientists have found that identical twins are much more likely to share smoking or nonsmoking behaviors than fraternal twins. This leads researchers to believe that there is a genetic tendency to be a smoker.

The same study showed that a twin who smoked died earlier than a twin who did not smoke. It did not matter whether the twin was identical or fraternal. In this case, the environment caused health problems, regardless of genetics.

1. What is the difference between identical and fraternal twins?

2. Why are scientists interested in studying differences in identical twins?

3. What information about smoking was discovered by studying twins?

- Behavioral biology is the study of the behavior of living things. Ethologists are scientists who study behavioral biology.

- Behaviors can be inherited or learned. Some behaviors evolve within species and are favored by natural selection.

- An innate behavior is a behavior an animal is born with. Mating and feeding behaviors are often innate.

- Physical characteristics, such as bright coloring, can be combined with behavior to ward off predators.

- Imprinting is behavior learned by a young animal.

- Some behaviors, such as birds learning songs, are a combination of imprinting and learning.

- Animals interact with one another in social behavior. Examples of social behavior are aggression, courtship, and cooperation.

- Courtship behavior between animals ensures partners are the same species.

- Animals use aggressive behavior to protect against predators or to defend territory.

- Animals may communicate as a means of cooperating within their community. Communication is used to warn of danger, signal the location of food, or identify members of a community.

Vocabulary

aggressive behavior, 514
agonistic interaction, 521
behavior, 506
behavioral biology, 506
cognition, 524
communication, 520
competitor, 521
cooperation, 521
courtship behavior, 513
defensive behavior, 514

dominant, 521
ethologist, 506
external stimulus, 506
fixed action pattern behavior, 507
imprinting, 515
innate behavior, 507
instinct, 514
internal stimulus, 506
landmark, 515
learned behavior, 507

matched submission, 521
metacommunication, 522
mimicry, 514
observational learning, 515
parental care behavior, 513
pheromone, 524
predator, 514

prey, 514
releaser, 515
scent, 521
signal, 521
simulate, 513
social behavior, 520
sociobiologist, 520
spatial learning, 515
territorial behavior, 515
warning coloration, 514

Chapter 16 R E V I E W

Word Bank

aggressive
  behavior

agonistic
  interaction

behavior

cognition

competitor

cooperation

dominant

ethologist

innate behavior

learned behavior

matched
  submission

predator

releaser

scent

signal

sociobiologist

warning coloration

Vocabulary Review

On a sheet of paper, write the word or words from the Word Bank that best complete each sentence.

1. An animal that is _____ shows influence or control over other animals.

2. Knowledge or recognition of another organism or surroundings is _____.

3. A scientist who studies the behaviors of animals is a(n) _____.

4. Growling and showing teeth are examples of _____.

5. A(n) _____ is present at birth.

6. A(n) _____ is behavior that results from experience.

7. Some animals use pheromones to communicate using _____.

8. A(n) _____ hunts and eats another animal.

9. The way an organism acts is _____.

10. The bright colors or patterns on animals that scare off predators is _____.

11. A(n) _____ tries to obtain the same resources as another animal.

12. A scientist who studies the factors that determine the social behavior of animals is a(n) _____.

13. A behavior that causes a change in the behavior of another animal is a(n) _____.

14. A type of social behavior in which individuals have contests and show aggressive behavior is _____.

15. The result of animals that display _____ is that one animal gets all the resources.

Review continued on next page

16. A _____ is a stimulus that brings out a certain behavior in another animal

17. A type of social behavior in which animals work or act with another or others for a common purpose is _____.

Concept Review

On a sheet of paper, write the letter of the answer that best completes each sentence.

18. Imprinting takes place _____.

   A before an animal is born

   B when the animal is very young

   C when the animal matures

   D throughout an animal's life

19. An animal uses a courtship ritual to _____.

   A notify a mate or group of a food source

   B warn of danger

   C attract a suitable mate

   D protect its territory

20. A(n) _____ results from experience.

   A learned behavior

   B innate behavior

   C territorial behavior

   D courtship behavior

21. Learning in which an animal bonds with the first object it sees is _____.

   A spatial learning   **C** mimicry

   B defensive behavior   **D** imprinting

22. A fixed action pattern behavior is an action that _____.

   A sometimes changes   **C** always occurs the same way

   B always changes   **D** is a pheromone

Critical Thinking

On a sheet of paper, write the answers to the following questions. Use complete sentences.

23. Define fixed action pattern behavior. Give an example.

24. How does warning coloration help an animal survive predators?

25. Describe how inheritance and learning are both necessary for a bird to sing correctly.

Research and Write

Find an example of courtship behavior used by an animal species. Make a small presentation of the ritual. Use photos, audio sounds, or video. Explain how the ritual is accepted or turned down by the possible mate.

Test-Taking Tip If a question asks you to describe or explain something, try to answer the question as completely as possible. Use complete sentences.

Chapter

17 Populations and Communities

The school of fish in the photograph is part of a coral-reef ecosystem. The organisms depend on each other for survival. Algae that live in the coral grow using energy from the sun. The algae become food for crustaceans, which are eaten by fish. Decomposers break down crustaceans and dead fish. This releases nutrients into the water. Crustaceans and fish hide in the coral to escape being eaten. In Chapter 17, you will learn about the living parts of an ecosystem—populations and communities. You will find out how the living things are woven together by the transfer of energy and materials.

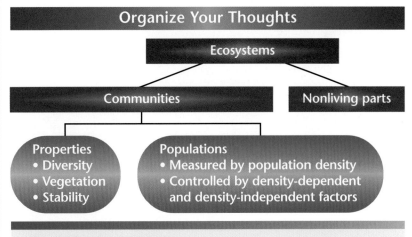

Organize Your Thoughts

Ecosystems

Communities   Nonliving parts

Properties
• Diversity
• Vegetation
• Stability

Populations
• Measured by population density
• Controlled by density-dependent and density-independent factors

Goals for Learning

◆ To explain the structure of populations and communities
◆ To describe factors affecting population growth
◆ To identify properties of communities
◆ To describe community interactions
◆ To explain how communities change

Objectives

After reading this lesson, you should be able to

◆ identify the levels of organization in life

◆ define population and community

◆ describe how populations are measured

◆ identify properties of communities

Interact

To act upon or influence something

Biosphere

The total area of the earth that contains and supports life

You have now learned about the different levels and types of organization in life, from organism to molecule, and from kingdom to species. Every level acts upon, or **interacts** with, other levels. The many types of life also interact with nonliving things in their environments.

Recall from Chapter 1 that ecology is the study of how organisms interact with each other. Ecology is also the study of organisms interacting with the living and nonliving things in their environment.

Levels of Organization

Ecologists organize the environment into five levels: **biosphere,** ecosystem, community, population, and organism. The higher the level, the more interactions there are. Each level has unique properties because of the interactions of its parts. Organisms interact at different levels.

Study Figure 17.1.1. Notice that the highest level of organization is the biosphere.

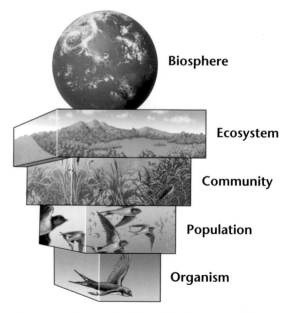

Biosphere

Ecosystem

Community

Population

Organism

17.1.1 *The environment is organized into five levels.*

The biosphere is all the areas of the earth where life can exist. These areas are the air, land, and water. All organisms are found in the biosphere.

Ecologists divide the biosphere into large areas called **biomes.** Biomes are areas of land or water that have similar weather conditions. Some biomes are oceans, forests, grasslands, wetlands, and deserts. Different biomes are found in different climates. You will learn more about the different biomes in Chapter 18.

Biomes are made of smaller units called ecosystems. Recall from Chapter 1 that an ecosystem is all the living and nonliving things found in a particular area. Ecosystems occur on land, in the water, and in the air. The interactions that occur in a pond make up an ecosystem. So do the interactions in a river or lake.

The third level of organization is the community. All organisms in an ecosystem are its community. Populations of different species that live in the same area make up a community.

Populations in a community interact with each another in many ways. In a forest, trees provide food and shelter for animals. Deer eat tree bark. Squirrels live in the trees. Squirrels eat the nuts from some trees. They also bury nuts, which then grow into new trees.

The next level of organization is a population. All the members of one species in an ecosystem are a population. The individual members of a population interact with each other. They interact when they mate or when they compete for food and water.

Notice that the lowest level of organization in Figure 17.1.1 is an individual organism. The place where an organism lives is its habitat. Every organism is adapted to live in its habitat.

Link to ➤➤➤

Language Arts

The word *ecology* comes from the Greek word *oikos,* which means "house." The word *biosphere* comes from the Greek words *bios,* which means "life," and *sphaira,* which means "globe."

Learning About Populations

Populations are made of members of one species that live in a particular place. A population is also the smallest unit that can evolve. Ecologists study how well a particular population survives in an ecosystem. They look at factors that affect a population's survival. Based on these data, ecologists can then determine the factors that cause a population or an entire species to evolve.

The number of individuals in a population is the size of that population. Size is an important property of population. Ecologists may be able to count a small population. However, the size of a large population can be difficult to measure. There may be too many individuals. Or, individuals may move around quickly, as with many species of insects and birds.

To measure size, ecologists often use **population density.** Population density measures how crowded a population is. It is the number of individual organisms of a particular species in a particular area of an ecosystem.

To measure population density, ecologists take **samples** of a population. A sample is a part that represents the entire population. Ecologists use samples to estimate the size of the population. To get a sample, ecologists count the number of organisms in a small area. Then they watch for changes in this number.

Population density

The number of individuals in a population in a particular area

Sample

A part that represents an entire population

Technology and Society

Scientists know that wild relatives of food crops, such as corn and wheat, have valuable genetic diversity. People need to preserve these wild relatives. Consumers value some varieties of corn for consistent size, yield, and quality. This consistency may increase the chance of disease. Saving older species of corn can preserve valuable genetic diversity for future food crops.

Learning About Communities

Communities are made of all of the populations that live in a certain area. Ecologists study communities to determine how populations of different organisms interact with each other. Every species has a niche, or a particular ecological role. The relationships between different species and their niches give each community its special properties.

For example, an ecologist counts 500 individuals in an area. This area is one-tenth of the area of an ecosystem. The ecologist then multiplies 500 by 10 to get an estimate of 5,000 individuals. In other words, 5,000 individuals make up the population in a certain ecosystem.

Ecologists study these relationships to understand common properties of communities. Two properties are the diversity of species and the interactions of these species. Diversity is the number of different species in a community. A third property is the **stability** of the community. The stability of a community shows how much it can resist change.

Link to ➤➤➤

Math

Ecologists usually cannot measure all the variables in an ecosystem. They often use mathematical models to better understand the structure and function of an ecosystem. Ecologists base their models on data obtained from observations.

Word Bank

community

diversity

niche

On a sheet of paper, write the word from the Word Bank that completes each sentence correctly.

1. All of the organisms of a particular species found in a certain area form a _____.

2. A _____ describes the role played by a species in an community.

3. In a community, _____ refers to the number of different species present.

On a sheet of paper, write the letter of the answer that completes each sentence correctly.

4. A scientist who studies the interactions of organisms with their environments is a(n) _____.

   A biologist   **B** zoologist   **C** ecologist   **D** botanist

5. Population density is a measure of the _____ of organisms in an area.

   A diversity   **B** health   **C** number   **D** niche

6. The smallest number of living things is found in the _____ level of ecological organization.

   A community   **B** population   **C** ecosystem   **D** biosphere

Critical Thinking

On a sheet of paper, answer the following questions. Use complete sentences.

7. Why are rain forests and deserts different biomes?

8. What is the difference between a population and a community?

9. Describe an ecological community in your area.

10. Order the following levels of organization from lowest to highest: community, organism, ecosystem, biosphere, population.

Growth rate

The amount by which a population's size changes in a given time

Carrying capacity

The largest density an ecosystem can support for a particular population

As you know, populations are made of organisms of the same species. These organisms have similar structures and functions. They behave in similar ways.

When ecologists study populations, they study characteristics that arise through adaptation. These characteristics may help the entire population to survive. Ecologists also study the characteristics of the ecosystems that populations live in.

Limits on Population Density

Recall from Lesson 1 that ecologists can estimate a population's size by measuring its density. Density increases if a population is surviving well in an ecosystem. This means more organisms are being born than are dying. Density decreases if a population is not surviving well.

If a population has all the resources needed for survival, density should increase forever. However, these resources are not always available. A population's ability to grow is limited by food and water supplies, disease, shelter, and other factors in the environment.

Factors Affecting Population Growth

Many factors affect the **growth rate** of a population. The growth rate is the amount by which a population's size changes in a given time. Factors that limit how much a population can grow are found in all ecosystems. Some factors, such as food and water supplies, are common among all populations. Other factors are unique to certain populations.

An ecosystem and its factors will not support population growth forever. At some point, a population reaches its **carrying capacity** for its ecosystem. The carrying capacity is the largest density an ecosystem can support for a particular population. At carrying capacity, the number of organisms being born equals the number of organisms dying.

Competition

When organisms try to use the same resources

Density-dependent factor

A factor related to the density of a population that affects population size

Different populations share the same resources, such as food and water. Plant populations are the main food for many animal populations. Both plant and animal populations need water and space. Organisms in the same population also share resources with each other.

Organisms are in **competition** for the same resources. Some organisms get more resources than others. As populations grow, competition for resources becomes greater. **Density-dependent factors** are resources that affect population growth. Density-dependent factors include food, water, and habitat. When the number of organisms increases in an ecosystem, the amount of available resources usually stays the same. This means organisms have access to fewer resources.

★ ★

Achievements in Science

Coevolution

Evolution shapes populations. If two species live together, the evolution of one species can influence the evolution of another species. Biologists call this coevolution. Coevolution means "evolving together." An example of coevolution is plants and the animals that pollinate them.

American biologists Paul Ehrlich and Peter Raven founded the study of coevolution in the early 1960s. Ehrlich and Raven worked together to study butterflies and their food plants. They observed that monarch butterfly larvae, or caterpillars, feed only on plants of the milkweed family. These plants produce bitter, poisonous chemicals. Insects do not eat milkweeds.

Monarch butterflies are different. Monarch butterflies have evolved to make a special enzyme. This enzyme lets caterpillars eat milkweed plants without being poisoned.

The poisonous chemicals give milkweeds an evolutionary advantage. Most insects do not eat them. However, monarch butterflies developed a method to overcome this advantage. The milkweed family and monarchs influenced each other's evolution, or coevolution.

Density-independent factor

A factor that affects population size, but does not depend on population density

Immigrate

To move into a population

Emigrate

To leave a population

Boom-bust cycle

A period in which the densities of populations increase or decrease at the same time

Uniform

When a population spreads out evenly through an ecosystem

Clumped

When a population spreads out in small groups through an ecosystem

Random

When a population has no order as to how it is distributed through an ecosystem

Density-independent factors do not depend on population density. These factors affect the same percentage of the population regardless of its density. Examples of density-independent factors are fires, freezes, droughts, and floods. Density-independent factors often are important in regulating the growth of a population. Both density-dependent factors and density-independent factors affect population size.

Other factors also affect population growth. Organisms **immigrate,** or move into a population. Organisms **emigrate,** or leave a population.

Some populations have **boom-bust cycles.** In these cycles, populations rely on other populations for survival. Their densities affect each other. As one population grows, the other population also grows. This is a boom period. As one population decreases, another population also decreases. This is a bust period. There are many causes of boom-bust cycles.

Boom-bust cycles respond to various factors. One factor is the changes in predator and prey populations. Other factors are the quality and amount of the prey's food.

Population Distribution

Factors that affect population growth also affect how organisms in a population distribute themselves throughout an ecosystem. Organisms in the same population spread out in three patterns: **uniform, clumped,** and **random.**

Science Myth

Myth: Experiments are the only way to gain scientific knowledge.

Fact: In addition to experiments, scientists can learn much from observations. Experimentation is not always possible in some fields of sciences such as ecology. Ecologists may not be able to control some variables like weather, for example. Ecologists often use observation and analysis to learn about populations.

UNIFORM

Study Figure 17.2.1. In a uniform pattern, organisms spread evenly through their ecosystem. A clumped pattern is when organisms of the same population form small groups through the ecosystem. In a random pattern, organisms of a population are distributed in no particular way.

CLUMPED

RANDOM

Figure 17.2.1
Population distribution patterns are uniform (top), clumped (center), or random (bottom).

Express Lab 17

Materials
◆ 6 index cards
◆ six-sided number cube
◆ 30 buttons

Procedure
1. With a pen, label the index cards from 1 to 6.

2. Make a rectangle with two rows of index cards. In row 1, lay out index cards 1 to 3. In row 2, lay out index cards 4 to 6. The rectangle represents an ecosystem.

3. Each button represents one organism in a population. Select a distribution pattern: uniform, clumped, or random.

4. Put the buttons on the rectangle to show the distribution pattern you selected.

5. Roll the number cube. Find the card with that number. The organisms on this index card represent your sample.

Analysis
1. Does your sample contain one-sixth of the organisms in your ecosystem? Explain your answer.

2. How do distribution patterns affect sampling?

3. Which pattern will give the best estimate of true population size?

On a sheet of paper, write the word or words from the Word Bank that complete each sentence correctly.

Word Bank

density-
  independent

immigrating

increases

more

1. Organisms that are _____ are entering a population.

2. As populations grow, competition _____ and resources become _____ scarce.

3. Fires and lack of rainfall are examples of _____ factors.

On a sheet of paper, write the letter of the answer that completes each sentence correctly.

4. When a population reaches its carrying capacity, _____.

   A the ecosystem cannot support more growth

   B diversity increases

   C organisms form random distribution patterns

   D new individuals will immigrate

5. A population that is evenly distributed forms a(n) _____ pattern through an ecosystem.

   A clumped   **B** random   **C** grouped   **D** uniform

6. An example of a density-dependent factor is a _____.

   A freezes   **C** food supply

   B droughts   **D** fire

Critical Thinking

On a sheet of paper, write the answers to the following questions. Use complete sentences.

7. Explain the role of competition in the use of density-dependent resources.

8. Wolves live in groups within their ecosystem. What kind of distribution pattern is this? Explain your answer.

9. How do immigration and emigration affect population density?

10. Compare density-dependent and density-independent factors.

Materials

◆ small paper bag containing dried navy beans

◆ red wax pencil

Estimating Population Size

To study a population, ecologists must determine its size. Ecologists usually cannot count all the members of a population. Instead, they use sampling methods to estimate the size of a population. In this investigation, you will use the mark-recapture sampling method to estimate the size of a population of navy beans. Ecologists often use the mark-recapture method to estimate the size of animal populations.

Procedure

1. Remove 10 beans from the bag. Use the red wax pencil to put a large dot on each of the 10 navy beans. **Safety Alert: Do not put the navy beans in or near your mouth.**

2. Return the marked navy beans to the paper bag. Close the bag. Shake the bag gently.

3. Remove 20 navy beans from the bag. This is your sample. Count the number of navy beans with red dots. The navy beans with red dots are your marked recaptures. Record this number.

4. Return the navy beans with red dots to the bag.

5. Count the total number of navy beans in the bag. This is the actual population size. Record this number.

Analysis

1. What does each navy bean represent?

2. What does the bag represent?

3. Use the following equation to estimate the population size, *N:*

$$N = \frac{M \times S}{R}$$

Where M = number marked
   S = total number in the sample
   R = number of marked recaptured

How close was your estimate of the population size to the total number of navy beans in the bag?

Conclusions

1. The mark-recapture method assumes that each marked individual has the same chance of being recaptured as each unmarked individual. What problems do you see with this assumption?

2. In a real population, what are some events or factors that could affect the accuracy of the mark-recapture method?

3. Write a new question about estimating population size that you could explore in another investigation.

Explore Further

Use a similar procedure to explore the effect of sample size on estimating population size.

After reading this lesson, you should be able to

◆ identify the major properties of communities

◆ describe a niche

◆ describe different interactions among organisms in communities

Interdependent

Having to rely on each other

Recall from Lesson 1 that the populations in an ecosystem make up the community of the ecosystem. A community is all the living members of an ecosystem. This includes animals, plants, bacteria, and fungi.

The organisms in a community are **interdependent.** The organisms rely on each other for survival. For example, some animals eat plants. Plants rely on bacteria to break down dead trees on the forest floor. The nutrients from the dead trees enrich the soil so that plants can grow. Bacteria live on or inside other organisms. Fungi use plants and trees as places to grow.

Community Diversity

When ecologists study communities in ecosystems, they observe and measure properties for each community. A property common to all communities is diversity. Diversity is the number of different species in a community. Diversity is also the number of individuals in each population. The more diverse a community is, the more types of organisms it has.

Species Interactions

The members of species in a community interact with each other. For example, bears eat honey made by bees. Bees collect pollen from flowers. Some animals eat flowering plants. Every species in a community uses living and nonliving resources. Every species also provides resources. All of these activities make up the niche of a species. Every niche is unique.

Species in a community must interact to live and survive. Different types of interaction exist among species, including competition, predation, parasitism, mutualism, and commensalism. These interactions determine the makeup of a community.

Competition

One type of interaction among species is competition. Members of a species compete with each other and with other species. They compete for food and water, for example.

Competition happens constantly in communities. Different species must share some resources. If two species had identical niches, they would compete for the same resources. Over time, one species would force the other species out of the ecosystem. Both species could stay if one species changed its niche.

Trophic Structure

The feeding relationships among the species of a community are called the **trophic structure.** In an ecosystem, all organisms that eat the same kinds of food are in the same trophic level. Look at Figure 17.3.1.

Figure 17.3.1 *How many trophic levels are in this ecosystem?*

Predation

Another type of interaction is **predation.** Predation is when one species eats another species. Recall from Chapter 16 that a predator eats an organism called the prey. There are many predator-prey relationships in any community. Deer are predators of grass. Snakes are predators of mice. Snakes are the prey of hawks. Species in predator-prey relationships often evolve different predator and defense, or prey, methods. Many big cats, such as lions and tigers, have long claws to catch prey. They can run fast, so they do not become prey. Mint plants use their strong flavor to defend themselves. Many animals dislike the taste of mint.

Many animals use defense methods against predators. As you learned in Chapter 16, some defend themselves by using warning coloration. Their bright colors and patterns scare off predators. Other organisms have colors or patterns that help them blend in and hide in their surroundings. Predators have difficulty seeing them. This is called **camouflage.** Another defense method is mimicry. In mimicry, one species looks like another poisonous or dangerous species. This causes predators to stay away.

Symbiotic Relationships

Other community interactions involve **symbiosis.** Symbiosis is the relationship between different species that live in close association with one another. **Parasitism** is a symbiotic relationship. In parasitism, one organism, the parasite, feeds off of another organism, the **host.** Fleas are parasites that feed off dogs and cats.

Mutualism is a symbiotic relationship in which two different organisms benefit from living together. Birds live on the backs of rhinoceros. The birds eat biting insects off of the skin of the rhinoceros. The birds get food, and the rhinoceros does not itch.

In **commensalism,** one organism benefits, and the other organism is not affected. Barnacles live on whales. Whales carry the barnacles around, which helps the barnacles feed. The barnacles do not hurt the whales.

Plant Life and Communities

Plant life, or **vegetation,** is a property of communities on land. Plants provide food for organisms. They also determine the structure of an ecosystem. Forest ecosystems have many tall plants such as trees. Trees provide homes for species such as birds and insects. Forest ecosystems have species that live in the **canopy,** or the tops of trees. These species are different than species living on the forest floor.

A desert ecosystem may have only a few plants, like cactus. A desert ecosystem may not support many species. The plant life in a community determines what other species can survive there.

▼◄▲▼◄▲▼◄▲▼◄▲▼◄▲▼◄▲▼◄▲▼◄▲▼◄▲▼◄▲▼◄▲▼

Science at Work

Demographer

Demographers study the size, growth, density, and distribution of human populations. They collect and analyze data on births, marriages, deaths, and diseases. Demographers examine population trends due to changes in birth rate, death rate, emigration, and immigration. They predict how changes in population will affect public services such as health care, housing, and education.

Demographers need training in statistics. Statistics is the collecting of and using numerical facts about people, business, health, and so on. Jobs in demography may also require training in geography, economics, public health, medicine, or marketing. Many demographers work for federal, state, or local governments. Some work for state colleges and universities. Others work for private companies.

A demographer must be observant, orderly, and accurate. Demographers need good analytical and communication skills. They analyze and interpret data and work as a member of a team.

Lesson 3   R E V I E W

Word Bank
camouflage
parasitism
vegetation

Link to >>>

Chemistry
Allelopathy is the natural secretion of harmful chemicals by certain plants. These chemicals discourage the growth of competitor plants of the same or another species. The black walnut tree is an allelopathic species. The buds, roots, and nut hulls of black walnut contain a poisonous chemical called juglone. Juglone causes many plants to wilt and die.

On a sheet of paper, write the word from the Word Bank that completes each sentence correctly.

1. The plant life in an area is the _____.

2. A symbiotic relationship in which one organism feeds off another organism is _____.

3. Animals with _____ have colors or patterns that help them hide from predators.

On a sheet of paper, write the letter of the answer that completes each sentence correctly.

4. A species that eats another species is _____.

   A competition   **C** predation

   B mutualism   **D** mimicry

5. Commensalism is a symbiotic relationship in which _____.

   A one organism benefits and the other is not affected

   B one organism captures and eats another

   C one organism feeds off of another organism

   D both organisms benefit

6. The trophic structure of a community describes its _____ relationships.

   A feeding   **B** mating   **C** symbiotic   **D** niche

Critical Thinking
On a sheet of paper, write the answers to the following questions. Use complete sentences.

7. What will happen if two species have identical niches?

8. Why are all organisms in a community interdependent?

9. Describe three methods animals use to reduce the risk of being eaten.

10. How does a predator-prey relationship differ from a parasite-host relationship? How is it similar?

DISCOVERY INVESTIGATION 17

Surveying an Ecological Community

An ecological community is made of all the biotic, or living, species in an ecosystem. Ecology is the study of the interactions among living things and the nonliving things in an environment. Living things are the biotic factors in the environment. Abiotic factors are nonliving things, such as air, temperature, light, and water. In this investigation, you will survey an ecological community in your area.

Procedure

1. Put on heavy gloves.

2. Using a meterstick, measure a 5 meter by 5 meter site. Put a stake at each corner of the site. **Safety Alert: Wear heavy gloves to push the stake into the ground. Stay only in the area as directed by your teacher.**

3. Make a border around the site by looping string around the first stake. Continue looping string around each stake until you have formed a border around the site.

4. To map your site, draw a 15 centimeter by 15 centimeter square on a sheet of paper. Draw the physical features of your site on your map.

5. Use a green pencil or marker to draw the plants in your site. Use blue to draw the animals. Use brown to represent evidence of animals, such as egg cases, animal tracks, or burrows. Use black to show dead organisms or parts of organisms, such as fallen leaves or twigs. Use orange to show decomposers.

6. Write a hypothesis, Safety Alerts, and procedure describing how to determine which organism in your site has the greatest population density.

7. Have your hypothesis, Safety Alerts, and procedure approved by your teacher. Carry out your experiment.

Analysis

1. List the abiotic and biotic features of your site.

2. Describe a distribution pattern—uniform, clumped, or random—for one organism in your site.

3. Which organisms at your site are producers? Which organisms are consumers?

4. Describe evidence of primary succession at your site.

Conclusions

1. Was your hypothesis supported by the results of your investigation?

2. Are consumers or producers found in the greatest number at your site?

3. What density-dependent and density-independent factors are likely to affect the organisms at your site?

Explore Further

What relationships exist among two or more different kinds of organisms at your site? Suggest a procedure to answer this question.

Disturbance

A large change in a community

Toxic

Poisonous

Succession

The process of ecological change in a community

Communities tend to be in a constant state of change. Natural **disturbances** such as fires, blizzards, freezes, floods, droughts, and storms affect communities. A disturbance is a major change in a community. Human disturbances such as **toxic,** or poisonous, spills also affect communities. For example, hurricanes and toxic spills can disturb marine communities. Disturbances destroy organisms. They also change the resources available to organisms that survive.

Stability

Ecologists study a community property called stability. Recall from Lesson 1 that stability is a community's ability to resist changes. Many disturbances happen regularly. Many large disturbances are density-independent factors that regulate populations and communities. Recall from Lesson 2 that a density-independent factor affects population or community size, but does not depend on population density.

Succession

A stable community can recover from some disturbances in a few years. Other communities may have to start over after a disturbance. A community that experiences major changes undergoes **succession.** Succession is the process of ecological change in a community.

Change is not necessarily bad for a community. Disturbances may remove some species and bring in new species. Sometimes, species struggling to survive are given a new chance. Major changes can open new niches and resources for them. For example, a fire destroys many trees in a forest. However, seeds of some plant species need high temperatures to sprout.

Communities that experience succession may take thousands or millions of years to become stable. However, disturbances continue to happen. Most communities never become completely stable.

Primary
succession

The changes in a lifeless environment that create a community

Secondary
succession

The changes in a community as it recovers from the effects of a disturbance

Link to ➤➤➤

Earth Science

The volcanic eruption of Mount St. Helens on May 18, 1980, created a natural outdoor laboratory. Mount St. Helens is in the state of Washington. Ecologists observed a succession following a major disturbance. They found that most early plant species thrived in nutrient-poor, disturbed areas. These areas had very little water.

Primary Succession

Communities can go through two types of succession. The first type is **primary succession.** Communities start in an area that had no life. These areas are usually made of nonliving rock and land. They are usually uncovered by melting glaciers or created by new rock from volcanic eruptions. For life to exist, the soil must build up nutrients that organisms need.

Primary succession begins with microorganisms, such as mosses and lichens. These small organisms perform photosynthesis. As these species take over the area, other plant species move into the area. As more plants move in, animals also start to move in. A diverse community has now formed. Primary succession creates a new community over a long period of time.

Secondary Succession

Secondary succession happens after disturbances have destroyed many populations in a community. Secondary succession often happens after a forest fire, or a human activity such as logging or mining. Secondary succession is more common than primary succession.

In secondary succession, soil nutrients remain in an area. Since vegetation supports all other organisms in a community, plants are the first species to appear. Plants include grass species and small, woody shrubs. These species make way for larger plants, including several species of trees. Eventually, the community grows into a large forest. As vegetation grows, the kinds and numbers of animal species also grow depending on the biome.

Figure 17.4.1 *A forest fire causes cones of Jack Pine trees to open and release seeds.*

Many communities remain stable. However, small areas are disturbed. These small areas experience secondary succession. A community can have several small areas undergoing secondary succession at one time. Like land communities, marine communities also experience disturbances and go through succession.

Biology in Your Life

The Environment: Choosing Native Plants

The next time you notice flowering garden plants for sale, take a closer look. You will see trays of healthy plants covered with colorful flowers. People buy them, plant them in their outdoor gardens, and then hope to enjoy months of flowers.

However, some garden plants fail to thrive. Why does this happen? In most parts of the United States, many flowering plants are non-native species. Non-native species are species originally from a different area. The ideal conditions for a non-native plant may be very different from those in an outdoor garden.

Flowering garden plants that die may be in an ecosystem that differs from their native ecosystem. Many gardeners choose favorite plant species. These species may be poorly suited for the local temperature, rainfall, and soil type.

Adding native plants to a garden boosts the chances of success. Because they occur naturally in the area, native plants are ideally suited for local conditions. In drier parts of the United States, many native plants are xeriscapic. The word *xeriscapic* comes from the Greek word *xeros,* meaning "dry." Xeriscapic plants do well in dry areas. They do not require extra watering. This is an advantage in areas where rainfall is scarce.

1. What are non-native plants?

2. Tony has just moved from Texas to Vermont. His family buys flowering garden plants like the ones they had in Texas. The plants soon die. Why?

3. A neighbor who has just moved into your area is planning a new garden. What gardening advice could you offer your new neighbor?

Lesson 4   R E V I E W

Word Bank

primary succession

stability

succession

Research and Write

With a partner, use Internet and print resources to write a report on Surtsey. Surtsey is a volcanic island off the coast of Iceland. Describe how organisms began to grow on this island.

On a sheet of paper, write the word or words from the Word Bank that complete each sentence correctly.

1. A property called _____ is a community's ability to resist change brought on by disturbances.

2. When a community experiences major changes, it undergoes _____.

3. A process known as _____ takes place when communities start in an area that has no life at all.

On a sheet of paper, write the letter of the answer that completes each sentence correctly.

4. Organisms such as _____ are among the first to appear during primary succession.

    A trees   **B** wildflowers   **C** shrubs   **D** mosses

5. After _____, secondary succession will occur.

    A a volcanic eruption produces a new island

    B a forest fire takes place

    C a parking lot is paved

    D a melting glacier uncovers new earth

6. A _____ is a likely location for primary succession.

    A forest floor   **C** mowed field

    B grassy hillside   **D** large boulder

Critical Thinking

On a sheet of paper, write the answers to the following questions. Use complete sentences.

7. Is primary or secondary succession more frequent? Why?

8. What kinds of organisms first appear during primary succession? Explain your answer.

9. Which takes longer: primary or secondary succession? Why?

10. What might happen if primary succession did not occur?

Friendly Predators

The insect in the photograph is a praying mantis. Its name comes from how it looks when it eats. The praying mantis uses its front legs to hold an insect as it eats. It looks like it is praying. Sometimes, this insect is called a "preying" mantis because it is a predator.

The praying mantis looks fearsome. However, it is harmless to people and it is very helpful. It eats small insects such as spiders and mosquitoes. It also eats beetles and aphids that attack garden plants. Gardeners and farmers sometimes find their tomato, rose, and other plant leaves full of holes. Insect pests eat these leaves.

To fight insect pests, some people use chemicals. Others use a natural method. They use natural predators of insect pests. For example, they plant praying mantis egg cases in their garden. The egg cases are small brown masses of eggs. Many garden supply stores and catalogs sell the egg cases.

Where do the egg cases come from? In autumn, a female praying mantis lays a mass of eggs. Then she dies. The eggs live over the winter because they are surrounded by protective material. In the spring, hundreds of tiny praying mantises hatch from the eggs. They gobble up harmful insects.

Using predators to kill harmful prey is called biological pest control. Other insect predators, such as ladybugs and lacewings, also control harmful insect populations.

1. Name two garden pests that are prey to praying mantises.

2. Why might a gardener use praying mantises to control pests rather than spraying plants with chemicals?

- Ecology focuses on the interactions of organisms with their environments.

- Ecologists organize the environment into five levels: the biosphere, ecosystems, communities, populations, and individual organism.

- All the organisms of the same species in a community form a population. A community is all the species in an ecosystem. Each organism has a role, or a niche, in its ecosystem.

- Population size is the total number of organisms of a particular species in an ecosystem. Population density is the number of individuals in a population in a particular area.

- Diversity and stability are properties of a community.

- Population growth is influenced by density-dependent factors, such as food and water. These factors are affected by density of the population.

- Population growth is also influenced by density-independent factors, such as fires, freezes, and floods. These factors are not affected by population density.

- Organisms in a community are interdependent. They rely on each other for survival.

- Species compete for resources. In predation, the predator eats an organism of a different species. Warning coloration, camouflage, and mimicry have evolved to reduce the chance of some species becoming prey.

- Symbiosis is the relationship between organisms living in close association. Parasitism, mutualism, and commensalism are three types of symbiotic relationships.

- Natural and human disturbances cause a community to change. Succession is the process of ecological change in a community. Primary and secondary succession occurs after different types of disturbances.

Vocabulary

biome, 537
biosphere, 536
boom-bust cycle, 543
camouflage, 550
canopy, 551
carrying capacity, 541
clumped, 543
commensalism, 550
competition, 542

density-dependent factor, 542
density-independent factor, 543
disturbance, 555
emigrate, 543
growth rate, 541
host, 550
immigrate, 543
interact, 536

interdependent, 548
mutualism, 550
parasitism, 550
population density, 538
predation, 550
primary succession, 556
random, 543
sample, 538
secondary succession, 556

stability, 539
succession, 555
symbiosis, 550
toxic, 555
trophic structure, 549
uniform, 543
vegetation, 551

Word Bank

biome

biosphere

camouflage

carrying capacity

commensalism

competition

density-dependent factor

density-independent factor

growth rate

mutualism

parasitism

population density

primary succession

secondary succession

stability

succession

symbiosis

trophic structure

Vocabulary Review

On a sheet of paper, write the word or words from the Word Bank that best complete each sentence.

1. Organisms begin to grow in a lifeless area during _____.

2. Organisms reappear after a disturbance has destroyed many populations during _____.

3. A growth factor not influenced by how many organisms are in a population is a _____.

4. A species that uses _____ has colors or patterns that help it hide in its surroundings.

5. The ability of a community to resist change is _____.

6. The total area of the earth that contains and supports life the _____.

7. The number of individuals of a particular species in a small area of an ecosystem is measured by a _____.

8. The largest number of individuals that an ecosystem can support is its _____.

9. Both organisms benefit from living together in a relationship called _____.

10. One organism feeds off of another organism in a relationship called _____.

11. One organism benefits while the other is not affected in a relationship called _____.

12. When resources such as food and water are in short supply, _____ occurs between species and organisms.

13. The amount by which a populations size changes in a given time is the _____.

Review continued on next page

14. The feeding relationships among the species of a community make up its _____.

15. A force that influences population growth and is affected by the number of individuals in the population is a _____.

16. A large area of land or water that has similar weather conditions is _____.

17. A close association between organisms of two different species is _____.

18. The process of ecological change in a community is _____.

Concept Review

On a sheet of paper, write the letter of the answer that completes each sentence correctly.

19. The regrowth of plants and trees after a forest fire is an example of _____.

    A competition   **C** emigration

    B succession   **D** parasitism

20. A community high in diversity _____.

    A has a uniform population distribution

    B contains many organisms

    C has few species

    D has few predators

21. A _____ is a density-dependent factor.

    A fire   **C** freeze

    B drought   **D** food supply

Critical Thinking

On a sheet of paper, write the answers to the following questions. Use complete sentences.

22. Both density-dependent and density-independent factors affect population size. Which factor involves competition? Explain your answer.

23. What happens when a population exceeds the carrying capacity of its ecosystem?

24. Compare primary succession and secondary succession. Give one example of each.

25. Compare parasitism, commensalism, and mutualism.

Research and Write

Write a report on the warblers observed by ecologist Robert H. MacArthur. Explain how the warblers he observed shared resources and reduced competition. Use both Internet and print resources for your report.

Test-Taking Tip   If a word on a test is new to you, take the word apart. Compare the parts to other words you know.

Ecosystems

The stream in this photograph is home to many living things. The stream is rich in nutrients released by the organisms that break down dead organic matter. The stream is rich in oxygen that dissolves in the water. The living things in and around the stream depend on the health of the stream, which is maintained by natural cycles. In Chapter 18, you will learn how living things exchange energy and materials with ecosystems.

Organize Your Thoughts

Ecosystems

- Energy flow
- Biomes
- Chemical nutrient cycling

Energy flow
- Controlled by trophic structure
  • Food chains, webs, energy pyramids

Chemical nutrient cycling
- Driven by organic and geologic activities
  • Includes carbon, nitrogen, water

Goals for Learning

◆ To describe feeding relationships in ecosystems
◆ To describe how energy flows through ecosystems
◆ To identify major nutrients and describe how they cycle through ecosystems
◆ To identify major biomes in the world

565

After reading this lesson, you should be able to

◆ name the different ways organisms get energy

◆ explain the feeding relationships in ecosystems

◆ identify the different roles in a food chain or web

◆ describe an ecosystem using an energy pyramid

Phototroph

An organism that gets its energy by capturing sunlight

Chemotroph

An organism that gets its energy from chemicals in food

Solar

Of or from the sun

In Chapter 17, you learned about lower levels of organization in ecology. The lower levels together form one of the largest and most important levels, the ecosystem. An ecosystem includes all the living and nonliving matter in an area. This matter includes organisms of different species and also nonliving things like rocks and rivers.

Ecologists study ecosystems to understand how living things interact with their surroundings and with each other. When ecologists look at an ecosystem, they examine how two major factors keep the ecosystem going. These factors are the flow of energy and the cycling of chemicals. In this lesson, you will focus on the flow of energy from the sun through different organisms in an ecosystem. In Lesson 2, you will look at how chemicals cycle through an ecosystem.

Phototrophs and Chemotrophs

Recall from Chapter 1 that the sun is the ultimate source of energy for the earth and all its ecosystems. The energy from the sun is transformed into food energy through photosynthesis. Ecologists label organisms based on how they get their energy. Plants and photosynthetic organisms get their energy directly from the sun. They are called **phototrophs.** *Photo* means "light." *Troph* means "the process of feeding."

Other organisms, such as animals and insects, get their energy from chemicals in food, like glucose. These organisms, which include humans, are called **chemotrophs.** *Chemo* means "chemicals."

Food Chains

The way organisms feed determines how they get their energy and chemicals. Recall from Chapter 17 that the feeding relationships in an ecosystem are called the trophic structure. Ecologists study the trophic structures of ecosystems to determine how **solar** energy is transferred to organisms.

To describe the trophic structure, ecologists create diagrams to represent different feeding relationships. A **food chain** arranges organisms that feed on each other in a sequence, or series. Look at Figure 18.1.1. Food chains are arranged in trophic levels. The first trophic level in every food chain is the **producer.** Producers are plants and other photosynthetic organisms that produce food that all other organisms eventually eat.

After the producers are the **consumers.** Consumers are chemotrophs that eat other organisms. Consumers that eat the producers are primary consumers. A primary consumer is eaten by a secondary consumer. There can also be tertiary (third) and quaternary (fourth) consumers. Every food chain ends with **decomposers.** Decomposers are organisms, usually bacteria and fungi, that feed by breaking down dead organisms. As they break down dead organisms, they return nonliving elements, like carbon and nitrogen, to the ecosystem.

Humans are consumers in food chains. Depending on what you eat, you can be at two or more consumer levels in just one meal. For example, if you eat a steak and a salad meal, you are both a primary and secondary consumer. Eating the salad makes you a primary consumer because you are eating producers. The steak comes from cows that were already primary consumers. This makes you a secondary consumer.

A Food Chain

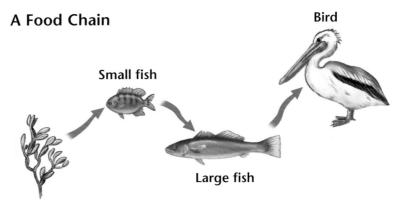

Figure 18.1.1 *A food chain shows the sequence of organisms that feed on each other.*

Aquatic

Growing or living in water

Plankton

Small organisms found in the ocean; usually at the beginning of a food chain

Food web

All the food chains in a community that are linked to one another

Organic matter

A compound that contains carbon

Every ecosystem is made up of many food chains at any one time. Food chains can be found on land and in water. Many **aquatic** food chains start with small organisms called **plankton.** Some plankton perform photosynthesis. Other plankton and larger organisms, like fish and whales, eat photosynthetic plankton. Ecologists studying a certain ecosystem work to define all of the food chains in that ecosystem. Many organisms are part of two or more food chains.

Food Webs

To better understand food chains, ecologists combine an ecosystem's food chains into a **food web.** Study the food web in Figure 18.1.2. A food web shows all the trophic levels that organisms are part of in an ecosystem. A food web can show that an organism can be a primary consumer in one food chain. It can also be a tertiary consumer in a different food chain.

After ecologists identify the feeding relationships in an ecosystem, they can understand how energy flows through that ecosystem. Recall that all energy in an ecosystem ultimately comes from the sun. Phototrophs capture that light energy. Through photosynthesis, they store it in **organic matter.** Organic matter is made up of compounds containing carbon. Phototrophs make enough organic matter, like sugars and proteins, to feed the rest of the ecosystem.

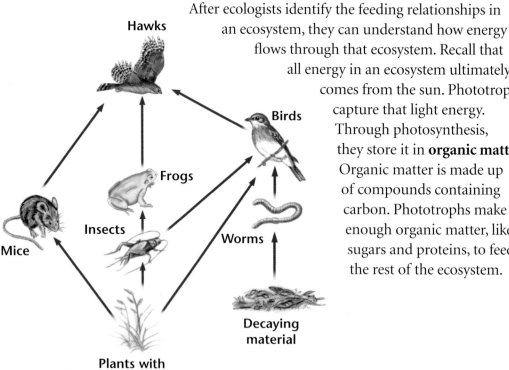

Figure 18.1.2 *A food web shows all the trophic levels that organisms are part of in an ecosystem.*

Primary productivity

The speed at which photosynthetic organisms produce organic matter in an ecosystem

Energy pyramid

A diagram that compares the amounts of energy available to the populations at different levels of a food chain

Science Myth

Myth: Bacteria are bad and useless.

Fact: Bacteria play an important role as decomposers. Decomposers break down dead organisms and recycle chemical nutrients.

Ecologists study how fast these phototrophs make organic matter. This is called **primary productivity.** How much organic matter is produced determines how much energy is available for the ecosystem. Energy in an ecosystem moves through different organisms and trophic levels according to feeding relationships.

Energy Pyramids

How much energy gets transferred during each feeding activity? As energy moves through the trophic levels, much of it is lost. Much of the chemical energy in food gets transformed into heat. Heat is the most random form of energy. It cannot be used for work or to do work. About 10 percent of the energy in one trophic level is transferred through to the next trophic level. Phototrophs must produce a lot of organic matter to support an ecosystem.

Look at Figure 18.1.3. Ecologists create diagrams called **energy pyramids** to represent the transfer of energy through trophic levels. The bottom of an energy pyramid is very large due to the large number of photosynthetic producers. Only a small amount of energy passes to each higher level. Because of this, the top of an energy pyramid is very small.

Figure 18.1.3 *The energy pyramid represents the low percentage of energy transfer from one trophic level to another.*

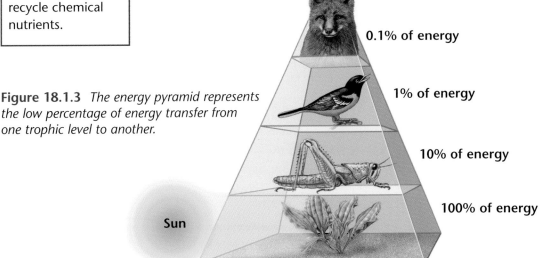

0.1% of energy

1% of energy

10% of energy

100% of energy

Sun

Word Bank

bottom

decomposers

secondary

On a sheet of paper, write the word from the Word Bank that completes each sentence correctly.

1. When people eat meat, they are _____ consumers in an ecosystem.

2. Every food chain ends with _____.

3. The _____ is the largest part of an energy pyramid.

Critical Thinking

On a sheet of paper, write the answers to the following questions. Use complete sentences.

4. Compare and contrast phototrophs and chemotrophs.

5. How does a food web differ from a food chain?

Link to ➣➣➣

Home and Career

Solar energy is radiation from the sun. Collection devices capture solar energy. Captured solar energy can then be converted to heat or electricity for home use. Some solar collectors contain a black metal plate. When sunlight strikes the plate, heat is transferred to air or water behind the plate and stored for later use.

Express Lab 18

Materials

◆ 3 index cards

◆ marker

◆ photographs of organisms

Procedure

1. Label one index card "P" for producer. Label a second index card "C" for consumer. Label a third index card "D" for decomposers.

2. Put the cards in a row. Put each photograph under the correct index card to show the role the organism plays in its ecosystem. Some organisms may play more than one role.

Analysis

1. Which organisms are producers? Which are consumers? Which are decomposers?

2. Why is each trophic level necessary in an ecosystem?

Materials
◆ organism cards

Building a Food Web

Ecologists observe the feeding relationships among organisms to study how energy moves through an ecosystem. In this investigation, you will build a food chain. The food chain will show a sequence, or series, of feeding relationships. You will then combine your food chain with other food chains to build a food web.

Procedure

1. Your teacher will give you a set of organism cards. Separate the cards into three groups to represent each trophic level: producers, consumers, and decomposers.

2. Begin your food chain by putting a producer card at the lower edge of your desktop.

3. Put a consumer card just above the producer card. A consumer eats a producer. Put the other consumer cards on your desktop in the correct sequence.

4. Add one or more decomposer cards to complete your food chain. Copy your food chain on a sheet of paper.

5. Combine your food chain cards with a classmate's cards. Use your knowledge of trophic structure to arrange the cards into a food web. On a sheet of paper, copy your food chain.

Analysis

1. How was your food chain similar to your classmate's? How was it different?

2. What is the difference between a food chain and a food web?

Conclusions

1. What would happen to your food chain if sunlight no longer existed? Explain your answer.

2. Write a new question about the role of each trophic level you could explore in another investigation.

Explore Further

Use the procedure above to discuss the differences in the numbers of individuals at each trophic level.

Objectives

After reading this lesson, you should be able to

◆ describe how energy and chemicals travel together in an ecosystem

◆ discuss different ways chemicals cycle through an ecosystem

◆ relate chemical cycling to geological processes

◆ trace the cycles of carbon, nitrogen, and water

Phosphorous

An element that cycles through an ecosystem and is used by organisms to make ATP

Atmosphere

The air that surrounds the earth

Ecologists study ecosystems to understand how energy and nutrients are used by different groups of organisms. Energy travels through ecosystems as it is passed to different trophic levels. But energy does not make this journey by itself. Energy gets transferred through food. Food also moves another major ecosystem factor, chemical nutrients. As you know, chemical nutrients are substances that organisms need to live.

Cycles of Nutrients

You have probably heard of the importance of nutrients, like vitamins and minerals, in foods you eat. When ecologists study nutrients, they look at molecules like water and carbon compounds. Organisms need water to survive. Organisms also need carbon to build molecules. Plants need carbon to make sugars that other organisms eat. As food is broken down and used, chemicals are rearranged into new molecules. These new molecules are returned to the ecosystem and can be used again.

Nutrients move through the living parts of an ecosystem. They also journey through the nonliving parts of an ecosystem. Water is an ecosystem nutrient. It is in organisms, rivers, and rain. Nutrients such as water and carbon move through ecosystems in different ways.

Some nutrients, like the element **phosphorous,** cycle within a single ecosystem. Phosphorous is found in soil and rocks. Phosphorous can also be dissolved in water and then transferred back to land. Land and some water sources stay in a particular area. Because of this, phosphorous used by organisms usually comes from their local ecosystem.

Other nutrients are available in the form of gases. These gases are found in the **atmosphere.** The atmosphere is the air that surrounds the earth.

Nutrients in gases can travel from one ecosystem to another. Because ecosystems share these nutrients, all ecosystems are connected. They rely on each other. Nutrients found in the atmosphere include carbon, nitrogen, and water. Water and the nutrients dissolved in it are also cycled through different ecosystems by the movement of rivers and oceans.

The Importance of Geological Processes

Chemical nutrients cycle through the living and nonliving parts of an ecosystem. **Geological** processes control the nonliving parts of an ecosystem. Geological processes have to do with different parts of the earth, like land and water. Any process that changes the earth affects the nutrient sources available to ecosystems. Geological processes include volcanoes, ocean currents, and weather. Weather moves gases in the atmosphere.

Another geological nutrient source is fossil fuels such as coal, oil, and natural gas. Recall that fossil fuels are made over millions of years. They are made from the breakdown of skeletons and organic waste deep inside the earth. Fossil fuels provide chemical nutrients such as carbon and nitrogen to ecosystems. When people burn fossil fuels, carbon dioxide gas is released into the atmosphere.

The Carbon Cycle

Now we will look at the cycles of three nutrients. Carbon cycling is very important to any ecosystem. Carbon is a main element in organic matter. The main source of carbon in any ecosystem is the atmosphere. Photosynthesis is the process that changes carbon dioxide into organic molecules. These molecules are used to build cells and tissue and to provide energy for organisms.

Organic molecules pass through different levels in a food chain, including decomposers that eat dead organisms. Eventually, cellular respiration breaks down organic molecules. Recall that cellular respiration produces carbon dioxide, which cycles back into the atmosphere.

The Nitrogen Cycle

Ammonium

A nitrogen-containing compound used to cycle nitrogen into an ecosystem

Nitrate

A nitrogen-containing compound used directly by plants

Nitrogen-fixer

Bacteria that convert nitrogen gas into ammonium

Nitrifying bacteria

Bacteria that convert ammonium into usable nitrates

Another main nutrient cycle involves nitrogen. Study Figure 18.2.1. Animals need nitrogen to build proteins and nucleic acids. Ecosystems use the atmosphere as a source for nitrogen. Most gas in the atmosphere is nitrogen gas. Organisms cannot use this form of nitrogen. To use nitrogen gas, it must be changed into **ammonium** or **nitrates.**

Bacteria in the soil, called **nitrogen-fixers,** take in nitrogen gas and change it to ammonium. The ammonium is changed to nitrates by other bacteria called **nitrifying bacteria.** Nitrates dissolve in water in the soil, where they can be absorbed through the roots of plants. Plants use nitrates to build amino acids and nucleotides.

Nitrogen-containing molecules cycle through the food chains in an ecosystem. Decomposers return nitrogen to the soil in the form of ammonium. Once nitrogen is cycled into an ecosystem, it usually stays there without returning to the atmosphere.

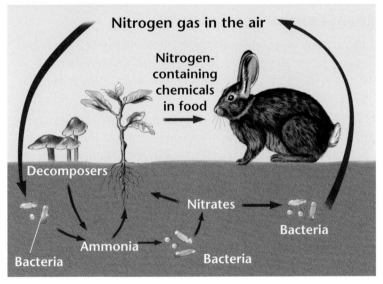

Figure 18.2.1 *Nitrogen is a main nutrient in ecosystems.*

The Water Cycle

A nutrient necessary for life is water. Water is involved in most metabolic reactions. As a human, you need to drink a certain amount of water every day to stay healthy. Water is in lakes, rivers, and oceans. Water is also in the atmosphere and underground. The water cycle depends on energy from the sun.

As solar energy warms bodies of water, **evaporation** occurs. During evaporation, water molecules become water vapor, a gas. As water vapors build up in the atmosphere, they form clouds. Clouds move through the atmosphere, constantly gaining more water. Eventually, clouds carry too many water molecules. These molecules return to their liquid form. Then clouds release **precipitation** as rain or snow. Rain and snow returns the water to the land and aquatic ecosystems. The weather that ecosystems experience is greatly influenced by the water cycle.

Cycles in Ecosystems

As you have seen, the different cycles in an ecosystem are linked to one another. Scientists sometimes study one cycle at a time. This makes it easier to understand that cycle. However, each cycle is a small part of a system of cycles in ecosystems. These cycles interact with one another.

★ ★

Achievements in Science

Nutrient Cycling in an Ecosystem

Ecologists study nutrient cycling to learn how chemical elements are recycled in an ecosystem. To do this, they must measure everything that enters and leaves the ecosystem. How is this possible outdoors?

In 1963, American ecologists Herbert Bormann and Gene Likens began a long-term study of nutrient cycling. Their study was at the Hubbard Brook Experimental Forest in New Hampshire. A layer of bedrock, or solid rock, lies under the forest's shallow soil. Water cannot seep through the bedrock. A creek drains each valley within the forest. All water leaving the Hubbard Brook ecosystem exits through these creeks.

To measure the loss of water and nutrients from the ecosystem, the ecologists built a dam at the bottom of each creek. They found that most mineral nutrients cycled within the forest ecosystem. In one valley, the researchers cut down all trees and plants. They let the dead materials remain in place. Large amounts of water and minerals were lost. Bormann and Likens concluded that plants keep nutrients within an ecosystem.

Lesson 2 REVIEW

Word Bank

carbon

carbon dioxide

precipitation

On a sheet of paper, write the word or words from the Word Bank that complete each sentence correctly.

1. Rain and snow are examples of _____ in an ecosystem.

2. Cellular respiration produces _____, which cycles back into the ecosystem.

3. A main element in organic matter is _____.

On a sheet of paper, write the letter of the answer that completes each sentence correctly.

4. The process of liquid water changing into gas due to heating is _____.

   A precipitation   **C** evaporation

   B nitrogen-fixing   **D** carbon cycling

5. Bacteria changes _____ from the atmosphere into a form that plants can use.

   A oxygen gas   **C** carbon dioxide

   B phosphorus   **D** nitrogen gas

6. Nutrients found in the atmosphere include all of the following except _____.

   A carbon   **C** phosphorus

   B nitrogen   **D** water

Critical Thinking

On a sheet of paper, write the answers to the following questions. Use complete sentences.

7. Describe how carbon cycles through an ecosystem.

8. How do plants obtain nitrogen?

9. Describe how phosphorus cycles through an ecosystem.

10. What is produced when fossil fuels are burned?

Materials

- safety goggles
- lab coat or apron
- gallon glass jar
- pond water
- pond plants, such as *Elodea*
- pond animals, such as protozoa or *Daphnia*
- four 250 mL beakers
- high-phosphate detergent solution
- eyedropper

Phosphate in Aquatic Ecosystems

Phosphorus is an element needed by organisms. In most ecosystems, phosphorus occurs in the form of phosphate, which can be found in soil and rocks. Too little phosphate can limit plant growth.

Procedure

1. Put on safety goggles and a lab coat or apron.

2. Fill the glass jar half-full with pond water.

3. Add the pond plants and animals to the water.

4. Put the glass jar on a sunny windowsill for several days.

5. When the water in the glass jar has begun to turn green, divide the pond water and plants equally among the four beakers. Each beaker will represent an aquatic ecosystem. **Safety Alert: Be sure to wash your hands immediately after handling the pond water.**

6. Write a hypothesis and procedure describing how you can determine the effects of phosphate on aquatic ecosystems.

7. Have your hypothesis, procedure, and Safety Alerts approved by your teacher.

8. Set up your experiment. Observe and record your results after several days.

Analysis

1. Describe the appearance of each beaker after several days.

2. List the control group and the experimental group in your experiment. What is the variable?

Conclusions

1. What is the effect of adding phosphate to aquatic ecosystems?

2. Why do you think many states have banned phosphates from household laundry detergents?

Explore Further

What will eventually happen to the plants and animals in an aquatic ecosystem that contains a lot of phosphate? Suggest a procedure to answer this question.

Climate

The average weather of a region over a long period of time

Terrestrial

Having to do with land

Weather influences ecosystems by driving the water cycle. The weather in an area also determines the overall **climate** of that area. Climate is the average weather conditions for a region over a long period of time. This includes temperature and precipitation. Climate also determines what kind of organisms, especially plants, can exist in an area. The type of plants in an area influence the community found in an ecosystem.

Factors that Control Weather and Climate

What controls weather and climate? One factor is land features. The weather on one side of a mountain can be very different from the other side. One side of a mountain often gets more rain and wind than the other side.

Weather and the water cycle move together. Both are driven by energy from the sun. Each area of the earth does not get the same amount of solar energy. This is due to the curve of the earth's surface and the tilt of the earth's axis. For example, areas near the equator are physically closer to the sun than areas farther north or south. These areas receive more sunlight. They stay warmer than areas closer to the poles of the earth. The larger amount of sunlight also means more solar energy is being used to drive the weather.

These differences in sunlight cause different weather and water cycles. Different cycles create different climates. This leads to different types of ecosystems.

Ecosystems that experience the same climate conditions are grouped together into larger regions called biomes. Recall from Chapter 17 that a biome is a large area of the earth that has similar ecosystems and weather. Ecosystems in the same biome share some of the same kinds of organisms. They may also share some of the same kinds of species.

The rest of this lesson will describe the different kinds of land and aquatic biomes found on the earth. Climate and typical communities are discussed for each **terrestrial,** or land, biome.

Terrestrial Biomes

Tropical forests are the main type of biome near the equator. Temperatures are high here. Some tropical forests receive large amounts of rain. They typically have many species of plants. Many of these plants are large trees and other species that grow on them. Other tropical rainforests have less rainfall and more shrubs mixed in with trees. Tropical forests often have very diverse communities with many different species.

Savanna biomes are usually large areas of land that have many grass species with trees scattered throughout. The grass in these areas can grow tall. Some grasses grow taller than three feet. The climate in savannas includes a rainy season and a very dry season. Animals in these biomes are usually large, grazing animals and their predators, like zebras and lions.

Deserts are another biome caused by low rainfall. Temperatures in deserts can be very hot, mild, or very cold. Plants and animals live in many deserts. One key feature of these organisms is their ability to save water. To survive in this biome, organisms must use water carefully.

Chaparrals are biomes with rainy winters and long, dry summers. Instead of grasses, these areas have many shrubs along with a few pine and oak trees. Fires often control the ecosystems in this biome.

Temperate grasslands are biomes with large areas of grass species. Grazing animals and seasons of drought prevent larger plants from growing there. These biomes have fertile soil. People have converted many temperate grasslands into farmland.

Tropical forest

A terrestrial biome with many trees and organisms

Savanna

A terrestrial biome with grasses and grazing animals

Desert

A very dry terrestrial biome

Chaparral

A terrestrial biome with many shrubs

Temperate grassland

A terrestrial biome with fertile soil and tall grasses

Science Myth

Myth: Decay is an event caused by nonbiological processes.

Fact: Decomposing agents, such as bacteria and fungi, perform decay.

❋ ❋

Technology and Society

Aquaculture, or fish farming, is the commercial raising of fish. People grow fish in freshwater or marine environments. The fish are raised in artificial ponds. They are given food and protected from predators. For example, aquaculture is used to produce fish such as catfish for the commercial market. Government agencies use aquaculture to raise sport fishes for restocking lakes and rivers.

Temperate deciduous forests are biomes that experience hot summers and cold winters. These areas also receive a lot of rainfall. This allows for many different animal species to live in these forests. During fall and winter, deciduous trees shed their leaves. Mammals hibernate for the cold season.

Coniferous forests are biomes found in northern parts of the world. They have only a few kinds of cone-bearing trees. They experience heavy snowfall during the winter. The climate is drier and colder than the other biomes. Trees are the main plants in this land. Large mammals, such as moose, live in these forests.

Tundras are the coldest and driest biomes. They are also the furthest north biome on the earth. No trees grow in tundras because much of the soil is frozen. This permanently frozen soil is called **permafrost.** The vegetation is typically shrubs and small trees. Some animals migrate here during the summer, when water and vegetation become available.

Aquatic Biomes

Aquatic biomes include rivers and lakes. These are examples of **freshwater** biomes, meaning that the water does not contain salt. Aquatic biomes in oceans are called **marine** biomes. The area where an ocean meets land is called an **intertidal zone.** Another biome is formed where freshwater meets saltwater. It is called an **estuary.** Estuaries support a diverse group of organisms. These areas are often subjects of concern because of their unique communities.

All aquatic biomes are divided into three zones based on light exposure. The tops of these aquatic biomes receive the most solar energy. This area is called the **photic zone.** Photosynthesis takes place in the photic zone. The area under this zone does not receive sunlight. It is called the **aphotic zone.** The floor of an aquatic biome is called the **benthic zone.** Each zone has a unique collection of organisms.

Environment: Organic Farming

Organic farming is a unique form of agriculture. Unlike conventional farming, organic farming does not use synthetic (man-made) fertilizers or pesticides. These chemicals can hurt the environment. Instead, organic farmers use natural methods to grow plants and  control insects. They add compost to soil instead of synthetic fertilizer. Compost is decayed organic material. Compost improves the soil and nourishes plants. As a result, the soil produces stronger plants that resist insects and disease.

To control weeds, organic farmers use tilling, mulching (covering the soil surface with organic materials), and hand weeding. To control insect pests, they use traps, stop insect mating, or introduce insect predators. Organic farmers also rotate crops. They switch the kinds of plants grown in a field from year to year. Crop rotation changes the ecology of a field and controls weeds and insects.

Organic products are grown and harvested without artificial chemicals, irradiation, or genetically engineered ingredients. Organic farms and processing facilities are regularly inspected to ensure that foods are grown and processed without artificial ingredients. Organic farms must be separated from nearby conventional farms by buffer zones. This prevents contamination from synthetic fertilizers or pesticides.

1. How does organically grown food differ from conventionally grown food?

2. How do organic farmers control insects?

3. Why might you prefer organic food instead of conventionally grown food?

Lesson 3 REVIEW

Word Bank

coniferous forests

deserts

tropical forests

Link to ➤➤➤

Health

Weather conditions in very populated cities may be affected by smog. *Smog* comes from the words *smoke* and *fog*. Brown colored smog forms when vehicles release nitrogen oxides and hydrocarbon vapors. These gases react with sunlight to produce ozone, a toxic gas. Smog irritates the eyes and can cause respiratory problems.

On a sheet of paper, write the word or words from the Word Bank that complete each sentence correctly.

1. Near the equator, _____ are the main biome.

2. Biomes that have little or no rainfall are _____.

3. Found in the north are biomes known as _____.

Critical Thinking

On a sheet of paper, write the answers to the following questions. Use complete sentences.

4. What key features do desert plants and animals share?

5. Why does differences in sunlight lead to different ecosystems?

▼◄▲▼◄▲▼◄▲▼◄▲▼◄▲▼◄▲▼◄▲▼◄▲▼◄▲▼◄▲▼

Science at Work

Soil Scientist

Soil scientists study the composition of soils. They research the response of soils to fertilizers, crop rotation, and other farming practices. Soil scientists also help farmers and landowners find solutions to soil-related problems.

Many soil scientists work for federal, state, or university research stations. They may conduct soil surveys to classify and map soils in different areas. Soil scientists work with others to ensure environmental quality and effective land use. They may work with researchers who study the growth of plants in natural ecosystems. Soil scientists may work with ecologists to help them better understand how nutrients cycle within an area.

Soil scientists must be patient and observant. They must work well with others in project teams or research groups.

Water: Conserving a Scarce Resource

How much water does your household use every day? The average single-family home in the United States uses 350–400 gallons of water daily. Are you surprised at this amount? More than half of this water is used for watering lawns and gardens. Indoors, toilets are responsible for a fourth of this amount. Think about the water you use for drinking, cooking, showering, and washing dishes and clothes. It all adds up.

Most of us take water for granted. But if you live in an area where rainfall is scarce, you are aware of the need to conserve water. The fastest growing states in the United States are Nevada, Arizona, Colorado, Utah, and Idaho. Many cities in these states have very low rainfall.

As new residents move to these areas, population growth can strain the local water supplies. In many cities, ground water is pumped to the surface from deep within the bedrock. Lakes, springs, and wetlands may dry up if groundwater is removed faster than it is replaced.

Many communities provide rebate programs that pay homeowners who reduce water use. Some cities offer rebates for adding timers to sprinkler systems.

They may also offer rebates for installing toilets, washing machines, and dishwashers that use low amounts of water. Other programs reward people for planting a certain percentage of their yard with desert plants that need little or no extra water. Local laws often do not allow outdoor watering during the hottest times of the day. That is when water evaporates most easily.

The city of Albuquerque in New Mexico has used programs like these to reduce water use. In the last 10 years, this city reduced its overall water use by 27 percent.

1. How can timers on sprinkler systems save water?

2. Suggest three ways that people can reduce indoor water use.

- The sun is the ultimate source of energy for the earth and all of its ecosystems.

- Phototrophs capture sunlight energy and store it as chemical energy. Chemotrophs get energy from the chemicals in food.

- The trophic structure of an ecosystem describes the flow of energy within the ecosystem. An ecosystem has producers, consumers, and decomposers.

- Producers are phototrophs. Consumers and decomposers are chemotrophs.

- Food chains and food webs show the feeding relationships within an ecosystem. Energy pyramids show the flow of energy from one trophic level to the next.

- Nutrients such as carbon, nitrogen, water, and phosphorus move through the living and nonliving parts of an ecosystem. Carbon compounds, nitrogen, and water are found in the atmosphere as gases. Phosphorus is found in soil and water. The carbon cycle, nitrogen cycle, and water cycle move these nutrients within and between ecosystems.

- Ecosystems with the same climate conditions are grouped together to form biomes. Each biome has characteristic plants and animals.

- There are several terrestrial biomes around the world. Aquatic biomes are freshwater or marine. Aquatic biomes are divided into zones based on the amount of light each zone receives.

Vocabulary

ammonium, 575
aphotic zone, 582
aquatic, 568
atmosphere, 573
benthic zone, 582
chaparral, 581
chemotroph, 566
climate, 580
coniferous forest, 582
consumer, 567
decomposer, 567

desert, 581
energy pyramid, 569
estuary, 582
evaporation, 576
food chain, 567
food web, 568
freshwater, 582
geological, 574
intertidal zone, 582
marine, 582
nitrate, 575

nitrifying bacteria, 575
nitrogen-fixer, 575
organic matter, 568
permafrost, 582
phosphorous, 573
photic zone, 582
phototroph, 566
plankton, 568
precipitation, 576
primary productivity, 569

producer, 567
savanna, 581
solar, 566
temperate deciduous forest, 582
temperate grassland, 581
terrestrial, 580
tropical forest, 581
tundra, 582

Word Bank

atmosphere

chemotroph

climate

consumer

decomposer

energy pyramid

estuary

evaporation

food web

freshwater

intertidal zone

marine

nitrogen-fixer

permafrost

phototroph

plankton

precipitation

primary
productivity

producer

terrestrial

Vocabulary Review

On a sheet of paper, write the word or words from the Word Bank that best complete each sentence.

1. An organism that gets its energy by capturing light energy is known as a(n) _____. A(n) _____ is an organism that gets its energy from chemicals in food.

2. All of an ecosystem's food chains can be combined to form a(n) _____.

3. The _____ is the average weather an area experiences over a long period of time.

4. The first trophic level in a food chain is the _____.

5. Permanently frozen soil is _____.

6. In a food chain, an organism called a(n) _____ gets energy by eating other organisms.

7. An organism that breaks down dead organisms is called a(n) _____.

8. Water vapor that becomes concentrated and changes back into liquid as snow or rain is _____.

9. In an aquatic ecosystem, _____ are at the beginning of food chains.

10. Ecologists use a(n) _____ to show the movement of energy through trophic levels.

11. A bacterium that is a(n) _____ can change nitrogen into ammonium.

12. Biomes found on land are called _____ biomes.

13. The air that surrounds the earth is the _____.

14. A(n) _____ is a biome found where freshwater meets saltwater.

Review continued on next page

15. When the sun heats bodies of water, molecules of water escape their liquid form to become water vapor during _____.

16. Aquatic biomes lacking salt are _____ biomes. Oceans contain salt and are examples of _____ biomes.

17. The production of organic matter by phototrophs is _____.

18. The ocean meets the land in the _____.

Concept Review

On a sheet of paper, write the letter of the answer that completes each sentence correctly.

19. A(n) _____ is an example of a phototroph.

    A elephant   **B** tree   **C** hawk   **D** fungus

20. The burning of oil and coal produces _____.

    A nitrogen gas

    B phosphorous

    C water

    D carbon dioxide

21. A very dry terrestrial biome with low rainfall is a _____.

    A chaparral

    B savanna

    C desert

    D temperate grassland

Critical Thinking

On a sheet of paper, write the answers to the following questions. Use complete sentences.

22. Explain the relationships among producers, consumers, and decomposers.

23. What does an energy pyramid represent? Explain why it is shaped like a pyramid.

24. Describe how carbon cycles through an ecosystem.

25. Which biome has the largest number of species? Explain your answer.

Research and Write

Write a report on plant fertilizers. Include information on the three main chemical nutrients found in most plant fertilizers.

Test-Taking Tip If you know you will have to define certain terms on a test, write each term on one side of an index card. Write its definition on the other side. Use the cards to test yourself, or use them with a partner.

19

Human Impact and Technology

In some parts of the United States, fields of wind turbines, or wind farms, produce electricity. Electricity made by wind farms is clean energy. The process releases no pollutants, but it has some drawbacks. Turbines can slightly alter the local climate. Scientists look for ways to obtain resources while protecting the environment. In Chapter 19, you will learn how people affect ecosystems. You will also learn how technology can help us keep the earth's ecosystems healthy and productive.

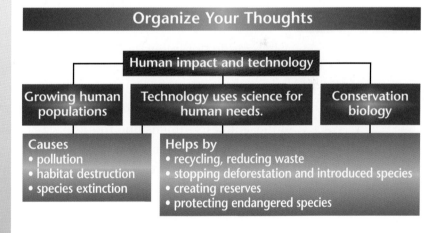

Organize Your Thoughts

Human impact and technology

| Growing human populations | Technology uses science for human needs. | Conservation biology |

Causes
• pollution
• habitat destruction
• species extinction

Helps by
• recycling, reducing waste
• stopping deforestation and introduced species
• creating reserves
• protecting endangered species

Goals for Learning

◆ To recognize that some human activities damage some ecosystems

◆ To discuss how changing human activities can help the environment

◆ To describe conservation efforts to reduce damage

◆ To describe how technology helps people and to understand how science and technology work together

Humans are one species of organisms. Humans coexist with many different species in many different places in the world. Humans affect every ecosystem in the world. This is true even though they are not part of every ecosystem. Like other organisms, humans have basic needs that must be met, such as having food, water, and space. These resources usually limit how large a population of organisms can grow. However, this is not true for humans.

Growth of Human Population

Most populations eventually reach carrying capacity for their ecosystem. Recall from Chapter 17 that the carrying capacity is the largest density an ecosystem can support for a particular population. At carrying capacity, populations are using all of the limited resources that are shared with other populations. Populations usually stay at carrying capacity unless a major disturbance happens.

Humans do not follow this pattern. Scientists do not know the carrying capacity for the human population. Human populations use their knowledge to find ways to expand their carrying capacity. When food runs short, humans find other food sources. Humans find more space or build more in the space they have when space becomes limited. When resources become limited, humans find solutions for their needs.

Today, the world population is more than 6,000,000,000 people. The human population adds about 100 people every minute of the day. More than 70 million people are added to the population every year. The activities of this growing population of humans affect the ecosystems in which they live. Natural resources are limited. To get more resources, humans often harm other organisms in their ecosystems. Humans change ecosystems every day, in many different ways.

Impact of Trash

Humans damage many ecosystems by destroying habitats. Remember that a habitat is an area where an organism naturally lives. Many habitats make up an ecosystem. Many factors cause habitats to be destroyed. As humans go through their daily lives, they produce a large amount of trash and waste. These waste products are often disposed of in certain areas that were once habitats. Humans do not use some of these areas. Instead, they litter the land and water around them. This trash can harm or kill other organisms.

Science at Work

Park Ranger

Every day is different for a park ranger. A ranger may work for a local, state, or national park system. The tasks of a park ranger can include supervising or performing conservation work and protecting forests. Park rangers may also watch for and fight fires. Rangers may work with the public by demonstrating outdoor skills, preparing exhibits, and promoting safety and conservation. They may lead nature walks, enforce laws, and operate campgrounds.

Park rangers must be able to work independently. A love of nature is important for this job because much of the work is outdoors. Rangers must be able to think clearly in emergencies. They may rescue lost hikers and mountain climbers or provide first aid.

Most park ranger jobs require a bachelor's degree in park and recreation management or a natural science, plus on-the-job training. Other positions allow people with work experience or a combination of work experience and college courses to qualify for jobs. Completion of police academy or peace officer training could be helpful, because some park rangers are also peace officers.

Impact of Pollution

Pollution also destroys habitats. Pollution is anything added to the environment that is harmful to living things. Factories, cars, trucks, boats, and many other machines that burn fuels give off chemicals as waste. These chemicals move into the air, land, or water. There they can build up to levels poisonous to many organisms.

Chemical runoff is liquid chemical waste from factories and other sources that enter into water sources. Chemical runoff usually contains high concentrations of nitrogen compounds. These chemicals cause fast growth of algae. Remember from Chapter 15 that algae are water plants. The algae soon take over and force other organisms out of that ecosystem. This process is called **eutrophication.**

Waste gases enter the atmosphere and cause pollution in many ways. Sulfur dioxide dissolves in water vapor in the air. The water vapor falls to land as rain, carrying those chemicals with it. This polluted rain is called **acid rain.** It can damage ecosystems and poison many organisms, especially plants.

Machines that burn fuels give off carbon dioxide gas. This is the same gas humans breathe out. Plants remove carbon dioxide from the atmosphere during photosynthesis.

However, humans and industry are giving off carbon dioxide faster than plants can use it. The extra carbon dioxide traps solar energy in the atmosphere. As this energy gets trapped, it causes the temperature to rise around the world. This warming of the atmosphere is called the **greenhouse effect.**

Link to >>>

Earth Science

The greenhouse effect is a natural process that warms the earth. Radiant energy from the sun is absorbed by the earth's surface. The warmed surface gives off heat. Most of the heat radiates back into space. Some is trapped in the earth's atmosphere by gases such as carbon dioxide. This trapped heat maintains the earth's temperature and makes life on the earth possible.

The earth is also being harmed by another gas, **ozone.** Ozone is a form of oxygen. Look at Figure 19.1.1. Ozone makes up a tiny but important part of the atmosphere. A thin layer of ozone high in the atmosphere absorbs ultraviolet radiation from the sun. The ozone layer prevents most of the ultraviolet radiation from reaching the earth. Ultraviolet radiation can cause sunburn and skin cancer.

Humans have damaged this protective ozone layer. For example, certain gases released from spray cans drift high into the atmosphere and break down ozone. Holes have appeared in the ozone layer over Antarctica.

Ozone is also an ingredient in smog. This hazy mixture of gases damages the lungs and can worsen heart disease. Ozone collects at ground level because vehicle exhaust releases ozone. Factories make and use ozone for cleaning flour, oil, fabrics, and water.

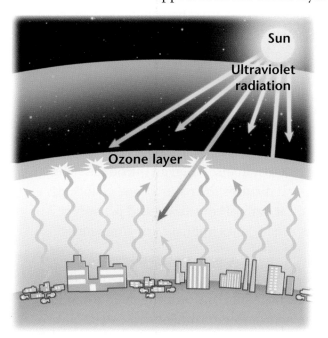

Figure 19.1.1 *The ozone layer prevents most ultraviolet radiation from reaching the earth.*

Impact of Land Development

The growing human population must have space and food. These needs drive **land development.** Land development is when humans change natural land to land used for farming or living space. This change disrupts and sometimes destroys ecosystems.

Deforestation

The removal of forest ecosystems for land development

Introduced species

A species taken from its natural ecosystem and placed in another ecosystem

For example, **deforestation** clears out forested areas to make room for buildings or farmland. Land development in deforested areas can greatly harm the natural ecosystem. New buildings may give off waste and pollute the environment. Humans removed most or all of the trees and plants in the area. Fewer trees and plants are available to remove carbon dioxide from the atmosphere. Farmers may overwork the land and remove important nutrients from the soil. Topsoil may be lost because of construction or bad farming practices.

To make room for humans, natural ecosystems and their many different organisms are removed. The original organisms may not have other ecosystems to go to. They often die. Species then become extinct. Remember that extinction is when all the members of a species are dead. Almost 100 species become extinct every day around the world.

Impact of Introduced Species

Extinction is caused by another damaging human activity, **introduced species.** Introduced species are species that are introduced into new ecosystems. When an introduced species enters an ecosystem, it disturbs the natural food chains. Its members hunt and eat natural consumers and producers. An introduced species usually does not have any competition.

Because of this, the introduced species can take over an ecosystem. It may eventually destroy the ecosystem. Introduced species usually come from humans carrying them from their natural environments. Many governments have strict laws to stop the spread of introduced species.

An example of an introduced species is kudzu, a vine. It grows quickly, up a to foot a day. Kudzu was introduced into the United States from Japan in 1876. Farmers in the South planted kudzu to reduce the loss of topsoil. In 1972, the United States Department of Agriculture declared kudzu a weed.

Link to >>>

Health

Smog is a type of air pollution found mostly in cities. The exhaust from vehicles and factories react chemically in sunlight to form ozone. Because ozone is a pollutant, breathing smoggy air can harm people. It can damage the lungs and cause lung diseases such as emphysema and bronchitis. Smog can also make it harder for people to resist lung infections.

Today, kudzu is common throughout much of the southeastern United States and some northern states. Kudzu can destroy valuable forests by preventing trees from getting sunlight. Scientists are developing chemicals to stop its growth.

Summing Up

The human population continues to grow. This growth is taking resources away from other species and ecosystems. However, not all human activities hurt the environment. By understanding ecology and the environment, humans are also performing activities to help ecosystems. You will learn more about these activities in Lesson 2.

Express Lab 19

Materials

◆ rainwater sample
◆ small jar with lid
◆ forceps
◆ 2 pieces of pH paper
◆ 2 eyedroppers
◆ pH chart
◆ distilled water

Procedure

1. In a small jar, collect a small sample of rainwater from a clean puddle or directly from the air. Put the lid on the jar and bring it to class.

2. Put on safety goggles and a lab coat or apron.

3. Use the forceps to pick up a piece of pH paper. Use an eyedropper to put a drop of distilled water onto the pH paper.

4. Compare the color of the wet pH paper to the pH chart. Record your observations.

5. Using a new eyedropper, repeat Steps 3 and 4 with a drop of rainwater.

6. When you are finished, wash your hands well.

Analysis

1. What is the pH of distilled water?

2. What is the pH of the rainwater? Is this acid rain?

Word Bank

eutrophication

greenhouse effect

chemical runoff

On a sheet of paper, write the word or words from the Word Bank that complete each sentence correctly.

1. The warming of the atmosphere caused by trapped solar energy is the _____.

2. A process in which algae growth chokes out other water ecosystems is _____.

3. The chemical waste produced on land that enters water sources is _____.

Critical Thinking

On a sheet of paper, write the answers to the following questions. Use complete sentences.

4. How do waste gases enter the atmosphere and cause problems?

5. Human populations do not have a carrying capacity for their ecosystems. Explain why.

★ ✦ ★

Achievements in Science

Bringing Back the Whooping Crane

About 1,500 whooping cranes once lived in the North American wetlands. As people drained the wetlands, the number of these great white birds decreased. By the 1940s, the worldwide population was only 14. Members of other crane species were also decreasing. Thanks to a unique conservation effort, there are 320 whooping cranes in the world today.

In 1973, two graduate students, George Archibald and Ron Sauey, realized cranes were nearly extinct. They founded the International Crane Foundation near Baraboo, Wisconsin. There they developed methods to breed and raise the 15 crane species.

Whooping cranes are bred at the International Crane Foundation. When the chicks hatch, they first see puppets that look like cranes. The chicks are raised by volunteers who wear crane costumes. This is done so the chicks form social attachments to other cranes. This is important for releasing them into the wild.

Materials

- safety goggles
- lab coat or apron
- 2 microscope slides
- 2 petri dishes
- marker
- petroleum jelly
- 2 petri dish lids
- microscope

Measuring Particulates in the Air

Particulates are a form of air pollution. They are tiny particles suspended in the air you breathe. Particulates come from fires, tobacco smoke, vehicle exhaust, plants, and animals. In this investigation, you will collect two air samples and count the particulates in each sample. Where do you think you will find the most particulates?

Procedure

1. Put on safety goggles and a lab coat or apron.

2. Make a data table like the one shown below.

3. Get two microscope slides and two petri dishes with lids. Using a marker, label a corner of one slide A. Label a corner of the other slide B. **Safety Alert: Handle glass microscope slides with care. Dispose of broken glass properly.**

4. Choose two locations to test for particulates. Using a marker, label the bottom of a petri dish A. Write its location. Label the bottom of the other petri dish B. Write its location.

	Slide A	Slide B
Location		
Number of particulates—first field of view		
Second field of view		
Third field of view		
Fourth field of view		
Fifth field of view		
Total number of particulates		

5. Use petroleum jelly to lightly coat the unlabeled side of each slide. Put the slide, with the petroleum jelly side up, in the petri dish with the same letter. Wash your hands well.

6. Put the uncovered petri dishes containing the slides in the chosen locations. Do not disturb them for 24 hours.

7. Cover the petri dishes with the lids.

8. Use a microscope to observe slide A. Use low power and then high power. Count the number of particulates in each of 5 different high-power fields of view. Record your data. Find the total number of particulates counted for slide A.

9. Repeat Step 8 for slide B.

Cleanup/Disposal

When you are finished, wash the slides and petri dishes thoroughly with detergent and warm water. Wash your hands well.

Analysis

1. What is the purpose of the petroleum jelly?

2. Make a graph comparing the total number of particulates counted from your two locations. What kind of graph would best compare your data?

Conclusions

1. Which location had the largest number of particulates?

2. Where do you think the particulates in your locations came from?

3. Write a new question about particulates that you could explore in another investigation.

Explore Further

If you know someone who smokes, repeat the investigation by placing a slide in his or her home. Place a slide in the home of a nonsmoker for comparison.

After reading this lesson, you should be able to

◆ define conservation biology

◆ describe how people are reducing air and water pollution

◆ discuss how people are protecting threatened and endangered habitats

Conservation biology

The science of using ecological information to help reduce damage to the environment

Landfill

An area where trash is collected and stored

As you learned in Lesson 1, humans can cause major problems in ecosystems. The human population is threatening the lives of many organisms.

People Helping the Environment

Today, many people work to help threatened organisms. Recall that a threatened species is a species that has many fewer members today than in the past. Many people are trying to correct or limit factors that harm these species.

Some people belong to organizations that fight pollution and ecological damage. Government agencies also help by passing laws to reduce pollution and habitat destruction. Government agencies and environmental organizations rely on scientific knowledge to make their decisions.

This knowledge comes from a branch of biology called **conservation biology.** Conservation biology uses ecological information to understand how to rescue and restore damaged ecosystems. Conservation efforts are targeted in several areas. These include controlling pollution, limiting habitat destruction, and protecting species.

Controlling Pollution

Efforts to control pollution are aimed at reducing the amount of waste people produce. People produce large amounts of trash that must be placed somewhere. Local governments usually collect trash in areas called **landfills.** However, landfills are becoming full.

In modern landfills, garbage is deposited in shallow layers, then covered with six inches of soil. This process is carried out every day. This seals in the garbage and prevents the spread of insects, mice, rats, and other rodents. Rodents carry diseases.

Trash is often made of substances that do not naturally break down quickly. To reduce trash in landfills, people are **recycling.** Recycling is a process of using certain kinds of trash to make new products. Most trash made of paper, plastic, or metal can be recycled. Many local governments have public recycling programs. Does your community have a recycling program? If not, maybe you could help start one.

Another source of pollution is chemical waste. Chemical waste has many forms, including chemical runoff and smoke from factories. Vehicles give off carbon monoxide and carbon dioxide. Carbon monoxide is poisonous. Both waste gases contribute to the greenhouse effect. Waste gases released in the environment are called **emissions.** Many countries have laws that limit the amounts of emissions and chemical runoff that factories can produce. Companies that break the laws pay fines. They also must fix the problem quickly.

Many governments have emissions standards for vehicles. If a vehicle does not meet these standards, the vehicle cannot be driven. The owner must fix the vehicle before driving it.

Limiting Habitat Destruction

Efforts to reduce pollution also help reduce habitat destruction. Deforestation makes more space for people. It also provides materials for making paper. By recycling paper products, companies can make more paper products without cutting down trees. You can help by buying paper products that are made of recycled paper.

Organisms in water ecosystems threatened by chemical runoff and litter must move to clean water. These areas also supply clean water for people. Reducing the amount of water people use helps these ecosystems survive. You can help by not wasting water. Turn the faucet off while you brush your teeth. Use water only when you need it. Do not throw trash on the ground or in a stream. Use a trash can. Recycle trash.

Reserve

A protected area that cannot be used for building or growth

Landscape ecology

Using ecological information to help balance human and environmental needs

Research and Write

Use both Internet and print resources to research and write a report about how paper is made. Trace the path from a tree to a sheet of paper. If you wish, make a poster showing the process. Label each step on your poster.

Creating Reserves

Ecosystems in danger get help in other ways. Governments create natural areas called **reserves.** These areas are left in their natural state. Their ecosystems are not disturbed. Many reserves have unique species. Companies and people are not allowed to use these areas for building or growth. Many of these areas are used as parks. Parks allow people to see plants and animals in their natural environments.

Most local governments require that builders be mindful of local ecosystems. Many governments do not allow companies to build in an area if it threatens a natural ecosystem. Builders often rely on **landscape ecology** to help them balance their needs with an ecosystem's needs.

Landscape ecology uses scientific knowledge to help develop land and design buildings without damaging natural ecosystems. This knowledge is also used to change existing buildings so they have less impact on their surroundings. Landscape ecology can also be used to identify and create more reserves.

Protecting Threatened Species

Protecting unique ecosystems helps protect the species that live in them. However, some threatened species do not live in protected areas. These organisms are being threatened in several ways. People hunt some species to use their skins for clothes or their bones for jewelry. Other threatened species are hunted for food, like many fish species. However, they are being hunted too much. As a result, populations cannot reproduce fast enough.

Governments help by creating hunting seasons. These seasons are the only times when certain animals can be hunted or fished. People who hunt out of season may pay fines. They may also go to jail.

Protecting Endangered Species

Some populations of species become so small that they are considered endangered. Endangered species have only a small number of individuals. These species are nearly extinct. Many governments have laws that do not allow anyone to harm these species.

The United Nations has created a list of endangered species. The United Nations is a world government body with representatives from many countries. Most countries have laws that protect the species on this list. People who break these laws are fined and may be put into jail.

Areas where endangered species live are often turned into reserves. Conservation biologists help the population of these species grow. Ecologists study the factors causing the greatest harm to these species. They also identify what these species need to better survive. Using this information, **recovery plans** are designed to restore endangered species and prevent extinction.

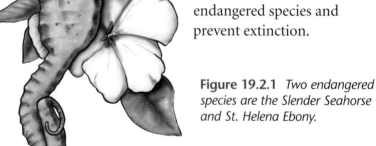

Figure 19.2.1 *Two endangered species are the Slender Seahorse and St. Helena Ebony.*

Protecting Biodiversity

Conservation biology's main goal is to help protect the **biodiversity** threatened by human growth. Biodiversity is all the different types and systems of life that exist, from organisms to ecosystems. People can protect the earth's biodiversity by changing or stopping destructive activities. People can use scientific knowledge to help improve their lives and the environment.

Biology in Your Life

Technology: Municipal Water Treatment

The water that comes out of your kitchen or bathroom faucet is from rivers, lakes, or reservoirs. A reservoir is a place where water is collected and stored for use. Many water sources have been exposed to pollutants. How is water made safe for drinking and cooking?

Municipal (city) water treatment plants purify the water supply to make it safe for human use. Water treatment often occurs in five steps: coarse filtration, sedimentation, sand filtration, aeration, and sterilization. First, water passes through a screen that removes large pieces of solids. This is coarse filtration. The water then flows into a settling tank. Medium-sized particles settle out. This step is sedimentation. Chemicals are added to cause the smallest particles to clump together and settle out. After settling, the water passes through a sand filter. This step, called sand filtration, removes any remaining particles.

The filtered water is then sprayed into the air. This is aeration. During this step, oxygen from the air is added to the water. Oxygen combines with certain pollutants and changes them into harmless substances. Finally, chlorine is added to the water for sterilization. Chlorine kills disease-causing bacteria. The water is now safe to use.

1. Why are chemicals needed to remove the smallest particles?

2. If water looks clean after filtration, why are aeration and sterilization needed?

3. Treatment processes can vary. What are the processes used for your household water?

Lesson 2 REVIEW

Word Bank

biodiversity

conservation
 biology

recovery plan

On a sheet of paper, write the word or words from the Word Bank that complete each sentence correctly.

1. All the types of life that exist is _____.

2. The science that uses ecological information to reduce damage to the environment is _____.

3. A _____ is designed to bring species back from possible extinction.

On a sheet of paper, write the word in Column B that best matches the phrase in Column A.

Column A

4. waste gases

5. where trash is collected

6. reduces the amount of trash

Column B

emissions

landfill

recycling

Critical Thinking

On a sheet of paper, write the answers to the following questions. Use complete sentences.

7. Why are landfills becoming full?

8. How can the amount of trash in landfills be reduced?

9. Describe two ways governments are protecting species.

10. Describe three ways people can protect water, land, or species.

After reading this lesson, you should be able to

◆ define technology

◆ discuss how technology supports science, and vice versa

◆ compare the goals of science and technology

◆ give examples of science and technology

Geology

The study of the nonliving parts of the earth

Biogeology

The study of the interaction between living and nonliving parts of the environment

Engineering

The use of math and science to create methods and machines to help solve problems or make life better

Engineer

A person who works in engineering

Scientists try to understand the world. They want to make it a better place to live for humans and other organisms. To do this, scientists use historical and current information about the world. This information is based on scientific evidence gathered by conducting investigations. Scientific knowledge influences the design and understanding of investigations.

Science is made up of many different areas, including biology, **geology,** chemistry, ecology, genetics, and more. These different areas focus on different pieces of the world. For example, biology focuses on the living parts of the earth. Geology focuses on the nonliving parts of the earth. To understand the world better, scientists from these different areas bring their information together. As they combine their knowledge sometimes new areas of science are created, like **biogeology.** Biogeology is the study of the interaction between living and nonliving parts of the environment.

Engineering and Technology

An important area of science that uses knowledge from many other areas is **engineering.** Engineering is the use of math and science to create methods and machines to help solve problems or make life better. **Engineers** are people who work in engineering. Engineers use the resources of matter and energy to design solutions to problems.

The products of engineering designs are called **technology.** Technology is any device, machine, or method designed to solve a problem or improve a situation. People use technology constantly in their daily lives. You may have used technology to get to school. Did you use a bus, bicycle, car, or other vehicle? You probably use telephone technology. You use both computer and Internet technology to browse the Internet.

Technology helps people live. Doctors use special machines and methods to help people who are sick. **Medical technology** is designed to solve medical problems.

Engineers do performance testing on new technology. Performance testing determines how well or, how fast a system process, or product performs. Performance testing is often done to help reduce the chance of a system failure. For example, software engineers performance test the system design of new software. To test performance, engineers sometimes use models, computer simulations, or similar systems.

To solve a problem, someone has to understand the problem. Medical knowledge helps doctors and engineers understand the causes of medical problems. Once the causes are known, engineers can design technology to stop or limit the causes. Designing new medical technology often results in the discovery of new scientific knowledge.

The Relationship Between Science and Technology

The relationship between science and technology is important. They rely on and influence each other. One could not exist by itself. As scientists try to understand life better, they become limited by the tools they can use to explore it. When scientists cannot explore further with these tools, engineers then design new technology. This new technology drives more scientific exploration. This leads to new scientific discoveries. Sometimes, these discoveries open new fields of science and technology.

As science and technology develop, they follow some of the same steps. Recall from Chapter 1 that the scientific method begins by observation and questioning. Technology development uses the same steps. Engineers observe current technology. They also observe people's problems, needs, and desires. Then they ask how a new technology might solve a problem or meet a need or desire. Scientists design and create experiments to answer questions. Engineers imagine and design new technology to help answer these questions. Both scientists and engineers rely on success that can be repeated with experiments or inventions. Scientists and engineers must be creative and work from a good knowledge base.

Technology and Society

Many hospital operating rooms have surgical robots. They cannot operate without human guidance. However, robots offer many advantages. Surgeons located far away from their patients can perform surgery by remote control. Robotic surgery is precise. A robotic arm can make smaller cuts than those made by surgeons. Smaller cuts means a patient recovers faster, with less pain.

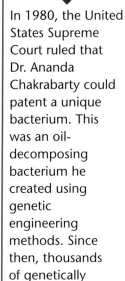

In 1980, the United States Supreme Court ruled that Dr. Ananda Chakrabarty could patent a unique bacterium. This was an oil-decomposing bacterium he created using genetic engineering methods. Since then, thousands of genetically modified organisms have been patented.

The Goals of Technology and Science

Although science and technology work together, the goals of each are different. The main goal of engineers designing technology is to make people's lives better, solve their problems, and meet their needs and desires. Since people are the focus, people are often affected more directly by technology than science.

People usually accept new technology since it benefits them. Some technology is only necessary because people desire it, such as improved televisions. Sometimes technology is not free to the public. Businesses use technology to make money. Many businesses get **patents** for new technologies they develop. A patent is a government notice of ownership for a piece of technology.

The main goal of scientists is to understand the natural world. People are not always the focus of scientific questions. They are not always affected by scientific discovery. People do not always accept new scientific information.

Scientific information is usually shared freely with the public. Scientists publish their findings in magazines called **scientific journals.** They hold meetings to tell other people about their findings. Funds for science research come from federal government agencies, industry, and private foundations. These funds often influence the areas of scientific research and discovery.

Science and Technology Working Together

Sometimes technology can be harmful to the environment while helping people. For example, factories make products and pollution. Ecologists are beginning to understand the damage that technology causes. Engineers use this scientific knowledge to design better technology. These activities have created factories and machines that produce less waste and less pollution.

In this way, science and technology work together in a cycle. Solving technical problems often results in new scientific knowledge. New technologies often extend current scientific understanding and open new research areas.

Lesson 3   R E V I E W

Link to ➤➤➤

Social Studies

Some people think a patent gives its owner the right to use, make, or sell an invention. This is not true. A patent only excludes other people from using, making, or selling the invention. To patent an invention, it must be useful. It also must be something that no one has created before.

On a sheet of paper, write the word that completes each sentence correctly.

1. Inventors protect their ownership of a technology by getting a(n) _____.

2. An area of science that creates methods and machines to solve problems is _____.

3. A machine or method designed to solve a human problem is _____.

On a sheet of paper, write the letter of the answer that completes each sentence correctly.

4. All of the following are examples of technology except _____.

   A bicycles   **C** rocks

   B the Internet   **D** computers

5. The goal of _____ is to understand the natural world.

   A science   **C** engineering

   B technology   **D** engineers

6. Any device, machine, or method designed to help a situation is _____.

   A science   **C** a patent

   B technology   **D** a factory

Critical Thinking

On a sheet of paper, write the answers to the following questions. Use complete sentences.

7. Give an example of technology that is harmful.

8. How are science and technology related?

9. What is medical technology?

10. How are the main goals of science and technology alike? How are they different?

Materials

- ◆ 2 small aluminum pans, each with 6 holes punched in one end
- ◆ garden soil
- ◆ large aluminum pan
- ◆ turf to fit in a small aluminum pan
- ◆ watering can
- ◆ graduated cylinder or metric measuring cup
- ◆ water
- ◆ 2 or 3 books or wooden boards to raise end of pan

Conservation of Soil

One of the most important natural resources is soil. Soil provides nutrients to plants. Plants are the base of almost all food chains on the earth. In this investigation, you will compare the effect of running water on the soil of a bare slope and on a slope planted with grass. What causes soil erosion? What happens to a bare slope and a grassy slope during a rainstorm? How can soil be conserved? You will investigate these questions.

Procedure

1. Discuss the questions in the first paragraph with your group. Write a hypothesis to answer this question: How does planting a slope with grass affect the amount of soil erosion caused by a rainstorm? The hypothesis should be one you can test.

2. Design an experiment to test your hypothesis. Make a table for the data you will collect. **Safety Alert: Be sure to include any Safety Alerts such as protecting your clothing and not touching your mouth or eyes with your hands.**

3. Have your hypothesis, Safety Alerts, experimental design, and data table approved by your teacher.

4. Carry out your experiment.

Cleanup/Disposal

When you are finished, clean up your materials and wash your hands with warm, soapy water.

Analysis

1. How much water ran off the bare slope? What did the water look like?

2. How much water ran off the slope with turf? What did the water look like?

Conclusions

1. Was your hypothesis supported by the results of your experiment?

2. How does this experiment model soil erosion?

3. How could a farmer practice soil conservation?

Explore Further

Design an experiment to determine how the steepness of a slope affects erosion. Carry out the experiment. Record your results.

Restoring the Prairies

Prairies once covered most of the North American Midwest. Tall grasses and beautiful wildflowers grew on the flat and gently rolling land. Not many trees grew in this area. Prairies were once home to huge numbers of bison, prairie dogs, deer, and wolves. As settlers came to this area after the Civil War, they plowed the prairie for farmland. The grasses and wildflowers began to disappear. Cities grew where animals once roamed.

Today, only one percent of the prairie exists. Many species of prairie animals are endangered or extinct.

Natural fires once played an important role in prairie life. Fires caused by lightning burned the grasses and prevented trees from taking over. Although fire destroyed the upper parts of the grasses, it did not harm their roots. The ashes added nutrients to the soil. New grasses soon sprouted. However, the settlers put out natural fires to protect their homes. As a result, trees took over parts of the prairies.

Today, people are beginning to appreciate the value of prairie ecosystems. Many former prairie areas in the United States and Canada are being restored. To do this, workers cut down trees. Then they plant the seeds of native prairie plants. To keep the restored prairies healthy, controlled fires are set every few years. The fires kill trees and nonnative plants growing in the prairie. Without fire, dead plant material piles up and gradually chokes out new growth. Prairie plants need sunlight to grow. Shade from trees stops their growth.

Americans probably will never again see the "sea of grass" that the pioneers saw. However, people are preserving and restoring small prairie areas and their unique plants and animals.

1. Why did prairie plants disappear?

2. Why do you think prairie animals disappeared?

3. Why must restored prairies be set on fire? How often are the fires set?

Chapter 19 SUMMARY

- Like all organisms, humans have basic needs. The carrying capacity of human populations is unknown. The human population is growing rapidly.

- Expanding human populations harm ecosystems. They destroy the habitats of other organisms and pollute the environment.

- Chemical runoff is liquid pollution that damages ecosystems. It can result in eutrophication.

- Air pollution by waste gases causes acid rain. Buildup of carbon dioxide from emissions causes global warming. Pollution harms the ozone layer.

- Deforestation results when a forest is cut down. This results in habitat loss.

- Species may become threatened, endangered, or extinct if their habitats are destroyed and they cannot move away. Introduced species disrupt food chains and threaten native species.

- Conservation efforts to reduce pollution include recycling and preventing chemical runoff and emissions from cars and factories.

- Conservation efforts such as creating reserves limit habitat destruction and protect species. Recovery plans restore endangered species.

- Conservation biology protects biodiversity. People can help by changing some destructive activities.

- Engineers use math and science to create methods that solve problems or make life better.

- Patents provide ownership of technology. Some technologies create pollution. Solving technical problems often results in new scientific knowledge. New technologies open new areas of scientific research.

Vocabulary

acid rain, 594
biodiversity, 604
biogeology, 607
chemical runoff, 594
conservation biology, 601
deforestation, 596

emission, 602
engineer, 607
engineering, 607
eutrophication, 594
geology, 607
greenhouse effect, 594
introduced species, 596

land development, 595
landfill, 601
landscape ecology, 603
medical technology, 608
ozone, 595
patent, 609
pollution, 594

recovery plan, 604
recycling, 602
reserve, 603
scientific journal, 609
technology, 608

Word Bank

acid rain

biodiversity

chemical runoff

conservation
  biology

deforestation

emission

engineering

greenhouse effect

landfill

landscape ecology

medical
  technology

ozone

patent

recovery plan

recycling

reserve

technology

Vocabulary Review

On a sheet of paper, write the word or words from the Word Bank that complete each sentence correctly.

1. The warming of the earth by trapped solar energy is the _____.

2. Most trash is collected and stored in a(n) _____.

3. The science that uses ecological information to prevent or reduce damage to the environment is _____.

4. Water sources can be polluted by _____ that contains nitrogen compounds.

5. The process of cutting down trees to make room for buildings and farms is _____.

6. The _____ of plastics and paper can slow the growth of landfills.

7. A thin layer of _____ prevents most ultraviolet radiation from reaching the earth.

8. Precipitation that is polluted is known as _____.

9. Human activity is not allowed in a(n) _____ to protect the land and the organisms in it.

10. Any technology designed to help human medical problems is _____.

11. A waste gas produced by cars and factories is a(n) _____.

12. A government notice of ownership for a piece of technology is a(n) _____.

13. The total of all the living things on the earth is _____.

14. When people talk on a telephone or ride in a car, they are using _____.

Review continued on next page

15. The use of math and science to create methods and machines to solve problems or make life better is _____.

16. A builder may use _____ to balance people's needs with the needs of the environment.

17. An idea that uses scientific knowledge to bring species back from possible extinction is a(n) _____.

Concept Review

On a sheet of paper, write the letter of the answer that completes each sentence correctly.

18. Conservation practices include _____.

    A reducing pollution

    B limiting habitat destruction

    C protecting species

    D all of the above

19. Science often advances when _____ design new technology.

    A eutrophication   **C** engineers

    B introduced species   **D** scientists

20. All of the following are good conservation practices except _____.

    A turning off the water when brushing your teeth

    B recycling glass jars and bottles

    C buying products with a lot of packaging

    D walking short distances instead of riding in a vehicle

21. Many governments have _____ standards for vehicles.

   A reserve   **C** science

   B emissions   **D** habitat

22. Eutrophication occurs in a pond when rapidly growing algae _____.

   A use up all the water in the pond

   B force other organisms out of the pond

   C use up all the nutrients in the pond

   D all of the above

Critical Thinking

On a sheet of paper, write the answers to the following questions. Use complete sentences.

23. A scientist wants to study the structures of organelles in a cell. How can technology help the scientist?

24. Explain how introducing a new kind of fish into a lake might damage the lake's ecosystem.

25. How does the United Nations protect endangered species?

Research and Write

People do not agree on whether to reintroduce wolves into the environment. Research both sides of this issue. Organize your information. Choose one side of the argument. Pair up with classmates who have chosen the other side. Conduct a debate for the rest of the class.

Test-Taking Tip When choosing answers from a Word Bank, complete the items you know first. Then study the remaining answers to complete the items you are not sure about.

Appendix A: The Periodic Table of Elements

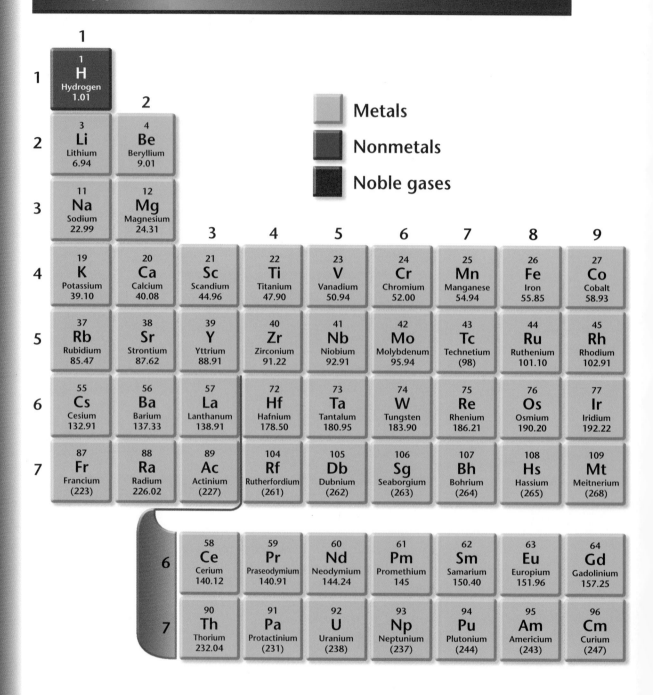

Metals
Nonmetals
Noble gases

1								
1 **H** Hydrogen 1.01	**2**							
3 **Li** Lithium 6.94	**4** **Be** Beryllium 9.01							
11 **Na** Sodium 22.99	**12** **Mg** Magnesium 24.31	**3**	**4**	**5**	**6**	**7**	**8**	**9**
19 **K** Potassium 39.10	**20** **Ca** Calcium 40.08	**21** **Sc** Scandium 44.96	**22** **Ti** Titanium 47.90	**23** **V** Vanadium 50.94	**24** **Cr** Chromium 52.00	**25** **Mn** Manganese 54.94	**26** **Fe** Iron 55.85	**27** **Co** Cobalt 58.93
37 **Rb** Rubidium 85.47	**38** **Sr** Strontium 87.62	**39** **Y** Yttrium 88.91	**40** **Zr** Zirconium 91.22	**41** **Nb** Niobium 92.91	**42** **Mo** Molybdenum 95.94	**43** **Tc** Technetium (98)	**44** **Ru** Ruthenium 101.10	**45** **Rh** Rhodium 102.91
55 **Cs** Cesium 132.91	**56** **Ba** Barium 137.33	**57** **La** Lanthanum 138.91	**72** **Hf** Hafnium 178.50	**73** **Ta** Tantalum 180.95	**74** **W** Tungsten 183.90	**75** **Re** Rhenium 186.21	**76** **Os** Osmium 190.20	**77** **Ir** Iridium 192.22
87 **Fr** Francium (223)	**88** **Ra** Radium 226.02	**89** **Ac** Actinium (227)	**104** **Rf** Rutherfordium (261)	**105** **Db** Dubnium (262)	**106** **Sg** Seaborgium (263)	**107** **Bh** Bohrium (264)	**108** **Hs** Hassium (265)	**109** **Mt** Meitnerium (268)

6	**58** **Ce** Cerium 140.12	**59** **Pr** Praseodymium 140.91	**60** **Nd** Neodymium 144.24	**61** **Pm** Promethium 145	**62** **Sm** Samarium 150.40	**63** **Eu** Europium 151.96	**64** **Gd** Gadolinium 157.25
7	**90** **Th** Thorium 232.04	**91** **Pa** Protactinium (231)	**92** **U** Uranium (238)	**93** **Np** Neptunium (237)	**94** **Pu** Plutonium (244)	**95** **Am** Americium (243)	**96** **Cm** Curium (247)

18
2 **He** Helium 4.00

13	14	15	16	17
5 **B** Boron 10.81	6 **C** Carbon 12.01	7 **N** Nitrogen 14.01	8 **O** Oxygen 16.00	9 **F** Fluorine 19.00	10 **Ne** Neon 20.18
13 **Al** Aluminum 26.98	14 **Si** Silicon 28.09	15 **P** Phosphorus 30.97	16 **S** Sulfur 32.07	17 **Cl** Chlorine 35.45	18 **Ar** Argon 39.95

10	11	12						
28 **Ni** Nickel 58.70	29 **Cu** Copper 63.55	30 **Zn** Zinc 65.39	31 **Ga** Gallium 69.72	32 **Ge** Germanium 72.59	33 **As** Arsenic 74.92	34 **Se** Selenium 78.96	35 **Br** Bromine 79.90	36 **Kr** Krypton 83.80
46 **Pd** Palladium 106.42	47 **Ag** Silver 107.90	48 **Cd** Cadmium 112.41	49 **In** Indium 114.82	50 **Sn** Tin 118.69	51 **Sb** Antimony 121.75	52 **Te** Tellurium 127.60	53 **I** Iodine 126.90	54 **Xe** Xenon 131.30
78 **Pt** Platinum 195.09	79 **Au** Gold 196.97	80 **Hg** Mercury 200.59	81 **Tl** Thallium 204.40	82 **Pb** Lead 207.20	83 **Bi** Bismuth 208.98	84 **Po** Polonium 209	85 **At** Astatine (210)	86 **Rn** Radon (222)
110 **Uun** Unununilium (269)	111 **Uuu** Unununium (272)	112 **Uub** Ununbium (277)		114 **Uuq** Ununquadium (289)		116 **Uuh** Ununhexium (289)		

65 **Tb** Terbium 158.93	66 **Dy** Dysprosium 162.50	67 **Ho** Holmium 164.93	68 **Er** Erbium 167.26	69 **Tm** Thulium 168.93	70 **Yb** Ytterbium 173.04	71 **Lu** Lutetium 174.97
97 **Bk** Berkelium (247)	98 **Cf** Californium (249)	99 **Es** Einsteinium (254)	100 **Fm** Fermium (257)	101 **Md** Mendelevium (258)	102 **No** Nobelium (259)	103 **Lr** Lawrencium (260)

Note: *The atomic masses listed in the table reflect current measurements.*
The atomic masses listed in parentheses are those of the element's most stable or most common isotope.

Appendix B: Body Systems

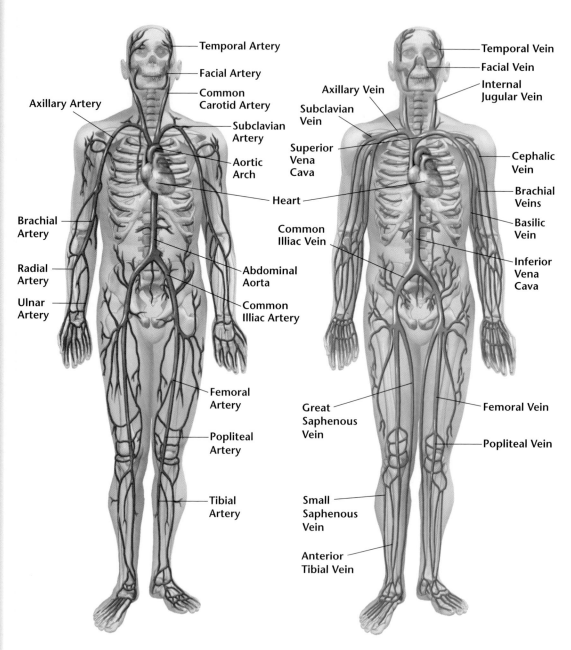

Temporal Artery

Facial Artery

Common Carotid Artery

Axillary Artery

Subclavian Artery

Aortic Arch

Brachial Artery

Radial Artery

Ulnar Artery

Femoral Artery

Popliteal Artery

Tibial Artery

Temporal Vein

Facial Vein

Internal Jugular Vein

Axillary Vein

Subclavian Vein

Superior Vena Cava

Cephalic Vein

Brachial Veins

Basilic Vein

Heart

Common Illiac Vein

Abdominal Aorta

Common Illiac Artery

Inferior Vena Cava

Great Saphenous Vein

Femoral Vein

Popliteal Vein

Small Saphenous Vein

Anterior Tibial Vein

The Circulatory System

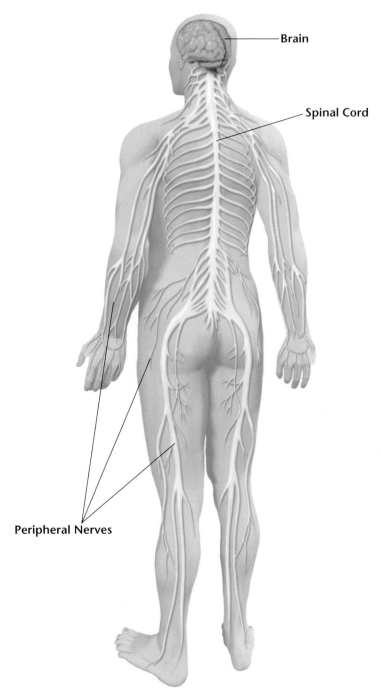

Brain

Spinal Cord

Peripheral Nerves

The Nervous System

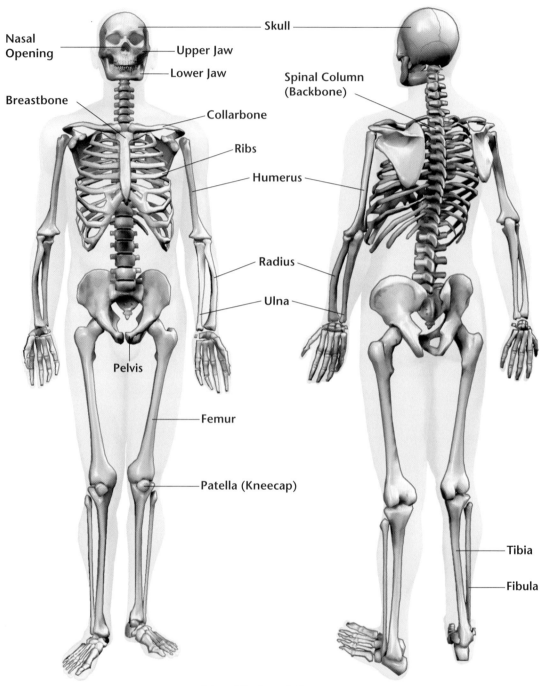

Nasal Opening

Skull

Upper Jaw

Lower Jaw

Spinal Column (Backbone)

Breastbone

Collarbone

Ribs

Humerus

Radius

Ulna

Pelvis

Femur

Patella (Kneecap)

Tibia

Fibula

The Skeletal System

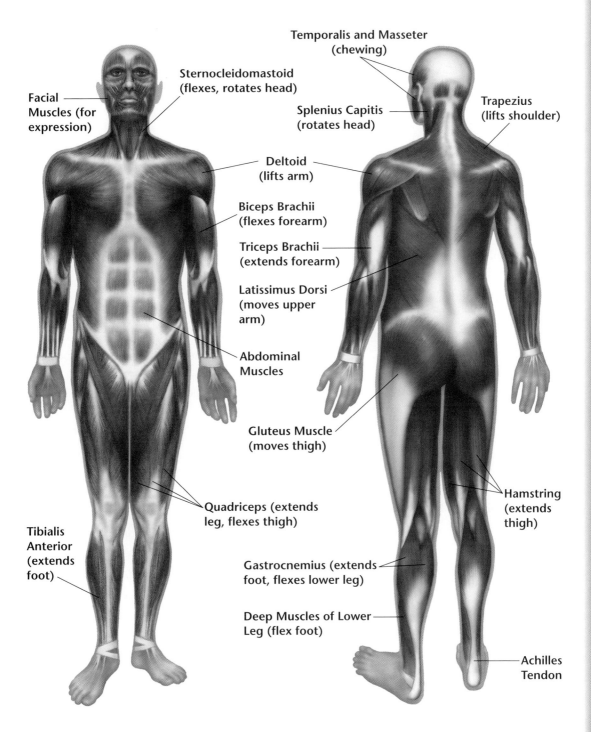

Temporalis and Masseter
(chewing)

Sternocleidomastoid
(flexes, rotates head)

Facial
Muscles (for
expression)

Splenius Capitis
(rotates head)

Trapezius
(lifts shoulder)

Deltoid
(lifts arm)

Biceps Brachii
(flexes forearm)

Triceps Brachii
(extends forearm)

Latissimus Dorsi
(moves upper
arm)

Abdominal
Muscles

Gluteus Muscle
(moves thigh)

Hamstring
(extends
thigh)

Quadriceps (extends
leg, flexes thigh)

Tibialis
Anterior
(extends
foot)

Gastrocnemius (extends
foot, flexes lower leg)

Deep Muscles of Lower
Leg (flex foot)

Achilles
Tendon

The Muscular System

Appendix C: Measurement Conversion Factors

Metric Measures

Length
1,000 meters (m) = 1 kilometer (km)
100 centimeters (cm) = 1 m
10 decimeters (dm) = 1 m
1,000 millimeters (mm) = 1 m
10 cm = 1 decimeter (dm)
10 mm = 1 cm

Area
100 square millimeters (mm^2) = 1 square
   centimeter (cm^2)
10,000 cm^2 = 1 square meter (m^2)
10,000 m^2 = 1 hectare (ha)

Volume
1,000 cubic meters (m^3) = 1 cubic
   centimeter (cm^3)
1,000 cubic centimeters (cm^3) = 1 liter (L)
1 cubic centimeter (cm^3) = 1 milliliter (mL)
100 cm^3 = 1 cubic decimeter (dm^3)
1,000,000 cm^3 = 1 cubic meter (m^3)

Capacity
1,000 milliliters (mL) = 1 liter (L)
1,000 L = 1 kiloliter (kL)

Mass
100 grams (g) = 1 centigram (cg)
1,000 kilograms (kg) = 1 metric ton (t)
1,000 grams (g) = 1 kg
1,000 milligrams (mg) = 1 g

Temperature Degrees Celsius (°C)
0°C = freezing point of water
37°C = normal body temperature
100°C = boiling point of water

Time
60 seconds (sec) = 1 minute (min)
60 min = 1 hour (hr)
24 hr = 1 day

Customary Measures

Length
12 inches (in.) = 1 foot (ft)
3 ft = 1 yard (yd)
36 in. = 1 yd
5,280 ft = 1 mile (mi)
1,760 yd = 1 mi
6,076 feet = 1 nautical mile

Area
144 square inches (sq in.) = 1 square foot
   (sq ft)
9 sq ft = 1 square yard (sq yd)
43,560 sq ft = 1 acre (A)

Volume
1,728 cubic inches (cu in.) = 1 cubic foot
   (cu ft)
27 cu ft = 1 cubic yard (cu yard)

Capacity
8 fluid ounces (fl oz) = 1 cup (c)
2 c = 1 pint (pt)
2 pt = 1 quart (qt)
4 qt = 1 gallon (gal)

Weight
16 ounces (oz) = 1 pound (lb)
2,000 lb = 1 ton (T)

Temperature Degrees Fahrenheit (°F)
32°F = freezing point of water
98.6°F = normal body temperature
212°F = boiling point of water

To change	To	Multiply by	To change	To	Multiply by
centimeters	inches	0.3937	meters	feet	3.2808
centimeters	feet	0.03281	meters	miles	0.0006214
cubic feet	cubic meters	0.0283	meters	yards	1.0936
cubic meters	cubic feet	35.3145	metric tons	tons (long)	0.9842
cubic meters	cubic yards	1.3079	metric tons	tons (short)	1.1023
cubic yards	cubic meters	0.7646	miles	kilometers	1.6093
feet	meters	0.3048	miles	feet	5,280
feet	miles (nautical)	0.0001645	miles (statute)	miles (nautical)	0.8684
feet	miles (statute)	0.0001894	miles/hour	feet/minute	88
feet/second	miles/hour	0.6818	millimeters	inches	0.0394
gallons (U.S.)	liters	3.7853	ounces avdp	grams	28.3495
grams	ounces avdp	0.0353	ounces	pounds	0.0625
grams	pounds	0.002205	pecks	liters	8.8096
hours	days	0.04167	pints (dry)	liters	0.5506
inches	millimeters	25.4000	pints (liquid)	liters	0.4732
inches	centimeters	2.5400	pounds advp	kilograms	0.4536
kilograms	pounds avdp	2.2046	pounds	ounces	16
kilometers	miles	0.6214	quarts (dry)	liters	1.1012
liters	gallons (U.S.)	0.2642	quarts (liquid)	liters	0.9463
liters	pecks	0.1135	square feet	square meters	0.0929
liters	pints (dry)	1.8162	square meters	square feet	10.7639
liters	pints (liquid)	2.1134	square meters	square yards	1.1960
liters	quarts (dry)	0.9081	square yards	square meters	0.8361
liters	quarts (liquid)	1.0567	yards	meters	0.9144

Appendix D: Geologic Time Scale

Era	Period	Epoch	Years Before the Present (approximate) Began	Ended	Forms of Life	Physical Events
Cenozoic	Quaternary	Recent	11,000		Humans dominate	West Coast uplift continues in U.S.; Great Lakes form
		Pleistocene	2,000,000	11,000	Primitive humans appear; mammoths	Ice age
	Tertiary	Pliocene	7,000,000	2,000,000	Modern horse, camel, elephant develop	North America joined to South America
		Miocene	23,000,000	7,000,000	Grasses; grazing animals thrive	North America joined to Asia; Columbia Plateau
		Oligocene	38,000,000	23,000,000	Mammals progress; elephants in Africa	Himalayas start forming; Alps continue rising
		Eocene	53,000,000	38,000,000	Ancestors of modern horse, other mammals	Coal forming in western U.S.
		Paleocene	65,000,000	53,000,000	Many new mammals appear	Uplift in western U.S. continues; Alps rising
Mesozoic	Cretaceous		145,000,000	65,000,000	Dinosaurs die out; flowering plants	Uplift of Rockies and Colorado Plateau begins
	Jurassic		208,000,000	145,000,000	First birds appear; giant dinosaurs	Rise of Sierra Nevadas and Coast Ranges
	Triassic		245,000,000	208,000,000	First dinosaurs and mammals appear	Palisades of Hudson River form
Paleozoic	Permian		280,000,000	245,000,000	Trilobites die out	Ice age in South America; deserts in western U.S.
	Pennsylvanian		310,000,000	280,000,000	First reptiles, giant insects; ferns, conifers	Coal-forming swamps in North America and Europe
	Mississippian		345,000,000	310,000,000	Early insects	Limestone formation
	Devonian		395,000,000	345,000,000	First amphibians appear	Mountain building in New England
	Silurian		435,000,000	395,000,000	First land animals (spiders, scorpions)	Deserts in eastern U.S.
	Ordovician		500,000,000	435,000,000	First vertebrates (fish)	Half of North America submerged
	Cambrian		540,000,000	500,000,000	Trilobites, snails; seaweed	Extensive deposition of sediment in inland seas
Precambrian			4,600,000,000	540,000,000	First jellyfish, bacteria, algae	Great volcanic activity, lava flows, metamorphism of rocks; evolution of crust, mantle, core

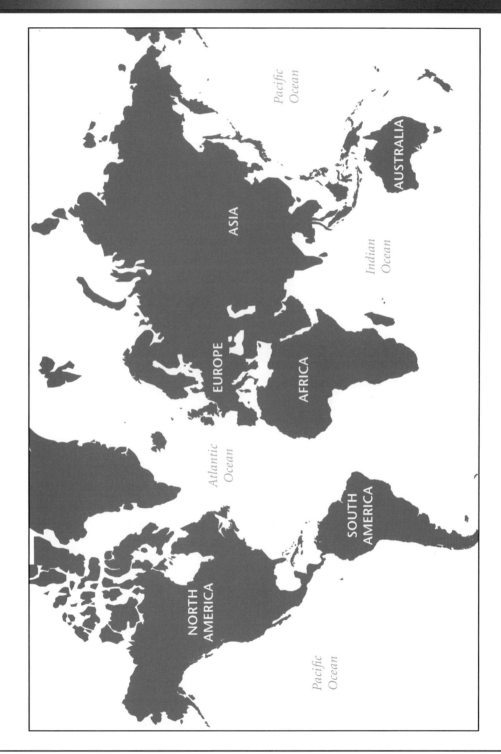

Fossil Fuels

We fly through the air in planes. We roll down highways in cars. On the coldest days, our homes are warm. Our stores are full of products to satisfy our needs and wants.

The power that runs our lives comes from fossil fuels. A fossil is the remains of ancient life. Fossil fuels formed from the remains of dead matter—animals and plants. Over millions of years, forests of plants died, fell, and became buried in the earth. Over time, the layers of ancient, dead matter changed. The carbon in the animals and plants turned into a material we now use as fuel. Fossil fuels include coal, oil, natural gas, and gasoline.

Fossil fuels power our lives and our society. In the United States, electricity comes mainly from power plants that burn coal. Industries use electricity to run machines. In our homes, we use electricity to power lightbulbs, TVs, and everything else electric. Heat and hot water for many homes come from natural gas or oil, or from fuels that come from oil.

Of course, cars and trucks run on gasoline, which is also made from oil. Powering our society with fossil fuels has made our lives more comfortable. Yet our need for fossil fuels has caused problems. Fossil fuels are a nonrenewable source of energy. That means that there is a limited supply of these fuels. At some point, fossil fuels will become scarce. Their cost will increase. And one day the supply of fossil fuels will run out. We need to find ways now to depend less and less on fossil fuels.

Fossil fuels cause pollution. The pollution comes from burning them. It is like the exhaust from a car. The pollution enters the air and causes disease. It harms the environment. One serious effect of burning fossil fuels is global warming. Carbon dioxide comes from the burning of fossil fuels. When a large amount of this gas enters the air, it warms the earth's climate. Scientists believe that warming of the climate will cause serious problems.

Renewable Energy

Many people believe that we should use renewable fuels as sources of energy. Renewable fuels never run out. They last forever.

What kinds of fuels last forever? The energy from the sun. The energy in the wind. The energy in oceans and rivers. We can use these forms of energy to power our lives. Then we will never run out of fuel. We will cut down on pollution and climate warming. Using renewable energy is not a dream for the future. It is happening right now—right here—today.

Energy from the Sun

As long as the sun keeps shining, the earth will get energy from sunlight. Energy from the sun is called solar energy. It is the energy in light. When you lie in the sun, your skin becomes hot. The heat comes from the energy in sunlight. Sunlight is a form of renewable energy we can use forever.

We use solar energy to make electricity. The electricity can power homes and businesses. Turning solar energy into electricity is called photovoltaics, or PV for short. Here's how PV works.

Flat solar panels are put near a building or on its roof. The panels face the direction that gets the most sunlight. The panels contain many PV cells. The cells are made from silicon—a material that absorbs light. When sunlight strikes the cells, some of the light energy is absorbed. The energy knocks some electrons loose in the silicon. The electrons begin to flow. The electron flow is controlled. An electric current is produced. Pieces of metal at the top and bottom of each cell make a path for electrons. The path leads the electric current away from the solar panel. The electric current flows through wires to a battery. The battery stores the electrical energy. The electrical wiring in a building is connected to the battery. All the electricity used in the building comes from the battery.

Today, PV use is 500 times greater than it was 20 years ago. And PV use is growing about 20 percent per year. Yet solar energy systems are still not perfect. PV cells do not absorb all the sunlight that strikes them, so some energy is lost. Solar energy systems also are not cheap. Still, every year, PV systems are improved. The cost of PV electricity has decreased. The amount of sunlight PV cells absorb has increased.

On a sunny day, every square meter of the earth receives 1,000 watts of energy from sunlight. Someday, when PV systems are able to use all this energy, our energy problems may be solved.

Energy from the Wind

Sunlight warms different parts of the earth differently. The North Pole gets little sunlight, so it is cold. Areas near the equator get lots of sunlight, so they are warm. The uneven warming of the earth by the sun creates the wind. As the earth turns, the wind moves, or blows. The blowing wind can be used to make electricity. This is wind energy. Because the earth's winds will blow forever, the wind is a renewable source of energy.

Wind energy is not new. Hundreds of years ago, windmills created energy. The wind turned the large fins on a windmill. As the fins spun around, they turned huge stones inside the mill. The stones ground grain into flour.

Modern windmills are tall, metal towers with spinning blades, called wind turbines. Each wind turbine has three main parts. It has blades that are turned by blowing wind. The turning blades are attached to a shaft that runs the length of the tower. The turning blades spin the shaft. The spinning shaft is connected to a generator.

A generator changes the energy from movement into electrical energy. It feeds the electricity into wires, which carry it to homes and factories.

Wind turbines are placed in areas where strong winds blow. A single house may have one small wind turbine near it to produce its electricity. The electricity produced by the wind turbine is stored in batteries. Many wind turbines may be linked together to produce electricity for an entire town. In these systems, the electricity moves from the generator to the electric company's wires. The wires carry the electricity to homes and businesses.

Studies show that 34 of the 50 United States have good wind conditions. These states could use wind to meet up to 20 percent of their electric power needs. Canada's wind conditions could produce up to 20 percent of its energy from wind, too. Alberta already produces a lot of energy from wind, and the amount is expected to increase.

Energy from Inside the Earth

Deep inside the earth, the rocks are burning hot. Beneath them it is even hotter. There, rocks melt into liquid. The earth's inner heat rises to the surface in some places. Today,

people have developed ways to use this heat to create energy. Because the inside of the earth will always be very hot, this energy is renewable. It is called geothermal energy (*geo* means earth; *thermal* means heat).

Geothermal energy is used where hot water or steam from deep inside the earth moves near the surface. These areas are called "hot spots." At hot spots, we can use geothermal energy directly. Pumps raise the hot water, and pipes carry it to buildings. The water is used to heat the space in the buildings or to heat water.

Geothermal energy may also be used indirectly to make electricity. A power plant is built near a hot spot. Wells are drilled deep into the hot spot. The wells carry hot water or steam into the power plant. There, it is used to boil more water. The boiling water makes steam. The steam turns the blades of a turbine. This energy is carried to a generator, which turns it into electricity. The electricity moves through the electric company's wires to homes and factories.

Everywhere on the earth, several miles beneath the surface, there is hot material. Scientists are improving ways of tapping the earth's inner heat. Some day, this renewable, pollution-free source of energy may be available everywhere.

Energy from Trash

We can use the leftover products that come from plants to make electricity. For example, we can use the stalks from corn or wheat to make fuel. Many leftover products from crops and lumber can fuel power plants. Because this fuel comes from living plants, it is called bioenergy (*bio* means life or living). The plant waste itself is called biomass.

People have used bioenergy for thousands of years. Burning wood in a fireplace is a form of bioenergy. That's because wood comes from trees. Bioenergy is renewable, because people will always grow crops. There will always be crop waste we can burn as fuel.

Some power plants burn biomass to heat water. The steam from the boiling water turns turbines. The turbines create electricity. In other power plants, biomass is changed into a gas. The gas is used as fuel to boil water, which turns the turbine.

Biomass can also be made into a fuel for cars and trucks. Scientists use a special process to turn biomass into fuels, such as ethanol. Car makers are designing cars that can run on these fuels. Cars that use these fuels produce far less pollution than cars that run on gas.

Bioenergy can help solve our garbage problem. Many cities are having trouble finding places to dump all their trash. There would be fewer garbage dumps if we burned some trash to make electricity.

Bioenergy is a renewable energy. But it is not a perfect solution to our energy problems. Burning biomass creates air pollution.

Energy from the Ocean

Have you ever been knocked over by a small wave while wading in the ocean? If so, you know how much power ocean water has. The motion of ocean waves can be a source of energy. So can the rise and fall of ocean tides. There are several systems that use the energy in ocean waves and tides. All of them are very new and still being developed.

In one system, ocean waves enter a funnel. The water flows into a reservoir, an area behind a dam where water is stored. When the dam opens, water flows out of the reservoir. This powers a turbine, which creates electricity. Another system uses the waves' motion to operate water pumps, which run an electric generator. There is also a system that uses the rise and fall of ocean waves. The waves compress air in a container. During high tide, large amounts of ocean water enter the container. The air in the container is under great pressure. When the high-pressure air in the container is released, it drives a turbine. This creates electricity.

Energy can also come from the rise and fall of ocean tides. A dam is built across a tidal basin. This is an area where land surrounds the sea on three sides. At high tide, ocean water is allowed to flow through the dam. The water flow turns turbines, which generate electricity. There is one serious problem with tidal energy. It damages the environment of the tidal basin and can harm animals that live there.

The oceans also contain a great deal of thermal (heat) energy. The sun heats the surface of the oceans more than it heats deep ocean water. In one day, ocean surfaces absorb solar energy equal to 250 billion barrels of oil! Deep ocean water, which gets no sunlight, is much colder than the surface.

Scientists are developing ways to use this temperature difference to create energy. The systems they are currently designing are complicated and expensive.

Energy from Rivers and Dams

Dams built across rivers also produce electricity. When the dam is open, the flowing water turns turbines, which make electricity. This is called hydroelectric power (*hydro* means water). The United States gets 7 percent of its electricity from hydroelectric power. Canada gets up to 60 percent of its electricity from hydroelectric plants built across its many rivers.

Hydroelectric power is a nonpolluting and renewable form of energy—in a way. There will always be fresh water. However, more and more people are taking water from rivers for different uses. These uses include drinking, watering crops, and supplying industry. Some rivers are becoming smaller and weaker because of the water taken from them. Also, in many places dams built across rivers hurt the environment. The land behind the dam is "drowned." Once the dam is built, fish may not be able swim up or down the river. In northwestern states, salmon have completely disappeared from many rivers that have dams.

Energy from Hydrogen Fuel

Hydrogen is a gas that is abundant everywhere on the earth. It's in the air. It is a part of water. Because there is so much hydrogen, it is a renewable energy source. And hydrogen can produce energy without any pollution.

The most likely source of hydrogen fuel is water. Water is made up of hydrogen and oxygen. A special process separates these elements in water. The process produces oxygen gas and hydrogen gas. The hydrogen gas is changed into a liquid or solid. This hydrogen fuel is used to produce energy in a fuel cell.

Look at the diagram on page 377. Hydrogen fuel (H_2) is fed into one part of the fuel cell. It is then stripped of its electrons. The free electrons create an electric current (e). The electric current powers a lightbulb or whatever is connected to the fuel cell.

Meanwhile, oxygen (O_2) from the air enters another part of the fuel cell. The stripped hydrogen (H+) bonds with the oxygen, forming water (H_2O). So a car powered by a fuel cell has pure water leaving its tailpipe. There is no exhaust to pollute the air.

When a regular battery's power is used up,

the battery dies. A fuel cell never runs down as long as it gets hydrogen fuel.

A single fuel cell produces little electricity. To make more electricity, fuel cells come in "stacks" of many fuel cells packaged together. Stacked fuel cells are used to power cars and buses. Soon, they may provide electric power to homes and factories.

Hydrogen Fuel Cell

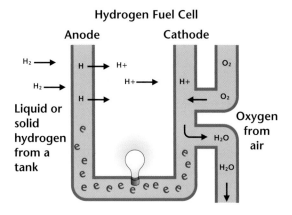

Hydrogen fuel shows great promise, but it still has problems. First, hydrogen fuel is difficult to store and distribute. Today's gas stations would have to be changed into hydrogen-fuel stations. Homes and factories would need safe ways to store solid hydrogen.

Second, producing hydrogen fuel by separating water is expensive. It is cheaper to make hydrogen fuel from oil. But that would create pollution and use nonrenewable resources. Scientists continue to look for solutions to these problems.

Energy from Atoms

Our sun gets its energy—its heat and light—from fusion. Fusion is the joining together of parts of atoms. Fusion produces enormous amounts of energy. But conditions like those on the sun are needed for fusion to occur. Fusion requires incredibly high temperatures.

In the next few decades, scientists may find ways to fuse atoms at lower temperatures. When this happens, we may be able to use fusion for energy. Fusion is a renewable form of energy because it uses hydrogen atoms. It also produces no pollution. And it produces no dangerous radiation. Using fusion to produce power is a long way off. But if the technology can be developed, fusion could provide us with renewable, clean energy.

Today's nuclear power plants produce energy by splitting atoms. This creates no air pollution. But nuclear energy has other problems. Nuclear energy is fueled by a substance we get from mines called uranium. There is only a limited amount of uranium in the earth. So it is not renewable. And uranium produces dangerous radiation, which can harm or kill living things if it escapes the power plant. Used uranium must be thrown out, even though it is radioactive and dangerous. In 1999, the United States produced nearly 41 tons of radioactive waste from nuclear power plants. However, less uranium is being mined. No new nuclear power plants have been built. The amount of energy produced from nuclear power is expected to fall. People are turning toward less harmful, renewable energy sources: the sun, wind, underground heat, biomass, water, and hydrogen fuel.

Fuel That U.S. Electric Utilities Used to Generate Electricity in 2004

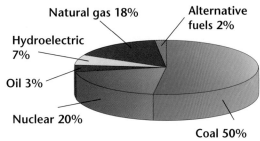

Source: U.S. Dept. of Energy Information Administration

Appendix G: Plant Kingdom

Spore Plants

Group	Description	Examples
Bryophyte *Division**	Nonvascular (no tubes for carrying materials in plant); live in moist places	liverwort, hornwort, moss
Club Moss *Division*	Spores in cones at end of stems; simple leaves	club moss
Horsetail *Division*	Spores in cones at end of stems; hollow, jointed stem	horsetail
Fern *Division*	Spores in sori; fronds	fern

Seed Plants

Group	Description	Examples
Palmlike *Division*	Naked seeds in cones; gymnosperm (nonflowering seed plant); male and female cones on different trees; palm-shaped leaves	cycad, sago palm
Ginkgo *Division*	Naked seeds in conelike structures; gymnosperm; male and female cones on different trees; fan-shaped leaves; only one known species	ginkgo
Conifer *Division*	Naked seeds in cones; gymnosperm; male and female cones; most are evergreen; needlelike or scalelike leaves	pine, fir, spruce, yew
Angiosperm *Division*	Produce flowers; seeds protected by ovary that ripens into a fruit; organs of both sexes often in same flower	
Monocot *Class*	One cotyledon; parallel veins; flower parts in multiples of three	grass, palm, corn, lily
Dicot *Class*	Two cotyledons; branching veins; flower parts in multiples of four or five	cactus, maple, rose, daisy

*For plants, biologists use *Division* instead of *Phylum*.

Glossary

A

Absorb (ab sôrb´) to retain (p. 230)

Acetic acid (ə sē´ tik as´ id) a sharp-smelling, colorless acid formed from the breakdown of pyruvic acid (p. 201)

Acetyl CoA (ə sē´ tl kōā) a compound made from the bonding of coenzyme A and acetic acid (p. 201)

Acid (as´ id) a substance that can donate a proton (H^+) or accept an electron pair (p. 59)

Acid rain (as´ id rān) rain that is caused by pollution and is harmful to organisms because it is acidic (p. 594)

Acquired trait (ə kwir´ d trāt) a trait that comes from an organism's behavior (p. 389)

Actin (ak´ tən) a ball-shaped protein used to make microfilaments (p. 154)

Activation energy (acti va´ tion en´ ər jė)the amount of energy needed to start a chemical reaction (p. 184)

Active site (ak´ tiv sīt) the area on an enzyme where the substrate fits in shape and chemistry (p. 185)

Active transport (ak´ tiv trans pôrt´) the movement of molecules across a membrane when the movement requires energy (p. 138)

Adapt (ə dapt´) to change genetically over generations to become more suited to the environment (p. 390)

Adaptation (ad ap tā´ shən) an adjustment to environmental conditions (p. 10)

Adenine (ad´ n ēn) a nitrogen-containing compound found in ATP, DNA, and RNA (p. 170)

Adolescence (ad l es´ ns) the teenage years of a human (p. 266)

ADP (ā dē pē) adenosine diphosphate; a molecule converted to ATP by the addition of a phosphate (p. 174)

Aerobic (âr ō´ biks) requiring oxygen (p. 208)

Aggressive behavior (ə gres´ iv bi hā´ vyər) a behavior that warns predators not to approach (p. 514)

Agonistic interaction (ag nos´ tik in ter ak´ shən) a type of social behavior in which individuals have contests and show aggressive behavior (p. 521)

Algae (al´ jē) a protist that makes its own food and usually lives in water (p. 464)

Allele (ə lēl´) one form of a gene (p. 279)

Allopatric speciation (a lə pa´ trik spē shē ā´ shən) when similar organisms do not interbreed due to physical barriers (p. 431)

Alternation of generations (ol tər nā´ shən ov jen ə ra´ shən) a life cycle of mosses, algae, and some protists that alternates between a haploid phase and a diploid phase (p. 473)

Alveolus (al vē´ ə ləs) a tiny air sac at the end of each bronchiole that holds air (plural is alveoli) (p. 349)

Amino acid (ə mē´ no as´ id) a molecule that makes up proteins (p. 72)

Ammonium (ə mō´ nē əm) a nitrogen-containing compound used to cycle nitrogen into an ecosystem (p. 575)

Amniotic egg (am nē ot´ ik eg) the egg of a vertebrate that lives on land (p. 491)

Amoeba (ə mē´ ba) a protozoan that moves by pushing out parts of its cell (p. 465)

Amphibian (am fib´ ē ən) a vertebrate that lives at first in water and then on land (p. 398)

Anaerobic (an ə rō´ bik) not requiring oxygen (p. 208)

Analysis (ə nal´ ə sis) making sense of the results of an experiment; also the fifth step of the scientific method (p. 20)

Anatomy (ə nat´ ə mē) the structure of an organism (p. 394)

Angiosperm (an´ j ə spėrm) a flowering seed plant (p. 472)

Anticodon (an ti kō´ don) a three-base sequence complementary to the codon, found in tRNA (p. 318)

Antidiuretic hormone (ADH) (an ti dī yu̇ re´ tik hôr´ mōn) a hormone that controls the absorption of water back into the body (p. 360)

Antigen (an´ tə jən) a foreign molecule that activates the immune system (p. 334)

Aorta (ā ôr´ tə) a large vessel through which the left ventricle sends blood to the body (p. 353)

Aphotic zone (ā fō´ tik zōn) an area in aquatic biomes that does not receive solar energy (p. 582)

Aquatic (ə kwat´ ik) growing or living in water (p. 568)

Arachnid (a rak´ nid) a class of arthropods that includes spiders, scorpions, mites, and ticks (p. 484)

Archaea (är kē´ ə) the domain of prokaryotic organisms that are not bacteria (p. 436)

a	hat	e	let	ī	ice	ô	order	u̇	put	sh	she	ə	a	in about
ā	age	ē	equal	o	hot	oi	oil	ü	rule	th	thin		e	in taken
ä	far	ėr	term	ō	open	ou	out	ch	child	ᴛʜ	then		i	in pencil
â	care	i	it	ȯ	saw	u	cup	ng	long	zh	measure		o	in lemon
													u	in circus

Artery (är′ tər ē) a blood vessel that carries blood away from the heart (plural is arteries) (p. 353)

Arthropod (är′ thrə pod) a member of the largest group of invertebrates; this group includes insects (p. 484)

Artificial selection (är tə fish′ əl si lek′ shən) a process of changing a species by people who select the breeding of certain traits (p. 410)

Asexual reproduction (ā sek′ shü əl rē prə duk′ shən) reproduction that involves one parent and no egg or sperm (p. 431)

Asthma (az′ mə) a condition that narrows or blocks the airways and makes breathing difficult (p. 350)

Atherosclerosis (ath ər ō sklə rō′ sis) a disease that harms the arteries by narrowing them (p. 355)

Atmosphere (at′ mə sfir) the air that surrounds the earth (p. 573)

Atom (at′ əm) the basic unit of matter (p. 32)

Atomic mass (ə tom′ ik mas) the average mass of the atom of an element (p. 40)

Atomic number (ə tom′ ik num′ bər) the number of protons in the nucleus of an atom (p. 39)

ATP (ā tē pē) adenosine triphosphate; a molecule in all living cells that acts as fuel (p. 105)

ATP synthase (ā tē pē sin′ thās) an enzyme at the end of the electron transport chain that helps drive the bonding of a phosphate to ADP to create ATP (p. 203)

Atrium (ā′ trē əm) a heart chamber that receives blood returning to the heart (plural is atria) (p. 353)

Auditory nerve (o′ də tôr ē nèrv) a bundle of nerves that carry impulses from the ear to the brain (p. 369)

Autosome (o′ tə sōm) a chromosome other than a sex chromosome (p. 292)

Autotroph (o′ tə trof) a self-nourishing organism that makes its own food (p. 224)

Axon (ak′ son) a long extension of the nerve cell that carries information to other cells (p. 364)

B

Bacteria (bak tir′ ē ə) the simplest single cells that carry out all basic life activities (p. 33)

Bacteriophage (bak tir′ ē ə) a virus that infects bacteria (p. 310)

Base (bās) a substance that can accept a proton (H⁺), release OH⁻, or donate an electron pair; an alkali (p. 59)

Behavior (bi hā′ vyər) the way an organism acts (p. 506)

Behavioral biology (bi hā′ vyər əl bi ol′ ə jē) the study of the behavior of living things (p. 506)

Benign tumor (bi nin′ tü′ mər) a tumor that is only in the area where it began (p. 252)

Benthic zone (ben′ thik zōn) the floor of an aquatic biome (p. 582)

Bilateral symmetry (bi lat′ ər əl sim′ ə trē) a body made of left and right halves that are the same (p. 483)

Bilayer (bī′ lā ər) two layers (p. 134)

Bile (bīl) a substance made in the liver that breaks down fats (p. 345)

Binary compound (bī′ nər ē kom′ pound) a compound that contains two elements (p. 45)

Binary fission (bī′ nər ē fish′ ən) reproduction in which a bacterial cell divides into two cells that look the same as the original cell (p. 117)

Biochemistry (bī′ ō kem′ ə strē) chemistry that deals with the chemical compounds and processes in organisms (p. 429)

Biodiversity (bī ō di vėr′ sə tē) the total of all life on the earth (p. 604)

Biogeography (bī ō jē og′ rə fē) the study of the geographical distribution of fossils and living organisms (p. 393)

Biogeology (bī ō jē ol′ ə jē) the study of the interaction between living and nonliving parts of the environment (p. 607)

Biological evolution (bī ə loj′ ə kəl ev ə lü′ shən) the change in the gene pool of a population over time (p. 388)

Biological species concept (bī ə loj′ ə kəl spē′ shēz kon′ sept) a principle that defines a species as populations that can interbreed and produce offspring (p. 430)

Biologist (bi ol′ o jist) a person who studies life (p. 2)

Biology (bi ol′ ə jē) the study of life (p. 2)

Biome (bī′ ōm) a large area of the earth that has similar ecosystems and weather (p. 537)

Biosphere (bī′ ə sfir) the total area of the earth that contains and supports life (p. 536)

Biotechnologist (bī o tek nol′ ə jist) a scientist who studies biotechnology (p. 325)

Biotechnology (bī ō tek nol′ ə jē) the use of organisms and their genetics in industry to make products (p. 325)

Bipedal locomotion (bi ped′ əl lō kə mō′ shən) the ability to walk upright on two feet (p. 497)

Blastula (blas′ chə lə) a hollow ball of cells formed by cell divisions of a zygote (p. 479)

B lymphocyte (bē lim′ fə sit) a white blood cell that produces antibodies (p. 333)

Boom-bust cycle (büm bust sī′ kəl) a period in which the densities of populations increase or decrease at the same time (p. 543)

Brain stem (brān stem) the part of the brain that controls automatic activities and connects the brain and the spinal cord (p. 362)

Bronchiole (brong′ kē əl) a tube that branches off the bronchus (p. 349)

Bronchitis (brong ki′ tis) an inflammation of the bronchial tubes (p. 350)

Bronchus (brong´ kəs) a tube that connects the trachea to a lung (plural is bronchi) (p. 349)

Buffer (buf´ ər) a solution that can receive moderate amounts of either acid or base without significant change in its pH (p. 61)

C

Calorie (kal´ ər ē) a unit used to measure the amount of energy food contains (p. 171)

Calvin-Benson cycle (kal´ vən ben´ sun sī´ kəl) a process in photosynthesis that produces sugar (p. 233)

CAM plant (kam plant) a plant that takes in CO_2 only during the night (p. 239)

Camouflage (kam´ ə fläzh) the colors or patterns on animals that help them hide in their surroundings (p. 550)

Cancer (kan´ sər) a condition in which a cell grows without control and divides too much (p. 252)

Canopy (kan´ ə pe) the tops of the forest trees (p. 551)

Capillary (kap´ ə ler ē) a blood vessel through which oxygen and food molecules pass to body cells (p. 348)

Capsid (kap´ səd) the protein shell of a virus (p. 321)

Carbohydrate (kär bō hi´ drāt) a sugar or starch that living things use for energy (p. 72)

Cardiac (kär´ dē ak) relating to the heart (p. 352)

Cardiovascular disease (kär dē ō vas´ kyə lər də zēz´) a disease of the heart and blood vessels (p. 355)

Carotenoid (kər ot´ n oid) any yellow, orange, or red pigment found widely in plants and animals (p. 232)

Carrier (kar´ ē ər) an organism that carries an allele but does not show the effects of the allele (p. 294)

Carrying capacity (kar´ ē ing kə pas´ ə tē) the largest density an ecosystem can support for a particular population (p. 541)

Cartilage (kär´ tlij) a soft material found in vertebrae skeletons (p. 489)

Catalyst (kat´ l ist) a chemical that helps in a chemical reaction, but is not consumed or changed in the reaction (p. 180)

Cell (sel) the basic unit of life (p. 7)

Cell cycle (sel si´ kəl) the life cycle of a cell from its beginning until it divides (p. 248)

Cell theory (sel thē´ ər ē) a theory that all living things are made of cells, that cells are the basic units of structure and function in living things, and that cells only come from already present cells (p. 107)

Cellular respiration (sel´ yə lər res pə rā´ shən) the process in which cells break down food to release energy (p. 147)

Cellulose (sel´ yə lōs) a woody polymer of glucose (p. 78)

Cell wall (sel wol) the rigid layer of cellulose outside the plasma membrane of plant cells (p. 159)

Central vacuole (sen´ tral vak´ yü ol) a large membrane sac in the center of a plant cell used for water storage (p. 159)

Centromere (sen´ trə mir) the area where two sister chromatids are tightly joined together (p. 249)

Cephalaspidomorphi (sef ə las pə də môr´ fi) a class of fish with a cartilage skeleton and no jaws or scales; lampreys (p. 490)

Cerebellum (ser ə bel´ əm) the part of the brain that controls balance (p. 362)

Cerebral cortex (sə rē´ brəl kôr´ tex) the part of the brain in which most of the high-level functions take place (p. 362)

Cervix (sèr´ viks) an opening that connects a female's uterus and vagina (p. 265)

C_4 plant (sē fôr plant) a plant that photosynthesizes in hot, dry weather (p. 239)

Chaparral (shap ə ral´) a terrestrial biome with mostly shrubs (p. 581)

Chemical bond (kem´ ə kəl bond) the force holding atoms together in a compound or molecule (p. 34)

Chemical formula (kem´ ə kəl fôr´ myə lə) a set of symbols and subscripts that tell the kinds of atoms and how many of each kind are in a compound (p. 42)

Chemical process (kem´ ə kəl pros´ es) a rearrangement of atoms or molecules to produce one or more new substances with new properties (p. 33)

Chemical property (kem´ ə kəl prop´ ər tē) a characteristic that describes how a substance changes into a different substance (p. 34)

Chemical reaction (kem´ ə kəl rē ak´ shən) a chemical change in which elements are combined or rearranged (p. 34)

Chemical runoff (kem´ ə kəl run ôf) the chemical waste produced on land that enters water sources (p. 594)

Chemistry (kem´ ə strē) the study of matter and how it changes (p. 33)

Chemotroph (ki´ mō trof) an organism that gets its energy from chemicals in food (p. 566)

Chlorophyll (klôr´ ə fil) a molecule in chloroplasts that traps energy from the sunlight (p. 146)

Chloroplast (klôr´ ə plast) an energy organelle in plants that harvests energy from the sun (p. 146)

Chondrichthyes (kän drik´ thē əz) a class of fish with a flexible skeleton made of cartilage (p. 490)

a	hat	e	let	ī	ice	ȯ	order	u̇	put	sh	she	ə	a in about
ā	age	ē	equal	o	hot	oi	oil	ü	rule	th	thin		e in taken
ä	far	ėr	term	ō	open	ou	out	ch	child	ᴛʜ	then		i in pencil
â	care	i	it	ȯ	saw	u	cup	ng	long	zh	measure		o in lemon
													u in circus

Chordate (kôr´ dāt) an animal that, in its embryo stage, has a dorsal nerve cord, a notochord, pharyngeal slits, and a tail that goes past the anus (p. 489)

Chromosome (krō´ mə sōm) a structure in the nucleus made of individual DNA molecules folded and coiled together with proteins (p. 143)

Chyme (kīm) the liquid food in the digestive tract that is partially digested (p. 345)

Cilia (sil´ ē ə) small, hair-like structures made of microtubules; found on the outside of some cells to aid in movement (p. 155)

Circulatory system (sėr´ kyə lə tôr ē sis´ təm) a collection of organs, including the heart, which moves blood and gases throughout the body (p. 124)

Classify (klas´ ə fī) to group (p. 428)

Cleavage furrow (klē´ vig fur´ row) a structure that is formed when fibers pinch in the membrane of a dividing cell (p. 250)

Climate (klī´ mit) the average weather of a region over a long period of time (p. 580)

Clumped (klumpt) when a population spreads out in small groups throughout an ecosystem (p. 543)

Cnidarian (nī da´ rē ən) a group of invertebrates, including jellyfish, corals, and hydras (p. 482)

Co-adaptation (kō ad ap tā´ shən) one species becoming dependent on another species (p. 448)

Cochlea (kok´ lē ə) the organ in the ear that sends impulses to the auditory nerve (p. 369)

Codominance (kō do´ mə nəns) two different alleles come together and produce both trait forms (p. 286)

Codon (kō´ don) a specific sequence of three consecutive nucleotides that is part of a gene (p. 90)

Coenzyme A (kō en´ zīm ā) an organic molecule that helps move the products of glycolysis into mitochondria (p. 201)

Cognition (kog nish´ ən) knowledge (p. 524)

Cold-blooded (kōld blud´ əd) having a body temperature that changes with the temperature of the surroundings (p. 491)

Commensalism (kə men´ sə liz əm) a symbiotic relationship in which one organism benefits and the other is not affected (p. 550)

Common descent (kom´ ən di sent´) a theory that present organisms descend from past organisms (p. 389)

Communication (kə myü nə ka shən) sending information (p. 520)

Community (kə myü´ nə tē) a group of different populations that live in the same area (p. 447)

Comparative anatomy (kəm par´ ə tiv ə nat´ ə mē) the study of the anatomy of different species (p. 394)

Competition (kom pə tish´ ən) when organisms try to use the same resources (p. 542)

Competitor (kəm pet´ ə tər) an animal that tries to get the same resources as another animal (p. 521)

Complement protein (kəm plēt prō´ tēn) a protein that breaks the membranes of pathogens (p. 333)

Complementary base pairing (kom plə men´ tər ē bās pâir´ ing) the pairing of the nitrogenous bases adenine to thymine and cytosine to guanine in DNA strands (p. 308)

Complete metamorphosis (kəm plēt´ met ə môr´ fə sis) the changes in form during development in which earlier stages do not look like the adult (p. 485)

Complete protein (kom plə ment´ prōtēn) a protein source that provides the body with the essential amino acids (p. 91)

Compound (kom´ pound) a substance that is formed when atoms of two or more elements join together (p. 38)

Concentration (kon sən trā´ shən) a measurement of the amount of dissolved substance in a fixed amount of solvent (p. 112)

Concentration gradient (kon sən trā shən grā´ dē ənt) a difference in the concentration of a substance across a distance (p. 113)

Conifer (kon´ ə fər) a cone-bearing gymnosperm (p. 475)

Coniferous forest (kō nif´ ər əs fôr´ ist) a dry, cold terrestrial biome with cone-bearing trees (p. 582)

Connective tissue (kə nek´ tiv tish´ ü) the supporting framework of the body and its organs (p. 354)

Conservation biology (kon sər vā´ shən bī ol´ ə jē) the science of using ecological information to help reduce damage to the environment (p. 601)

Consumer (kən sü´ mər) an organism that feeds on other organisms (p. 567)

Continental drift (kon tə nen´ tl drift) a theory that the major landmasses of the earth move (p. 399)

Contractile (kən trak´ təl) able to become shorter or longer (p. 89)

Control group (kən trōl grüp) the setup in an experiment that has no factor, or variable, changed (p. 19)

Cooperation (kō op ə rā´ shən) a type of social behavior in which two or more individuals work or act together (p. 521)

Coordinated stasis (kō ôrd´ n ə tid stā təs) a pattern where most species appear at about the same time (p. 442)

Cornea (kôr´ nē ə) a clear layer of the eye that light passes through (p. 368)

Courtship behavior (kôrt´ ship bi hā´ vyər) a behavior that helps attract a mate (p. 513)

Covalent bond (kō vā´ lənt bond) a bond resulting from the sharing of one or more pairs of electrons between two atoms (p. 49)

Cristae (kris´ tē) the folded layers of the inner membrane inside mitochondria (p. 148)

Cross-fertilization (krȯs fėr tl ə zā´ shən) a process in which pollen from one type of plant fertilizes the eggs in a flower of a different plant (p. 278)

Crossing over (krȯ´ sing ō´ vər) the process of homologous chromosomes in a tetrad trading pieces of similar DNA (p. 257)

Crust (krust) the outer layer of the earth (p. 400)

Crustacean (krus tā´ shən) a class of arthropods that includes crabs, lobsters, crayfish, and pill bugs (p. 484)

Crystalline (kris´ tl ən) a substance with a regularly repeating arrangement of its atoms (p. 55)

Culture (kul´ chər) the languages, religions, customs, arts, and dress of a people (p. 497)

Cycle (sī´ kəl) a course or series of events or operations that repeats (p. 3)

Cynobacterium (sī nə bak ti´ rē um) a blue-green algae (p. 469)

Cytokinesis (sī tō kə nē´ səs) the process of dividing the cytoplasm of a cell into two (p. 250)

Cytoplasm (sī´ tə plaz əm) the area inside a cell; contains organelles and cytosol (p. 136)

Cytosine (C) (sī´ tə sēn) a single-ringed nitrogenous base found in DNA and RNA (p. 307)

Cytoskeleton (sī´ tə skel´ ə tən) a group of fibers running throughout the inside of a cell that supports the cell and helps the cell move (p. 154)

Cytosol (sī tə sol) the fluid base of the cytoplasm; contains molecules used and made by the cell (p. 136)

Cytotoxic T cell (sī tə tok´ sin t sel) a lymphocyte that scans for antigens and then destroys infected cells (p. 334)

D

Data (dā´ tə) information collected from experiments (p. 20)

Decomposer (dē kəm pō´ zər) an organism at the end of a food chain that feeds by breaking down dead organisms (p. 567)

Defensive behavior (di fen siv bi hā´ vyər) a behavior to avoid or protect against predators (p. 514)

Deforestation (dē fôr ist a´ shən) the removal of forest ecosystems for land development (p. 596)

Dehydration synthesis (dē hi drā´ shən sin´ thə sis) the process of joining monomers by removing a molecule of water (p. 73)

Deletion (di lē´ shən) a mutation in which one or more nucleotide bases are removed from a DNA sequence (p. 319)

Dendrite (den´ drit) a thin branch out of the cell body that receives information from other cells (p. 364)

Density-dependent factor (den´ sə tē di pen´ dənt fak´ tər) a factor related to the density of a population that affects population size (p. 542)

Density-independent factor (den´ sə tē in di pen´ dənt fak´ tər) a factor that affects population size, but does not depend on population density (p. 543)

Deoxyribose (dē ok sə rī bōs) the five-carbon sugar in DNA (p. 95)

Dermis (dėr´ mis) the thick layer of cells below the epidermis (p. 360)

Descent with modification (di sent´ with mod ə fə kā´ shən) the theory that more recent species of organisms are changed descendants of earlier species (p. 389)

Desert (dez´ ərt) a very dry terrestrial biome (p. 581)

Diabetes (di ə bē´ tis) a genetic disease in which a person has too much sugar in his or her blood (p. 181)

Diencephalon (dī ən se´ fə lon) the front part of the brain (p. 362)

Differential reproduction (dif ə ren´ shal rē prə duk´ shən) when individuals leave more offspring than other individuals (p. 418)

Diffusion (di fyü´ zhən) the movement of molecules from an area of high concentration to an area of low concentration (p. 112)

Dihybrid cross (dī hī´ brid kros) a cross between two plants that differ in two traits (p. 280)

Dipeptide (dī pep´ tīd) two amino acids joined by a peptide bond (p. 90)

Diploid (dip´ loid) having two copies of each kind of chromosome (p. 256)

Disaccharide (dī sak´ ə rīd) a sugar formed from two monosaccharide molecules (p. 77)

Disturbance (dis tėr´ bəns) a large change in a community (p. 555)

Diversity (də vėr´ sə tē) differing from one another (p. 33)

DNA (dē ēn ā) deoxyribonucleic acid; a chemical in an organism that contains the instructions for life (p. 7)

DNA ligase (dē ēn ā lī gās) an enzyme that bonds all pieces of newly made DNA to make one strand (p. 312)

DNA polymerase (dē ēn ā pol´ ə mə rās) an enzyme that adds new nucleotide bases to a new strand during DNA replication (p. 311)

Dominant (dom´ ə nāt) having the most influence or control (p. 521)

a	hat	e	let	ī	ice	ȯ	order	u̇	put	sh	she		a	in about
ā	age	ē	equal	o	hot	oi	oil	ü	rule	th	thin	ə	e	in taken
ä	far	ėr	term	ō	open	ou	out	ch	child	ᴛʜ	then		i	in pencil
â	care	i	it	ȯ	saw	u	cup	ng	long	zh	measure		o	in lemon
													u	in circus

Dominant gene (dom´ ə nāt jēn) a gene that shows up in an organism (p. 279)

Dorsal (dôr´ səl) the back part of an animal (p. 489)

Downs syndrome (dounz sin´ drōm) a medical condition caused by cells having an extra chromosome 21 (p. 327)

Dysentery (dis´ n ter ē) a disease of the intestines (p. 465)

E

Eardrum (ir´ drum) a thin tissue in the middle ear that vibrates when sound waves strike it (p. 369)

Ecological species concept (ē kə loj´ ə kəl spē´ shēz kon´ sept) a principle that defines species as populations that can interbreed and produce offspring based on their niche (p. 431)

Ecologist (ē kol´ ə jist) a person who studies ecology (p. 12)

Ecology (ē kōl´ ə jē) the study of interactions among living things and the nonliving things in their environment (p. 12)

Ecosystem (e´ kō sis təm) all of the living and nonliving things found in any particular area (p. 12)

Ectotherm (ek´ tə thərm) an animal whose main source of body heat is its environment (p. 491)

Effector cell (ə fek´ tōr sel) a muscle or gland cell that carries out the body's responses to stimuli (p. 357)

Egg (eg) the female gamete (p. 256)

Ejaculation (i jak yə lā´ shən) the release of semen from the penis (p. 261)

Electromagnetic radiation (i lek trō mag net´ ik rā dē ā´ shən) radiation that is made up of electric and magnetic waves (p. 230)

Electromagnetic spectrum (i lek trō mag net´ ik spek´ trəm) the range of wavelengths of electromagnetic radiation (p. 231)

Electron (i lek´ tron) a tiny particle in an atom that moves around the nucleus; it has a negative electrical charge (p. 39)

Electron carrier (i lek´ tron kar´ ē ər) a molecule that carries electrons from one set of reactions to another (p. 198)

Electron cloud (i lek´ tron kloud) the space effectively occupied by electrons in an atom (p. 39)

Electron shell (i lek´ tron shel) a specific energy level in which electrons orbit the nucleus (p. 48)

Electron transport chain (i lek´ tron tran spôrt´ chān) the third stage of cellular respiration (p. 202)

Element (el´ ə mənt) a substance that cannot be separated into other kinds of substances (p. 34)

Element symbol (el´ ə mənt sim´ bəl) one, two, or three letters that represent the name of an element (p. 38)

Embryo (em´ brē ō) an early stage in the development of an organism (p. 263)

Emigrate (em´ ə grāt) to leave a population (p. 543)

Emission (i mish´ ən) a chemical waste given off as gas (p. 602)

Empirical formula (em pir´ əkəl fôr´ myə lə) the simplest formula for a compound (p. 42)

Endangered (en dān´ jərd) a condition in which there are almost no members of a certain species left (p. 407)

Endocytosis (en´ dō sī tō səs) a process in which a cell surrounds and encloses a substance to bring the substance into the cell (p. 139)

Endomembrane system (en´ dō mem brān sis´ təm) a group of organelles that help a cell make and use different molecules (p. 150)

Endoplasmic reticulum (ER) (en dō´ plaz mik ri´ ti kyə ləm) an organelle that makes different molecules (p. 150)

Endoskeleton (en´ dō skel´ ə tən) an internal skeleton (p. 487)

Endotherm (en´ dō thėrm) an animal that creates its own body heat through metabolism (p. 492)

Energy (en´ ər jē) the ability to do work; found in many different forms (p. 5)

Energy pyramid (en´ ər jē pir´ ə mid) a diagram that compares the amounts of energy available to the populations at different levels of a food chain (p. 569)

Engineer (en jə nir´) a person who works in engineering (p. 607)

Engineering (en jə nir´ ing) the use of math and science to create methods and machines to help solve problems or make life better (p. 607)

Environment (en vī´ rən mənt) an organism's natural and man-made surroundings (p. 11)

Enzyme (en´ zīm) a protein that brings about a chemical reaction in an organism (p. 89)

Epidermis (ep ə dėr´ mis) the thin outer layer of skin (p. 360)

Epithelial cell (ep ə thē´ lēəl sel) a skin cell (p. 123)

Epithelium (ep ə thē´ lēəm) a thin layer of cells forming a tissue that covers body surfaces and lines some organs (p. 348)

Equilibrium (ē kwə lib´ rē əm) a state where concentrations are equal in all parts of an area (p. 114)

Estrogen (es´ trə jən) the female sex hormone (p. 262)

Estuary (es´ chü ər ē) a marine biome where freshwater meets saltwater (p. 582)

Ethologist (i thol´ ə jist) a scientist who studies the behaviors of animals (p. 506)

Ethyl alcohol (eth´ əl al´ kəhol) a colorless liquid waste produced by anaerobic fermentation (p. 209)

Euglena (yü glē´ nə) a protist that makes its own food (p. 464)

Eukarya (yü kar´ ē ə) the domain of eukaryotic organisms (p. 436)

Eukaryote (yü kar´ ē ōt) a cell with several internal structures, including the nucleus, that are surrounded by membranes (p. 117)

Eutrophication (yü trə fə kā´ shən) a process in which chemical runoff causes algae growth that chokes out other organisms in a water ecosystem (p. 594)

Evaporation (i vap ərā´ shən) the process of liquid water changing into gas due to heating (p. 576)

Evolution (ev ə lü´ shən) the changes in a population over time (p. 10)

Evolutionary (ev ə lü´ shə ner´ē) of or relating to evolution (p. 440)

Evolutionary biology (ev ə lü´ shə nerē bī ol´ ə jē) the study of genetic changes within and among populations of organisms (p. 419)

Evolve (i volv´) to change biologically (p. 321)

Exocytosis (ek´ sō sī tō səs) a process in which a substance is released from a cell trough a pouch that transports the substance to the cell surface (p. 139)

Exon (ek´ sän) a part of mRNA that has protein-making instructions (p. 317)

Exoskeleton (ek sō skel´ ə tən) an external skeleton (p. 484)

Experimental group (ek sper ə men´ tl grüp) the same group as the control group, except for one factor, or variable, to be tested (p. 19)

External stimulus (ek stèr´ nl stim´ yə ləs) a stimulus that occurs outside of an organism (p. 506)

Extinct (ek stingkt´) when no members of a species are alive (p. 10)

Extinction (ek stingk´ shən) the death of all members of a species (p. 407)

Extracellular matrix (ek strə sel´ yə lər mā´ triks) a sticky coating outside the plasma membrane of animal cells that joins cells together (p. 136)

F

Facilitated diffusion (fə sil´ ə tā td di fyü´ zhən) passive transport that involves membrane proteins (p. 138)

FADH$_2$ (fad āch tü) an electron carrier produced by the Krebs cycle (p. 201)

Fallopian tube (fə lō´ pē ən tüb) a tube through which eggs pass from an ovary to the uterus (p. 262)

Fat (fat) a chemical that stores large amounts of energy (p. 73)

Fatty acid (fat´ ē as´ id) a long hydrocarbon with a carboxyl group at the end (p. 73)

Fatty layer (fat´ ē lā´ ər) the layer of skin that protects organs and keeps in heat (p. 360)

Feces (fē´ sēz) the solid waste material remaining in the large intestine after digestion (p. 346)

Feedback inhibition (fēd´ bak in hi bish´ ən) a process used by cells to control metabolic pathways (p. 214)

Fermentation (fèr men tā´ shən) an anaerobic process for making ATP (p. 208)

Fern (fèrn) a seedless vascular plant (p. 472)

Fertile (fèr´ tl) capable of producing offspring (p. 429)

Fertilization (fèr tl ə zā´ shən) the joining of male and female gametes to create a new organism (p. 257)

Fetus (fē´ təs) an embryo after eight weeks of development in the uterus (p. 266)

Fibrinogen (fi brin´ ə jen) a protein in the platelets that forms into threads, creating a clot (p. 355)

Fixed action pattern behavior (fiksd ak´ shən pat´ ərn bi hā´ vyər) a behavior that always occurs the same way (p. 507)

Flagella (flə jel´ ə) long, tail-like structures made of microtubules; found on the outside of some cells to aid in movement (p. 155)

Flatworm (flat´ wèrm) a simple worm that is flat and thin (p. 483)

Fluid mosaic model (flü´ id mō zā´ ik mod´ l) a plasma membrane model where proteins float freely through the phospholipid bilayer (p. 136)

Follicle (fol´ ə kəl) a ball of cells with a growing oocyte found inside (p. 262)

F$_1$ generation (ef wun jen ə rā´ shən) the offspring that result when two different kinds of pure plants are cross-pollinated (p. 279)

Food chain (füd chān) the feeding order of organisms in a community (p. 567)

Food web (füd web) all the food chains in a community that are linked to one another (p. 568)

Fossil (fos´ əl) the remains or impressions of an organism that lived in the past (p. 388)

Fossil fuel (fos´ əl fyü´ əl) the fuel formed millions of years ago from the remains of plants and animals (p. 475)

Fossil record (fos´ əl rek´ ərd) the history of life on the earth, based on fossils that have been discovered (p. 392)

Frequency (frē´ kwən sē) the rate of occurrence (p. 416)

Freshwater (fresh´ wot ər) an area of water with no salt (p. 582)

Frond (frond) a large, feathery leaf of a fern (p. 475)

---

a	hat	e	let	ī	ice	ȯ	order	u̇	put	sh	she	ə	a	in about
ā	age	ē	equal	o	hot	oi	oil	ü	rule	th	thin		e	in taken
ä	far	ėr	term	ō	open	ou	out	ch	child	ᴛʜ	then		i	in pencil
â	care	i	it	ȯ	saw	u	cup	ng	long	zh	measure		o	in lemon
													u	in circus

Fructose (fruk´ tōs) a form of sugar found in fruit and honey (p. 77)

F₂ generation (ef tü jen ə rā´ shən) the offspring that result when two hybrid plants are crossed (p. 279)

Functional group (fungk´ shə nəl grüp) a group of atoms within a molecule that causes the molecule to react in a specific way (p. 71)

G

Gallbladder (gôl´ blad ər) the digestive organ that stores bile (p. 345)

Gamete (gam´ ēt) a sex cell, such as sperm or egg (p. 256)

Gametophyte (ga mē´ tō fit) in alternation of generations, the phase in which gametes are formed; a haploid individual that produces gametes (p. 474)

Gap junction (gap jungk´ shən) connections between cells made for support and communication (p. 140)

Gene (jēn) the information about a trait that a parent passes to its offspring; a section of DNA (p. 90); a section of DNA that carries instructions to make a specific protein (p. 143)

Gene flow (jēn flō) the movement of genes into or out of a population (p. 406)

Gene pool (jēn pül) the genes found within a population (p. 388)

Genetically modified food (jə net´ ĭ kal ē mod´ ə fīd füd) a food product with genes that have been changed (p. 327)

Genetic code (jə net´ ik kōd) a specific code used to translate base sequences in RNA into amino acid sequences in proteins (p. 317)

Genetic drift (jə net´ ik drift) the random changes in the gene pool of a small population (p. 407)

Genetics (jə net´ iks) the study of heredity (p. 284)

Genome (jē´ nōm) the entire DNA found in a cell (p. 143)

Genotype (jen´ ə tīp) an organism's combination of genes for a trait (p. 284)

Genus (jē´ nəs) a group of similar species (p. 434)

Geological (jē ə loj´ ə kəl) having to do with the solid parts of the earth (p. 574)

Geologic time (jē ə loj´ ik tīm) all the time that has passed since the earth formed (p. 397)

Geologic time scale (jē ə loj´ ik tīm skāl) a table that divides the earth's history into time periods (p. 398)

Geology (jē ol´ ə jē) the study of the nonliving parts of the earth (p. 607)

Germinate (jėr´ mə nāt) to start to grow into a new plant (p. 477)

Gestation time (je stā´ shən tīm) the period of development of a mammal, from fertilization until birth (p. 265)

Gill (gil) a structure used by some animals to breathe in water (p. 490)

Glomerulus (glə mer´ yə ləs) a group of capillaries that make up a tiny tube in nephrons (p. 360)

Glottis (glot´ is) the opening to the windpipe (p. 348)

Glucose (glü´ kōs) a monosaccharide used as a source of energy in animals and plants (p. 77)

Glycerol (glis´ ə rol) a sweet, syrupy alcohol with three hydroxyl groups (OH) (p. 73)

Glycogen (glī´ kə jən) the main storage form of glucose found in animal cells (p. 78)

Glycolysis (glī kol´ ə sis) the first stage of cellular respiration in which glucose is first split (p. 200)

Golgi apparatus (gol´ jē apə rat´ əs) an organelle made of stacked membrane sacs that makes final changes to and packages molecules made in the cell (p. 151)

Gonad (gō´ nad) an organ that makes gametes (p. 260)

Grana (grä´ na) stacks of thylakoids inside chloroplasts (p. 147)

Greenhouse effect (grēn´ hous ə fekt´) the warming of the atmosphere because of trapped heat energy from the sun (p. 594)

Growth factor (grōth fak´ tər) a protein that helps control the growth and division of cells (p. 327)

Growth rate (grōth rāt) the amount by which a population's size changes in a given time (p. 541)

G3P (jē thrē pē) a sugar molecule (p. 233)

Guanine (gwä´ nēn) a double-ringed nitrogenous base found in DNA and RNA (p. 306)

Gymnosperm (jim´ nə spėrm) a nonflowering seed plant (p. 472)

H

Habitat (hab´ ə tat) the place where an organism lives (p. 408)

Haploid (hap´ loid) having one copy of each kind of chromosome (p. 257)

Heat (hēt) a form of energy resulting from the motion of particles in matter (p. 6)

Helix (hē´ liks) a twisted shape like a spiral staircase (p. 94)

Helper T cell (hel´ pər tē sel) a lymphocyte that scans for antigens (p. 335)

Hemoglobin (hē mə glō´ bən) an iron-containing protein in red blood cells that carries oxygen (p. 89)

Hemophilia (hē mə fil´ ē ə) a genetic disease in which a person's blood fails to clot (p. 293)

Heredity (hə red´ ə tē) the passing of traits from parents to offspring (p. 278)

Heterotroph (het´ ər ə trof) an organism that cannot make its own food (p. 479)

Heterozygous (het ər ə zī´ gəs) having chromosomes that contain an identical pair of genes that do not code for the same trait form (p. 280)

Homeostasis (hō mē ə stā′ sis) the ability of organisms to maintain their internal conditions (p. 111)

Homologous chromosome (hō mol′ ə gəs krō′ mə sōm) one of a matching pair of chromosomes that comes from each parent (p. 256)

Homologous structure (hō mol′ ə gəs struk′ chər) the body parts that are similar in related animals (p. 394)

Homozygous (hō mə zī′ gəs) having chromosomes that contain an identical pair of genes for a particular trait (p. 280)

Hormone (hôr′ mōn) a chemical signal used to control body function (p. 105)

Host (hōst) an organism that is food for a parasite (p. 550)

Host cell (hōst sel) a cell infected and used by a virus (p. 322)

Hybrid (hī′ brid) the offspring of two different true-breeding plants (p. 279)

Hydrocarbon (hī drō kär′ bən) a molecule that contains carbon and hydrogen (p. 72)

Hydrogen bond (hī′ drə jən bond) a weak electrical attraction between the slight positive charge on a hydrogen atom and a slight negative charge on another atom (p. 54)

Hydrolysis (hī drol′ ə sis) a chemical process in which a molecule is separated into two parts by adding a molecule of water (p. 73)

Hydrophilic (hī drə fil′ ik) water-loving; polar molecules are hydrophilic (p. 55)

Hydrophobic (hī drə fō′ bik) water-hating; nonpolar molecules are hydrophobic (p. 55)

Hypertension (hī per ten′ shən) high blood pressure (p. 355)

Hypertonic (hī pər ton′ ik) a solution whose solute concentration is higher than the solute concentration of another solution (p. 114)

Hyphae (hī′ fā) threadlike fibers containing membranes and cytoplasm (p. 468)

Hypothalamus (hī pō thal′ ə məs) a part of the brain that regulates hormones, the pituitary gland, body temperature, and other activities (p. 363)

Hypothesis (hī poth′ ə sis) an educated guess; also the third step of the scientific method (p. 19)

Hypotonic (hī pə ton′ ik) a solution whose solute concentration is lower than the solute concentration of another solution (p. 114)

I

Immigrate (im′ ə grāt) to move into a population (p. 543)

Immune system (i myün′ sis′ təm) the body's most important defense against diseases (p. 323)

Immunity (i myü′ nə tē) the ability of the body to fight off a specific pathogen (p. 335)

Imprinting (im prin′ ting) learning in which an animal bonds with the first object it sees (p. 515)

Incomplete dominance (in kəm plēt′ dom′ ə nəns) two different alleles that come together and produce a trait that is neither dominant nor recessive (p. 286)

Incomplete metamorphosis (in kəm plēt′ met ə môr′ fə sis) the changes in form during development in which earlier stages look like the adult (p. 486)

Infect (in fekt′) to cause disease or an unhealthy condition by introducing germs and viruses (p. 322)

Infectious disease (in fek′ shəs də zēz′) an illness that can pass from person to person (p. 332)

Inferior vena cava (in fēr′ ēər vēnə kā′ və) a large vein that carries blood from the trunk and legs to the heart (p. 353)

Inflammatory response (in flam′ ə tôr ē ri spons′) an increase in blood flow to infected body tissue (p. 333)

Ingestion (in jes′ chən) the intake of food; the first stage of digestion (p. 344)

Innate behavior (i nāt bi hā′ vyər) a behavior that is present at birth (p. 507)

Insertion (in sėr′ shən) a mutation in which one or more nucleotide bases are added to a DNA sequence (p. 319)

Insoluble (in sol′ yə bəl) not able to dissolve in water (p. 92)

Instantaneous speciation (in stən tā′ nēəs spē shē ā′ shən) a new species formed in one to several generations (p. 448)

Instinct (in′ stingkt′) a pattern of innate behavior (p. 514)

Interact (in tər akt′) to act upon or influence something (p. 536)

Interbreed (in tər brēd′) to breed together (p. 429)

Interdependent (in tər di pen′ dənt) having to rely on each other (p. 548)

Intermediate filament (in tər mē′ dēit fil′ ə mənt) a rod-like cytoskeleton fiber used to strengthen the cell's shape; organelles anchor themselves to these rods (p. 154)

Internal stimulus (in tėr′ nl stim′ yə ləs) a stimulus that occurs inside of an organism (p. 506)

Interphase (in′ tər fāz) the phase of a cell cycle in which a cell grows to mature size and carries out typical activities (p. 248)

a	hat	e	let	ī	ice	ȯ	order	u̇	put	sh	she		a	in about
ā	age	ē	equal	o	hot	oi	oil	ü	rule	th	thin	ə	e	in taken
ä	far	ėr	term	ō	open	ou	out	ch	child	ᴛH	then		i	in pencil
â	care	i	it	ȯ	saw	u	cup	ng	long	zh	measure		o	in lemon
													u	in circus

Interstitial fluid (in ter stish´ əl flü´ id) a fluid that fills the space around cells and exchanges nutrients and wastes with blood (p. 353)

Intertidal zone (in tər tī´ dl zōn) an area where an ocean meets land (p. 582)

Introduced species (in´ trə düsd spē´ shēz) a species taken from its natural ecosystem and placed in another ecosystem (p. 596)

Intron (in´ tron) a part of mRNA that does not have protein-making instructions (p. 317)

Invertebrate (in vėr´ tə brit) an animal that does not have a backbone (p. 398)

Involuntary muscle (in vol´ ən ter ē mus´ əl) a muscle that a person cannot control (p. 377)

Ion (ī´ ən) an atom that has either a positive or a negative charge (p. 42)

Ionic bond (ī on´ ik bond) a type of bonding in which ions are held together by the strong attraction of their opposite charges (p. 50)

Ionic compound (ī on´ ik kom´ pound) two or more ions held next to each other by electrical attraction (p. 42)

Iris (ī´ ris) the part of the eye that controls the amount of light that enters (p. 368)

Isomer (ī´ sə mər) one of two or more compounds with the same molecular formula but different structures (p. 78)

Isotonic(ī sə ton´ ik) a solution whose solute concentration is equal to the solute concentration of another solution (p. 114)

Isotope (ī´ sə tōp) one of a group of atoms of an element with the same number of protons and electrons but different numbers of neutrons (p. 40)

K

Kinetic energy (ki net´ ik en ər jē) energy of motion (p. 170)

Kingdom (king´ dəm) a group of similar phyla or divisions (p. 434)

Krebs cycle (krebz sī´ kəl) the second stage of cellular respiration (p. 201)

L

Lactic acid (lak´ tik as´ id) an organic waste produced by anaerobic fermentation (p. 209)

Lagging strand (lag´ ging strand) the side of the replication fork where the newly made DNA is in several small pieces (p. 312)

Land development (land di vel´ əp mənt) the changes people make to natural land so it becomes land for farming or living space (p. 595)

Landfill (land´ fil) an area where trash is collected and stored (p. 601)

Landmark (land´ märk) an object used to mark a location or position (p. 515)

Landscape ecology (land´ skāp ē kol´ əjē) using ecological information to help balance human and environmental needs (p. 603)

Larva (lär´ və) the immature form of an animal that looks different from the adult form (p. 491)

Larynx (lar´ ingks) the voice box (p. 348)

Law of conservation of energy (lô ov kon´ sər vā shən ov en´ ər jē) energy cannot be created or destroyed (p. 6)

Law of independent assortment (lô ov in di pen´ dənt ə sôrt´ mənt) a law that states that each pair of chromosomes separates independently of other pairs of chromosomes in meiosis (p. 280)

Law of segregation (lô ov seg rə gā´ shən) a law that states that the pairs of homologous chromosomes separate in meiosis and each gamete receives one gene of a pair (p. 280)

Leading strand (lē´ ding strand) the side of the replication fork where the newly made DNA is in one piece (p. 312)

Learned behavior (lėrnd bi hā´ vyər) a behavior that results from experience (p. 507)

Lichen (lī´ kən) an organism that is made up of a fungus, a green alga, and cynobacterium (p. 469)

Life span (līf span) the number of years an individual lives (p. 497)

Ligament (lig´ ə mənt) a strong tissue that connects bone to bone (p. 376)

Limbic system (lim´ bik sis´ təm) the part of the brain that registers feelings (p. 362)

Linkage map (ling´ kij map) a map that shows distances between linked genes on a chromosome (p. 287)

Linked gene (lingkt jēn) a gene close to another gene on a chromosome, causing their alleles to be inherited together (p. 287)

Lipid (lip´ id) a macromolecule that is not soluble in water (p. 72)

Lipid bilayer (lip´ id bī lā´ ər) two layers of phospholipids (p. 84)

Lymphocyte (lim´ fə sīt) a white blood cell that has receptor proteins that recognize antigens (p. 333)

Lymph system (limf sis´ təm) a human organ system that transports hormones and human immune cells throughout the body (p. 332)

Lysogenic cycle (lī sə jen´ ik sī´ kəl) a cycle in which a virus hides its genetic information in the host cell until it switches to the lytic cycle (p. 323)

Lysosome (lī´ sə sōm) a membrane sac with special enzymes used to break down large molecules (p. 152)

Lytic cycle (lit´ ik sī´ kəl) a cycle in which a virus uses a host cell to make more virus particles until the host cell is destroyed (p. 322)

Macroevolution (mak rō ev ə lü´ shən) the large-scale changes in a population over long periods of time (p. 416)

Macromolecule (mak rō mol´ ə kyül) a molecule composed of a very large number of atoms (p. 72)

Macrophage (mak´ rō fāj) a large white blood cell that eats pathogens and cellular waste (p. 335)

Magma (mag´ mə) hot, liquid rock inside the earth (p. 400)

Malaria (mə ler´ ē ə) a disease that causes bouts of chills and fever (p. 411)

Malignant tumor (mə lig´ nənt tū´ mər) a tumor that has spread from its original site to other body areas (p. 252)

Mammary gland (mam´ ə rē gland) a milk-producing structure on a mammal (p. 428)

Marine (mə rēn´) an area of water that has salt (p. 582)

Marker (mär´ kər) a material, such as an atom, used to mark an item (p. 310)

Marsupial (mär sü´ pē əl) a mammal with a pouch (p. 493)

Mass (mas) the amount of material an object has (p. 32)

Mass extinction (mas ek stingk´ shən) the dying out of large numbers of species in a short period of time (p. 447)

Matched submission (macht səb mish´ ən) a type of social behavior in which a threatened animal yields to a dominant animal (p. 521)

Matrix (mā´ triks) a thick fluid inside mitochondria (p. 147)

Matter (mat´ ər) anything that has mass and takes up space (p. 32)

Medical technology (med´ əkəl tek nol´ ə jē) any technology designed to help human medical problems (p. 608)

Meiosis (mī ō´ sis) a process that results in sex cells (p. 257)

Membrane (mem´ brān) a wall made of different molecules that separate a cell from its surroundings (p. 79)

Memory cell (mem´ ər ē sel) a lymphocyte that is activated if an antigen causes a second infection (p. 335)

Menopause (men´ ə pôz) the period when menstruation naturally stops; usually occurs between the ages of 45 and 55 (p. 263)

Menstruation (men strü ā´ shən) the process during which an unfertilized egg, blood, and pieces of the lining of the uterus exit the female body (p. 263)

Mesophyll (mes´ əfil) the green tissue inside a leaf (p. 225)

Messenger RNA (mRNA) (mes´ n jər är en ā) an RNA molecule that carries instructions for the order of amino acids in a protein (p. 316)

Metabolism (mə tab´ ə liz əm) the collection of the chemical reactions that occur in the cell (p. 170)

Metacommunication (met ə kə myü nə kā´ shən) a signal that changes the meaning of the next set of signals (p. 522)

Metamorphosis (met ə môr´ fə sis) a major change in form that occurs as some animals develop into adults (p. 485)

Metaphase plate (met´ ə fāz plāt) the middle of a cell where chromosomes line up during metaphase (p. 249)

Metastasis (mə tas´ tə sis) the process of cancer cells spreading from one body area to another (p. 252)

Microevolution (mī krō evə lü´ shən) the minor changes in a population's allele-frequencies from generation to generation (p. 416)

Microfilament (mī krō fil´ ə mənt) a long cytoskeleton fiber used to move the cell (p. 154)

Microscope (mī krō skōp) an instrument used to magnify things (p. 106)

Microtubule (mī krō tü´ byül) a tube-like cytoskeleton fiber used by organelles to move around (p. 155)

Mimicry (mim´ i krē) a method of defense in which a species looks like another poisonous or dangerous species (p. 514)

Mitochondrion (mī tə kon´ drē ən) an energy organelle that converts energy from bonds in glucose into ATP (plural is mitochondria) (p. 146)

Mitosis (mī tō´ sis) the process of dividing a cell's nucleus to make two identical nuclei (p. 249)

Modern synthesis (mod´ ərn sin´ thəsis) a theory that states evolution involves changes in a population's gene pool over time (p. 390)

Mold (mōld) a fungus that grows quickly on a surface (p. 468)

Molecular (mə lek´ yə lər) related to molecules (p. 33)

Molecular biology (mə lek´ yə lər bī ol´ ə jē) the study of the biochemical and molecular processes within cells (p. 395)

Molecule (mol´ ə kyül) the smallest particle of a substance that has all the properties of the substance (p. 32)

Mollusk (mol´ əsk) an invertebrate that has three body parts (p. 483)

Molting (mōlt ing) the process by which an arthropod sheds its exoskeleton (p. 484)

Monohybrid cross (mon ə hī´ brid kros) a cross between two plants that differ in only one trait (p. 279)

Monomer (mon´ ə mər) a small molecular structure that can chemically bond to other monomers to form a polymer (p. 72)

Monosaccharide (mon ə sak´ ə rīd) a carbohydrate made of one sugar (p. 72)

a	hat	e	let	ī	ice	ô	order	ů	put	sh	she	ə	a	in about
ā	age	ē	equal	o	hot	oi	oil	ü	rule	th	thin		e	in taken
ä	far	ėr	term	ō	open	ou	out	ch	child	ᵀH	then		i	in pencil
â	care	i	it	ȯ	saw	u	cup	ng	long	zh	measure		o	in lemon
													u	in circus

Morphology (môr fol´ ə jē) the study of differences in body forms of organs (p. 428)

Moss (mos) a nonvascular plant that has simple parts (p. 472)

Multicellular (multi sel´ yə lər) made up of many cells (p. 479)

Multiple allele (mul´ tə pəl ə lēl´) one of more than two forms of a gene (p. 285)

Mutagen (myü tā´ jən) a physical or chemical material that causes changes in DNA (p. 319)

Mutation (myü tā´ shən) a change in the sequence of DNA (p. 319)

Mutualism (myü´ chü ə liz əm) a symbiotic relationship in which both organisms benefit (p. 550)

Mycelium (mī sē´ lē əm) the underground feeding network of a fungus (p. 468)

Mycorrhiza (mī´ kə rī zə) a closeness in which a fungus and the roods of a plant live together and help each other (p. 473)

Myxini (mik´ sī nē) a class of fish with a cartilage skeleton and no jaws or scales; hagfish (p. 490)

N

NADH (en ā dē āch) nicotinamide adenine dinucleotide; the main electron carrier involved in cellular respiration (p. 198)

Natural selection (nach´ ər əl si lek´ shən) the process by which organisms best suited to the environment survive, reproduce, and pass their genes to the next generation (p. 389)

Nectar (nek´ tər) a sweet liquid that many flowers produce (p. 477)

Nephron (nef´ ron) a small tubule that is the excretory unit of the kidney (p. 360)

Nervous tissue (nèr´ vəs tish´ ü) nerves made from a collection of nerve cells (p. 123)

Neuron (nûr´ on) a nerve cell (p. 364)

Neurotransmitter (nûr ō tran smit´ ər) a substance that transmits nerve impulses across a synapse (p. 364)

Neutral solution (nü´ trəl sə lü´ shən) a solution that has a pH of 7; it is neither an acid nor a base (p. 60)

Neutron (nü´ tron) a tiny particle in the nucleus of an atom; it has the same mass as the proton and no electrical charge (p. 39)

Niche (nich) the way of life of a species (p. 431)

Nitrate (nī´ trāt) a nitrogen-containing compound used directly by plants (p. 575)

Nitrifying bacteria (nī´ trə fī ing bak tir´ ē ə) bacteria that convert ammonium into usable nitrates (p. 575)

Nitrogen-fixer (nī trə jən fiks´ ėr) bacteria that convert nitrogen gas into ammonium (p. 575)

Nitrogenous base (nī troj´ ə nəs bās) a nitrogen-containing molecule attached to a nucleotide (p. 306)

Nondisjunction (non dis jungk´ shən) chromosomes that do not separate during anaphase, resulting in extra chromosomes in some cells (p. 327)

Nonspecific defense (non spi sif´ ik di´ fens) the use of a skin barrier, complement proteins, and the inflammatory response to defend against pathogens (p. 333)

Nonvascular plant (non vas´ kyə lər plant) a plant that does not have tubelike cells (p. 473)

Notochord (nō´ tə kôrd) a rod found in the back of embryo chordate (p. 490)

Nuclear envelope (nü´ klē ər en´ və lōp) the membrane surrounding the nucleus of a cell (p. 142)

Nucleic acid (nü´ klē´ ik as´ id) a large macromolecule that stores important information in a cell (p. 72)

Nucleolus (nü klē´ ə ləs) a ball of fibers in the nucleus that makes ribosomes (p. 142)

Nucleotide (nu´ klē ə tīd) the repeating monomer in nucleic acid; consists of a nitrogen base, a sugar, and a phosphate group (p. 73)

Nucleus (nü´ klē əs) an atom's center; made of protons and neutrons (p. 39)

O

Obesity (ō bē´ sə tē) a condition of being greatly overweight (p. 181)

Observational learning (ob zər vā´ shə nəl lėr´ ning) learning by watching or listening to another animal (p. 515)

Oocyte (ō´ ə sīt) an early egg cell that has not finished meiosis (p. 262)

Oogenesis (ō ə jen´ ə ləs) the process of creating an egg cell (p. 262)

Operculus (ō pėr´ kyə ləs) a protective flap over gills that allows a fish to breathe without swimming (p. 491)

Optic nerve (op´ tik nėrv) a bundle of nerves that carry impulses from the eye to the brain (p. 369)

Organ (ôr´ gən) a group of different tissues that work together to perform specific functions (p. 124)

Organelle (ôr gə nel´) a tiny membrane-bound structure inside a cell (p. 117)

Organic compound (ôr gan´ ik kom´ pound) a compound that contains carbon (except carbon dioxide, carbon monoxide, and carbonates) (p. 70)

Organic matter (ôr gan´ ik mat´ ər) a compound that contains carbon (p. 568)

Organism (ôr´ gə niz əm) a living thing; one of many different forms of life (p. 2)

Organization (ôr´ gə nə zā´ shən) the arrangement of parts into a whole (p. 33)

Organ system (ôr´ gən sis´ təm) a group of organs that work together to perform specific connected tasks (p. 124)

Origin of replication (ôr´ ə jin ov rep lə kā´ shən) a site where DNA replication begins (p. 311)

Osmosis (oz mō´ sis) the movement of water through a cell membrane (p. 113)

Osteichthyes (os tē ik´ thē ēz) a class of bony fish with jaws and scales (p. 490)

Osteoporosis (os tē ō pə rō sis) a disease in which bones become lighter and break easily (p. 375)

Ovary (ō´ vərē) the female organ that makes egg cells (p. 262)

Overproduction (ō vər prə duk´ shən) when organisms produce more offspring than can survive (p. 418)

Ovulation (ov´ yə lā shən) the process of releasing an egg from an ovary (p. 262)

Oxidation (ok sə dā shən) a chemical reaction that results in a loss of electrons (p. 197)

Ozone (ō´ zōn) a form of oxygen (p. 595)

P

Paleontologist (pā lē on tol´ ə jist) a scientist who studies fossils (p. 397)

Parasite (par´ ə sīt) an organism that absorbs food from a living organism and harms it (p. 321)

Parasitism (par´ ə sī tiz əm) a symbiotic relationship in which one organism feeds off another organism (p. 550)

Parental care behavior (pə ren´ tl cār bi hā´ vyer) the caring for offspring by a parent (p. 513)

Passive transport (pas´ iv tran spôrt´) the movement of molecules across a membrane when the movement requires no energy (p. 138)

Patent (pat´ nt) a government notice of ownership for a piece of technology (p. 609)

Pathogen (path´ ə jən) a germ (p. 332)

Penis (pē´ nis) the male organ that delivers sperm to the female body (p. 261)

Pepsin (pep´ sən) an enzyme produced in the stomach for digestion (p. 182)

Peptide (pep´ tīd) a compound made up of two or more amino acids; peptides combine to make proteins (p. 90)

Peptide bond (pep´ tīd bond) a covalent bond between two amino acids (p. 90)

Peristalsis (per ə stôl´ sis) the movement of digestive organs that pushes food through the digestive tract (p. 345)

Permafrost (pėr´ mə frôst) permanently frozen soil (p. 582)

Perspiration (pėr spə rā´ shən) a liquid waste made of heat, water, and salt released through skin (p. 360)

PGA (pē jē ā) phosphoglycerate; a three-carbon molecule formed in the first step of the Calvin-Benson cycle (p. 238)

P generation (pē jen ə rā´ shən) parental generation; the first two individuals that mate in a genetic cross (p. 279)

pH (pē āch) a number that tells whether a substance is an acid or a base (p. 59)

Phagocyte (fag´ ə sīt) a cell that eats infected cells and pathogens (p. 333)

Pharyngeal slit (fə rin´ jē əl slit) an opening in the wall of the pharynx of a chordate embryo (p. 490)

Pharynx (far´ ingks) the passageway between the mouth and the esophagus for air and food (p. 345)

Phenotype (fē´ nə tīp) an organism's appearance as a result of its combination of genes (p. 284)

Pheromone (fer´ ə mōn) a chemical signal produced by an animal (p. 524)

Phloem (flō´ em) the vascular tissue in plants that carries food from leaves to other parts of the plant (p. 473)

Phospholipid (fos´ fə lip id) a lipid with two fatty acid molecules joined by a molecule of glycerol (p. 82)

Phosphorous (fos´ fər əs) an element that cycles through an ecosystem and is used by organisms to make ATP (p. 573).

Phosphorylation (fos fôr ə lā´ shən) the addition of a phosphate group to a molecule (p. 174)

Photic zone (fō´ tik zōn) an area in aquatic biomes that receives solar energy (p. 582)

Photon (fō´ ton) the smallest unit of light (p. 230)

Photosynthesis (fō tō sin´ thə sis) a process that chloroplasts use to convert energy from the sun into chemical energy stored in glucose (p. 146)

Photosystem (fō tō sis´ təm) an assembly of proteins and pigments through which electrons are transferred to reaction centers (p. 234)

Phototroph (fō´ tō trof) an organism that gets its energy by capturing light energy (p. 566)

Phylogeny (fī loj´ ə nē) the origin and evolution of a species (p. 482)

Phylum (fī´ ləm) a subdivision of a kingdom (plural is phyla) (p. 434).

Physical property (fiz´ ə kəl prop´ ərtē) a characteristic of a substance or an object that can be observed without changing the substance into a different substance (p. 33)

Pistil (pis´ tl) the female organ of reproduction in a flower (p. 477)

a	hat	e	let	ī	ice	ô	order	ů	put	sh	she	ə	a in about
ā	age	ē	equal	o	hot	oi	oil	ü	rule	th	thin		e in taken
ä	far	ėr	term	ō	open	ou	out	ch	child	ʈH	then		i in pencil
â	care	i	it	ȯ	saw	u	cup	ng	long	zh	measure		o in lemon
													u in circus

Pituitary gland (pə tü′ ə ter ē gland) a gland in the brain that produces secretions that regulate basic body functions (p. 363)

Placenta (plə sen′ tə) a tissue that provides the embryo with food and oxygen from its mother's body (p. 266).

Plankton (plangk′ tən) small organisms found in the ocean; usually at the beginning of a food chain (p. 568)

Plasma (plaz′ mə) the liquid part of blood (p. 354)

Plasma membrane (plaz′ mə mem′ brān) the membrane that surrounds a cell and separates it from the environment (p. 135)

Plasmid (plaz′ mid) a small, circular piece of DNA, usually found in bacteria (p. 325)

Plasmodesmata (plaz mə dez′ mətə) openings in the cell wall used for communication and transport of molecules (p. 159).

Plastid (plas′ tid) a small, special part of a plant cell (p. 79)

Plate (plāt) a large section of the earth's crust that moves (p. 400)

Platelet (plāt′ lit) a tiny piece of cell that helps form clots (p. 354)

Plate tectonics (plāt tek ton′ iks) a theory that the earth's surface is made of large sections of crust that move (p. 399)

Pleiotropy (plī o′ trə pē) one gene that affects many traits (p. 286)

Polar molecule (pō′ lər mol′ ə kyül) a molecule with an uneven distribution of electron density (p. 54)

Pollen (pol′ ən) tiny grains containing sperm; the male plant gamete (p. 278)

Pollination (pol ə na′ shən) the process by which pollen is transferred from the stamen to the pistil (p. 477)

Pollution (pə lü′ shən) anything added to the environment that is harmful to living things (p. 594)

Polygenic trait (polē jē′ nik trāt) a trait controlled by two or more genes (p. 287)

Polymer (pol′ ə mər) a very large molecule made from simple units (p. 72)

Polypeptide (pol ē pep′ tīd) several amino acids joined to form a chain (p. 90)

Polysaccharide (pol e′ sak′ ə rīd) a carbohydrate that can be broken down by hydrolysis into two or more monosaccharides (p. 73)

Polyunsaturated fatty acid (pol ē un sach′ ə rā tid fat′ ē as′ id) a fatty acid containing many double or triple bonds (p. 83)

Population (pop yə la′ shən) a group of organisms of the same species that live in the same area (p. 388)

Population density (pop yə la′ shən den′ sətē) the number of individuals in a population in a particular area (p. 538)

Pore (pôr) a hole in the nuclear envelope used to send and receive messages (p. 142)

Potential energy (pə ten′ shəl en′ ər jē) stored energy (p. 170)

Precipitation (pri sip ə tā′ shən) the moisture that falls to earth from the atmosphere (p. 576)

Predation (prē dā′ shən) a relationship in which one species eats another species (p. 549)

Predator (pred′ ə tər) an organism that eats another organism (p. 514).

Pregnancy (preg′ nən sē) the development of a fertilized egg into a baby inside a female's body (p. 265).

Prey (prā) an organism that is eaten by another organism (p. 514)

Primary productivity (prī mer′ ē prō duk tiv′ ətē) the speed at which photosynthetic organisms produce organic matter in an ecosystem (p. 569)

Primary succession (prī mer′ ē sək sesh′ ən) the changes in a lifeless environment that create a community (p. 556)

Producer (prə dü′ sər) an organism that makes its own food (p. 567)

Product (prod′ əkt) a substance that is formed in a chemical reaction (p. 51)

Prokaryote (prō kar′ ē ōt) a cell with only one outside membrane and no nucleus or other internal structures (p. 116)

Promoter (prə mō′ tər) the sequence of DNA at the beginning of genes (p. 317)

Protein (prō′ tēn) a chemical used by cells to grow and work (p. 8)

Proton (prō′ ton) a tiny particle in the nucleus of an atom; it has a positive electrical charge (p. 39)

Protozoan (prō tə zō′ ən) protists that ingest food and usually live in water (plural is protozoa) (p. 464)

Pseudopod (sü′ də pod) a part of some one-celled organisms that sticks out like a foot and moves the cell along (p. 465)

Punctuated equilibrium (pungk′ chü āt əd ē kwə lib′ rē əm) a theory that states species stay the same for a long time, then new species evolve suddenly due to global changes and mass extinctions (p. 441)

Punnett square (pun′ it skwer) a model used to represent crosses between organisms (p. 281)

Pupil (pyü′ pəl) the black circle in the center of the iris (p. 368)

Pyruvic acid (pī rü′ vik as′ id) a major product of glycolysis (p. 200)

Radial symmetry (rā′ dē əl sim′ ə trē) an arrangement of body parts that resembles the spokes on a wheel (p. 482)

Radical (rad′ ə kəl) a group of two or more atoms that acts like one atom (p. 43)

Radioactive (rā dē ō ak′ tiv) the property of some elements (such as uranium) or isotopes (such as carbon-14) to give off energy as they change to another substance over time (p. 40)

Radioactive element (rā dē ō ak′ tiv el′ əmənt) an element that decays to form another element (p. 398)

Radioisotope (rā dē ō ī′ sə tōp) a radioactive isotope (p. 40)

Radula (raj′ ủ lə) a tonguelike organ covered with teeth that is used for feeding (p. 484)

Random (ran′ dəm) when a population has no order as to how it is distributed through an ecosystem (p. 543)

Reactant (rē ak′ tənt) a substance that is altered in a chemical reaction (p. 51)

Reaction center (rē ak′ tənt sen′ tər) a special molecule of chlorophyll a in which electron transfer occurs (p. 233)

Recessive gene (ri ses′ iv jēn) a gene that is hidden by a dominant gene (p. 279)

Recombination (rē kom bə nā′ shən) the creation of new combinations of alleles in offspring (p. 405)

Recovery plan (ri kuv′ ər ē plan) a plan using scientific knowledge to help bring endangered species back from possible extinction (p. 604)

Rectum (rek′ təm) the lower part of the large intestine where feces are stored (p. 346)

Recycling (rē sī′ kəl ing) using waste products to create new products (p. 602)

Red marrow (red mar′ ō) the spongy material in bones that makes blood cells (p. 375)

Redox reaction (rē′ doks rē ak′ shən) a chemical reaction in which electrons are transferred between atoms (p. 197)

Reduction (ri duk′ shən) a chemical reaction that results in a gain of electrons (p. 197)

Reflex (rē′ fleks) an automatic response (p. 344)

Releaser (rē lēs′ ər) a stimulus that brings out a certain behavior in another animal (p. 515)

Replication (rep lə kā′ shən) the process DNA uses to copy itself (p. 310)

Replication bubble (rep lə kā′ shən bub′ əl) an area in which DNA replication is occurring with both strands unwound and being used as templates (p. 311)

Replication fork (rep lə kā′ shən fôrk) the end of a replication bubble in which DNA polymerase is actively adding nucleotide bases to a new strand (p. 311)

Reproduction (rē prə duk′ shən) the process of making new life (p. 7)

Reproductively isolated (rē prə duk′ tiv lē īsə lāt əd) a division between populations that once mated, but can no longer mate and produce fertile offspring (p. 429)

Reptile (rep′ tīl) an egg-laying vertebrate that breathes with lungs (p. 398)

Reserve (ri zėrv′) a protected area that cannot be used for building or growth (p. 603)

Respiration (res pə rā shən) the process by which living things release energy from food (p. 196)

Restriction endonuclease (ri strik′ shən en dō nü′ klē ās) an enzyme that cuts DNA molecules at specific sequences (p. 326)

Retina (ret′ nə) the back part of the eye where light rays are focused (p. 369)

Rhizoid (rī′ zoid) a tiny rootlike thread of a moss plant (p. 473)

Ribose (rī′ bōs) the five-carbon sugar in RNA (p. 95)

Ribosomal RNA (rRNA) (rī bə sō məl är en ā) an RNA molecule found in ribosomes that positions mRNA during translation (p. 317)

Ribosome (rī′ bə sōm) an information organelle that uses the instructions in DNA to make a protein (p. 142)

RNA (är en ā) a molecule that works together with DNA to make proteins (p. 94)

RNA polymerase (är en ā pol′ ə mə rās) an enzyme that adds RNA nucleotides to a new RNA molecule (p. 316)

RNA splicing (är en ā splīs′ ing) the removal of introns from an mRNA (p. 317)

Roundworm (round′ wėrm) a worm with a smooth, round body and pointed ends (p. 483)

RuBP (rü bē pē) ribulose bisphosphate; a five-carbon carbohydrate that combines with CO_2 in the first step of the Calvin-Benson cycle (p. 238)

S

Saccharide (sak′ ə rīd) a simple sugar (p. 77)

Saliva (sə lī və) a liquid produced by glands in the mouth that helps in chewing and starts digestion (p. 182)

Sample (sam′ pəl) a part that represents an entire population (p. 538)

a	hat	e	let	ī	ice	ȯ	order	ủ	put	sh	she	ə	a	in about
ā	age	ē	equal	o	hot	oi	oil	ü	rule	th	thin		e	in taken
ä	far	ėr	term	ō	open	ou	out	ch	child	ᵵᵜ	then		i	in pencil
â	care	i	it	ȯ	saw	u	cup	ng	long	zh	measure		o	in lemon
													u	in circus

Saturated fatty acid (sach´ ə rā tid fat´ ē as´ id) a fatty acid containing no double carbon bonds and the maximum number of hydrogen atoms (p. 82)

Savanna (sə van´ ə) a terrestrial biome with grasses and grazing animals (p. 581)

Scent (sent) having a smell or odor (p. 521)

Scientific journal (sī ən tif´ ik jėr´ nl) a scientific magazine (p. 609)

Scientific method (sī ən tif´ ik meth´ əd) a series of steps used to test possible answers to scientific questions (p. 17)

Scrotum (scrō´ təm) a sac that holds the testes (p. 260)

Secondary succession (sek´ ən der ē sək sesh´ ən) the changes in a community as it recovers from the effects of a disturbance (p. 556)

Secrete (si krēt´) to make and then give off (p. 151)

Sedimentary rock (sed ə men´ tərē rok) the rock formed from pieces of other rock and organic matter that have been pressed and cemented together (p. 392)

Seed (sēd) a plant part that contains a beginning plant and stored food (p. 472)

Segmented worm (seg´ mentəd wėrm) a worm whose body is divided into sections (p. 483)

Selectively permeable membrane (sə lek´ tiv lē pėr´ mē ə bəl mem´ brān) a membrane that allows some molecules to pass but blocks other molecules from coming through (p. 113)

Semen (sē´ mən) a mixture of fluid and sperm cells (p. 261)

Semi-conservative replication (sem´ ē kən sėr´ va tiv rep lə kā´ shən) a model of DNA replication in which an old strand of DNA is used to make a new strand of DNA (p. 310)

Seminiferous tubule (sem ə nif´ ər əs tü´ byül) the tissue in the testes where spermatogenesis happens (p. 261)

Sensory receptor (sen´ sər ē ri sep´ tər) a specialized neuron that detects sensory stimuli, then converts them to nerve impulses that go to the brain (p. 367)

Sequence (sē´ kqəns) a continuous or connected series (p. 90)

Sex chromosome (seks krō´ mə sōm) a chromosome that determines the sex of an organism (p. 292)

Sex-linked inheritance (seks lingkt in her´ ə təns) the passing on of traits with genes located on the X chromosome (p. 295)

Sex-linked trait (seks lingkt trāt) a trait determined by an organism's sex chromosomes (p. 293)

Sickle-cell disease (sik´ əl sel də zē´) a genetic disease in which a person's red blood cells have a sickle shape (p. 286)

Signal (sig´ nəl) a behavior that causes a change in the behavior of another animal (p. 521)

Simple dominance (sim´ pəl dom´ ə nəns) one allele is dominant to a recessive allele (p. 284)

Simulate (sim´ yə lāt) to make the same conditions as the natural or original conditions (p. 513)

Sister chromatid (sis´ tər krō´ mə tid) one of a pair of identical chromosomes created before a cell divides (p. 249)

Skeletal system (skel´ ə təl sis´ təm) the network of bones in the body (p. 375)

Sleep apnea (slēp ap´ nē ə) a condition in which short periods of not breathing occur during sleep (p. 350)

Slime mold (slīm mōld) a protist that lives as an individual cell, then joins other slime mold cells to form a community that produces spores (p. 466)

Social behavior (sō´ shəl bi hā´ vyər) the interaction between two or more animals (p. 520)

Sociobiologist (sō sē ō bī ol´ ə jist) a scientist who studies how animals communicate and interact with each other (p. 520)

Solar (sō´ lər) of or from the sun (p. 566)

Solute (sol´ yüt) a dissolved substance (p. 114)

Solvent (sol´ vənt) a substance capable of dissolving one or more other substances (p. 55)

Somatic cell (sō mat´ ik sel) a non-sex cell (p. 256)

Sori (sôr´ ē) the clusters of reproductive cells on the underside of a frond (p. 475)

Spatial learning (spā´ shəl lėr´ ning) learning by recognizing features (p. 515)

Speciation (spē shē ā´ shən) the process of making a new species (p. 10)

Species (spē´ shēz) a group of organisms that can reproduce with each other (p. 10)

Specific defense (spi sif´ ik di fens´) the use of lymphocytes to recognize antigens and attack infected cells based on antigens (p. 333)

Specimen (spes´ ə mən) a sample; an individual item or part considered typical of a group or whole (p. 17)

Sperm (spėrm) the male gamete (p. 256)

Spermatogenesis (spėr ma tō jen´ ə sis) the process of making a sperm cell (p. 260)

Spermatogonia (spėr ma tō gō´ nēa) early gamete cells that have not grown into sperm (p. 261)

Spindle (spin´ dl) a network of fibers that move chromosomes during mitosis (p. 249)

Spore (spôr) a reproductive cell of some organisms (p. 466)

Sporophyte (spôr´ ə fit) in alternation of generations, the diploid individual or generation that produces haploid spores (p. 474)

Stability (stə bil´ ə tē) the ability of a community to resist change (p. 539)

Stamen (stā´ mən) the male organ of reproduction in a flower, which includes the anther and filament (p. 476)

Starch (stärch) a polymer of glucose found in plants (p. 78)

Stasis (stā´ sis) showing little change over time (p. 441)

Steroid (ster´ oid) a lipid containing four attached carbon rings (p. 82)

Stigma (stig´ ma) the upper part of the pistil on the tip of the style (p. 477)

Stimulus (stim´ yə ləs) anything to which an organism reacts (p. 12)

Stoma (stō´ mə) an opening on the underside of a leaf for gas exchange (plural is stomata) (p. 225)

Stroma (strō´ mə) a thick fluid inside chloroplasts (p. 147)

Subatomic particle (sub e tom´ ik pär´ tə kəl) a proton, neutron, electron, or other particle smaller than the atom (p. 39)

Subpopulation (sub pä pyə lā´ shən) a division of a population (p. 432)

Subspecies (sub´ spē shēz) a division of a species (p. 431)

Substitution (sub stə tü´ shən) a mutation in which one nucleotide base is replaced with another (p. 319)

Substrate (sub´ strāt) a reactant molecule; the molecule on which an enzyme reacts (p. 185)

Succession (sək sesh´ ən) the process of ecological change in a community (p. 555)

Sugar-phosphate backbone (shüg´ ər fos´ fāt bak´ bōn) the negatively charged backbone of a nucleic acid molecule (p. 306)

Superior vena cava (sə pir´ ē ər vē´ nə kā´ və) a large vein that carries blood from the head, neck, and arms to the heart (p. 353)

Swim bladder (swim blad´ ər) a gas-filled organ that allows a bony fish to move up and down in water (p. 491)

Symbiosis (sim bē ō sis) a relationship in which two different species live in close association (p. 550)

Sympatric speciation (sim pa´ trik spē shē ā´ shən) when similar organisms live nearby, but do not interbreed due to behavioral differences (p. 431)

Synapse (si naps´) a tiny gap between neurons (p. 364)

Synthesize (sin´ thə sīz) to make into a whole substance (p. 91)

T

Taxonomist (tak so´ nə mist) a scientist who classifies and assigns scientific names to organisms (p. 458)

Taxonomy (tak son´ ə mē) the science of classifying organisms based on the features they share (p. 458)

Technology (tek nol´ ə jē) any device, machine, or method created to solve a human problem or question (p. 608)

Temperate deciduous forest (tem´ pər it di sij´ ü əs fôr´ ist) a terrestrial biome with wet forests that change activity during winter (p. 582)

Temperate grassland (tem´ pər it gras´ land) a terrestrial biome with fertile soil and tall grasses (p. 581)

Template (tem´ plit) a pattern used for copying (p. 311)

Tendon (ten´ dən) a tough tissue that attaches muscles to bones (p. 377)

Tentacle (ten´ tə kəl) an armlike body part of cnidarians that is used to capture food (p. 482)

Terminator (tėr´ mə nā tər) the sequence of DNA that signals the end of transcription (p. 317)

Terrestrial (tə res´ trē əl) having to do with land (p. 580)

Territorial behavior (ter´ ə tôr´ ē əl bi hā´ vyər) a behavior that claims and defends an area (p. 515)

Testcross (test´ kros) a test that determines an unknown genotype of an organism by crossing it with a homozygous recessive organism (p. 285)

Testis (tes´ tis) the male sex organ that produces sperm cells (plural is testes) (p. 260)

Testosterone (te stos´ tə rōn) a male sex hormone (p. 260)

Tetrad (tet´ rad) a pair of homologous chromosomes joined together (p. 257)

Thalamus (thal´ ə məs) a part of the brain that directs sensory messages (p. 363)

Theory (thē´ ə rē) a well-tested explanation that makes sense of a great variety of scientific observations (p. 21)

Three-domain system (thrē dō mān sis´ təm) a system that classifies all living things into three broad groups (p. 436)

Thrombus (throm´ bəs) a clot of blood formed within a blood vessel (p. 354)

Thylakoid (thī´ lə koid) membrane sac that contains chlorophyll (p. 147)

Thymine (T) (thī´ mēn) a single-ringed nitrogenous base found in DNA (p. 307)

Tissue (tish ü) a group of cells that are similar and work together (p. 123)

T lymphocyte (tē lim´ fa sit) a specific defense cell that signals and destroys infected cells (p. 333)

Toxic (tok´ sik) poisonous (p. 555)

Trachea (trā kē ə) the tube that carries air to the bronchi (p. 349)

Trait (trāt) a characteristic of an organism (p. 278)

Transcription (tran skrip´ shən) the creation of an RNA molecule using the bases in a DNA molecule as a template (p. 316)

a	hat	e	let	ī	ice	ô	order	ů	put	sh	she		a	in about
ā	age	ē	equal	o	hot	oi	oil	ü	rule	th	thin	ə	e	in taken
ä	far	ėr	term	ō	open	ou	out	ch	child	ᴛʜ	then		i	in pencil
â	care	i	it	ȯ	saw	u	cup	ng	long	zh	measure		o	in lemon
													u	in circus

Trans fat (tranz fat) an unsaturated fat that has been changed to a saturated fat (p. 83)

Transfer RNA (tRNA) (tran sfér är en ā) an RNA molecule that brings in amino acids during translation (p. 317)

Transform (tran sfórm´) to change form or makeup (p. 5)

Transformation (tran sfər mā´ shən) the process of adding foreign DNA to a bacterial cell (p. 326)

Translation (tran slā´ shən) the creation of a protein using the bases in an RNA molecule as a template (p. 316)

Transport (tran spôrt´) to move molecules from one side of a membrane to the other (p. 112)

Transport protein (tran spôrt´ prō´ tēn) a protein in the plasma membrane that helps move molecules across the membrane (p. 136)

Triglyceride (trī glis´ ə rīd) a lipid made of three fatty acids and one molecule of glycerol (p. 82)

Trophic structure (trō´ fik strək´ chər) the feeding relationships between species in a community (p. 549)

Tropical forest (trop´ ə kəl fôr´ ist) a terrestrial biome with many trees and organisms (p. 581)

Truncate (trung´ kāt) to shorten (p. 91)

Tube foot (tūb fút) a small structure used by echinoderms for attachment and movement (p. 486)

Tubulin (tü´ byə lən) a ball-shaped protein used to make the hollow tube structure of microtubules (p. 155)

Tumor (tü mər) a ball of cells made from the extra divisions of a cancer cell (p. 252)

Tundra (tun´ drə) a cold, dry terrestrial biome with shrubs and small trees (p. 582)

U

Umbilical cord (um bil ə kəl kôrd) the cord that connects an embryo to the placenta (p. 266)

Uniform (yü nə fôrm) when a population spreads out evenly through an ecosystem (p. 543)

Unsaturated fatty acid (un sach ə rā tid fat´ ē as´ id) a fatty acid containing double or triple bonds and less than the maximum number of hydrogen atoms (p. 83)

Uracil (U) (yü´ r ə səl) a single-ringed nitrogenous base found only in RNA (p. 307)

Ureter (yủ rē´ tər) a tube that carries urine from the kidney to the urinary bladder (p. 359)

Urethra (yü rē´ thrə) the tube that carries urine and semen out of the body (p. 261)

Urine (yủr´ ən) liquid waste formed in the kidneys (p. 359)

Uterus (yü tər əs) an organ in most female mammals that holds and protects an embryo (p. 262)

V

Vaccine (vak´ sēn) a material that causes the body to make antibodies against a specific pathogen (p. 323)

Vacuole (vak´ yü ol) a membrane sac that transports and stores molecules (p. 151)

Vagina (və jī´ nə) the tube-like canal in the female body through which sperm enter the body (p. 265)

Variable (ver´ ēə bəl) the factor that is tested in an experiment (p. 19)

Vascular bundle (vas´ kyə lər bun´ dl) a vein in a leaf that transports water and food (p. 225)

Vascular plant (vas´ kyə lər plant) a plant that has tubelike cells (p. 473)

Vascular tissue (vas´ ky ə lər tish´ ü) a group of plant cells that form tubes through which food and water move (p. 473)

Vas deferens (vas def ər enz) the tubes that connect the testes to the urethra (p. 261)

Vegetation (vej ə tā´ shən) the plant life in an area (p. 551)

Vein (vān) a blood vessel that carries blood back to the heart (p. 353)

Ventricle (ven´ trə kəl) a heart chamber that pumps blood out of the heart (p. 353)

Vertebra (vȇr te bra) one of the bones or blocks of cartilage that make up a backbone (plural is vertebrae) (p. 489)

Vertebrate (vȇr´ tə brit) an animal that has a backbone (p. 398)

Villi (vil´ ī) the tiny, fingerlike structures in the small intestine through which food molecules enter the blood (p. 345)

Virus (vī´ rəs) a type of germ that is not living (p. 310)

Voluntary muscle (vol´ ən ter ē mus´ əl) a muscle that a person can control (p. 377)

W

Warm-blooded (wôrm blud´ id) having a body temperature that stays the same (p. 492)

Warning coloration (wôr´ ning kul ə rā´ shən) the bright colors or patterns on animals that scare off predators (p. 514)

Wavelength (wāv´ lengkth) the distance between repeating units of a wave pattern (p. 230)

White blood cell (wit blud sel) a cell of the immune system (p. 333)

X

Xylem (zī´ lem) the vascular tissue in plants that carries minerals from roots to stems and leaves (p. 473)

Z

Zygote (zī´ gōt) a fertilized cell (p. 257)

Index

high-tech medications, 151
hydrogenation, 84
industrial fermentation, 208
LASIK surgery, 370
organisms, classification of, 484
organisms, discovery of, 437
physiological saline, 115
radon, 40
skin cancer, 404
surgical robots, 608
Temperate deciduous forest defined, 582
Temperate grassland defined, 581
Temperature and heart rate, 354
Template defined, 311
Tendon defined, 377
Tentacle defined, 482
Terminator defined, 316, 317
Terrestrial biome defined, 580, 586
Territorial behavior defined, 515
Testcross defined, 285, 289
Testis defined, 260
Testosterone defined, 260
Tests, preparing for, xv
Tetrad defined, 257, 259
Thalamus defined, 362, 363
Theory defined, 21, 27
Thermoreceptors described, 368, 371
Threatened species defined, 601
   protecting, 603
Three-domain system of species classification defined, 436, 458
Thrombus defined, 355
Thylakoid defined, 147, 225
Thymine defined, 307, 311, 338
Thymus gland, function of, 372
Thyroid gland, function of, 372
Tinbergen, Niko, 515–16, 517
Tissue culture described, 118

Tissue defined, 123, 128, 480
T lymphocyte defined, 333, 334
Touch, sense of, 370
Toxic defined, 555
Tracers. *See* Radioisotope defined
Trachea defined, 349
Traits
   defined, 278
   inheritance, sex-linked, 293
   See also Heredity
Transcription, 316–17, 319, 320, 338
Trans fat defined, 83
Transformation defined, 5, 325, 326
Translation
   defined, 316
   overview, 317–18, 319
Transport
   active, 138
   defined, 112
   within organisms, 155
   passive, 138, 164
   proteins, 136, 138
Transport protein defined, 136, 138
Trash, impact of on ecosystems, 593, 631
   See also Pollution
Triclosan described, 140
Triglyceride defined, 82, 98
tRNA (transfer RNA) defined, 317, 318
Trophic structure defined, 549, 552, 566–67, 586
Tropical forest defined, 581
Truncate defined, 91
Tube foot defined, 486
Tubulin defined, 155
Tumors
   defined, 252, 253
   removing, 252
   See also Cancer
Tundra defined, 582
Twins, behavior studies of, 529
Tympanic membrane defined, 369

U

Umbilical cord defined, 265, 266
Uniform pattern of population distribution defined, 543, 544
United Nations described, 604
Unsaturated fatty acid defined, 82, 83
Uracil defined, 307, 338
Ureter defined, 359
Urethra defined, 261
Urine defined, 359
Uterus defined, 262, 263

V

Vaccines
   defined, 323
   delivery, 336
   polio, 341
Vacuole defined, 151
Vagina defined, 265
Variable defined, 19, 27
Vascular bundle defined, 225
Vascular plant defined, 472
Vascular tissue defined, 472, 473
Vas deferens defined, 261
Vegetarian diets, 91
Vegetation defined, 551
Vein defined, 353
Venn diagrams, using, xviii
Ventricle defined, 353
Vertebra defined, 489
Vertebrates
   defined, 398, 480, 500
   overview, 489–94
Villi defined, 345
Viruses
   classification of, 460
   defined, 25, 310, 324, 338
infection, mechanism of action, 322–23
   structure of, 321–22, 324
Vitamin A and blindness, 97
Voluntary muscle defined, 377

W

Warm-blooded defined, 492
Warning coloration defined, 514
Wasp behavior, 515–16
Water
   absorption of, 360
   balance, regulating, 359
   chemical bonds in, 49
   conserving, 585
   cycle, 575–76, 581
   heat capacity of, 54
   in organisms, 53, 56, 59
   properties of, 53–55, 56
   surface tension in, 54–55
Watson, James, 307, 308
Wavelength defined, 230
Weather, factors affecting, 580
Wegener, Alfred, 399–400
White blood cells. *See* Macrophage defined
Whooping crane recovery, 598
Wind energy, 629–30
Windmills described, 629
Wireless communications, 525
World map, 627

X

X-rays, 412
Xylem defined, 472, 473

Y

Y chromosome, 409
Yeasts and sugar fermentation, 210

Z

Zygote defined, 256, 257

Photo and Illustration Credits